Psycholinguistics
Introduction and Applications

Psycholinguistics
Introduction and Applications

Lise Menn, PhD

PLURAL
PUBLISHING
INC.

SAN DIEGO
OXFORD
BRISBANE

PLURAL PUBLISHING
INC.

5521 Ruffin Road
San Diego, CA 92123

e-mail: info@pluralpublishing.com
Web site: http://www.pluralpublishing.com

49 Bath Street
Abingdon, Oxfordshire OX14 1EA
United Kingdom

FSC
Mixed Sources
Product group from well-managed
forests and other controlled sources

Cert no. SW-COC-002283
www.fsc.org
© 1996 Forest Stewardship Council

Library of Congress Cataloging-in-Publication Data

Menn, Lise.
   Psycholinguistics : introduction and applications / Lise Menn.
        p. ; cm.
   Includes bibliographical references and index.
   ISBN-13: 978-1-59756-283-6 (alk. paper)
   ISBN-10: 1-59756-283-1 (alk. paper)
   1. Psycholinguistics—methods. 2. Language Development. 3. Phonetics.
I. Title.
   P37M357 2010
   410.1'9—dc22

                                                                2010025512

Contents

6 Analyzing Aphasic Speech and Communication: The Psycholinguistics of Adult Acquired Language Disorders — 205

7 Developmental Psycholinguistics: Studies of First Language Acquisition — 251

Foreword

Psycholinguistics can be defined as the psychology of language; this definition is deceptively simple. Psychology, as the study of behavior, is an ever-expanding field, embracing new theories, research methods, and data. The formal study of language is rooted in linguistics, one of the oldest domains of scholarship and one that is continually renewed by efforts to understand the structure of language. Psycholinguistics is the hybrid offspring of psychology and linguistics, and, like many hybrids, it is vigorous and fruitful. A proper understanding of psycholinguistics requires a deep knowledge of its parent fields, but it can be a daunting effort to gain even a basic understanding of either psychology or linguistics, let alone their intersection. The challenge to the learner is clear. Fortunately, the answer to that challenge is now clear as well.

In this remarkable book, Lise Menn lays out the field of psycholinguistics like a feast on the table of knowledge. Moving deftly between theory and experiment, she reviews contemporary understanding of basic questions on the use of language, such as: How do we acquire a first or later language? How do we understand and produce sentences? How do our brains process language? What causes errors in language production and what do these errors tell us about the neural organization of language? How do neurologic disorders such as stroke lead to impairment of language? Menn's deep knowledge of the subject matter is beautifully matched with her verbal skills to produce a book that is inviting and rewarding to read. Above all, this extraordinary book carries the reader along a journey that explores the excitement of research accomplishments in the field of psycholinguistics. Readers who may have been frustrated in previous attempts to fashion an understanding of psycholinguistics from other books or journal articles are well advised to read this book for a clear and comprehensive account of the field. Readers who know little about either psychology or linguistics should not be intimidated, as this book will escort them through discovery after discovery and hypothesis after hypothesis. Instructors who have searched for a book that will encourage and educate their students need not look any further.

Psycholinguistics: Introduction and Applications is authoritative in its command of knowledge and enjoyable in its exquisite use of words to talk about words. What better way to learn about psycholinguistics?

Ray Kent

Introduction

How Psycholinguistics Can Help Understand the Kinds of Problems That People Have With Language

0.1 Everyday Language Problems

Think about language problems: What comes to mind? If you are a clinician or a language teacher, or a close relative of someone with a language disorder, if or you are studying or working outside your home country and still stressed by understanding the language around you, most of your everyday life probably floods into your mind at the thought of language problems.

If you are not in one of those situations, language problems may be a more remote idea; probably, you will think of children or foreigners struggling to be understood. Or, perhaps, of yourself trying to remember words in a technical course or foreign language, or the names in a novel set in an unfamiliar or imaginary world. Perhaps you may think of older people trying to remember names of people, places, or even fairly common objects, like *pliers*; parents calling children by the name of their brother or sister, or even the name of a pet (I did that once; my son was not amused). Accidentally saying the opposite of what you mean, in a way that feels like a blend of two things you wanted to say at the same time: for example, "everything under the world" when what you wanted to say was either "everything under the sun" or "everything in the world" (a real example from a published collection of speech errors). Words that you see sneaking into what you are saying when you are talking on the telephone and looking at a computer screen at the same time (*Do you have time to go to a carpet sale—I mean a movie—tomorrow?*). Hearing somebody say something that, in fact, is not what they said; misconstruing unfamiliar words in titles, song lyrics, or prayers (*Do you know who painted the ceiling of the sixteenth chapel?*).

All of these are "normal" language problems; much worse are the problems of people who have had strokes or other injuries affecting the language areas of the brain, and the problems of children with developmental language disorders. In this book, we develop the descriptive and conceptual tools for understanding how these language problems seem to happen. Gradually, we see how those tools can help with the design of second language curricula and programs, with language testing and therapy, and how they can simply provide us with a feeling of insight into our own language behavior and that of people around us—insight that will help us deal with everyone's language problems with as much grace and humor as possible.

0.2 What Is the Difference Between Linguistics and Psycholinguistics?

The boundary is fuzzy, but basically, linguistics is about describing languages—their sounds, grammar, the differences between formal and informal language, and many other properties that we look at in Chapter 1. (Incidentally, Chapter 1 puts more emphasis on phonetics, the description of language sounds, than most other short psycholinguistics books do, because sounds are so important in applications like speech-language pathology, teaching literacy, teaching second languages, and computer speech recognition. Speech sounds also get ignored by many psycholinguists and language development researchers, who would rather study written language or take grammatical morphemes like the *-ed* past tense ending as their smallest units. But I've taught phonetics for many years, and I love it.) Linguistics gives us the concepts and vocabulary that we need to describe language problems accurately. It also lets us catalogue the differences and similarities between languages or dialects in ways that don't make (or thinly conceal) value judgments.

PSYCHOLINGUISTICS, in contrast, tries to discover how we manage to actually DO all the things that go into speaking and understanding, reading and writing: How do sound waves hitting your ear become, in less than half a second, your understanding of what another person means? How, in speaking a modest two-second sentence, have you managed to find the dozen or so words that you need to express your meaning out of the tens of thousands of words stored in your mind, put them in the right order so that they make sense, and get them all pronounced clearly enough for your hearer to understand, even though, in order to do this, your tongue and lips had to perform a complicated ballet involving hundreds of individual instructions? Psycholinguistics uses experiments and intense laboratory observations to break into these incredibly fast, highly skilled language performances, and to study the accumulation of the experiences that have built up those unconscious skills over our lifetimes. It also uses the current findings of NEUROLINGUISTICS about how language is remembered and deployed by our brains; that is the subject of Chapter 2.

0.3 What's an Example of a Psycholinguistic Explanation of a Language Problem?

We haven't yet developed our promised tools, so I can't give you a completely worked out example of a psycholinguistic explanation of a language problem; but here's a sketch of one (which I hope you haven't run into personally). Imagine that your new sweetheart, Chris, suggests that the two of you eat dinner at a restaurant that you used to go to with your previous partner, Sam, and you accidentally say, *Sure, Sam, I'd love to!* How did the wrong name get in there—and furthermore, how did it get into the exact place in the sentence where a name belongs, instead of perhaps replacing the verb, making you say, *Sure, Chris, I'd sam to?* And why was it "Sam" rather than the name of someone else, and why was it a personal first name rather than any of the dozens of categories of words that are stored in our minds?

Chris naturally feels that you made this mistake because you still have Sam on your mind as a romantic partner. That's possible, but it doesn't have to be true. However, even an anxious or angry Chris knows that you haven't confused the *people*; you've just confused their *names*. This makes one of our first psycholinguistic points: Words (including names) are not the same mental objects as the things or people they refer to. Yes, the word and the person or thing that it refers to are usually closely connected in your mind. However, the connection between them can be weak (maybe you just met the person at a party) or nonexistent (you never heard the name in the first place). That's fairly obvious. What is less obvious is that the name of someone you know can come into your conscious mind without thinking of the person consciously—or that the name can come to awareness first, dragging the concept of the person behind it. In Chapter 3, we present some evidence supporting these ideas.

A psycholinguistic explanation of a "wrong name" error has to start from two basic theories: first, a *general psychological theory* of how information is stored in your mind and retrieved when you need it and, second, a *specific psycholinguistic theory* of how sentences are formed in your head before they are spoken, and how the words in those sentences get put in the right order and given the right accent to convey what you meant by saying them.

0.4 The Plan of This Book

After we introduce language in Chapter 1 and the brain in Chapter 2, we present evidence in Chapter 3 that the concepts in our minds are linked by a huge and mostly subconscious network of similarities and information about whether things are close or far apart in real or imagined worlds of space and time. (Even if you hate Sam by now, and even if Chris and Sam are totally different in every way you can think of, they are linked together in your mind because of the similarity in their relationship to you. You knew that; so did Chris.)

In Chapter 4, we present evidence to support the statement that the words in your mind are also linked by a huge and mostly subconscious network that includes not just what they mean and how they sound, but also their grammatical properties—because grammar, like a set of blueprints for construction, is what organizes a sentence and specifies the proper place for each of its words.

Chapter 5 introduces you to experimental studies of psycholinguistics and neurolinguistics, which are necessary when the questions about how language works in our brains can't be answered just by observing errors. Chapter 6 presents the spoken language of people with the rather common and often disabling language disorder called APHASIA, and shows how what we've learned in the first five chapters can help us to understand their problems. Chapter 7 looks at what has been discovered about how children learn to speak their first language, starting from before they are born.

In Chapter 8, we study what our minds do when we are reading, and what that implies for how reading should be taught, and in Chapter 9, we explore some of the similarities and differences between learning a first language and a second language, and why a learner's age affects how quickly and how well they learn a second language. Finally, in Chapter 10, we show how thinking about language and communication psycholinguistically can help in the language classroom and the clinic.

At the ends of chapters, you will find exercises based on clinical and/ or language classroom situations so that you can get practice in applying your new concepts to analyzing real-world language behavior.

The text has a glossary; all words and phrases that are printed like THIS in the text are defined there.

On the CD, there are audio and video materials that will help you get closer to the experience of being an observer or a participant in an experiment, suggestions for further reading, links to useful Web sites, and, for most chapters, an optional "Challenge" section with additional material and exercises for advanced and ambitious readers.

Instructors Note: Because Chapter 1 is so long, it may be broken up into Section 1A and Section 1B, as indicated in its outline. Chapter 2 may be read between Section 1A and Section 1B, but Section 1B is necessary before reading Chapter 3, and Section 1A is necessary before reading Chapter 4. Chapters 1 through 4 are needed for Chapters 5 through 10; 1A is especially important for sections on reading, accents, and spoken language comprehension.

0.5 In Defense of My Writing Style: *Apologia pro stilo suo*

I have written this book in the plainest English (although I'm sure there's still room for improvement). I'm not doing this to be cute or folksy, but on psycholinguistic principles. Understanding a description or an explanation means building a clear mental model of it. Passive voice, nominalizations (like the word *nominalization* itself) instead of clauses with real verbs, and terms that make readers go back to see what they mean (like *the former* and *the latter*) all take extra work for our brains to process. That work slows them down when they are trying to figure out what the writer means so that they can build their mental models.

Real or realistic examples also are essential for building a clear mental model of what the writer is trying to communicate; names and a few exclamation points keep readers alert and focused. Personal pronouns also encourage sharper mental model building, I think; I don't have hard evidence for that claim, but there are plenty of hints in the mental-model and **MIRROR NEURON** literature that we understand what others are doing by subconsciously imagining doing something of the sort ourselves. By saying *The tip of your tongue* instead of *The tip of the tongue*, I'm trying to jump-start that process.

Letting readers know what a barrage of new information is good for gives them not only a reason to care about learning it, but a way to remember it when the time to use it finally arrives. We don't have to teach the "pure" science in a vacuum and then teach its applications separately. And after 40 years in the profession, most of them working in interdisciplinary settings, I find that combining linguistics with its applications invigorates it as well as making it more understandable, because applying any science to the real world challenges its theoretical assumptions and demands accountability.

Unfortunately, the habit of reading and writing in standard disembodied academic style is so deep that some people think it is unscientific and less rigorous to write simple active declarative sentences like *We asked 10 people with aphasia to name these pictures* than *Ten aphasic persons were instructed to label the stimuli.* And someplace we researchers also got the idea that descriptions of research should contain as few references to human beings as possible, as if science were untouched by human hands or minds. But good professional science journalists (and researchers who write well) know that science is created by people, even if a few of them hide behind wizards' masks, and that people who are learning science deserve to know where knowledge comes from, so that they don't feel betrayed when new discoveries upset what they learned previously.

If you're not sure about all this yet, I hope you will be by the time you're a few chapters into this book.

Acknowledgments

Many colleagues, students, and other friends have contributed to this book, providing materials, suggesting resources, and giving feedback on various chapters; others have simply listened to my ideas and shared theirs with me. I especially thank Bruce Kawin, who read and edited the whole book, giving me unfailing encouragement; Ray Kent and Audrey L. Holland, who gave me feedback on chapter after chapter; and, in alphabetical order, Mary Beckman, Giulia Bencini, Chuck Bigelow, Suzanne Boyce, Carolyn J. Buck-Gengler, Robin Smith Chapman, Jill Duffield, Susan Fischer, Julia Fisher, Michael Flahive, Barbara Fox, Francis Ganong, Jean Berko Gleason, Harold Gray, Sarah Hawkins, Alice Healy, Pui Fong Kan, Bill Labov, Vicky Lai, Brian MacWhinney, David McNeill, Stephanie Meissner (my editor at Plural, who helped materially with the illustrations), Laura Michaelis-Cumming, Brett Miller, Kevin Munhall, Bhuvana Narasimhan, Joe Perkell, Ann Peters, Carol Pfaff, Gail Ramsberger, Joe Redish, Joe Salvucci, Rebecca Scarborough, Isla Schanuel (who wrote the code for the CD), Larry Shriberg, Ronnie Silber, Ken Stevens, Will Styler (who engineered the recordings for the CD), Hiromi Sumiya, Maria Thomas-Ruzic, Walter Taylor, Ron Tikofsky, João Veloso, Glenys Waldman, Dick Wexelblat, Doug Whalen, and Arthur Wingfield.

Much of what I have learned outside my own fields has come from participating in interdisciplinary courses, research groups, and seminars at the University of Colorado and abroad; for those opportunities at home, I would like to thank Tim Curran, Al Kim, Walter Kintsch, Tom Landauer, Clayton Lewis, Jim Martin, Dick Olson, Barbara Wise, and also Marie Banich, Director of the Institute for Cognitive Science; elsewhere (within the last 15 years), Merrill Garrett and Audrey Holland at the University of Arizona, Joan Bybee at the University of New Mexico, Jared Bernstein of Ordinate Corporation in Menlo Park, Matti Laine and Jussi Niemi in Finland, Leonor Scliar Cabral and Ana Cláudia Souza in Brazil, Xiaoxiang Sophy Chen and Qingguo Jimmy Li in Hunan, Ovid Tzeng and Daisy Hung in Taiwan, Yumiko Tanaka Welty in Japan, and all the people who participated in my classes and presentations. Some of my doctoral students led me into new areas of psycholinguistics and neurolinguistics which are now reflected in this book, notably Debra Biasca, Holly Krech Thomas, and Valerie Wallace. I am also grateful to the children I have studied (my own and Jacob Hankamer), and to many people with aphasia, including my late co-author and dear friend Shirley Kleinman and her family, for countless examples of aphasia and how to live with it.

Thanks also to my life-support system: the friends, tenants, neighbors, and graduate students who have looked after me since 2006; they include most of the people I already thanked above. Special gratitude to my family (all of you—born, step, adopted, in-law, and out-law), Chris Tanz, Shirley Brice Heath, Jane Hill, Ginny Redish, Geri Walther and her family, Kris Holmes, Chuck Bigelow, Eve Sweetser, Judy Aissen, Dan Jurafsky, Laurel Rodd, Martha, Neil, and Derek Palmer, Martha Polson, Liz and Dave Abbott, Ingrid and Ted Becher, Will Vanderveer, Chelsea Porter, Kailin Yong, Ellen Yong, Takanori, Caitlin, and Kiryu Sugishita, Isla Schanuel, Leonardo Alves-Soares, Miranda Wilson, Sarah Wood, George Figgs, Jena Hwang, Jenny Davis, Brent Nicholas, Roy Warnock, Alison Hilger, Scott Duffield, Mike Thomas, Jeff Stebbins, Zoe Tribur, Jule Gómez de García, Patrick Juola, and the rest of the Fellowship of the Wug Mug (you know who you are), and of course the ladies from the warm-water pool at Mapleton Rehab Hospital, Allie Cash and Merry Sue Clark. And my Fb friends who kept cheering each bit of progress that I posted, especially Karen Emmorey and Natasha Warner.

The invitation to write this book came as a lovely gift in a time of grief; I had lost my beloved husband and colleague of 20 years, the linguist William Bright, in October 2006. The chance of creating a work that would say to a larger world what I had been teaching in classes, workshops, and lectures has been one of the main things that has kept me going, but actually starting to write turned out to be hard. I thank the late Dr. Sadanand Singh, Stephanie Meissner, and everyone at Plural Publishing for their patience; also Audrey Holland for impatiently nipping at my heels. This book would not have come into existence without her.

For Bruce, Audrey, and the Fellowship of the Wug Mug

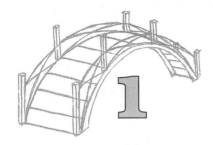

Basic Linguistics: How to Describe Language Use and Language Knowledge

1.10.1 Some important differences
between languages
1.10.2 Being similar and being related

1A. INTRODUCTION, PHONETICS, AND PHONOLOGY

1.0 Terminology: Strategy for Learning About Language

As adults, we usually take our first language for granted, and the effort of describing it in detail seems like a waste of time. If you already know how to speak English, what's the good in worrying about whether *on* is a preposition or an adverb, or whether *hot dog* (the sausage) is one word or two?

On the other hand, if you've had some experience with language problems like the ones discussed in the Introduction—for example, if you've tried to explain to someone who is not a native speaker of English why you say *on the 20th of February* but *on 20th Street* (rather than *on **the** 20th Street*), or if you've tried to help an elderly friend who has had a stroke find a needed word—you might feel that language is so hopelessly complicated that it's not possible to learn a useful amount about how it works in a reasonable amount of time. And if you've taken an ordinary linguistics course, it might have seemed very far removed from what you would need for language teaching, international Web page design, or speech-language therapy.

The terminology may have been a barrier, too. In this book, I will keep linking the materials on linguistics and psycholinguistics to examples of real-world language problems that they can help us understand. Our basic strategy for dealing with technical terms is to define terms as we need them for describing real or realistic examples of language problems: normal slips of the tongue, children's errors, second language learners' errors, aphasic errors, and so on. We'll start by introducing basic linguistic terms in this chapter because they are key tools for describing language as it is produced by skilled as well as unskilled or disabled speakers and hearers. (Most of the ideas here are also applicable to signed languages.) The terms that are presented in BOLDFACE SMALL CAPITALS are also defined in the Glossary. If you run into any technical term that you're not sure of, check the Glossary or the Index.

1.1 Divide and (More or Less) Conquer: Levels of Spoken Language

The usual way to organize language for study is by the size of the various kinds of pieces it can be divided into, from small to large; the small units are the low-level ones. The small units that we'll start with are the sounds that make up spoken words, or the letters that make up written ones. Then we'll go on to bigger units: WORDS, PHRASES, SENTENCES, and PARAGRAPHS (for written language) or CONVERSATIONAL TURNS (for spoken language).

As you've just noticed, some of these terms (word, phrase, sentence) are used for both written and spoken language, but others can only be used for describing writing, or only for describing speaking. In particular, people don't speak in "letters," so we will talk about people speaking in *sounds*, not letters. One reason for doing this is that the letters of the English alphabet are a poor tool for describing any kind of speech, so it's important to start thinking in terms of sounds (and to stop thinking in terms of letters) as soon as possible; section 1.2.1 will get you started in that direction. Another reason is that speech sounds are related to each other like nodes in a network; they aren't just items in a list. Understanding these relationships among speech sounds is the key to understanding, for example, why people have foreign accents and why children make characteristic errors in learning to speak and to read. More about that soon, in section 1.2.4.

Our list of levels of language above skipped some important items. SYLLABLES in spoken language, SYLLABARY symbols in Japanese and several other written languages, and CHARACTERS in written Chinese and Japanese are some that you may have thought of. Another important level for language teaching and error analysis is one that doesn't have a common name; it's the one involved in errors like *I was get inning the car*. Here, it looks like the speaker has treated the construction *get in* as if it were the verb, right? The whole phrase *get in* seems to have slipped into a SLOT where just the verb *get* should have gone, just before the *-ing* ending. We'll get to these errors in Chapter 4.

1.2 The Level of Speech Sounds: The Sounds of Spoken Words

People who are interested in language rarely start out with an interest in the level of SPEECH SOUNDS, also called the PHONETIC level, because it seems both so mechanical and so detailed. But it's "where the rubber meets the road": if someone's speech articulation is poor, or if they can't distinguish the sounds of speech reliably, it doesn't matter how brilliant they are; they are cut out of full participation in spoken conversation. Speech is our basic tool for connecting with friends and family, except in Deaf communities that use a signed language fluently. Because social isolation is deadly for mental and even physical health, the quality of speech matters.

Phonetics is often seen as a difficult subject for two reasons: You are supposed to learn to make and hear unfamiliar speech sounds, and you have to learn a new writing system, the **INTERNATIONAL PHONETIC ALPHABET (IPA)**, in order to write down and discuss even the sounds of languages that you know. Learning the IPA is mostly a matter of practice. If you've ever studied a spoken language other than your native one and learned how to write and pronounce it more or less correctly, you have already done the same kind of thing: learning that, for example, in French, the letter combination *eau* is pronounced close to American *oh*, but without pulling your lips into a *w* at the end of it the way Americans do. Or learning that in Russian, the letter Я is pronounced *ya*. But learning to make and hear unfamiliar speech sounds correctly can indeed be a real challenge. Understanding why this is hard will lead us from linguistics to psycholinguistics, and also (in Chapter 7) to the study of how speech sound perception develops in young children.

1.2.1 What's wrong with letters for describing speech sounds?

1.2.1.1 Inconsistency of English spelling

As you know, the English spelling system is not user friendly. Here's an example to make this point, the first 10 lines of a comic poem called "The Chaos."

The Chaos, Lines 1–10

Gerard Nolst Trenité   (Netherlands, 1870-1946)

   1 Dearest creature in creation,

   2 Study English pronunciation.

   3 I will teach you in my verse

   4 Sounds like corpse, corps, horse, and worse.

   5 I will keep you, Suzy, busy,

     6   Make your head with heat grow dizzy.

     7   Tear in eye, your dress will tear.

     8   So shall I! Oh hear my prayer.

     9   Just compare heart, beard, and heard,

    10   Dies and diet, lord and word,

Spelling is a nationally televised competitive sport in English because the same sound can be spelled by different letters. (Compare *busy* and *dizzy* in lines 5 and 6; *tear* meaning "rip" and *prayer* in lines 7 and 8.) Plus, one letter or combination of letters can spell different sounds. (Compare *tear* "teardrop" and *tear* "rip" in line 7; *horse* and *worse* in line 4.) A good first exercise in thinking phonetically is to compile all the examples of these two types of inconsistency in the 10 lines of the poem.

    Because English letters are so bad at matching sounds, using letters as names for sounds constantly requires saying "i as in *smile*" or "long i." This is good enough for school, but it is too clumsy for professional language work. For example, if you need to organize sets of words by their length (in number of sounds) or by complexity of pronunciation, which is important for creating testing and teaching materials for oral language, it is nasty work when *Joe* looks just as long as *Zoe* (*zoh-ee*), and both of them look much shorter than *though* or *dough*. And if you (or your students) are going to teach reading to children or adults, you need to be able to think separately about the sounds and the letters in a word, so that you have a clearly organized mental picture of which words (or parts of words) new readers can safely be asked to sound out, and which ones they will have to learn with less help from PHONICS. If you don't have practice in thinking in terms of sounds, it is quite easy to let the letters in a word persuade you that you pronounce things the way they are written, even when you don't; for example, you may be fooled by the spelling into thinking that the first vowel in *pretty* is a "short e." (What is it? Does *pretty* rhyme with *Betty* or with *bitty*?) If your students are not native speakers of your language, or speak a very different dialect of your language, you also need to be able to think about how the words of your language sound to them (see Exercise 1.1, and Chapter 8, section 8.4.).

1.2.1.2 Coarticulation: Anticipating and continuing each speech sound

When we speak, we don't make sounds one at a time, the way we type or write letters of the alphabet. We give information about what the upcoming sounds are going to be well before we actually get to them (the way prizefighters may "telegraph" their upcoming moves), and other information may linger well after we feel that a sound has been made. Lay your fingers lightly on your mouth; say first *steel* and then *stool*. You may be able to feel your lips spreading sideways toward the smiling shape needed for the *ee* as early as the beginning of the *s* in *steel*, and you will almost certainly feel them pushing outward toward the kissing shape needed for the *oo* of *stool* before you make the *t* sound. This kind of articulatory anticipation (and lingering; the L sounds in these two words are also made with different mouth shapes) is called COARTICULATION. Using just the right amount of coarticulation at the right time for each speech style and speaking rate in a native speaker's repertory is essential for normal-sounding fluent speech. Unsurprisingly, given the huge number of combinations of possible sound sequences, styles, and speech rates, simulating normal coarticulation is one of the huge problems for getting computer speech to sound human and for getting animated movie speech to look real, although there are now phonetically correct simulations of mouth movements that are used in computer-assisted speech therapy; links to some sites are on your CD under Materials for Chapter 1.

1.2.1.3 Phonotactics: Sound sequence patterns

Finally, we speakers can't make sounds in any order that we please, although we can write letters in any old order. English speakers struggle with Russian words like *lba* "of the forehead," *rta* "of the mouth," and *vzglyad* "glance." Every language has its own permitted and disallowed sequences of sounds, and makes its own demands that children and adult learners must master. English allows words to begin with the sounds *st*, but you probably know that Spanish and Portuguese don't, and that German doesn't either; in German, this sequence of letters is pronounced as what we have to write in English as *sht*. These PHONOTACTIC (sound sequencing) restrictions seem understandable if putting several consonants in a row is somehow inherently difficult (and it probably is), but many phonotactic constraints have no such explanation. For example, English speakers have a hard time pronouncing the perfectly ordinary sound of *e* in *pet* when it's at the end of a word, as in the name of the Japanese drink *sake* (*sah-keh* is about as close as I can get to spelling it for you at this point).

So there are three major reasons to get away from the English alphabet: its unreliability, the fact that speech sounds are not actually produced discretely one after another, and the fact that producing new sequences of sounds is just as much a challenge as mastering new individual sounds. A fourth reason, of course, is that English is just one of the many languages in the world that use the Roman alphabet. And as you know if you have studied almost any other spoken language, we use it in a very peculiar way, because the pronunciation of English changed drastically in the 1400s, long after the language began to be written, and the spelling didn't change along with the pronunciation.

The unreliability problem is solved fairly well by using a more reliable alphabet, the **INTERNATIONAL PHONETIC ALPHABET (IPA)**, which will be introduced in the next sections of this chapter; this solves the fourth problem as well, because the IPA is not based on the way English uses the alphabet. This simple change of notation will not solve the problems of dealing with coarticulation and phonotactics, but we will keep them in mind every time that we discuss the challenges of learning pronunciation or analyzing the speech sounds that novice and skilled speakers really make.

1.2.2 How speech sounds are made: The vocal tract

Here are two pictures of the vocal tract in cross-section. The first (Figure 1.1A) shows clearly where we have bones (spongy-looking in cross-section), cartilage (black), and the shaded hollows of our nasal passage, mouth, and some of our sinuses; it will help you visualize the structure of your head and how the cartilage at the back of your mouth (labeled "soft palate") hangs down, so that air can flow between your lungs and your nostrils when you are breathing normally through your nose, with your mouth closed.

The second picture (Figure 1.1B) is a more standard two-dimensional diagram that focuses on the parts of our mouth (aka oral cavity) that we use to make speech sounds. If you look carefully, you'll see that the velum in this one is in a different position: it's raised, blocking off the connection between your pharynx and your nasal passage, so that air can't get out through your nose. This is the position of your velum when you make most (but not all!) speech sounds; more about that soon. Materials for Chapter 1 on your CD has color images of these figures.

You'll need to learn the names of the parts of the vocal tract, because they are used to describe speech sounds in terms of how they are made. Pure memorization, so just do it and get it out of the way; there's an unlabeled diagram in Materials for Chapter 1 on your CD, so you can print out and fill in the labels. If you do that a few times, you should be fine. Watch the spelling and pronunciation of the anatomic words listed below; especially, don't confuse the alveolar ridge and the velum, which unfortunately sound like they are related words (they aren't). To help you remember and be comfortable with the new terms, which were perfectly ordinary words

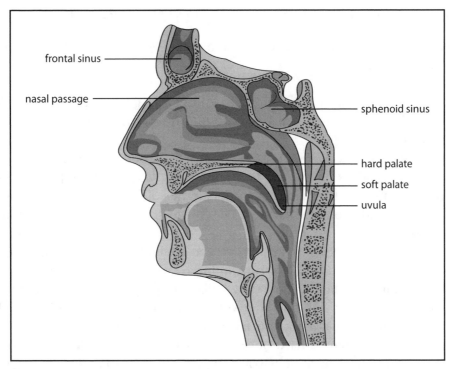

A

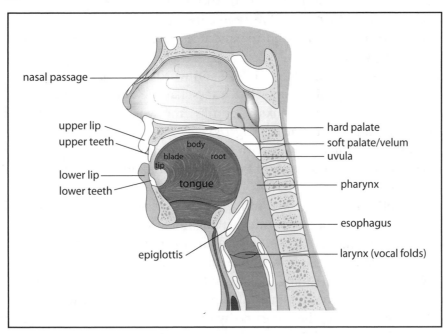

B

Figure 1.1. A. Vocal tract; soft palate (velum) lowered to let airflow in and out through the nose. **B.** Vocal tract, velum (soft palate) raised to block airflow through the nose. (Images adapted from Shutterstock®. All rights reserved.)

in ancient Greek and classical Latin, I'm giving you some of their original meanings, too.

ALVEOLAR RIDGE (al–VEE-o-lar) [æl.ˈvi.o.lɝ], the gum ridge. Alveolus is Latin for "little pocket," in this case referring to the sockets that hold your teeth.

PALATE (PAL-et, [ˈpælət], the same as *pallet*), the roof of your mouth. (Linguists and phoneticians use *palate* to mean just the bony part of the roof of your mouth, and *velum* to mean the soft part behind that—look at the definition of *velum* and you'll see why that's the convenient thing to do.)

VELUM (VEE-lum) [ˈvi.ləm], also called the **SOFT PALATE** as in Figure 1.1A. Velum is from a Latin word meaning a sail or other hanging fabric, because it does start to hang down, like a tarp, forming the back of the roof of your mouth. To find your velum, run the tip of your tongue back along your palate, curling it as far back as you can. The front two-thirds or so of the palate is hard bone—this part is called the **HARD PALATE**. But just about as far back as you can get with your tongue, you may be able to feel that the roof of your mouth is softer—it's now made of cartilage instead of bone. We won't use the term **SOFT PALATE** in this book, because *velum* is shorter, and it has a convenient corresponding adjective, **VELAR**.

UVULA (YOU-view-luh) [ˈju.vju.lə], a Latin word meaning "little grape," the plump little bulge that hangs like a tassel at the end of the velum.

LARYNX (LARR [as in Larry]-inks) [ˈlær.ɪŋks], the "voice box" (adjective form *laryngeal*; inflamed form *laryngitis*).

PHARYNX (FARR-inks; rhymes with larynx) [ˈfær.ɪŋks], the air tube leading from the lungs to the back of both the mouth and the nose.

We'll also need to be able to talk about parts of your tongue in order to describe some speech sound articulations accurately: from front to back, we'll distinguish the tongue **TIP**, **BLADE**, **BACK**, and **ROOT**. Figure 1.2 is a close-up diagram to show where those regions are.

When you're breathing quietly, airflow through your whole vocal tract is essentially noiseless; the airflow is like a stream flowing without obstructions. A stream becomes noisy when the flow becomes turbulent, for example, when it has to go over rocks or through a narrow channel; many speech sounds involve a similar kind of turbulent flow of air. And the vocal tract has another kind of sound generator that you won't find in a stream channel: a gadget that can generate a musical sound as well as a noisy sound.

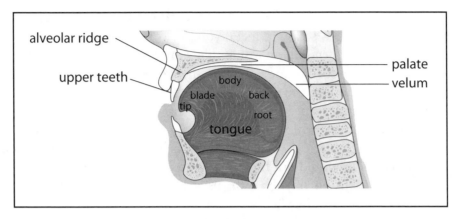

Figure 1.2. Mouth close-up. (Image adapted from Shutterstock®. All rights reserved.)

A Note About Sound Waves

Musical sounds—for example, singing and humming as well as the sounds of melodic instruments—are made when your ear is struck by sound waves that have regular, repeating patterns. Musical sounds from your voice and from almost all instruments have many tones, not just one: above the basic pitch, there are higher tones called **HARMONICS** in acoustic analysis. Noisy sounds—for example, hisses, bangs, and pops—are made by soundwaves that have irregular, nonrepeating patterns, which don't have harmonics. Examples of these two kinds of sound waves, with graphs of the corresponding air pressure variations, are on your CD in Materials for Chapter 1; they are the speech sounds "mmm" and "sss."

1.2.2.1 The larynx: Voice pitch and voice quality

Your larynx is the only source for the musical sound you make when you hum or when you sing a vowel sound (and some consonant sounds, as in the syllables *ma* and *la*). If you've got a good singing voice, your larynx can produce very regular-looking sound waves. If you tend to croak and creak, as I do, it's because your vocal folds tend to vibrate irregularly. The outside of your larynx is easy to feel if you put your fingers lightly on your throat. But it's what is going on inside that's important. Inside your larynx are two flaps of tissue, properly called the **VOCAL FOLDS** (they are *not* cords, so we will not use the more common term). When someone's voice becomes really unpleasant to listen to, or is badly matched to their social role—a breathy "baby" voice in a woman running for public office, or a way of using voice pitch that sounds too masculine in a newly transgendered woman who would not be safe advertising her past life as a man— voice therapy focusing on how she uses her vocal folds can save her career, or possibly even her life.

The opening between the vocal folds has its own name: the **GLOTTIS**. The glottal opening can be widened, narrowed, or shut tight, like the opening between your two lips. Figure 1.3A shows the vocal folds, taken peering down someone's throat; the glottis is open in the left-hand picture, and almost but not quite closed in the right-hand picture (Figure 1.3B). The back of the person's neck would be at the top of these pictures. The tube that you can see below the vocal folds when they are held apart is the trachea ("wind-pipe"); it's going down toward the person's lungs.

The sound between the two vowels of *uh-oh* is made by closing your glottis tightly, so that no air can get from your lungs into your mouth. Sensibly, it is called a **GLOTTAL STOP**. Try holding that middle sound (which English has no letter for), and you'll feel that the airflow is completely choked off. In fact, a glottal stop is a silence, and not a sound at all. In the IPA, glottal stop is written using a question mark without the dot under it: [ʔ]. (The

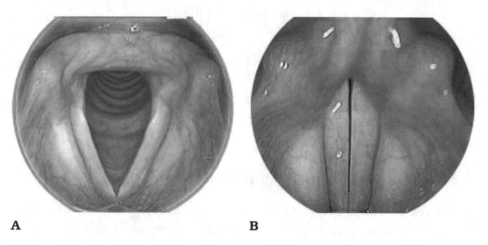

A   **B**

Figure 1.3. A. Vocal folds apart. **B.** Vocal folds together. (Both from *The Vocal Instrument* by S. L. Radionoff, p. 104). Copyright © 2008 Plural Publishing, Inc. All rights reserved. Used with permission.)

square brackets around IPA symbols are to make clear that we are refer-ring to speech sounds, not to letters in the English or another alphabet.)

In some languages, the glottal stop functions like any other conso-nant, for example, in Hawai'ian (that's what the apostrophe between the two i's means). In the Roman type font used in the islands, it's actually written with a backward apostrophe, like this: *Hawaiʻian*.

When your vocal folds are held just the right distance apart—more or less as shown in Figure 1.3B—and air from your lungs is pushed through the glottal opening between them at the right speed, the vocal folds will vibrate just the way your lips do when you make a "raspberry," only much faster. There's a link to a video of vocal fold vibration on your CD in the Materials for Chapter 1 folder.

For each vibration, the air blows the vocal folds a little farther apart; then they fall back loosely together, and are immediately blown apart again as the airflow continues. A deep male voice might have about 80 of these blow-open-and-let-lightly-close-glottis events (called **GLOTTAL PULSES**) in one second. A faster rate of vibration produces a voice pitch that's higher on the musical scale, and a screeching small child's vocal folds might have 800 vibrations per second or more. (Orchestras usually tune to the note *A* at 440 vibrations/second; every octave is a doubling of vibration rate [also called the **FREQUENCY**], so the next higher A is 880 vibrations/second.) Vocal fold vibration, often called **VOICING**, happens during almost all Eng-lish vowels and many of the consonants; the "mmm" that you heard and saw graphed on your CD is voiced, but the "sss" is not.

1.2.2.2 The mouth: Articulated speech sounds

All four of the consonants [p], [t], [k], and [ʔ] are silences, so how do hearers know which one has been said? Make each sound by itself—for example, say just [p], not *puh*. A good way to do this is to say a syllable like *ip*. When you feel that you are into the [p], hold onto the closure part of the sound as long as you can. Feel and listen to what's happening. You'll find, in fact, that there is nothing to hear; and, furthermore, that you can't breathe dur-ing the actual period of silence.

All four of these sounds, reasonably, are called **STOPS** because the air that's coming from your lungs is stopped before it gets out of your mouth (which is why you couldn't breath during the [p]). But as you have discov-ered, the place where the stoppage occurs is different for each one. We can tell these sounds apart because we can hear their coarticulation with the sounds that come before and/or after them; that is, how the shape of your mouth or the nature of your vocal fold vibration changes (or fails to) as you move into and out of the closure itself.

[ʔ] chokes off the air when you hold your vocal folds tightly together, closing your glottis. When you close your glottis, the vocal folds keep the air from your lungs from getting through your larynx, so it doesn't get to your mouth at all. Closing your glottis doesn't change the shape of your mouth or your pharynx, so the coarticulation that tells your hearer that this particular silence was made by closing your glottis tightly comes from slowing down the vocal fold vibrations as you close down your glottis, and starting them up quite sharply as you let it blow open again.

[p] is the easiest of these four speech sounds to see: air from your lungs gets all the way to your tightly closed lips, and is blocked there, so it's called a **LABIAL** stop. Visualizing your mouth as a hollow place with a complicated shape—to be precise, visualizing the oral cavity, as it looks in Figure 1.1A—becomes really useful now: we can say that we hear the difference between [p], [t], and [k] because we hear the effect of the different ways each of them changes the shape of the oral cavity. If your hearer can't see you, she can still tell that you are making a [p] because closing your lips changes the shape of the air cavity in your mouth just the way a "wa-wa" mute changes the shape of the air cavity in a trumpet. We'll talk about how this and other **COARTICULATIONS** work in section 1.2.3.

[t] is harder to see, but almost as easy to feel: your tongue is making tight contact all around the inside of your upper and/or lower gum ridges, from behind your front teeth to inside your molars. In particular, the **BLADE** of your tongue—the part of your tongue just behind the very tip—is touching the alveolar ridge behind your front teeth; the tip of your tongue is probably in contact with those teeth, but it might be on the alveolar ridge a bit behind them. (Look at Figure 1.2 to check the where your tongue blade and alveolar ridge are.) English [t] is called an **ALVEOLAR** stop; but in making Spanish, French, and Italian [t] the tongue has much less all-around contact with the upper alveolar ridge and definitely touches the back of the upper front teeth, so it is a **DENTAL** stop in those languages and many others.

[k] may be harder to feel; usually, the whole back half of the tongue humps up and touches the velum, and the sides of this hump touch your upper molars to complete sealing off your airflow. (You might want to re-read the information about how to find your velum.) [k] is called a **VELAR STOP**. Try feeling this contact point for the velar stops in the words *book* and *coo.* The exact position of [k] is a little different; it depends on what vowels are next to the [k]. Try saying *beak* and then *book,* holding onto the [k] each time, and feeling where your tongue hits the roof of your mouth—if you can't feel a difference with these two words, try *key* and *coo.* Where your tongue hits for *beak* and *key,* which have the *ee* vowel (IPA symbol [i], as in *pizza*) is probably on your hard palate, in front of the velum, because the [i] is made with your tongue further front than any other English vowel. But we don't have to worry about that yet.

Lips, alveolar ridge, velum, and glottis are the four PLACES OF ARTICU-
LATION for English stops—that is, the points where the vocal tract is closed
off. [b], [d], and [g] are made at essentially the same places as [p], [t], and
[k]—they are considered to be the three VOICED (ORAL) STOPS of English,
because they do have more vocal fold vibration connected with them than
the corresponding totally VOICELESS STOPS [p], [t], and [k] do. But there
are some complications in the details of the way that these three pairs of
sounds [p-b, t-d, k-g] contrast with each other, which we'll talk about in
section 1.2.3.

For another class of sounds, the friction sounds or FRICATIVES, the
vocal tract isn't closed off, but instead narrowed just enough to produce
turbulent, noisy airflow, just as when a river pours through a narrow
gorge. So the fricatives bring us another sound source to think about:
airstream friction. English has eight fricatives. Four of them, including [f]
and [s], are made by friction alone—these are the VOICELESS FRICATIVES.
The other four, the VOICED FRICATIVES, including [v] and [z], are made at
the same places of articulation as the first four, but with vocal fold vibration happening at the same time as the friction noise. Make these four
sounds—hold each one as long as you can—and feel what's happening in
your mouth. Also, press your finger lightly on the your throat where your
larynx is, and switch back and forth between saying [fff] and [vvv] or [sss]
and [zzz]; you should be able to feel the vocal fold vibration or at least
some increase in laryngeal tension while you are making the voiced fricatives, but there's no larynx action during the voiceless ones.

The place of articulation for fricatives (and other sounds where the
vocal tract isn't closed off) is defined as the place where the vocal tract is
narrowest; for fricatives, that's where the airflow is fastest, most turbulent,
and so makes the most noise. The fricatives [s] and [z] have their narrowest place just about where [t] and [d] have the front part of their contact,
at the alveolar ridge, so they are called alveolar fricatives.

The other three pairs of fricatives are made at three new places of
articulation. [f] and [v] are more or less labial, but they really only use the
lower lip; if you watch yourself say [p] and [f] in a mirror and feel yourself
switch between them, you'll see that when you say [f], you pull your lower
lip back so that the narrowest place in the airstream is between your
lower lip and your upper teeth. When we need the details, we say that [f] is
a LABIODENTAL fricative, but when we can afford to speak loosely, it's just
referred to as a labial fricative—a voiceless one, of course. [v] is made the
same way, with voicing added, as you noticed earlier when you were switching between [f] and [v]. If you don't learn Spanish until after childhood,
one of the Anglo accent problems you'll have to overcome is the habit of
making a labiodental [v] (whether the Spanish word is spelled with *b* as
in *Cuba* or *v* as in *vaca*), because in Spanish, this sound is a true BILABIAL

(two-lipped) voiced fricative: the narrowest place in your airstream has to be between your lips. As you see, in this case (and many others), comparison of pronunciation across languages is a place where the details matter. In IPA, the voiceless bilabial fricative is spelled with the Greek letter phi, [ɸ], and the voiced one with the Greek letter beta, [β].

What about the other four English fricatives? The four fricative sounds we've discussed so far have the same (single) symbol in IPA as they have in English spelling, but I've delayed introducing the other four because their IPA symbols are probably new to you. The first one of them is easy enough: the sound spelled "sh" in English is represented in IPA by the symbol ʃ, called "esh." If you make the sounds [sssʃʃʃsssʃʃʃ], you can feel the blade of your tongue sliding back to make the [ʃʃʃ] and front again for the [sss]. The narrowest place in the airstream for the fricative [ʃ] is at the front of your hard palate where it starts to slope down into the alveolar ridge, so this place of articulation for this sound is usually called ALVEOPALATAL. But on some phonetics Web sites, it's called POSTALVEOLAR, and you may also see the terms "palatoalveolar" and "prepalatal." If you're not sure you can feel this place, try saying [ʃ] and then, without moving any part of your mouth, breathing in; the cool spots on your tongue and the roof of your mouth are where the airflow is fastest, so that must be where the airstream is narrowest.

The voiced counterpart for [ʃ] is the fricative in the middle of the words *pleasure* ['plɛʒr], *treasure* ['trɛʒr], or at the beginning of Chinese family names like *Zhong*. In IPA it's [ʒ], called "ezh." By the way, the IPA vowel symbol [ɛ] that I've just used stands for the vowel of *red*; also, you may have noticed that IPA puts the accent mark ['] at the beginning of the stressed syllables of a word rather than over its vowel. (If you speak a Southern, New England, or urban New York variety of English, you probably don't have an [r] as the second syllable of *pleasure* or *treasure*; instead, you probably have almost the same vowel as you do in the second syllable of *Martha*, which is written with the symbol [ə], called "schwa." Did you notice that this vowel sound is quite different from the one in the first syllable of *Martha*, even though they are both spelled *a*?)

The name *Martha* brings us to the last pair of English fricatives, which are famously hard for children learning English and also for almost all adult learners of English as a second language. This pair can also be a problem for skilled English speakers to think clearly about, because they are spelled the same, with the letter pair *th*. But *th* really does spell two entirely different speech sounds, just as the letter *a* did in *Martha*. One of the sounds is the voiceless fricative in the middle of *Martha,* the beginning of the words *think*, *theater*, and *thigh*, and the end of the nouns *broth*, *bath* and *teeth*. IPA uses the Greek letter theta [θ] for this sound; try saying it by itself, [θθθ].

Its voiced counterpart is in the beginning of the words *this*, *the*, and *thy*, the middle of *brother*, and the end of the verbs *bathe* and *teethe* (as in "The baby's fussy because he's teething" = his new teeth are coming in). In IPA, this voiced fricative is spelled with the Icelandic letter [ð]. Try it by itself, also: say *the* but hold onto the friction sound spelled by the *th* instead of moving on into the vowel. (If you do it for more than few seconds, saying [ððð] will probably tickle your tongue!) You can call this sound "edh"; make sure to pronounce its name [εð] and not [εθ] or [εd]! Listen to and feel the similarities and differences between the two sounds when you say [θθθððð θθθ ððð], as you've done with the other three voiceless/voiced fricative pairs. The position of articulation that [θ] and [ð] share is a new one: your tongue sticks out a little bit between your upper and lower front teeth, and the bottleneck in the airflow is between your tongue and your upper front teeth. Try the breathing-in trick again if you want to feel this really clearly. The usual name for this place of articulation is **INTERDENTAL** (between the teeth), but occasionally you'll see the term "linguadental" (*lingua* is Latin for "tongue"). It's not at all clear why these two sounds are so rare and so difficult—especially when you think about the fact that [ð] is the commonest sound in English!—because it's easy to see and to describe how to say it. However, their sounds are very close to the sounds of [f] and [v] respectively, so maybe it's partly a perception problem—in fact, in some varieties of English, such as Cockney (spoken in parts of London), they have been replaced by [f] and [v]. Also, you have to move your tongue farther front than for any other speech sound, and then keep it just the right distance from your upper teeth so that you make the airstream friction. Counting the places of articulation for English stops and fricatives brings us to a total of seven. From front to back, they are: labial, labiodental, interdental, alveolar, alveopalatal, velar, and glottal. Make sure you know which sounds are made at each place! We'll start to organize them into a chart in section 1.2.3.

An equally hard and rare sound in the other direction (so to speak) is one found in Arabic, a voiceless pharyngeal stop; to make it you have to pull the root of your tongue straight back till you've squeezed your pharynx closed. (They have voiced and voiceless pharyngeal fricatives, too.) If you want to listen to speech sounds not found in English or to make sure that you understand the English sounds correctly, go to http://www.phonetics.ucla.edu/course/chapter1/chapter1.html and click on a symbol; if you do this, you can listen to each sound.

English also has the voiceless/voiced pair of alveopalatal sounds usually spelled *ch* as in *church* and *j* as in *judge*; these sounds are written in IPA as [tʃ] and [dʒ]. They are both hybrid sounds, which is why each one takes two symbols. As you would guess, [tʃ] begins with a voiceless stop—although it's not exactly an alveolar one (you can probably feel the difference between where your tongue starts for saying *twos* as compared to *choose*; for *tease* versus *cheese*, the difference may not be detectable). Then your tongue moves a little away from the back-of-the-gum-ridge position so that [tʃ] ends with the alveopalatal voiceless fricative [ʃ].

The stop [tʃ] begins with is alveopalatal, but alveopalatal stops don't exist by themselves in English. The symbol *t* is pressed into service for the stop part of the sound, instead of making up a whole new symbol. As the *t* is written right next to the [ʃ], there's no confusion, and the combination lets us waffle on the question of whether this should be considered one complex speech sound, as we've introduced it, or as a sequence of two speech sounds. The story for [dʒ] is just the same, except that your vocal folds are vibrating during the [ʒ] and maybe during part of the [d].

1.2.3 Families of speech sounds: Sound features and sound waves

Even though we are only halfway through the English speech sounds at this point (we've done 7 stops, 8 fricatives, and 2 affricates), we've gained tremendous descriptive power. To see this, let's organize what we've learned already, beginning by putting the sounds we've learned into the standard IPA organizational chart (simplified a little, because we're just doing English speech sounds for now).

Like the periodic table of the elements in chemistry or the color wheel in art, a good chart is much more useful than a list like the alphabet, because it shows many of the relationships among its entries. The standard IPA chart for consonants is organized so that the principal places of articulation for consonants go from the front of the mouth to the back of the mouth; sounds that have the same places of articulation are in the same column. From top to bottom, the sounds are arranged in terms of how open the mouth is, which also separates them according to their types of airflow (also called their MANNER OF ARTICULATION). Right now we have only two manners of articulation, but we'll be adding more (Table 1.1A). The row and column labels (bilabial, labiodental, etc.) that we are using to pigeonhole English consonants are called ARTICULATORY FEATURES.

Notice that voiced and voiceless pairs of sounds that have the same place and airflow, like [p] and [b], or [s] and [z], are put in the same box, voiceless first. Affricates, because they are complex segments, having two manners of articulation combined, aren't usually put into the chart, but if you wanted to add them, it would seem sensible to put them in between the stops and the fricatives, like this (Table 1.1B). Now let's put those features to work. For example, suppose we're describing a fairly typical toddler

Table 1.1A. IPA Chart for English Stops and Fricatives

	Bilabial	Labiodental	Interdental	Alveolar	Alveopalatal	Palatal	Velar	Glottal
Stop	p b			t d			k g	ʔ
Fricative		f v	θ ð	s z	ʃ ʒ			

Table 1.1B. Modified IPA Chart for English Stops, Fricatives, and Affricates

	Bilabial	Labiodental	Interdental	Alveolar	Alveopalatal	Palatal	Velar	Glottal
Stop	p b			t d			k g	ʔ
Affricate					tʃ dʒ			
Fricative		f v	θ ð	s z	ʃ ʒ			

who says something like *bat* for both *bad* and *bag*, *tat* for *cat*, *dough* for *go*, and *dawt* for *dog*. Oh, and *tea* for *see*, *Pete* for *piece*, *pit* for *fish*, *dat* for *that*, *do* for *zoo*, *bat-tomb* for *vacuum* (as in "vacuum cleaner"—little kids *hate* that noise and learn the word pretty early), and also for *bathroom*.

Suppose we were still stuck with thinking in terms of letters, and had no way of organizing these changes (and the kid's correct sounds) except alphabetically. For the consonants that we've learned so far, we'd have to say something like: the toddler's *b* is okay; *c* in *piece, cat,* and *vacuum* turns into *t*, *d* is okay, *f* turns into *p*, *g* turns into *t* at the end of a word, but becomes *d* at the beginning of a word; the *h* is left out of *bath*, *th* in *this* turns into a *d*, *p* is okay, *s* turns into *t*, *t* is okay, *v* turns into *b*, and *z* turns into *d*. Hard to make any sense out of that! And do you really think the *s* in the middle of *Susie* will become a *t*?

But assuming that his other words follow the same patterns as the ones I've given you (things are always a bit more complicated with real kids than with the ones in textbook examples; never assume that a few words like this will give you a child's whole system), that whole list of changes in letters boils down to just three changes in sounds: velars are replaced by alveolars; fricatives are replaced by the nearest possible stop; and all final voiced consonants become voiceless. Check it out. What does this set of descriptions predict about how *Susie* will be pronounced?

Now, as for the complications in the voicing process: There are some unexpected details in the timing of when the articulators for a voiced sound like [b] or [v] get close to each other and when the vocal fold vibrations start and stop. And the timing is also dependent on how fast people are speaking, how relaxed they are, the neighboring sounds, and what language they are speaking. We're not going to even try to cover all that here, but the important thing to know is that in English, at the beginnings and ends of phrases, and next to voiceless sounds, these "voiced" sounds may actually lose part or all of their voicing—that is, the vocal folds may not be vibrating during some or even all of the time that your lips are closed for [b] or partly closed for [v]. A lot of what gives us English speakers our "Anglo" accents when we speak other languages is that we carry over these same timing patterns for vocal fold vibration, but each language has its own tiny variations on the way it does vocal fold timing, so these transferred patterns are rarely if ever correct.

If you go to http://www.chass.utoronto.ca/~danhall/phonetics/sammy .html, you can click on descriptions of speech sounds and see the articulation; if you go to http://www.phonetics.ucla.edu/course/chapter1/chapter1 .html and click on a symbol, you can hear each sound. But those sites may be a bit confusing until we get through all of section 1.2. (These links are also on Materials for Chapter 1 on your CD so you can just click on them from there.)

1.2.4 The sonorant sounds and /h/

1.2.4.1 The nasal cavity: Sinus is not just a headache

There's a lot of empty space in the area labeled "nasal cavity" on your vocal tract pictures, and in the sinuses themselves, which are near it (and that's what *sinus* means: a hollow place). (Look at Figures 1.1A and 1.1B again.) The nasal cavity itself is not really empty, though; it contains structures that act like baffles, making the air follow a complex route through the nose, so that there's time en route for it to be filtered and moisturized before it gets to your lungs. If you understand musical instruments, you know what hollow spaces connected to a sound-maker are good for: adding resonance to the sound, which will make at least some of the harmonics (see A Note About Sound Waves on p. 11) louder, and, depending on the material and shape, will make others softer.

People without training in speech science or linguistics tend to describe almost any speech whose sound they dislike as being "nasal," but language professionals can't afford to be so casual with technical terms. A speech sound is NASAL if the passageway between the mouth (aka the ORAL CAVITY) and the nasal cavity is open, as in Figure 1.1A, so that the nose and the sinuses provide a lot of resonance to the sound. It's ORAL (or NON-NASAL) if this passageway is closed, as in Figure 1.1B.

When you looked back at Figures 1.1A and B, you saw that in 1.1B, the velum is raised so that it touches the rear wall of the pharynx; only the uvula hangs down at its end. This is the position for all speech sounds *except* the nasal ones like [m], [n], [ŋ], and the nasal vowels as in French or Portuguese. (Actually, English also has nasal vowels; we'll discuss that in the Challenge section for this chapter on your CD.) In Figure 1.1A, a lot of velum is hanging down, which is the position for normal breathing and for nasal sounds.

Think of the velum as a trapdoor in the ceiling, leading to an attic: Pull down to open the trapdoor, push up to close it. To see how this works, look in a mirror and say a good long /aaa/. No air comes out of your nose when you say this, because the trapdoor is closed, as in Figure 1.1A. You'll see your uvula hanging at the back of your mouth—for the moment, think of it as the rope to a closed trap door. Now make the nasal vowel [ãããã]— if you're not sure how to do this, get a friend who speaks some French to say the preposition *dans* "inside," or else imitate the [aaa/ãããã] example on your CD. If you do it right, some air will come out of your nose—remember, that's what it means for a sound to be nasal. (Wet your finger and hold it right under your nose while you switch between the oral and nasal vowels—you should be able to feel the air flowing over your finger during the nasal one, but not the oral one.) In the mirror, you'll see your uvula move

DOWN when you switch from [aaa] to [ãããã], because you had to *lower* your velum to let air go out of your nose. But it's very hard to feel what the velum is doing—it doesn't seem to have the proper nerves for reporting its movements to our brains in a way that we can become aware of, even though our automatic control of it for breathing, speaking, and swallowing is superb. However, try holding the blade of your tongue tight to your alveolar ridge and saying [dnndnndnn], not letting any air come out of your mouth, but only (during the [n]), out of your nose. You can probably feel the wiggly part of your velum moving, or at least the sense of the air not being able to leave your mouth during the [d] and something at the back of your mouth changing so that it can leave your mouth during the [n].

The best way to describe whether the passageway between your nose and your mouth is open (attic trap door down) or shut (attic trap door up) is to say that the velum is **lowered** for nasal sounds and **raised** for oral sounds. Try to avoid saying that the velum is "open" or "closed," because the velum is the hunk of cartilage that moves to cover or uncover the passageway; it's not the opening itself. This is important because it will help you keep a sharp mental picture of how nasal airflow is controlled. You need that picture to understand many developmental speech problems, what happens to speech sounds when someone has a stuffed-up nose, and some of the historical language changes that give us some peculiar-looking modern language patterns (like why there's a [b] in *remember,* but not in *memory.* (See the Challenges for Chapter 1 on your CD to read about these and other applications of what you've just learned.)

We can add the English nasal consonants very quickly to the IPA chart, now (Table 1.1C). In this new version, there's a nasal row, with labial [m] and alveolar [n] in their appropriate columns—on the voiced side of their boxes, of course, because they are made with vocal fold vibration, as you can feel by putting your finger lightly on your larynx when you hum them: /mmm/, /nnnn/.

What's new here is the velar nasal [ŋ], called "eng" or "angma." Remembering this new symbol is easy, because it's an *n* with a *g* tail. Zeroing in on the sound in your mind may be harder, because in some words *ng* spells [ŋ], but in other words it spells [ŋg]—and there are dialect differences in where that [g] shows up and where it doesn't. Try this: say "drink" slowly, and then do it going all the way through the sound spelled with the letter *n* as if you were going to say the [k] too, but leave the [k] off, and keep making the nasal sound (which you can do because the air will come out of your nose). Feel where the back of your tongue is humped up—it will be way back of the alveolar position for a real [n]. In fact, it's in the same velar position as the [k] which you were about to say, but the movable part of your velum, just behind where your tongue is hitting the

Table 1.1C. IPA Chart for English Stops, Fricatives, Affricates, and Nasals

	Bilabial	*Labiodental*	*Interdental*	*Alveolar*	*Alveopalatal*	*Palatal*	*Velar*	*Glottal*
Stop	p b			t d			k g	ʔ
Affricate					tʃ dʒ			
Fricative		f v	θ ð	s z	ʃ ʒ			
Nasal	m			n			ŋ	

23

roof of your mouth, will be down to let the air out your nose. This velar nasal is the [ŋ]—hold on and hum it, [ŋŋŋŋ]. You make the [k] after it simply by raising the movable part of the velum to seal off your nasal opening—nothing else has to move. Try it slowly: [drɪŋŋŋŋk]. You can switch back and forth between the two velar sounds, [ŋŋŋŋkŋŋŋŋk], and feel your velum's wiggly part go up for the [k] and down for the [ŋ].

1.2.4.2 The semivowels

[Note: you might prefer to do the vowels in section 1.2.4.3 and then come back to the semivowels.] Three of the SEMIVOWEL sounds in IPA, [l], [r], and [w], have approximately the same values that they typically do at the beginnings of words in the English alphabet. The fourth English semivowel is the sound at the beginning of *you*; the International Phonetics Association chose the symbol [j] for this sound, because in quite a few languages of northern Europe (e.g., Dutch, Swedish, German, Finnish), "*y*" is how the letter *j* is pronounced. This can be hard for English speakers to get used to, and some American authors don't go with the IPA at this point. But the major speech pathology and phonetics journals are international, and most textbooks are written for international audiences, so we will use [ju] to spell *you,* and [jɛt] to spell *yet.* (Remember, IPA has [dʒ] for the first sound of *jet* [dʒɛt].) The best way to train yourself to stay with IPA is to practice making phonetic transcriptions and then check them, but it's a big help if you NEVER use *jay* as the name for the IPA symbol [j]. From now on, when you see it in the text, think of the name for the symbol [j] as YOD, which is approximately the name for whatever symbol spells the "*y*" sound in several alphabets, including Hebrew and Arabic.

You've probably figured out that calling the consonants [j] (*yod,* remember!), [l], [r], and [w] "semivowels" implies that they are in some way "in between" vowels and consonants. One of the ways that they are in the middle involves the size of the air channel that you use to make these four sounds. All the consonants in the earlier sections of this chapter involve closing your mouth or glottis, or else narrowing the air channel enough to make airstream friction. But the four semivowels have openings that are too wide to cause friction, though they aren't as wide as the openings for true vowels. (We'll modify that statement later in this section, but it'll do for now.) And like vowels, as we'll see soon, what distinguishes each of these sounds from the others is the way each different tongue shape changes the sound that comes into the pharynx and mouth from the vibrating vocal folds (did you notice that all four of them are voiced?). Another term you'll see a lot for [l] and [r] is the rather poetic descriptive term LIQUIDS, and for [j] and [w], GLIDES. We'll explain that one shortly.

As for their positions of articulation, each of these sounds involves a mouth and pharynx shape that we haven't seen yet (more than one, actually—the shapes for [l] and [r] vary tremendously, depending on where they are in a word and what other sounds are next to them). MRI scans (on your CD) show that there are an amazing number of different tongue positions that will result in saying [r], and each person seems to use several different ones in different contexts. This wasn't known until recently, because it is terribly difficult to feel where your tongue is unless it is touching some other part of your mouth. In [r], [j] (*yod!*), and the vowels, your tongue is mostly arching itself into a complicated shape in the middle of your mouth (there may be a little contact with your molars), and at the same time, your tongue root may move forward or backward to change the shape of your pharynx. For making English [r], a lot of your tongue is raised up through most of the middle of your mouth (Figure 1.4A) and your tongue root may be pulled back, which makes the opening of your

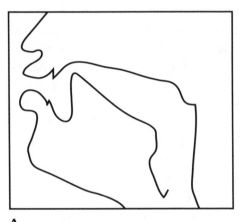

A

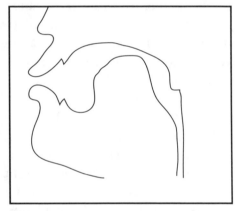

B

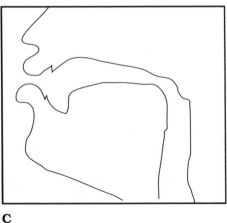

C

Figure 1.4. A. An alveoplatal [r] articulation, tongue root pushed forward. **B.** A bunched, almost velar [r] articulation, tongue root pulled back. (A and B based on MRI scan in Zhou, X., Espy-Wilson, C. Y., Boyce, S., Tiede, M., Holland, C., & Choe, A. (2008). A magnetic resonance imaging-based articulatory and acoustic study of "retroflex" and "bunched" American English /r/. *Journal of the Acoustical Society of America, 123*(6), 4466–4481.) **C.** [w] articulation.

pharynx narrower. Most textbooks ignore the tongue root movement, which is a bit hard to feel, and they choose just one of the possible ORAL (mouth) tongue shapes for [r] to describe. That's why you'll sometimes see that [r] is put in the alveolar column, and sometimes in one of the columns further back in the mouth. When I make an [r], the narrowest part of the air channel is alveopalatal, and that's the column I'll use. This must be a fairly common air channel shape, because a lot of children who sound words out for themselves spell *train* as *chrain.* That makes good sense if the sound at the beginning of *train* is very close to the alveopalatal affricate [tʃ] sound at the beginning of *chain.* Try it yourself and see if *train* and *chrain* are almost identical for you, too. If they are, your [r] is probably alveopalatal.

It takes more than your tongue to make [r], and [w] as well (Figures 1.4B and C). Both of these sounds—[w] more than [r]—require pursing your lips towards a kissing position, as you can see in Figure 1.4 (put your fingers on your lips or look in a mirror to check this out). Making the kissing lip shape is called LIP ROUNDING, and it's also needed for making the vowels [u] as in *clue,* [o] as in *know,* and the sound spelled *oo* in *cook* or *u* in *put,* nowadays written with [ʊ] (the Greek letter upsilon) in IPA. [w] requires pursing your lips and raising the back of your tongue towards the velum at the same time (see Figure 1.4C), so it's sensibly called a LABIOVELAR semivowel, or a labiovelar glide. Because it has two positions of articulation at the same time and would have to go in two columns at once, [w] isn't entered on the official IPA chart, but Table 1.1D shows how we enter it and the other three semivowels. You'll see other unofficial versions, depending on what users are trying to communicate by using an IPA chart, and you can find the current official version on the International Phonetic Association Web site, www.langsci.ucl.ac.uk/ipa/

As for my promised explanation of the term *glide,* as well as an explanation of the PALATAL position for [j] (*yod*), first try these two feel-and-listen exercises:

1. Say *woo* [wu] slowly several times and track what your lips and tongue do. You should be able to tell that each of them moves only a little in moving from [w] to [u]: your lips open a bit wider and the back of your tongue moves down a tiny bit. Now say [wwww] and listen carefully: it should seem to turn into a [u] (as in *true*) even if you don't move your mouth at all! So here's the modification I warned you about: the semivowel [w] can have exactly the same mouth shape as the vowel [u], which means that the air channel for some pronunciations of the semivowel [w] is the same size as the air channel of the semivowel [u].

Table 1.1D. IPA Chart for English Stops, Fricatives, Affricates, Nasals, and Semivowels

	Bilabial	Labiodental	Interdental	Alveolar	Alveopalatal	Palatal	Velar	Glottal
Stop	p b			t d			k g	ʔ
Affricate					tʃ dʒ			
Fricative		f v	θ ð	s z	ʃ ʒ			
Nasal	m			n			ŋ	
Semivowel	(w)			l	r	j	(w)	

2. Do the same thing with *ye* [ji], and then with holding onto the yod by itself. When you say *ye* [ji], you might not have to move your tongue at all—the yod will just seem to turn into an *ee* [i]. Or you may feel small tightening movements at the sides of the back of your tongue. The highest part of your tongue is just below the hard palate when you make [j], which is why the yod is called a palatal glide; it's in pretty much the same position as that front-shifted [k] in *key* that we talked about in the section on velar stops.

So: we can only hear [w] and yod when they are transitions between two sounds or a sound and silence. When they are held, the perception morphs into the perception of *oo* [u] and *ee* [i]! That's an amazing phenomenon, and it also explains why these sounds are called glides: They only seem to exist as transitions between two other speech sounds, or between a speech sound and silence. The near-identity of [w] with *oo* [u] and of yod with *ee* [i] also helps to understand the problems that speakers of many languages—for example, Chinese (and Japanese, which is a totally unrelated language)—may have with distinguishing between [wu] and [u], or between [ji] and [i]: their language doesn't happen to make this tiny distinction. The common Chinese names spelled Wu (or Woo) and Yi (or Yee) in English may be pronounced with the glides at the beginning, but they usually are not. This makes it hard for English learners from those languages to hold onto the difference between *year* and *ear*. But they have no problem with saying the [w] in *weird* or the [j] in *you*, where the glide is in a very different place of articulation from the following vowel and can't just blend into it.

The sound English writes with the letter "L" is a wonderful sound—in fact, it's a whole family of sounds. At the beginnings of syllables—well, first start saying [ta] only don't actually say it; stop during the [t] and feel what your tongue is doing. Then do the same thing with [la]. Feel the difference? Switch back and forth between the [t] and [l] tongue positions quietly a few times and feel what seems to be moving. Also, in the [l] position, breathe in through your mouth for a second and see where your tongue gets cool. (In [t] position, you can't breathe either in or out.) For both the [t] and the [l], you're touching the blade of your tongue to your alveolar ridge, but for this [l], instead of the rest of your tongue making a tight seal against your teeth and gums all around your mouth, one or both of the sides of your tongue drop down below your upper teeth so that air can flow over the tongue-sides and out of your mouth. Because the position of the sides of the tongue is critical to making an [l] at the beginning of a syllable, [l] is called a LATERAL semivowel; it's the only lateral sound that English has. (Spanish, in many dialects, has two: the alveolar one and a palatal one, which is spelled [ll] in Spanish and symbolized by [λ] in IPA.

In some dialects of Spanish, though, the [ll] isn't a palatal lateral semi-vowel any more; it's just the palatal semivowel [j], the sound that we've learned to call "yod.")

If you try saying [la, li, lu] but stop during the [l] for each one, you'll feel big differences in what your lips are doing, and also substantial differences in your tongue position; it probably feels as if the whole rest of your mouth except for the blade of your tongue is starting to say the vowel while the blade is still doing the [l]'s alveolar contact. In other words, the coarticulation of [l] with the following vowel sounds is very strong.

[l] at the ends of (most) syllables in English is an entirely different sound, different enough to have its own IPA symbol, [ɫ], often called "dark L," or sometimes "velar L." What's velar about it? Say *all* (or any word that rhymes with it) as naturally as you can, and hold onto the [ɫ] at the end. You will probably find that your tongue isn't touching the roof of your mouth anywhere, so this sound is even closer to being a vowel than the word-initial [l]. For some speakers, the back of the tongue is humped up a bit towards the velum, which is why the dark [ɫ] is called velar. But it's not humped up like that for me. What about you? Can you tell? The sound is very different from the sound of word-initial [l]; listen to the pair of words *all/law* and the same two words reversed on your CD for a startling demonstration of this fact.

If you try saying different words spelled with the letter L (making sure that they actually do have some kind of [l] sound—there are quite a few silent L's in English, for example, in *calf*), you'll discover other variations in its tongue position and sound.

1.2.4.3 Vowels and /h/

VOWELS are the last major category of English sounds—and they are indeed major: English has more different vowel sounds than most other languages, even though there are also many vowel sounds that other languages have and we don't. Spelling of vowels is the least reliable part of English orthography, and reforming it, if we ever do, will be a huge mess because variation in pronunciation from one English dialect to another is greater for vowels than for any other class of sounds (although the cross-dialect variation on when and how /r/ is pronounced is just as bad). All through this section, we've been using English-based vowel spellings like *oo* and *ee* as a temporary measure, although I've put in the IPA symbols occasionally. Now let's learn the IPA that we need.

Table 1.2 gives you a standard list of American English vowels, adapted a little from the great phonetics textbook, *A Course in Phonetics*, by Peter Ladefoged (which is the book you should work through if you really want to learn phonetics from a linguistic point of view). The symbol names are

Table 1.2. IPA Chart for (almost all) American English Vowels

i	heed, he, beat, heat	lowercase *i*	ʌ	Hudd, mud	wedge; turned *v*
ɪ	hid, bid, hit, kid	small capital *I*	ɜ	herd, hurt, bird, curd	reversed epsilon
eɪ	hayed, hay, bade, hate	lowercase *e*+ɪ	aɪ	high, hide, bide, height	lowercase *a*+ɪ
ɛ	head, bed	epsilon (Greek)	aʊ	how, cow, cowed	lowercase *a*+ʊ
*æ	*had, *bad, hat	ash	ɔɪ	(a)hoy, boy, Lloyd	open *o*+ɪ
**ɑ	**hard, bard, hod, cod	script *a*	**iɾ	**ear, beard	lowercase *i*+r
**ɔ	**haw, bawd, caw	open *o*	**ɪɾ	**ear, beard	small capital *I*+r
oʊ	hoed, hoe, code	lowercase *o*+ʊ	**ɛɾ	**ber(ry), mer(ry)	epsilon+r
ʊ	hood	upsilon (Greek)	**eɾ	hare, bare, mare, Mar(y)	lowercase *e*+r
u	who, hoot, booed	lowercase *u*	aɪɾ	hired, hire	

Note: Asterisks mark places where speakers whose dialects vary from the model that Ladefoged used. See text on pp. 31–32 for explanation of individual sounds.

also given; "Greek" means that the symbol is taken from the Greek alphabet. If there are two symbols together, it means that the position of your tongue and lips changes during the course of making the vowel; these complex vowels are called **DIPHTHONGS**. (And you'll notice that the list ends with a triphthong.) These are the vowels that can appear in stressed syllables. We also need one more symbol, for a vowel that only appears in unstressed syllables like the second syllable of *sofa* or the first syllable of *about*. This is the [ə], called "shwa."

The list in Table 1.2 works well for people from most of the Middle Atlantic states. If you are from somewhere else, you'll need more time with the CD to get some of the sound distinctions, and to figure out what symbols are more accurate for you. We'll discuss some likely problems below, and there are others in the exercises for this chapter. Once you've mastered these symbols, you should practice IPA by transcribing that sample of the Chaos poem I gave you in section 1.2.1; there are two recordings of it on your CD, one with my Middle Atlantic accent and the other with a "General American" accent. Then you should be ready to think clearly about the speech sound aspect of whatever phonetic problem is part of your life: teaching reading, accent reduction, computer understanding of human language, and so on.

The asterisks in Table 1.2 mark places where my students and I over the years have had problems because our dialects differed from the American model that Ladefoged chose. You'll need to listen carefully to the CD to understand the discussion of these problems, so you'll find most of the material of this section (1.2.4.3) on the CD as well.

*1. The problem with /æ/ is that in the Northeast and some neighboring areas, it has moved towards /i/ and also developed into the diphthong /ɪə/, at least in some contexts. The word *bad,* for example, is pronounced /bɪəd/ by many millions of people, so there's no point in complaining about it if you don't happen to be one of them.

2. The major problem with /ɑ/ and /**ɔ/ is that more than half of all Americans can't easily hear the difference between them. If you ask a friend to say the names *Don* and *Dawn* naturally while you're not looking, and you can't tell the difference between them, one or both of you is in that half. On the other hand, if you're American and it's never even occurred to you that these names (and the word pairs *cot* and *caught, tot* and *taught, rot* and *wrought*) could be pronounced and sound the same for some people, you're probably from the Northeast or Middle Atlantic states. A second problem is the symbol /ɑ/ itself; keeping it distinct from the symbol /a/ is almost impossible, because the Roman alphabet simply treats them as alternative ways of writing lower case A. And a third problem is that almost no American English dialect has the distinction that the IPA makes between the sound it writes as /a/ and the sound it writes as /ɑ/, so I'm not going to try to teach or make that distinction in this text. If you want to learn IPA absolutely properly, study the IPA chart on the Web using the IPA's sound examples (link on your CD)

3. The problem with /ir/ and /**ɪr/ is that most American English speakers say *ear, beard,* and words like them with a vowel sound somewhere between /i/ and /ɪ/, so if you are already sensitive to speech sounds, neither of these spellings will make you happy. Don't worry about it; there's no dialect of English where the difference between [ir] and [ɪr] matters.

4. Finally, the problem with /ɛr/ and /**er/ is like the problem with /**ɑ/ and /**ɔ/, only more complicated. For some people in the United States, especially people from the Northeast like me, the vowel sound in *merry* is /**ɛr/ (the same ɛ as in *mess*y), and it's not at all confusable with the vowel sound /**er/ in *Mary* (which is the same as the vowel in *mare*). Furthermore, neither of these vowels is confusable with the vowel in *marry*, which is very close to—and best transcribed as—/æ/, because it's almost the same as the vowel in *Mattie*.

But if you are from California, the last paragraph was total garbage to you: *Merry, marry*, and *Mary* are pronounced identically, as it is by the two Western speakers on the CD. When you listen to the way I say them on the CD, you'll be able to tell the difference, but it will still be almost impossible to tell which word I say corresponds to which meaning—except that, luckily, the pronunciation of the vowels actually corresponds to their English spellings: respectively, in school grammar terms, they are short *e*, short *a*, and long *a*. Depending on where you grew up, you might also distinguish one of these three words from the other two, but which one's the distinct one for you may be different than it is for the person sitting next to you.

Does this matter? Well, people who make distinctions get very annoyed if they are forced to overlook them in making transcriptions, and people who don't make them really have to sweat to learn to hear them. So if the people who are studying phonetics and the people who are grading them have different dialects, some kind of agreement will have to be reached. Beyond the short term of learning phonetics, though, there's a lesson here: Reading teachers will be able to tune their advice to their students' questions better (particularly in judging whether or not the advice to "sound out" a particular word is going to work) if they understand that sound differences which are clear to them may not exist in their students' dialects, and that their students might be puzzled by how to spell sound differences which aren't easily heard by the teacher. The opportunities for mismatches like these are multiplied dozens of times, of course, if the teacher and the student are native speakers of different languages. We'll come back to this in Chapter 8.

A worse scenario occurs if a child who moves from a different dialect area is falsely judged to have a speech disorder because of pronunciation differences, and the most politically sensitive situation of all for phonetics is trying to decide fairly whether a child who is not a native speaker of English (or of the teacher's dialect of English) should have speech therapy. We'll talk about the psycholinguistic basis of speech perception when we look at experimental studies in Chapters 5 and 8.

1.2.5 Contrasting classes of sounds: Phonemes and minimal pairs

1.2.5.1 Phonemes

If you've heard the term PHONEME before, you may be wondering why we haven't used it yet, because you know that it is commonly used as we have used the term "speech sound": to avoid the misleading term "letter" when what you mean is in fact a speech *sound*, and not the letter that may be used to write it. But linguists and psycholinguists have something more in mind when we use the term "phoneme."

Think about what you've just learned about the ways the sound we hear as "L" varies in different contexts: Isn't it amazing that we hear them as "the same speech sound" until our attention is focused on the articulatory and auditory differences among them? How can people not notice such big differences? Of course, one reason is that they are all spelled with the same letter "L," which makes it harder to think about the differences—that's the same problem you may have had in learning to hear the difference between the two sounds that English spells *th*, but that IPA distinguishes as theta [θ] and edh [ð]. But for theta [θ] and edh [ð], we have at least one pair of words, *thigh* [θai] and *thy* [ðai], which are kept from being homonyms only because one has theta [θ] where the other has edh [ð] (another such pair is the noun *teeth* and the verb *teethe*). In linguistic terminology, we say that the words *thigh* and *thy* CONTRAST (mean different things), and furthermore, that they are a MINIMAL PAIR: What keeps them apart is only a single sound (and in this case, only a single feature: voicing). We can also say that the sounds theta [θ] and edh [ð] CONTRAST: that is, if you choose to say one of them rather than the other, then you are choosing between two different words (*thigh* [θai] and *thy* [ðai]) or between a real word and a nonword—for example, [beið] *bathe* and [beiθ] *beith*. So they are separate phonemes.

But the many "L" sounds that we discussed in section 1.3.2—including the two that IPA distinguishes routinely, [l] and [ɫ]—never contrast in English. If somebody says the word *like* as [ɫaik], we hear them as mispronouncing an [l], but not as saying a different English word or as saying a sound that could be an English word but doesn't happen to be. So the various "L" sounds all belong to the same phoneme in English; the technical linguistic way to say this is that they are all ALLOPHONES of the phoneme /l/.

Understanding whether two speech sounds belong to the same phoneme or not in the first language of someone learning English can make a big difference in an ESL instructor's effectiveness. If that's a concern of yours, you might like to look now at section 5.5 on speech sound perception in Chapter 5, as well as the phonetics/phonology materials in Chapter 9, sections 9.1.1 and 9.2.1.

1.2.5.2 An English consonant that isn't a phoneme

One important English consonant has been left out of our discussion because it tends to vanish when you try to find it, and also because it's a speech sound, but it's not a phoneme. How is that possible? Well, if you say *water* in a relaxed way (put it where it's not the most important word in a sentence: try rapidly saying *When're ya gonna water the LAWN?*), you probably feel that the consonant spelled with the *T* is more like a /d/ than a /t/. The same sound is in the middle of all sorts of familiar words that are spelled with a *T* or a *D* between two vowels (or between a vowel and an *R*), but it only occurs when speech is natural and relaxed. As soon as you start to say the words distinctly, the /t/ or /d/ shows up. That elusive in-between sound is called an alveolar FLAP or a TAP, because you make it by flipping the tip or blade of your tongue up to the back of your alveolar ridge, often not even making a tight contact. Its IPA symbol is [ɾ], and we never put it in angle brackets / /, because it's not a phoneme on its own in English; it's just one of the ways of saying either the phoneme /t/ or the phoneme /d/. (Remember, if a speech sound is "one of the ways of saying a phoneme" it's called an ALLOPHONE of the phoneme.)

Here are some pairs of words that you probably pronounce identically when you're not paying attention to your pronunciation, but that separate out when you try to think about them. Trying to hear yourself say the flap [ɾ] is a bit like trying to see the back of your own head. To see the back of your head, you need mirrors held at the proper angle, and to hear yourself say the flap in these words, you need to record yourself saying them at the right tempo. Listen to them on the CD before you try. (If you speak a variety of British English, you may have a different pattern for using the flap speech sound. Or you may use a different sound for the /t/, perhaps a glottal stop, so this whole discussion may not make any sense to you.) Here are the words on the CD: *Ladder, latter; madder (than a wet hen), matter; padder, patter; kiddies, kitties; biddy, bitty.* When you record yourself, you might well do what I suggested for *water:* Put each one in a casual-sounding sentence where another word near it is the one that is carrying the most stress.

For some people the words *rider* and *writer* are another pair that are identical when they are both pronounced with that flap allophone in the middle; for other speakers, the stressed vowels in these two words are a little different depending on which one is intended, so they aren't quite homonyms even when they both have the flap sound. Try recording and listening to yourself saying these two words, too, if you're curious.

1.2.5.3. Minimal pairs and language testing

We often turn to minimal pairs of words to test the language abilities of people (and machines). Can someone with hearing loss point to a picture of a rat versus a rack, which differ only in their final consonant sound? Can a young child with immature pronunciation point to a picture of a ring versus a wing, even though she says them both [wɪŋ]? Can a child with difficulty in learning to read tell you, when you say the words aloud, whether it's the first sounds or the last sounds that differ in *coat* and *goat*, *cone* and *comb*? (If not, you know that you know you have to help him with PHONEMIC AWARENESS before he is going to be able to understand how letters are used in spelling.) Can a speech synthesizer produce the difference between *peace* [pis] and *peas* [piz] clearly enough so that native English listeners can tell them apart even in a noisy situation? Can an American trying to learn Japanese hear the vowel length differences between /tori/ *bird*, /toori/ *street*, and /torii/ *shrine gate* (Figure 1.5)? Can she imitate those three different words successfully? Can she remember which sound goes with which meaning? (Listen to those three words on your CD and see if you can do it. Be careful—the /oo/ is not pronounced like the "oo" in *boot* or in *took*—it's almost the same sound as /o/ in *code*.)

Can an English learner whose first language is Spanish hear the difference between *sick* [sɪk] and *seek* [sik]? Produce it? Remember which sound goes which meaning? In Spanish, those two sounds never contrast, and speakers don't have to learn to produce and remember them until they try to learn a language like English. So they're facing the same problem that you have when you try to hold onto the Japanese short /o/ and long /oo/ sounds, which don't contrast in English.

1.2.6 Special sounds in unskilled and disordered speech

The speech sounds made by children who are learning their first language, whether normal or delayed, are often not good matches for anything on the IPA chart. Speech may sound "wet" because there's too much saliva in the child's mouth, or it may be hypernasal—the /b/'s sounding sort of like [m] and the /d/'s sounding sort of like [n]—because the child doesn't raise her velum enough to shut off all the nasal airflow when she's trying to make these sounds. Or her tongue may touch too much of the roof of her

A

B

Figure 1.5. A. Torii (shrine gate). Artist: Kenta Honda. **B.** Toori (street). Artist: Nozomi Okamoto. *continues*

mouth, or the place of articulation that she uses for some sound may be in between two nearby places that the target language uses. On your CD in the Materials for Chapter 1, there are three short sound files from four-

Figure 1.5. *continued* **C.** Tori (bird). Artist: Nozomi Okamoto.

C

year-olds who were being seen at a major speech clinic. In the first pair of files, a little boy has problems with the /s/'s in the words *sister* and *parents*; it's difficult to figure out exactly what is odd about his fricative. In the third file, a little girl replaces the /ð/ in brother with an /l/-like sound that's fairly close to the standard European Spanish palatal lateral liquid [ʎ] (called *elye,* spelled *ll,* as in *llamar* "to call").

Children who are born deaf and adults who have speech problems because of brain injury also make many unusual speech sounds; so, of course, do people who have physical problems with their mouth or face after injury or because of incompletely repaired birth defects like cleft palate, and people with many kinds of muscle control problems that produce "slurred" speech.

Sounds made by speakers with all these kinds of articulatory problems can be wickedly difficult to transcribe, partly because it's hard to hear them accurately, and partly because we seldom have appropriate symbols for them. As we'll say many times throughout this book, we learn to hear the sounds that our own language (or languages) use, and we have a hard time with new ones. Individual clinics and research groups have to decide how much detail they want to add to the IPA for English by adding sounds used in other languages and by adding additional marks, called DIACRITICS, to the basic IPA chart.

1.3 Syllables and How to Count Them

English speakers are taught rules for dividing written words into syllables, but unfortunately, those rules aren't very good for dividing up spoken words. Let's start with counting the number of syllables in words, and then worry about exactly where the division between the syllables goes.

(A funny thing about counting syllables: Most of us, including linguists, have to use our fingers to get the count right if a word has more than two syllables. It's hard to count and to think about the sounds of a word at the same time.) For most words, it's easy to count the syllables if you use your fingers to tally them; starting with the first sentence of this section, *English* has two syllables, *speakers* has two, the four words *are taught rules for* are all monosyllables, *dividing* has three syllables, and so does *syllables* itself. The only longer word in this paragraph is *monosyllables*, with five.

Let's put some of those words into IPA, and then we can see a few less obvious points more clearly: /ˈɪŋglɪʃ/, /ˈspikrz/, /dəˈvaɪdɪŋ/, /ˈsɪləblz/. (The IPA accent mark ', annoyingly, goes right before the first consonant of a stressed syllable instead of over the vowel, probably because vowels often have to carry other marks like nasalization and pitch, so that the airspace above it gets crowded. That forces us to decide which sound actually is the first consonant of the stressed syllable, and that's often a pain, though these four words don't cause trouble. (I'll show you what "'trouble" means in the Challenge section.)

Almost every syllable has a vowel in it, which seems to form its heart —the technical way to say this is that the vowel is the SYLLABLE NUCLEUS. But the final syllables of /ˈspikrz/ and /ˈsɪləblz/ have liquids at their hearts —as their nuclei, that is. With /ˈsɪləblz/ it's especially easy to be sure of this, because you can feel that the blade of your tongue stays glued to your alveolar ridge during the entire /blz/ sequence—it's right there while you're saying the /b/ and it stays there for making the /l/ and the /z/. With /ˈspikrz/, your tongue has to move to make the /krz/ sequence—the back has to come down from the velum to stop making the /k/ and the blade has to go up at the end to make the /z/—but you don't have to make any sound in between them besides the /r/. So: liquids can be syllable nuclei, at least when the syllable is unstressed, and so can nasals in words like *bottom, button, baking.*

But with some words, the syllable count seems to depend on how you say the word, or even just how you think of it. Think about how you say the words *fire, hire, higher, towel, owl.* You and your friends may well disagree about these and other problem words, which mostly involve glides next to liquids at the ends of words; the question is whether that liquid is a syllable nucleus, or whether it belongs to the stressed syllable that makes up the rest of the word. (The *hire/higher* pair is from the superb introductory but fast-moving phonetics textbook by Peter Ladefoged, which, as I've already mentioned, is what you should read next if you're starting to enjoy phonetics. Get the 6th edition [by Ladefoged and Johnson], unless a newer one has come out, and if you buy it used, make sure your copy has the CD.)

1B. MEANINGFUL UNITS OF LANGUAGE

1.4 Morphemes: The Meaningful Units of Speech

Until now, the only time we've talked about meaning has been when we talked about minimal pairs or sets of words. But the rest of this chapter is all about meaning—although not always about the kind of meaning you can give a definition of. We're still going to have to continue working through a big load of definitions in the rest of this chapter, but to keep it from being totally indigestible, I'm putting some of the very basic ones only in the glossary. So if you don't find a definition of a term shortly after you see it in GLOSSARY format and you want to be sure you know what it means, look it up. Words from this chapter that I'm postponing to the glossary are the terms NOUN, VERB, ADJECTIVE, and ADVERB, and a few other PARTS OF SPEECH.

Think about the difference between the words *girl* and *girls*. Of course you know that the second one has the plural ending, and it means there's more than one girl being referred to. So *girls* has two meaningful parts: the main one, *girl*, which can also stand by itself, and the noun plural marker, spelled *s*, which has to be attached to something—in fact, quite specifically, to a noun (or another kind of word doing the job of a noun). These two meaningful pieces are called MORPHEMES. The word *girl* by itself is just one morpheme; because it can stand alone, it's called a FREE MORPHEME. But the ending, because it has to be attached to something, is called a BOUND MORPHEME. In this section, we'll look at two kinds of bound morphemes and two kinds of free morphemes. These distinctions are important, even though there are gray areas along the boundaries between the kinds of morphemes, because people's minds treat the different kinds in different ways, whether we're looking at aphasia, normal speech errors, first or second language learning, or at producing and understanding spoken and written language. Even a computer-based reading machine or search engine needs to be programmed to respond to the differences we're going to talk about next.

1.4.1 Free morphemes I: Content words

CONTENT WORDS—at least the kinds of content words that are labels for people and animals (*daddy, Susie, cat*), things (*milk, teddy*), properties (*hot, nice*) and actions (*throw, eat*)—are one of the two main kinds of words that children learn early. (Social-emotional words like *hi, no, bye-bye* are the other main kind. These words are also free morphemes, because they can be said without being attached to any other word, but they are neither content words nor function words. We won't say any more about them.)

We'll say that a **CONTENT WORD** is a word with a meaning that can be defined by referring to things and events in the real or imagined world, like the labels we've just listed, but also going on to include abstract concepts like *wish* or *justice* and fictional concepts like *wizard*. In school grammar terms, content words include almost all **NOUNS**, **VERBS**, and **ADJECTIVES**, plus many of the **ADVERBS**. The content words are bolded in this sentence from the *New York Times* (April 30, 2009); the non-bold-faced words are **FUNCTION WORDS**, which we'll talk about in section 1.4.2.

> To **inaugurate** the **new baseball season**, the **tasting panel sampled 18 pilsners** from **American craft breweries**.

1.4.2 Free morphemes II: Function words and words in the "gray area" between content words and function words

As challenging as it would be to define all the content words in that example sentence, it's nothing compared with the impossibility of defining essentially meaningless words like *the* and *to* (when it's used as it is here, as an **INFINITIVE MARKER**). Look in a dictionary and you can see the problems that these words cause for lexicographers. They are typical examples of **FUNCTION WORDS**—the "little words," people with **NONFLUENT APHASIA** sometimes call them, when they are trying explain which words drive them crazy because they can't remember how to say them or when to use them.

DEFINITE and **INDEFINITE ARTICLES**—in English, the words *the, a, an,* plus, in informal speech, *some* as in *some girl I know says . . .* and *this* as in *this guy you said you'd introduce me to . . .* ; in Spanish, *la, el, las, los, uno, una, unos, unas*—are hard-core function words. Instead of defining them, you have to explain and demonstrate their functions (which is why they are called function words, or in some books, **FUNCTORS**): that is, you have to explain how they are used and give examples. Many languages, including Russian, Polish, Chinese, and Japanese, have no articles; when someone whose first language is one of these learns a second language that does have them, like English or French or German or Hawaiian, learning where to put articles is a major challenge, because there are no rules that can be trusted completely.

Other central examples of function words are **CONJUNCTIONS** (English *and, or, but, if, because,* and several others), the English infinitive marker *to,* the **EMPTY PREPOSITIONS**—the ones that don't tell you where something is or is going—(*of, for, by* when it links a work to an author or an artist, and many others in various expressions), and PRONOUNS (*I, me, we, it, you, they, us, our, ours*). We'll mention others as we need them, later in the book.

There's a broad gray boundary area between clear examples of content words and clear examples of function words. Major inhabitants of this boundary zone are DIRECTIONAL PREPOSITIONS like *from, in, near*, and *under*, which often have quite clear meanings but which, as we'll see in section 1.6, have a lot of the same grammatical functions as the empty prepositions. A good English grammar resource, like one of those listed at the end of this chapter, will give you more information about all of these words, though it may not classify them in the same practically oriented way as in this book.

1.4.3 Bound morphemes I: Inflectional morphemes

We began section 1.4 by talking about plural markers being BOUND MOR-PHEMES—that is, morphemes that have to be attached to some other morpheme. Plural markers get added to almost all nouns when you're talking about more than one (the exceptions are words like *sheep*), although a handful of nouns are IRREGULAR and use their own special plural markers: *man/men, woman/women, child/children, ox/oxen*. When we talk about the English plural morpheme or marker, we mean the whole family of forms that can mark the plural, regardless of how they are spelled or pronounced. Look again carefully at *man/men* and *woman/women* [wʊmən/wɪmɪn]: In these two words, the past tense marker isn't an ending, it's the change in the vowels. A morpheme doesn't have to show up as a SUFFIX (or a PREFIX) that you can cut off; sometimes it's another kind of change in the form of a word. In *children*, the plural marker actually has two parts: the vowel change from /aɪ/ to /ɪ/ and the *-ren* ending.

The most widespread bound morphemes in English (and in many other languages) are called INFLECTIONAL MORPHEMES, a term that is annoying at first, because in everyday language, *inflection* is used to mean the rise and fall of voice pitch. It's never used that way in linguistics or psycholinguistics, though; when we talk about changing voice pitch, we use the terms INTONATION or TONE. We'll discuss why these very common bound morphemes form a category that need a name after we look at the rest of them—English has only a few, but if you know any other language of Europe or India, you know that some languages have quite a lot of them.

Another inflectional morpheme that you know is the PAST TENSE MARKER. The regular one, for example the one added to *walk, climb,* or *pet* (the verb), is made in writing by adding *-ed*, which, if you think about it, is pronounced /t/ in *walked* but /d/ in *climbed* and /əd/ in *petted*. This pattern is important to think about when you are teaching reading to children or English to foreigners—for example, in explaining why *naked* doesn't rhyme with *raked*. The *-ed* family of past tense markers gets added to most English verbs, but there are a lot more irregular verbs than there are irregular nouns. The irregular verbs—the exceptions to the "add *-ed*" pattern—are among the commonest verbs of all: *be, do, come, go, bring, take, sing,* and so on. The past tense marker in those words can be a vowel change, or it can be more drastic. (Isn't it annoying that the most irregular words in any language are also the ones that are so common that you have to learn them first? More about why that's true in the Challenge section for Chapter 9.) We've also got a few verbs—all ending in *-t*, so that they already sound like good past tenses if they are used to mean a past event—that never change: *put, let*, and *set* are the most common.

The English **THIRD PERSON SINGULAR MARKER** (spelled *-s* at the end of the verb in *he gives*, *-es* in *she kisses*) is an ending that has no meaning at all; it's just required by the grammar. It's very regular; even the irregular cases, which we hardly notice except for *is* and *was*, are still all written with *-s* or *-es* and pronounced /s/, /z/, or /əz/ in a totally predictable way. (Our other irregular third person singular-marked verbs are *has* instead of *haves*; *does*, pronounced [dʌz] instead of [duz]; and *says*, pronounced [sɛz] instead of [sɛiz].)

The most important other inflectional morphemes in English are the **POSSESSIVE** ending that's written *'s* for nouns, and the *-ing* added to verbs to make **PROGRESSIVE** forms like *is walking, was going*. They are completely regular, and almost completely predictable from the rest of the grammar of the phrases in which they are used.

Now, why do these five bound morphemes deserve to be put in this special category called "inflectional"? That'll be easier to explain when we can compare them with the other main kind of bound morpheme in English, **DERIVATIONAL MORPHEMES**.

1.4.4 Bound morphemes II: Derivational morphemes and how to take long words apart

Let's look at some familiar long words: *possibility, oxygenation, magnify, marvelous, prototype, semitrailer*—that will do to start with. One of the neatest things about words is that many of them, like these six, seem to come apart into reusable pieces. Or, looking at it the other way, many long words seem to have been built up from shorter parts, as if they were made with a big construction toy. Bound morphemes that are used to make new words are called **DERIVATIONAL MORPHEMES**. These prefixes and endings change the meaning of the basic word to some extent, and the endings often change its grammatical class as well. Think how hard it would be to learn new words if you couldn't find familiar parts inside a great many of them, like *possible* in *possibility* or *marvel* in *marvelous*. It's true, however, that you can't usually figure out the meaning of a new word like *containerization* completely. That's because derived words are often built on one very particular meaning of the base form. In the case of *containerization*, as you probably know, it's built on the sense of *container* referring to a huge steel box, exactly the size of the back part of a standard semi-trailer truck, which can be loaded onto ships, trains, and trucks with all its contents safe inside. So it would be a joke if you used *containerization* to mean putting your leftovers into little plastic containers.

Even when we can't take a word apart completely because some of its pieces don't exist in English, like *possible*, it may have a recognizable ending like the *-ible/-able* that makes it an adjective, or the *-tion* or the *-er* that makes it a noun, or the *-ize* or *-ify* that makes it a verb. These endings are all derivational morphemes.

Now we can look back to section 1.4.3 and compare derivational to inflectional morphemes. With very few exceptions, when we add an inflectional morpheme like a plural or a past tense marker or the progressive *-ing*, we don't feel that we have a new word—we'd think it was silly to have a dictionary that had separate definitions for, say, the singular and plural forms of nouns. That's because the meaning of the plural form is completely predictable from knowing the meaning of the singular combined with the idea of having more than one of something.

But adding derivational morphemes (in clear cases) creates combinations that feel like new words. Why do they seem to be new? Because we don't necessarily know exactly what the combined forms mean just by looking at what their parts mean. In other words, the less predictable the meaning of the combination of two morphemes, the more we need to have a new dictionary entry for the combination, as we do for *containerization*.

So now we can define both inflectional and derivational morphemes. **INFLECTIONAL MORPHEMES** are bound morphemes that intuitively feel (to ordinary folks and to dictionary makers) like they don't make a new word when they are added to a base form, and **DERIVATIONAL MORPHEMES** are bound morphemes that do seem to make a new word when they are added to a base form.

Another difference between these two categories that you often find stated in linguistics or grammar textbooks is that inflectional morphemes don't change the part of speech (a plural noun is still a noun) but derivational morphemes do (*possible* is an adjective, *possibility* is a noun). This statement, although true most of the time, has three problems. First, it applies only to suffixes, not prefixes (*semitrailer* and *trailer* are both nouns). Second, some inflections can perfectly well be considered to change a word's part of speech: the *-ing* form of a verb can be freely used as an adjective and sometimes as a noun (*the singing children, the children's singing*), and the possessive form of a noun behaves grammatically very much like a definite article; have you noticed that we can say *the cat* or *George's cat* or *the black cat* or *George's black cat*, but not *the George's cat?* And third, even some derivational suffix morphemes DON'T change the part of speech: *Child* and *childhood* are both nouns, although they are very different kinds of nouns.

Because many English derivational morphemes (for example, *-tion, -ity, -ous, in-*) originated in words borrowed from Latin or from French, which is descended from Latin (English itself is not), the modern languages that developed from Latin have those morphemes too, in very similar or even identical forms. So second language learners whose first language is Italian, French, Spanish, Portuguese, or a few others have an easy time learning how these derivational morphemes are used, and English speakers learning the Romance languages have an easy time learning their equivalents like Spanish *-cion, –idad, -oso, in-*. But speakers of Chinese, Japanese, and other languages that work rather differently from the major languages of Western Europe benefit very strongly in English classes by being shown how derivational morphemes give us related sets of words like *derive, derivation, derivative, derivational*. Even though you can't tell exactly what the meaning of the new word will be by knowing the meaning of the base form, you can almost always use the meaning of the base to help you remember the meaning of the derived form, and vice versa.

By the way, we English speakers can use some words that were originally nouns as verbs, and the reverse as well, without putting any derivational ending on them to change their part of speech: *a light, to light something*; *a house, to house someone*. Chinese speakers can do the same kind of thing with many of their nouns and verbs, but in many other languages, this kind of simple shift of a word's PART OF SPEECH isn't possible.

1.4.5 Compound words: Taking more long words apart

English speakers also make new words by joining other words together—that is, using our new terminology, by joining existing free morphemes to make COMPOUND WORDS, like *webmail, inbox, hovercraft, payback*. (Many other languages do this too.) And, of course, some of these words can then have derivational and/or inflectional endings added to them, as in *sleep-*

walker-s or *birdwatch-ing*. Sometimes, though, it's difficult to decide whether the name of a new object or institution, like *compact disc* or *day-care*, is one word or two, which takes us to the next topic: words.

1.5 Words

Everybody who can read a language written in an alphabet knows what a word is: a meaningful string of letters that has white space or a punctuation mark before and after it (unless it's in a Web address). But we've started to see that defining "word" is not quite that simple—in fact, as philosophers, psychologists, and linguists will tell you, it's very difficult, and we're not even going to try it here.

What we've said about "word" so far is this: If you add an inflection like plural or past tense to a base word form, like *books* from *book*, it isn't a different word, just a different form of the same word, because the meaning of the inflected form is almost 100% predictable from the uninflected form, so it doesn't need a separate dictionary entry or subentry. The same is true for the *-ing* form of most verbs, like *seeing*: if you know what *see* means, you know what *seeing* means. But you can't quite predict the meanings of words that are formed by adding derivational morphemes, like *cookie* (from *cook*). You also can't fully tell the meaning of the verb *book* from the noun *book*, so those—even though they are exactly the same sets of letters—are treated by dictionary makers as separate words. (Amazingly, there are people with aphasia who will look at a picture of a comb and tell you that they can't think of what it's called, but it is used to comb your hair with. So the dictionary makers are right about noun and verb pairs with identical forms, like *a book/to book* and *a comb to/comb*, being different words!)

All we'll add to this discussion of "word" is how to decide whether or not a particular combination of two words should be considered to make one new word. Dictionary makers do, sensibly, continue to follow the principle of predictability, although rather roughly. If the meaning of the combination is not predictable from its parts (plus a bit of common sense), as in *hot dog* or *keyboard* or *greenhouse*, the combination is a compound word, and it is relatively likely to be listed in the dictionary. If the meaning of two words together gives pretty much what you'd expect from combining their meanings (or some of their meanings), like *white horse*, then the combination isn't considered a compound.

What makes life interesting is that there are probably thousands of two-word combinations whose meaning isn't fully predictable, but which are not listed in even the largest dictionaries—although true unabridged dictionaries like the *Oxford English Dictionary* (the one that takes up 20 fine-print volumes) do include very large numbers of them. As far as how they are written, as we hinted at the end of section 1.4.2, combinations of two words are a complete grab-bag. Dictionary makers follow the usage of high-prestige print sources like major newspapers (which could just as well have become standardly written as *news papers* or *news-papers*). There is no principle for deciding how to write a compound word.

Being able to take apart compounds is important for beginning English readers, whether they are English-speaking children or adult second language learners, and it's not only because disassembling a word helps to figure out its meaning. Looking to see whether a word could be a compound can be essential to sounding it out correctly—for example, you'd never be able to connect the written words *chophouse* and *goatherd* to any words you have ever heard if you tried /f/ as a reading for the *p + h* sequence and /θ/ or /ð/ for *t + h*. In the same way, being alert for prefixes (which are derivational morphemes) can keep a reader from saying *misled* as /maizld/—an error that some people miserably recall making when they were reading the word aloud for the first time.

1.6 Utterances: Phrases, Clauses, and Sentences in Speech

1.6.1 What's an utterance?

If you look at a transcript of a real conversation like the one in Materials for Chapter 1 on your CD, you'll see that people say lots of things (UTTER-ANCES in linguistic terminology) that are treated as complete in spite of being only phrases, not complete sentences. The idea that people do or should talk to each other in complete sentences is just silly; the question *Where's my mittens?* can be answered equally well by *They're on the bed* or just *On the bed*. Even just *bed* is possible, though grumpy-sounding. Only some language textbooks for foreigners and some programs for children with language difficulties insist on complete sentences all the time. This is rather poor preparation for understanding what native speakers are likely to say, although it might be a good model for a second-language learner to use for speaking until her accent is no longer very strong.

For analysis of conversations, then, we divide speech into utterances, which may or may not be sentences. But as listeners, we start to interpret words as soon they come to our ears, and as readers, we start to attribute a meaning as quickly as possible after we see a word. We don't wait to get to the end of the utterance, even though that sometimes leads us to misunderstand the speaker or the writer temporarily, if the beginning of a sentence is ambiguous, like this one: *The truck unloaded at the rear door was rented*. (In case you're not quite getting it: This sentence has to mean *The truck that was unloaded at the rear door was rented*, but until you get past *door*, you're probably expecting *unloaded* to be the main verb, as it is in *The truck unloaded at the rear door and drove off*.)

With the elegant piece of laboratory equipment called an **EYE-TRACKER**, which makes a millisecond-by-millisecond record of exactly where a person is looking as they read or as they look at a picture, you can see that someone who is reading this kind of sentence usually stops when they hit the second verb—in our example, the word *was*—because that's when they discover that the first verb—in our example, the word *unloaded*— can't be the main verb of the sentence. They then go back to the beginning of the sentence and choose the right interpretation: that the first verb (*unloaded*) is being used as an adjective to describe the truck. We'll have a lot more to say about experiments like this in Chapter 5, section 5.5.2.

1.6.2 Pieces of utterances: Phrases and clauses

It's a good thing that long, complicated sentences are made up of smaller sequences of words, or we'd never be able to figure them out. That's partly because the details of what most words mean can't get filled in until we see them in their context; for example, you can't make a good mental picture of what *push* means in a sentence until you know whether what's being pushed is a door, a swing, a button, or a pencil. Other reasons will become clearer as we move through the next several chapters.

We need to take sentences apart into two kinds of groups of words: phrases and clauses. We could get pretty far just using the term "phrase" informally, to mean a few words that intuitively seem to go together. But we also need the formally defined terms **NOUN PHRASE** and **PREPOSITIONAL PHRASE**, because the words in these particular kinds of phrases become tightly bound together in our minds—we know this because whole noun phrases and whole prepositional phrases can move around together in speech errors like *The Grand Canyon went to my sister*, where the two noun phases *the Grand Canyon* and *my sister* have obviously switched places. Linguists and grammarians use these terms this way: a **NOUN PHRASE** is a **NOUN** or a **PRONOUN,** plus perhaps other words or groups of words that tell you more about it in order to help you identify it (in grammar school terms, that modify its meaning; this definition isn't perfect, and you can try to improve it once you feel that you understand the idea.)

Prepositions are words whose job is to link noun phrases—and only noun phrases—to the rest of a sentence, and a **PREPOSITIONAL PHRASE** is a noun phrase with a **PREPOSITION** in front of it. So, if you understand what a noun phrase is and isn't, you're also all set to deal with prepositional phrases. (There are two other important categories of words—conjunctions and relative pronouns—that are used to link other kinds of multiword units into a sentence. We'll get to them when we look at clauses.) Just one more grammar term here: in a prepositional phrase, like *to the Grand Canyon*, the noun phrase (*the Grand Canyon*) that follows the preposition (*to*) is called the **OBJECT OF THE PREPOSITION**.

Some examples will help: the groups of words in the first column of Table 1.3 are noun phrases, the ones in the second column are prepositional phrases with the prepositions **bolded**, and the ones in the third column are neither noun phrases nor prepositional phrases. Why not? What's wrong with each of them? Which ones seem to be some kind of unit, and which ones are just a sequence of words?

We'll also find it useful to talk about **VERB PHRASES**, even though a verb phrase is probably not such a tight mental unit as a noun phrase or a prepositional phrase. A verb phrase is defined as a **VERB**, its **OBJECTS**, and any **ADVERB**ial words or phrases that tell you more about it (modify it).

Table 1.3. Noun Phrases and Prepositional Phrases

Noun Phrases	Prepositional Phrases	Neither Noun Phrase nor Prepositional Phrase
She		she saw
them	**for** them	gave them
Susannah	**by** Susannah	Susannah called last night
our house	**under** our house	painted our house
the brick house down the street	**after** the brick house down the street	house down the
the blonde twins your brother had a crush on	**of** the blonde twins your brother had a crush on	that your brother had a crush on
Joseph and Samantha	**from** Joseph and Samantha	and Samantha

Okay, what are the objects of a verb? First of all, they are noun phrases, just like the objects of a preposition. But objects of a verb are noun phrases that are hooked into the sentence directly by the verb, without needing a preposition to introduce them. So, in English, the objects of a verb are the noun phrases that come right after that verb, like *the boys* in *He's picking up the boys after school lets out* (or noun phrases that would be fine coming right after the verb if you moved them there, as in *The boys, he's picking up after school lets out*).

Table 1.4 gives you some verb phrases, with the objects of the verb **bolded**. Remember that we are talking about syntax here, not about meaning: *took **a gift** for them* and *took **them** a gift* have the same meaning (specifically, the same semantic roles, which we'll talk about in section 1.7), but they have different grammatical forms: The verb phrase *took **a gift** for them* has an object and a prepositional phrase, but the verb phrase *took **them** a gift* has two objects—in school grammar terms, it has a direct object and an indirect object.

And, to get ready for our discussion of clauses, the last column has verb phrases with subject noun phrases, in *italics*. Remember that the objects of a verb are considered part of the verb phrase, but the subject is not. Instead, the combination of a SUBJECT with the verb phrase that gives information about it makes the last important unit that we need to talk about: a CLAUSE.

The CLAUSE is the most important multiword chunk for linguistic and psycholinguistic analysis. In lawyer-speak, a clause is a single provision in a law or a contract, no matter how complex its grammatical structure, but linguists and psycholinguists define a clause as a verb phrase with an

Table 1.4. Verb Phrases and Simple Clauses

Verb Phrase, No Object	Verb Phrase, One Object	Verb Phrase, Two Objects	Clause
go			*You and George* go
see clearly	see **Susannah**		*I* see clearly now
brings up	brings **a cake**	brings **her a cake**	*Jon* brings her a cake
took	took **a gift** for them	took **them a gift**	*My folks* took them a gift
boil for five minutes	boil **it** for five minutes		*(you)* Boil it for five minutes

implicit or explicit **SUBJECT**. And what's a subject. You already know that it's a noun phrase, and the examples in Table 1.4 remind you of some of the different kinds of noun phrases. But there's something special about the subject noun phrase: In English (and in all the languages that are closely related to English), it is different from object noun phrases, because it affects the form of the verb. The most dramatic example of these changes in the verb form, as you know, are those that happen to the present tense of the verb *to be* when it's combined with different subjects: *I* **am**; *he, she, it* **is**; *you, we, they* **are**. *Sam is, people* **are**, *George and Susanne* **are**. And in the past tense, *to be*, unlike any other English verb, has two different forms: *I, he, she, it, Sam* **was**; *you, we, they, people, George and Susanne* **were**. The standard way to talk about this is to say that the verb must **AGREE** with its subject noun phrase, even though for all the other verbs in English, the only **AGREEMENT** change is putting on the third person singular marker *–s* that we talked about in section 1.4.3 (plus, for *have, do,* and *say,* as we mentioned in that section, a change in the pronunciation of the sound that comes just before that -s).

A very large number of languages don't have any kind of agreement between subjects and verbs. So for people whose first language has no subject-verb agreement, remembering to put that third person singular marker *–s* where it's needed in English is a pain. Even for people who are learning English as a second language who grow up with subject-verb agreement in their first language, the third person singular marker is a nuisance. It takes a while for children whose first language is English to learn it, too, especially children with developmental language disorders.

Now, what about that "(you)" listed as the subject for the instruction, *Boil it for five minutes*? Obviously, in instructions and in orders like *Stand up!, Don't slam the door!,* or *Please take off your hat*, the person who is being instructed or given an order is expected to do (or not do) what the verb phrase says. So school grammar says that the sentence has an "understood" *you* subject, which is what the "(you)" is supposed to mean. For the subjectless sentences of casual speech, like, *Come here often? Looks like he's had a few*, or *Had a bad night, I'm afraid*, which are especially common as the first words of a new conversation or topic, some linguists say that they also have a kind of a pronoun subject (*You, he,* or *it, I*) that gets omitted. Other linguists would prefer to say that these verb phrases simply have no subject, and that the information about whom the verb phrase applies to is supplied by the context. (Remember that utterances don't have to be complete sentences or complete clauses.) We'll stay away from this controversy, and just use the school grammar term "the understood subject" if we need to.

There are some other roles that we'll need for our analyses, too—not ones that are central to the action, but nevertheless, roles we use all the time: MODIFIERS of nouns (ADJECTIVES like *red* or *terrific*, numbers, POSSESSIVES like *mine* or *their*), ADDRESSEE—the person or people you are talking to (*Hey, **Joe! Mom**, where are my sneakers? **Congregation**, please rise*), PREPOSITIONS (***under*** *the bed;* ***after*** *midnight*), OBJECTS OF PREPOSITIONS (*under **the bed**; after **midnight***), and ADVERBS, the large miscellaneous collection of words that modify sentences, adjectives, and verbs: ***Frankly**, I don't care; He's **really** sweet; It's full **enough**; Do it **now***).

1.7 Basic Syntactic and Semantic Roles: The Jobs That Words Do In Clauses

There are two ways of looking at how words work in clauses, and we need both of them in the classroom, the clinic, and in any application in which a computer is supposed to act as if it understands spoken or written language. One way is to look at the SYNTAX of the clause, as we have started to do already: which word is the subject, which words are adjectives, which words are in prepositional phrases, and so on. We need these concepts in order to be able to explain why a sentence sounds grammatical or ungrammatical.

The other aspect of clause structure is how the noun phrases contribute to its meaning, and this is very different from what we've done so far. The noun phrases in a clause have different SEMANTIC ROLES or FUNCTIONS: some of them refer to the AGENT (the person, animal, or person-like entity who carries out an action), and others to the UNDERGOER (the person or entity that is affected by an action). In section 1.7.2, we'll see why syntax isn't enough, and why we need to think about semantic roles in order to communicate who did what to whom.

1.7.1 Basic syntactic roles in a clause

We introduced the basic syntactic roles when we discussed clauses in section 1.6.2, so we can keep this section short; we only need it to help us compare syntactic roles with semantic roles. A clause is normally composed of a subject noun phrase and a verb phrase. The verb phrase may contain one or two object noun phrases; some verbs can have objects, others can't, some must. The whole clause and any part of it can have a prepositional phrase modifying it. Really complex sentences can be built up when we use a clause to modify part or all of another clause, or to be its subject or object. Here are some examples to refer to:

> *George gave me an idea yesterday.*

Subject *George*, verb phrase *gave me an idea yesterday*, objects *me* and *an idea*. *Yesterday* is an adverb that modifies the whole verb phrase.

> *Chris will be okay by tomorrow.*

Subject *Chris*, verb phrase *will be okay by tomorrow*, no object. *Okay* is an adjective (in school grammar, a **PREDICATE ADJECTIVE**) that modifies *Chris*. *By tomorrow* is a prepositional phrase that modifies the verb phrase.

> *Sam thinks that Chris will feel okay by tomorrow.*

Subject Sam, verb phrase *thinks that Chris will feel okay by tomorrow;* object *that Chris will feel okay by tomorrow*, which is the clause *Chris will feel okay by tomorrow* preceded by the connecting word *that*. (The usual linguistic term for the *that* when it's used this way is "complementizer." We won't need it in this book, so I'm not putting it in the Glossary.)

1.7.2 Basic semantic roles

We can't tell who did what to whom just by looking at the subject and the object (or objects); we also have to look at the verb itself quite carefully. This may seem odd—isn't the subject of the sentence the **AGENT**, the person who's doing what the verb phrase says? In sentences like *Joe kissed Samantha*, yes, the subject is the Agent (we're going to Capitalize semantic role terms to make them easier to spot). But what about who-did-what-to-whom in the sentence *Samantha was kissed by Joe*? In syntactic terms, *Samantha* is now the subject, but in semantic terms, she's still the **UNDERGOER**, the person affected by the action. And *Joe*, even though he's stuck out there on the end as the object of the preposition *by*, still did the kissing—he's still the Agent. So there's a big difference in the way the two sentences work to convey meaning. The reason for this difference, of course, is that the verb *kissed,* in the first sentence, is in the **ACTIVE VOICE**, but the verb *was kissed,* in the second sentence, is in the **PASSIVE VOICE**. So to understand and explain the difference between how clauses work when their verb is in the active voice and when it's in the passive voice, we need to separate the syntactic terms "subject" and "object" from the semantic roles like Agent and Undergoer that are played by the people and things being mentioned.

For some verbs, the subject is the Undergoer even when the verb is in the active voice. Here are some examples of sentences like that; if you think about it, you'll see that they have no Agent noun phrase at all, just an Undergoer, plus some other semantic information, mostly about where the Undergoer went.

The ball rolled under the car.

His cell phone fell into the water.

I accidentally tripped over that stone.

Her hat blew off.

My computer crashed again.

Stock prices dropped in early trading, but rose again before the market closed.

It often takes real-world knowledge to decide which semantic role the subject is playing. In a sentence like *I got my car totaled*, the subject is almost certainly the Undergoer, but in *I got the jar opened*, the subject is probably the Agent (although she might have gotten someone else to turn the lid for her: the sentence doesn't make that clear). It's not the grammar that tells us this; it's the probability that in real life, we don't want our cars smashed but we do want our jars opened.

So in sections 1.7.1 and 1.7.2, we've seen that an essential part of understanding what is happening around us is organizing events in terms of their causes and effects, including human (and animal) agents' intentions (or lack of them). We've also seen that language encodes this understanding by somehow linking each thing that we talk about with a semantic role, and that semantic roles are about meaning, while syntactic roles are not. School grammar often mixes these two aspect of clause structure together, but people who work with language need to keep them separate: A computer program that is near-perfect at figuring out the object of a clause may be nowhere near accurate at figuring out who the Undergoer is, and an aphasic person may know perfectly well who the undergoer of an action is but be quite unable to make that person's name be the subject of a verb phrase.

1.7.3 Combining words: Using syntax and semantics in understanding language

When beginning readers read sentences aloud one word at a time, we worry whether they are getting any meaning out of the way the words are combined. A very simple sentence, for example, *Joe likes Sam,* can probably be understood pretty well that way, in fact—let's see how it might be done. Suppose a reader assumes that a sentence that starts with *Joe* is about Joe, which means that it's likely to tell us about how Joe looks or what he feels or does. (A child with no experience of being read to could fail to have even this starting assumption—she could fail to realize that words in a line of text are not a list to be learned like spelling words, but are supposed to represent sentences. This is one reason that reading aloud to children is important for their success in school.)

After reading *Joe*, our beginner encounters *likes*, and if she expects the words written in a line of text to mean something, as the words that she hears one after another in conversation do, she can recognize that *likes* could mean a way that Joe feels, so that the two words start to make sense as a statement *Joe likes*. But what is it that Joe likes? A typically developing child over the age of three knows that after *Joe likes* comes at least one more word, containing information about what or who it is that Joe likes, whether it's ice cream, skateboarding, or one of his friends. Or at least, there must be an object pronoun like *it*, *us*, *you*, or *her*. In school-grammar terminology, the verb *likes* is TRANSITIVE—that is, it begins a verb phrase that must be completed with an object noun phrase, which could be the name of a person or a thing, or an activity, like *to go fishing* or *flying kites*. Psycholinguists would describe the word *likes* as being represented in our minds as being attached to two possible FRAMES: a TRANSITIVE FRAME with a SLOT for a noun after it, and another kind of transitive frame with a slot for a verb form that names an action (like *to go* or *flying*). (There's a linguistic term for these action-naming verb forms, although you don't have to know it: they are nominalized verb forms, which simply means that they have been made into nouns.)

A useful technical way of describing the same thing is to say that the word *likes* PROJECTS a noun phrase or a verb phrase. What this means, at least in this book, is simply that English speakers expect to hear a noun phrase (which might be a verb form that has been made into a noun) after *likes*. *Sam* will do very nicely to fill that slot.

Linguists often use TREE DIAGRAMS for representing sentence structures; Figure 1.6 shows you a typical tree diagram for the structure of *Joe likes Sam.*

In English, a verb frame also can be thought of as projecting the slot for its subject (although this isn't standard terminology). This is a useful

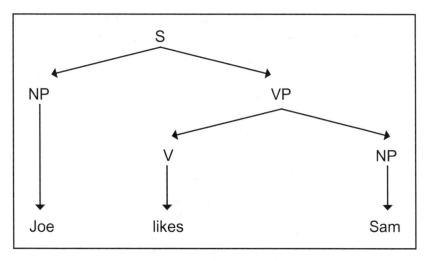

Figure 1.6. Tree diagram for *Joe likes Sam.*

description of something you know about verbs, because if you see just *likes Sam* at the top left of a page of text, you'll automatically assume that there was a word or phrase referring to the person who likes Sam at the end of the previous page (even if LIKES SAM is in all capital letters, so that you can't tell just from looking at the letters that the beginning of the sentence was missing). And if a sentence in Yoda-speak is read to you, you know where really belongs the noun phrase that shows up at the end of the sentence.

Most sentences have richer structures than *Joe likes Sam*. Readers have to be able to hold onto several possibilities for the sentence structure until they find out which one accounts for all of the words. And this is where reading one word at a time falls apart as a description of what a reader needs to do. Let's compare the structures of two sentences that are simple enough for a child's book, a beginning ESL reader, or a reading test for people with aphasia, and see why we don't just read words and combine their meanings—in other words, why readers need (subconsciously, of course) to compute sentence structures. Look at these example sentences:

Example 1.7.3A. *Sally took her to the zoo.*

Example 1.7.3B. *Sally took her shoes off.*

These two sentences begin with the same three words, but their structures are quite different, except for the fact that Sally is the subject of both of them. When you read the first one, you understood that the word *her* is referring to another female creature for whom Sally arranged a trip—to the zoo, as it turns out. But the same word *her* in the second sentence is referring to someone who owns something—in this case, shoes. (Maybe it's Sally, maybe it's someone else.)

Figure 1.7 shows you trees for first parts of each of them, which should make it easy to see the differences in sentence structure that go along with these two meanings: in Example 1.7.3A, *her* is the whole

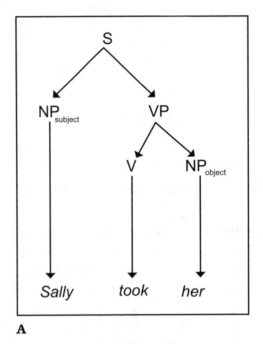

A

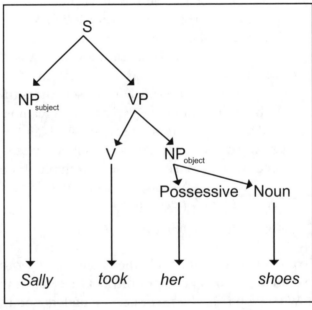

B

Figure 1.7. A. Partial tree for example 1.7.3A.
B. Partial tree for example 1.7.3B.

object of *took*, but in Example 1.7.3B, it's only part of the object; the whole object is *her shoes*.

(These trees are modified from what you'll see in most linguistics text-books, so that we can focus on what's essential for this pair of sentences.)

We're not quite done with figuring out how these two sentences work because the verb *take* has several different frames it might be used in, cor-responding pretty well to its several meanings. In addition to the object slot, the frame for both of these sentences has a **LOCATIVE** slot (LOC) for indicating a change of place for that object. (The meaning of *take* in our examples is something like *cause to change location*.) Now Example 1.7.3A has the locative prepositional phrase *to the zoo*, and Example 1.7.3B has the **LOCATIVE PARTICLE** *off*. Figure 1.8 gives you the completed trees that repre-sent what the hearer has to know in order to understand these sentences.

In natural speech, the pacing of our words and the rises and falls of our voice pitch—the **PROSODY** of the sentence—gives our listeners some information about how words are to be grouped together (listen to these two sentences on your CD under Materials for Chapter 1). This helps lis-teners decide which structure they are in the middle of hearing.

But in reading, there's no prosody on the page, so we often have to hold onto a word in our minds and wait for more information before we know how to interpret it. In these two sentences, the syntactic job of the word *her* becomes clear when we hear or read the word after it. If that next word is the preposition *to*, we know that *her* must be the object of the verb. But if the next word is a noun meaning something that could belong to Sally, like *shoes*, we know that *her* must modify it, and that the object must be the noun phrase *her shoes*. (However, we don't know whether the *her* in 1.7.3B. *Sally took her shoes off* means Sally or some-one else—we'll need more information to figure out its semantic job.)

In some sentences, readers must wait a bit longer to deal with a word that might belong to two different structures. If we make up our minds too quickly and are wrong, we may have to go back and see how else the sentence could work, as in the example *The truck unloaded at the rear door was rented.* (Misinterpretation of a sentence's structure can happen when we're listening, too.) An unskilled reader working one word at a time might be trapped into the wrong interpretation by a sentence like one of these, and need help in retracing her decisions about what it means. All this may seem like an unbelievable amount of work to go through in order to understand such simple sentences, and it would be if we had to do it deliberately and consciously. But we do it unconsciously most of the time, except when we've really gotten off on the wrong track. We'll see more about sentences that lead us off the right track in Chapter 5; they are called **GARDEN PATH SENTENCES**.

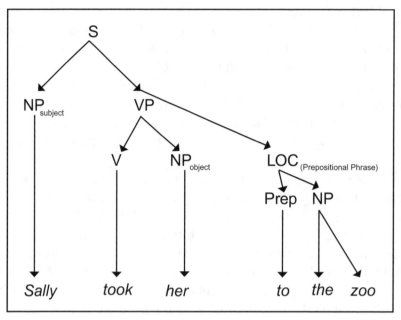

A

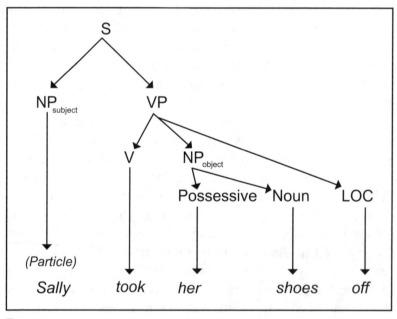

B

Figure 1.8. A. Completed tree for example sentence 1.7.3A.
B. Completed tree for example sentence 1.7.3B.

1.8 Pragmatics

PRAGMATICS is the part of linguistics that's sometimes called "how to do things with words." How do people choose words to have the effects that they want on other people—to be polite, to be understood, to make other people feel like insiders or outsiders, to make them feel good or ashamed, to encourage or console, impress or inform? The topic of pragmatics is huge but easy to understand, so you can read about it for yourself—there are some suggested readings in Materials for Chapter 1 on your CD.

Here's a pragmatic consideration for practical use in adult second language teaching: People need to know polite ways to ask for things in their new language, even if the polite forms are complex. For example, English learners need to be able to use, *Could I please have* instead of *I want*. It's hard enough to be a foreigner; one doesn't also want to be perceived as rude.

A lot of the differences between written and spoken language are also matters of pragmatics. Expressions that make fine, lively colloquial narratives like, *So then this guy comes up to me and says . . .* won't do in a formal report of an incident, and the formal alternatives like, *At that point a man I didn't know came toward me and said . . .* may have to be taught explicitly. People with aphasia, as we'll see later, typically have most of their sense of pragmatics spared by their brain injuries, but if they can't find the syntax or the words that they need to express themselves, what they say may nevertheless strike the people listening to them—including clinicians—as being pragmatically inappropriate.

1.9 The Gap Between What People Know and What They Do: Kinds of Linguistic Knowledge

1.9.1 Tacit knowledge and how you find out about it

By now you might be rather tired of being told things about your language. You knew how to speak it, so did all this stuff about tongue position, word endings, and sentence formation have anything new in it besides the terminology? If it's inside your head (and where else could it be?), why can't you just know it by thinking about it? Well, you can't see inside your eye, or hear what's happening inside your ear, or taste how the taste buds in your tongue work, either. People have to study them scientifically to know how they work.

You are quite right, though, that simply knowing about linguistics won't, by itself, help you speak. Knowing the mathematics of forces and trajectories doesn't help you with scoring a home run or a touchdown, either, and being a skilled ball player doesn't help you with physics. Knowing about things in a way that you are aware of (**EXPLICIT KNOWLEDGE**) and knowing how to do them (usually called **TACIT KNOWLEDGE**—*tacit* is a Latin verb form meaning *he/she/it is silent*) are very different kinds of knowledge. (And as the late and well-loved linguist Jim McCawley of the University of Chicago pointed out, there are still more kinds of knowledge, like knowing how particular things taste, look, smell, and sound—think of how you recognize cinnamon by its taste and smell, or snare drums by their sound.)

So how can you find out what you or someone else tacitly knows how to do with language, if you can't do it by asking them things like, "What is the right order of words in an English question?" You do it the same way you do any other science: by observing, recording your observations, making a sensible guess about the pattern formed by the events you've observed (in formal language, by making a **HYPOTHESIS** about the what the pattern is), figuring out some new things that should be true if you were right about the pattern, and then seeing if those new things are in fact true (formally, "testing the hypothesis"). It's no different from detective work, except that, in testing a scientific hypothesis, you're not solving a single case, but a whole class of similar cases. And you probably can't do it in time for the final commercial—but then, neither can real detectives, only the ones on television.

1.9.2 Spelling and speaking: The eyes fool the ears (and the tongue)

Sometimes, your explicit knowledge about your language—or rather, what you think you know about it—is actually wrong, and it can mislead you in your attempts to observe your tacit knowledge in action. We'll look briefly at how knowledge of spelling can distort the way you hear your own pronunciation. It's not really your eyes that are fooling your ears when this happens, of course; what's misleading you are the connections you have been making between letters and sounds since you learned to read English. Those well-learned associations between letters and sounds are competing with your actual perception of the sounds you make, and with your perception of what your vocal tract is doing when you are making those sounds. In the first part of this chapter, you had to work hard to build new connections between IPA symbols and sounds, so that you could think in terms of sounds rather than of spelling. What was hardest about this process probably wasn't making the new connections; it was keeping the old and by-now-automatic connections between sound and letter from interfering with the new ones. For example, remembering that *think* and *this* begin with two different English phonemes, respectively theta /θ/ and eth /ð/, is hard because those two sounds are both spelled the same way. Remembering that the symbol /e/ is pronounced in IPA only like the main part of the vowel in *eight* is hard because seeing it also calls up the other sounds English uses *e* for, like the /ɛ/ of *head* and the /i/ of *heed*.

So it's pretty common for speakers to think that they are pronouncing words in CITATION FORM (a super-distinct pronunciation like a person running a spelling bee uses), when, in fact, we rarely use such forms for the common function words of our language. People also often think that they are pronouncing words differently that are spelled differently, even when they are actually pronounced the same (or are usually pronounced the same). For example, we make a pronunciation distinction between the citation forms of *than* /ðæn/ and *then* /ðɛn/, but when we actually say *She's a lot taller than me* and *So then is that okay?* they are both usually pronounced /ðn/, with the /n/ doing the job of the vowel. Listen to these examples on your CD; we'll discuss this problem more in Chapter 8, section 8.5.1.

Another good example of how spelling fools us is with the word *that*; listen to the CD example showing how it's produced in some common contexts: *I told you about that time that I met him/The one that I bought/ I bought that one.* Using a sound wave analysis program like Praat (introduced on your CD) to cut up speech into pieces is immensely helpful in finding out facts like these.

Surprisingly, people who are not good at reading aren't actually better off at thinking about sounds than those of us who have been brainwashed by the alphabet. Usually, they have even less practice at thinking about speech sounds than those of us who can pretty much sound out unfamiliar words. They keep getting distracted by their connections between sounds and meaning, probably because they can't use alphabet letters—as limited as those are—to help keep their minds focused on the sounds instead of the meanings.

1.9.3 Right and wrong: Tuxedos at the gym

Another way that what we believe about our language is different from how we actually behave has to do with our ideas about speaking "correctly." Educated people often think, first, that speaking colloquially is wrong, and second, that they don't do it themselves. But what's appropriate pragmatically has little to do with correctness, and everything to do with where you are, who you're talking to, and what role you're playing. "Talking like a book" with friends at a bar is as out of place as wearing formal dress at an exercise class. (If you've grown up with your nose in a book, like a lot of us who have grown up to be professors and scientists, the patterns of language in what you have been reading may have gotten inside your head so seriously that you have to work very hard to talk like people who weren't quite so nerdy when they were young.) Language teachers and remediators have to think about what level or levels of formality their students or clients need to use or avoid. Everyone needs to be able to understand and use *gonna* and *wanna*, because those forms surround us on all but the most formal occasions. But most of us also need to know when not to use them.

Understanding the ways that people are expected to talk in different social settings is part of the topic of SOCIOLINGUISTICS; you may have seen books or newspaper articles by sociolinguists Deborah Tannen or William Labov. Sociolinguists also study dialects, the way that people feel about their own dialect, and what people think about those who speak various other dialects of their language. (Almost every language, even those with few speakers, has several dialects, and usually one of them is spoken by people who are (or were) politically dominant, so that one gets to be considered the "correct" way to speak in formal settings.)

1.10 Language Families and Language Types

If you are almost any kind of language professional (a language teacher, clinician, translator, or someone who works on international Web sites) you need to know the basics of LANGUAGE TYPOLOGY—the study of how languages are alike and different—because you never know what kind of language may walk into your life. The way children and adults read, write, speak, and understand English can all be affected by what other languages they learned first, so the more you know (or can find out) about how those other languages are like and unlike English, from the details of their sounds and writing systems to their ways of signaling politeness or intimacy, the better you can deal with whatever comes up.

1.10.1 Some important differences between languages

Languages, like personality types or cultures, can differ and be similar in many different ways. If you know only one or two languages, you may be startled at some of the big differences out there. For example, one of the biggest differences (although interestingly, it doesn't cause a lot of trouble for second language learners) is whether the object of a verb comes after the verb (*I found my wallet!*) as it does in English and Chinese, or before it (*I my wallet found!*), as it does in Japanese and Turkish and Hindi (just to name a few), or whether it sometimes come before it and sometimes after it, depending on the construction that the verb phrase is in, as is true for German, Dutch, Swedish, and their close relatives. (Learning to switch between two word orders is much more of a problem than just learning to use a new order). There are other possible word order and construction order differences, too: do you say *My red coat is in the closet* or *My coat red is in the closet* (as you would in French)? *The girl I met yesterday is from Kyoto* or *Yesterday I met girl Kyoto from is* (as you would in Japanese)?

Another substantial difference is whether you need to have a subject in every (or almost every) sentence as English, French, and German do (we even have to say *It's raining, Es regnet, Il pleut* when there's no "it"), or whether you can leave out meaningless subjects and just say the equivalent of *Is raining*, as you can in Portuguese, Spanish, and Italian (*Esta chovendo, Esta llovendo, Sta piovendo*), not to mention Russian and many other languages. In Chinese and Japanese (and again, in many other languages), you can leave out both subjects and objects if the person you are talking to can perfectly well figure out what they are, or doesn't need to know, but in English, we can only leave out the objects of a few transitive verbs like *eat* and *drink* (*We ate already*, *We drank all night*). It's moderately difficult to remember to leave words out in a new language; it's much more challenging to remember to put them in if your own language wouldn't need them.

Although all languages have nouns and verbs, lots of words can be either a noun or a verb depending on the construction they are being used in (*light* is a verb in *light my fire*, a noun in *light of my life*), as we've already seen for English in section 1.4.4. In Chinese, the situation is more confusing; in some constructions, people can disagree about whether a word is being used as noun or as a verb. Here's another difference: Many languages (for example Russian, Finnish, and Japanese) don't have any indefinite and definite articles that would correspond to *a* or *the*; some, like Hebrew, have only definite articles.

In section 1.6.2, we mentioned verb AGREEMENT (the way the form of a verb can depend on the person and number of its subject—*I was/you were* or *we sing/she sings*) and how some languages don't have it. But you probably know that in the languages English speakers are most likely to learn in school, Spanish or French (and others closely related to them, like Portuguese and Italian), every verb has several different forms, depending on its subject. In English, only the verb *be* has a whole suite of different forms (*I am, you are, he/she/it is, we are, they are*), but for Spanish and French, every verb has at least this many forms and you have to choose the right one depending on its subject. And you probably also know another typological difference between the morphology of English and those languages: They have GRAMMATICAL GENDER. All nouns are either MASCULINE or FEMININE (whether or not they can have biological gender, though nouns referring to male creatures are usually masculine and those referring to female creatures are usually feminine). Articles and most of the adjectives that modify a noun also have masculine and feminine forms, and they have to AGREE with the noun they modify—that is, they have to have the same gender as the noun. We'll come back to some of these differences between languages and the problems they make for second language learners in Chapter 9 and for multilingual aphasia evaluation in Chapter 10.

1.10.2 Being similar and being related

Now we have to take a step back and talk about two different ideas: languages being *similar* and languages being *related*. Languages change over time; grandparents have been complaining about the way their grandchildren talk, undoubtedly, since language began. A language that's spoken by people who lose contact with each other—settlers in two different mountain valleys, for example, or colonists who settle new countries across oceans—will change in different ways in the separate places. Very quickly, then, within a generation or two, different ways of speaking develop in the new places, and these become recognizably different DIALECTS in another generation or two. If changes keep accumulating to the point where people from the different groups can barely understand each other, so that translators and language lessons are necessary, the two forms of the original language are now separate languages. (Unless politics intervenes: If they both have the same government, they will probably still be called dialects of the same language. Everybody who is interested in how language is affected by politics should know the famous saying by Max Weinreich [originally stated in Yiddish, a dialect of German]: "A language is a dialect with an army and a navy.")

The situation is pretty much the same for languages as it is for people, except that languages (usually) have only one "parent": Two languages are related if they have descended from the same language, somewhere back in time. All the descendents of one language are, unsurprisingly, called a language family. Languages that separated only one or two thousand years ago may still look a lot alike, like the languages of Europe that came from Latin (the ROMANCE LANGUAGES and dialects: French, Provençal, Italian, Portuguese, Spanish, Catalan, Romanian, Romansh, and so on, some of which have never been completely separated from the others).

But we can trace back relationships that are much older than that. Latin itself is part of the huge INDO-EUROPEAN FAMILY of languages, whose common ancestor (which we call Proto-Indo-European) must have been spoken about 6,000 years ago. Three thousand years later, the Indo-European family included not only the immediate ancestor of Latin, but a number of Latin's rather distant cousins. One of those distant cousins is called Proto-Germanic, because it was the ancestor of the **GERMANIC FAMILY** of languages (which includes English, German, Dutch, and the languages of western Scandinavia). Another cousin, called Proto-Slavic, was the ancestor of the **SLAVIC LANGUAGES** (including Russian, Polish, Czech, and Bulgarian); still another was the ancestor of the **INDO-IRANIAN** languages of Iran, Afghanistan, and northern India. As the time gulf widened over the next three millennia, the descendents of these distantly related languages, like cousins who share one great-great-great-grandparent, eventually came to look very different indeed, like modern-day English (in the Germanic branch of the family), Italian (Romance branch), Russian (Slavic branch), Hindi (Indo-Iranian branch), and Irish (**CELTIC** branch).

In contrast, unrelated languages sometimes look a lot alike. How can that happen? Often, it's because their speakers have been in contact, and there once were (or still are) many bilingual speakers. When two languages are spoken by the same group of people (who might be neighbors, traders, scholars, soldiers, or missionaries), at least one of the groups is likely to have learned a lot of words and constructions from the other. That's true for Japanese and for Korean, which both borrowed a lot of vocabulary and morphology from Chinese. (They also borrowed the oldest parts of their writing systems—the original forms of the kanji in Japanese and the hanja in Korean, which we'll say more about in Chapter 8.)

And then, there's the equivalent of marriages between, say, third cousins. English and French come from different branches of the Indo-European family (Germanic and Romance) and so they shouldn't look much alike. But after the Norman Conquest about a thousand years ago, English absorbed a huge amount of French vocabulary and phonology, though it kept most of its Germanic-type syntax.

Finally, languages that are completely unrelated and that had no contacts as far back as we can trace them, like English and Japanese before the modern era, may still have one or two striking things in common (Japanese uses a present progressive tense almost the same way English does). It's a coincidence, just as you may find one friend who looks sort of like another of your friends, perhaps around the eyes or with the same little gap between his front teeth. Coincidences like that arise in languages because all languages are solutions to the same great problem: how to communicate about human needs with human brains and human vocal and auditory apparatus, (or, for signed languages, with human eyes and hands).

One more thing: there's a lot of folklore about languages that's not true, but is believed almost passionately by their speakers. If someone tells you that his or her language is a gift from God, or is the oldest in the world, or is exactly the same as was spoken by a religious leader thousands of years ago, just be polite about it. Even if the language has been written pretty much the same way for all that time, the spoken form will have changed, but there's no point in arguing.

Exercises for Chapter 1

Section 1A

1.1 When will sounding out words work, and when will memorizing spelling be needed?

Could you sound out the spelling difference between *merry*, *Mary*, and *marry*, or are they pronounced the same in your dialect of English? How about *caught*, *cot*? *Ann* and *Ian*? If you were teaching spelling, how could you find out whether your students should be able to hear the difference between two words that are spelled differently or whether they need to just memorize the spelling for each word, as we all do for *meet* and *meat*?

1.2 When can you use spelling to help someone learn grammar and pronunciation, and when will spelling mislead them? (I am not making this example up, by the way. I wish it hadn't happened, but it did.)

In a kindergarten-age classroom for children with slow language development, a teacher is using a multichannel approach. These children omit some unstressed words, and her lesson goal is to get them to attend to the unstressed words in some simple model sentences. So she writes some of the words that they tend to omit on the blackboard after she says a model sentence, and then she goes over these words one at a time, emphasizing the sounds and the letter names. After saying a short sentence containing the word *is*, she writes I S on the board, and then says the names of the letters and then the word again, emphasizing all the sounds: *I S, is*. Transcribe what she said (the two letter names and then the word *is* itself) into IPA.

Now imagine you are her supervisor. Explain diplomatically but accurately why her strategy was not likely to be helpful to the children for this particular word. What is another word that you could use as an example of where the same problem would arise? What would you suggest that she try instead of the strategy that she is using?

1.3 (Figure 1.9) If you are from California, you can immediately understand the joke in this cartoon by Joe Chiappetta.

Figure 1.9. Hairy potter. Silly Daddy cartoon copyright Joe Chiappetta, used with permission from www.joechiappetta .blogspot.com .

But most people from the Northeast have to think a minute to get it. Look back at the *merry, marry, Mary* story in section 1.2.4.3, note 4 of the vowel chart, and explain why people from the Northeast will be slow to understand this joke.

Section 1B

1.4 How can you explain what makes a sentence ambiguous? Here are examples of three different kinds of ambiguity to think about:

A. Referent ambiguity
    Sarah insulted Amy, and then she kicked her.

B. Syntactic ambiguity
    Kissing cousins can be serious trouble.

C. Temporary syntactic ambiguity ("garden path" sentence)
    The truck unloaded at the rear door was rented.

1.5 More English derivational morphemes. English has a good number of derivational morphemes that are not borrowed from Latin (or Greek). How would you show a young reader or a second language learner where the "joints" between the morphemes are in words like *wilderness, wonderful, bewitch, carrier, funnier, lively,* and how would you explain the way that taking these words apart can help your student understand them?

1.6 Your computer's grammar checker can recognize a lot of grammatical morphemes and what they do. For example, your grammar checker "knows" that *-s* is a plural ending on nouns, but that not all word-final *s*'s are endings, so it doesn't "think" that *kiss* or *basis* is plural, and doesn't mistakenly tell you that *A kiss is sweet* is incorrect.

However, your spellcheck program is dumb: if you give it a new word like *morpheme*, and then you write *morphemes* for the first time, it will tell you that *morphemes* is a spelling error. Why? What would the spellcheck have to "know" about a new word to avoid annoying you this way? How could it "find out" that information?

Note on English Grammars. There are hundreds of English reference grammars, but if you have a choice, consider the series of larger and smaller grammar books edited by Quirk, Swartvik, Leech, and Greenbaum (in various orders of authorship), published by Longman. The largest is *A Comprehensive Grammar of the English Language*.

References

Ladefoged, P., & Johnson, K. (2010). *A course in phonetics* (with CD-ROM). Boston, MA: Wadsworth.

Zhou, X., Espy-Wilson, C. Y., Boyce, S., Tiede, M., Holland, C., & Choe, A. (2008). A magnetic resonance imaging-based articulatory and acoustic study of "retroflex" and "bunched" American English /r/. *Journal of the Acoustical Society of America*, *123*(6), 4466–4481.

How Brains Work

2.1 Thinking About the Brain: A Quick History

Western medicine took many centuries to figure out that the brain is used for thinking, and several more centuries to have some clues about how something made of meat could have anything to do with ideas, dreams, and feelings (this is the "mind-body problem"). In fact, it is still a very hard question (search the Internet for "mind-body problem" if you are interested; most of the discussions are by philosophers). How does a few of pounds of cells and blood inside the hard shell of our skull—the only part of our body that *is* encased in a shell—make us human beings instead of robots? In this chapter, we will consider only how our brains make it possible for us to use language: to hear, speak, sign, read, write, and understand. The neurophysiology of love, ambition, and dreams are also products of those few pounds of meat, but much further beyond the reach of our understanding.

When Latin was the common language of learning in Europe, anatomists gave simple descriptions as names for the parts of the brain, and those are still used today, as you see in Figure 2.1. (If you want to remember those names better, or just not to feel mystified by them, it's helpful to know their meanings; they're in the Glossary.) Looking at the brain at the level

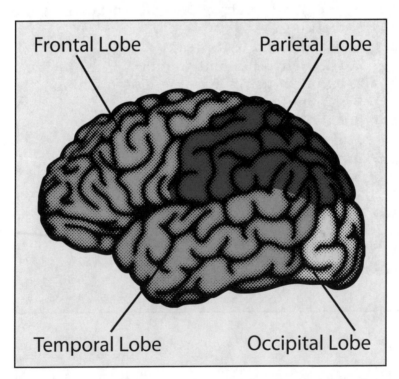

Figure 2.1. Viewing the left side of a brain; extra-deep grooves divide the outer layer (cortex) into four lobes. Image adapted from Shutterstock®. All rights reserved.

of these larger structures is essential for understanding the long-distance connections that make it possible for the different parts of our brains to synchronize their activities and work together so that we can go about our everyday activities. But information processing (including language information processing) begins at the level of individual brain cells, so to understand language processing and how we learn to do it, we have to look at a microscopic level: at small neighborhoods of brain cells and how they interact.

Since about the 1500s, people have thought about the brain as being like the most complicated machinery they knew about at the time; hydraulic pumps were the first (and not very useful) guess. In the 1800s, scientists and engineers figured out how to transmit information by electricity (first the telegraph, then the telephone); by 1900, this gave physiologists their first halfway useful model: brain as telephone switchboard (Figure 2.2). (To see more images of what a telephone switchboard or a telephone exchange was like a hundred years ago, search the Internet.)

Figure 2.2. Telephone switchboard. Image adapted from Shutterstock®. All rights reserved.

The "brain as telephone switchboard" metaphor was usable because the effects of some brain injuries can be explained fairly well using the idea that the brain has parts that do particular jobs—for example, a part where memory for word sounds is stored—and that brain injuries could destroy some of those parts, or just disconnect them from some other part. For example, the part that was supposed to store memory for word sounds could be disconnected from a part that was supposed to store information about how to move your mouth to make speech sounds. A disconnection like this would explain why a person with brain damage might be able to understand words but not say them.

As it turns out, the brain as telephone switchboard is not good enough to explain what we now know about the effects of brain injury. And it only deals with the collective effects of thousands of neurons working together to say or understand a word. The switchboard model has no way to explain how information is learned and stored in your brain, or how it is forgotten. It has no way to explain how learning that certain creatures, toys, and pictures are called "dog" leads to having a concept of what a dog is; and no way to explain that certain patterns of sounds are "music," others are "speaking," and still others are "laughing."

Since the 1950s, when the public began to hear about the first electronic computers (developed during World War II), it seemed obvious that the brain was like a computer. Well, it isn't—at least, it isn't like any computer that exists or has been designed. But the "brain as computer" is an idea that is helpful enough to be worth studying; for one thing, brains and computers both process information. We also have some reasonably clear evidence about the ways that your brain and your laptop are different kinds of information processors, which is helpful, too.

2.2 What Does it Mean to Say That the Brain Processes Information?

"Processing information" is a phrase that immediately builds a wrong subconscious image: that some kind of raw products are dumped into a machine that changes them into a new form. This image shoves us back to the pre-telephone days, in which the brain was (at best) some kind of assembly line or bread-making device. No good.

Try this image instead: The brain is a huge, bustling, complicated city. It's busy day and night, although its patterns of activity vary depending on the time. The city has docks and railroad lines, manufacturing districts and storage terminals, streets full of traffic—pedestrians, pushcarts, and delivery vans. There are short neighborhood streets, and there are freeways full of express traffic, essential for moving heavy traffic and large shipments across town. The population—the nerve cells, or NEURONS—have varied skills and varied access to the goods that are being transported. Thousands of transactions (perhaps hundreds of thousands!) are taking place all the time, but only a few of these can be seen happening; the bulk of the work that the inhabitants do must be painstakingly inferred from collecting statistics on shipping and traffic, imports and exports, as observed at hundreds of points in the city.

Enough metaphor? Here's an introduction to basic information about the brain as of 2010, which you can use when you are interpreting the dozens of new articles and Web posts about the brain that appear every month. But keep that "city" idea in the back of your mind, because most articles about what the brain does in reading, counting, remembering, or whatever, focus on a very small part of the huge silent roar of the hundreds of thousands of NEURAL EVENTS taking place at any one time.

Start with a close-up: What is a single neural event? Anything happening in a brain cell, which probably looks like one of these diagrams of neurons (Figure 2.3) (although much of the brain is composed of another kind of cells called GLIA or GLIAL cells; researchers are just starting to realize that they probably play an important role, too).

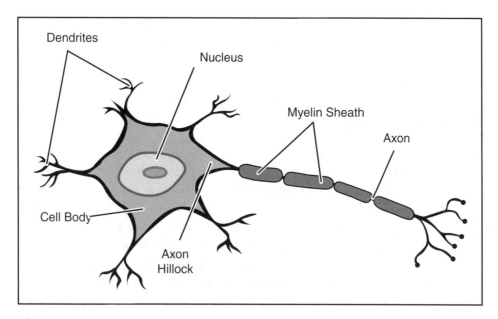

Figure 2.3. A single neuron. Adapted with permission from *Acquired language disorders: A case-based approach* by E. R. Klein and J. M. Mancinelli (p. 1). Copyright © 2010 Plural Publishing, Inc. All rights reserved.

You can see that neurons have complex branches (in fact, much more complex than Figure 2.3 shows). The **DENDRITES** are the multiple branches that bring information into the neuron, and the **AXON** is a single longer branch that carries information to the next neuron in line. Tips of the axon of each neuron come close to the tips of the dendrites of other neurons, but these tips never actually touch. Such near-contact points between axon and dendrite are called **SYNAPSES** (Figure 2.4). If some event causes one neuron to become active (more about this notion soon), it releases **NEUROTRANSMITTER** molecules from the tip of the axon on its side of the synapse. Activity in a neuron starts when it gets enough molecules of several neurotransmitter chemicals from a neighboring neuron or perhaps from several neighbors at the same time. If it gets enough neurotransmitter molecules, it becomes active too, and after a very short delay, it starts sending out its own neurotransmitter molecules from its axons to the dendrites of other neurons. In this way, activity can be passed along a chain from each neuron to many others.

Neurons that excite their neighbors are called **EXCITATORY NEURONS**. We need this term because at some synapses, something different happens: your brain also has neurons that reduce the activity in the neurons that they send neurotransmitter molecules to. These are called **INHIBITORY NEURONS**, and their activity is what keeps neural activity from turning into a neural explosion in which a person would be trying to do everything at once. Inhibitory neurons don't just keep our minds from exploding, though: Delicate interactions of excitation and inhibition are needed to give us precision in all sorts of perceiving, thinking, and acting.

2.3 How Can a Bunch of Cells Learn or Know Something?

All those neurons are sending information to one another, but what makes anything useful stick in your head? And how do you find it (if you can) when you need it again? This much is clear: If information (someone's name, the taste of a particular kind of cheese, as much as you can recall of a gorgeous sunset, etc.) or a skill (how to tie a bow, how to parallel park a car, etc.) is going to stay in your brain, it must change your brain a little. Otherwise, it would really be like water rolling off a duck's back.

And in fact, this is what happens: every experience, conscious or unconscious, makes tiny changes in the *strengths* of the synaptic connections between some of your neurons; that is, it changes how many bunches

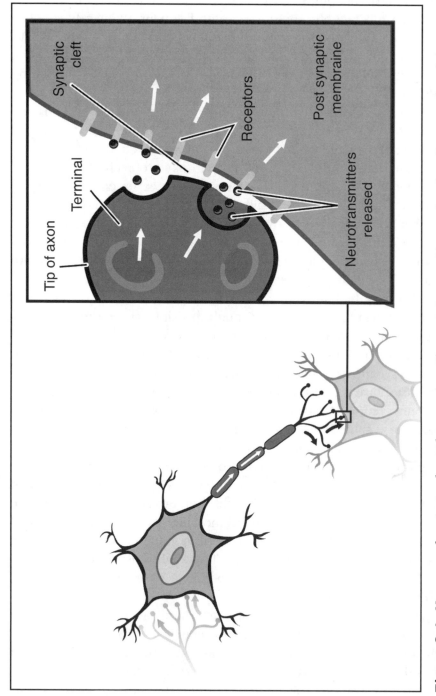

Figure 2.4. Neurons showing enlarged synapse with neurotransmitter molecules. Reprinted with permission from *Acquired language disorders: A case-based approach* by E. R. Klein and J. M. Mancinelli (p. 2). Copyright © 2010 Plural Publishing, Inc. All rights reserved.

of neurotransmitter molecules will be sent from a neuron to its neighbor if the first neuron becomes active. You've got billions of connections, so small changes in a few of them don't destabilize your brain and make you lose what you've already stored. But those small changes do modify what's there. When you pet an unfamiliar cat, the texture of its fur and the way it reacts to your touch get linked to all your previous experiences of petting cats, adding to your understanding of cat fur textures and the ways cats behave. When you learn a word, its sound, meaning, and the grammatical and social contexts for its use, as well as the voice of the person who said it or the look of the page where you read it, all get linked up to other information of the same kinds, as well as staying linked to each other.

The idea that the brain keeps changing with experience as synaptic connections change strength is called brain **PLASTICITY**. Brains are much more plastic than we used to think: in deaf people, neurons that would have been used for sound perception are used for processing visual language, and in blind people, the area for processing sounds expands into the area that normally processes vision. With enough intensive practice, people who have had strokes can start to regain more use of paralyzed arms and legs than had even been thought possible, and more use of language; this is an exciting research frontier to keep watching.

So your brain's knowledge exists, at least in large measure, as an enormous set of synaptic connection strengths. And these connections mean something because they are ultimately linked to parts of the brain that are tightly connected to **SENSORY NEURONS** and **MOTOR NEURONS**. When you remember how something looks, sounds, or feels, you are picking up a small part of the sensory activation caused by original experience. (If you are hallucinating or dreaming, you're probably getting activation of scraps that have come together from many different original experiences and imaginings to make a weird whole.) If the memory is not quite true to the original event—and memories can be modified by time, emotions, and later experience—it's because the synaptic connections that stored the original information have been changed. That's why false memories unfortunately feel just as real as true ones, sometimes causing terrible problems with eyewitness testimony.

When you remember how to do something—to say your name, or break a raw egg into a bowl—your motor neurons get **ACTIVATED**: chemical changes happen inside them that make them ready and able to send signals to the muscles you would need to carry out that action. What activates them? Your wanting (or being prompted) to do this thing, plus your memory of having done this thing before. The memory of all the times you have said your name or broken an egg has been formed from signals that came back to your brain from your mouth and your ears, or your hands and your eyes, as you learned to do these highly skilled acts. Some of these were sensory signals (sound, sight, touch, pressure) that became linked to the motor signals you had just sent out. Importantly, those memories of speaking or egg-breaking were linked to something else that was happening at the same time: your intention to say your name or to use the egg, and the context (e.g., introducing yourself, or making scrambled eggs) that aroused that intention. So the intention to use a skill has a (subconscious) link to the stored motor memories that are the skill itself, and to the sensory memories that allow you to compare what you are doing to what doing it right should look and feel like.

When these long-distance links between intention and all the motor and sensory memories are weak or missing, a person's intentions are cut off from his or her ability to carry them out. Strokes can cause this kind of disconnection in a brain, but another way we get weak links is more familiar; as you know, people who are taught to say a phrase in the clinic or classroom, like *I would like to buy a newspaper*, often fail to use that phrase when they need it in the real world. Why? Because the memory of how to say the phrase is too strongly linked to the room where it was learned and the need to satisfy the teacher, and barely if at all linked to the situation where it will really be needed. So it doesn't get retrieved when you're a tourist standing in front of a strange clerk at a newsstand in a foreign country with money in your hand and the actual desire to read the news from home; instead, you smile, point, grunt, and hold out the money hopefully.

Imaginative teaching techniques are needed to help beginning students or disabled clients form strong and usable links between language and what they will need to use language for. Think about how you could teach language skills so that people could really use what you've taught them; discussion exercises at the end of this chapter will help you develop your ideas.

2.4 Activation and Its Spread

Having a strong link between your intention and your stored motor and sensory memory is important if you want to do something without the help of the context in which you learned to do it, whether it's something you learned to do in the real world and now have to perform in some kind of test, or whether it's something you learned in a class and now have to use for real. When some of the many stages of linkage between intention and stored motor memory are damaged or broken, as in some types of brain injury, people may have one kind of APRAXIA, the inability to carry out an action even though you understand what you are supposed to do and have no paralysis of the muscles you'd need to do it with. People with ORAL APRAXIA—apraxia affecting actions we do with our mouths—may be unable to follow the request to blow out an imaginary candle. Instead, they say *Blow, blow!* with a sort of intense, breathy voice, while the expression on their face suggests that they are trying to follow the examiner's instruction. That breathiness in their response shows that they understood, in some sense, what they were asked to do, yet they can't do it. But if the examiner shows them a real lit candle, they may be able to blow it out perfectly well. (If they can't, the apraxia is extremely severe.) How is it possible that a person who understands the examiner's request can be unable to demonstrate blowing out an imaginary candle, but can blow out a real one?

To understand this paradox, we need to explore further two of the most important concepts in this book: the concept of the ACTIVATION of a neuron or group of neurons, and an understanding of SPREADING ACTIVATION (i.e., how activation spreads from one group of neurons to other groups). We started developing these concepts in section 2.2, and now that we have some idea of what they're good for, we'll go on.

ACTIVATING a neuron means building up chemical changes inside it to the point where it starts sending out signals to the other neurons that it is connected to. We already know that the brain is a signal relaying system: If one neuron gets stimulated enough, it becomes activated, and passes that stimulation along to one or more neighbors. In somewhat more detail: Each neuron has a RESTING LEVEL of activity (think of the neuron as being asleep), where it stays when it is getting only a few neurotransmitters stimulating the synapses of its dendrites to send electrical signals toward the CELL BODY. But when enough neurotransmitters from active neighbor neurons barge into the dendrites of the sleeping neuron at about the same time, the resulting barrage of electrical signals starts to arouse it, to wake it up.

Continuing impacts from neurotransmitters make activity inside this neuron build up; if the activity increases to a THRESHOLD LEVEL, the neuron wakes up fully and passes on the activation. That is, it sends out new electrical impulses out along its axon, and when these impulses get to the end of the axon, they force neurotransmitters to move across the axon's synapses to the dendrites of neighboring neurons. If the connection is EXCITATORY, the neighbor will start to become active, but if it is inhibitory, the activity level in the neighbor will be reduced. (Whether it's excitatory or inhibitory depends on what kinds of neurotransmitters the neuron sends out.) Connections across synapses vary in strength: if a connection is strong, the number of packets of neurotransmitter that is released at the synapse is greater, and the amount of excitation or inhibition that the first neuron causes in its neighbor is greater, too. Neurons also vary in how much activation is needed to move them from the resting level to the threshold level. Some are very easily aroused, but others won't become fully awake until they've had a lot of excitatory input from their neighbors.

Different areas of the brain are specialized for handling different kinds of information, so activation must spread over long-distance networks, not just between neighbors, using major pathways between the brain regions. These pathways become more and more efficient highways for neural electrical activity as children learn and develop, and that long-distance information transmission is essential for the intricate brain coordination that we need to deal with the huge amount of information that keeps bombarding us all the time we are awake. Children with developmental problems like ADHD and autism seem to have poorer long-distance brain coordination, but we are a long way from knowing whether that is a cause or just a symptom of their information processing problems.

2.4.1 Activation and memory

We can remember huge amounts of information because of how this neural network mechanism works: Each memory is not a completely separate item, like a photograph in a drawer or a file in your computer would be, so you don't have to worry about running out of storage space. Perhaps a good analogy would be the huge wardrobe store of a theater company, because each memory, like an elaborate costume, is an assemblage of many parts; each assemblage is unique, but only some of its parts are; others get reused countless times. Each memory of something you have done is unique, but even your most extraordinary memory—perhaps a memory of being on top of a great mountain—reuses your memories of your own body and many other things that it must have had in common with more mundane events.

So everything we know or know how to do is stored in our brains as a set of synaptic connection strengths, and these strengths affect the way the information relay system works: a strong connection between two neurons means that activating the first neuron has a major impact on the second one. What good does that do, though? How does this relay of activations and inhibitions get translated into memories and actions?

Here's one way, starting from perception: Sensory responses to incoming stimuli send neural signals that reactivate memories of those stimuli (although that activation may not be enough to bring those memories to consciousness, especially if there are thousands or millions of them, as there would be for the memories of unremarkable daily events like brushing your teeth, and of using all but the rarest words.) Then, that activation propagates along the neurons from those memories to a wide range of others connected with them. This activation may not be enough to bring those others all the way up to their firing threshold, but if other connected stimuli are also perceived, the total activation will mount up to the point where action can begin. Below the level of consciousness, this spreading and summing of activation gets us through our daily lives almost seamlessly, as we prepare for each tiny component action of a familiar activity while still doing the one before it: Picking up the toothbrush with the dominant hand, we start to reach for the toothpaste with the other, at the same time tightening our dominant-hand grip on the toothbrush handle with the third, fourth, and fifth fingers, freeing up its thumb and forefinger to take the cap off the toothpaste . . . You can work through some of the steps of looking, visual stimulation, tactile feedback, and so on, as an exercise (how tight do you have to hold the toothbrush, the toothpaste tube, its cap?).

This activity is so common, dull, and easy (for two-handed people) that it has become deeply automatic; the only way to work through these steps is to actually get your toothbrush and toothpaste and pay minute attention to what your hands want to do. Your lifetime history of visual, tactile, and motor information relayed back and forth has become a skill, a special kind of knowledge. And it's more than "just a set of connections" because of where these connections end: in instructions that actually make your fingers move, on the motor side, and in the brain areas where the original information of touch and vision were interpreted, on the sensory side. All the connections in your computer wouldn't be of any use without the input (keyboard, mouse) and output (screen, Internet connection) interfaces, and all the connections in your head have to be anchored, eventually, to your own sensory and motor interfaces with the world.

Let's go back to the apraxia story now, and start working through the problem of being able to blow out a flame of a real match or a candle but not an imaginary flame. This seems much less automatic—and unless you are a smoker, much less practiced—than putting toothpaste on your toothbrush.

Have you been to a birthday party for really little kids? A one-year-old's birthday party is for the parents: Nobody expects the baby to have the faintest idea of what's going on, except when it comes to eating the cake; the party pictures usually feature the little person covered with splotches of chocolate frosting. A two-year-old's party is different; toddlers understand that tearing wrappings off what people give them at the party will reveal toys, and the parents coach the birthday child to do something new: to blow out the two candles on the cake before diving into it. Toddlers can imitate many actions that they see, thanks to months of observing and attempting actions, and of noticing the consequences of their own actions and those of others (and perhaps to some innate programming involving MIRROR NEURONS—neurons dedicated to stimulating an observer's brain and muscles to match what they see—this is still controversial). Probably putting the whole candle-blowing-out action together won't happen the first time, just a lot of huffing and puffing before the parents give in and do it so that the toddler and guests can get to the cake. But a three-year-old can handle the job, and a four-year-old has become an expert; she can even blow out imaginary candles on an imaginary cake, unlike the unfortunate brain-damaged adult with apraxia.

So, how has the four-year-old's brain actually learned this expertise, and exactly what has it learned?

2.4.2 Real-world learning: Establishing multimodal connections

Learning goes on all the time, whether we are conscious of it or not; every experience that leaves any subconscious or conscious memory is an instance of learning. We learn lots of apparently useless things; for example, people do better on an exam when they are tested in the same room that they had lessons in than they do when they are given the same exam in a different room, so they must have learned information about the room along with the lessons. Marketers know that we associate scents with products, even if the odor isn't the smell of the product, and that an odor plus an advertisement makes us remember the ad better. Clearly, our brains are not particularly selective. All the things that are going on at a given instant are linked together (and as we get older, we seem to hold onto more and more of this incidental information, which can compensate for some of the memory problems that come with aging). The links are usually weak at first, but if an event arouses strong emotions, strong ones may be forged immediately, probably by a rush of additional neurotransmitters at the synapses.

There's a good reason for our brains to work in such an indiscriminate way: Learners (including animals other than humans, of course) can't know from the beginning exactly what about an experience is going to end up being important: The sound of leaves when you walk through them tells you whether they would burn easily, the visual texture of a surface tells you a lot about how it would feel if you touched it (but not whether it'll be warm or cold), an –s or –z at the end of a word tells you that it's likely to be plural in English, but not in Hebrew.

When two sets of stimuli occur together many times (think of all the motor and sense impressions you get each time you eat an apple, open a package, or start up your computer), the connections among them get strengthened; one-time links, unless they were associated with a strong emotion, get swamped by the ones that are growing stronger, and become unable to contribute to remembering anything.

This unselective linkage idea is very different from our usual concept of learning, which concentrates only on the aspects of an experience that we know the learner is supposed to recall. When someone is learning a word, we normally think of them only as learning that a certain sequence of sounds has a certain meaning. But much more than that is being learned.

Suppose that between the ages of two and three, a particular child (call her Jenny) learns *blow*, *blow out*, and *candle*, and what *blow*, *out*, and *candle* mean together in that order. Let's analyze this seriously by considering some of the kinds of stimulating events that are likely to be linked up at each of the opportunities that Jenny has for learning what these three words mean, individually and together. At the level of sounds, she hears the word's sound in one or several adult and child voices; if she tries to say it, she hears its sound in her own voice and she feels the sequence of sensations in her mouth and chest when she is saying it. She sees how other people's faces move when they say *Jenny, blow out the candles!* She must also be recording the subconscious set of motor nerve impulses that get her oral tract in the right sequence of positions, or she'd never learn the skill of saying the words.

But if she's two, and hearing and developing normally, Jenny is not starting to learn this skill from scratch. She has been hearing words for two years, babbling for more than a year, and speaking, possibly for as much as a year already, in one or more languages. She has stored memories of thousands of speech events of varying degrees of similarity to this one, and those memories get activated as she listens—the auditory and visual ones first, and then those auditory and visual memories that rise above threshold activate the motor memories that they have co-occurred with in the past. The more similar the auditory and visual memories are to some or all of *Jenny, blow out the candles!*, the more activation they get.

Her mind is picking up everything else that is going on in the same way. Some things will be familiar and others different or combined in new ways, like singing before eating. In the exercises, you can try elaborating the scenario of just the few moments around *Jenny, blow out the candles!*

2.4.3 Spreading activation and the process of understanding a word

If Jenny's parents think she understands the word *blow*—and parents tend to be right about things like that—they expect her to blow air out of her mouth when they say it (unless she's in a contrary mood, being a two-year-old). Understanding the word *blow* is only part of understanding *Jenny, blow out the candles!* but Jenny's experience has also given her the basic grammatical tools to know that she is the person expected to do the blowing, and that she is somehow supposed to connect blowing with the candles over there on the cake. Working out how she has acquired these grammatical tools takes us well beyond the scope of this book, but I recommend Tomasello (2003). Let's go on with learning the word meanings, specifically the semantics of *blow* in this context.

So Jenny's parents also expect her to direct the air that she blows out at the candle flames, rather than at the candles themselves, which is not so reasonable when you think about it. On the other hand, birthday candles are small, so blowing on them hard enough will blow out their flames; when the flames go out people will celebrate her accomplishment, so she will find out how *blow out* is different from *blow away*, *blow over*, and *blow on*, not to mention *blow bubbles*, *blow Grandma a kiss*, and *blow your nose*. Like most if not all action verbs, precisely what *blow* means in motor terms depends on what, if anything, is being acted on (the direct object of the verb) and what the goal of the action is. Does it involve a change of position, a change of orientation, a transfer of object from one person to another, or just an action with no visible result?

The next time Jenny sees birthday candles is likely to be at another child's party. It's a fair bet that she will try to blow them out, and that she will be less than thrilled to be restrained from doing so. After all, she learned what to do with lit candles on a cake at her own party; you can easily work out the details of the series of arousals that will flow from the visual stimulus to her getting all set for performing the blowing-out again (sitting up straighter, taking a deep breath, holding it in, leaning forward . . .). Any stimulus that occurred at her own birthday party is connected to all the others (though with varying strengths), so any one of them may arouse any of the others.

Fast forward to Jenny at 80, having had a stroke that has left her with oral apraxia, and let's think about how it's possible that she understands the word *blow*, can't perform the activity of blowing out an imaginary candle, yet can blow out a real one. We can see now that understanding a word, though it takes place in a few tenths of a second, is not a single all-or-nothing event. It's a series of them, involving one set of activations after another, starting from hearing the sounds of the word *blow*, continuing through activation of the stored memory that there is such an English word, and spreading farther through links from the word *blow* to other words that can go with it, and to the properties that make it a verb, and to at least some of the specific motor and sensory associations of blowing on and into different objects and seeing other people do so.

So, Jenny at 80, asked to blow out an imaginary candle after her stroke, is saying *blow, blow* in a breathy voice with a look of effort on her face, but she hasn't pursed her lips and she's not exhaling enough air through her mouth fast enough to produce the sound of blowing; she's talking, with only a trace of the action she's supposed to carry out. Her stroke hasn't seriously damaged her memories of the word form, and she apparently still has access to the meaning, or some of it, because she still knows that it involves exhaling through one's mouth hard enough to make an air friction noise.

But the stroke must have damaged some connections in Jenny's brain between these memories and her memories of the motor program for blowing on an object. They have been weakened at least to the point where they can't compete with the activation of the motor pattern for saying the word, which is still spreading from having just heard the sound of the word itself, as she tries to concentrate on trying to do what she has been asked to do.

And maybe the word *candle* has lost its connections to her memories of how a candle flame looks, or maybe those visual memories are gone. We know that for some people with apraxia, seeing just an unlit match is enough to get them to blow on it correctly, so visual stimulation from the unlit match must be activating enough other memories to raise the activation of their motor program for blowing to the point where it can overcome the activation of the program for saying the word *blow*. And for others, although an unlit match won't work, seeing a real, moving flame will at last bring up enough associations to unleash the additional activation that they need to make the motor program for blowing strong enough to overcome the activation of the program for saying the word.

And sometimes the examining clinician's fingers get burned.

2.5 Top-Down and Bottom-Up Processing

Below the level of consciousness, our minds and our bodies are constantly working to deal with information about our surroundings. External and internal sensations bombard us—engine sounds, air currents, the normal pressure of a shoe or a chair back—the list seems endless. The enormous bulk of these sensory data has to be kept from driving us crazy so that we can concentrate on what we want to do—to cook dinner, to drive to work, to study; whatever. But when background information becomes important —an unfamiliar voice in the next room, a fire siren in the distance, a stone in your shoe—it has to get through so that we can respond appropriately. So the brain mechanisms that focus us on the traffic or on the page we're trying to read have to be screening devices, not shut-off devices.

Our minds and bodies have several ways of managing to keep bulk information under control; the most important one for language (and many other areas of sensory information) is prediction, based on activation spreading from one neuron to another along pathways that have become strengthened in the course of learning. A major part of becoming a skilled language user is learning what sounds and words are likely or unlikely to be what you hear or see in the next instant of listening or reading. This is what it really means to be learning the patterns of your language.

2.5.1 Language patterns

Suppose you are a native speaker of English, you are at a bus stop with a good friend, and a truck roars by just as she starts to say, without any particular context, *Hey, why don't you come over for dinner tomorrow?* All you actually hear might be something rather like *Hey, ay (something something something) inner uhmarruh?* (A sound file for this is in Materials for Chapter 2 on your CD.) The second word might have been *I* or *why*; you might have very little clue about the next couple of words, except that they were there; but *inner* will have been the accented word (linguists call it the stressed word because "accent" has too many other linguistic meanings). As for the final word, you heard that it had three syllables, that the middle one was stressed, and that that syllable was pronounced *mar*. Yet the chances are that if you heard this barely intelligible sentence, you would understand what your friend said, and be able to answer her appropriately as soon as she got to the end of it. On the other hand, if you have had only about a year of some other language, say French (or a few more years than that but you are way out of practice), you'd probably have to ask the speaker to repeat what she had said, even if you know all the individual words in the French version (listen to the example in Materials for Chapter 2 on your CD).

Why is there a difference between your ability to understand a sentence through noise in a language that you know natively and one that you don't know well (or haven't used lately)? Assuming you know all the words in the French sentence, why does the same amount of noise blot them out so badly?

The answer lies in the enormous amount of unconscious knowledge of English you have been accumulating since three months before you were born. (That is roughly when a normally developing infant becomes able to hear the rhythms and rises and falls of its mother's voice through the walls of her uterus.) You now carry in your head information about what speech sounds exist in English, which ones are likely to occur at the beginnings of clauses or next to certain others, and which ones are easily drowned out by noise. You know, unconsciously, which words are more frequent than others, which ones are likely to occur in a particular grammatical and social context, which ones are likely to be stressed, which words or parts of words will have to occur if certain others occur. For written words, we also have the same kind of unconscious knowledge of possible letter sequences, so that we can find words in "visual noise." To give yourself a sense of how strong this unconscious knowledge is of, for written English anyway, try reading the following word and word-part, clipped from a "Captcha" web security graphic (the correct letters to type into the security box are at the end of this chapter) (Figure 2.5).

If you are not a native speaker of English, that may have been a difficult task. A practical application of this: If you are photocopying some text for a classmate, student, or client who is not a native speaker of the document's language, be careful not to cut off any letters of any words, especially not their first letters! Here's what bad photocopying can do to a French newspaper article, with an English one for comparison. (Figures 2.6A and 2.6B). (The properly trimmed versions are on your CD.)

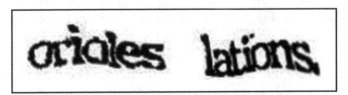

Figure 2.5. "CAPTCHA" graphic

première secrétaire du PS, qui était jeudi l'invitée d'«A vous de er» sur France 2, travaille sa stature de présidentiable.

peut le dire très simplement : Martine Aubry est en lice pour 2012. Dans son ourage, on a fait le compte, depuis longtemps, des cartes dont dispose la ire de Lille. La compétition pour l'investiture se jouera entre «Dominique ᴣuss-Kahn, Ségolène Royal et elle», dit-on, en excluant d'office François lande, Pierre Moscovici ou Manuel Valls.

dis que le directeur du FMI **a pour obligation de se taire** et alors que cienne candidate à la présidentielle **se bat pour le leadership de son ırant face à Vincent Peillon**, la première secrétaire a une obsession, dont fait une stratégie de communication : montrer qu'elle travaille au service du Exemple, jeudi soir : Martine Aubry était ainsi l'invitée d'«A vous de juger» France 2. Au menu : débat sur l'identité nationale, **immigration**, adoption ır les parents homosexuels, politique économique et sociale... Mais aussi la sidentielle.

n croire les sondages, **Dominique Strauss-Kahn serait le seul à pouvoir :tre Nicolas Sarkozy**. «Il y en aura d'autres au fur et à mesure que le temps nce», observe Martine Aubry. Mais DSK est-il le recours ? «Si c'est le meilleur didat, il faudra qu'il revienne», concède-t-elle avant d'ajouter : «C'est encore ɔ tôt.» Sur sa propre ambition, elle élude : «Je ne suis pas née pour cela, je ; née pour me battre.» Elle verra plus tard. Pour l'instant, elle ne veut pas ondre : «Ça me rase, cette question.» Dans la logique des institutions, le chef parti devrait être le candidat... «Cela l'est normalement, tranche-t-elle. Mais z nous, ce n'est pas ainsi.»

A

Figure 2.6. A. French news article with left margin cut off. *continues*

OSTON — Ask not how the Democratic candidates to succeed Senator
ward M. Kennedy would blaze a new path: most are too busy trying to
ove themselves his ideological twin as the Dec. 8 primary draws near.
presentative Michael E. Capuano, the only candidate with Congressional
perience, says his Washington seasoning makes him the obvious
nnedy heir. Electing someone who has not worked on Capitol Hill, Mr.
puano said in a recent debate, "would be to say to Senator Kennedy,
our 47 years of experience weren't worth much.' "

he debate took place at the Edward M. Kennedy Institute for the United
ates Senate, incidentally, next to the John F. Kennedy Presidential
orary, where Senator Kennedy lay in repose before his funeral.)

ephen G. Pagliuca, a co-owner of the Boston Celtics, has said he
cided to run because "Senator Kennedy would have wanted me to." And
an Khazei, co-founder of a national service program, says the Kennedys
ere his role models. Mr. Khazei's latest advertisement opens with the
sk not what your country" passage from John Kennedy's Inaugural
dress.

t playing the Kennedy card may not be a winning strategy after all.
tually every poll has put Martha Coakley, the state's attorney general
d the candidate least inclined to invoke Senator Kennedy, far ahead of
r three rivals.

. Coakley was the first to declare her candidacy (she did announce it at
e Omni Parker House, a hotel steeped in Kennedy lore), barely a week
er Senator Kennedy's death in August. Her haste drew some barbs.

B

Figure 2.6. *continued* **B.** English news article with same amount of left margin cut off.

Using knowledge of the patterns of a language to help compensate for noise is called TOP-DOWN processing: the "top" is your expectations of what should be there, and the bottom is what is in fact on the page or in the soundwaves. The same knowledge of language patterns also leads us to overlook errors in text that we are trying to proofread. Reading quickly, try to spot all seven errors in the following paragraph:

Text With Uncorrected Proofreader Errors

Many clinicians in English-dominant countries still see only monolingal English-speaking clients; and many clinicians in other countries or in overtly multlingual settings are used to taking information based on English and adapting it to a linguistically diverse clientele. But languages differ in ways in which directly affect the applicability of testing materials, the interpretation of aphasic response patterns, and the likely usefulness of remediation procedures (Menn et al., 1995). For example, "omission of a sentence subject" has less serious impact in Italian or Japanese than it does English or French. For the clinician in a non-English-speaking country, and indeed for every clinician and clinical researcher in world of mobile populations and empowered dialectal or linguistic minorities, it is esential to have access to neurolinguisitic research based directly on as many languages as possible.

A non-native speaker with a really good knowledge of English may actually do better at spotting some kinds of proofreader's errors, because she must rely more on the "bottom"—that is, on the information that is actually on the page. Using our new psycholinguistic terminology: If you are less able to rely on top-down processing, you must rely more on BOTTOM-UP processing—on the letters on the page, or the sound waves hitting your eardrum.

How does top-down processing of language work? It relies on subconscious knowledge of many kinds; we can illustrate a few of them here. Think about that bus-stop invitation: *Hey, ay (something something something) inner uhmarruh?* Why is *dinner* the word you reconstruct when you hear that those sounds? Because we have very good subconscious knowledge of the frequencies of words, and whether they are likely to occur in particular contexts. *Dinner* is the most frequent two-syllable word that rhymes with "inner," and it's hard to think of a context in which the most important word of a short sentence is *inner* itself. *Sinner*, maybe, or *thinner* or *winner*, but those would be odd things to find in a sentence that starts with *Hey* and no other context, such as glancing at a mutual acquaintance who seems to have lost 20 pounds (*thinner*), or being in a church (*sinner*) or at a race track (*winner*).

Knowing what words rhyme with *inner* is linguistic knowledge. Knowing which ones are probable in a particular grammatical context (which we don't have much of in this almost drowned-out utterance) is also linguistic knowledge, but knowing which ones are likely to occur between good friends at a bus stop with no more context than *Hey* is part of our social knowledge. You can imagine how socially based top-down processing might go badly astray in a place where people's manners are different!

A Reaction Letter to This Chapter from a Senior Chemical Engineer

Another example, your mind sees what it expects to see. I have found, on numerous occasions, very useful to have some one else proof read an important communication that I have drafted and feed back what it says to them. Some times I am astonished to find that their takeaway is very different than what I intended. In many cases only slight alterations are necessary to communicate what I originally intended.

Some time ago I was accountable for a major project in Europe where my company was trying to have a number of affiliates execute a common design for new production facilities and consumer products. Prior to this effort the affiliates were managed as separate entities. The stakes were very high; total investment was projected to be upwards of 500 million dollars for facilities and about 200 million in marketing and advertising.

On the project team were representatives from England, Belgium, France, Spain, Italy, Australia and the US. All spoke excellent English. Of the non-native English speaking countries, Belgium (Flemish-speaking, not French-speaking Belgium) had the best understanding, Spain had the poorest (fortunately, I speak a little Spanish), and English was the language used in the project. There were many examples of top down and bottom up understanding. You can just imagine the communication issues. One observation that may be of use to you is as follows. The non-native-English-speaking Europeans insisted that most major decisions be made in face to face meetings, not over the telephone as was more common domestically. Written communications were a second choice. At the time I thought it was because an important part of communication was non-verbal. Now I am wondering if it was because of their reliance on bottom-up communication.

2.5.2 How we learn language patterns

The story about Jenny learning the meaning of *blow out* dealt only with learning one kind of word, an action verb. How do we learn phonotactics, phonology, morphology, syntax, and the many levels of pragmatics that we touched on in Chapter 1? There has been intense controversy for many years between those who think that much knowledge of possible linguistic patterns is built into human minds genetically, so that what children need to do is figure out which of those patterns are used in the language around them, and those who think that what is built into our minds is not knowledge of language, but an extraordinary ability to respond to and extract the patterns that are present in the thousands of examples that we hear, examples of greetings and commands, questions and relative clauses, casual speech and prayers. We can't explore this LANGUAGE INNATENESS controversy in this short book, but don't worry; most of the psycholinguistics that this book is about depends only on the fact that intact adults know the patterns of at least one language, and not on where that knowledge came from.

2.6 Using our Knowledge of Language Patterns in Conversation

Of course, the major use for our knowledge of language patterns is to communicate (with ourselves as well as with others); as we'll see in the next chapter, we use grammar and morphology and phonology to comprehend and produce spoken, written, or signed messages. But our knowledge of language patterns is useful well beyond its obvious job of decoding and constructing nice clear messages. As we have seen by think-ing about the bus stop dinner invitation story and other examples, this knowledge is used by top-down processing to fill in the blanks and supply missing details; in other words, it allows us to predict part of what we hear or read, and so to make up for missing or distorted information.

Our syntax prediction ability, in particular, also allows us to prepare our responses to others before we have finished hearing their stories, questions, or commands. Part of this subconscious preparation, naturally, is the activation of the words and sentence patterns that we will need for responding. A less obvious but socially critical part is predicting precisely when our conversation partner is getting to a point where it will be per-missible for us to start speaking—because in a multipart conversation, if we actually wait until another person has paused, we're likely to miss our turn, and if it's just a two-way conversation, the other speaker may think that we're slow-witted, or wonder just what is really on our minds. One reason that normal conversation has so many utterances that begin with FILLERS like *oh*, *um*, and *well* is that we can quickly deploy a filler at just the right instant to stake our claim to a turn, gaining an extra half a sec-ond or so for planning and producing the first phrase of what we actually want to say.

2.7 Language Areas in the Brain

So far, we've talked mostly about how our brains deal with information. But how is the brain itself organized? News articles about the brain's organization tend to be about something that's a lot easier to visualize than the flow of information through it; they are usually about what areas of the brain we use to control our physical actions and our language, what areas are (somehow) responsible for seeing, hearing, tasting, and smelling, whether there's a particular area that's responsible for reading, planning, or long-term memory, and so on. The idea that different parts of the brain do different jobs is fairly old, and our ideas of what those jobs are have gotten much more sophisticated than they were 200 years ago. But they are still only approximate, and new refinements keep pouring in from research laboratories.

The basic evidence for this idea, which is called LOCALIZATION, is clear enough: If a person has a small brain injury from a bullet, a small tumor that's been taken out, or a small stroke, then in general, they'll have some of their abilities damaged but others intact or nearly so. Also, what will be preserved versus what will be impaired is roughly predictable from where the injury was. By the late 1800s, physicians knew that language problems were almost always consequences of damage to the left side of the brain, its left HEMISPHERE, and the idea of the brain containing areas whose sole job was to process language—the LANGUAGE AREAS—began to evolve. It's still evolving—and current research indicates that at least two things are seriously wrong with the traditional notion of "language area." First, the so-called language areas also process other kinds of information in addition to language; second, producing and understanding language also requires activity in some other areas of the brain, plus coordination of activities in several areas of the brain at once. (For these reasons, researchers are starting to use the term "language sensitive area" instead of "language area.") More about this in Chapter 6.

Information about a word's sound and meaning is widely distributed; some of it is in traditional language-sensitive areas, but some is in areas that are specialized for storing motor, sensory, and probably other information. Recent research from Carnegie Mellon (2010) suggests that our brains may have at least three specialized networks of meaning-related areas that make deep (prehuman, prelanguage) evolutionary sense: one network related to how we manipulate an object, one related to food, and one related to shelter. Another evolutionarily plausible special network that has considerable research support is one for information about living things. (They haven't yet checked to see whether this network also responds to words for natural forces that move or cause motion, and that an animal or human would have to reckon with in the wild, like wind, waves, or fire.)

2.8 Summary

Our brains are not computers, but they are an electrical network: an intricately structured, perpetually busy network of billions of branching nerve cells, called neurons. Neurons are linked locally by synapses at the ends of their branches, and over long distance by longer "neural superhighways." Knowing about the larger structures of the brain, including the language-sensitive areas, is critical for understanding the effects of brain damage, but we have to work at the level of the neurons to understand how we learn and process language.

If incoming information stimulates a neuron enough to make it active, it can pass that activation on to the neurons that are connected to it, and if they get enough activation, they in turn will pass activation further along the network. Neurons branch widely, so activation spreads out; and they interconnect, so activation from many sources can feed into one neuron and add up to help activate it.

Our brain's neurons are connected to our sensory and motor neurons, so that we can interpret what our senses bring in and develop movement skills, including speaking and signing. The basis of the neural network structure has developed by the time we are born, but our experiences play a major role in developing it, and it continues to change slightly with every experience we have. Neurons that are stimulated by events that occur together or in close sequence develop stronger connections that will pass activation more efficiently; connections between neurons that are not stimulated together or in some kind of coordinated fashion will wither away. The amount of this change in neural connection strengths can also be affected by our emotions. Every aspect of every experience, whether it seems to be relevant or not, contributes a small amount to changing the strengths of connections between our neurons—that's what learning is.

Learning language takes place in a rich setting of sensory and motor experiences of hearing, speaking, doing, smelling, tasting, and feeling, and using language appropriately. These complex experiences establish multimodal connections to the words in our minds, which we use in remembering and understanding.

Learning language is more than learning words: It's learning patterns of sounds, constructions, and probable sequences of words. The language patterns that we have learned enable us to fill in missing information in noisy signals—this is top-down processing, and it's essential so that we can communicate with each other at normal speeds in a busy real world.

Answer to Figure 2-5:

> "Captcha" words/letters:
>
> **orioles lations**

Exercises for Chapter 2

2.1. If you were teaching a second language to a beginning class of adults with normal social and cognitive skills, how would you teach words and phrases so that they will be most likely to be available when your students really need them? After you've thought about this, compare several textbooks and other language teaching resources and see which ones come closest to your ideal, and if some have better ideas than you were able to come up with.

2.2. If you have access to teaching materials for people with brain damage of any type, such as stroke, closed head injury, or developmental disorders, compare those to the ones for socially and cognitively normal students; what are the differences? Which materials among the ones that you have pay more attention to presenting and drilling material in contexts that resemble the ones in which the language would be used?

2.3. Elaborate the scenario of just the few moments around *Jenny, blow out the candles!* If you are working with others, you can divide up the task: auditory (speech and nonspeech) stimuli, auditory memories that will be aroused, motor and kinesthetic (speech, fine motor, gross motor) stimuli and memories, and other sensory modalities: touch, taste, and so on. Assume that Jenny has some idea of blowing (bubbles, balloons), but that she has never blown out a candle herself before and is going to need some coaching to do it. Be sure to include enough detail so that you can see how she could make the connection of the compound verb *blow out* with what one does in order to blow out a candle.

2.4. People with limited knowledge of the patterns of the language around them are clearly limited in their ability to predict what will be said or written or signed in the next few seconds. If you were training people to communicate with children or second-language learners, what are some communication guidelines that you might give them?

2.5. If you were responsible for the safety of a crew that included people who were native speakers of several different languages and needed to be able to communicate with each other in noisy and dangerous surroundings (factories, construction sites), how could you use what you've learned about language processing to set up guidelines and training to make sure they understood crucial warnings and instructions?

2.6. As middle-aged and elderly people gradually lose their hearing, they rely more and more on another source of bottom-up information about speech: the lip and jaw movements of the people they are speaking with. (Using this information is often called "lip reading.") Use what you've learned (in this chapter) about the brain's indiscriminate learning style, and (in Chapter 1) about how the mouth moves in making speech sounds, and create an information sheet or a Web page for the families of people with hearing loss, so that the family members can understand *why* it is important for them to make sure that their older relative can see their faces during a conversation. Also include one example of a pair of speech sounds that would look alike, so that they would still be confusing to people with hearing loss (in situations where they can't use top-down processing to help them, for example in hearing a family name from an unfamiliar part of the world).

Acknowledgments. A rigorous introduction to brain mechanisms is M. W. Dubin's *How the Brain Works*, 2002, Blackwell Science. Articles reviewed in preparing this chapter but not cited are listed on your CD, Materials for Chapter 2.

The letter in Box 2–2 is from Joseph Salvucci, who is currently Executive Director of the Delaware County (Pennsylvania) Regional Waste Water Control Authority.

References

Carnegie Mellon University. (2010, January 13). *Identifying thoughts through brain codes leads to deciphering the brain's dictionary.* Retrieved May 27, 2010, from http://www.sciencedaily.com/releases/2010/01/100112201347.htm

Klein, E. R., & Mancinelli, J. M. (2010). *Acquired language disorders: A case-based approach.* San Diego, CA: Plural Publishing.

Tomasello, M. (2003). *Constructing a language: A usage-based theory of language acquisition.* Cambridge MA: Harvard University Press.

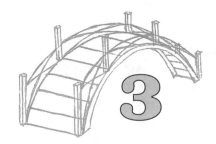

Normal Speech Errors and How They Happen: I. From Idea to Word

3.1 What is Normal? (and Why Don't We Say "Abnormal"?)

In clinical psychology, for abilities that can be measured, NORMAL means roughly, "not unexpectedly different from average." But this isn't what we mean when we use the term outside the clinic; what we do mean, although we don't want to admit it, is "approximately like us"—whoever "us" happens to be. A long and disturbing history of abusing people who were "not us" ("us" being whoever was in power in that particular time and place) lies behind the modern push to get rid of words like *abnormal*, a history that goes much deeper and wider than we can talk about here. (Look up *eugenics* if you would like to explore one aspect of it.) Let's assume we mean adult speakers who are using their native language and who rarely or never get noticed by the people around them as having a problem with speaking, hearing, reading, or writing that language. Being a normal speaker might be defined as being able to communicate what you mean and to understand what the people around you mean, at the rate and level of sophistication that brings you satisfaction in your personal and professional life. We'll talk more about who should be called a non-normal speaker or hearer in section 3.1.2.

So is it "normal" to make speech errors? Let's put it this way: All of us who are reasonably successful in speaking or signing, understanding spoken or signed language, writing, and reading nevertheless make errors in doing these things, because they are complicated processes with many component parts. Unless your setting requires near-perfect speech all the time (e.g., if you happen to be President of the United States), a modest number of speech errors won't attract unwanted attention or otherwise interfere with your life. If you do have to be near-perfect for part of the time—for example, if you are a teacher, a preacher, or a lawyer—then being able to understand speech errors, when they happen, may be useful, at least as consolation.

Studying speech errors has been a major way to look at how our brains create and understand meaningful language. In this chapter, we'll look at the kinds of speech errors that normal speakers make, and see, starting here and continuing throughout this book, that people who would not be considered "normal" speakers or hearers make errors that are very similar to those that normal speakers make. We'll start by building a model of speech production and perception that explains how speech errors occur, not just in normal speakers, but in learners and people with language disorders. For now, we'll assume that we know what it means for something to be an error; in the exercises for this chapter, after you've seen a good many examples, you'll be asked to come up with your own definition for what a speech error is.

3.1.1 Normal speech errors

First, we'll look at two kinds of production errors, and then at three kinds of perception errors.

The most common kind of speech error is a **SLIP OF THE TONGUE**: when we say something we didn't mean to, scrambling the order of the sounds or words or putting in a wrong word. Psycholinguists love to collect these errors because they give us all sorts of hints about the swift and mysterious process of making sentences. After all, whatever is inside our heads must be the kind of gadget that would fail in these documented ways, and not in ways that don't happen (for example, accidentally saying words backward). Here are some errors from my own collection that we'll analyze in this chapter and the next.

I'll move this over here until I can get things put awayed.

The problem is to find off [find ~ bite off] *a piece you can chew.*

I lost my track of thought [train of thought ~? got off the track]

Where'd I bring it when I put it in? [Where'd I put it when I brought it in?]

It's not tack deduckstible [tax deductible]

Psycholinguists also test their ideas about how sentences are made in the laboratory by asking volunteers to say tongue twisters or to do other speech tasks that are likely to provoke speech errors. We can get a great deal of information about sentence production by studying both natural and provoked speech errors.

Several other kinds of speech problems or errors are also normal, so we shouldn't fret about them (unless we make too many of them).

TIP-OF-THE-TONGUE STATE: This is the itchy mental state you are in when you can't find a word —especially a name—that you know and want, and can at best only come out with approximations to it. What's fascinating about these approximations is how close they can be to the word you want, and how the ways in which they are close to it vary from one attempt to the next. Looking at them gives us ideas about LEXICAL RETRIEVAL—how we activate a content word when we need it. Here's a search sequence I went through recently: Bhatnagar . . . , Baharav . . . , Bhuvana! What I was looking for was Bhuvana (BHOO-vuh-nuh), the given name of a woman friend and colleague of mine from India. The two other words are names of colleagues whom I hadn't seen for several years (although they are family names, not given names); Bhatnagar is also from India, though he's a man, and Baharav is a woman from Israel. All three names are stressed on the first syllable, and you can see lots of other similarities in both the sounds and the spellings.

The semantics of my intended message—my colleague's name— seemed to activate words that are related to the one I needed both in meaning (they were names, specifically names of colleagues), and in sound. (Searches for names always stay in the "names" category, have you noticed?) The only way to explain the arousal of names with similar sounds, as you'll see when we get into the later stages of sentence production in Chapter 4, is to propose that my memory for the name I was hunting for was activated enough to activate its phonological and semantic neighbors (the other two names). Yet, for some reason, it wasn't activated enough to get the information about the sounds in the word above the threshold that I needed to actually say the name I wanted just at the moment that I wanted to say it.

The next two kinds of errors aren't one-time problems. They happen when someone has apparently misperceived a phrase or a word, and then stored it with this incorrect information. Eventually, they may figure out that they must have made an error in perception (or storage), or they may never catch on; in that case, we only find out about their perception error when we notice it in their speaking or writing.

MONDEGREEN: misanalysis of a phrase that you have heard frequently, typically from a song. This error type gets its name from a report of hearing . . . *and lady Mondegreen* for the phrase . . . *and laid him on the green.* (According to Snopes, http://www.snopes.com/holidays/christmas/humor/

mondegreens.asp, the word is traced to a column by Sylvia Wright in 1954.). Probably the most famous recent example is *Excuse me while I kiss this guy* for the phrase *Excuse me while I kiss the sky*, from Jimi Hendrix' song *Purple Haze* (http://www.urbandictionary.com). You can see that mondegreens seem to be formed when the correct phrase originally occurred along with competing sounds (music, multiple voices), and when it contains very unfamiliar words or improbable combinations of words (have you ever kissed a sky?). This is the perfect setup for top-down processing, based on expectations, to overrule or fill in for bottom-up processing of the intended words (the terms "top-down" and "'bottom-up" processing were introduced in Chapter 2, section 2.5). We know that these errors were stored in people's memories because the people who confess to having made them tell us so.

MALAPROPISM: fusing or confusing two words that have similar sounds and using one of them where the other is appropriate. (The two words may also share a morpheme, like the *-ize* in the first example below.) Many famous examples are made up, including the ones spoken by the character Mrs. Malaprop in Sheridan's play *The Rivals*, but there are plenty of real ones, like these published by Arnold Zwicky (1980) in his useful book *Mistakes*:

> *I hereby jeopardize* [deputize] *you to handle my duties.*

> *The policemen threw an accordion* [cordon] *around the crowd*

As Zwicky says (p. 15), "It is important that the people who uttered these real-life examples often repeated their peculiar locutions and, when challenged, maintained that the word they used was the word they meant (usually indicating that they didn't see what the fuss was about)." So, according to Zwicky, these errors were also stored in memory, rather than being one-time events. And from the point of view of the speaker, they weren't even errors.

Here again, we can suspect that top-down processing interacted with the sounds that were heard back at the time when the needed word was originally (mis)learned, because it looks like the people who made these mistakes have substituted a similar-sounding word that they already knew for a less familiar one. The only psycholinguistic difference between a mondegreen and a malapropism is that a mondegreen is a embedded in the (mis)memorized lyrics of a particular song, but a malapropism is a word in a person's vocabulary (psycholinguists call this their **MENTAL LEXICON**), and might be used in any phrase where the correct word should go: *He was jeopardized to handle the job, She was blocked by the police accordion.*

Our last kind of error is different: these are one-time events, like slips of the tongue, only they happen in perception rather than in production.

SLIP OF THE EAR: misanalyzing a word or a phrase as you hear it. A collection of slips of the ear detected in conversations and reported by Sara Garnes and Zinny Bond (1975) includes mishearing *bridge cable* as *bridge table*, *recite* as *recycle*, and *I'm getting married* as *I'm getting buried*. We know about slips of the ear only if they are our own errors, or if they cause a misunderstanding in a conversation and the speakers eventually figure out that one of them has misanalyzed what the other has said.

If you track conversations that you overhear (hiding behind a newspaper in a busy coffee shop is a good way to eavesdrop), you will probably pick up a few more of these among the conversational backtrackings and corrections that happen around you.

Many mondegreens and malapropisms probably begin as slips of the ear that were never detected and got firmly lodged in a person's memory. There's a fine source of examples of malapropisms that look as if they might have started as slips of the ear in the librarian's weekly online humor post of questions that have been addressed to them by library customers. It's called *Funny You Should Ask*, sponsored by Gale Virtual Reference Library. (We can't be completely sure that these errors came from slips of the questioner's ear; the error also could have been created by something that happened to the words as they were being stored in the questioner's mental lexicon, or when they were retrieved from the person's mental lexicon at the moment that they were talking to the librarian.)

Some examples from *Funny You Should Ask* in 2008 and 2009 are:

I need to know who painted the sixteenth chapel.
(From a student beginning a unit on the Renaissance; presumably, the teacher had assigned him or her to find out who painted interior of the Sistine Chapel.)

Where is your gynecology department? I need to look up my family tree.

Do you have the "Genesis Book of World Records?"

Do you have any books on ESPN?
(From a 10-year-old wanting a book about extra sensory perception.)

Do you have "Little Richard's Almanac"? [Poor Richard's Almanac]

I can't find that Web site again—did you Barney Google it?
(A senior patron asking for Web assistance; Barney Google is an old-time comic strip character.)

Take a minute to look at the similarities between what each person asked the librarian and the word(s) he or she should have said; what part of each error is correct? You'll want to come back and consider the connections between errors and targets, because these connections give us valuable clues about the interconnected networks of information in our brains.

These three closely related types of errors are fun to think about because they give us hints about more aspects of language processing. Mondegreens are evidence for the fact that people mostly learn what new words mean from hearing speakers use them in context (as opposed to reading them or having them defined) because, as we've just seen, when the context is not helpful, it's easy to get words completely wrong. Malapropisms can arise from mishearing or from misreading, or from an error in storing what we have heard or read in our memory. Thinking through how they arise helps us to figure out what the steps in learning a word must be. Slips of the ear give us a real-time look at how we manage to find understandable words in the stream of sounds that pours into our ears as others talk.

So mondegreens, malapropisms, and slips of the ear all provide vivid evidence for how top-down processing (based on what we already know) interacts with bottom-up processing (based on what we are taking in at the moment—in these cases, what we hear at the moment of a first encounter with a word or phrase). And as you'll see, the interaction of top-down language processing and bottom-up processing in language comprehension will be one of our recurring themes, from Chapter 5 to the end of the book.

3.1.2 Who is a "normal" speaker, and who is not?

What researchers and clinicians mean when they call someone a "normal" speaker of a language is something like this: an adult speaker/reader with no detectable foreign accent and no detectable language comprehension or production problems other than occasional slips of the tongue. (A more accurate but clumsier term is "normal speaker/hearer.") A person who is a similarly fluent user of a signed language is a normal signer. It used to be that "normal" also implied "monolingual," but world migration patterns have made us aware of how many people are bilingual to varying degrees. Psycholinguistic researchers usually specify that the participants in their studies are monolingual unless bilingual speakers are the focus of the study, but classroom and clinical studies of the dominant language of a country may not have much information about what other languages their study participants speak, and how well they speak them.

Who is not a "normal speaker/hearer"? The answer depends on why the question is asked, and so do the ways of referring to the people in the answer, but here are the main groups of people who would not be considered to meet the clinical definition of "normal speaker."

First language learners

A child who is becoming a speaker or of at least one language within the statistically normal developmental time range is currently referred to as a "typically developing" child, because it will take many years before she is a normal speaker in the sense of being able to process language as skillfully as an adult. A child who is learning a signed language as a first language is a "typically developing signer" if she is meeting the typical developmental milestones. She may or may not also be a typically developing speaker: If she has more than a mild hearing loss and/or doesn't have much opportunity to learn a spoken language, her spoken language development is likely to be delayed. Deaf children with cochlear implants are currently under intense study, but very early implants (before the age of 1 year) generally result in spoken language development within a clinically normal timeline.

Second (or later) language learners

Someone who is learning a second (or third or fourth) language and who is a typically developing or normal adult speaker of a first language would be considered a normal second language learner, but again, it will take many years before she is a normal speaker of the second language in the sense of being able to speak and write it as skillfully as an adult native speaker of that language. Even people who are very skilled but not native speakers of a second (or later) language turn out to be slightly slower than native speakers at demanding tasks in the psycholinguistics laboratory. (In the real world, as we have already noted, people who are not bilingual from the beginning of speech need a little more time than native monolinguals for reading difficult material and understanding speech in noisy surroundings.)

People with developmental disorders, dyslexia, or brain damage

People who are not developing or learning normally, people with developmental language disorders, including dyslexia, are not fully language-normal speakers. People who have suffered brain damage, whether as infants, young children, teenagers, or adults, are also not "language-normal," but if their language disorder is very specific, or their brain damage is limited to a very small volume, they may be normal in every other measurable way. However, as clinicians know, children who have dyslexia very often also have attention deficit disorders, and in general, language and nonlanguage problems may compound each other in many ways. For this reason, people who have developmental cognitive/emotional disorders are also excluded from the "language-normal" group.

People with late-onset hearing loss

People who lose their hearing as adults, whether gradually or suddenly, are by definition no longer normal speaker/hearers. People who are losing their hearing must use more top-down processing in understanding spoken language, and they may also use more of the bottom-up visual information from lipreading (see Chapter 2, Exercise 2.6). People who have had a severe hearing loss as young adults, after many years of being unable to hear themselves and others speak, usually start to show abnormal patterns in the pitch and loudness of their voice.

3.2 Language Production: Describing the Basic Processes

Being a normal adult language user is the result of years of practice in comprehension and speaking (and reading and writing, for people in a large part of the world). When we try to figure out how to help improve the language of people who have a language disorder, or a cognitive disorder that produces language problems, or how to improve the language of computers and robots, we can draw on a rich understanding of how language-normal people use language and learn to use it. So, to start with, how do language-normal people speak? A lot happens when you talk, starting from having something that you want to express and ending with reasonably appropriate words coming out of your mouth about four-tenths of a second later. We're a long way from knowing all of what goes on, but the first steps toward working out the process were taken many years ago, as researchers tried to create a model of language production, that is, a rough description of a biological mechanism that could produce both correct speech and also the kinds of speech errors that we've talked about. (Many of the same processes are involved in signing and in writing, so we will focus on producing speech.)

It helps to divide the process of speaking into five rather different kinds of processes or levels; we'll base our description on one of the standard ways of doing this (from Bock & Levelt, 1994), although we'll be more explicit about a few of the steps. It's important to understand that there are a number of very similar, reasonable models. All of these speech production models are approximations to reality, and this version is not better than the others—it's just more explicit at some points. That will help you in making a mental picture of the process of sentence production, but it doesn't mean that the more explicit version is more accurate. On the contrary, the other models are deliberately vague for a good reason, which is that there's too much that we still don't know. So just consider this as the first-pass version; if language production modeling becomes important in your life, you'll undoubtedly use better ones.

The first level of production, then, is the **Message Level**: the processes concerned with choosing what, of all that's currently in your mind, you are going to try to put into words. The second is called the **Functional Level**: the processes of finding (arousing) the words you need to convey your chosen meaning, and getting the nouns and pronouns linked to the roles that the people and things played in the event you're talking about. The other three levels, which we'll talk about in Chapter 4, fill in the details: getting the phrases set up and getting the words into the right phrases in the right order (**Positional Level**), then getting the sounds of the words in the right order (**Phonological Encoding Level**), and finally, actually pronouncing them (**Speech Gesture Level**). Figure 3.1 gives you a schematic diagram of these five levels.

In this chapter, we'll focus on the first two kinds of processes, which involve choosing what to put into words, finding the needed words, and getting them linked to their roles in events. Put together, these levels will help us to imagine the thing in our head that gives us the power of speech.

Organizing these processes into levels and sublevels does not mean that each level is isolated from the others. As we said in Chapter 2, the assembly line metaphor is not a good approximation to what goes on in the brain. It's just that we can't describe everything at once, so we start by talking in terms of levels or steps.

3.3 Choosing What to Put Into Words and What to Focus On: The Message Level

We said that the Message Level is where our brains choose what we'll put into words: what our story will be. It's a conceptual level; that is, everything in it could happen without language (although the way it works is affected by your language, as we'll see later). You can think about this Message Level activity as having three parts: picking your story's angle, activat-

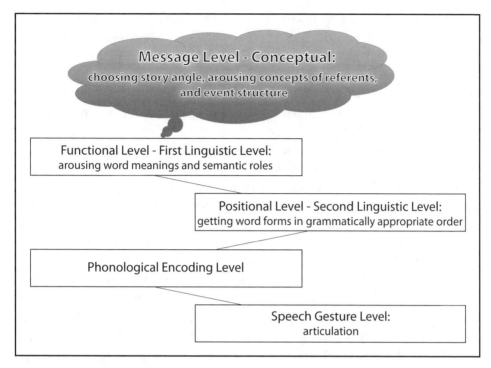

Figure 3.1. Levels of processing discussed in Chapters 3 and 4.

ing the concepts of the people and things you'll need to mention, and organizing what happened into event structures (the basic chunks of who did what to whom). At the end of Message Level processing, your brain has gotten a clause-sized chunk of this conceptual information organized well enough for actual language processing to begin. Let's look at an example to get a clearer idea of what this means.

Imagine an ordinary real-world scene, say a family—perhaps your own—interacting at a zoo, that something dramatic happened, and that you are starting to tell about it. Let's say that the story is about how your uncle handled a situation where your brother got too close to the lions. What parts of this complex event are you going to put into words? You have to organize the multiple simultaneous things that you might talk about. You have to decide which ones you need to tell your story and which ones are irrelevant, how detailed you want the story to be, how emotional you want to be, and whose point of view or emotions you want to convey. You usually make Message Level choices like this subconsciously, but one way you might become aware of those choices is if you first E-mail the story to a friend of your uncle's (with your quick-thinking uncle who distracted the lions as a hero and your brother as a total idiot), and then decide you had better also tell the story to your mother (who doesn't really need to know how close your brother was to getting mauled). That means you'll have to change a lot of details; even though you're telling about the same event, you're not telling exactly the same story (see Exercise 3.5). You'll recognize this process of organizing the Message Level of production as being part of what linguists call pragmatics (see Chapter 1, section 1.8).

The concepts of people and things that get activated will depend a lot on how detailed your visualization of the scene is—you may or may not activate details like the color of your brother's jacket or the size of the lion's teeth; if some of those details are too fussy or too scary for the angle that you chose, you'll have to inhibit them, and if your story angle calls for more vividness, you may have to wait a few tenths of a second so that more of the details can come to mind—that is, can reach threshold levels of arousal. Remember that the Message Level is prelinguistic processing: we're not talking about the words yet, just the concepts. But these concepts are the basis for finding your words, which will start to happen at the next processing level, the Functional Level.

The third aspect of Message Level processing is organizing the concept of the event into what we can call the EVENT STRUCTURE. What ideas will you pack into each clause, and what details of the action will you give? You might prepare to say, *My uncle distracted the lions*, or *My uncle got closer to the lions and started jumping up and down*, and probably dozens of other things that would build up your listener's mental picture of what happened. The event structure will be your basis for activating the appropriate verbs, and choosing the words that tell your hearer whether the action those verbs describe is stopping, starting, or continuing.

People with traumatic brain injury and right hemisphere strokes sometimes have problems with pragmatics. Using the ideas we've developed so far, we can describe part of their problems as trouble with organizing the Message Level of production in order to stay relevant and/or to find a diplomatic way to tell a story. People with aphasia don't have problems choosing an appropriate point of view, but they may have pragmatic problems for a different reason: they get badly tangled up because they can't find the syntax that they need to tell the story in a pragmatically appropriate way. (We'll look at a real example like this in the exercises for this chapter.) Young children often don't have the pragmatic skills to organize their messages in a way that another person can understand, as you know if you've listened to a kid retell a story or explain what happened on the playground. And normal speakers who get excited and plunge into the middle of a story may find themselves in pragmatic trouble, too, confusing our listeners or saying things we really shouldn't have mentioned.

3.4 The Functional Level, Part 1: Lemmas

3.4.1 What is a lemma, and why does our model need them?

Deciding to tell the zoo story with your uncle as a hero and your brother as an idiot means that activation will flow not only to their identities and word meanings like LION and CAGE, but to adjective meanings like SMART, BRAVE, QUICK, and STUPID, and to verbs of movement that were aroused by the event structure, and to adverbial meanings like CLOSER. Why am I suddenly using small capital letters here? Because the Message Level sends activation only to the MEANINGS of these words; that's the part of word retrieval that happens at the Functional Level. The retrieval of the sounds comes later. So I need a way to show you when we're only talking about a word's meaning, and not its sounds; that's what using the SMALL CAPS will mean. It's going to be helpful here and later to have a technical term for this concept "the meaning of a word, without its sounds": it's called the word's LEMMA.

If lemmas are, basically, word meanings, why do we need this obscure-sounding technical term for them? Why not just say "meanings"? One important reason is that the ideas of "meaning" and "concept" overlap a lot in the way we usually talk about language, so it would be confusing use those two words to mean two different things in our model. But a production model has to have some way to distinguish the prelinguistic level of concepts from the linguistic level of meanings, and also a way of distinguishing the level of word meanings from the level of word sounds.

Why do we have to distinguish prelinguistic "concepts" from linguistic "meanings"? We'll run into quite a number of reasons, but here's a good one to start from: A single concept can often be expressed by many different words and combinations of words. This is especially easy to see when you're talking about a person. So suppose you are telling a story about one of your linguistics professors, Prof. Barbara Fox. What your hearer needs is to be able to figure out is how the person you're talking about is connected to your story. If they know (or know of) the person, you can use her name, but if they don't know the person, a name might not be very useful. So depending on whom you're talking to and what happened in your story, you might want to refer to Prof. Fox as, *This woman who was buying a case of organic cat food* or *The prof I had for semantics last term*. And once you've introduced her in the story, if it's about her, you'll mostly refer to her with pronouns (*So I asked her . . .*) or shorter expressions (*The woman with the cat food*). All of these different expressions are ways of referring to the same person, who is just one concept in your mind. And each expression, by itself and outside of the context of your story, has a different meaning—after all, the meaning of the word *her* or of the phrase *this woman who was buying a case of organic cat food* isn't BARBARA FOX; it just happens to refer to Barbara Fox in the context of your story. Ditto for the phrase *the prof I had for semantics last term*.

A note about pronouns: We'll say right now that *he*, *him*, and *his* all have the same lemma, and also that *she*, *her*, and *hers* share a lemma, and so on with the case forms of other pronouns: *I*, *me*, *my*, and *mine* share the first person singular lemma, and *we*, *us*, *our*, and *ours* share the first person plural lemma. You'll see why in the next chapter when we look at mistakes that involve switching pronouns.

(Why do we need so many ways of referring to the people in our stories? Well, using pronouns and shortened expressions correctly makes a story sound more coherent, which in turn makes it easier to understand, at least for people (not for computers, however). If you keep using longer referring expressions (*This woman who was buying a case of organic cat food*), your listener may think that you're talking about someone new each time. When children, second-language learners, or people with aphasia can't use the language well enough to shift from longer to shorter referring expressions appropriately, it gets harder to follow their stories about what's happening in their lives. But for people who are trying to get computers to work as if they understand language, these natural ways of switching among different ways of referring to the same person [or thing] are an enormous headache.)

Agreed, now, that we need a term to separate a concept from the words used in referring to it. Why not just say we have "concepts" at the Message Level, and "words" when we get to linguistic levels of production, then? Why do we need this term "lemma" for the word's meaning? Because we're reasonably sure that finding a word in production has two separate steps: first, finding the lemma and second, going from the lemma to the sound.

What's the evidence for this? Here's some: Remember that, for people in the tip-of-the-tongue state (section 3.1.1), the meaning they need is activated, but the word form that they want hasn't gotten above the threshold required for speaking. And if you suggest a word to them, they can say whether the word you've suggested is the one they had in mind or not— they don't accept just any word that has roughly the same meaning as the one they were looking for. So it seems that what is aroused in their minds —what they are holding onto as they search for the word's form—is not only the concept, but the concept plus something more specific. In our model, this thing that they are holding onto is the word's lemma.

In our production model, a word's lemma is, more fully, its meaning plus the information that your mind needs to use it in making sentences (for example, for a verb, whether it's irregular, or whether it can have a direct object). This meaning-plus-grammatical-information is like what you'd find in a dictionary if you looked up a word, but the word's lemma in your mind is not the same thing as its definition in a dictionary. Why not? Because a definition is made of other words. So if we said that a word's lemma is its definition, that would lead to two problems. First, what's in a dictionary never captures all the nuances of what a word means, especially if its meaning contains a lot of direct sensory information, like *red* or *butter*. But a lemma is the meaning itself, as your mind has constructed it by reading and hearing the word, plus memories of the real world contexts that you've heard it used in, which may include visual memories, motor memories, taste memories, and so on (think back to Jenny learning about candles in Chapter 2). Those sensory and motor memories go beyond words.

Second, if we tried to define a word's lemma as made of other words, then we'd have to ask what those other words were made of, and we'd be in an endless loop. Not a good idea.

As we go on through this chapter, you'll get a better sense of how breaking up finding a word (or a phrase) into these three steps of concept (at the Message Level), lemma (at the Functional Level), and phonological form (at the Positional Level and the Phonological Form Level, which we'll discuss in Chapter 4) makes it easier to talk about a lot of things that happen when speakers make choices or errors.

3.4.2 Activating the wrong lemma

Let's look at some everyday speech errors.

1. *My dissertation is too short—long.*   (corrected by the speaker)

2. *. . . he's going downtown . . .*   (target: he's going *up*town)

3. *. . . before the place closes . . .*   (target: before the place *opens*)

4. *Look at the lady with the dachshund*   (target: Volkswagen)

5. *. . . he is a good magician*   (target: musician) (Fay & Cutler)

6. *Do you wash your Tupperware by hand or do you put it in the refrigerator?*   (target: *dishwasher*)

7. *. . . you have too many irons in the smoke.*   (target: you have too many irons in the *fire*)

8. *I really liked the original* Pink Panda.   (target: *Pink **Panther***, while discussing the movie *Kung Fu Panda*)

Examples 1–4 and 7 were collected and published by the late Prof. Vicki Fromkin of the UCLA Linguistics Department; Example 5 is from the collection of Fay and Cutler, and the others are from my collection.

Sometimes we catch an error as soon as it happens, as the speaker did in Example 3. Sometimes we don't catch it, but the people who are listening to us do, and sometimes nobody at all notices; yet, if the conversation was taped and you listened to it later, the error would be glaringly obvious. People with aphasia make similar mistakes, but much more often; we all make them more often when we are tired, or trying to do several things at the same time. (Should we call this "abnormal" behavior? Better to use it as a way of understanding that there isn't a clear boundary between normal and abnormal language errors.)

In the first three examples above, the speaker said the opposite of what she or he had intended. (For Examples 2 and 3, there's nothing in what's written to indicate that there was an error, but Prof. Fromkin realized from the context that the speaker had said the opposite of what he or she meant.) In these three cases, activation probably spread from the needed concept to its opposite, because words and their opposites are closely linked in our minds. (The best evidence for this is that if you ask people to say the next word that comes into their mind after you have said a word to them, and the word you say is one that has an opposite, they are very likely to say it.) And for opposites that are commonly produced in the same phrase, like *night and day* or *up and down*, our minds have plenty of opportunities to build direct connections between their lemmas, as well as the connections that already exist between the concepts.

How do concepts get connected so closely that activation can spread from one to another? And, besides opposites, which concepts get connected closely enough to make substitution errors likely? To answer that, we need to look at how we learn to group concepts into categories.

3.4.3 Relations between concepts

Children in middle-class families in mainstream Western society—and in many other cultures as well, although not in all of them—are taught names of things and people quite as deliberately as they are taught the basic words of politeness: to say *doggie*, *milk*, and *Grandma* as well as *please* and *thank you*. Not long after we teach the names of some kinds of things—and even before, in a few important cases—we teach the names of a few categories, in contexts like these: *Don't jump on the furniture! Don't play with your food! What's for dessert? Let's go see the animals; Here's some bread for the birdies; Don't squash the bugs! What color is it? Pick up your toys! Put on your clothes!* There are also plenty of categories that don't have an everyday name (that is, a name that we consider suitable for young children to learn): *Do you want something to drink? Look at all the cars and trucks! And trains and boats and planes! Pick up your crayons and markers and pens and pencils!*

So being a member of a SEMANTIC CATEGORY has nothing to do with whether our everyday language has a name for that category. What does create a category? Looking at the three examples (beverages, vehicles, and—what would you call them—drawing utensils?) in the last paragraph, the answer is easy: At least for these examples, it is what we *do* with the items in the category that defines them as belonging together, or what those items do in our lives. So a category seems to be a set of things that we use or interact with in a particular way, and our history of real or imagined interaction with those things must be what forms the category in our minds.

Category names, if we have them (and use them to teach, nag, or coax children), tell us how we can expect something to behave and how we are entitled to behave toward it: Will it bite? Are we supposed to take care of it, and if so, does that mean we feed it or that we polish it (or, as the wry army joke goes, salute it or paint it)? It's amazing to watch young children trying to figure out what to do with an item that might be in two categories that are to be treated very differently, like the small wooden horse in Figure 3.2: Is it to pat or to climb on?

Or for a child who already knows the story of the Gingerbread Man and now sees his first gingerbread man like the one in Figure 3.3 being taken out of the bakery bag: Is it going to run away when Mommy lets go of it? (Seeing the worried look on my 2-year-old's face and not wanting him to think we were cannibals, I immediately switched from calling it a *gingerbread man* to calling it a *gingerbread man cookie*.)

There is a lot of neat research on such semantic categories, how children learn them, how they differ across languages and cultures, and how they have unclear and somewhat flexible boundaries (people are more likely to agree that a chair is furniture than that a mattress on the floor is; and furthermore, if someone is sitting on the mattress, they are relatively more likely to call it *furniture* than if no one is there). But the importance of the idea of semantic category for this book is seeing how semantic categories are at work in our brains as we speak and listen to one another, bearing in mind that each of us has had our categories formed by slightly

Figure 3.2. *Is it to pat? to climb on?* Fifteen-month-old puzzled by merry-go-round horse.

Figure 3.3. Gingerbread man. Image adapted from Shutterstock®. All rights reserved.

different experiences, and that most things belong to several different kinds of categories, with and without category names (an aquarium inhabitant may be, simultaneously, a fish, a pet, a beautiful object, a vertebrate, something to keep the cat away from, and an expensive hobby).

3.4.4 Many are called, but few are chosen: Associative categories organize the pandemonium in our brains

3.4.4.1 Semantic categories and speech errors

So far, we've established that during the early part of time that we are formulating the message we want to say (maybe 100 or 200 milliseconds before the first word of the sentence emerges), the concepts that become active activate their lemmas, and they also activate some of concepts that are related to them. But we've only talked about errors arising from arousing opposites (**ANTONYMS**), and antonymy is just one kind of relationship among concepts. What kinds of errors seem to come from arousing unintended members of the sorts of categories we discussed in section 3.2.1? When people with aphasia try to name objects in pictures, they make lots of errors involving using the label of a different object in the same category, for example, calling a table a *desk*; we'll discuss those in Chapter 6. Let's look at normal speakers' Examples 4, 5, and 6 again:

4. *Look at the lady with the dachshund*   (target: Volkswagen)

5. *. . . he is a good magician*   (target: musician) (Fay & Cutler)

6. *Do you wash your Tupperware by hand or do you put it in the refrigerator?*   (target: dishwasher)

The category that *dachshund* and *Volkswagen* both belong to seems to be "things from Germany." You can figure out the shared categories for other two substitutions yourself—there are several of them. It's worth noting, by the way, that other factors may have been involved in these two cases. *Magician* and *musician* are a lot alike in both phonology (their sounds) and morphology (how they are put together from smaller meaningful parts), and we'll see in Chapter 4 how this would add to the activation of the unintended word *magician*. The *refrigerator/dishwasher* example was spoken by a friend helping me to deal with the dishes after we had eaten dinner; my dishwasher and my refrigerator are next to each other, so what she was looking at was arousing both words. And the small plastic containers she was talking about are usually used for storing food in the refrigerator.

What do category substitution errors like these add to our understanding of the process of arousing the words we need for saying something? We already knew that a message we want to convey typically involves the concepts of one or more people or things and something about how they act (the place closes) or how they are connected to each other (the lady has a Volkswagen) or about properties they have (long, good). And we knew that these concepts arouse the meanings—the lemmas—of one or more words that the speaker could use to convey them. What category substitution errors confirm for us is that concepts in the message indeed arouse other concepts that are members of some category that they both belong to, categories the speaker has created during a lifetime of firsthand and secondhand experiences (things from Germany, people whose skilled performances you enjoy watching, kitchen appliances). The "collateral lemmas" aroused by these other concepts may be activated enough, as we said in section 3.4.2, to compete with the lemmas for the words the speaker really wants. Sometimes that competition gets resolved in favor of one of the wrong words, and we get substitution errors.

When we analyze substitution errors, we often see other factors that probably contributed to the success of the wrong word, like the real-world link between small plastic food containers and refrigerators; this supports the idea that a lemma can be activated from several different sources. The most dramatic examples of this are Freudian slips, like substituting the name of your ex for the name of your current sweetie, as we talked about in the Introduction (section 0.3). How does our model of language production explain the way that the name of a person who is on your mind sneaks into a sentence that's supposed to be about someone else?

Well, if a person is "on your mind," that is a way of saying that their identity is activated pretty close to the threshold of consciousness most of the time, even when your current message has nothing to do with them. That background level of activation of their identity is enough to activate the lemmas you'd need for talking about them (including not just names, but titles like MOTHER) at the Functional Level, and those lemmas will compete with the lemmas for referring to the people you consciously intended to talk about. When will this competition tip in favor of a name or title of the person who's on your mind? Often, it's when the person you really want to talk about is in some semantic category that the person who is haunting your subconscious also belongs to.

How far does activation spread?

Activation spread among concepts while normal speakers are producing a sentence seems to be limited: it almost always stays within category boundaries. When it doesn't, the semantic links are still tight, as in this example: *She mentioned that she had lived in Hebrew for seven years* (target: *Israel*; LM). So there isn't a free-for-all competition among all the lemmas in our heads when we talk; it's only a struggle among close neighbors. This is also true for many aphasic speakers, but there are occasional exceptions among people with mild aphasias, and many dramatic exceptions for people with severe aphasias, often making it impossible to guess what they might have been trying to say. A moderately aphasic friend of mine said, of a family member who was planning to visit, "What about his delicious cats?" and then rephrased it as, "What about his cat deliciousness?" It turned out, after some guessing by the person he was speaking to, that he had meant to ask "What about his cat allergy?"

The model of language production that we are using explains errors of choosing a word that's related semantically to the one you really wanted as happening when something goes wrong during the production step in which activation spreads from concepts (at the Message Level) to lemmas (at the Functional Level). If you are a normal fluent speaker of the language you are using, activation will flow from the concepts in your message (like "lion" or "your uncle" or "distracting") to the lemmas LION or UNCLE or DISTRACT, which are very strongly connected to them. But activation will also spread from a concept like "lion" or "uncle" to related concepts like "tiger" or "aunt," and from there to your mental store of word meanings, so many lemmas that are related to the ones you really want also get activated.

Word substitution errors can happen this way for both normal speakers and those who have language problems or who are still language learners. (And we don't have to wait for speech errors to show that this kind of collateral lemma activation really happens. In Chapter 5, we'll sample more than 30 years laboratory experiments that explore it.) It's actually a good thing that this collateral activation of related concepts and lemmas happens, because if you can't find the exact word you want, you may be able to slip in a sufficiently close substitute without a hitch. Also, having several related lemmas activated often gives us the ability to patch up pragmatic errors before they happen—for example, if you suddenly realize that referring to someone who is very senior to you by her given name (*Barbara*) or a nickname (*Foxy*) is not appropriate because she has suddenly appeared within earshot, you can switch fluently to a politer form (*Professor Fox*).

This example also reminds us why it's useful to separate concepts from lemmas: it lets us say that the concept of this one person's identity is linked to all of the lemmas BARBARA, FOXY, and PROFESSOR FOX. That seems to be a sensible way to talk about people and their names.

3.4.5 Compromises don't work: Blend errors

Sometimes parts of two words or phrases seem to have tried to get out at the same time and gotten mixed together:

7. . . . *you have too many irons in the smoke.*   (target: you have too many irons in the fire)

8. *I really liked the original* Pink Panda.   (target: *Pink Panther*; commenting on an ad for the remake of the movie *The Pink Panther* while waiting for the movie of *Kung Fu Panda* to begin)

9. *I lost my track of thought.*   (target: train of thought; blended with *track*, aroused for use in something like *I lost track of what I was saying*.)

10. *The problem is to find off a piece you can chew.*   (*find* blended with *bite off*)

11. *Oh, help all you want*   (*help yourself* blended with *take all you want*)

12. *car dealsman*   (target: *car dealer* or *car salesman*)

13. *momentaneous*   (target: *momentary/ instantaneous*)

Examples 7, 12, and 13 are from Fromkin; the others are from my collection.

The subconscious struggle between two lemmas is even clearer in **BLENDS** than it is in substitution errors, because we can see that both of them were strong enough to call up their phonological forms at the same time. A wonderful thing about these errors is how beautifully they are formed: for example, the wrong nouns (*smoke, panda, track*) slip right in where the target nouns (*fire, panther, train*) should have gone. How do lemmas find the place in the sentence where they belong? How does the language production mechanism churning away in our brains almost always get words into the right order so that they mean what we intended to say? An essential step—probably the first one—in that process must be the one we'll turn to next: getting lemmas linked with the semantic functions that correspond to the roles in our message—AGENT, UNDERGOER, THEME, RECIPIENT, LOCATION, and so on (see Chapter 1, section 7). Just to recall some of other semantic roles introduced in that section that we'll need for our analyses, here they are again: MODIFIERS of nouns (ADJECTIVES, numbers, POSSESSIVES), SENTENCE ADDRESSEE (*Mom, where are my sneakers?*), PREPOSITIONS (*under* the bed), OBJECTS OF PREPOSITIONS (*under the bed*), and ADVERBS (*Frankly, I don't care; He's really sweet; It's full enough; Do it now*).

3.5 The Functional Level, Part 2: Semantic Functions

Why do we call the level where lemmas are activated the Functional Level? What is "functional" about activating the lemmas of needed words? Nothing, really. The name comes from another kind of information represented at the Functional Level: the semantic function or role of each word.

Semantic function

At the Message Level, your desire to tell a story didn't just activate concepts of people and things; if it did, the story you actually produced would just be a list of nouns, with nothing happening. The story you wanted to tell also activated EVENT STRUCTURES—what your REFERENTS (the people and things that you are talking about) did or what happened to them. The event structures are, basically, your concepts of who did what to whom in your story.

How does that information get into the sentence you produce? Each event structure has to arouse an appropriate verb lemma (TEASED, FRIGHTENED, DISTRACTED . . .). Verb lemmas, like noun lemmas, are their meaning plus the grammatical information needed to use them, and that includes the semantic roles or SEMANTIC FUNCTIONS that the nouns around them will play. In the sentence *My uncle distracted the lions*, illustrated in Figure 3.4, your uncle is the Agent and the lions are the Undergoers; in *My brother was frightened*, your brother is the Undergoer. These semantic role terms and several others were introduced in Chapter 1, section 1.7, if you want to look back there for a review.

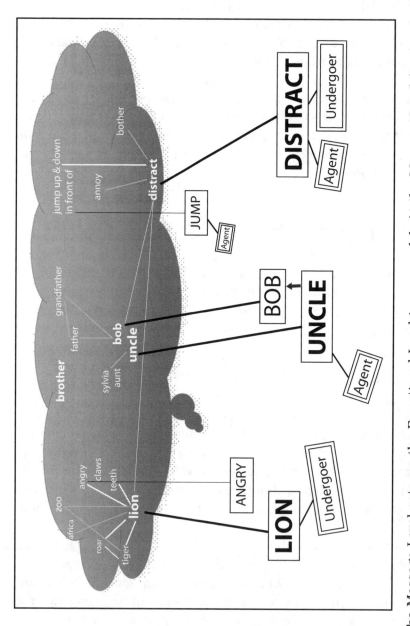

Figure 3.4. The Message Level sets up the Functional Level in our model. At the Message Level (*in the shaded cloud*), the real world events and referents activate their concepts; concepts are grouped into event structures, and activate other concepts as well. Concepts that were activated above threshold at Message Level activate their lemmas at the Functional Level (*the boxes*). The semantic roles that are part of the activated verb's lemma are attached as tags to lemmas of the participants in the event, according to their roles in the event structure. Lemmas don't have any order, so I've used a random order here.

At the Functional Level, the lemmas referring to the people, animals, and things in each event structure of your story get linked to the proper semantic functions of that event's verb lemma. This is a key step in making sure that your story will convey which person—if any—is the Agent of each verb, who is the Undergoer, what location is the source, what location is the goal, and so on.

What kind of thing is it in our heads that (usually) puts words in the right order to mean what we intend? In this section, we'll only discuss the steps involved in communicating information about actions, which is what has been studied most; feelings and sensations have different event structures, and they are probably slightly different.

We've seen how neat the blend and substitution errors are at putting words into grammatically appropriate slots. (Later we'll talk about errors that are not quite so neat. They do exist, so we have to explain them, too.) But when we mix up lists of numbers or of numbers and letters that don't spell anything (a telephone number, a license plate number), we are quite likely to get the numbers or letters in all sorts of wrong orders. So whatever we do in putting sentences together is not much like what we do in remembering a list of numbers. (Experiments on memory for sentences show this, too; see Chapter 5, section 5.2.4.)

As we've just said, language encodes our understanding of the events that are happening around us by somehow linking each thing that we talk about with a semantic function like Agent or Recipient or Undergoer—or, if no other semantic function fits, with Theme. Psycholinguists don't know how this linking works, so we duck by saying that during the construction of a sentence, each lemma is temporarily "tagged" with its semantic role. This idea of semantic role tagging is useful even though we don't know how to explain it in terms of how the brain does it. If we say that the lemma JON is tagged as Agent, SUSIE as Recipient, and CAKE as Theme (and MORNING could be called temporal Location) in the sentences here, then we have a way to talk about, for example, the link between the cake and its creator in all of these sentences regardless of their syntax or whether the baker and the recipient are explicitly mentioned:

Jon baked the birthday cake for Susie this morning.

Susie loved the cake Jon baked for her this morning.

The cake was baked this morning by Jon.

Activating lemmas and tagging each with its semantic function are two of the three main processes that create the Functional Level of sentence production. Sometimes, we don't even need a real lemma to refer to the agent of a sentence in English; there's no referring expression to say who the Agent is in *Bake a cake last night?* and no need for one, either, because you can only say that to the person whom you are guessing did the baking. Many other languages can leave out Agents even in formal speech, and some of them can leave out Themes, too, if they are unimportant, or if hearers can perfectly well figure out what was eaten, taken, seen, or whatever.

Clinical descriptions and tests show us that people with aphasia are usually clear on these semantic functions, even when they can't express them by putting words together in the right order. And children are very tuned into who-did-what-to-whom long before they can talk; as you'll see in Chapter 7, one of the first things children learning English understand about grammar, while they themselves are still only able to say one word at a time, is the meaning difference between *The dog pushes the baby* and *The baby pushes the dog*.

Here is a speech error that swaps semantic roles, from the Fromkin collection:

The Grand Canyon went to my sister. (Goal interchanged with Agent)

We'll talk more about this error in Chapter 4, as we'll need to introduce new concepts to understand how it might have happened in our model of speech production.

3.6 Summary of Language Production So Far

3.6.1 From ideas to lemmas and semantic roles

The first step in speaking is choosing what you're going to put into words. Usually, we do this without thinking about it, but if it's difficult for any reason, we may become conscious of parts of the process of trying to figure out how to say what we mean. The information that gets organized at this first step of language production, which we've called the **MESSAGE LEVEL**, is all concepts—it's not words yet. Setting up the Message Level means activating the concepts of our **REFERENTS** (whom and what to mention), and deciding who is the hero (or what is the topic) of our story. At the Message Level, we also decide (usually unconsciously) what sort of words we should use for referring—formal or informal, fully spelled out or abbreviated, or just a pronoun, or even no referring expression at all—and we organize the things that are happening into EVENT STRUCTURES, usually built around verb concepts.

Activation flows from the concepts at the Message Level to two kinds of information at the Functional Level, LEMMAS and SEMANTIC ROLES. The concepts for the REFERENTS activate the noun or pronoun lemmas (the meanings of the words without the sounds). At the same time, the event structure for the actions that the referents are involved in will activate two kinds of things: the verb lemmas that will describe the action, and the semantic roles that the referents will get TAGGED with. But the lemmas don't have any order; in fact, in our model, lemmas don't ever have an order—they just have tags that eventually will get them to their destinations, like checked luggage (we hope). The order that words come out in is created at the Positional Level, and we'll work on how that happens in Chapter 4. What we've done in this chapter is a little like the early part of preparing to stage a puppet show: at the Message Level, you've got the plot outline, and at the Functional Level, you've chosen the roles—a king, a queen, a villain, a wizard—and what they are going to do. However, you don't yet know exactly what they will look like or the precise order that they will appear in; that will be the next step.

3.6.2 Managing traffic without a cop, a play without a director

Speaking is different from putting on a scene in a very important way: Inside your head, there is *no director*. (We can't say that your mind is the director, because we're trying to explain how the mind itself works. If you explain the mind by putting another mind inside it, you'd have to explain how that inner mind worked, and so on . . .). This "choosing" that we've been describing doesn't happen because someone takes a concept out of a box; it happens, subconsciously, because some concepts are aroused by something we see, hear, and/or remember. In turn, activation automatically spreads from these concepts to some of the lemmas for the words that can be used to communicate information to someone. Again, *the spread of activation is automatic.* No one is responsible for it (although you may be concentrating on your language enough to be able to catch an error that has happened inside your head before you actually say it aloud). The concept of the person who can be called Professor Barbara Fox will activate all the possible lemmas for referring to her—and it will also activate the lemmas for some of your other professors, although not as strongly. And, when it is activated, the lemma BARBARA will activate concepts of some other people named Barbara, which in turn will link to the lemmas for the family names of these other Barbaras.

It's relative strength of activation that matters. Mistakes at the Functional Level can happen when two lemmas are activated to just about the same extent, so that we get blend errors like *I lost my track of thought* or *car dealsman* from trying to say both of them at once. They also happen when something else on your mind or happening around you adds to the activation of a concept or a lemma that isn't the one your conscious mind would have wanted, tipping the balance of activation in favor of the lemma for the wrong word, like REFRIGERATOR instead of DISHWASHER, PANDA instead of PANTHER, or DACHSHUND instead of VOLKSWAGEN.

3.7 Applying Our Model to an Aphasic Speech Production Problem

Shirley Kleinman, who told the story of her Broca's aphasia in *Shirley Says: Living with Aphasia* (online at http://www.spot.colorado.edu/~menn/docs/Shirley4.pdf), was trying, in an experimental test that I gave her, to describe what was going on in the picture shown in Figure 3.5).

Figure 3.5. Baseball hits baby.

Like most people with moderate Broca's aphasia, Shirley had lost the ability to make passive-voice sentences. What she said was *The baby—no (sigh)—the ball hit the baby*. We can use the ideas we've developed in this chapter to describe what happened here, based on what she started to say and how she revised it. First of all, the description she settles on is correct, so the picture must have activated the right concepts and event structure at the Message Level: a ball, a small child (baby), and a hitting event. The ball in this event hits the baby, and Shirley's not confused about that, either, even though people hit balls at least as often as balls hit people. Less important information—how the girls are reacting to the event—doesn't distract Shirley from focusing on the main event at the Message Level.

This information at the Message Level aroused two appropriate lemmas (BALL, HIT) at the Functional Level; we know that for sure because those two lemmas were then able to activate their phonological forms at the Positional Level. We'll talk about that process in Chapter 4. In the case of BABY, which doesn't seem to be the best possible word for a child who looks like he can walk, it's possible that the concept at the Message Level sent activation to the lemmas of more complicated referring expressions (like LITTLE KID), and/or a more precise but lower frequency word (like TODDLER), as well as to the lemma of the not-quite-accurate word BABY. But Shirley produced the word *baby*; why? Well, BABY is easier to activate than TODDLER) because it's much more frequent.

Why does higher frequency make a word easier to activate? We can't give the full story yet, but here's the main part of it: As you'll remember from Chapter 2, frequent words have a high resting level of activation. (Now we can say that more precisely: The lemmas of frequent words have a high resting level of activation.) That means that it doesn't take as much new activation to get those lemmas up to the threshold for sending activation on to their phonological forms. The lemma BABY would have gotten less activation from the picture than the lemma TODDLER, because the concept of a baby isn't a great match to the picture, but that small amount of input activation could get BABY up to threshold so it could activate its phonological form; the less frequent lemma TODDLER would have needed a lot more input to reach threshold.

The event structure at the Message Level also sent activation—and clearly, enough activation—so that the ball could be tagged as the inanimate Cause of the hitting event (we don't usually call inanimate causes Agents) and the baby could be tagged as the Undergoer.

And why did Shirley have a false start and a self-correction? We'll get the answer to that in Chapter 4, section 4.1.1.

Exercises for Chapter 3

3.1. Now that you've seen a lot of examples of speech errors, how would you define "speech error"? (I have deliberately not put a definition of speech error in the Glossary.)

3.2. Look back at the errors in the queries to librarians in section 3.1.1. Work out the details of how one of these errors might have occurred, in terms of spreading activation from the phonetic and syntactic information that was coming in when the customer heard his or her assignment, combined with expectations based on the words and the real-world information that the customer probably already had before they heard the teacher say the new name or book title. Consider how the sounds heard, the syntax, the semantics, and the pragmatics would activate stored information. What practical recommendations would you give to teachers and students (of any age) to reduce the chance that errors like these would happen, especially in a second-language setting?

3.3. Reading, like hearing, is also a mix of top-down and bottom-up processing, and we make errors of misreading when too little information comes from the letters, for whatever reason. Work out some of the similarities and differences between the processes that must be involved in understanding written words compared to those involved in understanding spoken language.

3.4. In an official written communication from a leader of an organization, the phrase "bottoms-up process" occurred not once but twice. (For non-native English readers and non-drinkers: "Bottoms up!" is a common alchoholic-beverage-drinking expression, used as a toast like, "To your health!" or "Cheers!") The context made it clear that his meaning was "a process originating in the membership of the organization, rather than in the leadership"—in other words, a bottom-up process.

After you finish chuckling at the implication that the author of this communiqué may have been drinking too many toasts, decide what kind of language production error this is, or whether you can't classify it, and why. Regardless of whether you can classify it, you can give a pretty full story of how it arose, in terms of spreading activation. Try doing that, step-by-step.

3.5. Pragmatics: Compose an E-mail telling a story, like the zoo event in section 3.2.1, to one person who would enjoy hearing the story in an exciting way and then telling the same story to person a who would be upset by the details, without lying to either person. After you've done this in as natural a way as possible, list the pragmatic differences between the two versions. If you using this book in a class, it would be best to work in pairs to do this, so that each person can analyze the other person's choices of messages, event structures, and words.

3.6. Analyzing a blend error: Explain the steps in creating the utterance *Did someone fly off the deep end?*, presumably a blend of *Did someone fly off the handle?* and *Did someone jump off the deep end?*

3.7. If you know a signed language, read some of the literature on "slips of the hand'" errors, and then consider the possibilities that Sign might offer for mondegreens and the other types of errors that we have discussed in this chapter.

Acknowledgments. The "Funny You Should Ask" quotes were forwarded to me by Glenys Waldman, PhD, Librarian, The Masonic Library and Museum of Pennsylvania, Philadelphia, PA. The librarians who posted the quotes to Gale Reference Library are Val Stark, Quincy Public Library, Quincy, IL; Susan Pitts, Lufkin Middle School, Lufkin, TX; Christie Hamm, Sacramento Public Library, Sacramento, CA; Jill Munson, Choteau County Library, Fort Benton, MT; Ellen Dunn, Wicomico Public Library, Salisbury, MD; and Carrie Damon, Rayburn Middle School, San Antonio, TX. I am grateful to Cengage Learning for permission to reproduce these contributions.

References

Bock, K., & Levelt, W. (1994). Grammatical encoding. In M. A. Gernsbacher (Ed.), *Handbook of psycholinguistics* (pp. 945–984). San Diego, CA: Academic Press.

Fay, D., & Cutler, A. (1977). Malapropisms and the structure of the mental lexicon. *Linguistic Inquiry, 8,* 505–520.

Fromkin, V. A. (Ed.). (1973). *Speech errors as linguistic evidence.* The Hague, Netherlands: Mouton.

Garnes, S., & Bond, Z. (1975). Slips of the ear: Errors in perception of casual speech. In *Papers from the Eleventh Regional Meeting of the Chicago Linguistic Society* (pp. 214–225). Chicago, IL: Department of Linguistics, University of Chicago.

Zwicky, A. M. (1980). *Mistakes.* Reynoldsburg, OH: Advocate Publishing Group.

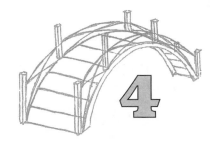

Normal Speech Errors and How They Happen: II: Saying Words and Sounds in the Right Order

4.0 High-Speed Grammar: Making Phrases and Sentences in a Few Tenths of a Second

Let's consider this set of errors from Fromkin and other published sources:

1. *Where'd I bring it when I put it in?*   [Where'd I put it when I brought it in?]

2. *the Grand Canyon went to my sister*   [my sister went to the Grand Canyon]

3. *turn to tend out*   [tend to turn out]

4. *a fifty-pound dog of bag food*   [a fifty-pound bag of dog food]

5. *stop beating your brick against a head wall*   [stop beating your head against a brick wall]

and, most spectacularly,

6. *Hey, joke, have you heard the Mike about . . . ?*

If you look back at the errors in Chapter 3, section 3.3, like *Look at the lady with the dachshund* (Volkswagen), *Do you wash your Tupperware by hand or do you put it in the refrigerator?* (dishwasher), or . . . *you have too many irons in the smoke* (. . . in the fire), you'll see that these examples are different. The errors here don't substitute an unintended word that's in the same semantic category as the intended target word, like *refrigerator* for *dishwasher*. Instead, they swap the places of two intended and semantically unrelated target words (or phrases), like *Mike* and *joke* or *the Grand Canyon* and *my sister*. So the resulting sentences are made with words that all really belong in them, but the words are in the wrong order. How could this have happened? In Chapter 3, section 3.5, we saw one way: A referent like *my sister* could get tagged with the wrong semantic role when the functional level was getting set up. In this chapter, we'll look at that possibility some more, and also at another one: Putting the word forms in the wrong order when the positional level is being created.

4.1 Getting Words Into the Right (and Wrong) Order

To answer this question, we need to see how the model we're using would get words into the right order—we're talking in terms of a "model," remember, because all this is a very simplified version of what's going on inside our brains. So at the end of Chapter 3, a sentence on its way from your mind to your mouth had gotten to the point where the lemmas for its words were activated, and each lemma was tagged with the semantic role that would be played by the person or thing it referred to. And you'd also chosen who was the hero of the story (or what the topic was), although we didn't say exactly how that affects matters at the Functional Level. We need to do that now.

4.1.1 Heroes, cascades, and buffers: Lemmas ready and rarin' to go

In Chapter 3, section 3.7, where Shirley, my friend with Broca's aphasia, started off describing a picture of a very small boy being hit on the head by a stray softball, you already see the problem. *The baby—no (sigh)— The baseball hits the baby.* Her first impulse was to mention the child first, as I just did two sentences ago. But as we saw, Shirley found that she couldn't continue her utterance the way she had started it. Her language comprehension ability was still plenty good enough for her to know that *The baby hit the baseball* was not at all what she meant, but her production ability wasn't good enough to come up with even the simplest kind of passive sentence, like *The baby is getting hit* or *The baby is being hit on the head.* So, reluctantly, she gave up and started again; she made the active voice sentence *The baseball hits the baby,* with correct grammar and meaning. But doing this forced her to sacrifice the pragmatic information that the passive voice would have let her convey: Her grammatically and semantically correct utterance lost the pragmatic information that the sentence is about the little boy and what happened to him, rather than being about the baseball and its flight path.

What does this mean for a model of sentence production? In Chapter 3, we said that we unconsciously make choices about who is the hero of a story (or what is the topic) at the Message Level; then the concepts activate the lemmas, and your conceptualization of the event (with some help from the verb lemma) tags the noun lemmas with their semantic (who-did-what) roles at the Functional Level. So how do we get the part about who is the hero into this model?

The Freudian slips we've discussed (plus laboratory experiments that we'll talk about in Chapter 5) have given us a strong suggestion: Not all the noun lemmas that we need to make the sentence we intend to say are activated at the same time or to the same extent. The concepts that are activated more strongly—for example, our concepts for the people that we have emotional reactions to—are faster in getting up to their threshold activation at the Message Level, and so they then activate their lemmas sooner at the Functional Level. Those activated lemmas, like BABY in Shirley's sentence, will be pushing and shoving to get into the sentence that is being constructed.

This idea—the idea that lemmas don't all politely wait for each other to be activated before a sentence-under-construction leaves the Message Level (and the later production levels, in turn)—is part of a **CASCADE MODEL** of processing. Cascade processing means that, when the activation for any step of processing a particular concept, event, or lemma reaches threshold, it starts to send activation to the next step of its production, regardless of whether other items at the same level are ready to go or not.

We're going to introduce one more useful term: We say that if an item is activated before it can be used in putting the sentence together, it's temporarily held in a waiting place, a **BUFFER**. (Human-life examples of buffers are waiting lines, waiting rooms, train platforms—anyplace you have to hang out because the thing that you are ready for is not ready for you.) If an item is activated but can't yet be put into the sentence being formed, we'll say that it's in a buffer.

In our model, getting the words of a sentence into their order happens at the third level of output organization: the **POSITIONAL LEVEL**. Here's an overall look at our model again, to help you keep track of where we are. Figure 4.1 is the same as Figure 3.1, except that now were emphasizing

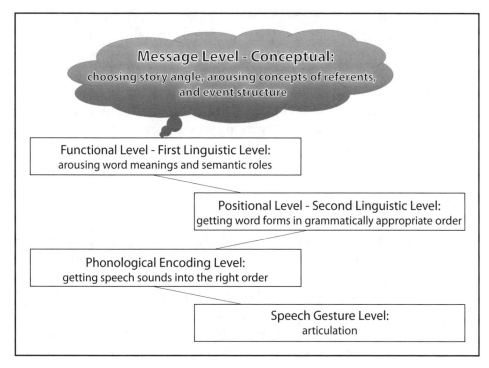

Figure 4.1. Processing levels in our speech production model.

the levels that we're focusing on in sections 4.1 and 4.2: the Positional and Phonological Encoding Levels, and the transition from the Functional Level to the Positional Level.

When the right words for the sentence go into the wrong order, the Positional Level has been constructed incorrectly, either because of switched tags at the Functional Level (as in *the Grand Canyon went to my sister*), or because phonological word forms activated by correctly tagged lemmas get put into the wrong places at the Positional Level. Errors where the right words go in the wrong order, by the way, are not particularly common in people with language disorders; they seem to be the kind of thing that happens when skilled normal speakers get to talking too fast.

But the processes of constructing the Positional Level are essential, and they can indeed go wrong in people with aphasia, as we'll see in more detail in Chapter 6. And in language learners, these processes will be in primitive shape until they know the grammar. If you've been a novice-speaker tourist, you know all too well the situation where the best you can do is say one noun and then another, plus a memorized phrase or two, instead of constructing even simple sentences. You have a whole lot of lemmas in a buffer, and you know their semantic roles, but you can't use that information to construct the Positional Level, so all the lemmas can do is activate their word forms. To communicate without syntax, you use gestures, facial expressions, and prosody: You point, raise your eyebrows, and use the pitch of your voice to indicate requests and questions. *Newspaper, please. Phone card? That one. How much?* No Positional Level, no syntax. So we might say that a large part of knowing the grammar of a language well enough to use it is equivalent to having the mechanisms for constructing its Positional Level working swiftly, smoothly, and automatically in your head.

4.1.2 Slots and fillers

It may already have occurred to you that the word and phrase exchange errors at the beginning of this chapter are like putting things in the wrong places in the real world, say, like putting the cereal box in the refrigerator and the milk carton in the cupboard on a bad morning. That's the metaphor our model uses: We say that the Positional Level has a SLOT for each word—more precisely, a slot where each lemma is supposed to send the phonological form that it activates. Each phonological form has to be put into the right slot, according to the tag that it gets from the lemma that aroused it. (We'll refine this statement a bit later.) But remember, the lemma tags were semantic (Agent, Recipient, Addressee, etc.), and said nothing about the syntax or the actual order of the words. So how does the proper order get computed? And what about those lemmas waiting impatiently in the buffer? Okay, one thing at a time.

Getting EVENT STRUCTURES turned into sets of slots and getting the lemmas to put their word forms into those slots is where syntax pretty much takes over from semantics. The best-studied part of this process is getting the main noun (or noun phrase) slots set up by the main verb, and getting the right phonological forms into those slots; the exercises at the end of this chapter will help you to think about the several other kinds of slots that are involved in the exchange errors we've seen.

Exchange errors

Two of our exchange errors involved the verb and the noun phrases it controls. As we saw at the end of Chapter 3, the two whole noun phrases in *The Grand Canyon went to my sister* have been so neatly interchanged that it seems like the error must have occurred in the process of putting the semantic tags onto the lemmas at the Functional Level, so that those whole noun phrases then got put into the wrong slots at the Positional

Level. Let's work through this using our sentence production model so far. (You might want to review the syntax and semantics sections in Chapter 1 before we do this.)

The speaker's concept of the whole story specifies, at the Message Level, the event structure which we could call {Person go (past, completed action) to Goal}. At the Functional Level, that event structure has activated the verb lemma GO, and the tense PAST. Because the speaker's concept of the story included concepts of the people and places involved, they were activated at the Message Level too. Those concepts activated the lemmas for FIRST PERSON SINGULAR PRONOUN, SISTER, and GRAND+CANYON at the Functional Level. Since GO is a verb lemma, it must also be linked to semantic roles that go with it at the Functional Level. What are they?

For GO and most motion verbs, the essential role is the person, animal, or thing that moves, and this "mover"' is the real-world item that is most affected by the action of the verb. That's one definition of **THEME**: the referent that's most affected by the action of a verb. (For transitive verbs, and some intransitive ones, Theme is pretty much equivalent to Undergoer, but it would seem really odd to call the subject of a voluntary motion verb an Undergoer.) So whatever moves to the Goal is the Theme, in our example, MY SISTER. The verb lemma plus the event structure should have tagged the lemma MY SISTER as Theme, and the lemma GRAND+CANYON as Goal—only, as we know, those tags got switched. Because GO is a motion verb, it can also have a Source, but in the sentence we're analyzing, the speaker hasn't said where his or her sister started from, so we'll say that GO only activated the Theme and Goal roles.

So far, this has all been semantic analysis, and all at the Functional Level. But now, at last, we have reached the Positional Level, and we can finally talk about syntax: subjects, objects, prepositional phrases, and word order. What the verb lemma does, then, in helping to create the Positional Level, is to set up a **SUBJECT SLOT** as the first noun phrase slot in the sentence. Almost every English verb does this, or can do it, because beginning sentences with subjects is our most frequent sentence pattern.

GO also sets up the Goal slot, in a prepositional phrase that comes right after its own slot. This is the slot where the phonological form that was activated by lemma THE GRAND CANYON should have gone, because the Grand Canyon is the place the speaker's sister went.

So far, in our model, the Positional Level, with the verb form in place but before the noun and preposition forms actually get into their slots, should have looked like this, if you work through the parentheses here carefully:

$$[\underline{\qquad}]_{\text{Theme, subject}} \ [go+\text{past}]_{\text{verb}} \ [\ [\underline{\quad}]_{\text{preposition}} \ [\underline{\qquad}] \ ]_{\text{Goal, prepositional phrase}}$$

If the lemmas had had the correct tags and their word forms had been sent where those tags told them to go, what the Positional Level should look like next is this:

[*my sister*]_{Theme, subject} [*go*+past]_{verb} [[*to*]_{preposition} [*the Grand Canyon*]]_{Goal, prepositional phrase}

But THE GRAND CANYON and MY SISTER had their tags switched while they were still lemmas at the Functional Level. So, instead, the speaker had this structure at the Positional Level:

[*the Grand Canyon*]_{Theme, subject} [*go*+past]_{verb} [[*to*]_{preposition} [*my sister*]]_{Goal, prepositional phrase}

The reason we analyzed this error as having started at the Functional Level is that the entire noun phrases *my sister* and *the Grand Canyon* were switched. Now let's work through one that must have happened during the construction of the Positional Level: *Stop beating your brick against a head wall.* Here, you can see that it's only the two nouns *brick* and *head* that got exchanged; the other words in their noun phrases, *your*, *a*, and *wall*, are where they belong. That could only have happened if, at the Functional Level, YOUR HEAD had gotten its correct tag, Theme, and if BRICK WALL was correctly tagged as Goal, so that's why the mistake must have happened later, as the speaker's brain was creating the Positional Level.

This verb's in the imperative, so its Agent—the person being spoken to—doesn't have to get a slot, and in this case, it doesn't. That means the slots at the Positional Level, after the verb phrase's phonological form gets filled in but before the noun phrases get their forms placed, look like this:

[*stop hit*+progressive]_{verb} [[___] [___]_{Theme, obbject} [[___]_{preposition} [_____]]_{Goal, prepositional phrase}

While the verb phrase *stop hit* was setting up those slots and activating the preposition *against*, the tagged lemmas YOU, HEAD, BRICK, and WALL were activating their phonological forms. Those four lemmas also carried additional tags (although we haven't taken the time to discuss this) that should also have told each of the forms where it should go within the two noun phrases: that YOU is supposed to modify HEAD (which means that its phonological form will have to be *your*), and that BRICK is supposed to modify WALL.

But for some reason, the form *brick* got too much activation to wait patiently in the buffer until it was time modify the object of the preposition. It shoved its way into the object noun phrase where *head* should have gone, leaving *head* to slip into the empty slot modifying WALL. So when all of these phonological forms send activation on to the Phonological

Encoding Level and from there to the Speech Gesture Level, the resulting sentence came out with its words scrambled, but its semantic structure still clear and its word forms intact.

STRANDING tense

Now let's look at a different kind of exchange error, one involving two verbs: *Where'd I bring it when I put it in?* The target was *Where'd I put it when I brought it in?* so the verb of the main clause (*where did I put it?*) got switched with the verb of the subordinate clause (*when I brought it in*). That seems very simple, but look again. You can't tell what tense the verb *put* is in, because it's one of those English verbs where the past tense and the present tense look identical. But the verb form in the main clause that the speaker actually said is *bring* without any tense marker. (That's because the main clause past tense is already marked on *did*—we don't say *Where did I left it?* or *When did you wanted it?*). Now in the target, it would have been *brought*, past tense, right? So why didn't the speaker say *Where'd I brought it when I put it in*? And why does that sound even odder than *Where'd I bring it when I put it in?*

To answer that question, we need to work at a finer level of detail, and at the steps involved in turning lemmas into words. We'll do that in section 4.2, after we look at one of the ways that people simplify the problem of putting sentences together: the use of formulas.

4.1.3 Formulas and clichés: Prefab word sequences (with a few options) reduce construction costs

Prefabricated units save construction costs in assembling sentences as well as houses. Completely ready-to-go units, including greetings like *'Sup?* (or the older version *What's up?*), clichés like *As dead as a doornail* and proverbs like *A stitch in time saves nine* seem to roll off our tongues, but more important in everyday language are FORMULAS: sequences of words with a slot or two for an additional word that you can choose, rather like a modular bathroom where you can choose the color of your sink and tub. Good examples are politeness formulas like *May I please have some (more)* [name of food/drink], standard information questions like *Are we at* [name of destination] *yet,?* and more complex formulas like [person] [form of verb *take*] [possessive pronoun for same person] *(sweet) time (about it)*. The "take time" formula that I just gave you covers a fairly large set of expressions, from the simple *He's taking his time* to expanded expressions like *He's certainly taking his own sweet time about it!*

Children pick up on many of these formulas early because of their frequency; second-language learners find them extremely useful to memorize because they help one sound more fluent; and for people with some kinds of aphasia, they may be among the few fluent word sequences that they can produce. Blend errors can occur when two relevant formulas are aroused at the same time: *Oh, help all you want!* was spoken at my dinner table by someone blending *Help yourself!* and *Oh, take all you want!* as I reached for a platter.

4.2 Errors in Word-Making: Word-Assembly Crashes

Now let's look at some errors involving parts of words—parts that aren't just sounds or syllables, but parts that are meaningful; to be precise, the MORPHEMES, which were introduced in Chapter 1, section 1.4.

4.2.1 Affixes on the loose

The first three are from Fromkin's error collection; the last one is from mine. I've used different typestyles to help you find the within-word morpheme boundaries (remember that many English words have only one morpheme). The first two are exchange errors, the third one is a blend, and the fourth one is a new kind: a deletion of one of two identical morphemes that seem to be coming too close together for comfort. Also, the first three errors all involve suffix morphemes, but the fourth error involves *out* in two different roles: as the second part of the compound noun *printout*, and as the particle in the verb+particle complex *turn out*.

a language neede*r* learn*s*	(target: a language *learn*er *need*s)
easy enough*ly*	(target: *easi*ly *enough*)
moment*aneous*	(targets: *moment*ary/*instant*aneous)
*Did the print*out *turn okay?*	(target: Did the print*out* turn *out* okay)

The first error, if you look closely, seems to involve switching the stems *learn* and *need*, while leaving their endings in the correct places, so that we still have the noun (ending in *-er*) and the verb (ending in *-s*) stranded just where they should be in a well-made sentence. The second error also involves a suffix getting detached from—or not getting attached to—the word it should have been on: the ending *-ly*, which should have been attached to the word *easy*, somehow attached itself to the next word instead.

Affix stranding errors like these—affix errors where suffixes get detached from their stems and left behind—are fairly common in normal English speakers. But it turns out that giving a complete account of how they might happen is quite complicated, so we won't try to work through the details. We'll just say that these two-morpheme words like *learner, needs,* or *easily* are stored in two parts, *learn* and *-er*, *need* and *-s*, *easy* and *-ly*, and that these parts are linked together like train cars that can become uncoupled when the train is derailed. If a word has three morphemes, it'll be like a three-car train, and so on.

When the assembly of *a language learner needs* goes wrong, how does this train-car idea help us to account for the fact that the suffixes *-er* and *-s* end up in places that give us good syntax while their stems, the words *need* and *learn*, are interchanged? It looks as if noun-ending morphemes like *-er* can be activated by slots that have been tagged to receive nouns (the subject slot and any object slots), and that verb-ending morphemes like the third person singular (*-s, -z, -ɔz*) can be activated by slots that have been set up for verbs (using the information coming from the subject's lemma about whether the subject is singular or plural). So they can be put into the subject and verb slots ahead of their content morpheme forms *need* and *learn*, like this:

[[indefinite]$_{\text{article}}$ [*language*]$_{\text{noun}}$ [[____]$_{\text{verb}}$+[*er*]] $_{\text{agentive noun}}$]$_{\text{noun phrase}}$ [[____]$_{\text{verb}}$ +[3rd sing. ending]]$_{\text{inflected verb}}$

The speaker's language-producing mechanism must have also known that it was looking for a verb to put before the *-er* suffix. The lemmas NEED and LEARN were both activated, they activated their forms *need* and *learn*, and somehow *need* jumped into that verb slot in front of the *-er* suffix instead of waiting in the buffer for its proper place before the *-s* suffix.

Affix errors are important in clinical and classroom settings: Speakers with aphasia often leave off suffix morphemes that are needed, or hitch up the wrong ones to the stem. And first- and second-language learners often have particular trouble learning certain kinds of affix morphemes; we'll have more to say about that in Chapter 9. Computer search engines need to be able to recognize affixes, too: If you search for *mummies*, you also want entries that have the word *mummy*, but if you search for the noun *pants,* you don't want entries with *pant*.

4.2.2 Stranding grammatical morphemes that aren't affixes

Morpheme problems, including stranding errors, don't always involve the kinds of morphemes that can be neatly thought of as detachable train cars. We just saw a tense-stranding error of that kind, *Where'd I bring it when I put it in?*, in section 4.1.2. Remember in Chapter 1 we discussed the English irregular plural morphemes, including those that are just changes in the vowels? These vowel-change morphemes can get stranded, too. Think about what must have happened to have the target sentence, *Where'd I put it when I brought it in?* actually get produced as *Where'd I bring it when I put it in?* and not as *Where'd I brought it when I put it in?*

If we break the verbs into morphemes at the lemma level, before their forms are activated, the target sentence is *Where* DO+past *I* PUT (no tense marker) *it when I* BRING+past *it in?* The mistake sentence, the one that was actually produced, has the two main verb lemmas PUT and BRING swapped, with the past tense information staying where it belonged. So this sharpens our understanding a little: It's not the forms of the endings themselves that stay where they belong; what doesn't move is the information about which tense or other form of the word should be chosen. The morphological knowledge in our heads isn't just about pieces of words, but also about the grammatical (tense, number) and the content (dictionary meaning) components of what they mean.

Does that make sense? Where understanding this comes in very handy is if you have to deal with mistakes in languages with a lot of irregularity, or in languages like Arabic and Hebrew that have a lot of their grammatical information distributed throughout a word (like our *sing, sang, sung* or *man/men* or *child/children*). Morpheme errors in those languages aren't describable in terms of moving pieces of words while other pieces stay in place, but only in terms of moving the content information while the grammatical information stays in place, or the opposite.

The most dramatic example of this kind of error in English, although it's not very common, is when a speaker switches two pronouns before they've been given their final form. I don't have a real example in my collection, but we can work with this made-up one: *They said **they** should come over to **our** place tonight*, target: *They said **we** should come over to **their** place tonight*. Here, the third person plural (*they, them, their*) and first person plural (*we, us, our*) meanings have gotten switched, but it's not the words themselves that moved—the error isn't the weird-sounding, *They said **our** should come over to **they** place tonight.*

Do you remember that in Chapter 3 we said that we'd treat each set of pronouns with the same person and number properties—each set like *they, them, their, theirs* or *we, us, our, ours*—as sharing the same lemma? Now you can see why that was a good idea: Using it, we can say that the hypothetical speaker here just switched the lemmas FIRST PERSON PLURAL and THIRD PERSON PLURAL when they were in the process of setting up the Positional Level. The information about which lemma would take the possessive form and which one would be the object of the preposition *to* was created separately, and it showed up in the right places. (Pronouns can also get switched after their forms have been filled in at the Phonological Encoding Level, but that produces awful-sounding ungrammatical sentences like *When I gave it to he—to him*, from Fromkin's collection.)

4.3 Errors in word sounds: A herrible mess at the level of phonological encoding or a foul-up in articulation?

4.3.1 Errors in phonological encoding: Planning the sequence of phonemes in a phrase

Everybody enjoys looking at error involving sounds—exchanges of vowel or consonant segment like (1) and (2), a shift of a segment from one word to another like (3) and (4), omission of a syllable that's too much like one or both of its neighbors as in (5), or something a little more bizarre, like (6)—I'll leave the job of describing that one to you, and you can also figure out the two words that were blended to make *herrible* in the title of this section. (Most of these errors, including *herrible*, are from the Fromkin collection; (4) and (7) are mine.)

1. odd hack /ad hæk/   (target: ad hoc /æd hak/)

2. *children interfere with your* /naif lait/   (target: . . . with your night life)

3. *a kice ream cone* /kais rim kon/   (target: an ice cream cone /ais krim kon/)

4. *It's not tack deduckstible* /tæk dədʌkstɪbl/   (target: . . . tax deductible /tæks dədʌktɪbl/) (LM)

5. *unamity* /ju'næmɪti/   (target: una'nimity /junæ'nɪmɪti/)

6. *smuck in the tid*   (target: stick in the mud)

7. *That's why you have full*   (target: *Finland*)
   Swedish-Finnish bilingualism in
   the area of Swinland . . .

What's important to note about these errors is, again, how neat they are. They create nonwords that obey English phonotactic patterns (Chapter 1, section 1.2.1), and most of the time, a sound moves from its place in the target syllable to a very similar if not identical kind of place in the error syllable. These are errors in planning the order of sounds in a word or in a phrase, not in actually articulating the sounds (as we'll see shortly); articulation happens at the final stage in production, the Speech Gesture Level, after a phrase has been pretty fully planned.

Psycholinguistic models for how sounds get into the wrong places are quite a bit like the models that are used for errors in the placement of words or morphemes, but in our production model, these exchanges have to happen after the Positional Level. At the Positional Level, word stems seem to be some kind of block of phonological information (in some related models, they are still lemmas, and grammatical morphemes are just pieces of information like "past" or "third person singular"). The level at which all the word sounds for all of the morphemes, including affixes, have been activated in the lexicon is, in the model we are using, called the **PHONOLOGICAL ENCODING LEVEL**. We use the term "encoding" here because meanings are what we want to convey to other people, but since we can't do it directly, we have to **ENCODE** those meanings in sounds (or in some other form that people can perceive).

Because the order of the sounds in a word is a crucial part of the information needed to produce it, psycholinguists often call these complete activated forms **ORDERED STRINGS OF PHONEMES**. Our model explains phonological errors that exchange or blend sounds across words (like the ones we've just been examining), by saying that these ordered strings of phonemes, after they have been aroused by their lemmas, have to wait around in a phonological **BUFFER** until we're on the point of producing the phrase that they are supposed to be in. So we could think of the Level of Phonological Encoding as the phonological buffer level. The phonological buffer holds about a phrase at a time; phonological errors that show sounds interacting over longer distances are rare (although semantic ones that go across phrase and clause boundaries are common).

When all goes well, each phoneme comes out in the right order and takes its place, but phonological errors happen when one of the phonemes is too strongly activated and pushes into the wrong place, or is too weakly activated and gets dropped out of the buffer. (There's lots more to say about how "the right order" is determined, but there's no perfect model yet.)

From the Positional Level to the Phonological Encoding Level

The lemma arouses the phonemes in the form of the word stem; the word stem as a block, plus the grammatical information to choose inflectional affixes with, is what we have at the completion of the **Positional Level**.

This information arouses the phonemes in the complete word, which go to the **Phonological Encoding Level**, which is a phonological buffer. In the buffer, the phonemes line up in the order they'll be needed in for actual production; this order basically determines which allophone of each phoneme will be produced.

In the clinic, one of the hard (and sometimes impossible) things to decide may be the problem of whether a pronunciation error is at the Phonological Encoding Level—choosing the wrong sound, but pronouncing it properly—or whether it's at the last level we'll talk about: the SPEECH GESTURE LEVEL, which is the level of actual phonetic production. But making this distinction is very important—you don't want to be having clients practice things that they can already do and failing to work on the things that really need work. And it's especially important to be able to understand this difference well enough to be able to explain it to clients and families, if they have the popular idea that something wrong with the client's mouth is what's making it hard for the client to say something (and of course, sometimes that idea is correct). If the aphasic person's speech sound errors are always clearly articulated, though, that means they are at the Phonological Encoding level, and not at the Speech Gesture Level.

4.3.2 Phonetic sound errors: Hitting an articulatory target

I like the term SPEECH GESTURE because it helps to draw our attention to the complex sets of muscle movements that get coordinated to make each sound, and to the ways that skilled speakers automatically make minute alterations in these movements—the COARTICULATION process—so that each articulation flows smoothly into the next one, like the movements of skilled gymnasts as they go through a routine. Some speech sounds could be made by moving only one articulator, but most of the time, many sets of muscles are brought into play, with exquisitely controlled timing: in your lips, your tongue, your jaw, your throat, and all the way down to your diaphragm (in the chest below your lungs) and in the chest wall, where the muscles push the air out of your lungs and through your vocal folds at just the right rate so that you can even get to the end of a long sentence like this one without running out of breath. Such a complex and automatized system is naturally vulnerable to damage at many points, and because it is automatized, it's hard to break in and teach it new ways of operation. Developing that automaticity is a major part of the work of first language learning, and trying to shift from the timing patterns needed for your first language to the ones needed for your second language is at least as much of a challenge as figuring out how to make the unfamiliar articulatory gestures and/or unfamiliar gesture combinations and sequences, as we'll see in Chapters 9 and 10.

From the Phonological Encoding Level to the Speech Gesture Level

The phonemes in the complete word are lined up in the phonological buffer at the **Phonological Encoding Level**. They line up in order, if all goes well. This order starts to determine which allophone of each phoneme will be produced.

The lined-up phonemes arouse the sets of neural instructions that go to the muscles needed to produce the articulatory gestures; this is the **Speech Gesture Level**. Coarticulation happens when any of the gestures needed to make one speech sound are being made at the same time as gestures for another speech sound; coarticulation also helps to determine which allophone of each phoneme will be produced.

Clear cases of errors at the Speech Gesture Level are those that listeners describe as "unclear," "slurred," or "mushy"; there are examples on the CD. Some of these errors may be caused by gestures that over- or undershoot their articulatory target, like making a full closure when a partial closure is needed or vice versa, for example, producing a sound that combines [p] and [f] when the target is one or the other of those sounds. Another kind of speech gesture error is mis-timing within a complex gesture set needed to produce a particular speech sound, for example, starting vocal fold vibrations too late or too early, relative to the tongue or lip closure, in making a voiced stop.

4.4 Double Whammies and Worse: Multiple-Source Errors Versus Self-Monitoring

In Chapter 3, we said that we'd come back to the error where the speaker said that someone was *a fine magician* instead of what they had wanted to say, *a fine musician*. Look at all the ways that these two words are similar: Semantically, they are both names of skilled occupations that involve performing for the pleasure of an audience. Syntactically, they are both nouns. Morphologically, they are both formed with a stem plus an affix that indicates a person involved in an activity, and furthermore, it's the same affix. And phonologically, they have the same number of syllables, the same stress pattern, and they start with the same sound, and contain several more sounds that are the same in their stems—they are almost a minimal pair. The two words could hardly be more alike, in fact. So activation could spread collaterally from one of them to the other at multiple points in the production process, all contributing to a buildup of activation for *magician*, which apparently gets into the buffer and shoves its way out at the point when *musician* should have gone into the final production stage.

You've probably had the experience of realizing that you are about to make a speech error but being able to stop it before actually saying it, or before saying all of it, like Shirley stopping herself from saying all of *The baby hit the ball*. Having enough awareness to stop your errors before they get to the Speech Gesture Level is called SELF-MONITORING; it takes attention and effort, so we don't do it well when we're tired or thinking about something else. The same multiple resemblances that made it easy for *magician* to slip into the buffer and supplant *musician* also make it harder for a speaker to catch the error on its way out. People with aphasia often seem to be making multiple-source errors; when you've analyzed a few of them, as we will in Chapter 6, and realized what a barrage of competing collateral activation a correct sentence has had to survive on its way to being produced, normal speech begins to seem positively miraculous.

4.5 Summary of Sentence Production: From Ideas to Articulation

If we go back through all the stages of sentence production starting in Chapter 3 and follow the whole complex of processes, it goes like this (in a simplified version): When we want to say something, what we see, hear, and feel (sensory input), plus what we think, know, and remember, combine to activate concepts of **events** and **referents** (the people and things being talked about: Grand Canyon, baby, ice cream) into a coherent package of what we intend to convey, including what we want to emphasize or downplay about it. This coherent package is the **Message Level**. To create it, the competition between many of the things we might have said has to settle down to **selecting** only as much can be put into coherent **event structures**. A lot of the messy semicoherent output that occurs when we're trying to think and talk at the same time happens because this competition-settling process doesn't go smoothly, especially when we're not quite sure what we really want to convey.

The second part of the process of putting each clause of the sentence together then flows through two streams: The concepts of the referents arouse the **lemmas** for the nouns and pronouns that will be needed to name them (GRAND CANYON, BABY, ICE CREAM), while the event structures arouse the verb lemmas and the specific **semantic role tags** (Agent, Source, Undergoer, and so on) that will have to be attached to the nouns. These streams recombine to make the **Functional Level**, where those tags specifying their semantic functions can get attached to the nouns and pronouns. If a lemma gets aroused before its tag is ready, it will have to wait in a **buffer** for awhile. (We are simplifying this story by leaving out other important kinds of words like adjectives, adverbs, and prepositions.)

The third set of processes starts at the Functional Level. The lemmas arouse the **phonemic forms** of their words (BABY arouses /beibi/), and the verb lemma also arouses the right **syntactic frame** for the event structure. The syntactic frame for a clause is mostly made up of the verb and labeled **slots** before and after it, plus information about the grammatical morphemes that the clause will need. (For example, if the event structure has called for the word *break* in a transitive active voice construction in the past tense, the lemma BREAK arouses a slot for Agent/subject before it and a slot for Undergoer/object after it, plus a past tense tag.) The semantic tags on the noun and pronoun lemmas match up with the ones on the slots to guide each noun or pronoun into the right place. If a lemma has aroused its phonemic form before its slot is ready, the form will have to wait in a **word-form buffer** until the slot has formed. When this assembly process is complete, we have the **Positional Level**, where we finally have syntax, including word order.

The syntactic, morphological, and phonological information at the Positional Level activates the rest of the phonological information that is still needed. In English, this is mostly the right case forms for the pronouns (/ai, mai, mi/ . . .), the right tense forms for the verbs (past tense -/t/, -/d/, -/əd/, or an irregular form like /browk/), the right number forms for the nouns, and similar choices. This gives us the **Phonological Encoding Level**, where all the phonemes are specified. Finally, as the beginning of a clause gets phonologically encoded, the phonemes send out activation to the articulators, and the person can begin to say the clause, perhaps while the phonemes at the end of it are still being specified. This final level of production is the **Speech Gesture Level**.

Exercises for Chapter 4

4.1. Nouns can set up slots for the adjectives and other words that modify them, and some other kinds of words also can (or have to) set up slots. For example, the adjective *fond* sets up a slot for a prepositional phrase beginning with *of*, because in modern English you can't just say someone is *fond*, you have to say *fond of* something.

Consider the following errors: What words are in the wrong slots, and what words set up the slots involved, or can't a controlling word be identified?

Hey, joke, have you heard the Mike about . . . ?

a fifty-pound dog of bag food

stops beating your brick against a head wall (MFG)

Every time I put one of these buttons off, another one comes on (MFG)

4.2. This morpheme blend error from Fromkin's collection is sneaky—it's easy to see what went wrong, but it's hard to analyze completely. Try it, and see if you can explain what is difficult about analyzing it.

car dealsman   (targets: car dealer/car salesman)

4.3. Outline how you would explain, to an English learner who doesn't know anything about grammatical morphemes but has been working hard to learn *I want, you want, they want, he she or it want***s**, why we don't say *Where does he want***s** *it*, or *She doesn't want***s** *it*.

4.4. Example 3 in Chapter 4, section 4.3.1 was *a kice ream cone* /**k**ais rim kon/ for target: *an ice cream cone* /ais **k**rim kon/. Did you notice that the form of the **INDEFINITE ARTICLE** in the error was *a*, as needed before /**k**ais/, instead of *an*, which you'd need before /ais/? What does that suggest to you about the point in processing at which the form of the indefinite article is chosen?

Below, you can see the point in assembling the Positional Level for the phrase *a language learner needs* before the exact forms (the **MORPHS**) for the indefinite article and the third person singular ending have been chosen:

[[indefinite]$_{article}$ [*language*]$_{noun}$ [[____]$_{verb}$+[*er*]] $_{agentive\ noun}$]$_{noun\ phrase}$
[[____]$_{verb}$+[3rd sing. ending]]$_{inflected\ verb}$

The information needed to decide between *a* and *an* is in place, so that morph could be chosen now, but the exact form of the third singular ending can't be chosen until after the stem of the inflected verb has been put into its slot. Why not?

Note: Popular books about speech errors, like Michael Erard's *Um . . . : Slips, Stumbles, and Verbal Blunders . . .* can give you many more examples, but most of them are stuck with using English spelling to communicate the phonological errors, which is tricky.

References

Erard, M. (2007). *Um . . . : Slips, stumbles, and verbal blunders . . .* New York, NY: Pantheon.

Fromkin, V. A. (1973). *Speech errors as linguistic evidence*. The Hague, Netherlands: Mouton.

Experimental Studies of Normal Language Production and Comprehension

An Introduction to Experimental Methods in Psycholinguistics and Neurolinguistics

5.0 The Plan for This Chapter

In this chapter, we'll look at experimental studies whose results have been helpful for understanding the basic language processing concepts that we've been talking about, and whose methods are easy to understand. Some of the studies here are famous; others are not (or not yet), but their findings are important for clinicians and teachers, and relevant for speech technology. If you enjoy reading about them and want to learn more, you'll find many more of them explained in the full-year psycholinguistics and neurolinguistics textbooks and handbooks listed under Further Readings in the Materials for Chapter 5 on your CD.

I am deliberately avoiding the usual styles of scientific writing and textbook explanation so that you get a better sense of what research is like: the fact that science is created by real people, not superhumans, and that what they are doing is just trying to figure out explanations for things and then seeing how well their explanations work. When you read research papers and typical textbooks, phrases like, "it was hypothesized that reaction times to competing stimuli would increase at points of ambiguity," you may have a hard time imagining the actual people who were really sitting around with their coffee mugs, frowning or grinning and saying, "Don't you think they ought to be slower at reacting to something else just after they see the ambiguous word?" Of course, you may not want to hear the full story—when you just want to know the results, and are not planning to do a similar experiment yourself, you may not care much how the researchers got those results, let alone how much trouble they had figuring out how to get them. So I won't ask you to slog through the history for all of the experiments that I'll describe. But textbook and Internet-based summaries of research have to skip over some details, possibly including the ones that you would need to know if you were trying to decide whether and how the original work applies to the problems you are really interested in. So you need to be able to read the original work that is published in print or online scientific journals. And that can be difficult, because journals demand that authors condense their articles heavily. Authors do this by using technical vocabulary and skipping explanations of points that would be familiar to their regular readers. (Journals also are also usually stuck in a severe tradition of pompous and impersonal writing; articles that were originally written rigorously but in a natural prose style may get rewritten using lots of passive voice and impersonal (no-Agent) constructions, so that they sound "scientific," even though this makes the information that they contain harder to process, as every psycholinguist knows.)

My goal in introducing psycholinguistic experiments is not to give you a large number of results, but to pick some that illuminate different levels of language processing, and use them as examples to introduce some of the vocabulary and concepts you will need for reading more standard sources. After working through them, you'll be ready to go on to standard textbooks like the ones at the end of the chapter, and from there to the journals. Psycholinguistic experiments are designed in the same way as experiments in other sciences, so if you already have a science background and don't need to learn about experimental design, you can read alternate shorter expositions of some of these experiments on the CD—although if your background isn't in experimental psychology, it might be a good idea to read both versions of a few of the experiments, starting with those in the text and then going on to read those on the CD. Also, the shorter versions on the CD are in a more standard "scientific" writing style, so that you can see how it's done.

5.1 Introduction to Psycholinguistic Experiments: Why Do People Do Them and How Do People Come Up With the Ideas for Them?

5.1.1 Psycholinguistic experiments and why we do them

What are psycholinguistics experiments like, and why do we have to do them? Why isn't observation enough? Psycholinguistic experiments can be as simple as asking people to rate sentences on whether they make sense or are grammatical, to repeat words and nonwords as accurately as possible, or to circle letters on a page. Or they can have complex designs and depend heavily on equipment: Some of them involve computing exactly where someone is looking (an EYE-TRACKER); others require computation of how many milliseconds after being flashed an image of a word or an object it takes a person to make a judgment about what they've seen (Is it a word? Is it a kind of animal?); still others record a person's brain waves in various laboratory situations that simulate everyday events (you have probably read many summaries of this kind of study, as they are often featured in the popular press).

The exasperating fact about all our skills and knowledge, including language and language processing, is that everything we know or know how to do is inside our own heads, so it seems as though we should be able to become aware of our knowledge by just thinking about it, the way philosophers traditionally have done. But if we ask ourselves how we remember words or make sentences (or how we remember faces or tie a bow), either we get nothing or we get an answer that is, at most, a very small part of the truth. Maybe this will seem less annoying if you imagine trying to use your own eye to see inside itself; you wouldn't expect to be able to discover your lens, your retina, or the BLIND SPOT where your optic nerve connects to the retina. In the same way, figuring out the workings of your brain can't be done by just thinking about them.

Observation of what people do when they are using language—especially, as we have seen, observation of errors—is one of the best places to start from. But figuring out how brains work just by looking at natural behavior is not going to get us to a deep understanding. Imagine figuring out how a computer works by looking at how people use it and what the screen shows when there's a crash—yes, it requires electricity and has a keyboard and a screen, but what's inside and what's actually happening there?

Psycholinguists use experiments to study language processes that happen too fast to grasp or that stay below the level of consciousness— and almost all language processes fall into those categories. We also use experiments to study language knowledge and processing in people who can't easily show us what they know, like young children or people with aphasia. In this chapter, we'll look at some experiments with normal monolingual adults and we'll include some studies of adults reading. In later chapters, we'll look at young children, bilingual adults, and classroom and clinical populations, and we'll look at reading in more detail.

5.1.2 Where do ideas for psycholinguistic experiments come from?

First, observation. Let's begin, then, as the most innovative experimenters do, with observations of people having real-life language problems, big or small. Like experimental psycholinguists, we analyze those problems using what we already know about linguistic structures and about psycholinguistic processing. Up until now, we've thought mostly about production of spoken language, but most psycholinguistic experiments and many kinds of clinical and classroom tests are about comprehension, and many of those are about comprehending written language. So let's consider some real-life places where normal language users are likely to make temporary errors in comprehending written language; for skilled readers, these are usually places where top-down processing happens to make false predictions.

We'll start with a familiar example of an error where top-down processing can cause a person to make mistakes. A PROOFREADER'S ERROR is a failure to notice a typing or a typesetting mistake when you are reading over something important (perhaps a job application or a wedding invitation) to make sure that it's perfect. Proofreading is still necessary in the computer age, because spell-checker and grammar-checker programs don't catch errors that make real words and don't violate any obvious grammar rule. And of course, people sometimes forget to use their spell-checkers. For example, the April 2009 New York Mets program said, *Santana was involved in the program in a triubute to Lynne Greenberg*; the error was caught by http://jalfredproofreader.blogspot.com/ .

A test for proofreading ability is to hand people an ordinary printed page and ask them to circle every *f* on it. If you try this, you'll see that they will miss many of the *f*s in the word *of*, because it's such a predictable word that we barely register it when we read. We do much better with catching the *f*s in other words. This isn't just a matter of skipping *of* as our eyes move across a page, as people used to think. What happens is that our top-down processing of syntax tells us that *of* should be in certain places, and we rely on that so much that we barely attend to bottom-up information: the actual marks on the page in those places. As you'd predict, then, when the word *of* is missing entirely from a spot where it belongs, we're more likely to overlook that omission error than we are to overlook a missing word that has more meaning, and is less predictable. Here's an example that escaped its proofreader on May 26, 2009, from an online science news article: *Traditional studies thus undermine this complexity by only accounting for the responses single neurons.* (How Does The Human Brain Work? New Ways To Better Understand How Our Brain Processes Information *Science Daily*, http://www.sciencedaily.com/releases/2009/05/090519152559.htm)

Here's a second example: a case of an error coming from top-down processing of semantics as well as syntax. Below is a pair of sentences that gave me a problem when I was reading an article in *The New York Times* on December 24th, 2008, about a particular very fancy version of the elegant French Yule Log cake called a *Bûche de Noel*. Try reading it quickly, and if you feel a problem as you read over the sentence, make a quick note of where you hit it, and what you thought about just as you were stumbling.

> The flavor is chocolate, sourced from Tanzania, Ghana and São Tomé and Príncipe, with a hint of Earl Gray tea. And it is swathed in chocolate colored and textured to look like maroon velvet.

Did you feel a little problem somewhere? I did. In the first sentence, I had to figure out the word *sourced*. The second sentence was worse: I had to do a double take and restart it somewhere around the words *and textured*. It felt as though this happened because when I read *chocolate colored*, I was expecting the next word to be a noun for some kind of frosting, like *butter cream*.

In other words, I must have been thinking subconsciously that *chocolate colored* was a phrase describing something that was the color of chocolate, and that a cake could be *swathed* in. So, soon after the word *colored*, I should have found the noun that would tell me what the chocolate-colored thing was. But no noun showed up! My expectation, based on top-down processing, had thrown me off this time, because this slightly weird sentence has to be understood as meaning . . . *it* (the cake) *is swathed in chocolate **that has been** colored and textured to look like maroon velvet.*

This is a real example of a general fact: In written language, readers are likely to have difficulty if the words in a sentence look like they might belong to one construction but, in fact, they belong to a different one. Sentences that mislead readers, making them do double takes like this, are called GARDEN PATH sentences, because they lead us "up the garden path" instead of putting us on the road to understanding.

The slips of the ear (or of our memory for what we've heard) that we discussed in Chapter 3, like the library user's request *I need a book about the sixteenth chapel*, are another kind of observation that has given rise to experiments on what happens when people are given slightly peculiar materials to listen to. Those experiments have given us a lot of insight about how speech perception works.

Observing how people hesitate when they speak, observing children trying to make past tenses for words that happen to be irregular, and observing one's own efforts to remember people's names or items on a shopping list have all been the starting points for illuminating experiments. And, of course, many experiments are inspired by theories that need testing, or by previous experiments, as psycholinguists think of new possible ways to explain the results of each other's experimental work.

5.2 Memory Experiments

The simplest psycholinguistic experiments are just systematic observations; they don't need any equipment, but they do require careful planning. If you already have a background in the sciences, you can read most of this chapter very quickly, and if you pass the "experimental design quiz" on your CD, you might prefer to read the condensed alternative versions of some of the experiments that are on your CD, instead of this print version. As I said earlier, I've written those in a more standard style, so that you can get some practice decoding it.

5.2.1 Experimental ethics: The first consideration

Psychologists and medical researchers used to call the people whose behavior we studied our **EXPERIMENTAL SUBJECTS**, but that phrase began to get nasty overtones, suggesting that we were treating them like laboratory rats. (By the way, even rats have to be treated humanely.) Because we want to emphasize that being in an experiment is voluntary and that people can opt out of being studied at any time, we call them **PARTICIPANTS** now. But what matters is not what we call the people in our experiments, it's keeping to the rules about letting them know what we're going to be asking them to do, and reminding them that they can drop out whenever they want and without giving us a reason. Hospitals, universities, and other research institutions have very strict **INTERNAL REVIEW BOARDS** that review all planned experiments; if you want to try something out on people (besides yourself), find out how to get it approved. If you are in a class and want to try out an idea on a classmate, ask your instructor about what's allowed. That can seem very silly for the kinds of experiments we'll talk about in this chapter—how could they possibly hurt anybody?—but anyone who has ever been on an internal review board will tell you that, although almost all the experiments that they review are just fine, when naïve people design experiments they sometimes have no idea of what might be risky for the folks who are participating in their studies. A review board never, in my experience, runs into anything evil, but it does sometimes run into ignorance and the failure to think carefully about how the participants will feel during and after the experiment.

5.2.2 A classic experiment on recalling words from long-term word memory

Let's get into experiments by looking at a study with a very simple method. It was published in 1944, long before we had a cognitive processing model as good as **SPREADING ACTIVATION** (see Chapter 2 if you need to review this concept), and before we had any idea of the amazing storage and processing capacity of the huge collection of different kinds of neurons in a human brain. On the other hand, for hundreds of years, people had recognized that associative links between words were important, even though they didn't have a way to explain how these links could form, or to show that there were links between ideas (which we now think are even more important than links between words. In fact, it took a long time to get clear evidence that ideas aren't just sets of words, but that's another story.) This study was a way of looking at associative links between words in various kinds of categories.

During World War II, a psychologist and a mathematician at the University of Connecticut, W. A. Bousfield and C. H. Sedgewick, chose several different categories of words, and asked students (probably students in their classes, and as it was wartime, probably mostly women, but their gender was not reported) to listen to the experimenter say the category labels, and then write down all the words that they could in each category. Bousfeld and Sedgewick tried several kinds of large categories, to see whether people seemed to think of the various kinds of words in different ways or pretty much in the same way. Some of the categories were rather ordinary conceptual ones, like "quadruped mammals" or "U.S. cities." Some were spelling based: "Words containing the letters M, T, or D," "5-letter words." Some were mixed, using both concepts and sounds or letters: "Friends—surnames beginning with S," "Animals—names with two or more syllables." Because Bousfield and Sedgewick were mostly interested in seeing if the same mathematical equation could describe the rate at which people run out of things to add to their various kinds of lists, every two minutes the person who gave the instructions told the participants to draw a line under what they'd written so far, and then keep going. (Bousfield and Sedgewick didn't have a good way to see whether this instruction itself affected the list-making; clearly, it might have.) They seem to have decided that their equation pretty much worked, and we'll leave it at that, because what we're interested in now is something else, which they also noticed: the subgroupings within each list. In their paper, they published only three of the many lists that they got, but fortunately, they did include this list of four-footed mammals from one participant. The slashes are at the original two-minute marks. The participant made some mistakes, by the way—one word is used twice, and the restriction to "four-footed" mammals seems to have been forgotten after a while:

> Horse, cow, pig, raccoon, mink, sheep, beaver, cat, dog, bear, donkey, woodchuck, tiger, lion, giraffe, leopard, wildcat, deer, goat / mule, squirrel, chipmunk, rabbit, bear, elk, seal, lynx, antelope, coyote / gopher, rat, oxen, wolf, whale, water buffalo, bison / ape, gorilla, chimpanzee, prairie dog / zebra, kangaroo, panther / otter, mole / muskrat.

You can see that the number of words between slashes keeps getting smaller—it looks like the person is gradually running out of names over the 14 or so minutes of sitting there! And you can also see that there are little bursts of words that seem related—twos, threes, maybe some fours—and that there are shifts in the kinds of relations: animals found in the same kind of place (including the zoo), animals belonging to the same biological category, animals with similar names, and so on. (If you wanted to make sure that you weren't just reading your own favorite categories into this list, you could ask a bunch of other people—preferably people from the Northeast of the United States, so that their experiences of animals would be somewhat similar to those of the original participants—to group the words; after that, you would focus on the categories that you all agreed were probably being used by the original participant.) It's these little bursts and the shifts between them that give us some clues as to how activation spreads in our brains. They suggest that we have different kinds of associative links, and that activation spreads from one concept or lemma to another along many different paths, running "in the background" while all that we are conscious of is trying to think of words (and perhaps of wishing we were doing something else). We'll pick up other clues about how activation spreads as we discuss the other experiments in this chapter.

5.2.3 Experimental variables and memory for lists

(About that quiz: if you are pretty sure that you know the standard terminology and design considerations for psychology experiments, go to the Materials for Chapter 5 on your CD and take the self-quiz. If you do well on it, you can go ahead and read the Alternative Versions for the next several sections on the CD instead of the ones printed here.)

In any experiment with human or animal participants, we do something that we think will affect their behavior—we provide a STIMULUS—and then watch to see what happens—their RESPONSE. But a properly designed experiment isn't just poking and watching, like a kid prodding a wasp's nest with a long stick. The idea that we start with, whether we get it from observation or from hearing about someone else's experimental study, has to be stated clearly, and it has to be testable: Just what is it that we think will happen in response to a particular stimulus, and why? What is special about that stimulus? In the Bousfield and Sedgewick experiment that we just looked at, the stimuli were the names of the categories that the participants were given, and the responses were, of course, the words that they wrote down. And even though we stayed away from the mathematical part of their experiment (which is still important to people actually making computational models of long-term memory), they were testing a specific idea about how memory might be described.

Let's design our own memory experiment, based on an everyday experience. Suppose you've tried to buy your groceries without a written list, and that you've come home with yogurt, lettuce, milk, and cream cheese, but what you really needed was yogurt, lettuce, cream cheese, and cottage cheese. You might reasonably feel that milk slipped in there instead of, say, celery, because you were trying to remember three dairy products but only one salad vegetable. How could you turn that feeling into a sensible, testable guess—a **HYPOTHESIS**? Your first step is to try to pare your hunch down to an essential idea: to make your hypothesis more general or more abstract. You've started with an idea about your groceries, but your hypothesis isn't really just about them (although food might turn out to be special in some way), or about you. It's really an idea about what kinds of errors you'd find when people try to remember lists that contain several items from the same category.

You haven't yet started to think about *why* having several items from the same category matters, and you'd want to do that eventually (by now you're ready to guess that it has to do with spreading activation). But before you go to work on *why* the structure of the list matters, you have to make sure that this kind of same-category substitution error really happens for different kinds of lists, and that it happens to other people, not just to you. And you want a cheap and easy test, not something that would involve going shopping over and over, and you want it to be something that other people probably won't mind doing for a small reward (like a chocolate bar or a beer), or in exchange for your participation in an experiment that they have designed.

And one more thing: you don't want your hypothesis to be obvious to your participants, because if they figure out what you're doing, whether they want to be cooperative or neutral or contrary, it's pretty likely to affect their behavior. If they have even an unconscious hunch about what you're after, that may affect what they do, and then you won't get a clear picture of how memory for lists behaves. So you need to camouflage your hypothesis until after your experiment is over; then you offer to explain what you were up to if your participant is interested.

All set to design the experiment? Not quite. You need to think about other possible explanations of your memory error. A **COMPETING HYPOTHESIS** —another reasonable guess—would be that the milk got in there because almost all the dairy items are near one another in your market. Let's call your first hypothesis the "category membership" hypothesis. This competitor—we could call it the "proximity" hypothesis—would claim that you got the *cottage cheese* because it was near the *milk*. And it's quite possible that both of these hypotheses are correct at the same time—at least, that they both are correct about mistakes made while grocery shopping.

How could you see whether just one of the hypotheses is true, or whether both of them are? You'd need to test each of them with a task where it is the only one of the two that could be relevant to what's happening. That often means looking for different examples of the phenomenon that you're interested in. For example, to make sure that the proximity hypothesis isn't the only reason that the cottage cheese slipped into your grocery list, you would need to use a category whose members are not sold near each other; if your supermarket doesn't have such a category, you may be unable to rule out the proximity hypothesis.

We'll walk through what you'd do to test the category membership hypothesis, and you can try figuring out how to test the proximity hypothesis—it's Exercise 5.1A. Here's the basic principle of experimental design: If you want to find out whether A affects B, you wiggle A and see whether B wiggles, too. (It's like trying to figure out which power cord of the six plugged into the power strip under your desk is the one connected to your printer. You wiggle the printer cord up near the printer, while keeping your eye on the power strip and seeing which cord is wiggling down there.) In scientists' terminology, to test the hypothesis that A affects B, you vary A systematically and see whether B changes.

We started with the hypothesis that a dairy product was the intruder on the list rather than a salad vegetable because you were trying to remember three dairy products but only one salad vegetable. And we've abstracted this to a more general hypothesis: When people try to remember a list that contains several items from the same category and only one item from some other category, their substitution errors will be new items from the category that had several members. How do you test this hypothesis?

Your basic idea is that having multiple items from the same category is what causes other items from that category to intrude. So to test it, you need to see whether you'd get just as many substitutions in lists that only have one item from each category. (You'll also have to figure out what counts as a "category"—that's not as easy as it seems, so do it carefully.) In psychologists' terms, the way your lists are composed—whether they have multiple entries from one category, or not—is your **INDEPENDENT VARIABLE**: the thing you are going to wiggle. And what you are going to keep your eye on is how many intruding items you get when your participants say the list back to you, or try to write it down for you, because if your hypothesis is correct, the number of intruding items is what should be affected by wiggling the way the list is composed. The formal term for this thing that you are going to measure or count to see whether your hypothesis is right is the **DEPENDENT VARIABLE**. If you are right, the dependent variable (what you are going to measure) will indeed turn out to depend on the independent variable (the thing that you are systematically varying).

So what you have to do is make up lists of the two kinds—some with multiple entries from a particular category and some that have no two items in the same category, making sure that you have lots of different categories involved to help camouflage what the independent variable is. Then you ask people to recall the lists (either writing them down or saying them while you make a sound recording). If the task is too easy for them to do— if they don't make any errors for you to analyze—you can make it harder by having them wait for a fixed amount of time before they respond, or even harder by making them carry out a **DISTRACTOR TASK**—that is, to do something else while waiting, like counting.

Now, look at the dependent variable: how many times participants substitute a new item that belongs to the same category as one of the items on the list. If you get a lot more substitution errors in a category when your list had several items from that category than when your list had only one item in that category, you were right. If you get fewer, you were probably wrong. If you get close to the same number, you can't be sure either way.

Is that all? If you've guessed correctly about how long the lists should be and how the items in them should be arranged, yes, probably. You could go ahead and try. You have a correct basic design. But there could be problems that would keep you from getting the results that you predicted, even if your hypothesis is correct.

In this experiment, there are at least two factors that aren't related to your hypothesis that might cause trouble. You have to **CONTROL** for possible **LIST EFFECTS**; that is, you have to make sure that you know whether there were any effects of the structure and order of the stimulus items you present. For example, it might matter whether your items that are all from the target category are near each other on each of your lists, and it might matter how well you've mixed up your different kinds of lists. You'll need to have several different list orders, to check and see if the order of items on a list makes a difference in the number of mistakes your participants make. Experimental stimulus orders that are properly mixed, by the way, are not truly random, because a true randomization may give long runs of the same type of stimulus, just by chance, like the throws of fair dice which the gambler thinks are "hot." Instead, your categories need to be **PSEUDORANDOM**—that is, the item order needs to feel random to your participants. Also, it almost certainly matters how long each list is; if it's too short, people won't make enough mistakes (unless you put in a distractor task). And if the list is too long, your participants may not be willing to try to remember it. Also, you might have to have more than three items from your target category in your list in order to get substitution errors.

There can be other problems, too. Designing an experiment that actually works takes a lot of patience and some lucky guesses, unless you are just running a minor variation on an experiment that has been successfully done by someone else. You may have to try several **PILOT STUDIES** to figure out a good set of stimulus lists before you can get enough substitution errors to analyze. And it simply might not work at all, at least not in the time that you have available to devote to the problem; that could be because your hypothesis is wrong, or because your method won't work for some reason that hasn't occurred to you. Science is really like this, but experiments that don't work don't usually show up in textbooks. If you'd like to learn about more kinds of memory errors, check out http://www .exploratorium.edu/memory/messingwithyourmind/index.html .

In the next section, let's look at two classic experiments that worked.

5.2.4 Memory for sentences

Here are two psycholinguistic experiments that successfully explored our memory for what we hear when we are listening more or less normally— that is, when we're listening to someone because we want to understand what they mean (or because we're going to be tested on what they mean). These experiments showed that that our memory of what we hear is dominated, after less than 30 seconds, by the meaning of what we heard, rather than by the exact words they used. This doesn't mean, as people have sometimes thought, that we don't remember the words at all—in Chapter 2 section 2.4.2 we discussed the disconcerting ways that unimportant details can in fact affect how well we remember information—but, fortunately, we don't remember the details nearly as well as we remember the important part: the content of the information, its message.

In the late 1960s, Jacqueline Sachs had people listen to ordinary-sounding accounts of events—for example, the discovery of the telescope —that were constructed to contain target sentences like *He sent a letter about it to Galileo, the great Italian scientist.* A few more sentences of the story (to be exact, either 80 syllables or 160 syllables more) were given after the target sentences; then Sachs interrupted the story, and played her listeners a test sentence. She had told them, before they started listening, that these test sentences would be either identical to one in the story or very similar to it, and she gave them an answer sheet, where they could circle, for each test sentence, whether they had recently heard exactly the same sentence in the story. If they thought that the sentence they heard wasn't exactly the same as the test sentence, she asked them to also circle "meaning and wording changed" or "wording changed but not meaning". Sometimes, the test sentence was indeed word-for-word identical, so the answer should have been "yes, same sentence"; sometimes there was a change in the form of the sentence that didn't change its meaning, including some changes from active to passive voice (*A letter about it was sent to Galileo, the great Italian scientist*), so the answer should have been "no; wording changed but not meaning"; and sometimes, there was a change that did affect the meaning (*Galileo, the great Italian scientist, sent him a letter about it*), so the participants should have circled "no; meaning and wording changed." (The exact instructions are on your CD under Materials for Chapter 5, so that you can imagine a little better what it might have been like to design this experiment or to participate in it.)

The participants, after 80 syllables or 160 syllables of delay, gave false "yes, same sentence" responses about half of the time to the sentences that had actually changed the wording but not the meaning (remember, those sentences should have had the response "no; wording changed but not meaning"). However, they only gave such FALSE POSITIVE "yes" answers about 10% of the time to the test sentences that had changed both the wording and the meaning; spotting meaning changes was much, much easier than spotting pure wording changes. As Sachs said, "very slight differences in the words of a sentence had vastly different effects on the experimental task, depending on whether or not the change affected the meaning."

Perhaps the participants never even registered the exact wording at all? Sachs also did another version of this experiment (in psychologists' standard terms, she also ran the experiment in another EXPERIMENTAL CONDITION): a no-delay condition, where she interrupted the story with the "Was this sentence in the story?" question immediately after each of those target sentences instead of playing them another 80 or 160 syllables of the story. In this no-delay condition, her listeners were 90% correct at detecting both kinds of altered sentences: the ones that changed only the form of the sentence and those that changed both the form and the meaning. So it looks like our memory for the exact words of a sentence that we hear in a story is indeed formed, but that it decays rapidly; our memory for the meaning is more durable.

The second classic memory experiment that we'll look at was done about four years later, and it showed something that was much less expected (and which has been followed up with FALSE MEMORY work that's extremely important in criminal cases). Bransford, Barclay, and Franks (1972) tested the idea that what we remember is not really the meaning of what we actually heard or read, but the mental picture that we constructed from what we took in. Here's how their experiment worked: They made up many sets of stimulus sentences that could give hearers clear mental pictures of slightly complicated events, like these four:

1(a)   Three turtles rested beside a floating log and a fish swam beneath them.

1(b)   Three turtles rested beside a floating log and a fish swam beneath it.

2(a)   Three turtles rested on a floating log and a fish swam beneath them.

2(b)   Three turtles rested on a floating log and a fish swam beneath it.

The four sentences in each set were, like these four, almost identical. But you can see that the words of the (a) and the (b) sentence in each pair differ from each other in the same way: both times, the last word changes from *it*, which has to mean the log, to *them*, which has to mean the turtles (or maybe the turtles plus the log). But 1(a) and 1(b) each give a slightly different mental picture of where the fish swam, right? Because the turtles are beside the log, in 1(a) the fish was under the turtles and not under the log; but in 1(b), the fish was just under the log, not under the turtles (see the diagrams in Table 5.1, which also gives a schematic presentation of the experimental design). But 2(a) and 2(b) both give the same mental picture, because the turtles are on top of the floating log, which means that if the fish swims under the log, it must have also swum under the turtles (and if the fish swims under the turtles, it must also have swum under the log; see the diagrams in Table 5.1 again).

We make these inferences rapidly, because of our real-world knowledge: what we know about water, floating, and swimming. So, in summary, our mental picture of the physical layout for 2(a) and for 2(b) is essentially the same (although these two sentences do focus our attention on it differently), but our mental picture of the layout for 1(a) is different from our mental picture of the layout of 1(b). (This research team made up their stimulus sentence sets very, very carefully, and it must have been a huge amount of work to make enough different sets for a good experiment.)

Now use what you learned about the Sachs experiment to figure out what Bransford's team did with these sentences. Try it for a minute and see whether you're right.

Table 5.1. Design Chart for Bransford et al. (1972) Experiment (showing only one condition per group)

	Participant in Group 1 hears "a" sentences:	*Participant in Group 2 hears "a" sentences:*
Step I:		
Listening to "them" sentences	1 (a) Three turtles rested *beside* a floating log and a fish swam beneath *them.*	2 (a) Three turtles rested *on* a floating log and a fish swam beneath *them.*
(Hypothetical) mental picture of the event after hearing the "a" sentence	(turtle) (turtle) (turtle) [log] →fish→ → → → →	(turtle) (turtle) (turtle) [log] fish→ → → → →
Step II:	*Participant in Group 1 hears matching "b" sentences:*	*Participant in Group 2 hears matching "b" sentences:*
Listening to "it" sentences, with judgement question: **Same** *sentence as I heard before or* **different** *sentence from what I heard before?*	1 (b) Three turtles rested *beside* a floating log and a fish swam beneath *it.*	2 (b) Thee turtles rested *on* a floating log and a fish swam beneath *it.*
(Hypothetical) mental picture of the event after hearing the "a" sentence	(turtle) (turtle) (turtle) [log] fish→	(turtle) (turtle) (turtle) [log] fish→ → → →
Comparison of mental pictures	1 (a) and 1 (b) are *different*	2 (a) and 2 (b) are *the same*
Response to "same sentence or different sentence" question	*Different*	*Same*

Okay, here's what they did (their **EXPERIMENTAL PROCEDURE**)—or rather, one condition of their experimental procedure. In Part I of this condition of the experiment, half of their participants heard many sentences like 1(a)—we'll call those participants Group 1. The other half of the participants, Group 2, heard many sentences like 2(a). (This part of a memory experiment is often called the "familiarization phase.")

Then, in Part II of each experiment, each group heard a list containing two kinds of test sentences: Half of them were: (a) sentences that they had actually heard before, and other half were the very similar (b) sentences, which they hadn't actually heard. So: if they'd had heard an (a) sentence, half of the time they now heard it again, and half of the time they now heard the corresponding (b) sentence instead. For each sentence, they were asked, like the people in the Sachs experiment, to say whether they'd heard it before. Table 5.1 will help you follow the experimental design; remember that for simplicity, we are just considering one of the experimental conditions, which is only part of what the participants in each group heard. (The full details are on the CD in the Challenge section for this chapter, in case you have time to work through what a complete experimental design is like and why it requires multiple conditions—in this case, four of them.)

What would you predict about which group gave false "yes" answers to the sentences that they hadn't actually seen? Go back and reread the description of this experiment if you're not ready to make that prediction.

Ready? Group 1 people, whose "false" test sentences gave them a different mental picture from the mental picture given by the sentences that they had actually seen, made very few errors in responding to their test sentence list: They were quite accurate about spotting and rejecting the new sentences as they heard them. But Group 2 participants gave lots of false positive (incorrect "Yes, I heard that one before") answers: They were quite poor at deciding which sentences in their test list were new and which they had actually heard before. Look at Table 5.1 again now: Bransford et al.'s explanation of the difference between Group 1 and Group 2 was that Group 1 could rely on their two different mental pictures to tell the old sentences from the new ones, but Group 2 didn't have that kind of difference to rely on.

Let's go back and think about these two sentence comprehension experiments in terms of the sentence production model we used in Chapters 3 and 4. What Sachs showed was that a short time after hearing a sentence (unless you are trying to memorize its words), what you remember best is not the form, which would be at the level of **PHONOLOGICAL**

ENCODING or maybe at the POSITIONAL LEVEL. What sticks in your mind is the meaning. In terms of our model, that would mean that you remember the information as LEMMAS and EVENT STRUCTURES, at the FUNCTIONAL LEVEL, or that you hold onto it as concepts and events, at the MESSAGE LEVEL, or even at a "higher" (or "deeper") visual mental image level.

And what Bransford et al. showed is that your long-term memory is most reliable at the Message Level (or even deeper) in your mental processing. What you remember best (at least for easily imaged sentences like these!) is the mental image that the sentence aroused, not the specific information that was explicitly mentioned in the sentence that you heard or read.

And after all, this is the way our minds should work. If someone's going to really understand what we're talking about, they need to be able to create and remember a mental picture of more of it than we put into words, or we'd never get done explaining things. For example, if your friend tells you that she's going to the beach for a vacation she expects you to infer that she probably won't be available by cell phone or e-mail for most of the day while she's gone. You can make that inference because you know that sand and water are bad for gadgets.

In fact, we can't help making INFERENCES. One serious real-world implication of the Bransford et al. result is that law courts have a good reason for excluding hearsay evidence: People can rarely tell the difference between what they actually heard and what they only *inferred* from what they heard.

Is this important in the classroom and the clinic as well as in a court of law? Absolutely. What students or clients have inferred from what you've said (or from what they think you said) will be in their minds as much the words you've said to them. Indeed, in most kinds of language disorders and for all kinds of learners, their minds will probably be more occupied by the concept that they've formed than by your words, and your words themselves will be even harder for them to remember than it would be if they were normal adult language users. We'll get into examples of this problem, and what it means in practice, throughout the rest of this book; a relevant Web site is called *Looking for the roots of "false memories"* (http://www.apa.org/monitor/oct99/cf11.html).

The failure to make inferences is an even bigger problem, though, than making inferences that might not be what the speaker intended to convey. If you know something about autism, you'll already have recognized that people with even mild degrees of autistic impairment have difficulty in making some kinds of inferences, especially inferences about what other people are going to do and why they are going to do it.

5.3 Production Experiments I: Finding Needed Words—Or Not

5.3.1 How long does it take to come up with the name of an object in a picture, and why?

Oldfield and Wingfield and word frequency effects

In Chapters 3 and 4 we began to talk about the process of coming up with words when we need them in producing a sentence: First, lemmas get aroused by concepts of objects, animals, or people (or by more abstract concepts like liberty, but we didn't try to deal with those), and then, in turn, the lemmas arouse their phonological forms. We usually feel that coming up with a word's form happens instantly (unless it gets stuck "on the tip of our tongues," of course). But quite a while back, in 1965, R. C. Oldfield and Arthur Wingfield decided to take a serious look at how long it takes a person to come up with a word for an object after seeing its picture, and they discovered something whose importance has become clearer over the years since then: The rarer a word is, on average, the slower people are at naming a picture of the object it means, from *cigarette* to *gyroscope* and beyond. So what seems an instant to the person doing the naming is indeed quick, around half a second, but if you measure the time in thousandths of a second from when the picture is shown to when the person looking at the picture starts to say its name, that time lag (the RESPONSE LATENCY) is much slower for rarer words than for common ones. In Oldfield and Wingfield's study, the participants averaged about eight-tenths of a second to start to say *cigarette* and about twice that long, about 1.6 seconds, to start to say *gyroscope*.

What's so important about the fact that less frequent words take longer to be produced? As long as a word is ready to say by the time you get to the place in a sentence where you're going to need it, why worry about tenths of seconds? One reason is that for many aphasic people, a noun's frequency is usually a pretty good predictor of whether they'll be able to come up with it at all, and their latencies for the words that they do manage to remember may be many seconds or even minutes; as a result, they don't have the word available when they need it. So word frequency really matters for the construction of tests and therapy materials. (We'll come back to this fact and its implications several times.) And the second reason to care about the relation between frequency and response latency is that it is central to our whole model of how knowledge of language gets into our brains in the first place: the idea that every time we encounter a piece of information, it changes our brains a little. If that information is a connection between two (or more) of your memories—for example, between your memories of what something looks like and its name—then the connections between those two memories get strengthened each time you hear and understand (or think of and say) that name. A postal or e-mail address that you use frequently becomes strongly connected to your other thoughts and memories about the person or organization it belongs to; every memory of visiting your favorite restaurant becomes closely linked to all the other memories of having been there (often to the point where all those memories start to blend together, and a couple might start to argue about whether they had ordered the chef's famous special on their anniversary or on one of their birthdays).

The stronger a connection gets, the more effective a stimulus that activates one of them will be at arousing the other one as that activation spreads. In this way, connections become more and more effective as channels for information flow. In general, the knowledge that any two things A and B belong together gets more accessible each time activation flows along the pathway between them, along with the information that they predict C, but not D, and are part of the same pattern as E, F, and G. All the information that we use becomes more and more a part of ourselves, each time we use it. This is a major key to understanding how we understand.

Confounding variables and experimental design

We need to stop here for a minute, and go back to the topic of how to design experiments. The Oldfield and Wingfield study gives us a good example of something that happens over and over again: It turned out that there was another possible explanation for their findings, a CONFOUNDING VARIABLE. If you looked at their word list, you'd see that their most frequent words were *book*, *chair*, and *shoe*, and their rarest words were *metronome*, *gyroscope*, and *xylophone*. (It seems to be easier to think of long rare words than it is to think of short rare words.) Maybe the only reason the rare words took longer to start to say was that it somehow takes more time to prepare to say longer words? Could this other variable, this POTENTIAL CONFOUND, have been the real reason that the rare words were slower? That would be a competing hypothesis. Fortunately, Oldfield and Wingfield thought of that problem before they finished their paper (although apparently not before they designed their stimuli and tested their participants), and they happened to have included a couple of common three-syllable words (*cigarette, typewriter*) and some rarer one-syllable and two-syllable words (like *dice* and *syringe*) in their list. So they were able to reanalyze their results statistically, and it was still true, when they just compared sets of words of the same length, that the rarer words were slower.

Later work has shown that in an experiment that's designed to compare words that are equally common but have different lengths, the longer words do indeed take longer to start to say, so the competing hypothesis is also true. So now, if you were going to try to check out whether "rarer is slower" in a different language, say, Russian, or in a different kind of population, for example, people with Alzheimer's disease, you know that you'd need to make sure that differences in the lengths of your target words wouldn't be a possible alternative explanation for your results. In the standard terminology that we used back in the grocery list experiment, you would have to control for the effect of word length.

And how could you control for the effect of word length—that is, make sure that "longer is slower" wouldn't be a possible alternative explanation for the "rarer is slower" pattern of results that you expect to get? The easiest way to do it would probably be to have all the words the same length; then, if the rarer words turn out to be slower, there's no way that the slowness could be due to length differences. But if you had all one-syllable words or all two-syllable words, it might be hard to find enough different words for which you could get pictures at the different word-frequency levels. So, instead, you could have a design like this:

	Common (High Frequency)	**Medium Frequency**	**Rare (Low Frequency)**
one-syllable	10	10	10
two-syllable	10	10	10
three-syllable	10	10	10

As long as you have equal numbers of words or each length, you'd be okay as far as controlling for the factor of length to see whether low frequency slows down responses. And as long has you have equal numbers of words of each level of frequency, you can compare the words of different lengths at each frequency level, to see whether length matters, too.

But why do we need more than one or two words in each section (psychologists call them CELLS) of this chart? Why 10 words per cell, and all the trouble of getting 90 recognizable stimulus pictures made, plus making sure that a group of people judges them to be fully recognizable before you start the main part of your experiment? Well, if we only had one or two words in each cell, there might be something about those particular words that would make them harder or easier to say; in other words, there might be other confounding variables that we haven't thought about. Maybe a word is slowed down by the particular combination of sounds in it, or made easier because it's associated with strong emotion, or something else we'd never guess. So we put enough words in each cell to hope that something special about a few of them can't affect our overall results.

And we also use at least 10 participants, more if we can, for the same kind of reason: Maybe there's something special about one of the people that we have no way of detecting, but if one person is wildly different from the others—maybe they were ill that day, who knows?—we can remove their data and still have enough to go on.

Designing an experiment to study the word frequency also has two preliminary problems that may have occurred to you by now. The first one, which we already mentioned in passing, is finding pictures that are easy to recognize; also, the pictures have to be ones that most people will call by the same name (for example, you can't use a couch, because for many people it's called a *sofa*, and for most people, both words will come to mind). Some useful sets of pictures have been published (e.g., Snodgrass, 1980; also at http://lifesciassoc.home.pipeline.com/instruct/humemory/ehm.htm), but you still need to pretest your pictures by getting a group of people whom you think are reasonably similar to your test population to name them for you. You could have this done all in one session by having a group of people write down their answers when they see your pictures projected on a screen, so it needn't take very long.

The second preliminary problem is deciding how to measure word frequency. These days, it's not so hard; there are computational algorithms that can look at large quantities of text on the Web and count the number of occurrences of each word. (The algorithms also have to specify that plural and possessive forms of nouns are to be counted as "the same word," and other such details.) This kind of frequency count won't match any particular person's experience with words, of course; for example, "abacus," used as a hard item in the Boston Naming Test, turns out to be relatively easy for an English speaker with an East Asian cultural background. That's another reason for using substantial numbers of participants and averaging their response times; you can't control for the variations in people's individual backgrounds.

Ethical issues again

The ethical issues in design are fairly obvious, once you think about them. The basic fairness principle is not to ask people to do things that are likely to upset them unless you have firmly established that there will be some real counterbalancing benefit. So you avoid asking them to name emotionally negative items like "skull" or "coffin." You also give them an accurate explanation of what they will experience, and make sure that they understand that they can opt out at any time. (This information will be stated in the consent forms that you must use, but you have to make sure that the participants understand what they are signing.) In the particular case of naming tests that contain words that your participants are likely not to know, you put the more frequent items first, so that if someone starts to miss a lot of them and feel discouraged about their abilities, you can quit the task very quickly. The positive side is that you can confidently assure them that practice in naming difficult words can't hurt them in any way, and is likely to help them with those words in the future.

Context and naming latency

Now let's look at a study done more than 40 years after Oldfield and Wingfield, and see something about how context affects **NAMING LATENCY**—that is, how long it takes people to come up with names. In case the idea of spreading activation (and of all that information churning and competing in your head even though you're not aware of it) still seems too weird to be plausible, maybe this study will help you to see why it's the best model of what's going on in our brains that we have so far.

In 2005, Eva Belke, Antje S. Meyer, and Markus F. Damian did some experiments that give us a better sense of how spreading activation happens when we're trying to speak and understand (although they only worked on the production of lists of picture names, which is still quite a distance from conversation). The first experiment in the set started with showing people a long sequence of pictures of things to name. But this time, the independent variable was something quite different from word frequency: it was the order that the pictures were shown in. Because the order of the pictures was the independent variable—the variable whose effects they wanted to study—Belke et al. needed to keep the effects of word frequency and word length from confounding their results. So they kept all the word frequencies quite similar, and they made sure the words all were just one syllable long.

Belke et al. chose their pictures from four familiar categories of objects: animals, tools, vehicles, and furniture. They had four pictures in each category, and were careful to choose objects/animals that don't look much alike, so there wouldn't be any confusion about which picture was which. They set up two main conditions in this experiment, and each person saw the stimuli in both conditions. Half of the time (let's call this Condition 1), each person saw pictures of all the items that were part of the same set clustered one right after another, like this: duck, mouse, fish, snake; saw, drill, rake, brush, and so on. The other half of the time (Condition 2), the order in which they saw the very same pictures was shuffled, like this: duck, chair, saw, bus, and so on. So, the important independent variable was whether pictures of items in the same category were clustered together, or whether they were shuffled and kept apart. Both groups of participants also saw some additional pictures (**FILLER STIMULI**), and each participant was asked to cycle through their entire set of pictures eight times in one session, naming them over again on each cycle, which must have been extremely boring. But there was a good reason for it, as we'll see in a minute.

The dependent variable—the thing about the participants' behavior that Belke et al. measured—was how long, on average, each person took to name each of the pictures (their response latency). What the team found was this: When the people were in Condition 1, the one where they were naming the pictures clustered into same-category sets (all the vehicles, then all the tools, then all the animals), they were slower to say the names of the pictures, on average, than they were when they were in Condition 2, looking at the pictures with the items from different categories shuffled and separated.

And one more detail: This difference between the two conditions wasn't there, or at least wasn't big enough to show up clearly, on each participant's very first cycle through naming the set of pictures. It only showed up on the second and later naming cycles. Here are the details: In that first cycle through naming the set of pictures, the participants averaged about 6.8 tenths of a second (680 milliseconds) latency to say each picture name, in both conditions—both in Condition 1, same-category items clustered together, and in Condition 2, same-category items shuffled. For all the rest of their cycles through the list, they were faster, in both conditions, than they had been in the first cycle, because the first cycle had given them practice at saying the words. However, the two conditions were different in *how much faster* the participants were on the second cycle (and the ones after it) than they had been on the first cycle. In the second and later cycles in Condition 1, when items in the same category were shown one right after another, the participants averaged about 640 milliseconds to say each name, so they were about 6% faster in the later cycles than in the first cycle. But in the second and later cycles in Condition 2 (pictures shuffled), the participants averaged about 600 milliseconds to name each picture; that means they were fully 12% faster on the second and later cycles than on the first cycle.

Why on earth could it be harder for you to say *duck, mouse, fish, snake, saw, drill, rake, brush, chair* . . . than to say the very same words when they are shuffled (*duck, chair, saw, bus* . . .)? And why didn't this difficulty show up on the first time through the list? Well, the four items in each category weren't very much alike (*saw, rake, brush, drill*) or very closely associated, so they wouldn't start out seeming particularly closely linked to each other. Probably activation wouldn't spread very strongly from one to another within a category until your brain began to subconsciously pick up on the fact that you were looking at sets that could be called tools, animals, vehicles, and furniture. But once these CATEGORY CONCEPTS were activated, they could start to send activation to all the concepts of the dozens or hundreds of other items in the same category, and then on to their lemmas.

At this point, when you start to try to name the picture of the duck and then immediately go on to the mouse, the animal concept gets even more activation, and so do all the other animal names in your mind. These unwanted names compete with the name you actually need; your mental picture of each animal that you actually need to name has to fight off all the competitors. This slows you down, because it makes the lemma for the name you need take longer to reach its activation threshold, and the lemma has to get to that threshold before it can send activation out to its phonological form.

Does the idea of that kind of invisible battle inside your skull still sound too fantastic? Well, there's more. Think about it: If this category-concept activation idea is right—if it's hard to say *duck, mouse, fish, snake* because you're fighting off the names of who knows how many other animals— then it should also be hard to name pictures of animals that you haven't seen recently, once the whole animal category has been activated. The particular animals to be named shouldn't matter. So Belke, Meyer, and Damian found four new items for each of their stimulus categories, and they created a complete alternative stimulus set of 16 pictures that didn't look too much alike, had one-syllable names, and were all about the same frequency (ant, frog, owl, pig; chest, clock, rug, shelf; axe, broom, nail, wrench; car, raft, ship, sled), and they started over again. I'm going to skip the details (they controlled for a lot of other factors that might conceivably have interfered), but here's their key step: They ran half of their participants in what we'll call Version A—the participants again named the pictures in the set eight times, cycling through them, and they all used the same 16 pictures in the same two conditions (category members together and category members shuffled), just as in the first experiment. But the research team ran the other half of the participants in a new version, Version B—these participants named just four cycles using one set of 16 pictures in the two conditions (category members together and category members shuffled), and then the stimuli were switched: they were asked to name four cycles through the *other* set of 16 pictures in those two conditions.

Remember that in the first experiment, the effect of category activation didn't show up until the second time through the list? If the whole category activation idea is correct, then when people in Version B switch from saying *duck, mouse, fish, snake* to saying *ant, frog, owl, pig*, there should continue to be a separation between the two conditions—it should show up on cycle 2 and just continue for all the rest of the cycles, even though there'd be 16 new words on cycles 5, 6, 7, and 8, right? Because the problem in the category-members-together condition is supposed to be that all animal names have gotten some activation and are competing to be the word that the participant actually says. (And the same for the other three categories, of course—the tool names are competing with other tool names and so on.) But if what is important is just repeating the specific animal (vehicle, tool) names that had been used already—if there is no activation of the animal vehicle, tool category as a whole—then when the 16 new pictures show up for the first time on cycle 5, the difference between the two conditions should go away; then it should come back on cycle 6, when people were seeing the 16 new pictures for the second time.

What happened supports the category activation idea really nicely: Switching to all the new pictures on cycle 5 temporarily slowed down the average naming speed for both conditions (category members together and category members shuffled), but the *difference* between the two conditions stayed there, bright and clear. On cycle 5, the very first cycle that they were shown in, the words *ant, frog, owl*, and *pig* were about 55 milliseconds slower to be spoken when their pictures were presented together than when their pictures were shuffled in with the other three categories. It looks as if ANT, FROG, OWL, and PIG were caught in the middle of the brain fight that DUCK, MOUSE, FISH, and SNAKE had started. And the same was true for the words in the other three semantic categories.

5.3.2 Where *is* a word when it's on the tip of your tongue?

It's somewhere below the level of consciousness in your brain, of course. But can we be more specific about what information about a word comes to consciousness before the whole word does? And about what goes on in our brains when we are searching for a word? Let's analyze a very different kind of word-retrieval experiment, studying the words people said when they were in the tip-of-the-tongue state (for a refresher, have a quick look back at Chapter 3, section 3.1.1). I was part of the group of six people who did this particular study in the early 1980s; the others were Susan

Kohn, Arthur Wingfield (of Oldfield & Wingfield), Harold Goodglass, Jean Berko Gleason, and Mary Hyde. The participants were 18 students at Brandeis University. Tip of the tongue (usually called TOT, pronounced T-O-T) is fun to think about as a clue to the mysteries of what's going on inside our heads, and it's also useful, because so much that goes on in language teaching and therapy is trying to help people retrieve the words that they need. The more we know about how skilled normal language users find words that they need, the better our chances of figuring out how to help people who are having trouble.

What we wanted to document was how much people in the TOT state can tell about the word they're looking for but haven't yet found. In terms of our model, if they have the lemma and are waiting for the sound pattern to be activated, is there some kind of partial activation of those sounds that can be strong enough to get to their conscious minds while the rest of the information needed to say the word is still stuck in some kind of mental murk? And do the words or fragments that they report as coming to their minds while waiting suggest that people in the TOT state have partial access to information about how long the target word is, and what sounds or letters are in it? My report in Chapter 3 about looking for *Bhuvana* and coming up with *Bhatnagar* and *Baharav* (all stressed on the first syllable) certainly sounds as if other names that were phonologically close to the form I needed had been activated, but was this typical, or was it a rare event?

And we also wanted to find out whether searching for a word is really like looking for something systematically, which is what we feel that we are doing, or if it's more like just waiting for water to boil. If the spreading activation model of how brains work is a good model, then searching is an illusion; what is happening below the level of our awareness when we feel as though we are hunting for a word is a lot more like water coming to a boil.

The first problem in designing a TOT study is to get enough people into a TOT state. The way that psycholinguists do this is to make up definitions for some moderately rare words as targets (making sure that the definition doesn't give any hint as to the sounds of the target word—for example, for a TOT study, you can't use the word "poor" in defining "poverty"). Then you ask people to give the word that matches the definition. They have to be interviewed one at a time, and it takes a rather long list of definitions (we had about a hundred of them), because even if you've chosen a good level of difficulty for your participants overall, for any particular person, the word you're asking for is likely either to be too easy and found right away, or too hard for the participant to come up with at all. We tried to vary how long the target words were, and the kinds of things they meant, so we could also see whether those variables had any effect on people's answers.

Here's a sample of our definitions (and the rest are on your CD)—see whether any of them put you in a TOT state!

#2. A professional mapmaker

#7. A term meaning reappearing or being reborn in another body after death.

#35. Pathologic enlargement of thyroid gland associated with iodine deficiency.

#80. A large seabird, sometimes used as a metaphor for a spiritual burden.

#93. The habit of repeated postponement.

We audio-recorded the responses, so that we had an accurate record of the sounds of any word fragments or non-words the participants might say. If they gave up before coming up with our target word, we told them what it was and asked if it was the one they were hunting for, because, in order to see any relationships between their attempts and the target, we needed be sure that they were actually hunting for it. (Of course, some of them might have been bluffing—either really looking for some other word, or having had no idea at all of what the target was, but there was nothing we could do about that.) After we got all the responses transcribed, we focused on the differences, for each word, between the responses of two kinds of participants who had spent time in a TOT state: the responses from the people who gave us one or more intermediate responses and then came up with the right word—the successful "searches"—and the responses from those who said that they had been looking for that target when we told them what it was, but who hadn't been able to come up with it themselves—the unsuccessful "searches."

What did we learn? Three main things: First, participants who turned out to be about to succeed in their "search" gave us more bits of words that sounded like the target than those who were in the unsuccessful TOT state, so it does seem as though the activation process, before it got all the way to arousing the form of the target word, can sometimes get to the lemma and then to part of the target word's sounds before it gets to all of them. Second, something we hadn't thought about before the study started: If a target is the kind of word that's composed of several morphemes, like #2, *A professional mapmaker*, then people who can't yet come up with the target may be able to come up with some of the morphemes that could be in it, like *geo-* or *graph*, and even use these to make up a word that *could* be a real one with the intended meaning, like *geographist*. From this we learned that a good model of word retrieval also needs lemmas for morphemes that are not whole words (bound morphemes) like *geo-*.

Third, and most important for our curiosity about what goes on in our heads when we're looking for a word, if an eventually successful person happened to give us a series of responses while they were in the TOT state, it didn't seem as if their brain was doing anything that brought them systematically closer to their target. For example, for definition #7, *A term meaning reappearing or being reborn in another body after death*, here's one person's successful sequence of responses: *euthanasia, revival, v- rec- reincarnation*. To the extent that this response sequence reflects what has been brought up to the conscious level by spreading activation, what goes on in our brain during a word search doesn't seem like anything systematic or controlled by the person trying the remember the word; it seems more like something that happens to them. So "searching" for a word is indeed an illusion; probably all we can do is wait for it to come to us and, meanwhile, gesture or find other ways to say what we mean.

5.4 Production Experiments II: Planning Sentences

Studying how we come up with words is just the beginning of understanding how we talk to each other. How do we come up with sentences and longer utterances? One of the first experiments, published by Frieda Goldman-Eisler (Goldman-Eisler, 1968), gave people cartoons to describe, and looked at how long and where they hesitated. Goldman-Eisler found that people hesitated more when they were asked to explain the cartoon than when they were just asked to describe it. That makes sense in two ways. First, if you are looking at a picture of something, it should be faster to come up with its name than with a word that can't be pictured; second, it takes more thinking to explain something than it does just to describe it, and thinking and talking at the same time is hard work. (So is talking and driving a car: see your CD for a link to an article about that.)

Lots of good experiments have been done on the details of timing of hesitations and the order in which people say words when they are asked to describe different pictures or layouts of items, but in recent years, a piece of laboratory equipment called an eye-tracker has made it possible to look even more closely at what people do in describing pictures of more than one thing. An eye-tracker is a computer-based gadget that bounces a low-intensity infrared beam off a person's cornea, captures the reflection, and computes what they are looking at. Human eyes move from one angle to another in quick jumps (called SACCADES, [sə'kadz]), and they take around a fifth of a second to change angles. If you set up a computer screen with a rather large picture on it and track which objects in the picture participants tend to look at while they are talking about what's happening, you can see more details of how what they say is related to what they've been looking at.

Zenzi M. Griffin and Kay Bock (2000) used eye-tracking to observe where people looked while describing events shown in pictures, particularly pictures of people interacting with animals, objects, or other people. They had several conditions in their study, but we'll focus on the one where they asked their participants to describe what was happening in a picture while it was still on the screen in front of them, and on the pictures that had one human in them and were likely to be described with a sentence whose syntax had a subject, a verb, and an object (or prepositional phrase). Figure 5.1 is one of those pictures, showing a dog chasing a mailman.

The participants usually started with glances at all of the items in the picture, but then they would settle into looking at the person for most of the time. About 900 milliseconds after that, they would use a word for that person as the subject of the sentence (*the mailman*), and at about the same time, they would start to look mostly at the other items in the picture (an animal or a thing). While they were doing that, they'd start to say the verb phrase (*is running away from*), and then they would finish up the sentence with the word for that second item in the sentence (*the dog*).

What's going on here? The sequence of events suggests this story: When people describe a picture like this one, they first quickly size up who-did-what-to-whom. In terms of the sentence production model that we've been using, what's happening in their brains is that the picture activates the event structure and the concepts for the referents, and that forms the Message Level. When each of the concepts at the Message Level reaches

Figure 5.1. Dog chasing mailman, from Griffin, Z. M., & Bock, K. (2000). What the eyes say about speaking. *Psychological Science*, *11*(4). Reprinted with permission from Sage Publications.

its activation threshold, it in turn sends activation to all the lemmas that might be used to refer to it (the MAN, the GUY, the MAILMAN; the DOG, the TERRIER; CHASES, RUNS AWAY FROM, RUNS AFTER, GETS CHASED BY). The concept for the person is likely to be important to participants (remember Shirley trying to describe the picture of the small child being hit by the baseball in Chapter 3, section 3.7), and according to Griffin and Bock's data, it seems that the participants committed very early to starting the sentence by mentioning the person—in this case, the mailman—because they first looked mostly at his picture.

That makes sense, but then why did they almost stop looking at him 900 milliseconds before they say a word referring to him? Putting this experiment together with other research on gaze and naming, this seems to be the story, and it supports the cascade model of word activation that we introduced in Chapter 4, section 4.1.1: People look at the picture of the thing they're going to mention first, and they keep looking at it until its concept has activated an appropriate lemma to use for talking about it, and until the event structure has aroused a verb lemma and tagged the lemma referring to the person with the right semantic role. (If the verb lemma is CHASE, the MAILMAN's semantic role is Undergoer, but if the verb lemma is RUN AFTER, the MAILMAN's role is Goal; if the verb lemma is RUNS AWAY FROM, the MAILMAN's role is Agent.) Once the activation for appropriate lemmas (say THE MAILMAN and RUNS AWAY FROM) and the verb's semantic frame have reached threshold and the mailman's noun lemma has been tagged, those lemmas should automatically arouse their forms. The Agent tag plus the verb's syntactic frame should tell the Positional Level that mailman is going to be the subject, and continuing to look at the mailman won't help with transmitting that information. So now, while the lemma THE MAILMAN activates its phonological form /ðə ˈmejlmn/ and the verb phrase gets set up with the mailman as the subject at the Positional Level, the speaker can switch her gaze to the dog to help arouse its lemma and get it tagged as Source. Sure enough, about nine-tenths of a second after she's stopped looking at the picture of the mailman, the speaker actually says *the mailman*, and goes smoothly on to say *runs away from*. So during that 900 milliseconds, the lemmas for the verb phrase RUNS AWAY FROM have gotten aroused, the Positional Level has been created, and the phonological forms *runs away from* for the verb phrase must have gotten ready in an output buffer, so that they were ready to come out as soon as the speaker said *the mailman*. And because she had shifted to looking at the dog as soon as she was done looking at the mailman, arousal of the lemmas for /ðə dɔg/ got underway while the speaker was saying the verb phrase *runs away from*. This means that, by the time that she's done saying *runs away from*, she'll be ready to say *the dog*.

All this seems to be what happens when speaking about a picture runs smoothly. But every step takes a bit of time, and if one or more of them get slowed down—arousing each needed lemma, settling on one of the possible competing verbs, retrieving its semantic frame and tagging the lemmas to create the Functional Level, creating the Positional Level with the corresponding syntax, arousing each phonological form—then we get dysfluencies. A few short ones are normal, but if they get to be too many or too long, the speaker has a problem.

5.5 Comprehension Experiments I: Discriminating Between Similar Speech Sounds and Recognizing Words

5.5.1 Sounds and boundaries

In Chapter 1, section 1.2.5, we spent quite a bit of time talking about phonemes and phonemic contrast; take a look at that section again if you feel fuzzy on those concepts. Now suppose we take syllables beginning with a contrasting pair of similar sounds, like [ba] and [da], with no context around them, and ask what the differences are in the sound waves. What makes a [ba] a [ba], and what makes it different from a [da]? It's not easy to tell if you just record it and look at the sound waves, because there's so much redundant information in natural speech sound waves, but well before the 1970s, researchers, especially a group at Haskins Laboratories (http://www.haskins.yale.edu; a very early publication is Liberman et al., 1957) figured out that the key to hearing a [b] or a [d] at the beginning of a syllable is the way the consonant changes the beginning part of the vowel; in fact, there doesn't actually have to be any sound that corresponds to the consonant. This is a good thing, because the oral stop consonants (the ones that don't let air out through the speaker's nose) make little or no sound. (Remember that with your mouth closed off by the velum and either your lips or your tongue, someone else trying to hear you say a non-nasal stop consonant [b,d,g] is like trying to hear a sound through a closed door. And there's no sound produced at all during the actual articulatory contact part of [p,t,k].)

After analyzing the differences in the sound waves between the way [ba] syllables begin and the way [da] syllables begin, researchers figured out how to make synthetic syllables (using an analog method) and they made one that seemed to be on the borderline exactly halfway between [ba] and [da], because 50% of the time listeners said that it was a "ba" and 50% of the time that it was a "da." They also made several intermediate syllables, two on the "ba" side of the borderline syllable, and two on the "da" side. The amount of acoustic change from each syllable to the next one was equal. So there was the original [ba], call that stimulus 1; then 2 and 3 that moved successively closer to the borderline syllable. Stimulus 4 was the borderline syllable, and then stimuli 5 and 6 that moved successively closer to the original [da], which was stimulus 7. Now they had seven steps, evenly spaced and dividing up the acoustic difference between [ba] and [da]; in technical terms, they had seven steps dividing up the "ba-da continuum" (Figure 5.2). You can hear modern ones that are somewhat like them in the Materials for Chapter 5 on your CD.

Using their ba/da continuum of seven steps, the Haskins group found out something new about how sound perception works, which you can try out yourself with the ones that you have. If you play any two different sounds on the [ba] side of the borderline 50/50 stimulus, even the pair #1 and #3, it's very hard to tell them apart, because they both just sound like [ba]—they are very difficult to discriminate (naturally, #1 and #2 or #2 and #3 are even harder to tell apart). The same thing is true for any two sounds that are both on the [da] side, like #5 and #7—they will both just sound like [da]. But if you take the #3 [ba]-side sound and the #5 [da]-side sound, the two that are closest to the 50/50 borderline sound but on opposite sides of it, it's much easier to discriminate between them than the pair #1 and #3 or the pair #5 and #7, even though the acoustic difference between them isn't any bigger. One sounds like [ba] and the other like [da]: We hear them as members of different categories. Does this seem obvious? Well, it wouldn't have to be that way. We could just get more and more confused about whether two sounds were the same or different when we get close to a category boundary—after all, if we hear a single syllable by itself and one of its sounds is close to a boundary, we do get more and more confused about what category it belongs to. But deciding what category a sound belongs to is not the same thing as deciding whether two sounds are the same or different. Bottom line: Humans (and other animals, too, by the way!) have a special sensitivity to differences that lie across some kinds of perceptual category boundaries. This special sensitivity to differences that lie on opposite sides of a category boundary is called CATEGORICAL

/ba/---#2---#3---#4---#5---#6---/da/

Figure 5.2. Seven equal steps on a ba/da continuum, with step #4 as the borderline point.

PERCEPTION. For most consonant sounds, very young infants have categorical perception, so for those sounds, categorical perception must result from the way the auditory system is constructed. But for other speech sounds, categorical perception seems to be learned by exposure to a particular language. And there are other types of speech sounds where people don't seem to show any increase in sensitivity to differences near their boundaries. After years of experiments, researchers are still uncertain about why people (and other animals) sometimes respond to speech (and musical) stimuli with increased sensitivity at category boundaries and sometimes don't.

In the second experiment of the next section, we'll come back to another set of stimuli made by putting synthesized steps between familiar speech sounds, and discover how their perception is affected by top-down processing.

5.5.2 Experiments inspired by slips of the ear: Evidence for top-down processes in auditory perception

Phoneme restoration

Read this rather dull sentence: *The state governors met with their respective legi#latures convening in the capital city.* What's the missing letter? How did you know? Okay, I didn't have to ask that; you already know that there's top-down processing in reading. And we talked about top-down processing for hearing in Chapter 2, section 2.5.1, but you didn't get to see any evidence there. Now let's look at some.

Back when editing speech sounds had to be done by actually cutting and splicing reel-to-reel audiotape instead of "cutting and pasting" audiofiles on a computer, Richard Warren (Warren, 1970) did one of the most elegant little experiments ever. He used a tape recording of that sentence *The state governors met with their respective legislatures convening in the capital city*, and then removed the 120 milliseconds of it that contained the first [s] in the word *legislatures*, plus the parts of the [ɪ] before it and the [l] after it that would tell a hearer that they had been coarticulated with [s]. As you can hear on your CD, a well-placed silence of 120 milliseconds does a very nice job of getting rid of all traces of the [s] while leaving the other two sounds quite clear.

Then Warren tape-recorded a cough and spliced it in where the [s] had been, and played those sentences to participants through headphones; he told them that there would be a cough on the tape, and gave them a printed version of the sentence, asking them to circle the exact position where the cough occurred, and also to note whether the cough had completely replaced the sound(s) they'd circled, or whether they'd been able to hear everything. Only one person out of 20 in the "cough" condition reported that anything was missing, and nobody located the cough or the tone correctly—about half of the participants didn't even place it in the word *legislatures*. (I've put a similar set of files on your CD for you to try on interested friends). "Hearing" a speech sound that isn't there is called the **PHONEME RESTORATION EFFECT**, and it's another great example of top-down processing. You have multiple cues as to what you should be hearing, and those cues activate the whole word *legislatures*; once it's activated, it activates your memory for all its sounds, and so it is usually impossible to tell the difference between what you heard and what was reconstructed by top-down activation.

When Warren played his tape in another condition, with just silence instead of an extraneous sound replacing the [s], his participants did notice the missing section, and they located it correctly. But only a little bit of noise is needed to give the illusion that you've heard an [s] in the spot where it should be. (That's especially true if you're over 60, because /s/ is a pretty quiet sound and it's mostly high-frequency noise, which is the first kind of sound that becomes hard to hear in normal aging.) Because one of the recordings on the CD was made with my computer humming audibly, you might feel that you hear the [s] even when there's no cough in the empty spot.

Top-down processing shoves category borderlines around

In 1980, W. Francis Ganong III investigated whether top-down processing would affect categorical perception, following up on the phoneme restoration effect and another top-down effect that had been discovered: People are faster to identify a consonant sound if they hear it in a familiar word than if they hear it in a nonsense syllable. (Skilled readers are also faster to identify a printed letter in a visual display if they see it in a familiar short word than if they see it by itself—in Chapter 8, we'll discuss why this *doesn't* mean that reading should only be taught by the whole-word method. Go have a look if you can't wait.)

Specifically, Ganong looked at whether there might be a top-down effect on where people put the category boundary between similar phonemes. If he took the 50/50 borderline alveolar consonant sound between /ta/ and /da/ and put it at the beginning of the syllable [æʃ] (*ash*), and asked people to say whether this new synthetic syllable was the real word *dash* or the non-word *tash*, would they still say that it was *dash* half of the time and *tash* the other half? Or would the fact that *dash* is a real word influence them to call it *dash* more often than half the time? He made sets of six-step gradations between the voiced/voiceless pairs of English stop phonemes b/p, d/t, and k/g. (He actually didn't use the sound that was exactly at the spot where the 50/50 borderline would have been if both of the ends of the continuum were nonsense—that's why there are only six steps.) And instead of putting his synthetic consonants in the (mostly) nonsense syllables [ba] or [pa], [da] or [ta], [ga] or [ka], he spliced the synthetic sounds so that they were followed by a vowel + consonant sequence like "ash" or "ark" or "arp." He set this up so that one end of his continuum made a real word and the other end didn't. For example, he made six steps starting with the word *dark* and ending with the nonword *tark*, and six steps starting with the nonword *darp* and ending with the word *tarp*. (Splicing could be done digitally by then, instead of by cutting audiotape, although it took room-sized computers and was very slow; it was possible only at the few most advanced phonetics labs in the world.)

Ganong made 28 sets like these; there were at least 8 sets for each of our three voiced/voiceless pairs of English oral stop consonants, and sometimes more. For each set, one end was a real word and the other was a nonsense word. He shuffled all 6 steps for all the b/p sets, played them through headphones to 18 participants, and asked each of them to type the syllable that they thought they heard, and he did the same thing for the d/t sets and the g/k sets. (He had them do some other tasks, too, but we won't deal with those.) You've probably guessed what he found, but let's go through it for two example continua, one between *dark* and *tark*, with the real word on the /d/ end, and the matching continuum between *darp* and *tarp*, with the real word on the /t/ end. Step 1 of both continua was made from a real /d/, and step 6 was made from a real /t/. The first finding (as in other experiments with synthetic speech and nonsense syllables) was that about 10% of the time even the endpoint nonword *tark* was identified as the real word *dark*, even though it had been made with a clear /t/ sound. And at the opposite end of the continuum, the nonword *darp* was reported as *tarp*. However, the participants made only about 1% misidentifications of the very same sounds when they heard them in the matching real words *tarp* and *dark*. So the participants were very strongly biased towards reporting that they heard real words even when what they heard was clearly a nonsense word.

Not impressed? Try this: the #3 step from *dark* to *tark*, which should still have been on the /d/ side of the usual borderline, was reported as the real word *dark* about 75% of the time, but the #3 step from *darp* to *tarp*, which started with exactly the same /d/-side sound, was reported as the nonsense word *darp* only 40% of the time. And the #4 step from *dark* to *tark*, which should have been over on the /t/ side of the usual borderline, was still reported as the real word *dark* about 50% of the time, while the #3 step from *darp* to *tarp*, with exactly the same /t/-side sound, was reported as the nonsense word *darp* only 35% of the time.

Results like these make a lot of sense in our spreading-activation framework (see Exercise 5.2), so they support that idea—that's their theoretical importance, as far as this book is concerned. But do they have any practical implication in the real world? Sure they do. Here's the simplest one: If you happen to have a rare name that is one feature different from a commoner one—if you are named Thallie instead of Sally, or Doans instead of Jones (or Menn instead of Mann!), forget about anyone *ever* hearing it right the first time. You have to spell it, slowly and carefully. Otherwise, no matter how carefully you say it, getting it across is hopeless. (And we're not even talking yet about the additional problems of having an unfamiliar accent; we'll get to those issues in Chapter 9.)

Getting people to understand your name is a nuisance, but there are worse problems. If you are stuck in a noisy tunnel or using a cell phone and trying to hear the name of a street in a strange part of town, or if you are hard of hearing and trying to catch the name of some new medication, then you know how miserable it is to have low quality bottom-up information about the sound of a word when there isn't much top-down information in the context that could compensate for it. And when someone's top-down processing is impaired (for example, people with aphasia, or second-language learners), or when the top-down information happens to be wrong, vital communication can be badly disrupted by just a little noise or a minor lapse of attention. The most dangerous cases are probably those that involve airplane-pilot-to-control tower communications (noisy radio channels, cockpit noise, and many second-language speakers and hearers; the international language of the air is English). One of the ways that air traffic safety regulations try to improve communication accuracy is to require pilots and control towers to use a highly standardized vocabulary, so that there are fewer words to guess among.

When you're communicating with aphasic people or other people who may not be getting clear input from you, do everything you can to improve both bottom-up information (avoid noise, speak as slowly and distinctly as you can without being insulting about it) and top-down or parallel sources of information (use gestures, move your lips, write things down, use familiar words if you can, and put them in a helpful context).

5.6 Comprehension Experiments II: How Understanding Unfolds in Time

5.6.1 Spreading activation, priming, and word recognition

For many years, psycholinguists have been doing experiments to explore how activation spreads when we hear or read a word or a phrase. We'll look at one of the classic types of experiment; it's basic because it's relatively simple to understand, and because people have used many variations of it to probe how our minds understand language. The experimental TASK—what the participants are asked to do—is to decide, as quickly as possible, whether a set of letters flashed on a screen for, say, 200 milliseconds (one-fifth of a second) makes a word or not; this is called a LEXICAL DECISION task. In a typical experiment, half the sets of letters make words, and the other half don't. The nonword sets of letters are chosen to look very much like real words (*dolk, purt*; not *czyx* or *aaaa*), so that the participants actually have to read the stimuli to decide whether they are words or not, and the words and nonword are mixed together in a pseudorandom way, so that the participants can't predict whether the next set of letters they see will be a word or not.

Usually, the participants are asked to push a button if what they see is a word, and to do this as quickly as they can. If the stimuli have been set up to make this easy—the letters easy to see and in a horizontal line near the middle of the screen, in a familiar typeface, making common short words—then it takes them, on average, a little over half a second—say 600 milliseconds from the instant at which the stimulus begins—to push the "yes" button when what they see is, in fact, a word. A new set of letters might be flashed about every 1.5 seconds, which means that the screen is dark for 1.3 seconds after each stimulus; that should be plenty of time for participants to press the button, if they are going to, and then get ready to pay attention to the next stimulus. (If the stimuli come along too quickly, people don't have enough time to respond; if they come too slowly, people zone out.)

So much for the task. How can it be used to study spreading activation? Here's one way: When you're setting up the lists of words and nonwords, include some pairs of words that you think should be related in meaning, and set up your stimulus list so that those words will be shown one right after the other. Remember to vary the mixture of words and nonwords in a pseudorandom way, just as if you were making up a true-false test. A small part of a sequence of stimuli and responses might look like:

Pseudorandom Mix of Words and Nonwords for a Lexical Decision Experiment

Stimulus	Response
prut	(no response)
knob	button push
door	button push
leng	(no response)
rice	button push
tolk	(no response)
thip	(no response)
leaf	button push
iron	button push
song	button push
wuts	(no response)

In this list, there are three places where one word comes right after another word: *knob-door, leaf-iron*, and *iron-song*. As you can see, *knob* and *door* are related, but the other two pairs aren't.

Decades ago, psycholinguists learned that if two words are associated in a participant's mind and one of them gets flashed on the screen first, the participant pushes the button faster when the second one appears than in any other condition. So of the five button pushes that would have been recorded for this subject, the fastest one probably would have been the response to *door*. (A real experiment to study the strength of different kinds of associations would have several hundred stimuli, with maybe 20% of the real words showing up in pairs like this, meaning that only 10% would be second members of a pair; that's done so that the participants won't notice the pairings.)

The spreading activation model, of course, predicts exactly this: When a skilled reader sees a word like *knob*, its meaning becomes activated, and then it automatically starts to spread activation to everything in his or her mind that is associated with it (even though the person is busy doing something else), including verbal concepts like "turn" and "pull," and object concepts like "door" So activation will have been spreading from the word *knob* to its meaning and on to all these associated meanings, and then on to their lemmas and their spoken and written forms. If the next stimulus the person hears after *knob* is one of the forms that has gotten some activation even before he or she has seen it, it will naturally reach its activation threshold faster. So the button will be pressed faster if *door* follows *knob* than if it had followed an unrelated word like, say, *song*.

Psycholinguists say that *knob* has PRIMED *door* (and other words closely related to knob), meaning that *knob* has given *door* (and, of course, those other words) some activation. In general, if making a particular response makes it faster for a person to make some other response, we say that the first stimulus has primed the second one. Hundreds of priming studies have been done with this task and several others, to try to see what kinds of words, ideas, and phrases are related in people's minds.

5.6.2 Figuring out how the parts of a sentence go together

Do you have to listen to all of a word before you understand it?

People have also used eye-trackers to try to figure out what is going on in language comprehension. If you set up a computer screen divided into four quadrants (top left, top right, bottom left, bottom right), put a different picture in each quadrant, and track which pictures participants look at while they listen to recorded words or phrases, you can see how long it is before what they hear has an effect on where they look. For example, an experiment on word understanding (Tanenhaus et al., 1995) used sets of simple pictures of objects that were chosen so that the names of two out of the four things started with the same syllable, like *fork, candy, bird, candle*. When participants just look at the screen, before they hear any of the words, they pretty much spend an equal amount of time looking at each of the four things, but when they hear the name of one of them, they look at it for a second or so and rarely glance at the others during that time.

What the Tanenhaus team showed is that participants don't always wait for the end of an object's name to start looking. How do we know this? Well, the average time to start a saccade (an eye-jump) to, say, the fork, if a person has been looking at another item on the screen, is about 145 milliseconds after the end of the word *fork*. Because it takes about 200 milliseconds to do a saccade, they must have started programming that movement about 50 milliseconds before *fork* ended. And there's more to the story: If the word they hear is, say, *candle*, and they've been looking at the fork or the bird, it takes them about 230 milliseconds after the end of the word to start moving. That extra 85 milliseconds of delay makes sense if that's the extra time it took them to decide whether the incoming word was *candy* or *candle*, because with a pair of words that are the same almost to the end, the participants had to wait longer before they would know where to look. So whether you listen to all of a word depends on whether you need all of it in a particular context.

How much of a sentence do you have to hear before you start figuring out what it means?

When the pictures are more complex, like Figure 5.3 (from Tanenhaus, Spivey-Knowlton, Eberhard, & Sedivy, 1995), we can get some clues to the process of sentence understanding. Notice that this picture has one apple on a towel and another on a napkin.

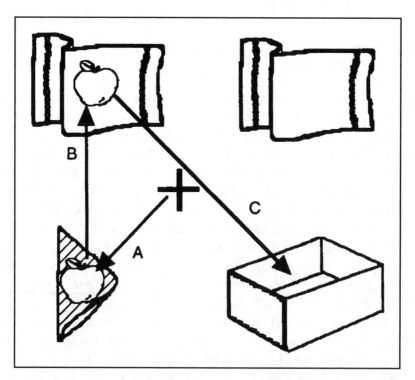

Figure 5.3. Eyetracking diagram 1: "Put the apple on the towel in the box"; two apples. (From Tanenhaus et al. (1995), Integration of visual and linguistic information in spoken language comprehension. *Science, 268,* 1632–1634, Fig. 2. Reprinted with permission from AAAS.)

Before the picture is put up on the screen, participants are told to start by clicking on the cross, which means they look at it first. Then they hear sets of instructions like, *Put the apple on the towel in the box* (which of course they can't actually carry out). What happens is that they start from the cross, look at one and perhaps the other of the two apples for a short time (glance A), settle on the one on the towel (glance B), and then look at the box (glance C). It seems that they almost never, with this sentence, look at the empty towel, even though they could have briefly interpreted the first part of the sentence *Put the apple on the towel* to mean that the apple is supposed to be moved to the towel. Because there were two apples and the word *the* had been used, they had been able to predict that a phrase like *on the towel* or *on the napkin* should be coming along to tell them which apple the sentence was about. So the participants were automatically tuning into the pragmatics ("They're going to have to tell me which apple!") and the syntax ("*on the* sounds like the start of a locative prepositional phrase, so it should tell me which apple they're talking about"). They didn't get lured into thinking that this first prepositional phrase was going to tell them the other thing that they could also predict that they would be needing after they heard the word *put*: where they were supposed to put the apple.

But in the condition shown in Figure 5.4, when the participants started by looking at the + and heard *Put the apple on the towel in the box*, their eyes followed the sequence A, B, C, D: apple, empty towel, apple, box. Why? Well, because there was only one apple, there was no reason, early on, to expect *on the towel* to mean anything except the apple's destination, so they first went to the apple (glance A) and then to the empty towel (glance B). But when *in the box* hit them, they typically went back to check that the apple was on a towel (glance C), and then they went to the box (glance D). (The study doesn't say anything about participants looking at the pencil; either they did this for an extremely small percentage of the time, or they identified it in peripheral vision, without ever looking at it directly.)

So people unconsciously start predicting what sort of information they should be hearing as soon as they get some relevant clues. Sometimes the predictions are wrong, but a normally working brain can go back and update the way it's interpreting an incoming sentence with only a short delay. On the other hand, people with some kinds of brain damage can't do this kind of thing very well, and it's probably also harder if you're trying to do it in a second language. One thing we can be sure of: If you're talking to someone whose comprehension is likely to be slower than that of a native speaker in top condition, you need to slow down and give them time to process what you're saying.

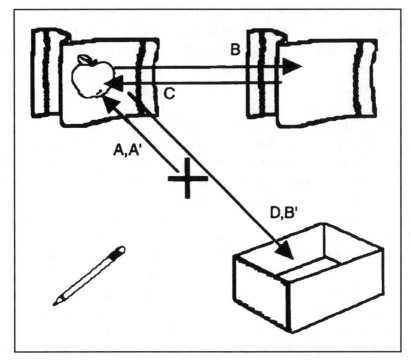

Figure 5.4. Eyetracking diagram 2: "Put the apple on the towel in the box"; one apple. (From Tanenhaus et al. (1995), Integration of visual and linguistic information in spoken language comprehension. *Science*, *268*, 1632–1634, Fig. 1. Reprinted with permission from AAAS.)

5.7 What Brain Imaging Adds to Psycholinguistic Studies: A First Look at Neurolinguistics

Figuring out what things mean can't always be a matter of understanding one word at a time and hooking it up with the words we've already heard using the predictions our brains have already made. Sometimes we hear friends tell stories with lines like, *I don't know how he'll get out of hot water this time.* Without even thinking, we know that *hot water* means "trouble." How come? It could be like figuring out the meaning of any ambiguous word, for example, *table* in *Look it up in the table of contents*: In our subconscious minds, activation spreads from a word to all of its meanings, literal or metaphorical, and then it bounces back and forth from possible interpretations of the sentence in the context to the different word meanings until the sentence interpretation that makes the most sense in the context rises above the others and reaches our consciousness as being "what the sentence means," carrying the right meaning of the ambiguous word along with it. Is understanding a familiar metaphor like this, too?

And suppose there's an unfamiliar metaphor, like *Every minute of my time was attacked*. The effort we have to put into understanding unfamiliar metaphors can be consciously noticeable, but is the difference just a matter of effort, or is what we do for unfamiliar metaphors really different? There are quite a lot of different ideas on both of these processes; the questions are far from settled, although researchers have been working on both of them for many years.

Psycholinguists have started to compare brain wave recordings of people when they are reading sentences that make sense literally with their brain waves when they read sentences with familiar and unfamiliar metaphors, and sentences that make no sense at all. Research using brain wave recordings goes beyond psycholinguistics, because in addition to looking at how people react to language (or language-like) stimuli, it's actually measuring the activity of various parts of the brain. That makes it **NEUROLINGUISTICS**, and neurolinguistics takes research beyond just thinking about how the brain might be working, which is all that we have been able to do in this book. Researchers need quite a lot of additional training in neurolinguistic techniques in order to run these experiments.

One advantage of doing neurolinguistic measurements of brain waves is that it can give us an idea of how hard someone's brain is working to figure something out, even when they're not aware of any effort. For example, a recent study, designed and carried out by Vicky Tzuyin Lai (Lai, Curran, & Menn, 2009) suggests that, when we are in the process of understanding familiar metaphors, our brains work a little harder but just as fast as they do in the process of understanding literal sentences. This would go along well with the idea that understanding a familiar metaphor is like figuring out an ambiguous word. But when we're in the process of understanding an unfamiliar metaphor, our brains have to work both harder and longer to figure it out. Does that make it "really different" from understanding a familiar metaphor? Well, we could be doing something different, but nobody is sure of the answer yet. Neurolinguistic methods, like all new scientific methods, answer some old questions, but not all of them, and they raise many new ones.

5.8 Summary

5.8.1 What we can learn about language processing from experiments

Psycholinguists design experiments to try to discover mental events that happen too quickly to be observed, like the spreading of activation from one word to the next; or that happen below the level of consciousness, like arousing multiple possible meanings for a word at the same time; or that happen when normal speakers are under mild stress, or when participants are immature or have brain damage. Experiments are also useful in cases where directly asking people about what they are thinking (for example, asking them whether they remember images or meanings or words) would be likely to influence their report, or when they can't give a report for some reason.

A properly designed experiment must be ethical. Even if it can't hurt or upset your participants, they should have a good explanation of what they will be asked to do. The experimental stimuli and the explanation need to be presented in a way that isn't disturbing or insulting. If your participants are fragile in some way—if they are children, aphasic, or very old, for example—then the experiment and its explanation shouldn't even make them uncomfortable, let alone put them at risk. But your experiment can still be a mental workout, as long as your participants know they can quit whenever they want to, and as long as you don't make any false promises about whether it will actually help them. Many people who have language problems are fiercely proud of what they still can do, and want very much to still be treated as valuable and important; participating in a study gives them a chance to be part of life.

To give useful information, an experiment needs to have a clear hypothesis that can be tested by comparing participants' responses to stimuli in at least two conditions, or by comparing the responses of two different types of participants in the same condition, so that you have both an independent variable and a dependent variable whose relationship you can look at. (Conditions aren't always different setups; sometimes the different conditions are just earlier and later parts of the same series of responses, as in the Bousfeld and Sedgewick word-finding study, and sometimes the independent variable is the stimulus itself, as in the TOT study). Competing hypotheses should be tested whenever possible, and the possible effects of confounding variables need to be controlled, or tested separately if they can't be controlled. An experiment needs enough stimuli or enough subjects (usually both) so that responses can be averaged, to allow for random variability that might be affecting the results.

We looked at several basic psycholinguistic experiments on memory, language production, and language comprehension, and here's a summary of what we learned: Studies of memory for sentences have shown that meaning and mental images are stored more accessibly than the words that originally conveyed those ideas. Studies of word and sentence production have shown that associative links help us recall words, and that more frequent words are produced faster (when word length is controlled). Patterns of people's responses in language production experiments have also suggested that the feeling of "searching" your memory in a TOT state is probably an illusion, and when we describe a picture, we stop looking at an object in it once a lemma for referring to it has been activated. Studies of comprehension have shown that for some kinds of phonemic categories (but not others), our perception is sharper near the category boundaries, but that the position of those boundaries, and the perception of speech stimuli in general, can be shifted by top-down processing.

All through this chapter, we've seen that spreading activation can explain many results: top-down processing in perception, unwanted items shoving their way into lists, similar items clustering together in lists, slower picture naming when pictures of items in the same category are clustered together, and faster "yes, it's a word" responses after seeing a related word (priming) in lexical decision. And we've also seen that we're far from being able to understand the details of any of these processes; even when we look at brain waves, many different hypotheses could explain why some processes take more time and/or more effort than others.

5.8.2 Why did you have to read all the details of these experiments?

Why didn't I just tell you what the researchers found out? For a couple of reasons. First, as I said in the introduction to this chapter, I want you to get a little sense of what science is like. Science isn't something created by superhumans, and it's not like some huge science-fiction machine that knows all the answers. It's a lot of people, many of them graduate students, who are reasonably smart and very hard working (including some geniuses, but there aren't a lot of those), trying to figure out explanations for things and then seeing how well their explanations work. They get rather fond of their own ideas and argue for them, and argue against other people who have different ideas. And over time, because people keep challenging each other with competing explanations, and because new ideas and new gadgets for doing experiments keep being developed, we get closer to understanding how minds work. Old ideas that turn out to have been wrong weren't "junk science" (except for some that were based on totally on politics and prejudice, and were never really tested in the first place); they were just the best that scientists could come up with at the time.

That leads into the second reason why I've given you so many details (though not nearly as many as the researchers give in their published papers): Whatever you learn from this book will not be the best ideas forever; even now, although they are what I think are the best, some people naturally disagree with me. If a particular research result is going to affect what you do in your work—if it's going to affect the advice you give or teaching you do or your own research—then before you use that result, you have a responsibility to your patients, students, clients, or customers to evaluate for yourself, if possible, the actual work that the researchers did. Did they really try out their ideas in a way that makes sense to you? Did they have a control condition where they did something else? Did they test any other possible explanations for their findings? Can you and your colleagues think of a different explanation for the results of their experiments? Are there published challenges to their work that seem valid to you?

5.8.3 Why do people have to do so many experiments?

You know one answer to this question already: Some experiments have been reworked for years to try to deal with competing possible explanations for their results. And you can guess another one: real-world questions, like why some people learn a second language better than others or recover their speech after a stroke better, or whether one teaching method is better than another, are hard to answer because there are so many variables that you can't control, and can't even get accurate information about. How many hours a day did this child hear which language, and how much of what she heard was addressed to her, and how much was complex explanatory language instead of just basic commands? Were the connections in this person's brain that are essential for syntax—assuming that there are such connections—located in a slightly different place from the connections in some other person's brain? To answer real-world questions, researchers have to be clever, patient, and able to make good use of the work that other researchers have done. That takes many, many experiments.

Exercises for Chapter 5

5.1A. How could you test to see whether substitutions in a remembered grocery list happened because the substitute and the original item were located near each other in the store, and that they did not just occur because several items on the list were in the same category as the substitute?

5.1B. How could you test to see if substitutions in a remembered grocery list happened both because the substitute and the original item were located near each other in the store, and that because several items on the list were in the same category as the substitute?

5.2. In Ganong's experiment, the #3 step from *dark* to *tark*, which should still have been on the /d/ side of the usual borderline, was reported as the real word *dark* about 75% of the time, but the #3 step from *darp* to *tarp*, which started with exactly the same /d/-side sound, was reported as the nonsense word *darp* only 40% of the time. And the #4 step from *dark* to *tark*, which should have been over on the /t/ side of the usual borderline, was still reported as the real word *dark* about 50% of the time, but the #3 step from *darp* to *tarp*, with exactly the same /t/-side sound, was reported as the nonsense word *darp* only 35% of the time.

Results like these make a lot of sense in our spreading-activation framework; explain why.

5.3. If you were testifying as an expert witness in a law court, what evidence would you present to convince the jury that hearsay evidence may be unreliable even when the people reporting it are honest, and are quite certain that they remember exactly what someone else said?

Acknowledgment. Thanks to Doug Whalen, Mary Beckman, and Ronnie Silber for material assistance in tracking down and interpreting some of the research articles on speech perception.

References and Sources Consulted

Association for Psychological Science. (2009, February 4). Differences in recovered memories of childhood sexual abuse. *Science Daily*. Retrieved June 1, 2010, from http://www.sciencedaily.com/releases/2009/02/090202175057.htm

Belke, E., Meyer, A. S., & Damian, M. F. (2005.) Refractory effects in picture naming as assessed in a semantic blocking paradigm. *Quarterly Journal of Experimental Psychology Section A, 58*(4), 667–692. DOI: 10.1080/02724980443000142.

Bousfield, W. A., & Sedgewick, C. H. W. (1944). An experimental analysis of sequences of restricted verbal associative responses. *Journal of General Psychology*, *30*, 149–165.

Bransford, J. D., Barclay, J. K., & Franks, J. J. (1972). Sentence memory: A constructive versus interpretive approach. *Cognitive Psychology*, *2*, 193–209.

Ganong, W. F., III. (1980). Phonetic categorization in auditory word perception. *Journal of Experimental Psychology: Human Perception and Performance*, *6*(1), 110–125.

Goldman-Eisler, F. (1958). The predictability of words in context and the length of pauses in speech. *Language and Speech*, *1*, 226–231.

Griffin, Z. M., & Bock, K. (2000). What the eyes say about speaking. *Psychological Science*, *11*(4), 274–279.

Kohn, S., Wingfield, A., Menn, L., Goodglass, H., Gleason, J. B., &. Hyde, M. R. (1987). Lexical retrieval: The tip of the tongue phenomenon. *Applied Psycholinguistics*, *8*, 245–266.

Lai, V., Curran, T., & Menn, L. (2009). Comprehending conventional and novel metaphors: An ERP study. *Brain Research*, *1284*, 145–155.

Liberman, A. M., Cooper, F. S., Shankweiler, D. P., & M. Studdert-Kennedy. (1967). Perception of the speech code. *Psychological Review*, *74*, 431–461.

Liberman, A. M., Harris, K. S., Hoffman, H. S., & Griffith, B. C. (1957). The discrimination of sounds within and across phoneme boundaries. *Journal of Experimental Psychology*, *54*, 358–368c.

Lisker, L. & Abramson, A. S. (1964). A cross-language study of voicing in initial stops: Acoustical measurements. *Word*, *20*, 384–422.

New York Mets Make Error in Media Guide. Retrieved June 1, 2010, from http://jalfredproofreader.blogspot.com/2009/04/new-york-mets-make-error-in-media-guide.html.

Oldfield, R. C., & Wingfield, A. (1965). Response latencies in naming objects. *Quarterly Journal of Experimental Psychology*, *17*(4), 273–281. DOI: 10.1080/17470216508416445

Sachs, J. S. (1967) Recognition memory for syntactic and semantic aspects of connected discourse. *Perception and Psychophysics*, *2*, 437–442.

Snodgrass, J. G., & Vanderwart, M. (1980). A standardized set of 260 pictures: Norms for name agreement, image agreement, familiarity, and visual complexity. *Journal of Experimental Psychology: Human Learning and Memory*, *6*, 174–215.

The Sunshine State. Retrieved June 1, 2010, from http://4.bp.blogspot.com/_-qP__B7vKI8/SeivguS_VXI/AAAAAAAAAXE/O9lyeIH-o1Y/s1600-h/TV+Guide+digital+cable+mistake+higlighted.jpg

Tanenhaus, M. K., Spivey-Knowlton, M. J., Eberhard, K. M., & Sedivy, J. E. (1995). Integration of visual and linguistic information in spoken language comprehension. *Science*, *268*, 1632–1634.

University of Leicester (2009, May 26). How does the human brain work? New ways to better understand how our brain processes information. *Science Daily*.

Retrieved June 1, 2010, from http://www.sciencedaily.com/releases/2009/05/ 090519152559.htm

Warren, R. M. (1970). Perceptual restoration of missing speech sounds. *Science, 167,* 392–395.

Where a Yule log is so much more than Christmas cake. *The New York Times,* Dec. 14, 2008. Retrieved June 1, 2010, from http://www.nytimes.com/2008/ 12/24/world/europe/24paris.html

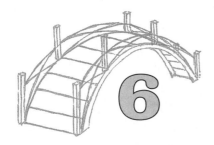

Analyzing Aphasic Speech and Communication: The Psycholinguistics of Adult Acquired Language Disorders

6.0 Why There's High Cost for Being Slow and Sounding Weird: Who Do They Think I Am?

Science news often has articles about how we unconsciously size up other people by what they look like. Based only on their looks, we react unconsciously to them as probably being smart or stupid, nice or sneaky, sexy or uptight, brave or timid, friendly or shy or standoffish, even though we are warned from childhood "not to judge a book by its cover." So we have to actively fight off the impressions we get from visual clues while we're trying to get valid information about what a new person is like. How people talk, what they say, and how they react to what we say is another major source of information, and we usually take it as a reliable guide to their personality, intelligence, and general competence; but, like physical appearance, it's an opaque surface, not a window. If a new person has slow (and possibly incorrect) responses to what we've said, and speech that's hard to understand or doesn't seem to make sense, it takes real work to discover whether they are still thinking and feeling normally, or whether they have some kind of cognitive problem or mental illness.

And every time they have to talk to someone new, people who have language disorders but normal intelligence and thought patterns fight grimly to have their competence recognized. (This also is often true for beginning and intermediate-level second language speakers who don't happen to look like students, business people, or tourists.)

Because confused ideas do produce confused language, even seasoned language clinicians can be fooled into forgetting the difference between being confused about words and being confused about concepts. How can we tell the difference between these very different kinds of problems when a speaker's language abilities are limited? As we look at language disorders, some answers to this question will emerge. Some of those answers will also be relevant to dealing with the problems faced by less skilled second-language users in schools and communities.

The language disorder that we focus on in this chapter is APHASIA, which we define as "an acquired language disorder caused by focal brain damage." Millions of Americans are stroke survivors, and about a million of them (25%–40%) have some degree of aphasia (for updates, visit the National Aphasia Association, http://www.aphasia.org/Aphasia%20Facts/aphasia_faq.html). Aphasia and its impact on people's lives can be reduced considerably by speech-language therapy; although therapy is best started as soon as the patient is able to interact with a therapist, it can be effective even years after the date when the brain damage occurred. The NAA Web site has good information about this, too.

6.1 Introduction to Aphasia

6.1.0 What's so interesting about aphasia?

To answer this in full, we'll need to unpack that definition of aphasia, and also get clear about two rather different ways that clinicians use the term, depending on the kind of clients that they see in their practice. But here's the short answer: Aphasia is interesting because, in many cases, it is language damage with minimal other cognitive damage, and so it gives us data that help us understand how language and thinking are actually related in our brains. And because, in a particular person, aphasia may have damaged some aspects of language while letting others escape, it gives us ideas about what aspects of language can be separated from others. If you go back to that single sentence *The baby, no, the ball hits the baby*, from Shirley in Chapter 3, section 3.7, and the discussion of Shirley's syntactic and semantic abilities in Chapter 4, section 4.1.1, you'll have a good example of what this "separation" means. All right, APHASIA is an ACQUIRED language disorder caused by FOCAL brain damage. Let's work through this definition, term by term: section 6.1.1 "language disorder," section 6.1.2 "focal brain damage," section 6.1.3 "acquired."

6.1.1 Language disorder: What's the difference between a language disorder and a speech disorder? Between a language disorder and a thought disorder?

We can use the language processing model that we've spent so much time developing to help us state a clear answer to this question: A LANGUAGE DISORDER is a problem that affects one or more levels of processing from the Functional Level to the level of Phonological Form, in comprehension or production. If the brain damage affects *only* the last stages of articulation, the ones that come after the retrieval and organization of the sounds needed to produce a word, that's a speech disorder; it's not aphasia. If someone has only a speech disorder, she can use writing to communicate normally, but people with a real language disorder have problems with reading and/or writing, because these are language functions, too (see Chapter 8).

If the brain damage affects the Message Level or concepts and thoughts, but does not affect the processes of language formulation or understanding, that's not aphasia either. It's a cognitive or thought disorder, although some thought disorders (like schizophrenia or severe temporal lobe epilepsy) seem to spill over and produce language disorders.

Many people with language disorders have a mixture of different degrees of damage at several levels of processing for both comprehension and production, although the proportions in that mixture can vary wildly, depending on what parts of the brain were injured, and how badly. So clinical testing is designed to figure out what's been damaged and what's in relatively good shape, at least well enough to plan rational treatment for clients, and communication coaching for them and the people who are important to them.

6.1.2 Focal: Does the brain damage really have to be focal for someone to have aphasia?

Focal (or local) brain damage is damage that still leaves a lot of the brain untouched. If a large part of the brain is damaged in addition to the areas that are directly involved in processing language (see Chapter 2, section 2.7), that is, if the brain damage is widely distributed or DIFFUSE, as it is in Alzheimer's disease, then many other things the brain has to do won't be working properly, either: maybe memory, planning, movement, sensation, or some part of the vital, complex, obscure activity that we call "thinking."

Now, here's where we bump into the "two rather different ways" that clinicians use the term *aphasia*. APHASIOLOGISTS (aphasia researchers and clinicians who specialize in clients with aphasia) use the term the way I defined it in section 6.1.1: the language problems of people who have no other major cognitive problem (although they may have motor and/or sensory impairments). These people usually do have a few cognitive problems (such as problems with arithmetic) that are detectable on clinical testing, but most of their brain is still working normally. (The National Aphasia Association says that there's *no* cognitive disorder in aphasia, but that's an overstatement. The NAA is trying to reach the general public— people who have no idea that language itself can be disordered, and who are likely to assume that disordered language always means disordered thinking.) Typically, people who have aphasia but no other cognitive damage have had relatively small strokes (from a problem with blood supply to a small volume of the brain), local head wounds, or small tumors that are in or very close to their brain's language areas.

But researchers and clinicians who work in a more general setting, quite reasonably, use "aphasia" to describe language problems that may only be a small part of their clients' difficulties: people with traumatic brain injury from closed or open head wounds; people with large strokes that include some or all of the language areas; people with Alzheimer's disease and other degenerative brain diseases that affect many abilities, including language; and people with tumors or cysts that cause pressure throughout their brains. Those aren't focal brain injuries; they are cases of widespread damage. And they can't be approached clinically without taking all that other damage into account.

So, when you talk to someone about aphasia, you need to make sure whether they are thinking about aphasia that's a client's major problem, or aphasia that's just one part of a much larger cognitive problem. In this book, we'll use the first sense of aphasia: a language processing problem with few or no other cognitive problems.

6.1.3 Acquired: Why does it matter when a language disorder starts?

Now, what about the word "acquired"? We need to make a distinction between language disorders that start very early in life—usually called **DEVELOPMENTAL LANGUAGE DISORDERS** or **DEVELOPMENTAL DYSPHASIA**—and those that are acquired—that is, those that start after someone has become a fully competent speaker of one or more languages. (There's also a gray area here: language disorders caused by brain injuries that happen after infancy but before late adolescence.) The symptoms and histories of developmental language disorders are different from those of acquired language disorders, because of **BRAIN PLASTICITY**: the brain's ability to change in response to what happens to it. Our brains, as you know by now, become finely honed language processing machines for the languages we use frequently and from early on. But because children haven't had as many years of practice at language use, children's brains haven't become organized to process language as efficiently as adult brains do. And infants' brains have only just begun to be organized by hearing the language around them. If an infant has a language processing problem before she can even talk, the way her brain processes language will be different from the start, and that means the language disorder won't look much like the problems of people who have had damage to part of a mature language processing system.

6.1.4 How to talk—and listen!—to people with aphasia

Before you go further in this chapter, listen to some of the conversations in Materials for Chapter 6 on your CD between people with aphasia and people who have normal language. At first, you'll probably be put off by the strangeness, by how hard the people with aphasia are working, and by your difficulty in understanding them, but keep trying; the subtitles and transcripts will help, when they are available. Here are some of the key things to remember when you are talking to people with aphasia:

1. Take it slow, and encourage them to do the same thing; act as if you have all the time in the world. You know enough about language processing now to be able to imagine how their brains are working overtime as they try to understand you and to speak to you. (As you get to know the person, you'll be able to judge the pace more accurately by watching and listening to their reactions to what you say.)

2. Look at your aphasic conversation partner; watch his or her face for indications of understanding or confusion; if they look confused by what you've said, ask if it's okay if you try saying it again.

3. Use multiple channels. Make gestures when you can think of them; write down words in nice clear letters if you think your aphasic conversation partner hasn't understood you; encourage them to gesture, write, or draw, if they can. If your conversation partner uses a word that doesn't make sense, and you have some idea what word they wanted, even if they can give you only its first letter, it will narrow down your range of guesses and make things much easier. But some people with aphasia can't use writing at all, so don't push it.

4. Say words in phrases or sentences, especially if you're repeating them because the person you're talking to apparently didn't understand them the first time. People with aphasia, just like the rest of us, rely on top-down processing to help identify a difficult word (although their syntactic top-down processing usually is less reliable than that of people without brain damage).

5. Check your understanding! Don't just say *uh-huh* if you didn't get it; try saying back to your partner what you think they said, and watch their reactions. You could be quite wrong about what they meant, and if you don't check up, you can come away from the conversation with a lot of misinformation.

6. Think about what you're going to say, and keep your sentences as simple as you can. Speaking slowly will help you do this, because you can monitor yourself better.

7. Treat your aphasic conversation partner like an intelligent adult: a person with valuable information and an interesting life that you could learn about.

6.2 Aphasic Language Is Not Like Child Language

Before there were easy ways to record sound, it was hard to make accurate studies of either aphasic language or young children's language, and the idea that aphasia was like a regression to child language was very appealing—almost poetic. The regression hypothesis was supported by two of the few genuine resemblances between children and aphasic people: First, some nonfluent aphasic speakers who can't reliably manage a range of morphology and syntax rely heavily on the verb and noun forms that are the most frequent and semantically clear, and those are the forms that are, in general, also the ones that are easiest for children to learn. Second, speakers with dysarthria (articulation problems) often have trouble with the same sounds that are hard for young children to pronounce.

But let's draw on what we know by now about brains and how they learn. We should expect language to be fundamentally quite different in people who had brain damage after they had fully developed language and in young children who are just learning to understand and speak. Why?

You might refer again to Chapter 2, sections 2.4.2 and 2.4.3, and our (made-up) example of "Jenny" learning to blow out a candle at the age of two and then, after a stroke at age 80, trying to show an examiner how she would blow one out. The point of those sections was that young children's brains are busy taking in huge quantities of information, and making the connections between new images, sounds, and all sorts of other sensory information, plus memories of previous collections of similar sensory information—connections that will enable them to extract the patterns of events (including what people around them say) and predict what's likely to happen when they're in a similar situation. Activation spreads out widely (although it may use rather specific channels when it has to travel over the long neural distances from one area of the brain to another). We might say that a young brain is like a landscape with lots of little footpaths (plus a few very important roads that were probably there before birth: the connections between a touch on the lips and starting to suck, and between vital stimuli—food, soft patterned sounds, faces, gentle touch—and pleasure).

Mature brains, in contrast, have an enormous network of connections that have already been made, and activation spreads along those very rapidly; we might say that your brain has been widening the most used paths, paving some of them into roads, and building some of those up into superhighways with major interchanges, a bit at time, over your entire lifetime. At the same time, many of the little footpaths, the ones that were rarely or never used, have become completely overgrown or washed away.

Now, what happens when a hurricane hits a mature brain? It's easy enough to imagine. If it doesn't obliterate everything, there will be a path of destruction, there will be a fringe of partial damage, and there will be substantial areas where the paths, roads, highways, and interchanges are still intact, whether or not traffic comes along to flow on them. Aphasic language production and comprehension are part of the traffic that still limps or runs through this partly ruined world; where it still happens to run, it is not at all like child language, but where it's limping through, it may be relatively childlike. And where the paths for activation are completely wiped out, language processing may even be poorer than a young child's.

6.3 Aphasic Language Production

6.3.0 How we'll approach analyzing aphasic speech production

After you've listened to the aphasic speech samples in Materials for Chapter 6 on your CD and gotten over your first shock or bewilderment, one of the first things that will strike you about the speech of people with aphasia is how different they are from one another. This means that different things must have gone wrong in their language processing. If we want to understand their disorders in terms of our model of language processing, and come up with appropriate treatments, the first step would seem to be to classify their production and comprehension problems: divide and conquer, again. But it turns out that this is not easy. Brain damage is quite different from one person to the next, and brain organization for language processing is at least a bit different, too, as you'd expect, once you think about how it develops from each person's individual experience with using language. The damaged area can be one large, irregularly shaped portion of the brain, or it can be several smaller areas with different shapes and sizes. And areas that aren't damaged still may not be functioning properly, because the information flowing into or out of them is impaired.

So it's hard to make psycholinguistic sense based on what part of the brain has been damaged, although researchers have tried to do it for over a hundred years. It may be possible to separate out areas of the brain that are particularly heavily involved in processing semantics and phonology, but a major 2007 study by a senior team from the Massachusetts General Hospital has found great individual differences in the parts of the brain that are damaged when people have trouble understanding sentences with complicated syntax, and it has also shown that many areas outside the "language areas" are involved in processing those complicated sentences. Other recent brain imaging studies have found multiple areas of the brain involved in other language tasks, and still others have found that the "language areas" are active when we listen to music. Perhaps the most interesting newer idea is that the major job of one of the traditional language areas, Broca's area, may in fact be to settle the competition among all kinds of items that have been aroused simultaneously, not just the competition among the constructions and words that your brain will use to put together or to understand a sentence. Because of these and similar findings, from now on I'm going to use the term LANGUAGE SENSITIVE AREA that's beginning to appear in professional publications, instead of the traditional term LANGUAGE AREA.

Classifying people's language disorders by describing everything that's wrong with each person's language and then sorting the disorders into types or SYNDROMES has problems, too, because there are so many possible mixtures of language difficulties. It's as problematic as classifying all the people you know into personality types—there are so many possible varieties and mixtures of human behavior that any simple classification (extrovert/introvert, optimist/pessimist, Meyers-Briggs . . .) only gets at a small part of the description of a person. In the same way, clinical experience with aphasia suggests that, if you have a system that's simple to use, it will lump people together who really seem, on closer examination, to be quite different. So we won't start out with the standard classification of aphasic disorders into syndromes, either; we'll postpone it until section 6.6.

For psycholinguistic analysis, the best way to start is with learning to see the evidence for language error patterns in people with aphasia; then we can use what we've learned about language processing to think about what their brains seem to be having trouble with. But observation still leaves us with many unanswered questions about what might be working or not working, especially about what a person really can understand, so after we learn something about language observation, we will follow up with some results from experimental work on aphasia, and, in Chapter 10, with a psycholinguistic analysis of some standard clinical aphasia test tasks.

When people with aphasia talk, what do you listen for and look for? Here's a list that comes from many years of studying aphasic language. You can use it as a checklist, for the most part, but the starred items are questions that are usually too hard to answer on the fly; to deal with them, you'd need to write down all the words and word-attempts that you hear in a transcription. The art of transcribing speech, normal or disordered, takes quite a while to learn, so basic transcripts are also provided on your CD. In section 6.4.2, we'll look more closely at just the words and grammar on some transcriptions of audiotapes.

Guide list

Below is a list of what to look and listen for on a video, in order to understand what parts of language processing are still available to a person with aphasia. The starred items are ones that can be evaluated by looking at an ordinary ("secretarial") transcript of a conversation; the others require audio or video records.

Comprehension

If it looks to you like the person understands what's being said, there are two things to document.

1. What's your **evidence** that the aphasic person really understood what they heard? If they just had an "understanding look," or responded with a nod or an *uh-huh*, is it possible that they thought they understood but really didn't? Look carefully at:

    a. What they said

    b. Their facial expressions

    c. Their gesture or posture

2. How **difficult** would it have been for a normal listener to understand the input? Could the meaning have been understood if the listener had understood:

    a. Just the intonation of interviewer,

    b. The separate words plus the intonation,

    c. Or would they have needed to do real syntactic processing?

Production

There are many things to notice and document about even a short production sample or its transcript; you'll need to listen to it/read through it several times to complete this checklist. The first five items are about speech, gesture, and cognitive matters; questions about language come later.

1. Nonspeech responses—gesture

    a. Are some/many/all responses just vocalizations plus gaze and gesture where words would be expected?

    b. Are there vocalizations without gestures? Do they still seem to be responses (or attempted responses) to the interviewer?

    c. Are gestures used to replace and/or clarify words? *What kinds of words?

    d. Do the gestures help you understand the speaker or are they too vague?

    e. Do gestures seem to help the speaker? Why do you think so, if you do?

2. Hesitations

    a. Are there many hesitations before words?

    b. Are they short (normal-seeming) or long?

3. Articulation and articulatory planning

    a. Are there struggles to articulate words, or misarticulated words?

    b. Are there nonwords (word-like sounds that don't seem to be real words)?

   c. If so, do they seem to be scrambled or shortened versions of real words?

   d. Are the nonwords blends of real words (as in Chapter 4)?

   e. Are the nonwords clearly articulated or mushy?

4. Fatigue or cognitive load effects

   a. Are there changes in the quality of the articulation during the time the person is speaking?

   b. Does the speaker seem to start to say things and then run into problems and restart? (Some of this is quite normal, and in a short video clip, you may be unable to tell whether there's enough of this to indicate a language problem.)

5. Non-speech responses—graphic

   a. Does the speaker use writing or drawing to help convey ideas?

   b. Is there any information about whether the speaker can read and write?

6. *Amount of speech

   a. Is the speaker's turn elaborate or minimal?

   b. Does the speaker seem eager to add information? (Minimal responses could be just be a normal personal style, or they could be a strategy that an aphasic person is using to stay out of linguistic trouble.)

   c. Does the speaker use descriptive phrases that seem to be substitutes for names and words they need but can't find (CIRCUMLOCUTIONS)?

7. *Word variety, CONVENTIONAL PHRASES, and syntactic structure of language

   a. Does the speaker use isolated single words or short phrases, without putting them into sentences?

   b. Is the person producing just 2 to different 5 words like *yes, no, uh-oh* (possibly repeated), or are there more different words than that?

   c. Are there conventional, formulaic phrases like *good morning, and that's all, you know, wait a minute, I don't know*? If so, does the person seem to rely on such phrases a lot? *If so, what percentage of their phrases are conventional phrases? Are the conventional phrases better articulated or syntactically more complete than the rest of what the speaker produces?

8. *Lexicon: Do words seem to be missing, or replaced with inadequate/odd substitutes?

   a. If there are missing or clearly substituted words, list the missing "targets" (if you can reconstruct them), and also list the words used as substitutes, if there are any.

   b. The words that seem to be missing: are they nouns, verbs, functors, and/or others?

   c. Compare the target words to the words used to substitute for them: Which substitutions seem to be phonological or phonetic (right target word in mind, wrong sounds produced)? Which ones seem to be semantic errors (words semantically related to the target? Are there unrecognizable "words"? Real but wildly unrelated words?

   d. When you compared the target words to the words used to substitute for them, did you feel that the substitutes have something in common with one another, or in their relationship to the target words?

9. *Morphology

   a. Are there verbs that are used with the wrong tense (or with the tense changing erratically from past to present during the speaker's turn)?

   b. Are there nouns that are plural when they should be singular or vice versa?

10. Numbers

   a. *Does the speaker have particular trouble with numbers?

   b. If so, do you see the speaker using a strategy to help say numbers?

   c. If so, is finger-counting used as a strategy?

6.3.1 A clinical tool for studying language production

To be able to study a person's language production, you have to get them to talk, and if you want to know how good a job they can do at getting information across, you need to know what that information is. (It's the same for language learners, or for anyone whose language ability needs to be evaluated, of course.) You can ask them about their families or their lives if you already know a lot about that from what is in their records, but if you want to compare people's abilities with one another and with some kind of standard criterion, you need a standard ELICITATION TASK—a standard story for them to tell. A very popular elicitation tool that clinicians and language disorders researchers use to get samples of people's speech is a picture used through all the editions of the Boston Diagnostic Aphasia Examination, the **COOKIE THEFT PICTURE** (Figure 6.1).

The Cookie Theft picture is a picture of 1960s suburban American kitchen gone haywire. A woman is drying a dish and looking off into space while water is overflowing her sink and splashing onto the floor at her feet; behind her back, a boy of about 10 is standing on a teetering stool trying to reach a container labeled COOKIE JAR. A girl about the same age is standing on the floor next to him with one hand reaching up—presumably to get a cookie from him—and the other near her mouth. What the hand near her mouth means isn't clear: She might be telling him to be quiet, or covering a laugh, or she might have suddenly realized that he's about to fall.

What makes this picture such a good one to use to get people to talk is that, first, there's a story here, and it's more involving than ordinary activity pictures because you can't be quite sure what the story is. Second, you can't tell the story properly without using verbs, without talking about the children's intentions and the mother's state of mind, or without

Copyright © 1983 by Lea & Febiger

Figure 6.1. Cookie Theft elicitation picture. From *Boston Diagnostic Aphasia Examination—Third Edition* (BDAE-3), H. Goodglass with E. Kaplan and B. Barresi, Copyright © 2001 PRO-ED. Used with permission.

relating the events to a timeline (some of the events are happening simultaneously, but the boy hasn't yet fallen off the stool). Many elicitation pictures are missing one or several of these demands on the speaker's morphology and syntax, so they can't give us as much information about their language limitations.

6.3.2 Using the checklist to analyze a transcript

Let's focus on the some of the words and grammar in three transcriptions of aphasic Cookie Theft narratives. Keep the picture in mind as you read these; you'll see that all three of these clients have understood the picture and are tuned into all of the things that are going wrong in that suburban kitchen. We can't count on these ordinary written transcriptions to give us information about articulation, gestures, and timing (although the dashes in the transcript do tell us that there were hesitations), so let's start with item 6 on the checklist, the amount of speech. On your CD's materials for this chapter, you'll find an analysis of a video using the full checklist, and you'll be able to see how the first five items on it work.

> **Client 1:** "Water spills. Turn it off. Cookie jar and he wanta give her that thing. Oh boy. A fall—fall." (Ex: "Anything else?") "Sink is full. Washing the dishes."

> **Client 2:** "This one's not right—not doing it right. That lady—tryin' to get things out but can't reach. That was the one I told you. That lady, she didn't get a chance to make that right. But this kid—you know—another thing—just spillin' all on the wall. She's not doing a good job. I don't know why she does it. She's doing pretty good now."

> **Client 3:** "A girl washin' dishes and uh—cookie jar—a drip ah—drips." (Ex: "What does?") "The water drippin'." (Ex: "Where?") "On the floor." (Ex: "What's she doing?") "She ain't doin nothing." (Ex: "Why?") "Because she's wipin' the rest of the dish. Uh over there—uh—he's ah trying to fall off the la . . . (?) trying to fall off the ladder and he's trying to get a cookie."

6. Amount of speech

Client 2 produces a lot more words than the other two; the examiners have felt that they needed to encourage Clients 1 and 3 to keep going.

7. Word variety, conventional phrases, and syntactic structure

All three of these clients have varied words. As for conventional phrases, Client 1 apparently uses the exclamation *oh boy;* Client 2 uses *you know*, and also several short sentences with good grammar that seem very non-specific and rather conventional, like *She's not doing a good job*. When he is using specific phrases that clearly refer to the picture—*tryin' to get things out* and *spillin' all on the wall*—he doesn't manage to give complete sentences with smooth syntax.

Clients 1 and 3 both have words and phrases that aren't integrated into sentences, like *a fall* and *drips*; you can find others.

8. Lexicon—missing or substituted words

Client 1 isn't providing subject nouns for several of his sentences (it looks like he can give at most one specific noun per clause), and he says *thing* where we expect *cookie*. Client 2 provides only the nouns *lady* and *kid*, which are appropriate to the story. However, when he seems to be combining them with the verb phrases *spillin' all on the wall* and *tryin' to get things out*, it looks like the wrong subject is being used—*kid* with *spilling* and *lady* with *trying*. *On the wall* appears where we expect *on the floor*. Client 3 is not producing the words that he would need to integrate *cookie jar* and *drip* into a sentence; he also seems to have one verb substitution and one noun substitution, when he describes the boy as *trying to fall off the ladder* instead of *going to fall off the stool*. These errors are semantically related to their targets (in standard technical terms, they are SEMANTIC PARAPHASIAS). None of these patients seems to have made a phonological error like saying /grɪpɪŋ/ for "dripping" (a PHONOLOGICAL PARAPHASIA), or to have sounds made with a badly controlled articulatory gesture (a DYSARTHRIC pronunciation).

9. Morphology

There don't seem to be any wrong number or tense uses in these three short narratives; normal speakers very often use the present tense in describing events in pictures.

In section 6.4.2, we'll look at these three narratives in terms of our psycholinguistic production model and see what that can add to our understanding of aphasic language problems.

6.4 Figuring Out the Psycholinguistics Behind (Some) Aphasic Speech Production Errors

6.4.1 Analyzing naming task errors

We have three main kinds of sources for information on naming errors in aphasia. The first one is published collections of errors on a standard clinical test like the Boston Naming Test. Naming test errors are good for spotting possible unusual language behavior patterns, because the objects to be named on clinical naming tests are quite miscellaneous and cover a wide range of word frequencies. This means that patients' naming abilities can be compared, and changes in their ability to come up with names can be followed. The second main source is the results of experimental studies using naming tasks that are designed to look for differences in the names of different categories of words: typically, the categories are objects of different kinds (for example, animate/inanimate), numbers and letters, picturable actions, and colors (which seem to be the only modifiers that can be shown without using pictures of objects). The third source is case studies that follow up on individual people with aphasia who seem to have extreme differences in the categories they can and cannot name.

Word errors

In general, most people with aphasia who are trying to remember a name sound a lot like the rest of us when we're stuck for a word: While they are looking for it, they say words and phrases that are associated with it, or come up with words that sound somewhat like the one they need, often commenting that what they have isn't quite right. All sorts of associated words and nonwords show up:

- semantically related words: *broccoli* for "asparagus," *coat rack* for "hanger," *brand* for "label"

- words that are commonly used together with the needed word: *ox* or *oxen* for "yoke"

- phonologically related words: *melon* for "medal," *leper* for "label"

- phonologically related nonwords: *trethil* for "trellis," *meller* for "medal"

People with aphasia also produce words that seem to come from first activating a semantically related lemma, which then activates a more frequent phonologically related word form: For the target "trellis," a patient said *lettuce*, presumably for "lattice." (All the phonemes in *lettuce* are also in "trellis," so a partly activated but below-threshold "trellis" word form could have helped to activate the phonemes in *lettuce*.) Words that have appeared earlier on the test list and that have a phonological and/or semantic link to the current target are particularly likely to shove their way into a patient's output processing: on the Boston Naming Test, that list effect accounts for the somewhat unlikely sounding errors *pencil* for "muzzle," *tree* for "flower," *canoe* for "igloo." Patients also make up words and phrases: *hanger around the clocker* for "pendulum." (All of these errors and many more are from the Boston CORPUS of naming errors, which was published in the journal *Brain and Language* in 1998.)

But aphasic people with more severe impairments also do some things that normal speakers don't do: They sometimes say words that seem to come from a long distance (*ping-pong* for "abacus," possibly linked by the little balls on the abacus rods and the concept "Chinese"—these data are from the period in the 1970s when China was best known in America for its championship ping-pong teams) or from nowhere, and nonwords that seem to have no connection to the target. Or they may say the right word but fail to recognize it as the one they need.

Word assembly errors

There's also another kind of problem that is fairly uncommon but worth analyzing in terms of psycholinguistic levels. It typically shows up in patients who take multiple stabs at saying words of three or more syllables, as is typical of people with the syndrome called CONDUCTION APHASIA. Here are some examples of one person's attempt to name a picture of a helicopter, from the Boston Naming Test: /hɛlipo/, /hɛlopɛt/, /pɛlo/, /hɛlətɪl/, /hɛlibl/, /hɛlətə/. And from another, similar patient: /kɛlə/, /kailətaptr/, /kilɪstaptr/, /kɛlɪstaptr/ (all of these were accented on the first syllable). These attempts contain so many correct target sounds that the target word form must have been activated, but the patients never actually manage to say it. Their problem isn't with articulating the sounds; they are produced quite clearly. They just keep coming out in the wrong order, and not all of the right sounds get into any one attempt. If you go back to normal slip-of-the-tongue errors in word sounds in Chapter 4, section 4.3, you'll also find nonwords that obey English phonotactic patterns, but there are differences: These aphasic speakers do not do quite as well at keeping sounds in the same place in the syllable, and, more importantly, their errors are within a single word, rather than involving switches between the sounds in two different words.

We'll follow the same reasoning that we used in Chapter 4 to analyze these errors; you might like to refer back to Figure 4.1. Because the right sounds and a lot of information about the word structure have been aroused, it looks like they occurred at a level below the Positional Level, which is where the sounds of the word (or at least the sounds of the word stem) were aroused as a block. We've said that the sounds get put in order at the Phonological Encoding Level, so in our model, that's the logical place for a problem with the ordering of the sounds to occur—either there, or in moving from there to the Speech Gesture Level, during some sort of word-assembling process. (The sounds come out clearly, so the mechanics of the articulatory gestures at the Speech Gesture Level—see Chapter 10, section 10.2.2—are also intact.)

It can be hard to convince people (including linguists!) who are not familiar with speech errors that an assembly process like this exists, because we don't have an intuitive understanding of it or of how it can go wrong. although we do intuitively understand "not remembering a word" and "not having clear pronunciation." Why should there be a complex process of word assembly between remembering (at the Positional Level) and pronouncing (at the Speech Gesture Level)? Why should a word need to be "assembled" when "remembering it" already must include remembering the order of its sounds as well as what they are? But what we have to conclude objectively (whether or not it seems logical in advance) is that the process of saying a word must have an assembly stage, because otherwise, we wouldn't get assembly errors. It's largely the job of psycholinguists to figure out how that assembly process works; we're still working on it.

Trouble with names in specific semantic categories

Let's move now from word forms up to semantics, and talk about two kinds of studies that show that our brains really make use of the kinds of semantic categories that we introduced in Chapter 3, section 3.3.1. One of the most fascinating findings from category naming studies is that, for some people with aphasia, words in one category may be significantly better or worse than words in some other category. People with nonfluent aphasias tend to be relatively poorer at naming actions like *running* or *smoking*, while people with fluent aphasias generally seem to have more trouble coming up with names for objects. In Chapter 5, section 5.3.1, I made quite a point of the importance of the general finding that more frequent words are faster/easier to retrieve, because it's strong support for our connection-strengthening view of learning. But that direct relationship between word frequency and word retrievability is obviously messed up when, for example, common action-naming words are harder to produce than less common object names.

While you think about this, we'll look at a case study of a man with aphasia who had an astounding difference between categories of nouns; after we've discussed his language, we'll see a way to account for both frequency and category effects on word retrieval. Our aphasia clinic saw a man who had been a civil engineer and who had had a severe stroke. After his stroke, he couldn't produce any personal names, not even those of his wife and grown children. Instead he used numbers to refer to them (*forty years old, six foot one*), and also to clinical personnel (using our birth dates, or sometimes our ages; always accurately, including making me a year older after my birthday came around). He also named colors perfectly, but his object naming was very, very poor—he couldn't name even the pictures of a house or a pencil (items 1 and 3 on the Boston Naming Test). He also seemed to be missing the ability to visualize an object; for example, he couldn't match the picture of an object that has a typical color (like a banana or a flamingo) with a square showing that color. However, he could correctly name any state in the United States, and on naming and other clinical tests, such as the Wechsler Adult Intelligence Scale, he would let us know, whenever possible, that he at least knew what things were, by giving appropriate numbers (and measuring units) related to the correct answer: *2,000 pounds* in response to the picture of a rhinoceros, *600 or 700 AD* in response to *What is the Koran?*

Researchers have put a great deal of effort into trying to figure out whether category-specific name problems and preservations happen because information that is crucial to activating words of different semantic and grammatical categories is stored in different places in the brain (at least in some brains), or whether there's something else that is different between different categories of words. In particular, perhaps what differs between categories is what kind of (or how much) stored visual information has to be available to arouse a concept strongly enough to start the process of arousing the lemma, and then the phonological form. If stored visual information about an object is wiped out or no longer linked to the concept, then even if you see a picture of it, your activation of that concept might be too weak to support naming it.

Both options may well be correct, for different people with different types of aphasia—and opinions are sure to change as more research is done over the next decade. The important thing to remember is this: Arousing a concept strongly enough so that it can activate an appropriate lemma, and so that the lemma can then arouse the word form, usually involves adding up activations that are being relayed in from several different parts of the brain to wherever the concept is stored. If your brain is working well, you don't need all of those sources of activation (you can recognize a drawing of a banana without cues from its color, let alone those you'd get from smelling and tasting it), but the worse trouble your brain is in, the more you need strong total activation of the concept coming in from somewhere. Damage to a large part of the brain may destroy or interrupt some sources of activation of a concept, so that its lemma can't be aroused, no matter how frequent the word is. Analogy: If you are just barely making a living by scraping together money from several jobs or other income sources, you can go broke by having any one of them taken away. Similarly, if you are just barely able to arouse a concept (or a lemma or a word form), your ability to name it can be wiped out by loss of any of the activation sources you have been depending on. So there are likely to be many ways in which naming can be impaired that are not related to a word's frequency. Some of them may relate directly to the semantics of a word, and others may be "pre-semantic," relating instead to how the real object looks or to some other sensory property, like whether it is something you are likely to have handled frequently during your lifetime. (Go back to the story of Jenny's attempt to show how to blow out a candle, Chapter 2, section 2.4.3 for another illustration of this idea.)

6.4.2 Analyzing problems and errors in connected speech in English

Now, as promised, we'll look psycholinguistically at the language problems in the three written narratives, the problems that we found using the checklist. More severely affected patients will have problems of types that we are not covering here; for a more complete listing, look at any of the aphasia books listed in this chapter's Further Readings in Materials for Chapter 6 on your CD.

Our thoughts about what might be behind these mistakes are speculations, but they do help us see the connections between normal and aphasic speech errors. Use the checklist structure again, starting from item 6, where the list really gets into language.

6. Amount of speech

If there is too little, the speaker could be having difficulty with almost any level of speech production from lemma arousal to phonetic control—or with all of them.

If there is too much speech, and much of it seems to be syntactically okay and well articulated but vague, as in Client 2's narrative, two things are happening. First, the speaker has difficulty in activating lemmas for the most specific words that are needed (GIRL, MOTHER, FLOOR, WATER, DISH, STOOL . . .). This is probably related to frequency—vague nouns like *thing* and vague verbs like *do* are very common—and also we probably have an automatic fall-back strategy of using *thing* any time that we can't find some specific word we need.

Second, the speaker probably also has the uncomfortable sense of not having said what she wanted. So she keeps on going with whatever she can manage to say, which leads us to the next section in our checklist.

Client 3 seems to be able to say more relevant words, but he needs to be coaxed to speak. We'll see that his problem seems to be at some very general level of overall speech production arousal.

7. Word variety, conventional phrases, and syntactic structure

In these small speech samples and with these three moderately language-impaired clients, we haven't noticed problems with word variety, but speakers with severely impaired language may be reduced to using very few words—perhaps only *yes* and *no*. For whatever reason or reasons, no other words in their brains are being activated enough to be produced.

Although our three clients are not severely impaired, Client 1 (as well as Client 2) is having trouble with word activation. Aphasic speakers who are trying to say something but who can't get specific words activated often fall back on various types of conventional phrases. Some of those are EVALUATIVE: They express the speaker's feelings about an event, like *This one's not right* and *She's not doing a good job*. Other conventional phrases may be more about their difficulty in speaking, like *Oh boy* and perhaps *I don't know why*. These phrases don't require activation of a specific concept (FLOOR, WATER, DISH, etc.) or the flow of activation from those concepts to their lemmas to their phonological forms. Instead, they are stored as wholes or as formulas (see Chapter 4, section 4.1.3), and they are probably aroused partly by emotions.

When we find isolated noun phrases, like *cookie jar* and *a fall* in Client 1's narrative, the problem could be activating the other words in the phrases and clauses that they should have been part of. Or it could be more complex: It could be a syntax problem, or a problem with coordinating the words and the syntax. Let's work this out, using what we said about semantics and syntax in Chapter 1, section 1.7 and sentence assembly in Chapter 3, sections 3.4 and 3.6, and Chapter 4, section 4.1. We're doing this not just for the fun of going through the logic, but because it could actually matter in choosing appropriate therapy materials, and in explaining to the clients' families (and to the clients) that they are not as confused about the world as they sound.

Let's review what's involved in coordinating words and syntax so that a whole sentence comes out with a correct meaning. First, the Message Level has to create the Functional Level. That process begins on the word side with the concepts activating the lemmas of words that could be used to refer to them (THE LADY, THE MOTHER, THE WOMAN, THE HOUSEWIFE; THE BOY, THE KID; THE GIRL, THE OTHER KID). On the syntax side, with the many possible event structures (boy will fall off stool, stool is falling, water is overflowing, water is spilling, faucet is running, woman is drying a dish . . .), it begins with calling up the verb lemmas (and tenses) and assigning the participants in the scene to their semantic roles. In this story, there's a particular event structure choice that must be made (or dodged) by everyone who narrates it: Will the verb that relates the girl, the boy, and the cookie be *give* (*The boy is giving the girl a cookie*) or *get* (*The girl is getting a cookie from the boy*)?

Already, then, during the formation of the Functional Level there is lots of competition among activated lemmas and event structures, and it has to settle out in a way that will tell a coherent story. So there could be problems with too much or too little arousal at these early linguistic processing steps, resulting in an incomplete or poorly constructed Functional Level.

The next job is constructing the Positional Level (which won't come out right unless the Functional Level was well done). To do this, the noun and verb lemmas have to arouse the phonological forms of their words, the role tags (Agent, Undergoer, Recipient . . .) have to get attached to the word forms, and the aroused words have to stay in a buffer, with their tags securely attached, until it's time for them to be used. The verb lemmas also have to set up the slots for the noun phrases that will be their subjects and objects; they may need to call up prepositions, as well, to make the prepositional phrases to express Source (*from the faucet, from the cookie jar, off the stool*) and Goal (*into the sink, onto the floor, into space*). If *give* was chosen at the Functional Level, there's yet another choice here: Will the slots around the lemma GIVE be set up with the recipient GIRL as the indirect object (BOY GIVES GIRL COOKIE) or as the object of a preposition (BOY GIVES COOKIE TO GIRL)? And then the words have to move from the buffer to the proper slots, according to the verb's specifications.

Look at all the new opportunities for things to go wrong; constructing a grammatical sentence whose meaning matches the picture begins to look like a miracle, doesn't it? It's no wonder that we get errors like *The boy gives to the girl a cookie* when the competition among possible ways to tell the story doesn't settle out quite right.

And finally, the Positional Level has to transmit all its information to the level of Phonological Encoding, and from there to the Speech Gesture Level—in other words, to the articulators and the vocal folds, so that the pronunciation and the rise and fall of the voice pitch come out properly.

At this point, you've realized that we can't possibly work through all the ways that things might go wrong in constructing the syntax for describing the Cookie Theft picture, or even all the things that might have gone wrong with the syntax used by our three sample clients. But let's start to look at Client 1, and you can do some more if you like; see this chapter's Challenge section on the CD.

Here again is the first part of Client 1's story: *Water spills. Turn it off. Cookie jar and he wanta give her that thing. Oh boy. A fall—fall.*

Because there's nothing wrong with *Water spills*, although it's abnormally minimal (and in this way, typical for a nonfluent aphasic speaker), let's start by analyzing *Turn it off.* Here's we see something that happens occasionally with nonfluent patients whose grammar seems limited. Instead of producing a full subject + verb-phrase utterance that would be usual in a narrative, they use a simpler construction, an **IMPERATIVE**—a command that would be appropriate if they were actually interacting with the people in the picture, like telling the mother *Turn it off* or telling the boy *Watch out!* Imperatives are syntactically simple to construct because they don't have to have a subject slot, and if they don't add one, there's no need to make the verb agree with anything. Imperative forms also seem to get some extra activation from emotional arousal, which helps the aphasic speaker to produce them.

Now, what about *Cookie jar and he wanta give her that thing?* First, why is *Cookie jar* off on its own, with no verb? Saying *cookie jar* is not a good way to start a sentence that would fit smoothly into this story; normal speakers use intransitive structures like *There's a cookie jar up on a shelf* or transitive ones like *The boy's trying to get cookies from a cookie jar.* If you just blurt out *cookie jar* (perhaps because you're afraid you'll lose it if you don't say it quickly, or perhaps because you can't hold it in) it's hard to figure out what to say next. So this could be a problem with a buffer that can't hold onto lemmas until they are needed, or a problem with assigning an appropriate Source semantic role tag to the lemma COOKIE JAR so that it "knows" to wait until a source is needed in a clause. Or the client may be unable—for many possible reasons—to make the rest of a complete clause that would have the cookie jar in it. (Maybe he can only activate *cookie jar* because he's reading its label in the picture.)

Let's turn to the clause *he wanta give her that thing*. The syntax is fine, but the semantics is a bit off target. The picture makes it clear that the boy wants a cookie, and probable that the girl wants the boy to give her one, but whether the boy wants to give her one is not so clear. We could make up a couple of ways to account for what our client has said, but one way or another, this clause looks like a blend of the materials that would have been aroused by the two event structures "boy wants cookie" and "boy will give girl cookie." You can compare it to the normal blend errors in Chapter 4, section 4.1.3.

Oh boy is a formulaic exclamation (see Chapter 4, section 4.1.3), and all the more interesting in that the client never manages to use the word *boy* in a construction. *A fall—fall* is even more interesting; we mentioned earlier in this chapter that nonfluent speakers usually have relatively more trouble naming verbs on test pictures (*falling, drinking*) than nouns, and here we see Client 1 using the noun phrase *a fall* instead of even the isolated verbal noun *falling*. We don't know whether this problem is because people with nonfluent aphasia have relatively more trouble getting their concept of an event to arouse a Functional Level event structure, with having the event structure arouse verb lemmas, or both of these, or possibly some other explanation. My guess is that it's both of these, because trouble arousing a verb lemma generally seems to go with trouble naming a picture showing *falling* when there's no story involved, and trouble arousing the event structure could explain why we don't get *boy—a fall* or *a fall—the boy*. But you and I both can come up with other stories about what might have gone wrong.

Client 2 looks very different in some ways—as we noted using the checklist, his syntax looks much better, and he has several short complete sentences. The problem we noted is that they are vague; worse, the last one, *She's doing pretty good now*, doesn't make any sense at all as a statement about the picture. And in his two utterances that are specific, *That lady—tryin' to get things out but can't reach* and *But this kid—you know—another thing—just spillin' all on the wall*, when apparently he tries to get relevant nouns integrated into sentences that actually specify events in the picture, something goes wrong.

Without access to the audio files, and without knowing where Client 2 was looking or pointing, we unfortunately have a problem before we can even get into analyzing these two utterances—and it's a problem that's all too frequent. What do those dashes mean? Is *That lady* the subject of the verb phrase *tryin' to get things out but can't reach*? In more general terms, is it part of the same construction as the verb phrase? Or did Client 2 find that he couldn't continue a sentence starting with *That lady*, break it off, and switch mentally to talking about the boy, without supplying the words *The boy*? The same question needs to be asked about *But this kid —you know—another thing—just spillin' all on the wall*, which is why I had to say that he "apparently . . . tries to get relevant nouns integrated into sentences." Maybe he wasn't trying any such thing.

But what we can say with confidence is that when Client 2 provides a specific noun that looks like it's going to be a sentence subject, he can't integrate it with an appropriate verb phrase to yield a complete sentence. Psycholinguistically, one story we could tell about this is that the picture has aroused enough words and syntax to make several partially constructed sentences, but that his brain might be unable to manage the competition among them. We all know the feeling of having too much to say and having our words tumble out in a rather messy way when some of them should be waiting in a buffer for their turn; perhaps Client 2 has the same problem, but much worse.

Some experimental studies have tried to look at what parts of syntactic processing are available in aphasic speech production. When a verb needs more noun phrases to fill its slots, that clearly makes producing a clause more difficult; in other words, if the verbs are of roughly equal frequency, a clause with a verb like *run*, which needs only a subject, is easier than a clause with a verb like *push*, which needs both a subject and an object; hardest is a verb like *put*, which needs a subject, and object, and a location. Also, verbs that have Agents as their subjects are probably easier, in general, than verbs that have any other kind of semantic role as the subject. Some experiments suggest that it is not just passive constructions (Undergoer or Theme = subject) that are difficult to produce, but also constructions using verbs like *sink* in sentences like *The ship sank*, where again the subject is the Undergoer, even though the verb is in the active voice.

8. Lexicon—missing or substituted words

We've already noticed that not one of the people in Client 1's story is referred to with a noun; he uses pronouns for boy and girl, but *Washing the dishes* has no subject—the mother is completely missing. As we know, Client 2 has managed to activate both of the lemmas LADY and KID, but he hasn't been able to put them in appropriate subject slots; if those utterances really were intended as clauses, then he had substitution errors for both clause subjects. That means that those two noun lemmas were both activated, and were twice in competition for the subject slot, the wrong one winning each time.

Client 3 has a verb substitution error; in *Uh over there—uh—he's ah trying to fall off the la . . . (?) trying to fall off the ladder and he's trying to get a cookie* it's pretty clear that the verb lemma TRYING TO was too strongly activated by the boy's evident effort in getting the cookie and muscled its way in where the future GOING TO was needed.

9. Morphological errors

Although these clients didn't make morphological errors, using *trying to* instead of *going to* is rather like a tense error (technically, it is an ASPECT error—see the Glossary). Although it's a word choice (lexical) error in English, there may be languages in which the same kind of error in meaning would be a matter of choosing the wrong affix for a verb. When we discuss test translation in Chapter 10, section 10.2 we'll come back to real examples where what is a word choice error in one language would be equivalent to a bound morpheme choice error in another language.

6.4.3 Cross-linguistic studies and the psycholinguistics of aphasic language production

As we began to see in Chapter 1, section 1.10.1, some other languages have much more complicated morphology than English. This means that their speakers have a lot more opportunity to make morphological errors. For example, German nouns can be masculine [der Wolf—the wolf], feminine [die Grossmutter—the grandmother], or neuter [das Rotkäppchen— Little Red Riding Hood], singular or plural, and they have different CASE forms—that is, different endings depending on whether they are subjects, objects, possessors, indirect objects, or objects of particular prepositions. Also, most nouns and the words that agree with them (adjectives, articles, and verbs) have different forms for the singular and the plural. In German, the definite article has six different forms, and the way those forms are used to agree with the nouns in the various gender-number-case combinations is quite complicated. What we find is that German speakers with aphasia may hesitate and switch back and forth among several forms; this means that those forms must all have been aroused and competing with each other in the speaker's brain while he was searching for the right one. Because adjectives have to agree in gender, number, and case with the nouns that they modify, a lot of work is involved in arousing the right forms and managing the competition when you are creating a German noun phrase!

More generally, if a noun, adjective, or article has many different forms in a language that has case marking, several of them will be aroused and be part of the competition to be spoken, at least when one of the less common forms is needed. For nouns, we know that the most common form, usually the nominative, is quite likely to be used instead of one of the less common ones—although not always. (People with fluent aphasias tend to make more wide-ranging errors; people with nonfluent aphasias are more likely to rely on the nominative case.) When there are many verb forms, the one that people with aphasia, especially nonfluent aphasia, often fall back on is the infinitive (e.g. French *chanter* "to sing," Italian *cantare*, Spanish *cantar*) if the language has such a form. In most European languages, the infinitive is very frequent, which makes its form easier to arouse, and it probably has some additional psycholinguistic advantages that researchers are still trying to understand.

If, on the other hand, there are few or no competing forms for some class of words in a language—for example, verbs in Chinese and Japanese, which you may remember have no person or number agreement to worry about—then choosing the wrong verb person or number form just can't happen in that language. Things do, however, go wrong with other parts of their grammars that are not like anything we have in English or other Indo-European languages.

Another difference between languages, as you know, is the order of words in clauses. In all of the Germanic languages except English, as we said in Chapter 1, section 1.10.1, there are two major required word orders —subject-verb-object for ordinary main clauses, and, usually, subject-object-verb for subordinate clauses. (These languages also have main clauses where the subject comes after the verb; the real form of the main clause requirement is that the verb has to be the second major item in the clause.) Aphasic speakers make errors when these different word orders compete with each other.

English has almost nothing analogous to such errors, except for a bit of competition in the syntax of "giving" events. In the Cookie Theft, as we saw earlier, errors seem to arise because the "give" event structure Agent-Theme-Recipient activates two slightly different constructions: subject-GIVE-object to recipient (which should result in *The boy gives a cookie to the girl*) and subject-GIVE-recipient object (which should result in *The boy gives the girl a cookie*). In some languages (like Italian), there's also a lot more freedom about word order than we have in English—you can pretty much start a clause with whatever noun phrase or verb phrase gets above activation threshold first. That should mean that nouns don't have to wait around in buffers so much, which might reduce some kinds of errors, but we don't have the right data to check out this idea yet—and in fact, surprisingly, people with nonfluent aphasia in languages with free word order usually seem to stick to subject-verb-object order even when they don't have to.

6.5 Psycholinguistic Considerations in Studying Aphasic Comprehension

6.5.0 The challenge of studying comprehension in people with aphasia

Just as there are different kinds of production problems, there are different kinds of comprehension problems. The comprehension problem may be mostly in understanding word meaning, or it may be in understanding morphology and/or syntax, or there may be substantial problems with both of these aspects of language.

There is a great range of severity of comprehension problems as well: A person who has aphasia may have comprehension that is nearly normal or seriously impaired. Sometimes there are specific problems in decoding the speech sound signal, which can complicate the aphasia. And the aphasic people almost always have trouble holding onto the exact words that someone has said to them, so that if there's something tricky about a sentence (like the misleading "garden-path" sentences of Chapter 5, section 5.1.2), they can't go back and reparse it the way you were able to do with those sentences. For older people, don't forget the extra burden of the ordinary problems of aging: Mild hearing loss and slower cognitive processing are "normal" as we get old.

Evaluating comprehension problems is much trickier than evaluating production problems, for two huge reasons. First, if you're trying to detect a comprehension problem from someone's conversation with you, they may be able to guess a lot of what you are saying from the context, your facial expressions, and your tone of voice, while picking up on just a few of your words and maybe almost none of your syntax. In that case (if their production problems aren't severe), they may give you very appropriate responses, and you may seriously overestimate how much of the actual language input they understand. That's how the false idea that most people with nonfluent aphasia have normal comprehension got started: They are often very good at compensating for it, which is of course very helpful to them.

Second, on the other extreme, if someone with aphasia has severe production problems—in the worst case, if he can't even reliably say *yes* when he means *yes* and *no* when he means *no*—he might actually understand a great deal and yet give verbal responses that would lead an observer to believe that he had understood nothing. (And experiments looking at brain responses in some people who seemed to understand almost no language even with careful clinical testing have shown that their brains still reacted differently to nonsense sentences and sensible ones.)

Because conversation has these serious limitations as a way to assess comprehension, clinicians and researchers have developed elaborate tests that ask people to carry out simple and then increasingly more complex instructions. We also check out comprehension of words and of different kinds of morphosyntactic structures, usually by asking the aphasic person to point to one out of two or more pictures that match a description, which can be as simple as "Point to the dog" or as complex as "Point to the clown that is being chased by the policeman." In Chapter 10, we talk more about test design, what tests test, and what you need to think about if you are trying to adapt a test created for one language to test comprehension in a different language.

In this section, we analyze just one kind of comprehension problem to show some of the things you might need to think about when a person with aphasia does badly on a comprehension test. This observation comes from a neurologist's demonstration at a teaching hospital. Imagine this scene: The doctor and the patient, both of whom wear eyeglasses, are sitting near each other with a small table between them. The doctor asks the patient to take off her glasses and put them on the table, and the doctor does the same thing, putting his glasses down so that they touch hers. The doctor says, *Point to my glasses*, and the patient does so; next he says *Point to your glasses*, and again, the patient responds correctly. The doctor says, *Put on your glasses*, gets a correct response, says, *Take off your glasses* and once again the patient gives a correct response. Then he gives the two pointing commands again, and the patient carries them out. Finally, the doctor says, *Put on my glasses*. The patient is stumped; perhaps she picks up and puts down one or the other pairs of glasses, and finally puts on her own glasses, not the doctor's.

What's going on here? Think about this in terms of top-down versus bottom-up language processing, and also in terms of a comprehension factor that I mentioned at the beginning of this section: Aphasia typically impairs the ability to mentally hold onto the exact words that someone has just said; in standard psychological terms, it impairs verbal WORKING MEMORY.

Does this patient understand the words *your* and *my* when they are the only words distinguishing the two pairs of glasses, even in an unfamiliar phrase like *Point to my glasses*? Yes. Does she understand *Put on your glasses*? Well, she does at least to this extent: If her glasses are sitting within view and the doctor says something about glasses, she puts them on or she points to them depending on what he said. So why, if she understands both *Put on* and *my glasses*, and can carry out the action of putting on a pair of glasses when she is asked to, does she seem to be unable to understand *Put on my glasses?* After all, her correct response to *Put on your glasses* wasn't just mechanical, as being the only thing the doctor could reasonably have been saying about glasses. We know that because we have seen that the patient has been able to take in the fact that there were two pairs of glasses on the table, and respond to the two contrasting pointing requests; furthermore, that she understands the difference between *point to* and *put on*. But at *Put on my glasses* (which could mean either *Put my glasses on your nose* or *Put my glasses on my nose*), her comprehension breaks down. The extra bit of top-down social inhibition—(*People, unless they are friends comparing vision problems, don't put on each other's glasses! And unless they are optometrists or helping an invalid, they don't put glasses on someone else!*)—combines with two other factors: First, both *my* and *your* are very close to their activation thresholds, because both of them have been repeatedly activated in this series of very similar requests (and on top of that, *my* and *your* activate each other because of their syntactic and semantic similarity—remember the pronoun-switching errors in Chapter 4, section 4.2.1). And second, the patient's impaired verbal working memory doesn't give her enough to fall back on—she can't replay the words of the doctor's request in her head. So she hesitates among the three possible *put on* _____ *glasses* actions (the way any of us might when we can't remember which of three similar grocery items we're supposed to bring home), and then she carries out the more plausible action.

Is she confused about the difference between what's hers and what's the doctor's? Of course not; if she were, she'd have no inhibition about putting on his glasses. But she is indeed confused, because she is caught in the competition among the meanings that were aroused by his words, while the words themselves have slipped away from her.

6.5.1 Language impairment and cognitive confusion

What I've just said might make it sound like people with aphasia only have language problems, not general cognitive problems. But that's false, for three reasons. The first two are anatomic: Probably the area of brain damage that caused the aphasia is large enough to damage at least a few areas of the brain that are crucial for other kinds of thinking. And second, even if the area of brain damage is all in the language sensitive areas, it will damage other kinds of thinking that happen to depend on activation of neurons in those same areas of the brain. For example, arithmetic ability is often impaired in people with aphasia (but not always—remember the civil engineer whom we discussed in section 6.4.1), so it may often depend on neurons in a language-sensitive area.

The third reason is psychological: Language is an important tool in many kinds of reasoning. To hold onto an idea (or at least all the kinds of ideas I can think of), we need to put it into words, pictures, musical notation, memories of movement, or some other form that can be aroused again when we need it. If language is impaired, some kinds of thinking— especially thinking about language itself—may become very difficult, even though others are still possible. And clients whose language seems to have recovered completely from aphasia may still find it extremely difficult, and perhaps impossible, to organize a business presentation or a lecture. They can construct all the sentences and recall all the words that they need, and yet organizing large quantities of information apparently makes demands on language abilities beyond what we currently understand—or on other abilities that depend on the same or adjacent areas of their brains.

6.5.2 Testing comprehension of words

For clients without much collateral brain damage from their injury, there are plenty of well-standardized test materials for comprehension of single words; they all involve pointing to one of several pictures in response to the name of one of them. Some tests are set up so that both spoken language and written language comprehension can be tested with the same pictures.

It's when brain injury is severe that comprehension testing gets complicated; the multiple pictures all will all partially arouse their names in the person's brain, and the additional arousal added by your written or spoken stimulus word may not be strong enough to shout down that competition. Sometimes clients have extremely poor comprehension when they are tested formally, but can do much better when the same words are used in their usual contexts. For example, a person who cannot reliably respond to an examiner's request *Point to the light switch* may respond to *Would you mind turning on the light?* by getting up and doing it quite normally. You can see why this would be the case: The context of an action request will provide just a bit of additional activation to the dozen or so kinds of things that people may reasonably ask others to do in a room—opening or closing a door or window, moving a chair, turning the lights or the heating off or on. In contrast, *point-to* questions (besides being a bit weird outside of an examination context) leave open all the visible people, things, and parts of things open as candidates that the examiner might possibly be referring to: the heating vent, his left eyebrow, someone else's hat. It's too much competition. (And another thing: Requests to get up and do something engage a person's motor system, and may set it up to carry out the whole task, even though the person can't hold onto the actual words of the request for more than an instant. Your motor system can remember things that your conscious mind has lost track of: If you've ever opened a familiar cupboard, lost track of what you had intended to get from it, allowed your hand to go where it wanted to, and realized that it was reaching for what you had meant to get, then you know this.)

6.5.3 Testing comprehension of syntax

Testing syntax comprehension is one of the most complicated—and actually, controversial—areas of aphasia testing. A major reason is that we can't just test syntax by itself, because the words in the syntactic structure— a minimum of two of them but usually three or more—also have to be understood and held onto. So we have multiple possible problems to consider, as we did when we looked at errors in syntax production.

How do we tell whether someone understands a sentence like *The man who kissed his wife was wearing an apron* or a noun phrase like *The bird outside the window*? Pointing to one of several similar pictures, or an item in a single complicated picture, is one way. For action sentences, making toy figures go through the action(s) in the sentence is another. A third, found in standard tests like the Boston Diagnostic Aphasia Examination, is reading a short story aloud and then asking questions about it ("Does this story tell how to hunt lions? Does this story tell how lions learn to hunt?"); of course, correct answers in this case depend both on having understood the story and having understood the questions.

In both child language and aphasia research and clinical practice, there's a long tradition of comparing comprehension of active and passive sentences that mean the same thing, like *The dog chased the cat* and *The cat was chased by the dog*. For young children and people with aphasia, the passive is harder and may be impossible to understand. Why? If you go back to Chapter 1, section 1.7.2 and think about this, you'll see one reason: For action verbs (like *chase* and *kiss*), English speakers expect the subject to be the Agent, but in the passive voice, the subject is the Undergoer.

Here are three more reasons. First, the perceptual difference between *The cat was chased by the dog* and *The cat was chasing the dog* is only a matter of three unstressed grammatical morphemes: *-ed*, *by*, and *-ing*. It's easy to miss them if you're not expecting them. Second, English—especially spoken English—uses active voice a lot more often than passive and when it does use passive voice, it tends to use a "short passive": the part without the Agent *by* + noun phrase. This frequency difference means that the full passive construction is harder to arouse than the short passive, and both are harder than the active voice construction. And third, we use passive for a reason (at least in conversation)—for example, when we don't want to say who did something—*Mistakes were made*—or when precisely who did it either doesn't matter or doesn't need to be mentioned—*Jones was arrested yesterday*. But in lists of test sentences, there's no reason, as far as the person being tested is concerned, to use the passive. So having it show up without its usual context is confusing.

For all of these reasons—word order expectations, frequency, and the fact that passive is used for specific reasons—the passive voice is in general harder to process than the active voice (which is why it is used so rarely— uh, why I am using it so rarely—in this book). (See Jorge Cham's *Ph.D.* cartoon at http://www.phdcomics.com/comics/archive.php?comicid=983 , and his paper at http://www.phdcomics.com/archive_journal.php?n=983). If a client can handle the passive voice and other less common constructions well, she has no syntactic problems. But if she has trouble with those constructions, you can't be sure that her problem is with syntax itself; it could be a problem with paying attention to or holding on to details in a test situation. Those problems can happen for many reasons, all based on what we've already said about the passive.

The real issue is this: When a person looks at picture of a cat chasing a dog and a picture of a dog chasing a cat, the pictures themselves start arousing the words and the syntax that could be used to describe them— with the normal active-voice construction of course being the most strongly aroused. So the incoming passive-voice syntax has to compete with the active-voice syntax bouncing around inside the hearer's head. This is a situation we've seen before: Unimpaired adult hearers can hold onto the actual words that they heard for a little while, and that word memory can overcome the mental noise that comes from looking at the pictures. But people with language problems may be unable to do this.

6.5.4 Experiments on comprehension of words and syntax in aphasia

For decades, experimenters have been trying to figure out what is going wrong when people with aphasia make errors in understanding passive sentences and other sentences where the word order (agent-action-undergoer) and real-world probabilities (dogs are more likely to chase cats than vice versa) are not enough to give the right answer. There is no consensus, and from what we have said in section 6.5.3, you can see why: There are too many possible explanations. On top of that, we don't have as clear a model for sentence comprehension as we do for sentence production. For production, researchers have had all those normal speech error databases to work from, but for comprehension, we have only the "slips of the ear," malapropisms, and the results of experiments like the ones in Chapter 5, sections 5.5 and 5.6.

But experimenters have established two strange facts about aphasic comprehension that seem like they ought to be related to each other, and that rule out some possible explanations of comprehension disorders. First, at the word level, most people with aphasia are fairly good at distinguishing between real words and nonwords (lexical decision, Chapter 5, section 5.6.1), even when they cannot correctly indicate what those real words mean. If they can do that, it means that they can at least recognize whether a sequence of sounds is a word or not, so the sounds must be activating the stored word forms even if that activation doesn't spread from the form to the word's lemma or to the concept. And at the sentence level, many people with rather severe aphasia are still fairly good at deciding whether a sentence is grammatical or not (though they have some trouble with certain kinds of sentences), even when they cannot understand that sentence. So they must be able to recognize grammatical constructions, but then they get stuck at some processing step that comes after that point.

Experimental studies of word comprehension using priming in people who have fluent aphasia and troubles with both naming and word comprehension suggest that their word comprehension problem might be a difficulty resolving the competition between the right and wrong answers, rather than a failure to activate them. And eye-tracking studies of some people with nonfluent aphasia who have syntax comprehension problems suggest that they actually start off with a correct analysis of who did what to whom, but that they can't hold onto it long enough to point to a matching picture. If that's true, then some later part of the comprehension process is messed up, probably whatever process holds onto the right answer in the face of competition from the other possibilities that were activated by the stimulus sentences and pictures. The story is made more complicated by experiments that look at the responses of each participant separately, which sometimes find that comprehending passives is harder than a particular kind of relative clause for one patient but the reverse for some other patient. This means that must be several different processes that contribute to understanding a complex sentence, and that sometimes one (or more) of those processes can be working fairly well while others are not.

6.6 Classifying Aphasias: The Boston Syndrome Categories and Some Reasons Why There are Controversies About Them

So far, we've stayed away from details about the types of aphasia—we've just talked about fluent and nonfluent speakers. But if you are going to work in aphasia, study more about it, or even just read about it in the popular science press, you absolutely have to know at least one of the widely used classifications of aphasic symptom patterns into types called **SYNDROMES**. The problem, as I said at the start of this chapter, is that sorting the disorders into syndromes is messy, because there are so many possible mixtures of the various specific language difficulties we've been talking about: with words and with syntax in comprehension and/or production of spoken language, plus articulation, reading, and writing, which we haven't even talked about). And with the kinds of errors—omission or substitution, and whether there's too much speech or too little.

Classifying patterns of symptoms that tend to occur together into syndromes (the Greek word that we get *syndrome* from means "running together") is like classifying personalities, mental illnesses, cultures, languages, political parties, ecosystems, or any other major natural or social phenomenon: You can recognize some recurring patterns that seem to make sense, but if you have a comfortably small set of types—say, from two to six or seven—there will either be a lot of individuals that aren't classified at all, or a lot of individuals that are in the same category (whether it's Democrats, extroverts, or ecosystems) but have very little in common with many of the other individuals that are in the same category.

Why look for syndromes (or political parties or ecosystem types) at all, then? Because, if we don't, we get too overwhelmed with details to make decisions. We need syndromes and other categories, even if they are messy, as handles, so that we can get a grip on a complex world. That's how human minds want to work. Also, we hope that there will be at least a few useful things that are true about all the items that are in each category. For aphasia, there is still some hope that classification will help us get a handle on what kinds of treatments are likely or not likely to work with people in a given group, just as we might divide infections into viral ones that cannot be treated by antibiotics and bacterial ones that can be (unless the bacteria have developed resistance . . .)

Pure cases—textbook examples—of the classical aphasia syndromes really do exist, just as pure colors in a rainbow exist even though they are part of a continuous spectrum. So let's see what the syndromes are in one of the classification systems, one that was developed in Boston by Harold Goodglass, Norman Geschwind, and Edith Kaplan in the 1950s and 1960s, based on earlier European ideas, and which became even more influential after the publication of the first version of the Boston Diagnostic Aphasia Examination in 1973.

The symptoms that are used as the basis for the "Boston" syndrome classification are fluency, comprehension (mostly content word comprehension, but also comprehension of simple syntax), production of content words, and repetition. So first, there's the major production-based division into fluent and nonfluent types of aphasia, which we've already been using: the people with good articulation who seem to use too many words, and the people who seem to work hard to produce speech and use too few. That seems simple, but there's a catch: FLUENT in the technical clinical sense doesn't mean what it does in everyday language. Client 2, even though he stops and starts and breaks off phrases, is fluent in the technical sense: He has long phrases, clear articulation, and a full complement of function words; he produces a fair number of sentences with smooth syntax but relatively little specific information (*That lady, she didn't get a chance to make that right.*)

People with nonfluent aphasias almost always have articulation problems (dysarthria); they don't hit some phonetic targets accurately, or have to work visibly hard to do so. One of the few correlations that is still holding between a person's symptoms and the area of his or her brain that is damaged is that people with nonfluent aphasias have more damage than people with fluent aphasias in the lower part of the area just in front of the deep groove labeled the CENTRAL SULCUS, which divides the FRONTAL LOBE from the PARIETAL LOBE (Figure 6.2).

But people with both kinds of aphasia usually have damage in many other areas of the brain as well.

The more common fluent aphasia syndromes are, in the Boston classification:

1. **ANOMIC APHASIA** (anomia): Good comprehension, good syntax in production, but difficulty in producing content words. Anomia can be very severe, but moderate and mild cases are common. (Anomia can be the only remaining problem for people who originally fit into one of the other syndromes but have recovered from all the rest of their language problems.) Client 2 appears to be anomic, though without comprehension test data, we don't know for sure. He could have a mild version of the next syndrome.

2. **WERNICKE'S APHASIA**: Poor comprehension and serious difficulty in producing content words; in more severe cases, producing nonsense words in place of content words, or using English content words in ways that make no sense, placed in syntax that seems smooth. (Because the

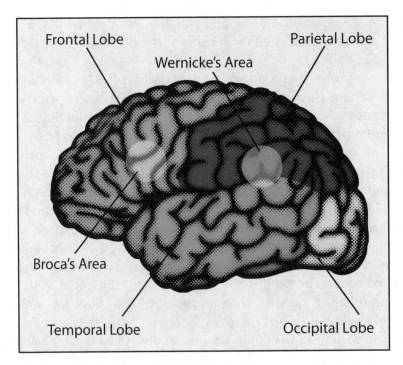

Figure 6.2. Brain with classical language areas. Image adapted from Shutterstock®. All rights reserved.

content words don't make much sense, the appropriateness of the function words is very hard to evaluate.) Because of the poor comprehension, Wernicke's aphasia has also been called "sensory aphasia" and "receptive aphasia." The Boston categorization avoids these terms, however, because the production problems of people with this syndrome are just as important and disabling as their comprehension problem.

3. **CONDUCTION APHASIA**: Good comprehension, good syntax, but serious problems with repetition and—although this is not part of the original definition—with getting the sounds of longer words in the right order; these are the people who made the word assembly errors we saw in section 6.4.1, like /hɛlipo/, /hɛlopɛt/, /pɛlo/, /hɛlətɪl/, /hɛlibl/, /hɛlətə/ for successive attempts at "helicopter." The name "conduction aphasia" comes from the classical theory of the cause of this disorder.

4. A rare fourth kind of fluent aphasia is called (because of the classical theory of its cause) **TRANSCORTICAL SENSORY APHASIA**. I have seen only one person with this disorder, but it was very dramatic: His speech seemed quite normal, but his comprehension was very seriously impaired, almost nonexistent. However, like other people with this syndrome, he could repeat words and sentences quite well.

The commoner nonfluent aphasia syndromes are

1. **AGRAMMATIC APHASIA** or **BROCA'S APHASIA** (the terms are not quite synonymous, but the difference between them is something people argue about, so we'll ignore it here): Comprehension of words is relatively good. Speech production is effortful, usually, but not always dysarthric; the speaker produces many isolated words and/or short phrases, and function words are often omitted. Comprehension of conversational speech seems fairly good, but there are usually problems with understanding complex syntax, such as the passive voice. Client 1 was diagnosed as having Broca's aphasia.

2. **MIXED APHASIA** (when severe, called **GLOBAL APHASIA**): Poor comprehension of words, combined with the production problems of Broca's aphasia.

3. A less common kind of nonfluent aphasia, called (because of the classical theory) **TRANSCORTICAL MOTOR APHASIA**, is what we see in Client 3: Comprehension is good, repetition is good, and the language that is produced has well-formed stretches, but the client seems to speak as little as possible and with effort.

If you are curious about who Dr. Paul Broca and Dr. Carl Wernicke were, and why they were important enough to have aphasia syndromes and parts of the brain named after them, you'll have no trouble finding good material on the Internet. But be careful: Web sources often just repeat old and/or oversimplified information, like the NAA's statement that people with aphasia have no cognitive impairment. Compare multiple sources of information, and look for ones that report on their own imaging studies or have links to contemporary research coming out of major universities' medical schools with leading neurology departments, such as UCLA, the University of Pennsylvania, Harvard, and McGill.

6.7 Aphasia in Native Bilingual and Second-Language Speakers

6.7.1 Which language comes back and which one should be treated?

Physicians and language researchers have published hundreds of papers on bilingual and multilingual people who become aphasic, and this seems to be the story: Most of the time, all of a person's languages are affected about equally, but that's not newsworthy. The cases that get noticed are the startling ones where one of the languages is much better preserved than the others. Sometimes the language that is preserved is the one the person first learned as a child, sometimes it is the one that she was using most around the time of the stroke, and sometimes it is the language that was apparently strongest before the stroke.

There is no way to predict what will happen, and no way to be sure of the explanation of what has happened, in a particular case. As for which language should be treated, or whether both should be, the ideal answer is clear: whatever language will help the client communicate best in her daily life. But it's not hard to see what can get in the way of supplying ideal services: If the language the person needs most is a minority language used in her family, there may be no trained person who can speak that language, and no materials available for therapy. And if the home language is the one that is most impaired, even if therapists and materials can be found for it, deciding what to do will involve family issues: Who will be taking care of the patient? Will the patient recover enough to make being able to communicate outside her ethnic community important again? The practical considerations may far outweigh the psycholinguistic ones.

6.7.2 Deciding whether a bilingual aphasic speaker's mistake is due to aphasia, the other language, or imperfect learning of a second language—and why it matters

If you go back to our quick look at some of the ways that languages differ in Chapter 1, section 1.10.1, you can come up with some of the problems that people face simply as second language users, especially if they learned the second language late in life or didn't have a chance to learn it very well because they were in jobs where skilled communication wasn't needed or encouraged (which is why they were given those jobs in the first place): as farm laborers, house cleaners, food-preparers, dishwashers . . . it's a long list.

If their first language had no grammatical gender or a very different gender system—Turkish speakers working in Spain, say—they will make lots of gender errors and agreement errors. If their second language marks first, second, and third person on main verbs, they may make verb agreement errors regardless of their first language, because the specific person-number morphemes are different in the two languages; that's true of both

English speakers learning French and French speakers learning English. There's a huge research literature on this kind of topic among journals that deal with second-language and bilingual education matters, especially in Europe, where the proportion of the population that crosses language boundaries for work is huge, and where there are many second languages to be learned, not just English.

Another thing that varies a lot from one language to another and is full of peculiarities is how prepositions are used (or their equivalents: Some languages, like Japanese, have POSTPOSITIONS (words that do the same kinds of job as prepositions but come after their noun or noun phrase instead of before it). Errors in the choice of prepositions, or simply omitting them, are common in second-language speakers no matter how closely the first and second languages resemble each other typologically.

So when you find an aphasic person who has a foreign accent (which you'll have to distinguish from dysarthria), and who is, say, leaving out articles or verb endings or omitting sentence subjects and objects, you have a problem: Are the language errors because she is aphasic, or because her English had never become nativelike? Or both? You need to consult with someone who knew her well before the stroke and can give you a good account of her language before it happened—a grandchild who speaks English natively, for example, might be a good source of information.

Why does this matter? Because it will help you set a realistic goal for treatment. If she hadn't mastered the use of articles before her stroke, this is not the time to get her to start putting them in the right places. Your responsibility is to help your patient communicate as close to her pre-stroke level as possible; it's not to improve her English beyond that. That would be an unattainable goal, and trying to get there would be frustrating and miserable for both of you.

6.8 Trying to Predict Communicative Success: Interaction, Gesture, and Communication

This chapter cannot be only about psycholinguistics, because the primary goal of aphasia therapy is not to restore language; it is to restore communication so that the person with aphasia isn't isolated from their family, friends, and the other people they need to interact with—plumbers, postal workers, and census takers; if they can return to work: employers, clients, and coworkers . . . the list is endless. Yes, if someone has only mild language impairment and is communicating well, then being able to use language fully

—reading and writing as well as spoken language—may be the remaining barrier to being normal again. But a huge proportion of aphasia cases have so much language impairment that getting all the way back to normal language is not realistic. Most people with aphasia need to supplement their language with gesture, drawing, and whatever amount of writing they can muster, and to pay attention to both the quality of their own speech and whether the people they are speaking to truly understand them or are just nodding their heads to be supportive. And their families need to learn how to encourage all of these strategies.

Brain damage can make doing each of these things more difficult, but therapy and counseling can help to bring some of them back within reach. Let's just spend a bit of time here talking about the problems that are the least obvious: keeping tabs on the quality of what you are saying and on whether the person that you are talking to is really understanding you. These are things that you have to do repeatedly while you are also trying to communicate (they are not communication itself) and so to do them, you have to shift your attention away from your topic, which is of course where it naturally goes when you're speaking.

Controlling what your attention is focused on is part of what psychologists call your **EXECUTIVE FUNCTION**. If two patients in a clinic have equal degrees and similar kinds of language difficulties, but very different communication abilities, then one of the main differences between them is likely to be that the one with better communication skills has better executive function. My aphasic co-author Shirley Kleinman, who was an excellent communicator, once sharply rebuked a physician who was interviewing her in front of an audience of medical students because he was just nodding *uh-huh* while she was talking, and she could tell that he hadn't really understood her. She had the executive ability to watch him and interpret what he was doing at the same time that she was fighting to produce words and short phrases. Other clients, with poorer executive function—for example, several of those whom Gail Ramsberger studied at our clinic at the University of Colorado—would spend minutes at a time not looking at the person they were talking to, with disastrous results for communication. However, clinicians can treat attention problems and get improvement in clients' ability to communicate even when the measures of their language alone are not showing any improvement.

The methods of Conversation Analysis, a painstakingly detailed transcription technique that records gaze and eye contact, gesture, facial expression, and language for all parties to a conversation, are a basic tool for studying how executive function affects communication; Goodwin's book *Conversation and Brain Damage* is the place to go for more information about how this is done.

6.9 Brain Plasticity and New Hopes for Therapy

For many years, no one had been able to observe new brain cell formation in adults, and researchers didn't know (and underestimated) how well our adult brains could form new synapses. Almost everyone thought that plasticity—the brain's ability to change as it learns from experience—was almost completely lost by the time we become adults. That picture changed abruptly late in the 20th century, and now we have plenty of evidence that an adult brain that works hard to do something new can reorganize itself to do it better. Although it's difficult, requiring hours and hours of training, new brain circuits can be created that will compensate fairly well for many losses due to strokes, although how well, of course, still depends on how much brain is left to work with. The big problem seems to be the time that has to be invested; computers are probably essential training tools, since they don't get tired and don't have to make a living. Considerable progress has been seen when clients use constraint-induced language therapy; that is, retraining regimens that require them to talk instead of using compensatory communication strategies. This approach is patterned on constraint-induced movement therapy, a successful procedure for restoring some control of hand and arm motion that had been impaired by strokes. We have good reason to hope that practicable methods will become available for clients who are motivated and can stand the frustration of spending hours trying to do things that seem to be impossible; social game-playing may be the best way to do this.

Another problem in aphasia therapy has been that patients often don't apply in the real world what they learned to do in the clinic: treatment fails to generalize. As we've said several times in this book, one thing that's necessary is to create links between a word or a construction that's being learned and the real-world situation that it should be used in, so that the right language gets activated when it's needed. As this becomes more widely understood, creative speech-language pathologists will come up with ways to make it happen—for example, perhaps by using virtual-reality mock-ups of places where people have to be able to talk to strangers, like banks and restaurants.

Exercises for Chapter 6

6.1. We often overestimate the speaking abilities of normal speakers because we are so used to mentally editing out minor dysfluencies. Record yourself, a friend, and/or a family member explaining what's happening in the Cookie Theft picture, and go through the recording carefully with the checklist. What kinds of normal speech problems do these speakers have? If you have access to AphasiaBank on the Internet, listen to some samples of aphasic and normal comparison speech there.

6.2. How would you help the family or friends of a person with aphasia understand the difference between confused language and confused thinking? Try to come up with a list of concrete examples from everyday life that you could get them to think about.

6.3. Why is it especially important to watch the person you're speaking to if you have language production problems? What can you "read" from your conversation partner's face that could help you?

References

Bates, E., Wulfeck, B., & MacWhinney, B. (1991). Crosslinguistic research in aphasia: An overview. *Brain and Language*, *41*, 123–148.

Caplan, D., Waters G., DeDe, G., Michaud, J., & Reddy, A. (2007). A study of syntactic processing in aphasia I: Behavioral (psycholinguistic) aspects. *Brain and Language*, *101*, 103–150.

Caplan, D., Waters G., Kennedy, D., Alpert, N., Makris, N., DeDe, G., . . . Reddy, A. (2007). A study of syntactic processing in aphasia II: Neurological aspects. *Brain and Language*, *101*, 151–177.

Dickey, M. W., & Thompson, C. K. (2009). Automatic processing of wh- and NP-movement in agrammatic aphasia: Evidence from eyetracking. *Journal of Neurolinguistics*, *22*, 563–583.

Ferreira, F. (2003). The misinterpretation of noncanonical sentences. *Cognitive Psychology*, *47*(2), 164–203.

Goodglass, H., & Kaplan, E. (1972, 1983). *The assessment of aphasia and related disorders (Boston Diagnostic Aphasia Examination)* (1st ed., 2nd ed.). Philadelphia, PA: Lea & Febiger.

Goodglass, H., Wingfield, A., & Hyde, M. (1998). The Boston Corpus of aphasic naming errors. *Brain and Language*, *64*, 1–27.

Goodwin, C. (2003). *Conversation and brain damage.* New York, NY: Oxford University Press 2003.

Hardin, K., & Ramsberger, G. (2004). *Treatment of attention in aphasia*. Poster, Clinical Aphasiology Conference, Park City, Utah.

Janse, E. (2006). Lexical competition effects in aphasia: Deactivation of lexical candidates in spoken word processing. *Brain and Language*, *97*, 1–11.

Kaplan, E., Goodglass, H., & Weintraub, S. (1983). *Boston naming test: Revised edition.* Philadelphia, PA: Lea & Febiger.

Kent, R. D. (Ed.). (2004). *The MIT encyclopedia of communication disorders.* Cambridge, MA: MIT Press.

Lee, M., & Thompson, C. K. (2004). Agrammatic aphasic production and comprehension of unaccusative verbs in sentence contexts. *Journal of Neurolinguistics*, *17*, 315–330.

Linebarger, M. C., Schwartz, M. F., & Saffran, E. (1983). Sensitivity to grammatical structure in so-called agrammatic aphasics. *Cognition*, *13*, 361–392.

Lorenzen, B., & Murray, L. (2008). Bilingual aphasia: A theoretical and clinical review. *American Journal of Speech-Language Pathology*, *17*(8), 299–317. doi: 10.1044/1058-0360(2008/026).

Menn, L., & Obler, L. K. (1990). *Agrammatic aphasia: A cross-language narrative sourcebook.* Amsterdam, The Netherlands: John Benjamin.

Ramsberger, G., & Menn, L. (2003). Co-constructing Lucy: Adding a social perspective to the assessment of communicative success in aphasia. In C. Goodwin (Ed.), *Conversation and brain damage* (pp. 283–304). New York, NY: Oxford University Press.

Ramsberger, G., Miyake, A., Menn, L., Reilly, K., & Filley, C. M. (1999). Selective preservation of geographic names and numerical information in a patient with severe aphasia. *Aphasiology*, *13*, 625–645.

Revonsuo, A., & Laine, M. (1996). Semantic processing without conscious understanding in a global aphasic: Evidence from auditory event-related brain potentials. *Cortex*, *32*(1), 29–48.

Schnur, T., Schwartz, M. F., Kimberg, D. Y., Hirshorn, E., Coslett, H. B., & Thompson-Schill, S. L. (2009). Localizing interference during naming: Convergent neuroimaging and neuropsychological evidence for the function of Broca's Area. *Proceedings of the National Academy of Sciences*, *106*(1), 322–327.

Spalek, K., & Thompson-Schill, S. L. (2008). Task-dependent semantic interference in language production: An fMRI study. *Brain and Language*, *107*, 220–228.

Stowe, L., Haverkort, M., & Zwarts, F. (2005). Rethinking the neurological basis of language. *Lingua*, *115*, 997–1042.

Resources (additional references in Materials for Chapter 6 on the CD)

Ahlsén, E. (2006). *Introduction to neurolinguistics.* Amsterdam, the Netherlands: John Benjamins.

Bedny, M., McGill, M., & Thompson-Schill, S. L. (2008). Semantic adaptation and competition during word comprehension. *Cerebral Cortex, 18,* 2574–2585. doi:10.1093/cercor/bhn018.

Goodglass, H., Kaplan, E., & Baressi, B. (2001) *The assessment of aphasia and related disorders (Boston Diagnostic Aphasia Examination)* (3rd ed.). Austin, TX: Pro-Ed.

January, D., Trueswell, J. C., & Thompson-Schill, S. L. (2009). Co-localization of stroop and syntactic ambiguity resolution in Broca's area: Implications for the neural basis of sentence processing. *Journal of Cognitive Neuroscience, 21*(12), 2434–2444.

Spalek, K., & Thompson-Schill, S. L. (2008). Task-dependent semantic interference in language production: An fMRI study. *Brain and Language, 107,* 220–228.

Developmental Psycholinguistics: Studies of First Language Acquisition

7.0 A Wealth of Studies, a Rich Topic

The number of textbooks, popular books, research books, and journal articles about children's language learning is enormous, as it should be: Becoming a normal language user is essential to living a full life as a member of our social species. We can't cover nearly all the ideas and findings that you would probably find useful or interesting, but there are plenty of good resources for you after you finish this chapter; suggestions are listed in this chapter's Further Readings section.

Infants and toddlers develop very rapidly, although it doesn't always seem that way when you're the person changing the diapers; Jenny at two is very different from Jenny at three. Understanding development takes patience, partly because the popular idea that children progress in discrete stages is a very clumsy simplification of reality. (After all, what stage are *you* in? A stupid question, right?) Many things change within each of us, on developmental time schedules that are partly related but partly independent of one another. And those schedules—if that's the right word at all—are continually being modified by our physical, emotional, and mental experiences. Of course, there are general correlations and correspondences and developmental norms; but because there is so much variation in what develops first and how fast, the biggest challenge is to understand that variability. And we need to understand it so that we can encourage ability of all kinds, instead of holding back the swift ones because it's easiest to have everybody do the same thing, and so that we can figure out when the slow ones are okay and when they need help, and what kind, and how to deliver it to them.

Because what you probably know the most about is the way toddlers talk, we'll work backward from about age three, beginning with morphology and syntax, until we get to the earliest evidence of the grammar in children's minds. Then we'll work forward again from when hearing is established, in the last trimester before an infant's birth, and study the development of phonetics and phonology. We'll work back up to the toddler level of phonological development, and then look at how toddlers learn the meanings of their words along with learning how to say them.

7.1 Output, Input, Intake, Imitation: How We Find Out What Toddlers Know About Language

7.1.0 A story and two questions

An astronomy-loving grandfather introduces Ryan (age 4) and Andrew (3) to the stars over Florida one clear, dark evening: *We looked up to see many stars and galaxies, with Orion the mighty hunter and his belt among the brightest. To Ryan, I said:* Look up there to see Orion (/o'rajan/ = O'Ryan). *Then Drew asked:* Where is O'Drewie? (E-mail communication from Harold Gray, 2008)

What does little Drew already know about language form and meaning that makes him think, after he hears /o'rajan/, that there must be a star (or a constellation) that's called O'Drewie? And how did he come to know so much by the age of three? Keep thinking about that, and we'll work toward the beginnings of an answer.

7.1.1 Observation of output and input: What young children say and hear

Unless you have infants of your own, or you care for or work with them professionally, you probably know quite a bit more about the language of two or three-year-olds than you do about babies—it's easy (sometimes too easy!) to hear TODDLERS (children between 12 and 36 months) talking in parks and supermarkets. So let's start there and work backward toward newborns. What do toddlers say, what do they really understand, and how do we figure out what they've learned about pragmatics, semantics, syntax, morphology, and phonology? If you try to write down a young child's utterance that flies past you as you listen, you can probably pick up accurately on its phonology or MORPHOLOGY or syntax—maybe more than one of those if it's short—but being accurate is a challenge (Did she say *I wan' dat* or [ʌ ˈaːvæʔ]?). And there's no way to check the details, especially because the child you're overhearing probably doesn't say things the same way each time. You need audio recordings to be sure of your transcription, and to figure what a word like *that* actually refers to, you need video (and you hope that whatever the child was pointing or looking at is actually in your picture).

Research using systematic audio recording of toddlers talking normally with their parents began in the 1960s for English, shortly after tape recorders became available, and spread to other languages; video-based studies began in the 1970s. To supplement your supermarket eavesdropping, one of the great resources for studying child language is the online Child Language Data Exchange (**CHILDES**), based at Carnegie-Mellon University, which has systematically collected audio and video materials from many languages that you can access after you register and agree to their terms (there's a link on your CD under Materials for Chapter 7).

Why am I emphasizing systematic collections? After all, single incidents like our O'Drewie story are very illuminating—and they are not to be dismissed, because they stimulate our thinking about what children must know in order to say the things that they do. But if you want to understand how development happens—for example, how Drewie actually came to know that words can have more than one MORPHEME—you have to follow individual children over time; that is, you have to do LONGITUDINAL studies. Otherwise, you can't trace the sounds, structures, and words that each child is using back to their earliest beginnings, and you can't watch how they change. To do this, in fact, you need to make the videos frequently, in settings that are similar from one recording session to the next, if you want to be able to compare them. And the recordings need to be made where there's not too much household noise, if you want to understand what's being said and what it means.

Also, because there are plenty of individual differences from one child to the next, researchers need to work with a library of systematically collected tapes of different children and their parents, so that we can see what stays the same across children and what doesn't. Quite a bit of comparison is needed to get an idea of the range of normal development, because there's a great deal of variation among children who are all developing quite normally. There are also differences from one language to the next, which makes collecting and comparing data from different languages very important; your CD has relevant links and information.

Giving parenting advice is a big industry, but a lot of it is based on the advice-givers' personal experience and culture-based beliefs. (Does baby-talk bug them? Are they upset by bossy-sounding language? Do they think that talking to children a lot is a good thing?) Much less is based on sufficient quantities of real data. That's not altogether the fault of the advice-givers, though: In spite of the hundreds of millions of children in the world, not a lot of longitudinal data sets are available for study. It takes a lot more determination than you'd think to fit a regular time for video recording into a busy family schedule. That's part of why CHILDES is so important.

And here's the really big picture: We already know that preschool language and cognitive development are huge predictors of how well children will do in school and in life, and that preschool and home-based intervention can improve children's chances of school success. So making good public policy decisions and good public and private investments in preschool education depend on understanding how children learn from their parents and caregivers.

7.1.2 Intake and imitation

If you are simply immersed in a foreign language and don't interact with the people who speak it (or if you are left in front of a foreign television), you'll only learn a few of the most striking forms and almost nothing about their meanings; the same is true for infants and children. Out of all the language around them, what do children actually learn from? What is their INTAKE, the part that actually sinks in? Researchers have been chipping away at the intake question for a long time. It has been slow work, because collecting data about what children say and what they hear is not enough; we also need to know what they have understood (and what patterns they've extracted) out of all that they hear.

The question of what children actually take in from the language around them has multiple answers, depending on what aspect of the language we are concerned with. Researchers have investigated different specific questions about intake with many neat (and some not so neat) experiments; for example, how much do toddlers understand out of the words that are addressed to them when there's no supporting context? How does context affect their interpretation of what they hear? We'll talk about some of these questions soon, and more when we analyze imitation in Chapter 10, section 10.1.2.

A lot of children's intake occurs during their unconscious pattern learning, which we'll talk about when we look at experimental studies of infants' phonological knowledge in section 7.5. But we'll start by using some famous data from an observational study. If you're planning to be a language teacher or a language clinician, read this section extra carefully, as well as section 10.1.2, because understanding the gap between input and intake is not just about toddlers; it's central to understanding a lot of what happens in the classroom and the clinic.

Let's look at a famous example of input that doesn't seem to result in much intake. It was originally published in 1966 by David McNeill of the University of Chicago, and it's been reprinted many times. (Even if you've read about it before, don't skip this discussion; what we're going to say about it is different from what you'll see in most textbooks.) A little boy, let's call him "Jimmy," says *Nobody don't like me*, and his mother says *No. Say "Nobody likes me."* Jimmy apparently tries to oblige her, but he keeps saying the same thing, and she keeps making the same correction. Finally, after about eight identical exchanges, she says: *Now, listen carefully: Say "Nobody likes me."* And he says: *Oh! Nobody don't like**s** me.*

What happened here?

Quite a lot, though it looks like almost nothing (eight repetitions and the kid still basically doesn't get it?). So let's think about it seriously, and in two different ways. Then we can try to answer the question of what Jimmy knows, and what his intake might have been—that is, what he might have learned about English grammar from this long exchange with his mother.

7.1.3 The sociolinguistics of correction

First, consider this as a communication story: Jimmy has made an announcement that sounds very discouraged. Even though it's not correct standard English, it's perfectly understandable. But instead of worrying about its content (Why would he say such a sad thing?) his mother is alerted by the wording. Like other sane parents, she doesn't usually correct her little son's deviations from adult language. (If adults regularly ignored the meaning of their children's messages to correct the wording, the children would probably give up trying to talk. Fortunately, the parents that we know about correct most errors, if they do it at all, by just rephrasing what their child said and then responding to what the child meant.)

But this error is different, almost certainly because of its SOCIO-LINGUISTIC importance to Jimmy's mother: *Nobody don't . . .* sounds like a variety of English that would be considered uneducated, and that's not the way this college-educated family and their friends want to be caught talking. (For them, it's as bad as wearing a bathing suit in a law court—see Chapter 1, section 1.9.3.) In their series of eight conversational turns, Jimmy's mother doesn't get him to change his utterance to the way she wants him to say it, but she probably has communicated the sense that there's something that she doesn't like about the way he said it. Eventually, he will find out that she doesn't want him to say *Nobody don't like me* because it makes him sound like one of the tough kids, which is not her idea of who he should be.

How quickly will he change? Well, how long will it take him learn to pick up his clothes? It will vary from child to child, and we have no proof one way or the other that nagging, setting an example, or any other strategy, will make a difference, although everybody has personal convictions on the matter. But learning to change the way you talk is more complicated than learning to pick up your clothes. In section 7.1.4, we'll see one of the reasons why.

7.1.4 The psycholinguistics of imitation

Let's look at this famous exchange again, this time as a psycholinguistic story. It happens that Jimmy was enmeshed in an intricate little snare of English grammar, involving two different problems: How to make the negative forms of verbs in standard English, and how to use them with the negative subject pronouns *nobody* and *nothing*. In the exercises for this chapter, you can work on formulating those grammatical patterns. What we need to think through here is why Jimmy obediently tries to imitate his mother seven times without managing to change one word of what he has said, and why, even when it looks as if Jimmy has finally noticed that what she is saying isn't the same as what he's been saying, he manages to make only one of the several changes between her version and his. In short, why doesn't he just imitate her? (By the way, as slow and painstaking as this analysis is going to be, it's still an oversimplification. We'll make one important improvement in it at the end of section 7.3, and more in Chapter 10.)

Psycholinguists who study children—DEVELOPMENTAL PSYCHOLINGUISTS—know a lot about imitation, because it's an obvious thing to try with children if you want to see whether they can say a word, a phrase, or a type of sentence that you want to study. And one thing we've learned is that pure imitation—repeating like an audio recorder, regardless of whether the item to be repeated is familiar or not—basically doesn't exist for input that's longer than one speech sound. In other words, our pure **AUDITORY MEMORY** can handle only a tiny amount of new information. Anything more complex than a single speech sound draws, at least partly, on arousing our memories of similar sounds; anything longer than a syllable draws on our memories of words that sound similar to it. We know this both from observations of dialogues like the one we're analyzing and from experiments over many years (see this chapter's Further Readings list on your CD). And, if you've studied a second language using tapes in a language lab, you also know exactly what I mean: Even when you can easily imitate a word that has a single non-English sound in it, you have to practice a word with two or more unfamiliar sounds over and over again until they both become familiar.

In general, the longer the material you are asked to imitate, the more you depend on arousal of forms and grammatical patterns that you have already stored in your memory. In other words, the more you have to hold in your mind, the more you depend on top-down processing to help you do it. Another way to demonstrate this is to notice that you can repeat a sequence of words that make a grammatical unit (*the bear that broke into the trailer ate all the peanut butter crackers*) much more easily than you can repeat a sequence that has the words but doesn't make a phrase or a clause (*trailer peanut the all that and into bear crackers the broke*). Try saying each of those sequences of words after just one quick glance back at them, and see for yourself.

When anyone, child or adult, tries to imitate an utterance, what comes out is a varying mixture of what they've understood and what they have re-created from their own syntax, morphology, phonology, and phonetics. Let's look at the details for McNeill's (1966) example. Jimmy's own brain created the sentence *Nobody don't like me*, and now he's being asked to listen carefully and repeat *Nobody likes me*. This gives him both a comprehension problem and a production problem. The comprehension problem is that he has to understand the meaning of his mother's sentence and also to register two differences between what his mother said and what he said: that she doesn't use the word *don't*, and that she adds an *-s* to *like*. His own grammar apparently doesn't have the construction *Nobody likes me*, so his top-down processing won't help him remember that that's what his mother said.

And with the best will in the world, his brain can't turn off the word forms and structures that have already been aroused by his own sentence. His top-down processing helps him remember what he already knows how to produce, but it's little help with what's new. So his mother's sub-tracted (*don't*) and added (*-s*) grammatical morphemes have to fight with his own wording. That gives Jimmy a heavy cognitive load trying to spot and remember those two differences. But he finally notices at least one of them, just before that eighth try, where he says, *Oh! Nobody don't like<u>s</u> me*.

Suppose that he has in fact finally managed to notice both of the differences between his mother's sentence and his. Now there's the production problem: Jimmy has to try to say what he remembers his mother as saying. To get the words out means another brain fight—a contest between the words he thinks his mother said and what he himself would normally say. He's making an effort—that is, he's trying to influence that brain fight by paying attention to those differences. But it's very hard to pay attention to two things at once in production, too. So even if he had actually noticed both the absence of the *don't* as well as the presence of the *-s*, he's over-loaded; the *-s* comes out, but that's as much as he can manage.

So: What did he know before this exchange with his mother, and what might his intake have been—what did he or could he have learned? Clearly, Jimmy doesn't know, when he says, *Nobody don't like me*, that English treats *nobody* as a singular noun. He probably hasn't figured it out even after he obligingly tacks the third person singular verb ending *-s* onto *like*, because if he had, he should have moved to saying *Nobody doesn't likes me* or *Nobody doesn't like me*. All that he's somewhat likely have learned —incorrectly, of course—is that the construction he needed was what he finally said: *Nobody don't likes me*. However, that could have been a temporary change; we'd have to be able to follow him until the next time he tried to put the same idea into words and see what he said. Probably the main thing he took in was the information that something about say-ing *Nobody don't like me* mysteriously bothers his mother.

Choosing to imitate

Imitation is so complicated that you might have started to wonder why children do it at all. Lois Bloom and her research team videotaped a sub-stantial number of children in a longitudinal study in the 1970s, and found that although some children rarely imitate without being asked to, others do it on their own quite a bit. However, the ones who imitate are quite choosy about *what* they imitate, and what they choose changes from one recording session to the next in an interesting way. When they looked at recording sessions of the toddlers who did like to imitate, Bloom and her team found that the imitated types of words or phrases would be ones that they were rarely saying unless they had just heard them. And typically, when the research team looked at the next recording session (if the timing between the sessions was right), the items that the little ones had been imitating during the earlier session had now become part of their spontaneous output repertoires. So imitation, when it's what the toddler herself chooses to do, seems to reflect what she's currently working on—it occurs at the leading edge of her language development. Yes, imitation is hard; but the children who use it do so to help them with something that's even harder: saying a word or a phrase that they don't feel confident about doing on their own. What their brains need is the little extra boost of activation from what they've just heard, stored in their **SHORT-TERM AUDITORY MEMORY**, to help them out with the bits that their own memory can't activate strongly enough. And their imitation isn't as accurate as a tape-recording; it's just a move in the right direction.

7.1.5 Being in the zone: The zone of proximal development

This brings us to one of the most useful concepts in all of the study of cognitive development: the **ZONE OF PROXIMAL DEVELOPMENT**, comfortably abbreviated as the **ZPD**. It means, basically, what your mind is ready to learn. So we can describe Bloom's observation like this: What toddlers choose to imitate is material in their ZPD.

The term Zone of Proximal Development comes from the writings of the Soviet psychologist Lev Vygotsky (say it [vɪ ˈgot ski], please, not [vaɪ ˈgot ski]!). We all know the ZPD idea intuitively, as teachers and learners: Whether you're trying to learn to cook, skateboard, or speak French, you need to see demonstrations or hear lessons or practice on what's just a little beyond your current skill level. If it's already well within your range, practicing it is boring, and you won't learn anything (although it might increase your speed, or your ability to do something else at the same time). And if it's too hard, you'll also learn very little, plus trying to do it is likely to make you (and/or your audience) miserable.

Because imitation has to draw so heavily on what a speaker already knows, asking children like Jimmy to imitate a word or phrase turns out to be a useful way of investigating their phonology or their grammar. What you get back has been filtered through the children's comprehension and their production processes, so if they actually repeat something exactly the way you said it, it must at least be in their Zone of Proximal Development, even if it's not something they've completely mastered. Let's look at some experiments that have used this method to figure out the child's grammatical abilities.

In the 1970s, a number of ELICITED IMITATION experiments (experiments where you ask participants to try to repeat exactly what you've said) provided lovely examples of how young children imitate structures that are a bit beyond their own grammar—sentences that they understand, but can't produce on their own.

One elicited imitation experiment was done by Thomas Thiemann when he was a doctoral student in 1975. He asked adults and children to repeat a variety of sentences with different structures, and some of these stimuli were deliberately awkward in phrasing. His adult control participants and his older children tended to repeat awkwardly phrased originals in shorter forms; for example, THE TRUCK HIT THE WALL AND THE CAR HIT THE WALL TOO sometimes became *The truck hit the wall and the car did too*; THE GIRL SAYS THAT THE CAKE IS GOOD became, for example, *The girl thinks the cake is good.* But the youngest participant, aged 3 years 8 months, apparently was still working on learning the structures in the sentences that he was asked to repeat. He often made his sentences longer, sticking to basic constructions and clear meanings. Other words also crept in, but as you can see, they are words that sound quite natural as completions of the model phrases. So they are not just junk, but evidence of the way his top-down processing was helping him to make these sentences. Have a look (stimulus sentences in small caps, child's responses in italics):

1. THE BOY TOLD HIS MOTHER A FUNNY STORY AND SHE LAUGHED.
   The boy told the story to his mommy and the mommy laughed.

2. THE BIRD SAT IN THE TREE AND IT SANG A SONG.
   The bird sat in the tree and the bird sang a song.

3. THE TRUCK HIT THE WALL AND THE CAR HIT THE WALL TOO.
   The truck hit the wall and the car hit the wall too.

4. THE CAT JUMPED OVER THE FENCE AND THE DOG DID TOO.
   The cat jumped over the fence and the dog jumped over there too.

5. THE GIRL SAYS THAT THE CAKE IS GOOD.
   The girl says that this cake is good.

6. THE TEACHER READ HER CHILDREN A STORY.
   The teacher read the story to the children.

In 1971, Dan I. Slobin and Charles Welsh studied a little girl they called "Echo," who was willing to try to repeat lots of sentences between the ages of 2 years, 3 months and 2 years, 5 months. Their study was very detailed, with a long, thoughtful discussion. We'll look just at the part of it that deals with the little girl's developing ability to imitate sentences with relative clauses. The first set of target sentences show Echo at 2 years, 4 months filtering three different complex structures with similar meanings through her language and memory.

7. THE OWL EATS CANDY AND THE OWL RUNS FAST.
   Owl eat candy and he run fast.

8. THE OWL WHO EATS CANDY RUNS FAST.
   Owl eat a candy and he run fast.

9. THE MAN WHO I SAW YESTERDAY GOT WET.
   I saw the man and he got wet.

10. THE MAN WHO I SAW YESTERDAY RUNS FAST.
    I saw the man who run fast.
    I saw the man and he run fast.

It's clear that Echo understands all four of these sentences, and in her immediate attempt to match sentence 10, she actually manages a relative clause, although it's the simplest kind: one where "who" is the subject of the relative clause (rather than the object, as in its model). Four of these five responses show her relying on a favorite slightly complex construction of her own: subject-verb-object-*and-he*-verb phrase.

But sometimes, the model sentences were too far ahead of the child —sometimes she had only understood parts of the adult sentence. We figure that out because what she said makes sense but doesn't match what the adult's sentence means. And sometimes, she hadn't understood the adult's sentence at all; we realize that because what she said doesn't make any sense, which means that she didn't create a coherent mental image from what she heard. The next three relative clause sentences, presented to Echo a month later, did not use the word *who* (or even the word *that*) to mark the beginning of the relative clause.

11. THE BOY THE BOOK HIT WAS CRYING.
    boy the book was crying

12. THE HOUSE THE BOY HIT WAS BIG.
    boy house was big

13. THE BOY THE CHAIR HIT WAS DIRTY.
    boy hit the chair was dirty.

Apparently, Echo didn't recognize that this new construction had two clauses; we can tell, because she didn't know what to do with their second noun phrase, the one that's the subject of the relative clause, or how to deal with the two verbs, even though she had done that nicely with the first four sentences.

So: Imitation tasks can be very useful as a way of pushing children to the limits of what they haves grasped of the grammar, so that we can see what they have mastered and what is (or is not) in their Zone of Proximal Development: A child who can imitate something reliably is probably just about ready to learn to use it on their own. (In speech-language pathology, if a speech sound or a phrase can be imitated but not said without help, it is said to be STIMULABLE.) But imitation has a lot of problems as a way to teach a person (of any age) to use language; go back to the tourist-buying-a-newspaper story in Chapter 2, section 2.3 to see one reason why this is true.

7.2 Building a Grammar: What Toddlers Say

Now we'll focus on children's spontaneous language production, and see what we can learn about how typically developing toddlers learn to combine words and morphemes in their speech before the age of three.

7.2.0 Theories

As we said in Chapter 2, there is intense controversy about language development—and especially about the development of grammar—between two groups of language researchers. One group thinks that people's knowledge of possible linguistic patterns is INNATE—that it's built into human minds genetically—which would mean that children just need to be able to figure out which of those patterns are used in the particular language around them. The other group (including me) thinks that what is built into our minds is not knowledge of language, but an extraordinary ability to find the patterns that are present in the hundreds of thousands of examples that children hear. Either way, though, we must be born with a tremendous potential to deal with communicative signals, and not only signals about what is happening now, but reports about the past, ideas about the future, and pure fiction—a communicative system that is much richer than any other animal has.

But whatever language capacity children are born with, it isn't something that can make them start out sounding like adults except for having small vocabularies. Inside each toddler's head are their own phonology, morphology, syntax, and semantics, none of which are yet adultlike. Also, each toddler catches on first to somewhat different aspects of the language around her (the AMBIENT LANGUAGE). But some of those aspects are harder to grab onto than others for everyone: Even a casual knowledge of toddlers will tell you that the [ð] and [θ] sounds of *the* and *think* are more difficult for them than the sound [m], and that regular plurals, as in *Hands cold,* are likely to be OVERGENERALIZED—that is, to be used incorrectly on nouns that in fact have irregular plurals (*Foots cold,* or *feets cold*). A good theory needs to be able to explain both what children do differently from one another and what they all have in common. You can make up your own mind about innateness when you think you know enough about it, or you can decide not to take sides.

7.2.1 Two ways that syntax gets started

For many children, syntax gets started gradually, and it happens in two different ways at the same time: They use both a WHOLE-PHRASE STRATEGY and a WORD-COMBINING STRATEGY. Some toddlers seem to rely very heavily on one or the other; some have a relatively even mix of the two approaches. The whole-phrase strategy, as you'd guess, means that the toddler uses phrases that seem to be modeled on whole adult two- or three-word utterances like *I like it, do it, Pick you up.* The phrases usually have at least one pronoun, which is often produced just as a schwa sound: [ə ˈwaikə], [ˈduə], [pɪkə ˈʌp]. Furthermore, the toddler doesn't seem to use the words in these phrases separately, or to give us any other evidence that she knows that the individual syllables in the phrases are actually words that have their own meanings. Sometimes we can even be certain that she is using a particular phrase as an unanalyzed whole: when the phrase contains the second person pronoun *you,* but the toddler uses the phrase about herself—for example, when she says, *Pick you up* as a request for someone to pick her up. What she has learned, apparently, is that this whole phrase goes with being picked up. Saying the phrase that goes with the picking-up event she wants is a kind of handle on getting it to happen again, just the way saying *milk* is a handle on getting some milk.

Another way we can get evidence that a phrase has been learned as a whole is to wait and see what happens to it. If *do it* later shows up in combinations like *do it button* and *do it shoe* (for "tie," "put on," or "take off" my shoe), where *do button* or *do shoe* would have meant the same thing, then the toddler probably hasn't realized that *do it* contains the words *do* and *it*. But this realization eventually does happen; the child's brain starts to recognize that the phrase has parts.

Starting off with phrases instead of single words is not a bad thing, as some child language experts used to think. After all, if the toddler is learning a language like Portuguese, where every verb form contains an ending, she'll figure out subconsciously that words like *falo* "I speak," *fala* "he/she speaks," *parto* "I leave," *parte* [partʃi] etc., are all ways of combining the morphemes *fal-* "speak," *part-* "leave"; *-o* "I," *-a* and *–e* "he/she," even though she won't ever hear any of those morphemes by itself. In the same way, a child learning English could learn the difference between *Pick you up* and *Pick me up* before she learned to say *you* or *me* as single words.

The word-combining strategy

The other strategy that toddlers use is to take two words they already know and combine them. If you watch toddlers when they first start to do this, you can see that it is a lot harder for them than we would imagine. Some toddlers start communicating combinations of ideas by, for example, shaking their head "no" and saying *good* in order to say that something isn't good. A gesture + word comment may also involve a combination of pointing and a word; for example, a little boy named Danny at two years and three months says *shopping* while pointing to himself and then to his mother, verifying that they were both about to go grocery-shopping. An even more dramatic illustration of gesture combination is an observation of an 18-month-old named Jacob at the one-word stage directing an adult in a well-practiced game of pretending to feed toy animals: He hands his caregiver a toy shovel (to use as a spoon), and points first to a pretend "dish" and then to the mouth of the animal he wants her to feed. In this familiar game, his Message Level contains the caregiver, the spoon, the dish, the toy animal, the idea that the animal should eat—and presumably, the imagined food as well. So one thing that we learn from multigesture and gesture + word combinations at the one-word stage is that what's keeping the children who produce them from combining words is not a conceptual problem: They obviously can hold onto and communicate two or more ideas at the same time. The reason why children who can combine a word with a gesture are stuck with saying only single words is probably a matter of their very limited, effort-laden word production skills.

Some of Danny's earliest two-word combinations were greetings and farewells, including ones that sound pretty odd: *Hi, hen!* The word-combining strategy tends to produce sequences that don't sound much like adults talking: *comb car, Mike home, mommy milk, tires on, Bob car.* Most of the utterances produced by the word-combining strategy are also strikingly different from the ones produced using the whole-phrase strategy; like the ones you've just seen, these early combinations almost never have articles, pronouns, prepositions, conjunctions, or the COPULAS (linking verbs) *is* and *are*. Instead, they are made of words that are likely either to be said by themselves, or in accented positions at the ends of sentences like the words *off* and *on* in the sentences *Take it **off**, Put it **on**!*

The two-word stage

Many—perhaps most—typically developing toddlers learning English spend a while making two-word combinations like these, so this period of time is called the TWO-WORD STAGE. (Remember not to take the term "stage" literally—a toddler who is making mostly two-word utterances will still have many one-word utterances, and probably a few longer ones.) To understand what a toddler's two-word combinations like *comb car* mean, we need to see them live or on video. We also make notes about whether she is asking what or where something is, demanding it, commenting, greeting, or perhaps just playing with the words. In adult language, after all, the same word or combination of words can mean different things depending on the context, including what the hearer thinks the speaker knows or doesn't know: *Sopranos tonight?* might be used to mean either "Is *The Sopranos* on tonight?" or "Do you want to watch *The Sopranos* tonight?" In the same way, *Daddy car* can be used to mean "Daddy's in the car," "Daddy's driving the car," "I want Daddy to get in the car," "That's Daddy's car," "Put the Daddy doll in the toy car," and so on.

Toddlers try to express a substantial range of semantic relations between people, things, and actions with two words. Here are some typical early semantic relations, and the usual terms for them:

Object-Location:	*Hat chair* (the hat's on the chair)
	Daddy car (Daddy's in the car)
	Mike home (Mike is at home)
Action-Location:	*Put chair* (put something on the chair)
Possession:	*Mommy sock* (that's Mommy's sock)

(See the note about Lois Bloom's famous *Mommy sock* in Materials for Chapter 7 on your CD.)

	Bob car (that's Bob's car)
Agent-Action:	*Mommy sock* (Mommy is putting my sock on, I want Mommy to put my sock on)
Action-Object:	*Eat cracker*

But children keep on pushing their own linguistic boundaries, wanting to say things beyond what they can quite manage to put into words. For example, a combination of two words and a gesture made up the following report from Danny: [gæk] (cracker) + (finger pointing into mouth) + *byebye* = "I've just eaten a cracker."

7.2.2 The conquest of morphology: Observations and experiments

We mentioned morphology just briefly in section 7.2.1, with Portuguese verb forms as an example. Now let's look at it more seriously. Children learning English don't have nearly as many verb forms to figure out as children who are learning a language that has extensive SUBJECT-VERB AGREEMENT, and English only has three noun forms: singulars, plurals, and possessives. So first-language English learners probably start figuring that words can have meaningful parts—that they can be made up of several morphemes—a little later than children learning, say, Portuguese, German, Russian, or Turkish, where there is much more AGREEMENT and CASE-marking. (You might want to review the names for the different kinds of morphemes, in Chapter 1, section 1.4, before you read the rest of this section.)

Observations

Some of those first observational explorations of toddlers' English done by Roger Brown and his students (many of whom became leaders of the next generation of child language researchers) tried to see whether there was a particular order in which children mastered basic English word endings, and how the discovery of those inflectional morphemes compared with the discovery of the function words—the articles, pronouns, and prepositions—that are also routinely missing in the two-word stage.

They discovered quite a bit of uniformity: The first bound morpheme that most English-learning children used reliably was the progressive *-ing* morpheme, and the first free grammatical morphemes were the prepositions *in* and *on*. (*In* and *on* as adverbs—that is, without a noun following them—were produced much earlier, as in *Shoe on!* or *Hat off!*) The regular noun plural ending (at least its /-s/ and /-z/ forms) came next after those two prepositions. After the plural, something a little unexpected happened: Children began to distinguish present and past tenses for a few of the common irregular verbs (not always the same ones): perhaps *sit* vs. *sat*, *go* vs. *went*, or *come* vs. *came*, even though they hadn't yet picked up on the regular past tense endings. (This is probably because the difference made by adding /d/, /t/ or /əd/ to a verb like *hug, walk,* or *pat* is a lot harder to hear than the difference made by the vowel change from *sit* to *sat.*) Toddlers caught onto the possessive *-'s* next, and after that, the first of the linking verbs, *is,* in some (but not all!) of its contexts. Articles *the* and *a* were next, then the regular past tense of verbs like *hugged* and *walked,* and, finally, tenth on Brown's list of 14 grammatical morphemes, came the third-person singular /-s/ and /-z/ endings of *runs* and *walks.* The reasons why these particular words are learned in this order are complex, but we know that it's not just a frequency order; if it had been, the definite article *the* would be the first grammatical morpheme learned. Several factors seem to affect the order in which children learn these English endings and function words: How much information you need to take into account to choose the correct form (there's only one –ing, but there are three different forms of each of the –s endings), how regular the form is, how frequent the form is, and how easy it is to perceive it. Another factor, probably, is how many different things a particular grammatical form means, that is, how many different morphemes it represents, because the child has to sort these out and it must be very confusing. (The English –s ending signals plural or possessive on nouns, third person singular on verbs, and it can also be the contracted form of *is* as in *it's here,* or of auxiliary *has,* as in *he's won!*) Some readings about the order of acquisition of grammatical morphemes are suggested at the end of this chapter.

Experiments

Now, do children really learn the rules for making these two-morpheme words? Or do they just memorize the fact that the plural of *cat* is *cats,* the same way that they must have to memorize that the plural of *child* is *children*? And when they start to use articles, do they understand the subtle difference between saying **a** cat and **the** cat, or between **a** *muffin* and **some** *muffin*? Brown and his students did the first experiments to try to answer these questions, and hundreds of others have followed, exploring dozens of languages and many types of language patterns. We'll look at the most famous of all those experiments, originally published in 1958, and you can work through several more in the Challenges for Chapter 7 if you like. It will take us out of the toddler age range; the children in these studies were four and older.

Here is a wug

Do children memorize all the inflected forms that they know, or do they subconsciously learn rules for making plurals and past tenses? Brown's doctoral student Jean Berko decided to settle the question of whether children just memorize regular plural noun forms (*dog, dogs*), regular past tense forms (*hug, hugged*), and so on, or whether they tune into the patterns of endings that we studied in Chapter 4. It was a pretty good bet that children did learn rules, because otherwise it would be very hard to explain why they sometimes used incorrect forms like *foots* or *feets* and *comed* or *camed*. But it was hard to prove it, and before 1958, there was no tool for studying just when this learning took place.

Here is what Berko figured out: "If a child knows that the plural of *witch* is *witches,* he may simply have memorized the plural form. If, however, he tells us that the plural of **gutch* is **gutches,* we have evidence that he actually knows, albeit unconsciously, one of those rules which the descriptive linguist, too, would set forth in his grammar."

Berko's brilliant insight and artistic talent produced a simple task, usually called the Wug Test, that has turned out to work very well with preschoolers and first-graders in many languages and cultures (as long as the parents in that culture have the habit of reading picture books to their children and encouraging them to name the pictures). She created a set of picture cards showing mostly imaginary creatures and objects, and people doing familiar and unfamiliar things. Here are about a third of the items she used, and two of the pictures she drew.

1. Plural. Picture: One bird-like animal, then two.

   "This is a wug /wʌg/. Now there is another one. There are two of them. There are two _____."

2. Plural. Picture: One bird, then two.

   "This is a gutch /gʌtʃ/. Now there is another one. There are two of them. There are two _____."

5. Past tense. Picture: Man swinging an object (Figure 7.1).

   "This is a man who knows how to rick /rɪk/. He is ricking. He did the same thing yesterday. What did he do yesterday? Yesterday he _____."

6. Diminutive and compounded or derived word. Picture: One animal, then a miniscule animal.

   "This is a wug. This is a very tiny wug. What would you call a very tiny wug? _____

   This wug lives in a house. What would you call a house that a wug lives in?" _____

This is a man who knows how to RICK.
He is Ricking. He did the same thing
yesterday. What did he do yesterday?
Yesterday he _____.

Figure 7.1. Rick-Ricked. (Version with original colors on CD.) Reproduced by permission of Jean Berko Gleason.

11. Past tense. Man doing calisthenics.

"This is a man who knows how to mot /mat/. He is motting. He did the same thing yesterday. What did he do yesterday? Yesterday he _____."

13. Plural. Picture: One animal, then two.

"This is a tass /tæs/ (Figure 7.2). Now there is another one. There are two of them. There are two _____.

18. Past tense. Picture: Man exercising.

"This is a man who knows how to gling /glɪŋ/. He is glinging. He did the same thing yesterday. What did he do yesterday? Yesterday he _____."

[*Gling* was created because it has several different reasonable answers: *glinged*, *glang*, or *glung*]

Berko put the real words that she wanted to compare with the nonsense words towards the end of the experiment, so that they couldn't influence

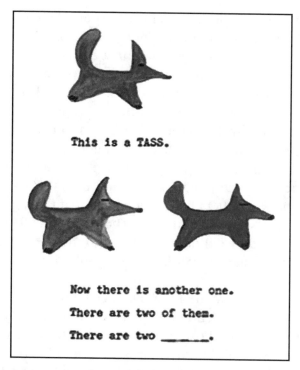

This is a TASS.

Now there is another one.
There are two of them.
There are two _____.

Figure 7.2. Tass-Tasses. (Version with original colors on CD.) Reproduced by permission of Jean Berko Gleason.

how the children answered the questions about the nonsense words: *Glass* came several turns after *tass*, *ring* came a while after *gling*, and *melt* came a while after *mot*.

17. Plural. Picture: One glass, then two.

"This is a glass. Now there is another one. There are two of them. There are two _____."

22. Past tense. Picture: A bell.

"This is a bell that can ring. It is ringing. It did the same thing yesterday. What did it do yesterday? Yesterday it _____."

26. Past tense. Picture: An ice cube, then a puddle of water.

"This is an ice cube. Ice melts. It is melting. Now it is all gone. What happened to it? It _____."

Berko's paper reported lots of comparisons between children of different ages and items of different types, as well as very thoughtful analyses, but we'll focus on the main results for the noun plural endings. Here are some of Berko's most important results about the plural: Three-quarters of preschool children aged 4 and 5 could put a correct /-z/ on the nonsense word *wug*, and about the same number could put a correct /-s/ on the nonsense word *heaf,* or change it to *heaves,* which is also correct. (In case you were wondering, Berko tested a bunch of adults on her materials before she used them with children; "correct" means what the adults did, which almost always matches what we would predict from having analyzed the patterns linguistically.) Three-quarters of the preschool children had also learned that the plural of *glass* has the /-əz/ ending. However, only about a quarter of them were able to put that ending on *tass*.

The first-graders had learned more: They could all fill in *glasses* as the plural of *glass,* and they did rather better than the preschool children on most of the other nonsense words, but still, only about 40% could give a correct plural for *tass*.

So what's the bottom line here? First, children do learn the rules for putting the commonest endings on English words, and they've got a good start on learning some of those rules well before they turn six. Second, if a morpheme has several different forms, like the plural morpheme with /-s/, /-z/, /-əz/, they may not all be learned at the same time; for the English plural, at least, the commonest forms are learned first. And third, tuning into the rules takes time, almost certainly because a substantial number of examples of a pattern has to be learned before your brain can sense the pattern and learn it well enough to use it in speaking. That's what we learn from the big age gap between the children who are only able to respond *two ... glasses* and the children who are also able to respond *two... tasses*.

If you like, you can look at what Berko found out about the details of the noun plurals and about the verbs, adjectives, and compound words that she tested. A copy of her original paper downloads automatically from the Internet if you Google "Berko 1958" and click on "The Child's Learning of English Morphology." (Watch out for some annoying little errors, though: Several of her nonsense words are sporadically changed to similar real words; for example, *tass* sometimes comes out *class* or *lass*. Too much top-down processing by a spell-checking Optical Character Recognition program!)

7.2.3 Back to observing toddlers: How does "real syntax" develop?

First, we'd better think about what it means to have real syntax: that is, to be able to combine words so that the pattern that they are combined in is meaningful. Linguists call a meaningful pattern of words a CONSTRUCTION; examples of constructions that you already know from Chapter 1 include TRANSITIVE CLAUSES and PREPOSITIONAL PHRASES.

What is a construction? How does a pattern have a meaning? This is a slippery idea.

The transitive clause construction

We'll start off with the clearest example in English, the TRANSITIVE CLAUSE construction—remember, that's the pattern of subject-verb-object that we know so well from textbook sentences like *The cat chased the mouse*, *The mouse chased the cat*, and, to take some less standard examples, *Chris misses Toby, Toby misses Chris*; *The ship sighted the raft, The raft sighted the ship*. In these REVERSIBLE SENTENCES, we are very aware that the order of the words is the key to understanding the speaker's meaning: if you interchange the subject and the object, you get a sentence that is grammatical but has the opposite meaning.

How does the word order tell is who is doing what? Well, we know that the noun phrase 1- verb- noun phrase 2 pattern is telling us something about the entity (the person, animal, or thing) that the subject noun phrase refers to. Depending on the verb, that "something" might be what it's doing, what has happened to it, what it feels, or what it's like.

The object noun phrase has a different role: Primarily, it gives us more details about the verb, although we do need knowledge of the world in order to be able to infer those details. Visualize chasing a rat; it's very different from chasing, say, a car, or a rainbow. Sighting a raft is different from sighting a star, or a whale. Really, a huge amount of the meaning we get from a sentence isn't "in" the sentence; it comes from the concepts that the words, combined into constructions, arouse in our minds. The approach to linguistics that explores this idea most fully is called COGNITIVE GRAMMAR.

So "verb-tells-about-subject; object-tells-more-about-verb" summarizes the meaning of the transitive subject-verb-object construction at its most general level, that is, for all of the kinds of transitive verbs we have in English. But young language learners probably don't start with learning this very general construction with its extremely vague meaning—or at least, that's not the main thing that they learn. Experiments suggest that toddlers learn specific meanings that are a lot more vivid, even though they don't apply to all English verbs, and that they might learn those specific meanings before they understand that there is a more general one. What they probably learn, for each verb or (more likely) for classes of verbs with related meanings, is its own particular way of connecting the SYNTACTIC ROLES of its SUBJECT and OBJECT to their SEMANTIC ROLES, such as AGENT,

THEME, and **UNDERGOER**. (Review Chapter 1, section 1.7, Chapter 3, section 3.2.2, or check the Glossary if you're not sure what these terms mean.) After we look at some major classes of English verbs, we can give a more precise version of this statement about what toddlers are probably learning early on.

TRANSITIVE ACTION VERBS are the class of verbs that describe someone really doing something to something or someone else, like *hit, kiss, pull, drink*, and so on. This is the verb type that's been studied the most, and for these verbs, the transitive construction means that:

1. The verb describes an action.

2. The thing that first noun phrase refers to is the subject, and its semantic role is the Agent; it does what the verb describes.

3. The thing that the second noun phrase refers to is the object, and its semantic role is the Theme or Undergoer; also, it is affected by that action: *The cat is chasing the mouse, The ball hits the baby, The rain flooded the highway.*

But for the sentence *Jimmy hears the doorbell*, what the verb affects is Jimmy, not the doorbell, right? *Hear* is not a transitive action verb, it's a **SENSORY VERB**; others are *see, hear,* and *smell.* When a verb is a sensory verb, children must learn a different specific meaning for the subject-verb-object construction, like this:

1. The verb describes a way of getting information about the world. The thing that first noun phrase refers to is the subject, and it's paying attention to that information (it's alive; it's not asleep); its semantic role is **EXPERIENCER**—that is, it is something that is consciously receiving a sensation. (An Undergoer is similar to an Experiencer, but the Undergoer doesn't have to be conscious of an event—it just has to be affected by it.)

2. The thing that the second noun phrase refers to is the object, and it is the source of that information, regardless of whether it's doing anything at all. Its semantic role is sometimes labeled Natural Cause, sometimes **SOURCE**.

Probably children start by learning some information about the individual sensory verbs (*see, hear, smell, feel, taste*), and then tune in subconsciously to the fact that the syntax of all these sensory verbs works pretty much the same way, and that it's different from how the action verbs work.

(English has other kinds of verbs that you can think about describing. For example, the relationship between the syntactic roles and the semantic roles of the noun phrases used in transitive constructions with emotion verbs—*love, hate, like, enjoy, resent*—are like action verbs in some ways, but like sensory verbs in other ways.)

Now we can give that promised more precise phrasing of our hypothesis about what toddlers learn about their early verbs: For transitive action verbs like *push* and *kiss*, they learn that the noun that comes before the verb refers to someone who does the verb action (the pushing or kissing) to someone else, and that the noun that comes after the verb is the person (or thing) that's acted on—the one that gets pushed or kissed. For sensory verbs like *see* and *hear*, toddlers probably learn that the person whose name comes before the verb is someone who is noticing and taking in information about something, and that the person, thing, or event mentioned after the verb is the one that's being noticed. This way of formulating what toddlers learn about different verb constructions is intermediate between saying that they learn each verb singly (for example, learning that the subject of *push* is someone doing the pushing and the object of push is someone getting pushed, making no connection between how *push* works and how *kiss* works), and saying that they learn very general constructions from the beginning.

The prepositional phrase construction

Let's work briefly through the prepositional phrase construction now, so you can see how gradually one child learned this construction. Instead of trying to figure out the meaning at a completely general level that would cover all prepositional phrases, which would give us another extremely vague construction meaning, let's focus on describing the meaning of the first kind of prepositional phrase construction that children learn, the LOCATIVE PREPOSITIONAL PHRASE, which, as you would expect, tells us where something is.

Take the made-up sentence *Your stupid cat is on the pillow on my bed again.* Suppose we compare the sequence of words *on the pillow* to the sequence of words *the pillow on.* You recognize that *on the pillow* is a prepositional phrase (and even if you hadn't known what to call it, you would know, as an English speaker, that the words seem to go together in that order). So you know that *on the pillow* is a construction, rather than being just a list of words. But what does the construction itself mean? Well, what's the difference between *on the pillow* and *the pillow on*? In this example, *on the pillow* tells you where the cat is. But although *the pillow on* looks like it's set to tell you where the pillow is, it's incomplete; it doesn't actually tell you anything. That's a major difference.

Now let's try to describe the meaning of the locative prepositional phrase construction explicitly.

1. The locative prepositional phrase construction is a locative **MODIFIER**; it describes or identifies (modifies) something by telling you where that thing is. (Annoyingly, there's no convenient grammatical term for this thing that is being modified.) In our example, the cat is the thing being modified by *on the pillow,* and the pillow is the thing that is being modified by *on my bed.*

2. The noun phrase that refers to the thing being modified (for example, *the cat*) is not part of the prepositional phrase. (Usually, the noun phrase comes before the prepositional phrase in English, but we can also say things like *Under the bed lurked the cat.*)

3. The locative prepositional phrase construction is made up of two parts: the preposition and a noun phrase that follows it. The noun phrase that follows the preposition is called the **OBJECT OF THE PREPOSITION**.

4. The object of the preposition names an entity (a person, animal, or thing) that is somewhere.

5. The preposition describes the spatial or support relation between the thing being modified and the object of the preposition.

Why didn't I just say "spatial relation"? Why "spatial or support"? Because some really common English prepositions—especially *on*, as it happens—are not just about direction. Think about the meanings of *on* in the prepositional phrases *on the wall, on the ceiling, on the airplane, on the bottom of your shoe. On* is really about what is supporting the thing being modified; we infer the directional information from our real-world knowledge of how things are normally oriented, just as we inferred the details of a verb's meaning in a particular sentence from our knowledge of the world.

Developing syntax: A longitudinal look at the development of prepositional phrases

Now let's go back to observing Danny, a toddler just beginning to put two words together in what sounds like a phrase, and see how his prepositional phrase construction developed. (Danny was a slightly late talker, but he grew up to be a journalist.)

Remember that being able to use a whole memorized phrase isn't syntax, and neither is just stringing together words that happen to be relevant to a situation; syntax is putting separate words into a construction. When Danny gets started on putting two words together in what sounds like a phrase, and in contexts where they make sense as phrases, some of them would be constructions for English-speaking adults. These include greetings (*Hi, foot*), possessives (*Mommy house, Mike's cucumber*), adjective + noun (*green pop* = green lollipop, *big soap*), locatives (*soap legs, books chair*), and action + object (*eat candy, drop roll*). (By the way, I've translated these from Danny's phonology to English spelling; more about how he actually said them is in this chapter's section on children's early phonology, section 7.5.) There's no way to prove that these are constructions for Danny. They could just be, as I just said, pairs of words that both happen to be relevant to what Danny is interested in.

However, they do seem to be quite different from some other word combinations from the same two weeks of the diary record, ones that are definitely not organized into constructions. Some of these are imitations or delayed imitation, and in all of them, Danny seems to be trying to say something that's syntactically way over his head. Here, for example, on a hot September day, he's all excited about getting into the plastic wading pool in the back yard along with his big brother:

In- in- pool- boys . . . in- too- tootoo- pool- pool

And here, he's pretending that he and other people are in a toy car:

truck - too - in - Dan - here.

Rehearsing the reassurance *The moon will be up before you go to sleep*, the diary notes say " . . . over the next half hour, long jumbles like *moon up sleep sleep moon; up moon sleep; sleep moon up.*"

So, although we can't always be sure whether a particular form is a construction, if it's part of a reliable pattern of combination, with each word used in a predictable place with a predictable meaning, it's reasonable to call it one.

When the missing free and bound grammatical morphemes—articles, prepositions, pronouns, linking verbs possessives, and so on—start to get filled in, so that we hear phrases like *Mommy's house* or *I eating a candy*, it becomes easier to see which of Danny's phrases are (and probably have been) constructions and which ones are just strings of relevant but syntactically unconnected words.

We can clearly see Danny's transitional period for learning locative prepositional phrases in these diary data, as he gradually moves from strings of relevant words to a stable construction for expressing location and change of location, because we have data from a period of some weeks when he only had one preposition that he could use in a prepositional phrase or in an adverbial phrase. His other locative preposition/adverb had not yet settled down to stable word orders. During that time, as he is putting away his toy cars and trucks, Danny sometimes says *table —off* and sometimes *off—table*, sometimes *truck—off* and sometimes *off—truck*. But during the same period, he says just *on table* (*on* + location) and *truck on* (object + locative adverb), without varying their word order. So these two phrases with *on* are now constructions, and not just "two words that happened to be relevant," because the words in them are each used in a predictable place with a predictable meaning. However, the phrases with *off* are not constructions yet—the location sometimes comes before and sometime after the *off*, and the object sometimes comes after and sometimes before it, with no difference in the meaning.

The theoretical question of where a child's syntax comes from, and how these transitions are relevant to that question, goes far beyond the scope of this book, but the question of whether a phrase is a construction for a given speaker is a very practical matter for people who are dealing with language disorders. Should a child who says *dog—mine* be scored as having a possessive construction? A sentence with a missing linking verb? Will making this decision one way or another affect whether she gets social services? How about a person with aphasia who is apparently talking about an important event: Does *doctor—call* mean that the doctor called someone or that someone called the doctor? You can imagine how getting the wrong interpretation can cause real-life trouble. (Those two words could also be an order or a request to call the doctor, but those meanings would be made clear by the rise or fall of the aphasic speaker's voice, tone of voice, and facial expression.) If you have enough data to see whether there could be a consistent pattern of the same word order being used with the same meaning, then you have evidence toward deciding whether your client has a construction.

Formulas: An early strategy for putting words together

One of the odder things that Danny (and many other children) do is to greet all sorts of objects as well as people and animals; you saw his *Hi, foot* earlier. Why would they do that? Well, young children (and beginning second language speakers and people with aphasia) know that normal speakers have lots of long utterances. And one of the ways that people with limited language production can sound more like normal speakers is to use a mix of memorized and new material. The memorized part, for example, *Will you now all please welcome tonight's special guest* . . . , is called a **FORMULA**, and the complete utterance, *Will you now all please welcome tonight's special guest, William Shakespeare!* is called a **FORMULAIC UTTERANCE**. You can think of a formula as being like a recipe that allows you to add one or two ingredients to customize it; with basic oatmeal cookie dough, you can add raisins, nuts, or chocolate chips. Here's an example of a formula being used by a little fellow just about to turn three; you can see how it lets him take a conversational turn. He had learned to say, about a rather small house cat, *Tanya's small, but she's not too small*. One night, he was sitting on a new high chair at dinner, and his mother exclaimed *Your chair is red!* The little boy immediately answered, *It's red, but it's not too red*.

With a greeting formula like *Hi* + <name>, a request formula like <food word> + *please*, or a command formula like *put* + <object name> + *down*, a toddler can make formulaic utterances like *Hi, daddy*; *Cookie, please*; and *Put teddy down*. These make him sound more like the bigger kids, so he becomes more socially competent. Some of children's constructions probably emerge from learning to vary these formulas a little more, or to recognize subconsciously that some of them are similar. For example, starting from the two formulas *put* + <object name> + *down* (**Put** *teddy* **down**) and *pick* + <object name> + *up* (**Pick** *teddy* **up**), a toddler could move to a more adult-like construction with many more options, like {Change-of-Position Verb} = <*put, pick, take* . . . > + <object name> + {Location word} = <*up, down, on, off, in, out*>.

What's the difference between a formula and a construction? There is no dividing line; that, in fact, is one of the main claims of Construction Grammar. But we tend to use the term "formula" for utterance recipes that seem to allow very little variation (one or two empty slots and a small set of things that can go into them), and "construction" for utterance recipes that have more flexibility.

As we said in Chapter 4, section 4.1.3, even skilled speakers use formulas to extend their sentences and to play for time while they are thinking of what to say next. Normal speakers (and people with milder types of aphasia) smoothly fill what would be gaps in our conversations and our monologues with idiomatic phrases like, *So then what happens next is* . . . , *Well, now that you mention it, in my opinion* . . . *Betcha can't wait to* . . . and many other stock phrases that go in and out of fashion over the years. Most skilled of all at using formulas in our society are ad-lib commentators, talk show hosts, and rap stars; in societies with less literacy, from Homeric Greece to today's indigenous cultures, traditional poets and storytellers use the same kind of strategies to keep their monologues flowing.

7.3 Do Toddlers Have Grammar in the First Year of Speaking?

Now let's step back before the two-word "stage," and consider the younger toddlers who are still only using one word at a time. What do they understand out of the grammar that surrounds them? Can we tell whether children understand the meaning of a construction before they can use it? We've seen that toddlers can memorize some phrases like *I want it* and use them without understanding how the parts were put together. So at least some of the time, the phrases that these toddlers produce sound as though they have a structure but probably don't. However, if children are going to get beyond a handful of memorized whole phrases and formulas and become able to use more flexible constructions, like the transitive clauses and the prepositional phrases that we worked through at the beginning of section 7.2.3, they have to understand what their formulas mean. So: When do children start to understand these basic constructions, and how do we know that they understand them if they can't use them? The one that has been studied the most, because it's so basic, is the transitive clause construction. Let's look at the evidence from one of these studies.

Preferential looking: A window into early comprehension of syntax

It turns out that toddlers do begin to understand the difference between *Daddy tickle Danny* and *Danny tickle Daddy* while they are still only using one word at a time. However, it takes laboratory techniques to show it, because toddlers at the one-word stage still need a lot of visual context to understand almost anything. Words alone (except maybe for their name and a shout of *No!*) can't produce enough activation to override all the things that their brains are busy processing; if you have experience with trying to get a toddler to change what she's paying attention to, you know exactly what this means. Regardless of what you say to them, you can't get children at the one-word stage to point to a picture of Big Bird tickling Ernie instead of Ernie tickling Big Bird. (Or even to reliably point to pictures of Ernie and Big Bird when someone asks them *Where's Big Bird? Where's Ernie?*).

The most influential studies of toddlers' language comprehension, starting in the late 1980s, have been done by the team of Kathy Hirsh-Pasek at Temple University in Philadelphia and Roberta Golinkoff at the University of Delaware. Instead of trying to get a wiggly toddler to point to one of two pictures, they set up a lab so that they could simply see which of two pictures the little one looked at more, and whether what she heard could influence what she looked at; this is the **PREFERENTIAL LOOKING** method. The lab is set up with two TV screens in front, a speaker between the TV screens, and the toddler on a parent's lap. A video camera is hidden between the TV screens, and the video recording is used later to score which TV screen the toddler was watching at each moment. The parent wears headphones playing music loud enough to drown out the sound of the speaker, and a blindfold, so he can't see the TV screens.

Two different scenes are shown on the TV screens. For example, to start by making sure that the toddler knows who's who, a clip of Ernie is shown on one screen, a clip of Big Bird on the other, and a recorded voice on the speaker says *Where's Big Bird?* for a while, then *Where's Ernie?* If the child looks more at the screen with Ernie when she hears *Where's Ernie?* and more at the screen with Big Bird when she hears *Where's Big Bird?*, she's good to go on to the main part of the study, which deals with the real issue: If one screen shows Big Bird tickling Ernie and the other shows Ernie tickling Big Bird, will she look more at the picture of Ernie tickling Big Bird when she hears *Ernie is tickling Big Bird?* And to make sure that it's not just because she likes looking at how Big Bird bounces and giggles when he is being tickled, the experimenters also check to see whether the toddler looks more at the other picture, the one with Big Bird doing the tickling, when the voice on the speaker switches to saying, *Big Bird is tickling Ernie.* (We're skipping some of the training and double-checking details here; a fuller description, taken from Hirsh-Pasek and Golinkoff's 1996 book, is on your CD.) About half the children in the young toddler age range (16 to 19 months) don't complete a typical experiment—too fretful, doesn't know and can't learn the Muppets' names, the parents peeked—and some of them don't in fact seem to pay attention to what they hear. But three-quarters of the children who stayed in the study averaged more time looking at the TV screen that matched what they were hearing than at the one that didn't. So even though they were just one-word-users themselves, those children had begun to know the meaning of the transitive verb construction: They knew that if they heard *Big Bird is tickling Ernie*, then Big Bird was the one doing the tickling.

Do notice the fact that I wrote "had *begun* to know" just above. The Preferential Looking paradigm is designed to pick up on a rather early stage of knowledge: when the children have started to expect that a name before a familiar action verb like *wash* or *tickle* or *feed* is the person doing that action. They have a long way to go before they are 100% sure of this, and before they also have the same expectation for other kinds of subject nouns, and before they can point to the right picture. They also don't yet know which verbs work this way and which ones, like *see* and *hear*, belong to a different construction (because their grammatical subject and object are connected to their semantic roles in a different way).

Now we can go back and put in that fix to the Jimmy *Nobody don't like me* story that I promised you at the end of section 7.1.4. I said, among other things, that Jimmy doesn't know that English treats *nobody* as a singular noun, and that he probably hasn't figured it out even after he tacks the *-s* onto *like*, because if he had, he should have moved to saying *Nobody doesn't likes me*. But we've just seen that learning is a gradual process, and that children start to learn syntactic constructions and get a vague idea of what they mean long before they can produce them or be completely sure of their meaning. So we have to modify what we said about Jimmy; instead of saying that he doesn't know something, if we're being careful, we have to say that he doesn't know it well enough for it to help his comprehension or affect his production. His intake from his famous conversation was probably somewhat more than the (likely temporary) ability to put an *-s* on the end of *like* in this particular sentence—he probably did pick up some subconscious information about the *Nobody likes me* pattern. But it's going to take him many more encounters with this pattern for it to be strong enough to compete with the *Nobody don't like me* pattern when he speaks, and then to take over. Most of the time, we can only measure intake by what children do in comprehension, imitation, and production, and that kind of measure doesn't take into account the partial knowledge that precedes their changes in how they speak. A new generation of longitudinal experiments looking at brain waves might be able to let us watch this gradual process as it happens.

7.4 Language From the Third Trimester to the Beginning of Speech: First the Sounds, Then Their Meanings

7.4.1 When does language begin?

Before birth, if you want the short answer. But as we've seen, it takes several years of hard work and practice to learn very much about language. What we should say is that language *learning* begins before birth. Fetal heartbeat monitors tell us that third-trimester babies are listening, because their heartbeat changes when they hear new sounds. And they are actually learning, not just listening: Newborns prefer to listen to their mother's voice rather than the voices of other women, so they must have learned some specific things about how her voice sounds. (Unsurprisingly, what they actually like best, given the choice, is a reproduction of her voice that's filtered to match the muffled sounds they were hearing before they were born.) Four-day-olds also have already learned something about the rise and fall of the pitch patterns of the ambient language, because they prefer its sound to the sound of foreign languages. And they have a little bit of control of their vocal fold vibration: Newborn cries are somewhat different in their pitch patterns depending on the language they heard before they were born. French phrases rise in pitch except at the ends of sentences, but German phrases mostly have falling pitch contours, and French infants tend to produce cries with a rising melody contour, while German infants mostly produce cries with falling contours.

A tremendous amount more about language is learned during the first six months, even before children visibly seem to respond differently to hearing their own names and other similar names. That's why newborn hearing screening has finally been provided for by state governments (at least in 38 states in the United States as of February 2008): Listening training and parent communication training that start before six months works much better than later intervention, and they make it much more likely for deaf and severely hearing-impaired children to succeed in the hearing world. Early cochlear implants work better; also, they need to be in place before the areas of the brain that are best for processing sound get co-opted for processing other kinds of information. We hope we are done with the days when children's hearing wasn't tested until two years or older, and then only if their speech seemed to be delayed.

But it took years of experiments to figure out that young infants were intently listening and learning the outer form of language, and its phonology. Observation was misleading, because young infants have such poorly controlled responses—they can't point or reach, or even turn their heads very well, so it's really hard to tell anything about what they are paying attention to. The first major breakthrough in studying infant perception came in 1971, when a research team led by Peter Eimas used one of the few actions that a newborn has under good control, sucking, and one of our basic human needs, entertainment. The idea was brilliantly simple, and it has been adapted for many other studies since then: Give a baby a pacifier to suck on that has a switch inside it; when the baby sucks, a sound plays. Babies get excited about this, and suck hard and often for a while, but then, as they hear the same sound over and over, they get bored, just like anybody else. So if you want to know whether babies like one sound better that another, you can see how long it takes them to get bored with it. That technique is what allows us to say what sounds they prefer.

But what Eimas's pioneering group did was something a little different, because they wanted to know whether infants could hear the single-
ARTICULATORY-FEATURE differences between speech sounds, for example,
between /t/ and /d/, and if not, whether this ability developed over
time. (If you don't remember this terminology clearly, review Chapter 1,
section 1.1, especially sections 1.2.3 on ARTICULATORY FEATURES through
1.2.5 on PHONEMES.) So, for example, the loudspeaker played /ta/ every
time the baby sucked the pacifier: /ta/, /ta/, /ta/ . . . until she got bored and
slowed down.

Now comes the fun part: The experimenters changed the sound, say
to /da/, /da/, /da/. If the baby could hear the difference in the sound, she
would pick up the pace so that she could hear this new noise; if she couldn't
hear the change, she'd continue to suck on the pacifier only once in a while.
It was fantastic; other labs joined in, and soon we knew that young children
are born able to distinguish essentially all the sounds they would need to
speak any language in the world.

Does this mean that our brains are wired for language? Well, yes and
no. Quite a number of other animals can also tell /ta/ from /da/—Patricia
Kuhl of the University of Washington got famous for being the first person
to show this, with chinchillas! The best way to think about it is that human
language takes advantage of our innate speech-sound processing abilities,
and that those are very impressive.

7.4.2 The importance of being human: The other prerequisite for learning language

Besides being able to perceive the differences in sounds that are needed for
spoken language (or the differences in hand shapes and motion needed
for signed language), babies—at least by the age of six months, probably
earlier—have another essential ability for learning language: the ability to
pay attention to people and figure out what they are doing.

By five months, babies can figure out what another person is looking
at and look at it, too. This ability will, before the baby is a year old, become
an important part of their basis for figuring out what people mean when
they are talking: If the other person is at least glancing at the same thing
you are looking at while they are talking, they are probably giving you
information about it (its name, whether you can eat it, etc.), but if they are
looking somewhere else, whatever they are talking about is not what you're
looking at. If infants didn't understand the idea that other people pay
attention to particular things in the world around them and that you can
find out what it is by following their gaze, they would have a much harder

time figuring out that *duckie* and *squeak* are about the yellow rubber bath toy they are chewing on, while *water* and *wet* and *Is it too hot?* are about the warm wet stuff they are sitting in. Of course, it also helps a lot that people talking to babies usually try to make sure that the baby knows what they are talking about—tapping, shaking, or showing the duck, moving the baby's hand through the water—and that they also use big voice pitch changes to attract the baby's attention, plus using extra-clear articulation and lots of repetition of the key words in what they are saying.

By six months, babies can figure out some things about our intentions, which is going to be another essential element in realizing that when we talk, we are talking about something. Six-month-olds react differently to a person who is not giving them a toy because the toy is apparently stuck so the person can't move it and a person who is teasing them and is unwilling to give them the toy. In other words, they have the concepts of "can't" and "won't," which they will need in order to learn when asking for something might get it for them and when asking is not going to make a difference. If they didn't have this "intention-reading" ability, their ability to learn the outer form of language would just leave them stuck as pure imitators; they wouldn't have the sense that language is for communication or any way of figuring out what people's mouth noises (or hand shapes) mean.

Imagine how hard it would be to teach someone the difference between *can't* and *won't* if they didn't already have the basic concept of other people's intentions! Being able to interpret the mental states of other members of your species is not only important for learning language, it's important for the survival of any animal, and humans are normally very good at it. It's this ability that is particularly impaired in autism.

7.4.3 Changes in perception

Between about 10 and 12 months of age, children learn something that seems very strange: They learn *not* to attend to small differences in sounds that will not be meaningful in their own language. In the technical terms that you learned in Chapter 1, section 1.2.5, just about when children are starting to recognize the meanings of some of the words of their language, they are also learning to ignore phonetic differences that are not phonemic. And if the ambient language doesn't use a particular sound difference as a way to keep two phonemes apart, for example, if they are learning Japanese or some other language that doesn't distinguish /r/ and /l/—they will come quite close to losing the ability to tell the difference between those sounds by the time they are a year old, even though they had it, originally. (The difference between English "r" and "l" is not meaningful in Japanese because Japanese has neither of these speech sounds. Instead, it has one speech sound that English speakers hear sometimes as "r," sometimes as "l," and sometimes as "d." You can listen to it on the Materials for Chapter 7 on your CD, and see what I mean.) Similarly, by the age of 12 months, English-learning babies who hear only English speakers have learned not to attend to the difference between the [t] of *top* and the [t] of *stop*, which are slightly different (see Materials for Chapter 7 on your CD for examples and details). But these sounds are separate phonemes in Thai, and children growing up speaking Thai won't lose the ability to tell them apart.

If children get a chance to spend time interacting with speakers of a second language while they are young enough, they will regain the ability to make small distinctions that their first language doesn't have. But the older we are, the harder it is to relearn to hear small sound differences that are not phonemic in our first language. So if you know a language other than the language of your community, speak it to your children when they are young; even if they don't want to learn it from you, if they decide to learn it later, the early start will improve their comprehension and probably their accent. More about this in Chapter 9, section 9.2.2.

7.5 Phonological Development in Toddlers

7.5.1 Early prespeech development

If you look at a movie of articulators moving while someone is speaking (see Materials for Chapter 1 on your CD), or think about all the positions of articulation that we learned about in Chapter 1, and then about how quickly we have to move from one to another of them in producing words at five syllables per second or more, you can see that children have to master enormously skilled control of their mouths and vocal folds. One of the very first problems is learning to get the speed of the air when they breathe out and the tension in their vocal folds adjusted so that they vibrate (**PHONATE**) in a way that will make a nice voiced sound—a coo or an *aah* —instead of the wails and screeches that come out automatically. After some weeks or months of playing around with their voicing and getting it under control, and more playing around, perhaps separately, with moving their tongue, lips, and jaw, infants learn to put these skills together—to make their vocal folds vibrate and to change their mouth shapes to modify the sound that comes out. For many children, this comes at the same time that they are getting into the fun of repetitive kicking and arm waving; repetitive jaw-wagging plus phonation is fun, too, and produces the *babababa* or *dadada* of CANONICAL BABBLE. Canonical babble doesn't just mean repetitive syllables, although; it refers to any utterance with at least one well-formed syllable—a syllable containing at least one cleanly articulated consonant that's not an /h/ or a glottal stop.

Beginning to make canonical syllables is a milestone on the way to speech, and it has a huge normal age range: as early as 6 months, as late as 10 months. Even deaf infants without hearing aids or cochlear implants do a little canonical babbling, but they soon stop. Hearing children, however, keep on playing with it, sometimes just in private, sometimes everywhere, and sometimes enough to be rather more than entertaining. So here we have a really neat developmental story: Canonical babble (or at least the jaw-wagging aspect of it) gets started as part of the general flowering of motion games at around six months, and when it's combined with phonation, it gives a hearing baby the excitement of making sounds that are much more like what the adults around her are doing when they are talking than anything she has been able to do before. If a baby is deaf and can't hear the neat sounds she's making, the game gets boring after a while. But if she can hear, her babble morphs from a mouth-movement game into a sound-making game, just as all the kicking and arm waving that started out as movement for its own sake morph into grabbing and reaching and kicking off blankets.

However, it takes a long time to develop the control and the understanding of cause and effect that turn an exuberant arm wave to a purposeful grab. It takes even longer to be able to control phonation and jaw-wagging, observe the effects that they have on other people, and become able to make speechlike sounds for purposeful communication.

7.5.2 Perspective: Why does language start and develop?

The story of children's cognitive, social, and emotional development isn't simple. This is partly because they have so much to learn, but also because we can see at least four major forces nudging them (and us!), with different strengths, sometimes interweaving toward the same goal, but often pulling in somewhat different directions: the restless urge to explore new sensations, the determined desire to control and master at least a part of the world, the social urge to be like and cooperate with others around us, and the fundamental need for security and comfort. Just watching a couple of toddlers in a daycare center for a few hours should convince you of the reality of all four of these basic drives, the likelihood that at least two of them are involved in most of what a child does at any moment, and how they vary in strength from child to child and moment to moment. Climbing as high as she dares on a jungle gym, trying to get a tower of blocks to balance, playing a following-orders game like "Simon Says," curling up under a favorite blanket with a thumb in her mouth, trying to get the teacher's attention, picking up a dropped crayon and handing it to the person who dropped it—toddlers are kaleidoscopes of patterns formed by these drives.

The desire to communicate might also be fundamental, but it seems to be so much a part of the drives for control, social belonging, and security that we won't treat it separately. Another reason for not separating out communication as a drive on its own is that there are many ways to communicate, and a lot of what needs exploring is why a child chooses one way rather than another. Other researchers have smaller or larger lists of fundamental drives that they use to account for a children's behavior, but four is enough to work with.

For convenience, let's give the items on our list short names: **excitement**, **control**, **belonging**, and **comfort**. All of these drives play roles in the development of language, and they help to explain some of the variability from child to child. (Psycholinguistics can't explain everything.) In section 7.5.1, thinking about the infant learning to babble, you can see that we've already talked in terms of the drives for excitement and belonging. Control—the thrill of being able to produce the sounds you like on purpose, when you want to hear them—and comfort—being able to make sounds that remind you of your parents' voices, or that just sound soothing to you —are probably also ingredients in the development of canonical babble.

What's *not* on this short list of reasons for why language starts and develops is the simplistic behaviorist "Say cookie—get cookie; don't say cookie, don't get cookie" attempt at an explanation. It's false as a description of how children and adults really interact (apart from specific cases like the "Say please" drill used in some families), and it can't explain how children progress from noises to narratives, from squeals to chatty fantasies. For a typically developing child, the psychological rewards for speaking—excitement, control, belonging, and comfort—are much richer and also much less adult-controlled than a cookie here and a hug there, and—we hope—they include cookies and hugs along with many other good things.

7.5.3 Starting to find and make meaning: From babble to words, and places in between

We'll break this section up into two parts. First we'll work through utterances that pretty clearly originate before the baby fully catches onto the idea that specific adult mouth noise patterns have particular meanings, and then the ones where the baby seems to realize that language actually consists of specific and CONVENTIONAL sound-meaning pairs, that is, it's made up of words (or to be more precise, morphemes).

Jargon and protowords

A baby's delight in babbling, *ah*-ing, squealing, making raspberries, and other mouth sounds doesn't satisfy her for long. By about 10 months, she starts to make her sound play more like the sounds of the adults around her (excitement wears off; belonging starts to become more important), and sometimes she links her sounds to specific settings. Some babies on the verge of talking (and some who already have a few words) respond to the sound of the doorbell or the telephone with a "hello"-like sound, and some of them produce long conversation-like monologues with elaborate rises and falls, often called JARGON. Jargon performances aren't just matching the sounds of speech, though; they also have eye contact, gestures, facial expressions, gaze shifts, pauses—everything that you might observe if you were watching a movie of a conversation in a foreign language without subtitles. A stunning example of a long jargon performance that made the rounds online in the first half of 2009 is at http://www.metacafe.com/w/2159468/ (the link is also in your CD materials for this chapter). When you listen to a florid performance like this, it's impossible to escape the sense that the baby thinks that what she is doing is exactly what the adults around her are doing. It's the complete outer form of conversation, without content. She's interacting, but what she's communicating is essentially "being there with you."

If conversation were an improvisational performance like a jazz jam session, the baby performing jargon would be a master of at least one style already; but as we know, that's not all there is to having a conversation. Language does have a lexicon; particular sequences of sounds do have particular meanings, and speakers don't get to just make them up. They exist already; in standard terminology, words are CONVENTIONAL. (Rebelling against the conventional straitjacket of the lexicon is the fun in songs and stories featuring nonsense words and monster pseudo-words like *supercalifragilisticexpialidocious*.) Babies usually come to realize the conventionality of words rather slowly; jargon, early conventional (= real) words, and solo sound play can all be in their repertoire at the same time. Some babies also produce another kind of prespeech: specific, recurring word-like or slightly longer utterances which have a recognizable form that isn't modeled on any adult word. Diary studies are full of them; an example is a repeated vowel-plus-glide sequence *ioioio* . . . that a 14-month-old said while he was making or watching wheels, knobs, records, toys' eyes, and other objects rotate. These invented recurring utterances are called PROTOWORDS, and sometimes they become part of the family's private vocabulary for months or years.

The challenges of saying words, and how to study them: Child phonology

In Chapter 1, section 1.2.3, we showed how describing words in terms of IPA instead of letters and thinking about speech sounds as being composed of features help us to see that at least sometimes, there's a system to the way children pronounce their early words. That example was fake "data," not from a real child; I invented it for you to illustrate typical CHILD PHONOLOGY—that is, some of the commonest patterns that English-learning children between the ages of one and three use for approximating the sounds that they have trouble saying. Let's call our example child "Jenny" again. Table 7.1 presents Jenny's word list, and this time I'll organize the "data" as if you were studying any talker whose articulation couldn't pass for a normal adult native speaker's pronunciation—it could be a child developing typically or atypically, a second language learner, or a person

Table 7.1. Fictional Child Language Pronunciation "Data"

	Original Description	*IPA for Adult Word*	*IPA for Jenny's Word*
1	*bat* for *bad*	bæd	bæt
2	bat for *bag*	bæg	bæt
3	*tat* for *cat*	kæt	tæt
4	*dough* for *go*	go	do
5	*dawt* for *dog*	dɔg	dɔt
6	*tea* for *see*	si	ti
7	*Pete* for *piece*	pis	pit
8	*pit* for *fish*	fɪʃ	pɪt
9	*dat* for *that*	ðæt	dæt
10	*do* for *zoo*	zu	du
11	*bat-tomb* for *vacuum*	ˈvækyum	ˈbæt-tum
12	*bat-tomb* for *bathroom*	ˈbæθrum	ˈbæt-tum

with an acquired speech disorder. First, we get everything into IPA. Then we line up the target words and their pronunciations in the way that most people do: treating the target word as the input to the speaker's system, and her pronunciation of that word as output.

Table 7.1 gives the list in English orthography, then in IPA (middle Atlantic states English), with the adult and child pronunciations lined up. (Exercise 7.7 will give you a chance to practice the same kind of reorganization for a set of real data.)

Now, examine the differences between the adult word and Jenny's word in terms of features, because that's how you'll find patterns if there are any. Refer back to Table 1.1D for our fullest IPA consonant chart to use as a quick reminder about features, or click on the link to the IPA in Materials for Chapter 1 on your CD and review Chapter 1, section 1.2.3, if you don't quite remember what the feature names mean. Remember that if there are two symbols in a cell of the chart, the one on the left is voiceless (has no vocal fold vibration) and the one on the right is voiced (has some vocal fold vibration, at least when it's between two vowels).

In the first word (Jenny's *bæt* for adult *bæd*), the difference between the two pronunciations is that Jenny has a [t] instead of a [d], right? So she doesn't have voicing where the adult does. That's a common pattern for consonants at the ends of words; it seems to take toddlers a while to figure out how to keep air flowing through their vocal folds when it can't get out through either their nose or their mouth, in other words, when they are making a stop consonant that isn't a nasal.

Since we're pattern hunting, as soon as we figure out something Jenny does, our strategy is to see whether she does it again. So we look to see whether there are other adult words that end in voiced stops, and see how Jenny says them. We find *bag* and *dog*, and we see that she ends them both with /t/. This looks like a pattern of making final voiced non-nasal stops voiceless, as well as specifically into /t/; we've confirmed our first pattern hunch (as well as we can with just these 12 words). This kind of pattern is so common, for both children and second language learners, that it has a name: **FINAL DEVOICING**.

But obviously, there's more to it: Jenny has changed the position of articulation of those final [g]s from velar to alveolar, as well as making them voiceless. Do we have another pattern? Look at all the velar consonants in the adult list, and see what happens to them. We find [g] or [k] in five words: *bag, cat, go, dog,* and *vacuum.* Jenny makes most of them into [t], but not all: Where adults have [g] at the beginning of a word, it looks like Jenny says [d]. So yes: She replaces alveolars with velars. This is common for children (though not for second language learners), and it has a name, too: It's called **FRONTING**, because you make alveolars with your tongue further front in your mouth than velars. And although it's common, there are quite a lot of children who don't do it. Some who are slow at catching on to how to make alveolars even use velars as substitutes for them, like a very young friend of mine who says [wɔga] for *water*.

We've now taken care of all the changes in the first five words (check and make sure). What's new in word 6 is the change of [s] to [t]: Jenny has rendered the alveolar fricative as an alveolar stop. This is very common, too: Fricatives require a very delicate adjustment of the space that lets the air out of your mouth, and children usually take a while to manage it (although some of them learn to say *sshhh!* quite early). Naturally, it has a name; since it's making fricatives into stops, it's called **STOPPING**. Looking at *piece*, we see that Jenny also changes word-final [s] to [t]; if you go down the changes in the rest of her words, you can see that they are all instances of stopping, plus changing the [kj] of vacuum to a simple [t].

So almost everything Jenny's phonology does is summed up by three patterns: final devoicing, fronting, and stopping. Of course, she's only a made-up example; real children's patterns are usually more complicated, for a variety of reasons that we can't cover in this chapter. But there are three more things you should know now. First, if there's going to be a pattern, it rarely becomes systematic until the toddler has 10 or 20 words. Second, early favorite words may hang on to their original versions instead of conforming to newer, more general patterns. For example, Danny's earliest words were approximations to *hi* and *hello*, and he began both of them with the [h] sound, but starting at about 10 words, he gave up on trying to match word-initial fricatives and liquids; the only word-initial consonants he used for many months were oral and nasal stops—except in those two words. And third, the opposite also can happen: An early word that was originally pronounced fairly well may become changed to match a new pattern. Danny originally pronounced *down* correctly and *stone* as /don/, but then he developed a pattern of making a whole word nasal if it ended in a nasal, and after a few weeks, *down* became *noun* and *stone* became /nõn/.

7.6 Learning About Word Meanings

Children start learning about word meanings before they can say recognizable words, and the Preferential Looking task can be adapted to help us learn what they know about word meanings at that early stage of development. We also can learn a lot from observing the words in that children in the CHILDES database use, parents' reports of what words their children know collected using the MacArthur Communicative Development Inventory checklist (which has been adapted for children learning many different languages), studies of how parents name new things for their children, children's mistakes in using words, and from other experimental studies.

Children learning English don't all start out saying the same kinds of words; some children are really into learning names for things very early, while others are more interested in people's names and words and short phrases that are useful for interacting with others: *bye-bye, look at me, look at that, want that, no,* and so on. This isn't just a matter of what parents teach them to say; children have their own preferences from the beginning. But parents are important language teachers, too; for example, they are sensitive to what children know. They seem to feel that some words and concepts are more basic than others, so that a young child at the zoo may be told that a tiger is "kind of a great big kitty-cat," but an older one may be told that it's a tiger; a still older child who knows something about tigers may be encouraged to say that this huge shaggy one is a Siberian tiger and that slightly smaller, sleeker one a Sumatran tiger. Families and cultures differ in exactly what words they think are basic and appropriate for children to learn first and what words or phrases they think are more elaborate or specialized, but there seems to be a general sense that some words and concepts are fundamental and that others should be built on those foundations. Eavesdropping at the zoo is a great way to get an informal introduction to how different families organize concepts about the animal kingdom for their kids.

Children's mistakes can tell us about what they expect new words to mean: English-speaking children, at least, are inclined to assume that a noun phrase describing a new object is in fact a single noun, the name of that object. For example, parents have reported that when they pointed to a new object and described it with a phrase (*Look, that's a flag flying!*), their child took the whole phrase to be the thing's name (*Wook, anovver fwagfwying!*). Making sure that their child knows that a particular animal is a tiger before they go on to the details of what kind of tiger it is a way that parents can avoid this "flag-flying" trap.

Experimenters have also explored children's expectations about what new words are likely to mean. One popular experimental method asks children to point to odd-looking toys and gadgets with made-up names. Some of the first experiments of this kind showed a young child a strangely shaped object made of an unusual substance like wire mesh or Styrofoam, and gave it a nonword name: *Here's the dax.* Then each child saw two more objects, one of the same shape but different material and one of different shape but the same material, and the experimenter asked the child to *Show me the dax.* Children usually pointed to the item that had the same shape as the original and was made of different material; apparently, English-learning children, at least, expect that the name given to an object is based on its shape, not on what it's made of. We say that they have a

SHAPE BIAS. But this is true only for objects that have neat, rigid shapes; if the first *dax* is a glob of gel or shaving cream, children are inclined to choose a different-shaped glob of the same stuff rather than a same-shaped glob of different stuff; they think that the word *dax* means the stuff itself, not the nondescript shape. It turns out that children's guesses about what a new word is likely to mean are parallel the way people tend to use names for "things" and "stuff" in the world around them: A hammer or a wrench is recognizable by its shape, regardless of its color, but applesauce and toothpaste are recognized by their consistency, smell, and color. Their shape (as opposed to the shape of the container they come in) gives no clue to what they are.

Children learn only a small (but probably important) percentage of their words from specific teaching like this, but their vocabulary starts to grow faster and faster over the first years until they average about 8 to 10 new words a day. Most of these words, clearly, are just picked up from listening to and taking part in conversations. And at some point, as we'll see in Chapter 8, reading needs to become another major contributor to developing a mature vocabulary.

7.7 Summary and Conclusion

We started this chapter with Harold Gray's story about taking his grandsons outside to look at the stars one evening. Here it is again: To four-year-old Ryan, he said: *Look up there to see Orion (/o'rajan/).* Hearing this, Ryan's three-year-old brother Drew asked: *Where is O'Drewie?*

Why does hearing that there is a star or a constellation in the sky called /o'rajan/ make little Drew think that there should also be a star or a constellation that's called O'Drewie? And how did he come to know so much by the age of three?

You know the answer to the first question now: Drew understands (unconsciously) that a word that he hears may be made of meaningful parts—of morphemes. When he knows what one part means, and what the whole thing means, he can figure out the meaning of the part that he doesn't know. Hearing the new word *Orion* activated the very familiar name *Ryan*, setting him up psycholinguistically to feel that the two words were connected; at the same time, his grandfather's pointing to the sky set him up cognitively to make a guess about what that connection might be: O'Ryan must be the name for Ryan's star. Now he was all set to make an analogy: to figure that this relation between Ryan and Orion could also apply to Drewie. So naturally, O'Drewie should be up there somewhere.

(Linguists avoid the use of the term "analogy" because it makes us think in terms of pairs of examples like this, rather than in terms of patterns and rules drawn from large sets of examples. But in this case, with Drew working from just one example, it is indeed the correct term.)

And how did Drew come to know so much by the age of three? First, he was born with a brain that has a magnificent statistical learning ability for all kinds of information; he not only learns from examples, but from patterns of examples—what's common, what's rare, what happens in what combination of real-word circumstances. He isn't restricted to learning rules that work every time; he can also learn rules or patterns that only work some of the time. When it comes to learning language, he doesn't change his unconscious ideas about how his language is patterned just because he hears exceptions to those patterns (like irregular nouns and verbs). And he generalizes cautiously, first learning specific little patterns and then building up gradually to great general ones.

Second, he has been listening to language since before he was born, with a very elegant mammalian auditory system, and with a developing and very human ability to understand the emotions and motivations of other humans. As a result, he can learn both patterns of sound (including patterns of voice pitch and timing as well as patterns of articulated speech-sound segments) and patterns of behavior, plus how they are correlated. His pattern-learning ability is strong enough to eventually find words and morphemes even when they are only parts of long utterances that he hears. The language around him has been varied—words have occurred in different combinations (and sometimes, by themselves), making it easier for him to find them when they recur. And its intonation contours and timing patterns have also helped him to find the component parts of long utterances. Because words tend to reappear in similar constructions over and over, he has also been able to recognize those recurring patterns of words and how each different construction combines their meanings.

Third, his drives for excitement, control, belonging, and comfort kept him practicing making those sounds himself, and then to start using them to interact with other people and to mean things. This probably helped him to remember the sounds better, and it also gave him a chance to register their effects on other people, which taught him more about their meanings and uses.

Drew has a lot more to learn about English (and hopefully, other languages) as he grows older; although the basic words and constructions are learned early, understanding, creating, and appropriately using really complex sentences requires both more grammar and more language processing ability than he has at three. Even at 13, he will not yet be a skilled writer or public speaker. But he should be able to talk up a storm.

Exercises for Chapter 7

7.1. Use the "Jimmy" example to explain the concept of the Zone of Proximal Development.

7.2. Describe the pattern for making *She likes me, They like me* into the corresponding negative forms *She doesn't like me, They don't like me* for standard English. If you are a fluent speaker of some other dialect, how are negatives made in that variety of English? If it's different from standard English, describe the difference.

7.3. For standard English, describe the pattern for making negative sentences with *nobody* and *nothing* as subjects, for example, relating the specific negative sentences, *She doesn't like me, It doesn't taste good* to the corresponding general negative statements, *Nobody likes me, Nothing tastes good.* Again, if you are a fluent speaker of some other English dialect, compare how it conveys these meanings to how it is done in standard English.

7.4. If a child says, *Sit on my lap* as a request or demand to sit on the adult's lap, what's the minimum that has she learned about the grammar of this phrase? What are you sure that she has not yet learned?

7.5. Some observational data from a three-year-old boy:

> Child: *Tanya's small, but she's not too small.* (talking about a small cat)
>
> then, at a later time
>
> Mother: *Your chair is red!*
>
> Child: *It's red, but it's not too red.*

What's the formula that this little boy is using? What are the slots, and what do you think he can put in each slot? Why do you think so?

7.6. We said that emotion verbs, such as *love, hate, like, enjoy, resent,* are like action verbs in some ways, but like sensory verbs in other ways. Using the semantic roles that we have discussed in this book (Agent, Undergoer, Experiencer, Theme, Source, Goal), describe the semantic roles of the subject and the object of these verbs (when they are in the active voice, as in *I love apple pie*), and compare this to the semantic roles of the subject and the object of active voice action verbs (*I baked an apple pie*) and sensory verbs (*I can smell apple pie!*), which were discussed in this chapter.

7.7. Reorganize the list in Table 7.2 of (selected and slightly simplified) real data (from Fey & Gandour, 1982) in a way that lets you see the patterns in the way this child changes adult words so that he can pronounce them; then describe what it is that he does to the words. When you see a nasal consonant after an oral consonant at the end of the child's words, he pronounced it as a separate syllable, the way adults do in saying "button" as /bʌtn/.
    Hint: Change the adult words into IPA before you start, and organize them by place of articulation and voicing of the final consonant in the adult word. Also organize by voicing of the initial consonant (if any) in the adult word.

Table 7.2. Data for Exercise 7.7

bed	/bɛdn/		feed	/vidn/
big	/bɪgŋ/		frog	/wɔgŋ/
broke	/bok/		had	/hædn/
bug	/bʌgŋ/		peep	/bip/
cook	/gʊk/		red	/wɛdn/
dad	/dædn/		read	/widn/
drop	/dap/		stub	/dabm/
egg	/ɛgŋ/		talk	/dɔk/
eat	/it/		up	/ʌp/
feet	/vit/			

References

Berko, J. (1958). The child's learning of English morphology. *Word, 14*, 150–177.

Bloom, L. (1970). *Language development: Form and function in emerging grammars*. Cambridge, MA: M.I.T. Press.

Bloom, L., Hood, L., & Lightbown, P. (1974). Imitation in language development: If, when, and why. *Cognitive Psychology, 6*, 380–420.

Brown, R. (1973). *A first language/the early stages*. Cambridge, MA: Harvard University Press.

Eimas, P., Siqueland, E. R., Jusczyk, P., & Vigorito, J. (1971). Speech perception in infants. *Science, 171*, 303–306.

Hirsh-Pasek, K., & Golinkoff, R. M. (1996). *The origins of grammar: Evidence from early language comprehension*. Cambridge, MA: MIT Press.

Kuhl, P. K. (1981). Discrimination of speech by nonhuman animals: Basic auditory sensitivities conducive to the perception of speech-sound categories. *Journal of the Acoustical Society of America, 70*, 340–349.

McNeill, D. (1966). Developmental psycholinguistics. In F. Smith & G. A. Miller (Eds.), *The genesis of language* (p. 69). Cambridge, MA: MIT Press.

Slobin, D. I., & Welsh, C. A. (1973). Elicited imitation as a research tool in developmental psycholinguistics. In C. A. Ferguson & D. I. Slobin (Eds.), *Studies of child language development* (pp. 485–497). New York, NY: Holt, Rinehart, and Winston.

Thieman, T. J. (1975). Imitation and recall of optionally deletable sentences by young children. *Journal of Child Language, 2*, 261–270.

Vygotsky, L. S. (1978). *Mind and society: The development of higher psychological processes*. Cambridge, MA: Harvard University Press.

Recommended Reading and Sources Consulted

Berman, R., & Slobin, D. I. (1994). *Relating events in narrative: A cross-linguistic developmental study*. Hillsdale, NJ: Lawrence Erlbaum Associates.

Bloom, L. (1991). *Language development from two to three*. Cambridge, NY: Cambridge University Press.

Colunga, E., & Smith, L. B. (2005). From the lexicon to expectations about kinds: A role for associative learning. *Psychological Review, 112*, 347–382.

de Villiers, J. G., &. deVilliers, P. A. (1973). A cross-sectional study of the development of grammatical morphemes in child speech. *Journal of Psycholinguistic Research, 2*, 267–278.

Fenson, L., Marchman, V., Thal, D. J., Reznick, S., & Bates, E. (2007). *The MacArthur-Bates communicative development inventories: User's guide and technical manual* (2nd ed.). Baltmore, MD: Paul Brookes.

Fey, M. E., & Gandour, J. (1982). Rule discovery in phonological acquisition. *Journal of Child Language, 9*, 71–81.

Gleason, J. B., & Bernstein Ratner, N. (Eds). (2009). *The development of language* (7th ed.). Boston, MA: Pearson.

Karmiloff, K., & Karmiloff-Smith, A. (2001). *Pathways to language: From fetus to adolescent*. Cambridge MA: Harvard University Press.

Kuhl, P. K., Williams, K. A., Lacerda, F., Stevens, K. N., & Lindblom, B. (1992). Linguistic experience alters phonetic perception in infants by 6 months of age. *Science, 255*, 606–608.

Mampe, B., Friederici, A. D., Christophe, A., & Wermke, K. (2009). Newborns' cry melody is shaped by their native language. *Current Biology, 19*, 1994–1997. DOI 10.1016/j.cub.2009.09.064.

Menn, L. (1971). Phonotactic rules in beginning speech. *Lingua, 26*, 225–241.

Menn, L. (1973). On the origin and growth of phonological and syntactic rules. *Papers from the Ninth Regional Meeting of the Chicago Linguistic Society* (pp. 378–385). Chicago, IL: Chicago Linguistic Society.

Menn, L., & Stoel-Gammon, C. (1995). Phonological development. In P. Fletcher & B. MacWhinney (Eds.), *The handbook of child language* (pp. 335–359). Oxford, UK: Blackwell.

Menn, L., & Stoel-Gammon, C. (2009). Phonological development. In J. B. Gleason & N. Bernstein Ratner (Eds.), *The development of language* (7th ed., pp. 58–103). Boston, MA: Pearson.

Mervis, C. B. (1987). Child-basic categories and early lexical development. In U. Neisser (Ed.), *Concepts and conceptual development: Ecological and intellectual factors in early categorization* (pp. 201–233). Cambridge, NY: Cambridge University Press.

Sachs, J. (2009). Communication development in infancy. In J. B. Gleason & N. Bernstein Ratner (Eds.), *The development of language* (7th ed., pp. 37–57). Boston, MA: Pearson.

Slobin, D. I. (1979). *Psycholinguistics* (2nd ed.). Glenview IL: Scott Foresman & Co.

Slobin, D. I. (Ed.). (1985–1997). *The cross-linguistic study of language acquisition* (Vols. 1–5). Hillsdale, NJ: Erlbaum.

Tomasello, M. (2003). *Constructing a language: A usage-based theory of language acquisition*. Cambridge, MA: Harvard University Press.

Werker, J. F., Gilbert, J. H. V., Humphrey, K., & Tees, R. C. (1981). Developmental aspects of cross-language speech perception. *Child Development, 52*, 349–355.

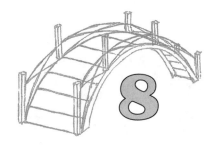

The Psycholinguistics of Reading and Learning to Read

8.0 Introduction: Why Teaching Reading Is Controversial

The English spelling system has been kicked around by more than a thousand years of history. Although it was largely standardized in the 1700s, it never got a decent overhaul to bring it into step with the drastic changes that had been happening in our spoken language since the Norman Conquest of England in 1066. As a result, English-speaking children have quite a hard time learning to read, and the longest lasting quarrels about our educational system have probably been the ones about how to teach reading. In fact, children who have to learn to read English do so more slowly than any other children who use a Roman- or Greek-based alphabetic system. All over Europe, and in other countries that use these alphabets, such as Turkey and Indonesia, children are lucky enough to be learning more consistent spelling systems than ours, and they learn to read faster than English learners, regardless of the system of instruction. (In Finland, children at the end of first grade are able to sound out 90% of the novel words they see). In section 8.1.3 we'll briefly look at how some of those other alphabetic systems work. But there's not much chance of a spelling reform for English, so we have to work with what we've got.

How our minds get meaning from written symbols depends partly on the writing system. There are many ways to use the ROMAN ALPHABET, and many alphabets besides the Roman alphabet: there are phonetically based writing systems whose symbols represent syllables instead of phonemes, or that mix alphabetic and syllabic symbols, and a few writing systems that are partly phonetic and partly semantic; there are also writing systems that mix more-phonetic and less-phonetic symbols. We can't cover them all, but we'll discuss the psycholinguistics behind three major points: First, phonetic regularity is extremely helpful for learners, both for pronunciation and for comprehension. Second, most learners eventually pick up on whatever phonetic regularities a spelling system has even if they are not taught to look for them, but in English, this is particularly difficult because of the unreliability of our system. And third, school children with reading problems exist in all languages, but at least in English, the problems with recognizing words are almost always problems with processing sounds, not with visual processing.

8.1 Reading as a Psycholinguistic Process

8.1.1 Comparing reading and listening

When we read, what we see on a page, a screen, or a sign has to arouse the right word forms in our brains. Then those forms have to arouse the words' meanings and some of the information about the constructions that the words are being used in, and those meanings have to give us the rest of the information about the constructions, so we know how to combine the meanings of the words. So although processing written words is different from processing speech, from its start (letters) almost to its finish (understanding), it's not *totally* different. Our goal, whether we are reading words or listening to them, is the same: to understand what someone means.

Unless we are reading a page with beautiful typography, reading poetry or fine prose to ourselves, or listening to someone else read poetry aloud, processing either letters or sounds is something to get through quickly, with as little attention and effort as possible. In one way, spoken language is harder to process than written language, because speech sounds come at us at a pace that we can't control and (as we saw in Chapter 1, section A) without spaces between the words. On the other hand, spoken language has a processing advantage that reading doesn't have: The rise and fall of a speaker's voice, plus tiny changes in speech rate (particularly a tendency to slow down at the ends of phrases), give hearers information about which words belong together and where new constructions begin—and rather more of that kind of information than punctuation does. So finding the constructions in reading takes extra effort.

One thing the antiphonics people legitimately worry about is that, if it takes too long to recognize each word, children won't have the extra resources they need to figure out the constructions. That's one reason that reading practice is necessary; it increases the strengths of all the connections, visual and phonetic, between a written word on a page and its lemma in your mind, and that makes word recognition easier. Easier word recognition then frees up more resources for finding the constructions that relate the words to each other. Children with classroom practice in oral reading get important experience not just in reading the words, but also in finding the syntactic and semantic relations among the words that they read. (There's experimental software for written materials that makes up for their lack of intonation and rate information by automatically leaving slightly smaller spaces between words that go together in low-level constructions like prepositional phrases, and bigger spaces after words at the ends of clauses. It improves reading speed and comprehension, so maybe someday, most reading materials will be prepared that way.)

8.1.2 The psycholinguistics of reading: Bottom-up, top-down, and interactive activation

8.1.2.1 Bottom-up activation in reading

In Chapter 5, section 5.6.1, we began looking at PRIMING: the way that sensing one stimulus increases our speed at reacting to other stimuli that are similar to it or linked with it by our experiences. Priming, in our model, is caused by activation spreading from neuron to neuron in our brains. When we, as skilled readers, see letters arranged to form a word, those letters activate two main kinds of stored information at the same time: letter-based and sound-based.

Visually, the letters we are looking at activate our stored whole words that share some of the same letters (actually, it isn't purely visual processing; we'll come back to this point later). Because activation from different sources adds up, the more letters that are shared between what you see and a word form that you have stored, the more activation gets to the stored word form.

Experiments and studies of readers' errors confirm the idea that reading, like listening and speaking, arouses competing possible words in our minds. But instead of competing to be spoken, the words we read are competing to be understood. The word forms that get activated above their threshold first are the ones that send activation off to their lemmas first, and the lemma that first gets its activation built up above its threshold is the one that first starts activating its concept. When the concept gets strong enough to reach your consciousness, you have understood the word that you have read. (We also have some SUBLIMINAL understanding—that is, there are cognitive effects of the meanings of words that get activated, but not activated enough to reach consciousness.)

The most frequent word forms have the highest resting level of activation (see Chapter 2, section 2.4.3, and Chapter 5, section 5.3.1), so they can get to their threshold with less activation coming in from the letters on the page. If you are looking briefly at an unfamiliar or unexpected word (like *systemic* or *astrobiological*), a similar but more frequent word (like *systematic* or *astrological*) can reach threshold level first and arouse its meaning. (I made both of those comprehension mistakes while I was skimming news articles.) In other words, you can think that you have seen a frequent word that looks like the one you're really looking at, which means you have misread what's on the page. (In a subjective sense, I really had "read" *systematic*: Its letters, lemma, and meaning were aroused by the letters I had seen.)

When the letters of a word directly arouse information about the word without first arousing its sounds, the process is called ORTHOGRAPHIC (spelling-based) arousal. In highly skilled readers, familiar written word forms and morpheme forms can directly arouse their lemmas orthographically. But do look carefully at how we're using this word. Many people use the term "orthographic reading process" only to describe looking at a whole word and going directly to its meaning, but that's too narrow to cover the range of events that happen when we see letters and perceive a word. For example, if you read a compound word like *mousetrap* or a word with derivational and inflectional morphemes like *vaporizers*, the morphemes that make up the word can be aroused directly, as well as the whole word.

The second kind of information aroused by seeing letters is sound-based—in other words, phonetic. The letters send activation to all of the sounds that they are likely to be linked to, but they don't necessarily do this one letter at a time. A useful idea in thinking about how phonetic activation works is GRAIN SIZE, that is, the number of letters that may be working together to arouse a sound (or a meaning). At the smallest grain size, for example, the single letter *P* arouses the sound /p/ a lot, but if an *H* follows it, the two-letter *PH* pair arouses /f/. You can probably feel the competition between those sounds if you look at a slightly unfamiliar compound like *chophouse*, where the words *chop* and *house* have to fight down the /f/ sound in your mind. At a four-letter grain size, the combination *OUGH* sends out activation to /u/ as in *through*, /o/ as in *dough*, /æw/ as in *plough* [plow], /ɔf/ as in *cough*, and /ʌf/ as in *enough*. At a five-letter grain size, *OUGHT* (and *AUGHT*) also arouse /ɔ/ as in *thought, naughty*.

Readers also get information about which syllable is stressed from multi-letter chunks of words (which may or may not be morphemes): Some word beginnings, like *eu-*, tend to be stressed, and others, like *be-* tend to be unstressed.

The most regular of the links between letters and the sounds they make, like the link between the letter *P* and the phoneme /p/ or between the sequence PH and the sound /f/, are called **GRAPHEME-PHONEME CORRE-SPONDENCES. GRAPHEME** itself is a useful word; it means a letter of the alphabet (like *P*) regardless of how it looks on a page—uppercase P and lower case p, through all the different fonts, size, boldness, italicizing, handwriting styles, and so on (Figure 8.1). So "grapheme" pretty much means the same as "letter" in the way that we normally use it; it is the class of letter forms that are all ways of writing the same letter of the alphabet. The concept of a grapheme is the writing-system parallel to the concept of a phoneme as we introduced it in Chapter 1—you recall, for example, that the L phoneme is the class of all the different L sounds that we described in section 1.2.4.2.

So: The orthographic and phonetic information from the letters (singly and in groups) is the bottom-up input to the process of reading a word. The top-down part is more complicated.

8.1.2.2 Top-down activation in reading

When we read something meaningful, instead of just words in a list, there's a flood of top-down information sending activation to words, constructions, meanings, and sounds. This information usually is helpful in getting the right words activated rapidly in your mind, just as it is when you are listening, but sometimes it can activate a word that isn't the page—for example, it's easy to think that you've seen a preposition that is grammatically required but actually missing. (I left one out in the last sentence; did you notice?)

Wait—where's the top? When we discussed speech production in Chapters 3 and 4, we didn't ask that question. The "top" for speech production pretty much had to be at the concept level—it was either what we wanted to say, or some other concept that we didn't intend to say but that managed to sneak in, like an ex-partner's name. When we talked about

Figure 8.1. Some ways of writing the grapheme P.

comprehension in various sections of Chapters 5, 6, and 7, we left the idea vague; we just treated any information that wasn't directly based on the incoming sounds as being top-down. But now we have to stop and take stock for a minute, because some of the sources of activation that help to arouse a concept in our minds when we look at the letters on a page are a lot "higher" than others—in other words, further from the word form, and closer to information and ideas that are already stored in our minds.

Let's walk "up" methodically from the very bottom, and survey the levels again, this time in the context of understanding reading. First, as I hinted earlier, the bottom is not really the letters. It's the marks on the page, which you once had to learn to interpret, but which now automatically activate letters. So we should treat our stored knowledge of the letters of our alphabet—of the graphemes—as the first level above the incoming visual stimuli. Without information from the grapheme level, we couldn't handle new typefaces; for a fairly extreme example, we'd be all bent out of shape by the missing crossbars on the letter A in NASA-script, as in Figure 8.2. And in fact, we do read this and other fancy fonts like the ones in Figure 8.2 more slowly, because we have to harness a lot of letter-down processing to recognize the marks on the page. That costs tiny bits of time for each letter.

8.1.2.3 Interactive activation

Much more obvious—and also playing a strong role in compensating for blurred ink, misaligned photocopies, and weird typefaces—is activation coming back down to the letter level from the word level. The basic phenomenon which tells us that this word-to-letter activation exists is probably the oldest fact that was discovered by an experiment in psycholinguistics: If skilled readers are shown a letter or a set of letters for a very short time (around a

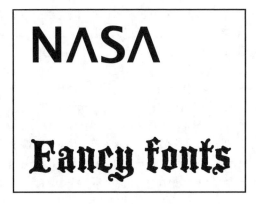

Figure 8.2. Fancy fonts.

tenth of a second), they can name letters that are shown in whole words faster than they can name letters that are shown one at a time. (This is called the **WORD SUPERIORITY EFFECT**, and it was reported by J. M. Cattell in 1886.)

Think about it—how could it be true? You have to recognize several letters in order to recognize a word, don't you? So how could you recognize a bunch of letters faster than you can recognize just one? Using what we know about spreading activation, we can solve the mystery. Remember that recognizing anything isn't instantaneous, even when we feel as if no time is needed. Activation of our neurons takes time to add up. As you look at a word, the marks on the page send activation to the letters that they might belong to; then, as some letters reach their threshold for passing on activation, they start to activate the written word forms that they belong to, and they also start to activate their individual letter-names. The activation that is going to a stored word form which contains all of the letters that you're looking at adds up fastest, so it soon reaches its threshold for sending on activation to its lemma. But activation doesn't just go "up" from the word form; it also comes "down": The activated word form sends activation back "down" to each of its letters.

The Classic Interactive Activation Model

In this schematic illustration of McClelland and Rumelhart's computer model of word and letter recognition, a letter is recognized when the activations coming into it from all sources add up to more than its threshold level. Each curvy connection line represents a neural connection, and each circle represents a node in the network. The nodes on the bottom layer represent a set of lines that can be combined to form each of the letters of the alphabet in the middle layer. If you look very closely, you can see that each of those lines ends either in an arrow, representing an excitatory connection, or in a round dot, representing an inhibitory connection, depending on whether the lower-level item is in the higher-level one. So, for example, the letter-top horizontal bar in the bottom layer excites all of the letters here except N, but it inhibits N, because if you (or the computer) see that bar, you might be looking at any of other letters, but you know you're not seeing an N. In the same way, the letter N inhibits all of the words at the top level because none of them contains an N, but A excites all of them except TRIP and TIME (Figure 8.3).

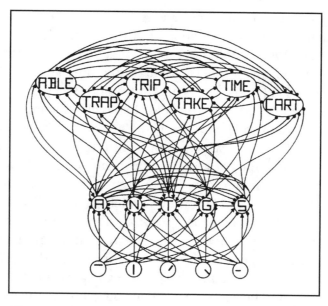

Figure 8.3. An interactive activation model for recognizing words and letters in words. From J. L. McClelland & D. E. Rumelhart. (1981). An interactive activation model of context effects in letter perception: I. An account of basic findings. *Psychological Review, 88*(5), 375–407, Figure 3, published by APA; Reprinted with permission.

So, letters in a word get a boost from the word they belong to—in other words, they get more activation than they would have if they were shown by themselves, so they get recognized faster. And that activation boost gets passed on to the names of the letters, so they get named aloud faster, too. There's a name for this tight mix of bottom-up and "top-down" activation that we see in word recognition: It's called **INTERACTIVE ACTIVATION**, and Figure 8.3 makes it easy for you to see why. By the way, I put "top-down" in quotes in the last sentence because the word form is not very close to the real "top" of our model of processing—it's only the next layer up after the letters. But that's the usual term, and I can't think of a better one. At least, it does describe the direction of the activation flow accurately.

8.1.2.4 Processing sequences of words

Cattell also found a sentence superiority effect: We read words in sentences faster than the same words in lists. Spreading activation and its top-down boosts explain this, too; in our model, when a word's lemma is activated, grammatical information about it is activated too, and that sends activations to the constructions it's used in, like noun phrase or prepositional phrase. Then those constructions can send activation to all the lemmas of the words that belong to the grammatical categories that are most likely to show up next. For example, after a verb (like *run* or *roll*) that describes movement, a prepositional phrase saying something about "where from" or "where to" is likely, so that means prepositions like *to, from, in, off, under* . . . that can describe Source and Goal will get some activation.

Reading a garden-path sentence like *Until the police arrest the drug dealers control the street* (which I got from http://www.fun-with-words .com/ambiguous_garden_path.html) dramatically demonstrates the force of the construction priming that is set in motion by the syntactic category that each word belongs to. *Until* is more likely to be followed by a whole clause than by just a noun phrase, so *until* starts you into this sentence with the wrong construction more highly activated. Then the word *arrest* (especially when it's preceded by a noun phrase like *the police* and fol-lowed by a noun phrase like *the drug dealers*!) is way more likely to be a transitive verb than to be a noun. So, when you get up to the word *control*, which could also be a noun but here has to be a verb, you have to work hard to reorganize the syntax, treat *arrest* as a noun, and understand the sentence as *Until the police arrest, the drug dealers control the street* (= Until the arrest that was made by the police, the drug dealers controlled the street).

The grammatical levels that we expect from our production model are the many levels of constructions, from little noun phrases like article + noun (*the Beatles*) up to clauses (*We all live in a yellow submarine*) and beyond. We can read nouns faster if they come right after articles, and verbs faster after nouns. But our minds don't just work in terms of grammatical levels; instead, they grab onto anything that's got a shred of even modestly reliable information and add it into the activation mix. From what you already know about spreading activation, you can predict that words that belong together in any sense—because they belong to the same semantic category, relate to the same topic, belong to same literary genre—are likely to activate one another. For example, we are faster at reading a particular verb that is more likely to occur after a particular noun (*baby cry*) than we are at reading a verb that is less likely to come after that noun (*baby fly*).

So the better we know a language (and the more we know about the topic), the more accurate our predictions are; in other words, the more top-down information we have to help us recognize the actual words on a page. As skilled readers, we aren't looking at words and "guessing": we are integrating activation from multiple sources, from the marks on the page on up. We're not guessing any more (or any less) than when we make other subconscious decisions based on a mixture of what we already know and what we see or hear in front of us—like what's the best buy for dinner or whether it's safe to turn left in traffic.

Until we had network models of neural processing, Cattell's Word Superiority Effect was often misinterpreted to mean that we read words but not letters, and this interpretation was part of the basis for the whole-word reading method. And indeed, given how the activation adds up, skilled readers do read familiar words as wholes. But that skill will develop with reading practice in people who are taught grapheme-phoneme correspondences. If people are only taught to read words as wholes, they are liable to have a lot of trouble reading words that they've never seen before, because they'll have to work out the grapheme-phoneme correspondences for themselves, and that is difficult if their language has a bad spelling system—for example, if it's English.

8.1.3 Shallow, deep, and irregular orthographies, and how English got this way

In Chapter 1, section 1.2.1, we looked at English spelling, but we didn't explain how it got so wild and crazy compared to the spelling systems of other languages that use alphabets. There are several kinds of reasons; some apply to all languages, and some come from the special history of the English language. In section 1.10.2, we talked about changes in language over time, including the fact that pronunciation shifts over just a few generations. When you talk, Grandma can scold you for mumbling, but unless she's a phonetician (and her hearing is still good), she has no idea exactly what about your pronunciation is making it hard for her to understand you. But when you write to her, she can easily catch your spelling mistakes and scold you for them. Because spelling is standardized and taught in schools, and spelling mistakes can be caught and corrected, it changes much more slowly than pronunciation. As a result, the pronunciation of a spoken language drifts away from the spelling of its written form.

Pronunciation drift by itself may not produce a huge amount of reading trouble, because such drifts tend to be systematic, and they mostly involve losing sounds, or losing distinctions between sounds that were once different phonemes (although we'll talk about another consequence of pronunciation drifts later in this section). If a distinction—like the one that once existed between "hoarse" and "horse"—is lost, it doesn't cause much of a reading problem: you just learn how to pronounce both letter combinations. It's mostly the spelling that's made harder by having many ways to spell the same sound, and that's because you have to memorize which way to spell it for each word, as we do for the /i/ sound, which can be spelled with *ee* as in *seed*, *e*-consonant-*e* as in *cede*, *ea* as in *read*, *i* as in *Tina*, *ei* as in *receive*, or *ie* as in *believe*—we saw lots of those variants in "The Chaos" in Chapter 1, section 1.2.1.

French is another good example of a language where spelling is a challenge. Like English, French is full of silent final letters that were once pronounced, and of different spellings for vowel sounds that no longer contrast. For example, what is now just the sound [ɛ] (for most speakers) may be spelled many ways, including *e* (*mettre*, to put/place), or *ai* (*aimer*, to love) or *aî* (*maître*, teacher) or *ê* (*même*, same). If the vowel [ɛ] occurs at the end of a spoken word, it may be followed by a silent consonant like *s* or *t*, giving still more possible spellings of this one sound. On the other hand, reading French isn't nearly as hard as reading English, because there's rarely more than one way to pronounce a sequence of letters, unless it's in a person's name. In French, you can rely on the spelling to tell you how to pronounce almost any word, but in English, you have no way of knowing whether *ea* will spell [i] or [ei]. etc.

There's another kind of drift that causes a relatively modest but very common problem for reading. We need a new technical linguistic term to explain it: a sound's **PHONETIC ENVIRONMENT** in a particular word. The phonetic environment of a sound in a word means all the phonetic information about where the sound occurs in the word: the nearby sounds, whether it's at the beginning or the end of the word, whether it's in a stressed syllable, and the other speech sounds near it. For example, the phonetic environment of the /k/ in /kip/ *keep* is that it's the first sound in the word, in a stressed syllable, and before the high front vowel /i/; the environment of the /k/ in /dʌnki/ *donkey* is that it's at the beginning of the second syllable, in an unstressed syllable, after a nasal consonant, and before a high front vowel (go back to the IPA chart if you need to). All of those facts about a sound's environment can affect the details of how it's pronounced—most sounds are longer in stressed syllables, for example, and as you saw in Chapter 1, section 1.2.3, because of coarticulation, /k/ is pronounced further front in your mouth when it's before a front vowel like /i/ than when it's before a back vowel like /u/.

Sounds often change, over time, in some phonetic environments but not others, or in different ways in different environments, and that's a major cause of letters ending up being pronounced different ways depending on the sounds around them and where they are in a word. Linguists call these changes **CONDITIONED SOUND CHANGES**, because whether the sound changes or not is conditional: It depends on the sound's environment. Portuguese is great for examples of conditioned sound changes. Here's one: The sound spelled by the letter *e* in Portuguese is usually /e/, as it is in Spanish, but at the ends of words it has drifted to /i/. So the word for "nine," spelled *nove*, is pronounced /ˈnovi/. Also, the sound /t/ has drifted to /tʃ/ before the /i/ sound (regardless of how the vowel is spelled or where it occurs in a word). This means, for example, that the word spelled *chocolate* is pronounced /ʃokoˈlatʃi/. But this pattern is completely regular, so it can be learned fairly easily: The letter combination *te* at the end of a word is always pronounced /tʃi/.

A spelling system that is consistent with the way things used to be pronounced rather than how they are pronounced now is called a **DEEP ORTHOGRAPHY**; French orthography is quite deep, Portuguese is less deep. A spelling system that has been fairly recently adjusted to match the pronunciation of a language, like Indonesian, Turkish, or Serbian, is a **SHALLOW** or **TRANSPARENT** orthography. (Often, those adjustments have happened as ways of solidifying major political changes; in the case of Turkish, this was particularly dramatic. The spelling system was created in 1928 in order to change from Arabic to Roman script, which helped both to symbolize and to establish Kemal Ataturk's secular government and educational system.) Turkish spelling, although it is not totally phonetic, is so closely attuned to the spoken language that children actually can learn to read by memorizing whole written sentences; their unconscious pattern-learning capacity apparently can do all the work of acquiring its shallow, regular grapheme-phoneme correspondences.

There's some fairly systematic deep orthography in English, too. For example, the regular *igh* = /ai/ as in *night* comes from a conditioned change in the /i/ vowel: Some hundreds of years ago, /i/ became long when it was before a voiced velar fricative that was, sensibly, spelled *gh*. The fricative sound disappeared from most varieties of English, but the letters remained in the written words. The vowel is still, as school grammar calls, it *long I*, and the letter sequence *igh* reliably signals this sound—it's a classic example of the three-letter grain-size for English grapheme-phoneme correspondences.

The long/short vowel pattern by itself is widespread in English, and it isn't too hard to learn. Keeping the same A, E, I, O, U symbols for the pairs of "long" and "short" vowel sounds actually has one advantage: it helps us to see the relationships between the semantically related words in hundreds of sets like *maternal* /məˈtɜrnəl/ and *matriarch* /ˈmeitriark/, *rabies* /ˈreibiz/ and *rabid* /ˈræbɪd/, please /pliz/ and pleasure /ˈplɛʒr/. So the long/short pattern is a clue to English morphological relationships. But it's weird that we use the letter *A* to spell both /ei/ in *rate* and /æ/ in *rat*, *E* to spell /i/ in *see* and /ɛ/ in *set*, and *O* to spell /o/ in *rote* and /a/ in *rot*, because the long vowel and the short vowel phoneme-grapheme correspondences are so different from each other, and also because it puts us way out of step with almost every other language that uses the Roman alphabet. Where did this peculiar spelling pattern come from?

It's due to a change in all of our vowels that swept over the southern English dialects sometime between Chaucer in the 1300s and Shakespeare in the 1500s. This change is called the **GREAT VOWEL SHIFT**. Before the

Great Vowel Shift happened, the sounds spelled with *A* in *hate* and *hat* really were almost the same, except that the stressed vowel sound in *hate* was longer and the one in *hat* was shorter; that's why they are still called "long *a*" and "short *a*." The Great Vowel Shift pulled those pairs apart, mostly by making big changes in the way the long vowels were pronounced. But the pattern of vowels that school grammar calls long *a* and short *a*, long *e* and short *e*, long *o* and short *o* is fundamentally regular. Learners can not only tell *rob* from *robe*, but also agree that a new name like *Dobby* probably has a short *o* (/a/) and not a long one (/o/). (There are exceptions to this short-vowel-before-single consonant pattern, as in the word Lego®.) As we've said, a deep orthography takes longer to learn to read than a shallow one, but once you've learned it, you can read, even if you may not be able to spell.

So what's different about English? Why is it harder to read than French, which also has a deep orthography? The problem for readers of English is not just that we have a deep orthography, as many articles on reading would leave you thinking. The problem is this: Our orthography is not just deep, it's IRREGULAR; that is, as you know very well by now, it's impossible to fully predict how a particular combination of letters will be pronounced. On top of the spelling problem of pairs like *bread* and *bred*, we have the reading problem of *steak* /steik/ and *streak* /strik/, *tear* /teir/ and *tear* /tir/, and so on. There is no way to predict whether the *ea* combination should be pronounced /ei/ or /i/; we just have to look up the pronunciations of most new words in the dictionary, and of course be able to interpret whatever system the particular dictionary uses to describe the pronunciation—it's rarely IPA, except in dictionaries meant to be used by people learning English as a second language.

There are two reasons for the horrible irregularity of English spelling. The first one is that our spellings come from many different English dialects. No single English dialect has ever had the political dominance and the policy priority that would have been needed to set up a phonetically-consistent spelling system that we could have started from; neither England nor any of its former colonies has an academy to reorganize the spelling system the way France and Spain do.

The second factor making English orthography irregular is that we have had a tremendous influx of words from other languages—first the Scandinavians who settled in the north of England from the early middle ages until 1066, then the huge impact of the French spoken by the Normans, and since then, the rich imports of words and things from perhaps a hundred languages around the world: Latin and Greek (via their written languages), Dutch (especially for shipping), and all of the language contact that got underway in the colonial era starting around 1500, and which has continued to increase in modern times. The words that were imported from (or via) languages that have alphabets brought along their spellings from their original languages: for example, from Greek the ch = /k/ of *school* and *charisma*, from French the ch = /ʃ/ of *chandelier*, *champagne*, from Spanish (and originally from Nahuatl) the ch = /tʃ/ of *chipotle*, *ancho*, and from Yiddish the ch = /x/ (voiceless velar fricative) of *challah*. (National Spelling Bee contestants are encouraged to ask for the language of origin for the words they are given because it gives them a better chance at guessing how to spell at least some of the word's sounds.)

Summarizing this section so far: across languages, the more reliable the phoneme-grapheme correspondence, the sooner children subconsciously rely on it; but in English, we always will have to look things up, because we are stuck with an orthography that is not only deep, but also irregular.

However, here's something else: Across languages, even when the orthography is regular enough so that the pronunciation of every word can be figured out from its letters, as in Spanish, Finnish, or Turkish, the more frequent words are read faster than less frequent ones. This means that regardless of the language or the writing system, sooner or later skilled readers acquire a large whole-word "sight" vocabulary. But the way that learners process an unfamiliar written word is different from the way skilled readers process a familiar written word. To understand reading research, we have to keep in mind that it may be better for beginners to use different processes than skilled readers do. If the beginners' brains are normal and they get enough practice in reading, their strategies will shift gradually to using multiple and more efficient processes, as connection strengths between sequences of letters and sequences of sound build up.

8.2 Reading for Meaning: What Happens After a Word Is Activated?

Because we had to talk about syntax and semantics in order to explore the top-down aspects of word recognition, we've already gotten a long way toward answering this "what happens next" question. We've seen that in skilled readers, getting to the constructions and the meanings overlaps with and affects the full arousal of the words in our minds, very much like what happens when we hear spoken words. Each word arouses its lemma, which has two kinds of information: semantic (including the link to concepts) and syntactic; they probably both send activation to the constructions the word can be used in. That information will help your brain to figure out how each word fits together with the ones that have already been aroused, or whether it is the beginning of some new sentence. This takes you "up" approximately to the Functional Level of our production model.

For beginning readers, this fitting-together is a slower and probably less accurate process. Practice in reading texts aloud for meaning helps children not to get hung up on word-by-word recognition, and the experience of being read to—which is highly predictive of school success—probably also helps, just by setting children up to expect that the words on a page will fit together into phrases that will combine to make sensible sentences. The great thing about practice in reading stories and other connected text, both aloud and silently, is that it increases reading speed; faster reading, in turn, means that the time that is spent in practicing will result in seeing even more text, and so arousing even more constructions and meanings, strengthening the connections needed to process written language more and more effectively. It's a "virtuous circle."

Comprehension isn't complete with the arousal of the Functional Level, though; to really understand something, our brains have to use information at that level to create a mental model of what a writer (or a speaker) is describing. We all have the experience of nodding along, reading the words on a page, apparently understanding them, and then realizing at some point that we remember little or nothing of what we read. Vivid writers (for example, popular novelists and bloggers) know how to keep getting our attention so that we don't do this; active voice syntax, action verbs, unusual adjectives, sound effects (onomatopoeia), and concrete nouns all help.

But even so, people vary. When we read a murder mystery, some of us build a fairly complete visualization of who was supposed to be in the dining room when the shot was heard in the attic, but other readers do much less of this and are likely to be a lot more surprised about who pulled the trigger. Building explicit, detailed mental models that integrate all the bits of information from what we are reading is optional when we're reading for fun, but as you've already realized, it's essential for getting usable information off a page.

8.3 Psycholinguistics and the Phonics Versus Whole-Word Teaching Controversy

Now that we've had a look at how reading works in English, let's look at the controversy about methods for teaching reading. On one far end of the rainbow of ideas for teaching English would be an extreme phonetic approach, requiring children to work entirely from the individual letters to the sounds. Probably nobody seriously advocates that, because it so clearly won't work for our deep, irregular orthography; deep orthographies require larger grain sizes, and irregular orthographies—well, you know all about that by now. **PHONICS** is used as the general term for a sound-based method; properly used, phonics teaches children to use letter-to-sound correspondences as much as possible, but it recognizes that these correspondences are complex for English, and that they sometimes can't be trusted at all (remember the poem "The Chaos" in Chapter 1).

At the other end of the reading instruction rainbow is the **WHOLE-WORD METHOD**, which argues that looking at individual letters distracts children from attending to word meanings, and that children should be taught to look just at whole-word shapes. (You can find an extreme version of this approach in workbooks where children are supposed to trace around the outlines of words. The outlines are what you'd see if you couldn't focus your eyes on the letters, and being unable to focus is not exactly good for reading, so it's hard to understand why these workbooks are used, except that they keep children quiet in class.)

The whole-word method advocates call skilled reading a "psycholinguistic guessing game," and I've already started to explain what's wrong with that way of looking at it. Their theory is at first attractive—we certainly do use context to decide among words that have been aroused simultaneously—but it has serious limitations. As we've seen, the way skilled readers actually use context involves an intricate interplay between bottom-up letter-based processing and many kinds of top-down information; it's not blind guessing. In practice, a lot of children who are taught whole-word reading (and quite a few who are not, but who get impatient) get a little phonetic information from the first letter of the word, and then jump off into saying almost any word that starts with the same letter or sound, whether or not the context gives enough information so that ignoring the rest of the letters could be a remotely successful approach. This is certainly not what skilled readers do.

Most children who are native speakers of any alphabet-using language *except English* learn to read their language at roughly the same average rate, regardless of how they are taught, because they can unconsciously learn the way that the letters represent sounds. But in English, look-and-say whole-word methods repeatedly have been shown to produce readers who are not able to figure out the sounds of words that they haven't studied. This is bad, because if you can't figure out how new words sound, you are running lame. After about third grade, and increasingly every year after that, you start to encounter words in your reading materials that you have never seen before, and you have to learn almost all of those words from the context that you read them in. As I'm sure you know, it is extremely difficult to acquire a college-quality vocabulary unless you can learn new words by reading them in novels, textbooks, Web pages, newspapers, and other contexts.

And learning new words requires more than understanding them. You can understand a word without knowing how it sounds, but if you don't know how a word sounds, you can't recognize it when you later hear it in a classroom or out in the world. And more than that: If you haven't formed some kind of image—even an incorrect one—of how it sounds, you probably have a hard time even recognizing it when you see it again. A purely visual mental image of the word is not good enough, because words—especially long words—look too much alike.

So children have to be able to do more than understand a new word that they see; their minds have to be able to hold onto it so they can recognize it the next time they see it or hear it. That's the only way that the information from seeing the word in different contexts can combine to build a real understanding of its meaning.

If you understand how a word is likely to sound when you learn it by reading, you'll store both its visual and its auditory information, in separate but linked areas of your brain, and your brain will be able to recombine that information when you see it again. Even if the visual information is incomplete and the auditory information is only partly correct, having this partly redundant information is better than just having a single kind of memory for the word's form to rely on. I'm not going to say any more about the history of phonics/whole word controversy—there's plenty of material available on that—but I'll say again what I think as a psycholinguist: In the English spelling system, letters give a great deal of information that is demonstrably useful to readers, especially for beginners. That information should not be thrown away in teaching reading. A lot of important information is also at the level of groups of letters, like the –IGH-complex that reliably spells the /ai/ diphthong. Those complexes can be taught, and doing this will increase learners' ability to deal with words that they have never seen before. But for many reasons—for example, the fact that so many vowels in unstressed syllables are reduced to [ə] and cannot be sounded out—memorization of spelling is also necessary.

Importantly, letter-level teaching and word-level teaching are not the only choices available to help overcome the challenge of English spelling. There is very useful information at the level of bound grammatical morphemes—the prefixes and suffixes that build up our words. Making this information explicit is especially helpful for L2 learners. (You'll see more about this in Chapter 10.) And auditory training can help people with dyslexia to overcome problems with auditory learning; we'll discuss that soon, in section 8.8.1.

Finally, studies of highly skilled readers are not a direct guide to how we should teach beginners to read, any more than studies of the way a concert pianist sight-reads and instantly performs complex music is a guide to the way we should teach beginners to learn to play the piano. Keep that in mind if you get involved in arguments about how reading should be taught. And of course, actual classroom studies are necessary; no theory is enough by itself. Lots of studies on teaching reading have been published in books and journals, and more need to be done.

8.4 Where Reading Errors Come From: Activation and Competition in Reading

As we've seen, reading involves both bottom-up processing of letters using grapheme-phoneme correspondences and "top"-down processing from different sources stored in our brains, ranging from knowledge of the graphemes up to knowledge of constructions, topics, and literary genres—as well as information about the real world. We already know about "seeing" missing words where we expect to find them—that is, when they have been activated by our subconscious knowledge of English grammar—and about misreading words that share a lot of letters with a word that is more easily aroused because it is more frequent than the one that's really on the page.

Let's look at the bottom-up side in more detail, now, to get a better idea of where many errors in reading come from. As I indicated when we talked about Cattell's word superiority effect, the letters in a written word don't only arouse the word-forms in your mind that happen to have all of the same letters. Experiments that look at readers' error patterns tell us that when the letters stored in your mind are activated, some of that activation probably spreads automatically to all the words that have any of those letters in them. If a word (like *systematic*) shares multiple letters with the one that's really on the page (like *systemic*), the activations from each of the shared letters add up; the more letters shared, the more the word form is activated. So, when we see a written word, it's not just the whole word that gets activation from the letters; some activation goes to all the other words that have some of the same letters in the same order, and especially to words that are only one letter different—its NEIGHBORS.

Then what starts to happen is competition: Words that have all the letters of the word you are looking at will be more strongly aroused than words that have only some of them, and the stronger words will send inhibitory signals to the weaker ones (*There's only room for one of us in this town, mister*). (If you look back at Figure 8.3, you'll see that each word at the top level has an inhibitory connection to each of the others.) Those inhibitory signals should insure that the word that's really in front of your eyes gets the most activation and is the one whose lemma is aroused first. Top-down processing usually also helps the competition to settle down to one of the aroused words by adding activation to words that are semantically and syntactically appropriate for the context. As a result, all that we are conscious of is seeing a sequence of words that makes sense, except when we are trapped by an ambiguous sentence, or a garden-path sentence that tricks you into making an incorrect guess about its syntax.

But the competition can go wrong if one of the competing words has a high resting level of activation (because it's frequent) or has been getting a lot of top-down activation because it's expected for semantic or syntactic reasons (like *house* in the context of the word *mortgage* or in the phrase *Come on over to my*). It won't take much additional activation from the "bottom" to bring such a predictable word from its resting level to its firing threshold level. So that's one important source of reading errors.

If the word form in your mind also has letters that are not in the word you are looking at—for example, when looking at *systemic* has activated *systematic*—then, if you don't take your eyes off the word too fast, the extra letters *A* and *T* in your mind will be confronted with the fact that there is no *A* or *T* in that spot on the page. The outcome of that confrontation should be that inhibition is sent to the word form *systematic*, reducing its level of activation. But if you're reading too fast, this may not happen; that's another source of errors. When you're skimming newspaper headlines, you're especially likely to make temporary reading errors, because headlines give fewer syntactic cues than regular text, and because you may not have looked at them directly for long enough to get all the letters right.

8.5 When Sounding Out Words Won't Work for You and Your Students: Orthographic Dazzle, Dialect Awareness, Speech Rate, and Hyperdistinct Speech

We already know that when their spelling is irregular, sounding out words to figure out how to spell them or how to read them won't work well and may not work at all. Unfortunately, it's easy to underestimate the difficulties that other people may have in sounding out words, because their pronunciation and speech perception may be different from yours. Unless you've heard recordings of your own voice a lot, you also may think you say things differently from the way you actually do. This doesn't mean that you can't use phonics, but it does mean that you'll be a better language professional if you know what kinds of problems may come up and can figure out strategies for dealing with them. In this section, we rely heavily on what you learned in Chapter 1 about phonetics and the disconnect between pronunciation and English spelling. I hope I've convinced you that teaching phoneme-grapheme correspondences is essential to producing competent readers of English, but you need to do it right; if there is no reliable correspondence in a particular situation, you need to deal with it. We are, after all, stuck with a spelling system in which *Ludacris* is a plausible way to spell *ludicrous*.

8.5.1 Orthographic Dazzle

All of us literate people have a problem in hearing our actual pronunciations of words. We think we say a /t/ in *fasten*, but we don't; we think we say, *Could you hold this for me* as /kʊd ju ˈhold ðɪs fɔr mi/, but what we really say is a lot closer to /khdʒəˈholðɪsfrmi/. Our knowledge of how words are spelled deludes us. If you are teaching reading, or using written words as part of a total communication approach in the classroom, your students will feel miserable and incompetent—unless they are very brave and sure of themselves—if you tell them that they say something in one way and either you or they in fact say it in another way. I like to use the informal phrase **ORTHOGRAPHIC DAZZLE** to describe the powerful top-down effect of spelling knowledge as it overrides people's ability to hear what they are actually saying unless it's played back to them on a tape recorder.

I had an unforgettably unpleasant experience as an observer in a private school for young children with language disorders, watching a special education teacher with a bad case of orthographic dazzle try to explain to a language delayed 4-year-old child that he should use the word *is*. She did this by writing on the chalkboard the letters *I S* and saying, very carefully and clearly, /ai ɛsss/—/ɪsss/—/ɪz/. This teacher apparently heard neither the disconnect between the letter names (/ai ɛsss/) and her "careful" version of how the word should be pronounced (/ɪsss/), nor between the letter-based pronunciation /ɪs/ and the actual pronunciation /ɪz/. (And she certainly didn't know that that /z/ becomes partly voiceless at the ends of sentences, adding to the complexity.) The moral of this story is that if you want to teach someone to sound out a word, or to use its written form to help them learn the spoken form, you have to be able to guide them accurately in seeing when the letters are a good match to the pronunciation and when they are ambiguous or misleading. If you leave your weaker students to figure that out for themselves, they are at risk for deciding that the whole business of reading is completely mysterious and beyond their capacities.

Here is a sample of the kind of problems that you can run into even at the beginning reading level: American English speakers (in the dialects I know of) rhyme *been* with *bin* or *ben*, not with *bean* (so the nursery rhyme *Pussycat, pussycat, where have you been, I've been to London to visit the Queen* is not a true rhyme on the west side of the Atlantic). Standard American English doesn't rhyme *says* with *days* (although some dialects may), and in the United States, in spite of what some instruction books say, the letter *y* at the end of adjectives like *lucky* and *pretty* is a "long e" (/i/), not a "short i" (ɪ). Oh, and as we implied in Chapter 1, *pretty* rhymes with *bitty*, not with *Betty*, regardless of the fact that it's spelled with an *E*. And for many English speakers, some or all of the time, the written E of *pretty* is completely gone: the word—especially when it's an unstressed adverb as in the phrase *pretty good*—is pronounced ['p r ɾ i], with the /r/ working as a vowel and the /t/ reduced to the flap [ɾ].

In short, using phonics does *not* mean closing your eyes and ears to the irregularities glaring off the page. And be prepared to fight orthographic dazzle by letting go of your memory of how a word is spelled, and using your hard-won ability to think about how it actually sounds.

8.5.2 Dialect awareness and phonics

Knowing your own pronunciation accurately isn't all you'll need to help people read, either in the clinic or in the classroom. Because not everyone pronounces words the same way, you need to know whether your students will be able to hear a difference between pairs of similar words. If there is no difference between two words in their pronunciation, they won't be able to figure out how to spell them just by sounding them out, any more than you yourself could have figured out how to spell *meat* and *meet* just from their sounds.

To be sure, if two words that are spelled differently sound identical, like *meat* and *meet*, you can still use phonics to pronounce them or to help narrow down the possibilities of how they might be pronounced (*EE* is always /i/, and *EA* is almost always either /i/ or /ei/). But phonics can't help anyone remember which of the two words is spelled which way. That's sheer memory work. Reading this book won't make you an expert on figuring out other people's dialects, but it may help you figure out your own. Make sure you know how you really pronounce words yourself— record your voice and listen.

By the way, if your students speak a lot more Spanish or Italian than they do English, the vowels /i/ and /ɪ/ probably sound the same to them— *to live* and *to leave* are just as homonymous to them as *meat* and *meet* are to you. And if you are teaching Spanish to English speakers, you already know that we can barely hear the difference between /r/ and /rr/, which makes it hard for us Anglos to remember which way an R-sound is spelled. In L2 teaching, the usual advice is to train listening, speaking, and spelling of such pairs of sounds all at the same time, because they all need to be learned and their interconnections will help each other. We'll say a bit more about this when we discuss second language teaching in Chapter 9, section 9.7.

8.5.3 Speech rate

We didn't emphasize this in Chapter 1, except when we introduced the flap [ɾ] allophone shared by the English phonemes /t/ and /d/, but the way we pronounce words depends a lot on how fast we are speaking, as well as on how formal the speaking situation is. In English, the vowels of unstressed syllables become very short in ordinary speaking situations, and many of them disappear altogether when we use what school grammar calls CONTRACTIONS and what linguists call CLITIC forms—that is, forms that have to be attached to other words in when we speak. Contracted spellings like *I've* /aiv/ for *I have, you'd've* /aidəv/ for *you would have* are accepted in novels (and I've been using them in this textbook because I think they are faster and friendlier). Comic strip spelling goes even further in recognizing how we normally talk, writing phrases like *Catch 'im! Wanna light? We oughta be there soon.* (Cartoonists also often go overboard and use nonstandard spelling where it wouldn't make any difference to the pronunciation, like writing *sez* for *says* and *wuz* for *was*, in order to make a character look uneducated or anti-intellectual, even though writing them *sez* and *wuz* is the nearest approach to the way we all say those words: /sɛz/ and/wʌz/ or, in faster speech /səz/, /wɔz.)

Our economical habit of contracting words and leaving out unstressed vowels in normal conversation means that most of us only learn from reading that the full form of *would've* is *would have*. We have almost no opportunities to hear the full forms in conversation. You yourself may have once written forms like *would of* for *would have, could of* for *could have, ought of* for *ought to have*—and if you didn't, just offer to help someone correct high school or freshman college writing assignments and you'll find plenty of folks who do. On the other hand, if we did learn the full forms like *would have* when we were quite young, we may be

324 PSYCHOLINGUISTICS: INTRODUCTION AND APPLICATIONS

completely unaware of the fact that we hardly ever say or hear them: Our knowledge of the written forms like *would have* overrides our ability to hear ourselves and each other saying /wʊdv/ all the time. It's orthographic dazzle again.

8.5.4 Hyperdistinct speech

At the opposite extreme from casual conversation is the **HYPERDISTINCT** or hyperarticulated speech style that we may use when we are consciously attending to our articulation, or when we are speaking over a noisy phone line. Our hyperdistinct forms can be affected by our knowledge of spelling, making them even less like our everyday speech; for example, we may say *informative,* normally /nˈfɔrmərɪv/, as /ɪnˈfɔrmætɪv/. This can be quite helpful to hearers, but if you are teaching non-native speakers, you have to help them get used to the more normal pronunciations as well. And again—are you getting tired of hearing this?—it's important to realize that we ourselves rarely speak hyperdistinctly. So if we are teaching children or other people who have not yet learned to read much English, the hyperdistinct form may be unfamiliar to them, which means that they won't be able to draw on their memory of it to help them with spelling. Teaching hyperdistinct forms and their corresponding casual form explicitly—especially for words like /nˈfɔrmərɪv/ that usually have flaps and unaccented vowels—is probably a good idea, but I don't think it has been tested yet.

Depending on where you are from and what pronunciations you have heard, you may be able to produce the distinctions between *Don* and *Dawn*, or between *pin* and *pen*, or between *Harry* and *hairy* easily, either only when you are speaking hyperdistinctly, sometimes, or not at all. If you can't make them easily, let it go.

8.6 Morphology and Reading

We said earlier in this chapter that if you read a compound word like *mouse-trap* or a word with common derivational and inflectional morphemes like *vaporizers*, the morphemes that make up the word are aroused, as well as the whole word itself. It makes sense that we would be able to tune into these word parts, because they are loaded with useful information. Knowing that English has a prefix *de-* that is pronounced /di/ and means something about removing or undoing helps you realize what *delouse* probably means, and that it isn't going to be pronounced /ˈdɛluz/.

If you see a set of newly coined words like *coralize, marblify,* or *quartzification*, your unconscious knowledge of the endings like *–ize, –ify, –ification* would tell you whether the words were nouns or verbs and which syllables would be stressed, and if you know the words *coral, marble,* and *quartz,* it would give you a very good guess as to the meaning of the new words. Morphological knowledge may not completely overcome conflicting bottom-up information from the letters when we encounter words like *hothouse* (the *th* in the middle arouses the sound /θ/ pretty strongly), *restenosis* (it's not *rest-enosis,* it's *re-stenosis*), or *misled* (many people report that they had thought, when they were children and encountered *misled* in their reading, that there must be an English verb *misle* /maɪzl/ meaning "to confuse," and that the person they were reading about had been /ˈmaɪzld/). But if we couldn't use morphology to go back and re-analyze these words, we'd be even worse off.

We know, from Berko Gleason's work and other studies that have extended her findings, that children from first grade through high school gradually acquire knowledge of English word endings and how those endings change the pronunciation of the words or word-stems they are added to (for example, the changes in the stress and the vowels that happen when *method* /ˈmɛθəd/ becomes *methodical* /məˈθadɪkl/). Like almost all linguistic knowledge, what children know about morphology seems to be mostly unconscious, learned from the semiregular patterns that they find over and over again as they listen and read. And children who have more unconscious knowledge about the morphemes of a long word read with better comprehension.

Explicitly teaching some morphological relationships improves English reading comprehension in children from ages 7 to 9, and has improved spelling in children with reading problems. Teaching morphology as part of "word attack skills" is especially useful for L2 learners whose first language does not have similar word formation patterns. And L2 learners whose first language is a Romance language (one that comes from Latin) should be able to improve both their English reading and their first language reading if they learn to connect the almost-identical derivational morphemes in their own languages and in English.

8.7 Reading Chinese, Japanese, and Korean

8.7.1 Comparing three very different writing systems

Important misconceptions about the Chinese writing system got into the reading literature in the 1970s. The most seriously wrong ideas were that Chinese characters are unanalyzable (have no component parts) and that they give no information about the sounds of the words that they represent. Most psychologists who are interested in reading have known about those misconceptions since the late 1970s, when actual experimental work on the psycholinguistics and neurolinguistics of reading Chinese and Japanese began, but some of that old misinformation is still being requoted. You can also find references to Korean "characters," but Korean is almost entirely written with an alphabet—a much better alphabet than ours! Understanding the writing systems of these three languages and the experimental work that has been done with them is worthwhile, even if you don't plan to learn them yourself, because they are very different from each other as well as from languages written with the Roman alphabet, and the comparison helps us to understand the psycholinguistics of reading English better. If you're teaching English as a second language to people who already read one of these languages, this section will be especially useful.

8.7.2 A little history of writing systems

Where East Asian writing systems started: Chinese

Let's start with some history of East Asian languages and writing to help anchor your understanding of how these three writing systems work. The Chinese writing system is one of the three (known) independently invented writing systems in the world; the other two were the Sumerian system in ancient Mesopotamia—which inspired Egyptian hieroglyphics as well as the writing systems of Hebrew and Greek—and the Mayan system in Yucatan. As far as we know, all other writing systems in the world were derived from one of these three—most from Sumerian via many different intermediaries, modern Chinese and Japanese from ancient Chinese—or were inspired by one of them, like Cherokee.

The units of these writing systems are not "little pictures," because pictures are not specific enough to convey the exact words of detailed messages. (Try to translate any sentence on this page unambiguously word for word into pictures!) But business and taxation records (which might be contested), astronomical records, and magical/religious formulas need to represent specific words without depending on the memory of a person who knows (or claims to know) what the person who sent the message intended. Otherwise, there might be some doubt about who paid what to whom on what date for what set of goods to be delivered by some other date, or the proper way to address a dangerous and powerful deity. As commerce and religion expanded in these early empires, their writing developed into sets of standardized symbols that could be written quickly, each symbol unambiguously representing a particular word. Now any trained scribe could read it, so written information could be carried for hundreds of miles and retained for hundreds of years, regardless of whether the courier or the curator could understand it.

A writing system that has an unambiguous (or nearly unambiguous) symbol for each word is called **LOGOGRAPHIC**: literally, word-writing. Some hundreds, perhaps, of its symbols will still be traceable as stylized pictures of the sun, the moon, a man, or a woman, and so on, used either with that original meaning or for another word that sounds like that word, the way we do in a rebus puzzle where a symbol that looks like an eye is used for the first person singular pronoun *I*.

But not enough words can be symbolized by easily readable stylized pictures or their homonyms—again, imagine trying to create a set of picture-based symbols to represent a sentence on this page! Most of the logograms in any logographic writing system are created by combining some information about a word's sound with some information about its meaning. It's like when we play charades: we use mime to show the meaning of our target word, plus the "sounds like" ear-cupping gesture and pointing to an object or miming something else, in order to narrow our audience down to our specific target word or phrase. In the same way, most Chinese characters are made up of two or more parts, called radicals. One of them (the phonetic component) is usually—or was historically—a single character representing a word that sounds like the target word, and the others (the semantic components) are (or were) single characters that represent some aspect of the meaning of the target word. (Sometimes, the meaning of a word has changed so much over the course of history that the semantic radical or radicals no longer give useful information.)

Chinese characters, then, except for the very simplest ones, are not stylized pictures, no matter what that "easy guide to learning the characters" might have told you. Except for the few hundred one-radical characters, they are not "unanalyzed wholes"; they are composites. Except for those one-radical characters, they are not "purely semantic," either; although the phonetic information is historically much older and more out of step with modern pronunciation than the worst of English spelling, it is there. In China (though not in Taiwan), children are taught to look for that phonetic information; it's still helpful for recognizing a word with the right semantics that's in your spoken vocabulary, although you might have to guess among three or more possible sounds. And none of the characters represent "ideas"; each one represents a specific word, or a morpheme in a compound word (most words in modern Chinese are two-morpheme compounds). To be minimally literate in Chinese, you need to know at least 5,000 characters.

Japanese

The Japanese writing system is a stunning example of what happens when a logographic writing system is borrowed to write a language that is neither similar to nor related to the language it came from (see section 1.10 if you want a refresher on the way languages can be similar or different). The Japanese language, as far back as it can be traced, has a wildly different structure from Chinese. Chinese has almost no "endings," almost all words are one or two morphemes long, and all morphemes have just one syllable. But Japanese verbs have inflectional tense endings, plus lots of derivational endings different from anything that we have in English. Some common ones are V-*tai* meaning "want to V," V-*nai* meaning "not V," V-*sase* meaning "cause to V," and V-*rare*, which is similar to the English passive. And it has plenty of morphemes that are several syllables long, like *minami* "south."

About 1,200 years ago, contact between the Chinese and Japanese cultures became intense for several centuries, and the Chinese writing system was borrowed for use in writing Japanese, along with many thousands of Chinese words. Many Japanese content morphemes, such as nouns like *mountain* and the stems of verbs like *push*, of course could be written with the characters that had the same meanings in Chinese. But the Japanese people had their own tools, customs, and ceremonies that didn't match any concepts in Chinese culture, and the Japanese inflectional and derivational morphemes didn't match any words in Chinese.

What happened, over time, was that about 50 of the thousands of Chinese characters were highly simplified and used just for their sounds, abandoning their meanings. Fortunately, Japanese had (and has) a very strict phonotactic system: no consonant clusters, fewer than 10 vowels, and only (/n/) or glottal stop allowed at the end of a syllable. So Japanese can be written phonetically with collection of about a hundred different phonetic vowel and consonant + vowel symbols. Each symbol is a KANA, and the whole set of kana is called a SYLLABARY. The Chinese characters that were used only for their sounds developed into the kana. (Strictly, these symbols don't always represent whole syllables; a word like *tai*—a kind of fish popular in sushi—is one syllable, but it needs two of the syllabary symbols, one for *ta* and one for *i*. The proper term for the phonetic unit that each kana represents is a mora.)

The kana were actually created in two ways, so that Japanese now has two completely parallel versions of its syllabary, as you see in Figure 8.4. One version is the square-looking *katakana* (now used mostly for writing foreign words, onomatopoeia, and sound effects); the other set is the more graceful *hiragana* which are used for all of those verb endings and other bound grammatical morphemes, for free grammatical morphemes, and for

Figure 8.4. Hiragana and katakana.

other words that have no characters or that have very rare ones that people are unlikely to know how to pronounce.

The kana syllabary is almost completely phonetic, completely regular, and very easy to learn; children are taught to read it early.

Learning to read the characters (which are called KANJI), however, is hard work—about 2,000 are required to graduate from high school, and much school time is spent in mastering them. (Learning them is harder than it would be for Chinese readers, for two reasons you can think about for the Challenge section if you are interested.)

In summary, Japanese depends on a hybrid writing system, where the 2,000 or so most common CONTENT morphemes—the commonest nouns, the commonest verb stems, and many adjective stems—are written with Chinese-based kanji (slightly modified from their original forms). All the other words, and the suffix morphemes on the common verbs and adjectives, are written using the symbols of the nice shallow katakana/hiragana syllabary.

Korean

Korean writing is mostly alphabetic, even though it doesn't look that way because of how the letters are arranged in the words. The history of writing in Korea starts out the same way as in Japan—by borrowing Chinese characters to use for Korean words with the same meaning. Korean is typologically similar to Japanese (and possibly related to it), but it has more consonants and vowels and a much more complex syllable structure than Japanese (there are lots of syllable-final consonants, plus consonant clusters). The Chinese writing system fit Korean just as poorly as it fit Japanese, for the same reasons: Korean had (and has) lots of polysyllabic words and lots of endings, as well as plenty of words that had no equivalent in Chinese.

Koreans originally adapted Chinese characters in ways similar to what was done in Japan. But the bad fit was recognized by Korean linguistic scholars, who designed a phonemic alphabet of 24 letters, called Hangul; it was officially adopted by royal proclamation in 1446. The Hangul has changed somewhat since then, but not fundamentally. Writing today may be all Hangul, or Hangul mixed with Chinese-based characters, called Hanja or Hanza. Korean high school students are expected to know about 1,800 Hanja by the time they graduate, but they are used much less than the Kanji are in Japan.

The scholars who created Hangul gave it two special features that were clearly based on linguistic analysis. One is how the letters in each word are arranged: They are organized into blocks, one for each syllable, which is probably quite helpful in learning to read. Each syllable contains one to four letters, which are altered in shape and size to make a neat square-ish block that superficially looks like a Chinese character. Figure 8.5 presents an example from the Internet (http://www.omniglot.com/writing/korean.htm), showing how to decompose the two syllables in the word Hangul (you may also see this word spelled Hangeul or Hankul).

The other linguistic feature of Hangul is that the letter shapes are systematically designed so that consonants with similar places of articulation have similar letters (and the consonant shapes are schematic representations of the shapes of the articulators). So remembering which letter means which sound is much easier for learners of Korean than it is for learners of any other alphabet.

8.7.3 Psycholinguistic studies of reading Chinese and Chinese-based characters

Learning to read Chinese characters is an enormous task, and Chinese-language educational systems are designed around coping with it. Children learn each character by writing it over and over, and because the phonetic information is much less predictable than is in English, visual/motor learning has to play a much larger role in learning to write each word. (As a result, second-language learners who are literate in Chinese may need extra

한(han) ㅎ(h) + ㅏ(a) + ㄴ(n) 글(geul) ㄱ(g) + ㅡ(eu) + ㄹ(l)

Figure 8.5. Example of Hangul.

encouragement to use the available phonetic information when they learn an alphabetic script.) Chinese pupils learn the more frequent characters more quickly and can read them faster. But as we said above, children learning to read Chinese characters do learn to use some of the partial phonetic information that is in the phonetic component of most characters—explicitly on the mainland, and without explicit teaching in Taiwan. And it seems that the better learners in Taiwan make phonologically based errors, showing that they are (probably unconsciously) learning, fairly early, to organize words by their sounds. Experimental studies also show that Chinese adult readers make highly automatic use of whatever phonetic information a character has, because they recognize words that have more regular phonetic components faster than those that have less reliable phonetic information. (More precisely, they do this if the words are infrequent. For frequent words, skilled adult readers are just as fast at reading the irregular ones as the regular ones. Does that sound familiar?)

In Japanese, because of the history of the spoken language and of the writing system, the phonetic information in the Chinese-based kanji characters is even less reliable than it is in Chinese (although it exists for many kanji when they are being used to represent words that were originally borrowed from Chinese). But even when a character does not itself contain phonetic information, readers learn how it sounds as well as what it means (except for rare characters that they have never heard anyone pronounce). Looking at a familiar character sends activation directly to both the word form and the word meaning; arousal of the word's sound does not have to wait until the meaning has reached threshold activation. Evidence for this is that elderly Japanese people with dementia can sometimes read familiar kanji characters aloud even when they no longer seem to know what the characters mean. So: People who apparently start by learning a direct visual-to-semantic connection also develop a visual-to-phonetic link. This is the flip side of something that we mentioned near the end of section 8.1: People who learn to read a regular orthography phonetically will eventually also develop a visual-to-semantic representation of the whole word. Our minds build all kinds of connections as efficiently as they can, and this includes developing shortcuts that pay no attention to the logic of how a writing system is constructed.

8.8 Reading and Language Disorders

8.8.1 Dyslexia

Children who are having difficulties learning to read are the ones who are most affected by the teaching method. After DYSLEXIA became widely recognized as a reading disorder in the later part of the 20th century, quarrels over teaching methods intensified. Many (and possibly most) dyslexia cases are caused by trouble processing the sounds of words efficiently, or with some other aspect of getting word lemmas activated in the brain, but the problem is seldom purely visual. An early phonological problem can be subtle or undetectable by the time a child gets to school, but it can have persisting effects; children who have trouble with pronouncing a difficult sound at age 3 can have problems with reading and spelling it at age 8. The more pervasive early language problem known as **SPECIFIC LANGUAGE DISORDER (SLI)** puts children at high risk for dyslexia, although the two disorders are not the same.

Why is the visual processing problem theory of dyslexia so popular? Partly, it seems to be easier to suspect visual problems than sound-processing problems, because most children with dyslexia can hear and understand spoken language well enough to seem normal. And partly it's because many of the dyslexic person's errors are getting the letters of a word in the wrong order. But here's a different explanation for getting letters in the wrong order: The problem isn't visual. What makes people with reading problems liable to scramble the letters in words is that they have trouble using their memory of word sounds to help them decide what the order of the letters should be; they are relying on visual memory only. They are "visual learners" by default, because their auditory processing doesn't work well enough to rely on.

Visual learning, although helpful to all of us, is not enough: None of us would be good at getting letters in the right order if we couldn't link at least some of the letters to their sounds, and had to rely just on pure visual memory for each word. That's why the "i-before-e or e-before-i" problem of *belief, receipt, weird*, and the rest of that *ie/ei* set is so intractable even for good spellers: The two vowel orders sound exactly the same, and the incorrect versions of the words look too much like the correct ones. Many children with dyslexia (and less severe reading problems) seem to be fighting the same kind of battle on a gigantic scale: Because they can't hold a clear, explicit memory of a word's individual sounds in mind (remember coarticulation? We don't get to hear the sounds in a word one at a time—that sequence is something that our minds construct), they are trying to remember the order of the letters in every word with relatively little help from the order of its sounds. With a lot of hard work and good teaching, people can compensate for dyslexia, but it absorbs a lot of time and effort. Intensive computer-game type training on attending to speech sounds helps; so does practice with grapheme-phoneme correspondences (at least for English), and so does practice in getting meaning as well as sounds from written words. However, there are still plenty of controversies about the subtypes of dyslexia, and about the proper ways to help people compensate for their reading problems.

8.8.2 Reading and writing in aphasia: Entangled language modalities

One of the questions people ask when they first learn about aphasia is: But if someone with aphasia can't talk, can he write? As you know by now, the answer (almost always) is "sometimes, but if it's really aphasia, they can't write they way they used to." That's because aphasia is damage to the language processing system, and we use our language processing system for written language as well as for spoken language and signed language.

Researchers use the word **MODALITIES** to mean the various different sensory and motor channels that we use for getting and giving information. For people who can hear and see reasonably well, listening and reading are their main language input modalities, and speaking, writing, typing, and texting are their language output modalities. Perceiving and producing a signed language is an additional pair of input/out modalities; lipreading and perceiving Braille are other input modalities.

For an analogy, think about the way information gets into and out of your computer. To input information, you can download from the Internet, receive e-mail, put in a CD or DVD, use a scanner, get a fax, or type. If your computer has a microphone, you can record sounds; if it has a camera, you can make pictures and videos. For output, you can send e-mail, post to a social networking page or some other Web site, print, or send a fax; if you have a microphone, you can make a phone call using Skype. If one of those input or output modalities isn't working, one of the others may be able to take over or supplement it—but if there's a central processing problem, it's going to show up in several or all of those modalities, not just in one.

The variety of ways that brain damage can interfere with reading and writing is astounding. Aphasia may affect all of a person's input and output modalities, or some of them may be relatively better off, as we saw for spoken language comprehension and production when we looked at the different aphasia syndromes at the end of Chapter 6. To the list of the way different language modalities may be affected differently, we can add people who can write the names of pictures on a test page but not say them, and others who can say them but not write them.

Aphasia tests are typically organized so that modalities can be compared—for example, at least some of the same pictures will be used to test naming, auditory comprehension (pointing to the right picture), reading (matching word to picture), and writing (writing the name of the pictured item). But as we go beyond standard tests with clients who are interested in participating in research, we find nearly endless variations in the individual details of problems with reading (acquired **ALEXIA**) and writing (**DYSGRAPHIA, AGRAPHIA**).

The big difference between human brains and most computers is that we are self-organizing systems, shaped by the ways that our experiences are connected to each other. Our memories of speech sounds, for example, are linked to our experiences of saying and hearing them, reading and writing them. And our present experiences are interlinked, too, not just our past ones; an aphasic person who has trouble articulating sounds and tries to supplement her speaking with writing may write some of the letters correctly from memory, but some of the mangled speech sounds that she is actually saying may trigger the writing of other letters that don't belong in the word at all.

All this supports our general model of the brain: It's a mechanism that forges many partially redundant connections among our memories of things that we see, do, hear, feel, and say. And we'll probably never know what all of the possible direct and indirect connections are. For literate computer-using adults, writing and typing are amazingly automatized— they are almost as easy as speaking, and you can do it fairly well while you are still listening to what someone is saying. You don't think about the mechanics of forming the letters or hitting the keys unless you have an injury to your hand or are using a keyboard that has the letters in unfamiliar places; you don't think about what the letters look like unless you are a calligrapher or have just learned a new writing system; and you don't think about the spelling of familiar words: It's stored, so that the word's lemma can directly activate the letter string as a whole. In addition, the word's sounds activate the letters, one or a few at a time. But remember, activation spreads automatically; in addition to the words you want to say, write, or type, activation will spread from the lemma you want to semantically related lemmas, and from the sounds of the word to various letter combinations that can be used to write them—not just to the ones you need. If you're multitasking or have a complex story to tell, lemmas for words that you don't need just at that moment will also be somewhat active, and sending some activation out to letters, sounds, and concepts. Looking at some errors in aphasic reading and writing will give you a sense of this intense bustle of activity in our brains, even when they are injured and limping along.

In reading aloud, some people with aphasia say words that are related to the written word in sounds or letters, like saying *touch* when they see the letters THOUGH. Someone making this kind of error seems to have gotten relatively little information from the meaning of the word; the written form either doesn't activate the lemma, or the lemma sends very little activation on to the word's stored spoken form. Other people with aphasia say words that are related in meaning but not in sounds to the one they are looking at, for example, saying *bird* or *cardinal* when trying to read the word ROBIN. This looks as though the grapheme-to-phoneme information from the letters on the page is very weak and the lemma is activated directly; or perhaps the phonological information is very transient, and can't hang around in their minds. In either case, there's not enough phonological activation from the letters, so nothing in the person's brain is able to check whether the lemma that gets the most activation is the one that really matches the written word, instead of being some other member of the same semantic category.

In writing picture names, people with aphasia sometimes make the same sorts of errors that they do in reading aloud. They may write a semantically related word, like *fork* for a picture of a spoon: Activation of the lemma for the wrong word has somehow gotten too strong. Importantly, errors like this are not consistent from one test run to the next, nor from one modality to the next, so they must be happening as accidents during language processing. Here are examples from some aphasia research centers: An American patient sees a picture of brush, writes <u>brush</u>, says *comb*; sees a picture of a knife, writes <u>spoon</u>, says *fork*. An Italian patient sees a picture of trumpet, correctly writes <u>*tromba*</u>, but says *orchestra*. A patient in Argentina, matching written words to pictures, pairs up the written word meaning <u>*sword*</u> to a picture of a shield; reads the written word <u>*vaca*</u> (cow) aloud as <u>*toro*</u> (bull), reads the written word <u>*cebolla*</u> (onion) aloud as *ajo* (garlic). He is unable to read the written word <u>*carreta*</u> (cart) aloud but draws a picture of one as his response, is unable to read <u>*sabana*</u> (sheet) aloud, but in response to the word, mimes sleeping. In writing to dictation, he again writes semantically related words about half the time: He hears *piloto* (pilot), writes <u>*avion*</u> (airplane); hearing *noche* (night), he writes <u>*luna*</u> (moon). And sometimes, he appears to be trying to write the correct word, but it comes out slowly, with phonological or orthographic errors like <u>c-o-t-a-r</u> for *cortar*, <u>c-e-p-o-c-a</u> for *cebolla*.

Some needed information is getting through, some is not, and the checking/inhibiting systems are either working badly, or being overridden because the patients want so intensely to show the examiner that their knowledge has not been completely wiped out.

8.9 Summary

Some research on reading is keen to tell you that the mind uses a particular method to get to a complex goal like understanding a written text. Well, the mind uses so many methods that any psycholinguistically reasonable claim that "the mind does X" is probably right—but be very skeptical if someone claims that their favorite avenue to text comprehension is the *only* one that will help you or your students or clients. Analyzing the error patterns from normal and less able readers shows us that reading and writing make use of multiple, interacting sources of information; our minds are greedy pattern-hunters, and they will use as many simultaneous avenues to activation as they can, both bottom-up and top-down.

Too much of the reading literature has been based on English. Work on other writing systems, alphabetic and nonalphabetic, shows the value of something English doesn't have: a reliable, consistent, simple pattern relating written forms to their pronunciation, and pronunciation to spelling. Such shallow or transparent orthographies, like the Spanish, Turkish, and Korean alphabetic systems and the Japanese kana syllabary (but *not* the kanji characters!) are easy to learn from exposure to writing, and need minimal teaching. Deep but fairly reliable orthographies, like French, are not much harder to learn to read than shallower ones, but they are harder to learn to spell with; in compensation, they give useful information about semantic relationships between words.

English spelling is a problem not so much because of its depth as because of its irregularity. Nevertheless, in English spelling (and even in Chinese characters), the available phonetic information is extremely valuable. English readers who cannot figure out how a new word is likely to sound will be hampered in their ability to learn new words from reading and to recognize them when they hear them spoken. Although the best learners will probably pick up the grapheme-phoneme correspondences of varying grain sizes unconsciously, the poorer ones probably won't, and need explicit teaching.

If you are teaching grapheme-phoneme correspondences across dialects and accents, be aware of both your actual pronunciation and that of your students. Listening to recordings of your own voice in casual conversation will probably reveal that how you really speak is different from the way you think you speak.

The art of reading doesn't end with sounding out words phonetically or recalling their sounds from memory. Learning basic morphology helps readers of all ages to break up long words into accessible parts and gives significant help with predicting their sounds. Practicing reading aloud for meaning helps children learn to combine words into phrases and larger constructions; beyond that, readers must learn to build up their mental pictures of what the text is telling them, using their common sense and their knowledge of the world.

Serious developmental reading problems usually involve phonological problems in processing sounds, although other factors may be involved also; reading can be improved, in many children, by intensive work listening to and becoming aware of speech sounds. Brain damage that causes aphasia in adults also impairs reading and writing, but because there are many ways that information about words is stored and activated, patients show many different patterns of damage and partial preservation of both spoken and written language.

Exercises for Chapter 8

8.1. Explain why the misspelling "rice patty" for "rice paddy," seen on the Web, is a plausible spelling error for someone using phonics to make. (Go back to Chapter 1, section 1.2.5.2 for a hint as to how to start.) Also describe some of the errors that a person *not* using phonics could make in spelling "paddy."

8.2. As we said in the text, here is no way to predict whether the *ea* combination should be pronounced /ei/ as in *steak* or /i/ as in *streak*. Foreigners just have to look up the pronunciation of these words in the dictionary. Many of the words spelled with /ea/ are common enough to be in the vocabulary of a first-grader, but they might not be familiar to some adult second-language learners of English from other cultures.

What would be different about the way you would teach first-graders and the way you would teach adult L2 learners to deal with figuring out how to recognize words like *break, steak, freak, teach, leak, meat, treat, bead* . . . when they encounter them in a story or a message that they are trying to understand? *Hint:* What kinds of knowledge of English are first-graders likely to have that new speakers of English might not have?

Important: Don't forget about the way our brains make associations whether we want them to or not. I have no empirical evidence for this, but everything I know suggests that, because there is no rule to follow, it would be a bad idea to teach the *ea* = /ei/ and the *ea* = /i/ words on the same day or even in a similar kind of lesson. Why?

8.3. Teaching morphology as part of "word attack skills" is especially useful for L2 learners whose first language does not have similar word formation patterns, such as Chinese.

And L2 learners whose first language is a Romance language should be able to improve both their English reading and their first language reading if they learn to connect the almost identical derivational morphemes in their own languages and in English. Create two parallel morphology lessons, one for speakers of Chinese and one for speakers of a Romance language like Spanish, French, Italian, or Portuguese, explaining how to find and use endings like *-tion*, *-ian*, *-ic*,*-ical*, *-ize*, *-ology*, and so on, in figuring out the meanings of many long English words. You may want to read some of the articles about morphology in the Sources Consulted for this chapter before you do this. (Obviously, you can teach a lot more in one lesson to the Romance language speakers, who have a head start, than to the Chinese speakers.)

Reference

Cattell, J. M. (1886). The time it takes to see and name objects. *Mind*, *11*(41), 63-65. Retrieved from http://www.jstor.org/stable/2247157

Suggested Readings and Sources Consulted

Aro, M., & Wimmer, H. (2003). Learning to read: English in comparison to six more regular orthographies. *Applied Psycholinguistics*, *24*, 621-635.

Berends, I. E., & Reitsma, P. (2006). Addressing semantics promotes the development of reading fluency. *Applied Psycholinguistics*, *27*(2), 247-265.

Carlisle, J. F. (2000). Awareness of the structure and meaning of morphologically complex words: Impact on reading. *Reading and Writing*, *12*, 169-190.

Carlisle, J. F., & Fleming, J. (2003). Lexical processing of morphologically complex words in the elementary years. *Scientific Studies of Reading*, *7*(3), 239-253.

Catts, H. W., Adlof, S. M., Hogan, T. P., & Ellis Weismer, S. (2005). Are specific language impairment and dyslexia distinct disorders? *Journal of Speech, Language, and Hearing Research*, *48*, 1378-1396.

Chan, C. K. K., & Siegel. L. S. (2001). Phonological processing in reading Chinese among normally achieving and poor readers. *Journal of Experimental Child Psychology*, *80*, 23-43. doi:10.1006/jecp.2000.2622

Cuetos, F., & Labos, E. (2001). The autonomy of the orthographic pathway in a shallow language: Data from an aphasic patient. *Aphasiology, 15,* 333–342.

Daniels, P. T., & Bright, W. (1996). *The world's writing systems.* New York, NY: Oxford University Press.

Deacon, S. H., & Kirby, J. R. (2004). Morphological awareness: Just "more phonological"? The roles of morphological and phonological awareness in reading development. *Applied Psycholinguistics, 25,* 223–238.

Friend, A., & Olson, R. K. (2008). Phonological spelling and reading deficits in children with spelling disabilities. *Scientific Studies of Reading, 12*(1), 90–105.

Gaab, N. (2007). Sound training rewires dyslexic children's brains for reading. http://www.scilearn.com/resources/brain-fitness/sound-training-rewires-dyslexic-childrens-brains-for-reading.php Source publication: Gaab, N.; Gabrieli, J. D. E.; Deutsch, G. K.; Tallal, P.; & Temple, E.; (2007). Neural correlates of rapid auditory processing are disrupted in children with developmental dyslexia and ameliorated with training: An fMRI study. *Restorative Neurology and Neuroscience, 25,* 295–310.

Hillis, A. E., Rapp, B. C., & Caramazza, A. (1999). When a rose is a rose in speech but a tulip in writing. *Cortex, 35,* 337–356.

Hotz, R. L. (2008). How the brain learns to read can depend on the language. *The Wall Street Journal.* May 2, 2008, p. A10.

Kintsch, W., & Kintsch, E. (2005). Comprehension. In S. G. Paris & S. A. Stahl (Eds.), *Children's reading comprehension and assessment* (pp. 71–92). Mahwah, NJ: Erlbaum.

Leong, C. K., & Ho, M. K. (2008). The role of lexical knowledge and related linguistic components in typical and poor language comprehenders of Chinese. *Reading and Writing, 21,* 559–586.

LeVasseur, V. M., Macaruso, P., Palumbo, L. C., & Shankweiler, D. (2006). Syntactically cued text facilitates oral reading fluency in developing readers. *Applied Psycholinguistics, 27*(3), 423–445.

McBride-Chang, C., Wagner, R. K., Muse, A., Chow, B. W.-Y., & Shu, H. (2005). The role of morphological awareness in children's vocabulary acquisition in English. *Applied Psycholinguistics, 26*(3), 415–435.

McClelland, J. L., & Rumelhart, D. E. (1981). An interactive activation model of context effects in letter perception: Part 1. An account of basic findings. *Psychological Review, 88,* 375–407.

McDonald, S. A., & Shillcock, R. C. (2003). Eye movements reveal the online computation of lexical probabilities during reading. *Psychological Science, 14,* 648–652.

Miceli, G., Benvegnù, B., Capasso, R., & Caramazza, A. (1997). The independence of phonological and orthographic lexical forms: Evidence from aphasia. *Cognitive Neuropsychology, 14,* 35–69.

National Reading Panel. (2000). *Teaching children to read. Reports of the subgroups.* Washington, DC: National Institute of Child Health and Human Development.

Nunes, T., Bryant, P., & Olsson, J. (2003). Learning morphological and phonological spelling rules: An intervention study. *Scientific Studies of Reading, 7*(3), 289–307.

Rapp, B., Benzing, L., & Caramazza, A. (1997). The autonomy of lexical orthography. *Cognitive Neuropsychology, 14*, 71–104.

Reichle, E. D., & Perfetti, C. A. (2003). Morphology in word identification: A word-experience model that accounts for morpheme frequency effects. *Scientific Studies of Reading* 7(3), 219–237.

Seva, N., Monaghan, P., & Arciuli, J. (2009). Stressing what is important: Orthographic cues and lexical stress assignment. *Journal of Neurolinguistics, 22*, 237–249.

Shelton, J. R., & Weinrich, M. (1997). Further evidence of a dissociation between output phonological and orthographic lexicons: A case study. *Cognitive Neuropsychology, 14*, 105–129.

Siok, W. T., Niu, Z., Jin, Z., Perfetti, C. A., & Tan, L. H. (2008). A structural–functional basis for dyslexia in the cortex of Chinese readers. *Proceedings of the National Academy of Sciences, 105*(14), 5561–5566. doi:10.1073/pnas.0801750105

Thomas, E., & Sénéchal, M. (2004). Long-term association between articulation quality and phoneme sensitivity: A study from age 3 to age 8. *Applied Psycholinguistics, 25*(4), 513–541.

Thompson, G. B., McKay, M. F., Fletcher-Flinn, C. M., Connelly, V., Kaa, R. T., & Ewing, J. (2008). Do children who acquire word reading without explicit phonics employ compensatory learning? Issues of phonological recoding, lexical orthography, and fluency. *Reading and Writing, 21*, 505–537. doi:10.1007/s11145-007-9075-9

Verhoeven, L., & Perfetti, C. (2003). Introduction to this special issue: The role of morphology in learning to read. *Scientific Studies of Reading*, 7(3), 209–217.

Winskel, H., & Widjaja, V. (2007). Phonological awareness, letter knowledge, and literacy development in Indonesian beginner readers and spellers. *Applied Psycholinguistics, 28*(1), 23–45.

Zaretsky, E., Kuvac Kraljevic, J., Core, C., & Lencek, M. (2009). Literacy predictors and early reading and spelling skills as a factor of orthography: Cross-linguistic evidence. *Written Language and Literacy, 12*(1), 52–81. doi:10.1075/wll.12.1.03zar

Ziegler, J. C., & Goswami, U. (2006). Becoming literate in different languages: Similar problems, different solutions. *Developmental Science, 9*(5), 429–453.

Zoccolotti, P., De Luca, M., Di Filippo, G., Judica, A., & Martelli, M. (2009). Reading development in an orthographically regular language: Effects of length, frequency, lexicality and global processing ability. *Reading and Writing, 22*, 1053–1079.

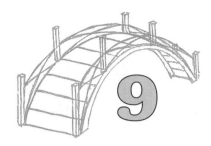

First and Second Language Acquisition

A Psycholinguistic Approach to Their Similarities and Differences

9.0 How Is Learning a First Language Different From Learning a Second Language, and Why?

Did you ever see the ads for the well-known company that teaches foreign language to adults that featured a close-up of the face of a meltingly beautiful little girl with huge dark eyes and a caption something like "She's only four years old and she speaks fluent Mandarin" (or Portuguese or whatever)? The implication was, of course, that if you went to their intensive language school, you (being an adult and therefore smarter than a child) could learn to speak a new language fluently, too, and in less than four years.

Good luck with that!

Infants who learn two languages at the same time become native bilingual speakers, and children who start intense interaction in a second language before they turn five usually become nativelike adult speakers. But very few people who start learning their second language after their early teens reach the elusive goal of becoming a nativelike speaker, although they can become very competent and effective speakers as teachers, politicians, and so on. If they are so good at their second language, what stops them from being just like native speakers?

Some people give simple answers to this question, some give complex ones. In this chapter, we'll look at it the problem psycholinguistically, without taking sides or claiming that we have the whole answer. Our approach lays the groundwork for Chapter 10, where we'll see how psycholinguistics can help us to understand many problems of second-language learning, teaching, and evaluation.

By way of introduction, here's a quick summary of the kinds of answers that you'll find to the question of why second-language (L2) acquisition is different from acquiring a first language (L1). As you probably expect by now, the answers come in two basic types: answers that assume that there is a strong innate component to grammar, and answers that assume that what's innate is a powerful learning mechanism, rather than a grammar or a blueprint for making grammars. There's more gray area between these schools of thought than there is for first-language learning, though, because it does seem that learning a second language after early childhood is rather more like learning other demanding skills (gymnastics, playing a musical instrument) than learning a first language seems to be. That still begs the question, though: Why?

You probably already know about the CRITICAL PERIOD HYPOTHESIS: the idea that there is a certain period of time, early in a child's life, when the brain can learn language "naturally," but that this period ends at some point, so that learning a language when you're older requires different processes. (Some researchers emphasize the claim that there are different processes by reserving the term language ACQUISITION for early language development and the term "language learning" for language development after this critical period.) Researchers argue a lot about whether there really is a critical period for language development and, if so, when it ends (the range of proposed "end ages" is from about age five to puberty), whether it applies to all aspects of language (phonology is clearly hard to master later, but vocabulary seems learnable all during our lives), whether it ends abruptly or gradually, and so on. A softer-edged version of this idea uses the term SENSITIVE PERIOD instead of Critical Period; the point of this change of name is to suggest that, although there's an optimal age for language learning, it can happen outside of that optimal period, only just not as well. By now, as you'll see in this chapter, it's clear that learning phonetics and phonology works best in infants and young children. But it's also clear that there are no sharp cutoff points to language learning abilities, and that that different aspects of language-learning ability (for example, the ability to learn general patterns vs. the ability to learn irregular forms) fade at different rates.

People who think that an infant's brain contains an innate grammar—or rather, an innate **UNIVERSAL GRAMMAR** that gives guidelines for the possible grammars of human languages—also think children use this universal grammar to guide them in discovering the patterns of their first language, which is why they learn that language so rapidly. If this claim about universal grammar is true, then because adolescents and adults rarely (if ever) learn a second language as rapidly or as completely as monolingual or bilingual native speakers, they must not be getting as much help from the universal grammar as infants do. So a possible reason that learning L1 and L2 are different could be that older learners have less access to this universal grammar. People who think this is true generally assume that what interferes with access to universal grammar is some kind of change in the brain (the brain certainly does change during maturation!), and that this change brings the critical (or sensitive) period to a close.

There are debates within this school of thought about whether L2 learners are getting any help at all from universal grammar and, if so, what kind and how much and for how long. However, modern researchers who take the universal grammar approach understand that second-language learners have processing difficulties in their second language, and they do take these processing difficulties into account in their research and theory making. (If you are wondering who the researchers are that take these different positions, check a few standard textbooks and journals on language learning. Also note that a number of researchers have changed their minds or modified their statements over the years as more evidence has become available.)

The people who think that language development depends on a powerful learning mechanism instead of a universal grammar of course have to give more complex answers to the question, "Why are learning L1 and L2 different?" Part of their answer may be in terms of primary changes in the brain as we mature, but they don't think that the critical period hypothesis is really an explanation of anything, and some of them have argued that there is no such thing as a critical period for language development.

So what explanation do these learning-mechanism people give for the question of why learning L1 and L2 differ? It has two main components. The first one is physiological-psychological: Learning L1 has actually changed your brain substantially, strengthening some connections greatly while weakening others or disrupting them entirely. (Learning anything changes your brain to some extent, of course—we talked about that in Chapter 2.) Those changes are a major part of what makes it harder to learn L2.

The second component of their answer is social-psychological: Learning L2 is different because older children and adults have different emotions, motivations, and opportunities to learn than infants and young children.

The ideas in this second component are certainly true: Sitting in a classroom, even in an intensive course, is not like being surrounded by a language 24/7. Also, if older children or adults are almost completely surrounded by a second language, their relationships and interactions with the speakers of that language are very different from the relationships and interactions that infants have with their caregivers. But it's not clear whether these social-psychological factors are strong enough to explain the difference between learning your first language and your second one.

Which of these issues can psycholinguistics help us to understand, and how? Unfortunately, we can't say much about the universal grammar idea, because psycholinguistics is about language processing, and the universal grammar hypothesis doesn't make clear predictions about processing. But both schools of thought need to use the idea that L1 changes how you process language to some extent. So let's consider how learning your first language might change your brain and how that, in turn, would affect learning your second language. In section 9.3 and in the Exercise section for this chapter, we'll think about the social-psychological component: how being, say, 5 years old or 12 years old or an adult affects the kind of language you get to hear and the kind you are expected to produce.

9.1 How Does Learning Your First Language Change Your Brain?

Let's recap the relevant material from Chapter 7 about what children learn during their first few years of listening and speaking, and add a bit to it, bringing up to age five; then we can think about what effects that skill and knowledge might have on learning a new language.

9.1.1 Phonetics and phonology in the first five years

Phonetics and allophones

In Chapter 7, section 7.4.2, we learned a startling pair of facts that are essential for understanding why the development of one or more first languages is different from learning a later language. First, children are born with the ability to distinguish all the pairs of sounds that languages use to keep two words apart—that is, all the possible contrasting phonemes (or at least all of the pairs of phonemes that have been tested, and that's quite a large number of similar pairs of sounds from many languages). Second, as they start to learn that words have meanings, they also come close to losing the ability to make speech sound distinctions that *don't* matter in the language(s) they are interacting in. We've already used the example of one of the Japanese phonemes that's very hard for English speakers to make and hear correctly. This sound is spelled /r/ in the Roman alphabet, but it's actually in between English /r/, /l/, and flapped /d/ or /t/. English listeners sometimes hear it as one of these three, sometimes as another. (You can hear it on your CD.) How is it possible that this is "one Japanese speech sound" if English speakers hear it as three different speech sounds?

Well, in Japanese, there's no meaning contrast between the [r]-like and the [l]-like versions of this phoneme—in other words, those sounds are **ALLOPHONES** (Chapter 1, section 1.2.5.1). That's because there are no **MINIMAL PAIRS** of words comparable to *road* and *load*, or *collect* and *correct*, or the hundreds of other English word pairs where the only difference in sound between two words with entirely different meanings is that one has an /l/ where the other one has an /r/. In English, we have to attend to that small difference in sounds to understand and be understood, but in Japanese, what a speaker has to learn is not to be distracted by that same difference in sound.

As a result, when adult or teen-aged native speakers of Japanese start to learn English (or any other language that has a phonemic contrast between /r/ and /l/), they have a great deal of trouble hearing the difference between all those minimal pairs of /r/-words and /l/-words, although if they have the time for putting in long, hard hours of practice, they can learn to control their mouths to produce them distinctly. (Recent experiments report success with training Japanese learners on hyperdistinctly pronounced /r/ and /l/ pairs of words like *light* and *right* first, and then moving them toward learning to choose between more normally produced pairs of L-words and R-words.)

In the first few years of speaking and hearing a language, then, children learn what aspects of a speech sound to pay attention to, and which ones to ignore. They have hundreds of thousands of opportunities to hone this unconscious knowledge, and it becomes deeply **ENTRENCHED**—that is, their brains have formed strong connections that spread activation from hearing these speech sounds to memories of all the words that contain those sounds.

Phonotactics

Over the first five years of life, children also learn a lot about phonotactics (Chapter 1, section 1.2.1)—that is, what sequences of sounds in their language are common in various positions in words (like /ta/ at the beginning of hundreds of words in English), which ones are rare (like English /ʃl/, as in *Schlitz*), and which ones are impossible in English at word beginnings (like /zl/, as in the unit of Polish money, the *zloty*). They learn to produce most of the common ones and some of the rarer ones. As adults, if we hear one of the "impossible" sound sequences, for example the /zg/ in a Czech name like Zgusta, it slows down our processing, and we'll probably mishear it as /sk/ or /zəg/ because it will activate the familiar sound sequences that are a bit like it. Only determined effort will allow us to say it more or less properly.

Intonation

Another aspect of phonology (one that this book can't spend enough time on) is **INTONATION CONTOUR**: the pattern of the rise and fall of people's voices as they speak. We can hear those patterns before birth, and we learn them by the time we are born; the evidence for this is that near-newborns prefer familiar ambient language pitch patterns to the pitch patterns of other languages. Our ability to use intonation like other speakers of our L1 seems to be deeply ingrained below the level of conscious control, because it is one of the things that is hardest for L2 speakers to master. Most of us never quite manage it unless we started to learn the second language while we were very young.

9.1.2 Morphology and syntax

In Chapter 7, section 7.2, we looked at morphology and syntax for English toddlers. By age three, typically developing children of all languages seem to have broken up the common phrases of their language into words. If their language has verb or noun endings, they've learned the basic ways that their language uses them to show things like who is the Agent or Undergoer in a sentence, whether the event was in the past or will happen in the future, and whether it's over or still happening. They know how to use prepositions (or equivalent function words) and pronouns, although they still make some mistakes.

This amount of knowledge includes some surprising information, because languages differ more than you might think. For example, although English toddlers have acquired the differences between the ways we use *in*, *on*, and *at* (*in a bowl, on a plate; at the store, in the store*), Korean children are learning to use two different words for what we would translate as *in*, depending on whether the fit is snug (*in his fist*) or loose (*in the box*). Similarly, English 5-year-olds have mastered the use of singular and plural, but Japanese, Chinese, and Thai learners, by the time they are five, know something quite different: that you have to count cars differently from the way you count kittens (although the word for car or for kitten doesn't change when you mean more than one of them). In Japanese, if we translated it awkwardly back into English, *two cars, two kittens* would be *car-two-machine, kitten-two-(small) creature*. Another example of how children learning different languages have different facts to learn: English 5-year-olds know when to say *a muffin,* **some** *muffin,* **the** *muffin,* **some** *muffins,* or **the** *muffins,* but Russian doesn't have any articles, so young Russians don't distinguish between *a muffin* and *the muffin.* On the other hand, they know that when you are counting muffins, you must change the ending of the noun. Clumsily retranslating back into English, Russian counts like this: *one muffin* (singular ending), *two* **of** *muffin* (possessive singular ending), *three* **of** *muffin, four* **of** *muffin, five* **of** *muffins* (possessive plural ending), *six* **of** *muffins, seven* **of** *muffins . . . twenty* **of** *muffins, twenty-one muffin, twenty-two* **of** *muffin . . . twenty-five* **of** *muffins . . .*

Five-year-olds can make the commoner kinds of constructions with transitive clauses (*I hit him, I saw him, I like him*). By the way, in some languages, the clauses that express these meanings don't look as much alike as they do in English—for example, if we translated the Greek equivalent of *I like him* back into English, it would come out roughly as *He pleases me.* Five-year-olds have mastered that form, too. They can also make intransitive clauses (*She's sleeping*), and if their language uses passive verbs a fair amount, they can make at least the common passive forms (*I got hit*).

The morphology that 5-year-old English speakers are still working on are many of the irregular forms of nouns and verbs (*oxen, wrung*), and the beginnings of how derivational endings make new words *(duck, duckling; choose, choosy; free, freedom)*; and in other languages, they are working on the corresponding items, if their language has them. However, if their language has a common DIMINUTIVE ending like English *-ie* (*doggie*), Spanish *-ito* (*perrito*) and so on, for small or cherished creatures, they're likely to know how to use that one already. The syntax they are still learning to understand and use seems to be the kinds of constructions that are used mostly in formal speech and in writing—for example, in English, sentences starting with SUBORDINATE CLAUSES (*Because you used up all the hot water, I couldn't take a shower!*).

9.1.3 Vocabulary, formulas, and probable sequences of words

Five-year-olds are expanding their vocabulary rapidly, especially if their parents read to them or if they have a rich preschool environment. This expansion comes partly from learning how new words are made in their language, as we've just seen, but also from learning more about the world and what is in it. They are also learning all sorts of useful formulas, like {*I'm sorry that I* <verb + Past> *your* <noun phrase>, name} (*I'm sorry that I stepped on your tulips, Mr. Woodstein*), or ways to start and end stories (*happily ever after*). Over their school years, they will continue to learn what sequences of words are more likely than others, and their ability to unconsciously predict what words are likely to come next will increase steadily—that is, activation will spread more efficiently from each familiar word to the ones that are likely to follow it. This knowledge—this change in their brains—will reduce the work that they have to do in understanding and producing sentences, because it will, on average, help to increase the activation that goes to the words that they are about to need to recognize or use. That will shorten the "brain fights," unless, of course, some unexpected word is actually what is coming next.

9.1.4 Pragmatics: Viewpoint, politeness, narrative information

Learning what to say goes along with learning when to say it, though we tend to notice this only when children make mistakes. (The Internet is full of jokes about children speaking too much too frankly; some of those probably started from true stories, although we'll never know which ones.) Children learn not only the expressions used in telling stories and in being polite, but also when to use them. They also (slowly!) learn to think about what the person they are talking to already knows or doesn't know. (Kids' narratives of playground incidents are notorious for using sentences like *He pushed him so she picked him up* without realizing that the person they are talking to doesn't know who on earth they are talking about. We didn't get into first language pragmatics problems in Chapter 7, but it's another very important topic, as you can imagine from our brief introduction to it in Chapter 1, section 1.8.)

When you learn a second language, you have many layers of pragmatics to master—for example, when it's okay for you to speak, when it's appropriate to use nicknames and informal pronouns, which words and expressions are polite and which ones are gross for you to be saying in a particular social setting, and whether it's friendly or invasive to ask a new acquaintance how old they are, whether their parents are alive, or whether they have children. Fortunately, outsiders are usually forgiven for not knowing what to say when, but the more nativelike you become in your speech, the less slack they'll give you for your bad manners.

9.1.5 "Thinking for speaking"

A famous study led by Ruth Berman and Dan Slobin (Berman et al. 1994) compared children and adults narrating a little story from a book of pictures without words, Mercer Mayer's *Frog, Where Are You?* Their international team compared the stories across many languages, and one of the things that they noticed is that speakers of the different languages gave slightly different information. In languages where words have the same form for singular or plural, nobody bothered to say explicitly that there was just one boy, one dog, and (for most of the story) one frog. In languages without definite articles, nobody used a form that made it explicit that the boy in the first picture is the same boy throughout the story. English speakers sometimes call the dog or the frog *it*, so they don't have to decide on whether the animals are male or female, but in French, a narrator has to decide this and let you know, because they must choose between the pronouns *il* (masculine) and *elle* (feminine). In Japanese or Chinese, as there's no gender difference in pronouns, the storytellers also don't have to say whether the animals in the story are male or female, and they don't.

But why not? After wondering about a host of such small details, Berman and Slobin realized that each language essentially trains its speakers to pick up on the particular kinds of information that they must put into choosing the words and the word forms. Speakers could of course put in unnecessary information, but ordinary storytellers rarely do. So: as we learn our language, we learn to subconsciously make the dozens of small decisions that its grammar requires about the characters and events in our stories. We learn to pay attention to the things our language encodes as we choose particular words or constructions, and to ignore many others that a different language might require, unless they play a special role in our story. Berman and Slobin call making these unconscious little decisions "thinking for speaking."

9.2 What Happens When a New Data Set Meets an Experienced Brain?

We've already begun to hint at the answer to this question in our sketch of what a speaker has learned by the age of five (not to mention the ages of 10, 15, or 20). By the age of five, and even more as we get older, *we have learned what to expect* when we listen to our native language(s), and *what to prepare to say* when we talk. This is because activation spreads strongly to sounds, words, and constructions that we have often heard in sequence and in the situation. It's the same reason that Jenny expects to blow out candles on another toddler's birthday cake. Unexpected sounds, words, and constructions, if we actually hear them or need to produce them, have to fight their way past the expected ones that already have begun to be aroused. So they take longer to understand or to say, and are more likely to be misunderstood or mispronounced because of strong interference from their competition.

In addition, our skill at thinking for speaking our first language means we notice (or invent!) the kinds of details about the world that our grammar forces us to encode (how many? what gender? tight fit or loose fit? flat support or concave support?). But our second language will have a somewhat different set of demands, which we'll have to learn to satisfy if we want to sound like competent speakers and to understand conversation at normal speeds.

9.2.1 Transfer

The greater our skills as speakers of our first language(s), the larger the set of expectations that we bring from those first languages to each later language. And we can't just turn those expectations off, because activation spreads automatically, whether we want it to or not. Learning a new language means forming a new huge set of expectations that are strong enough to compete with the earlier ones. This can be done only by building up new connections between subconsciously remembered events in our brains. Conscious learning can help us practice and monitor for errors, but *only repeated experience can set up the automatic spreading activation* that is necessary if we're going to be efficient processors of a new language. And the older we are when we learn our second language, the stronger the new links have to be to compete successfully with the old ones; in other words, the older we are when we learn our L2, the more practice we'll need to get good at using speaking and understanding it.

In studies of L2 acquisition, the result of the entrenched expectations that we automatically carry from our first language into our L2 is called TRANSFER. A lot of this transfer is useful; it means that we don't have to learn the new language from scratch. Some of the sounds, constructions, and usage patterns will be almost the same as what we already know, and more will be close enough to help us start to communicate, even if imperfectly. Some second-language acquisition textbooks treat the effects of transfer on learning second-language morphology and syntax as unimportant, but recent reviews of research tell a different story: For example, English articles are learned earlier by learners whose L1 is Spanish (which has them) than by learners whose L1 is Chinese (which doesn't).

As we become more advanced learners, however, the sounds and grammatical patterns that are close but not quite right may cause trouble. For example, definite articles are used slightly differently in Spanish than they are in English; getting them *mostly* right isn't hard, but getting them *all* right all of the time is. Or take a phonetic example: Making a Spanish /t/ is delicately different from making any of the several sounds that can express the English phoneme /t/. (In this book, we've only talked about the flap, but there are others; I've put some information about them in the Challenge section for this chapter.) It may be easier to master an entirely new sound, like the German or Russian voiceless velar fricative (**IPA** [x]), which doesn't exist in English, than to modify a familiar L1 sound toward a slightly different L2 version. After all, it's often easier to learn an entirely new skill (like using chopsticks) than it is to modify a familiar habit (if you were brought up to switch your fork to your right hand after it's been in your left hand for cutting meat at the table, it can be hard to learn to keep it in your left hand).

The biggest problems will be in learning to hear and make new distinctions. If you are an English speaker, it's hard to master the differences between Japanese long and short vowels (which really do differ in length) or Spanish single *r* and double *rr*. If the information can be memorized (like whether the vowel or the *r* in a particular word is long), or if there is a pattern that follows clear regular rules (like putting the third person singular /s/ ending on English present-tense verbs), diligent work will produce good results. But for patterns that defy explicit statement, like exactly where to use definite articles in each language that has them, it's rare for a late learner to reach near-native abilities. It probably requires a combination of dedication, immersion in the language, emotional identification with the new culture, and sheer talent. Probing studies of even the most splendid late learners—those who pass completely as native speakers in their adopted community—suggest that they still are slightly slower than fully native speakers in processing the late-learned language, and that they differ slightly in their judgments of what is and isn't grammatical, although no one outside the psycholinguistics laboratory would ever guess it from interacting with them.

9.2.2 Buried memories: The long-term effects of infants' language learning

Two dramatic demonstrations of how infant learning has long-term effects on the brain come from psycholinguistic studies of some **HERITAGE LANGUAGE LEARNERS**—native or nativelike speakers of English who were enrolled in university Spanish and Korean language classes and who came from those language backgrounds. The people who were studied had heard those languages when they were very young (five years old or less) but had rarely used the language since then, so they needed to study it in school in order to speak it. A research team at UCLA, Prof. Terry Kit-fong Au, Leah Knightly, Sun-Ah Jun, and Janet S. Oh, sorted these students not just by their own statements of how much they had heard or used their heritage language as young children, but also by how well they knew the usual informal household words for terms like *spanking, cry-baby, spoiled child, pacifier* —words that are used almost exclusively with or about young children.

Let's look at the Spanish study first. The participants were enrolled in second-year university Spanish classes. One group was made up of 11 students who had overheard Spanish (but had spoken it very little) for several hours per week for at least three years between birth and age six, and who had then heard it much less until they began taking Spanish at about age 14. These students were called the "Overhearers." The other group of students were twelve "Typical L2 Learners": no Spanish was spoken in their homes, and until they started taking Spanish in school (also at about age 14), they had had only the casual restaurant-and-bilingual-sign exposure to Spanish that is part of the general Southern California language environment. Ten native bilingual speakers of California Spanish who were students at the same university also participated as a comparison group.

The research team asked other native speakers of Spanish to judge the quality of all of these participants' pronunciation of Spanish on a scale from 1 (very strong foreign accent) to 5 (no foreign accent). They also recorded how the students pronounced words containing the consonant sounds /p,t,k,b,d,g/, which are rather different in Spanish and English, and measured some key details of the sound waves. (What they measured is explained in the Challenge section of this chapter, on your CD, in case you are interested and would like to try a similar study yourself, or would like to check on the accuracy of your own pronunciation of these Spanish sounds.) The research team also looked at how good their participants were at producing Spanish gender and number agreement, and at how quickly they could recognize agreement errors. (Spanish has four forms for most adjectives: masculine singular, feminine singular, masculine plural, and feminine plural: for example, *blanco, blanca, blancos, blancas* "white." Feminine adjective forms must be used with feminine nouns and masculine adjective forms with masculine nouns, singular adjectives with singular nouns and plural adjectives with plural nouns: *la vaca blanca*, the white cow; *los pianos negros*, the black pianos; etc.).

The results? On measurements of the sound waves of their consonants, the Overhearers were indistinguishable from the native Spanish speakers, and their accents overall were rated much better than those of the Typical L2 Learners (although not quite as good as the native speakers). So the Overhearers' home-based early exposure to Spanish had left them in possession of phonetic details that the Typical L2 Learners had not mastered in spite of several semesters of high school and college Spanish. (By the way, the Overhearers' English consonants matched those of the Typical L2 Learners, and so did the consonants of the native English-Spanish bilingual speakers. Learning a second language after infancy but before about age five, if you're interacting with native speakers of the L2 enough, produces just as good results as learning the L2 phonology from birth, as far as we can tell.)

Basic Spanish morphology, on the other hand, hadn't been picked up from listening. The Overhearers, who reported having spoken only a few words and phrases of Spanish as young children, were no better than the Typical L2 Learners in either how accurately they produced phrases requiring gender and number agreement or how fast they detected gender and number errors in recordings. And both the Overhearers and the Typical L2 Learners took twice as long as the native bilingual speakers to detect spoken morphological errors. So, early home exposure to a language does not affect all areas of language development equally. If you've heard the language but not really spoken it, you'll retain some important phonetic details, but not the morphology.

Next, the UCLA research team looked at several groups of students who were about four months into a college course in Korean. They were able to find two groups of heritage Korean L2 learners who had early exposure to the language: some students who had heard but not spoken Korean as young children ("Childhood Hearers") and some who had both heard and spoken it as their main language until about age five ("Childhood Speakers"). Both of these Korean groups, like the Spanish Overhearers, heard their first language very little after starting school in the United States. The researchers compared these two groups' ability to pronounce some of the sounds of Korean that are very difficult for English speakers to master (Korean alveolar stop consonants, which are hard because although English has only two kinds of stops, voiced and voiceless, at each place of articulation, Korean has *three*; one is similar to English word-initial voiceless stops, but the other two, called "plain" and "tense," are both slightly different from English voiced stops.)

The team also compared these two groups of Korean-language-background L2 students to Typical L2 Learners in the same classes (that is, students of Korean who had never been exposed to the language outside of the classroom), and also to other adults who were native speakers of Korean and were now studying in the United States. This time, the research team didn't look at morphology, but they did something new: They looked at the participants' perceptual abilities, asking all four groups of students to try to distinguish among words contrasting the three Korean alveolar stops. (So these were minimal triplets instead of minimal pairs. The details of the study are in the Challenge section for this chapter.) The results were neat: The Childhood Speakers—the students who had both heard and spoken their heritage language as children—were better than the Childhood Hearers or the Typical L2 Learners at producing those difficult Korean sounds. And both the Childhood Speakers and the Childhood Hearers were better than the Typical L2 Learners at distinguishing between them. In summary, unused or little-used phonetic skills in both production and perception, if they are established in infancy and maintained until age five, can be retained and re-activated in adulthood—at least for second-generation heritage learners like these, who would have continued to hear Korean-accented English from one or both of their parents and probably other family members.

In stark contrast, a brain-activity-imaging study showed that Korean-born adults who had been adopted by French families before they were three years old and who never heard Korean again couldn't recognize it at all, not even subconsciously. But perhaps if they had been studying Korean for a while as adults, some of its phonetics would have been re-activated. Or perhaps it's hearing accented speech while growing up that's essential to holding onto the phonetics of a language you heard as an infant. There is room for more research on this topic. And we do know, from this study and many others, that older children—and even adults—gradually lose their first language skills if they don't keep using them. It's exciting to know that some traces of a speaker's first language can remain for years, as the UCLA team showed, but having only traces of your L1 left is a pretty poor showing, considering that you could have become a fluent bilingual if you'd had even a few hours every week of conversation in your first language.

9.2.3 Transfer in learning L2 morphology and vocabulary

Transfer from L1 to L2 happens at all levels of linguistic (and cultural) knowledge, and just as in phonology, it can be helpful or it can complicate matters. When we talked about language typology in Chapter 1, section 1.10, we discussed a number of ways that languages can be different or similar, and we also talked about language relationships. If two languages are moderately closely related, like Russian and Polish or like Swedish and German, they'll still share a lot of their vocabulary, and that can be very helpful to

L2 learners. In an L2 English class with mixed L1 backgrounds, some of your students, for example, speakers of Dutch or Swedish, may be getting a major vocabulary boost from shared vocabulary, but others—say, Arabic, learners of English—are getting no help at all.

After the Norman Conquest, English borrowed a huge amount of vocabulary from French—so much so that we also effectively borrowed the Romance language patterns of word formation, including suffixes like -*age* and -*able*. And, like other languages of Europe, we took so many families of derived words from written Latin and Greek that we also incorporated dozens their prefixes and suffixes into our morphology, like Greek *auto-*, *pseudo-*, -*ize*, and Latin -*tion*, -*ify*, -*al*, and so on, as we mentioned in Chapter 1, section 1.4.4, and in Chapter 8 as well. These give a big automatic boost to English speakers who are learning Romance languages, and vice versa. (If you skipped Chapter 8, note that's important to teach those prefixes and suffixes to speakers of Chinese, Japanese, and other languages that work rather differently from the major languages of Western Europe. If you show them explicitly how these derivational morphemes give us related sets of words like *derive, derivation, derivative, derivational*, it cuts down on the amount of sheer memorizing that they'll have to do in acquiring English vocabulary.)

9.3 What Else Is Different About the Older Learner?

9.3.1 Identity

Remember the set of four motivations that we used to understand very young children—the drives for excitement, control, belonging, and comfort? Learning to talk gives you more fine-grained control over what happens to you (not just *No*, but *No, I want butter on it*), and sounding like the people around you brings you a sense of belonging and comfort (as do many other ways of matching their behavior); partly that's because you perceive that you are fitting in, and partly it's because you can see that they are accepting what you're doing and treating you as one of their group.

Older learners have a lot of experience in being successful at satisfying these needs (and more sophisticated ones as well) in their first language, so being a beginner again is a major setback. You are an outsider: you don't belong, you don't understand what's going on, you have lost power. It's humiliating. And to become like the people in the new environment, you have to let go of some of what has brought you successes in the past.

Depending on the social situation, you may have to let go of a lot of your identity. Some people are willing and able to do this, which usually gives them better results as L2 learners; others are not. If you haven't gone through this experience yourself, try to find someone who has, and who is willing to talk about it with you—it's an eye-opener.

9.3.2 How other people speak

When you are an older child, teen, or adult, what people expect of you is obviously very different from what they expect of a baby or a toddler, and the way they talk to you and listen to you is different, too. You now have responsibilities and tasks to carry out; people expect you to deal with lots of information, and it's not their job to take care of you day and night. Words come at you fast, and you feel always behind; your uptake is too slow, and may be fragmentary. Your own less-than-perfect efforts will warn them to slow down and to use simple syntax, but learning to talk effectively to foreigners is a skill, and most people that you run into don't have much practice at it.

From what you know now about how language processing works, you see why information in a new language is so much harder to understand than the same amount of information in a language that you know well: It's because your TOP-DOWN processing of the language is so limited, putting a huge burden on your BOTTOM-UP processing, and taking resources away from actually understanding the content of what you are hearing.

9.3.3. Literacy

Immigrant learners who are middle-school age or older are usually expected to manage to read and write in the second language at the same time that they learn to speak it (unless they are past school age and their jobs require no literacy), and the same is usually true for people who are learning a second language in a classroom. (In some teaching traditions, students only read and translate; they almost never get to practice speaking, or even listening to recordings of a native speaker.) Writing and seeing words can be a big help to learning vocabulary, morphology, and syntax—it gives additional ways to practice and to make memory connections between related items. However, it may not be much help for pronunciation. We'll say more about problems of learning to read your L2 in section 9.6.

9.3.4. Cognitive abilities

Older learners have some real advantages. Their greater experience of the world means that they can learn words faster, because they have more concepts to hook them up to. Their memory for idioms and phrases is better, so they can master longer formulas and formulaic expressions. They are also better at understanding explanations, and at SELF-MONITORING— deliberately watching their own performance. So adults and older children often learn the vocabulary and syntax of a new language faster than younger children at the beginning. But if the younger speakers stay in the new language environment, they will eventually catch up and surpass their elders, and their accent will become good even faster.

9.4 What First-Language Learners and Second-Language Learners Have in Common

In spite of all these differences, we shouldn't overlook the important similarities in first- and second-language learning. First, both kinds of learners make errors of OVERGENERALIZATION: For example, they tend to make irregular forms regular (*I sing, I singed*). After all, generalizing (and overgeneralizing) are things that we do in all kinds of learning, not just in language learning.

Second-language learners may overgeneralize more than L1 learners, however, if a pattern in their first language has made it hard for them to pick up the way an L2 rule works. Remember that Chinese has the identical form for a verb regardless of whether it is used with a first, second, or third person subject? Beginning Chinese learners of English, encountering the third person singular *-s* on our verbs, may take a while to get a sense of when to add that *-s* and when not to. Where it goes must seem quite arbitrary at first, just like an irregularity. So some of them, having learned to say *She goes*, also say *I goes* for a while.

Second, L1 and L2 learners both make ERRORS OF OMISSION—they leave out many words and grammatical morphemes that they haven't yet figured out how to deploy, or that seem to add a processing burden without adding much meaning, like subject pronouns and the third person singular *-s* verb ending. Again, this isn't necessarily a language-learning thing —you'd expect beginners learning any complicated process to leave out some of the steps.

And third, both kinds of learners tend to rely on long, memorized units before they have figured out how to analyze them and reuse their parts, so their language is full of FORMULAS and prefabricated sequences. Second-language learners apparently stick with this strategy longer than first-language learners, though, because even skilled late learners show less variety in their language use than native speakers do.

9.5 Language Processing in Bilingual Speakers

9.5.1 L2 processing by L2 learners

L2 learners, like L1 learners, unconsciously start to learn the patterns of their new language long before they can correctly answer explicit questions about those patterns. Remember the studies in Chapter 7, section 7.3, showing that toddlers who were only producing one word at a time were beginning to understand the word order of sentences? As we saw, when these children were hearing a sentence like *Big Bird is tickling Cookie Monster* and had a choice of looking at a video that matched this sentence and one that showed Cookie tickling Big Bird, they preferred to look at the matching video, although they did sometimes look at the mismatch video. But at that age, they can't answer questions about what a sentence means, even by pointing to pictures.

Here's a somewhat similar experimental result for beginning L2 learners of Spanish. When they were asked to judge whether Spanish sentences were grammatical or not, these learners seemed to be just guessing—they were correct only about 50% of the time. But when they just listened to those sentences while their brainwaves were being monitored, they showed "surprise" brain wave patterns more often when they heard the ungrammatical sentences than when they heard the grammatical ones. So their brains had begun to form expectations of the ways words go together in Spanish, even though this knowledge was still quite wobbly and not really usable.

Here's the flip side of that experiment, done with advanced L2 learners as well as with beginning and intermediate students. An eye-tracking study compared native speakers of Spanish with advanced L2 learners who had thoroughly mastered the gender agreement rules for Spanish adjectives, and with less skilled L2 learners as well. Both the native speakers and the advanced learners reacted to gender-agreement errors like *una casa pequeño* (*a house*-feminine *small*-masculine) by looking back at the feminine noun after reading the masculine adjective form, but only the native speakers reacted automatically to gender errors when there was a long distance between the noun and its adjective, as in the sentence *Una casa cuesta menos si es pequeño* . . . (*A house*-feminine *costs less if it is small*-masculine . . .). So learners who know the L2 grammar well still don't have the information as active and automatically available in their brains as L1 speakers of the same language. (The beginning and intermediate speakers hardly looked back at the noun at all.)

Experienced language teachers know that L2 learners rely on their knowledge of word meanings and tend to ignore the information in GRAM-MATICAL MORPHEMES like gender-agreement endings, which this study certainly confirms. But both these experiments show more than that: They both demonstrate the fact that language knowledge (of L1 or L2) is *not* "all or nothing." It is not a matter of either knowing a rule or not knowing it, of knowing a word or not knowing it. Instead, language knowledge grows slowly, from a vague and unconscious sense that there's something funny about an ungrammatical sentence or that a particular word or word order has a particular meaning to strong, fast, and reliable recognition of errors and use of L2 information. And even people who know a form or a rule well may not be able to use that knowledge for fast and effective information processing if they are processing a lot of other information at the same time.

9.5.2 Language processing by native bilinguals and near-native L2 speakers

Let's turn back to fluent bilingual and multilingual speakers and ask a basic question: How do they keep from mixing up their languages? Before we launch into this discussion, we need to make an important distinction. Speakers may *mix* their languages without being in the least *mixed up*. If you've studied Spanish and go into a restaurant that uses lots of words from that language on its menu, you know perfectly well whether you are using a Spanish word as if it were an English word or whether you are saying it the way you should in Spanish—whether you are saying [təˈmaliz] or [taˈmalɛs]. If your pronunciation is good enough, you also know whether you are using a Spanish /t/ or an English one when you order your [taˈmalɛs].

If your Spanish isn't very good, or the waitperson doesn't speak Spanish but you still want to sound like you respect the language, you might put the Spanish-pronunciation word in an English sentence, trilling your *r*s: *I'd like a* [taˈmal de ˈpwerko] *and a* [tʃile reˈjeno], *please*. That's mixing the languages; more formally, it's called CODE-SWITCHING or CODE-MIXING. In many of the communities around the world that are full of immigrants and their descendents who were born and educated in the new country, code-mixing is the normal way to talk, and it's not random—it's under control. Here's an example from a Belgian collection of bilingual French-Dutch conversations (Belgium being a French-Dutch bilingual country):

Les étrangers, ze hebben geen geld, hé?

The foreigners, they have no money, huh?

Bilingual speakers don't mix the languages when they are talking to people who only understand one of them. (Unless there is no word or expression for a needed concept, or they deliberately want to remind you that you are an outsider. If they don't know whether you understand both languages, they might also drop in a few words of the other one just to check you out.)

So, when bilingual people talk, how do they control which language a word comes out in? They don't just turn one of them off, because experiments show that both languages of a skilled bilingual speaker are activated at the same time. For example, experimental studies of English-Spanish skilled bilingual speakers suggest that seeing a picture of a table activates the word forms for the concept "table" in both English and Spanish. And for less skilled speakers of the second language, the picture probably activates the L2 word less strongly than it activates the L1 word. So if there's no "brain switch" that will turn off the first language, how can learners manage to speak their second language at all?

We already have some good hints about what's happening, because we've seen many examples of how speakers unconsciously form expectations about what is going to happen next. Remember that our brains keep track of the past by making connections between things that happen in sequence, strengthening those connections each time the sequence recurs, and weakening them (and building up rival connections) when something else happens instead. When we listen to a language (unless we grew up in a code-mixing community), one of the things we learn is that the other person is going to keep on using that language. So we expect that words in our new language are going to be followed by other words in that language. Since the way that expectation works in our minds is by spreading activation, this means that each word in L2 sends some activation to all of the others. (Yes, the brain is a very busy place!) And that activation gets added to the activation of the L2 word for whatever concept we're trying to talk about. But this may be just part of the story; it is likely that keeping to one language when you know several of them also requires you to inhibit the languages that you are not using at the moment.

It's not just the words that have to be controlled, it's the constructions, too: for example, adjectives go before nouns in some languages and after them in others, and in both places in still others; objects go before verbs in some languages, after them in others, and can be omitted in still others, as we saw in Chapter 1, section 1.10.1.

The story about how switching between languages is controlled needs to be somewhat different for people who grow up in a code-mixing bilingual community, because they do expect that words from both of their languages will be used in the same sentence some of the time. How do they learn not to mix their languages when they talk to a monolingual person? Their brains must be keeping track of which language is which, but we don't know exactly how that happens. We have some hints, though: Bilingual children seem to have, on average, better EXECUTIVE FUNCTION — better ability to keep track of what they are doing while they are doing it (see Chapter 10, section 10.2.5)—than monolingual children of the same age. So living a bilingual life probably exercises and depends on our executive functioning.

9.6 Accent Reduction: Psycholinguistics Meets the Sociolinguistics of Identity, Politics, and Prejudice

In our multilingual and multidialectal world, psycholinguistics can help us in understanding how people use language to communicate, but it doesn't deal with the question of what a learner's goals ought to be. A controversial area that involves many groups of language professionals—particularly language teachers, speech-language pathologists, and scientists trying to make computers that can respond to spoken instructions—is the problem of variations in how a language is pronounced. Every language professional should understand both the psycholinguistics of this problem and something entirely different: the SOCIOLINGUISTIC aspect (see Chapter 1, section 1.9.3).

The psycholinguistic part is the easy part: It's definitely easier to understand someone when they speak with a familiar accent—in other words, when they use the same phonetics that you do. The speech sounds they make will activate the words in your mind faster, you will process the syntax faster, and you'll have more mind power left over to deal with the message that they are giving you, whether it's how to troubleshoot your computer, land your airplane, or arrange for a payment. So people who want jobs that involve communication—and that's a lot of the jobs in a service economy—may decide to invest time and money in accent reduction: that is, in learning to speak like a large group of potential clients. They learn to sound more like white Americans from California, or like old-university-educated British. That's all very well from the point of view of people who already speak General American or British Received Pronunciation, but they are not the majority of English speakers on this planet, nor even the majority of native English speakers. Why should everyone else learn to speak one of those two ways? Why shouldn't we all learn to listen to and understand many different kinds of English? It's just a matter of practice.

Maybe we can work toward the goal of making exposure to a wide variety of English a part of everyone's education. (Movies from Australia and India have helped many of us learn to understand more varieties of English.) But in the meantime, economics and politics call the shots: Immigrants, foreigners, and speakers of less "standard" dialects are expected to lose most of their accent if they want to be successful, or even if they just want to be understood by the automatic speech recognition system at the other end of the telephone connection.

The same kind of thing holds for other languages with vast numbers of speakers from different areas and often with different first languages—Mandarin, Spanish, French, Hindi, and so on. In all these cases, people who speak a near-standard version of the language could be educated so that they could understand its other varieties more easily—it's not that hard to learn. But while we're working to make that happen, at least where it's politically possible, millions of speakers who didn't grow up with the standard variety will be trying to reduce their accents so that they can be part of the economic and social mainstream.

Changing your dialect or accent has penalties as well as rewards. As we mentioned in section 9.3.1, if you move to a new part of the country or a new social group, find that you speak with a different accent from the people around you, and try to change your speech so that you fit in better, you may feel like you're abandoning the people you really care about and the values you were brought up with. The PBS video *American Tongues* has some startling interviews about people's attitudes towards dialects and dialect change, including an interview with an African American speech-language pathologist who tries to manage a delicate balancing act: teaching clients to sound less African American for the sake of getting better jobs without making them feel that sounding African American is something to be ashamed of.

9.7 Psycholinguistics and Learning to Read and Write in a Second Language

By now you expect that what people have learned about reading in their first language affects how they start to read in their second language (and of course, other languages after that). In this section, we look at a few specifics about how first-language reading sets up top-down processing patterns that affect L2 reading. Have a quick look at Chapter 8 now if you haven't read it yet, and then you'll be ready for this final section of Chapter 9. You'll especially need section 8.7.2 on Chinese and other East Asian writing systems if you want to follow what I'm about to say on the difficulties of going from alphabetical to character-based writing systems and vice versa.

Assuming that you (or your students) are learning a second language in order to be able to speak and understand it, learning to make the new sounds is of course one of the major jobs—and there will always be some new sounds to learn. If you have started from an alphabetically written language and learn another one that uses the same alphabet, you will also have some new grapheme-phoneme correspondences to learn. Surprisingly, if you already are literate in a language that uses an alphabet, learning a language written in a different alphabet, like going from English to the Greek alphabet or to the Cyrillic alphabet (used for Russian and some other Slavic languages) is not hard. A few weeks of practice and you're writing the new letters instead of drawing them, reading them instead of puzzling them out. The Japanese kana syllabary is almost completely regular, and it's not hard to learn either. Making these new neural connections seems not to be difficult for people unless they already have L1 reading problems. In L2 teaching, the usual advice is to train listening, speaking, and spelling of sounds all at the same time, because they all need to be learned, and their interconnections will help each other.

Where the going gets difficult is if you move from an alphabetic or syllabic system to a logographic system like Chinese (and the Chinese-based kanji of Japanese or hanja of Korean), because so much memorization is involved. People who learn Chinese or Chinese-based characters when they are young do it by writing them over and over. They develop very impressive (and apparently direct) connections from each word in their mental lexicon to the sequence of hand movements needed to write its character or characters. (The order of strokes used to write each radical of a character and the order of writing the radicals is fixed—you can't start just anywhere in the character, any more than you can start writing a word from the middle.) Amazingly, to those of us who didn't grow up with this skill, they can also "read" that sequence of movements when someone else makes it. So, if you have two friends from China, one of them can trace a character in the air and the other can read it. Chinese people do that to clarify homonymous names, or spoken words that have two different meanings, just as English speakers may spell aloud for each other words and names that have commoner homonyms (/dʒonz/ J-O-N-Z-E, /tir/ T-I-E-R).

Spreading activation acquired from long practice is involved in all of these skills. A skilled reader of Chinese who is watching a friend writing a Chinese character in the air sees each stroke of each of its component radicals, one after another. Each stroke must be activating the radicals it belongs to, and those must in turn be spreading activation to the characters they belong to. So a skilled person "reading" a character made in the air doesn't have to remember all of the movements individually and try to imagine the pattern they would make on a page, any more than those of us who grow up hearing words spelled aloud have to visualize all of the letters at the same time in order to figure out what W-A-S-H-I-N-G-T-O-N spells. We find the syllables; Chinese readers find the radicals; and we both do it on the basis of what we already know about how words in our language are written.

Chinese learners of alphabetic languages—of English for sure, and probably other languages—have an unexpected problem, however. It turns out that they are not good at using phonetic information to help remember the order of letters. This is probably because the modest amount of phonetic information in Chinese characters has nothing to do with the order of sounds. As we said in Chapter 8, each Chinese character is one syllable, and it often contains a phonetic radical, but different characters might have their phonetic radical on the right side of the character, or the top, or the bottom (where it is has nothing to do with how the syllable sounds). So while native readers of Chinese have immense skill at remembering the order of the strokes and the radicals in a character, they aren't used to connecting that information to the order of sounds in a syllable, because it has no such connection in Chinese. Helping Chinese learners of English pay close attention to the order of letters in a written word needs extra work in an ESL classroom, and it might contribute to unusual spelling error patterns in a client with aphasia whose first language is Chinese.

Finally, you might remember that in Chapter 2, section 2.5.1 (where we first introduced the ideas of top-down and bottom-up processing) we talked about how people who are not native speakers of a language have more trouble compensating for missing information, because top-down processing of L2 is not as rapid and strong as it is in L1, and it's top-down processing that fills in the missing data. (The example we gave was L2 speakers' problems reading an L2 page with letters that are cut off by bad photocopying.) In Chapter 5, Section 5.1.2, I mentioned that it's harder to spot the F in the written word *of* than it is in other words, because the word *of* is so frequent and so predictable that we fill it in when we're reading on the basis of little (or no!) bottom-up information from the letters O and F. (The fact the F is pronounced /v/ instead of /f/ in this word might be adding to the problem—we can't hold onto the memory of its sound to keep our minds on finding the letter F, as we could if it always spelled the same sound.) Another word that plays the same trick is *the*; if you ask people to circle all the occurrences of the letter H in a paragraph, the ones in the word *the* are the most likely to be overlooked.

Some years ago, an experienced ESL and TESOL teacher named Maria Thomas-Ruzic was a student in my graduate psycholinguistics course. She decided to test the idea that people who were learning English as a second language had less automatic top-down processing happening during reading than native speakers do. My thoughtful student realized that if what I had been teaching about top-down processing was correct, then her English-learning adult students should do *better* at circling all the Hs in an English paragraph than native English speakers would—they wouldn't miss the ones in the word *the* nearly so often as the native speakers would, because they would be relying more heavily than native speakers on bottom-up information. So she created an experiment, and sure enough, her ESL students were more accurate than native speakers at spotting all the Hs. (Of course, it could just have been that they read English more slowly than the native speakers; to be sure of the explanation, she would have had to do a more elaborate experiment in which the English speakers were forced to slow down in their reading. Maybe you can design an experiment like that.)

9.8 Summary

In this chapter, we've taken what we know about how learning our first language (like learning any other skill) shapes the connections in our brains so that we can understand it and speak it efficiently. The effect of this entrenched knowledge of our L1 on how we process the sounds, grammar, and meanings of our second language is clear, whether or not you think that L2 processing is also affected by lack of access to an innate universal grammar of some kind. When we come to a second language, huge numbers of new connections need to be made in our brains, and the old connections will arouse sounds, words, and structures that may compete with the new ones—that's transfer. Although the old connections from L1 aren't too powerful before age five, they become stronger and harder to compete with as L2 learning starts later and later. It is especially difficult to start using kinds of information—phonetic, syntactic, or semantic— that our L2 needs but our L1 didn't, because our L1 trained our brains either to send that information to the wrong places for L2, or to treat it as background noise. Also, as we become literate, our first writing system affects the kinds of information about written symbols that we become skilled at noticing and using. Laboratory experiments show that late expert bilinguals—people who still use their first language but who are good enough to pass for native speakers of their second language—still process their L2 more slowly than real native speakers of that language.

Early language exposure, if it is interactive and not just exposure to TV, has a strong and lasting effect on how we sort sounds into phonemic categories. If a first language has not been used for a long time, for example after emigration, it may not be arousable, but speech sounds and sound distinctions that were heard in early childhood are likely to be relearnable with considerable accuracy. If you relearn a language you spoke as a young child, your pronunciation should be better than if you were learning it for the first time.

Many social factors also differ between child and adult language learners. Three important ones are: (1) how you are spoken to (as an adult, you will be expected to handle more complicated language than a child would), (2) how much you are willing to change the way your speech sounds (which is an important part of your identity), and (3) how good you are at memorizing (adults are better at it, which can give them a better start but won't lead to mastery in the long run). However, first- and second-language learning also have many things in common, because the same cognitive processes of pattern learning are involved in both cases.

People who speak with a foreign accent or with the accent of a "nonstandard" dialect of a language are often faced with the need to sound more like "standard" speakers; this can be difficult to do both because they have to master new sounds and because they may feel like they are betraying their family and their heritage. The need for this could probably be reduced by changes in social attitudes and by making learning to listen to many kinds of native and foreign accents part of our education, but neither of those things is likely to happen quickly.

Exercises for Chapter 9

9.1. Consider the situation of an L2 learner, in a setting and at a level of L2 ability that you are familiar with, and explain to someone with little experience the difference between language "input" to that learner and the learner's "intake."

9.2. If you can find a willing friend, explore how well you can recognize words spelled in the air and/or traced on the skin on the back of your hand.

9.3. How does being a preschool child, a middle-school child, a teen, or an adult affect the kind of language you hear and the kind you are expected to produce? Contrast two of these cases.

9.4. Why do we feel that people who are speaking a language we have just begun to learn are speaking much faster than people speaking our native language?

9.5. On the basis of what you have learned in this book as well as your own experience, create a poster or a web page of guidelines for use by employees in some commercial or government office on how to talk to foreigners; make sure it helps them to understand *why* they should talk in that way instead of just telling them what to do.

9.6. Give some real or realistic examples of generalization and overgeneralization in nonlanguage learning.

Reference

Berman, R., Slobin, D. I., Aksu-Koc, A. A., Bamberg, M., Dasinger, L., Marchman, V., . . . Sebastian, E. (1994). *Relating events in narrative: A cross linguistic developmental study.* Hillsdale, NJ: Erlbaum.

Suggested Readings and Sources Consulted

Abrahamsson, N., & Hyltenstam, K. (2009). Age of onset and nativelikeness in a second language: Listener perception versus linguistic scrutiny. *Language Learning, 59*(2), 249–306.

Au, T. K.-f., Knightly, L. M., Jun, S.-A., & Oh, J. S. (2002). Overhearing a language during childhood. *Psychological Science*, *13*(3), 238–243.

Beckner, C., Blythe, R., Bybee, J., Christiansen, M. H., Croft, W., Ellis, N. C., . . . Schoenemann, T. (2009). Language is a complex adaptive system: Position paper. *Language Learning*, *59*(Suppl. 1), 1–26.

Bialystok, E., & Craik, F. I. M. (2010). Cognitive and linguistic processing in the bilingual mind. *Current Directions in Psychological Science*, *19*, 19–23.

Birdsong, D. (2005). Interpreting age effects in second language acquisition. In J. Kroll & A. De Groot (Eds.), *Handbook of bilingualism: Psycholinguistic perspectives* (pp. 109–127). Cambridge, UK: Cambridge University Press.

Bresnan, J., & Ford. M. (2010). Predicting syntax: Processing dative constructions in American and Australian varieties of English. *Language*, *86*(1), 168–213.

British Medical Journal. (2008, September 10). Bilingual children more likely to stutter. *ScienceDaily*. Retrieved June 4, 2010, from http://www.sciencedaily.com/releases/2008/09/080908215938.htm

Chen, A. (2009). Perception of paralinguistic intonational meaning in a second language. *Language Learning*, *59*(2), 367–409.

Collins, L., & Ellis, N. C. (Eds.). (2009). Input and second language construction learning: frequency, form, and function [Special issue]. *Modern Language Journal*, *93*(2), 329–335.

Ellis, N. C. (2006). Selective attention and transfer phenomena in L2 acquisition: Contingency, cue competition, salience, interference, overshadowing, blocking, and perceptual learning. *Applied Linguistics*, *27*(2), 164–194.

Ellis, N. C., & Cadierno, T. (Eds). (2009). Constructing a second language. [Special section]. *Annual Review of Cognitive Linguistics*, *7*, 113–292.

Fennell, C. T., Byers-Heinlein, K, & Werker, J. F. (2007). Using speech sounds to guide word learning: The case of bilingual infants. *Child Development*, *78*(5), 1510–1525.

Flege, J. E. (1999). Age of learning and second language speech. In D. Birdsong (Ed.), *Second language acquisition and the critical period hypothesis* (pp. 101–132). Mahwah, NJ: Lawrence Erlbaum.

Flege, J. E., Frieda, E. M., & Nozawa, T. (1997). Amount of native-language (L1) use affects the pronunciation of an L2. *Journal of Phonetics*, *25*, 169–186.

Gardner-Chloros, P., & Edwards, M. (2004). Assumptions behind grammatical approaches to code-switching: When the blueprint is a red herring. *Transactions of the Philological Society*, *102*(1), 103–129.

Genesee, F., & Geva, E. (2006). Cross-linguistic relationships in working memory, phonological processes, and oral language. In D. August & T. Shanahan (Eds.), *Developing literacy in second language learners: A report of the national literacy panel on language minority children and youth* (pp. 175–184). Mahwah, NJ: Erlbaum.

Geva, E., & Siegel, S. (2000). Orthographic and cognitive factors in the concurrent development of basic reading skills in two languages. *Reading and Writing*, *12*, 1–30.

Guo, T., & Peng, D. (2006). Event-related potential evidence for parallel activation of two languages in bilingual speech production. *Neuroreport, 17*(17), 1757–1760.

Hakuta, K. (1976). A case study of a Japanese child learning English as a second language. *Language Learning, 26*, 321–351.

Healy, A. F. (1976). Detection errors on the word *the*: Evidence for reading units larger than letters. *Journal of Experimental Psychology: Human Perception and Performance, 2*, 235–242.

Healy, A. F. (1994). Letter detection: A window to unitization and other cognitive processes. *Psychonomic Bulletin and Review, 1*, 333–344.

Hernandez, A., Li, P., & MacWhinney, B. (2005). The emergence of competing modules in bilingualism. *Trends in Cognitive Sciences, 9*(5), 220–225.

Keating, G. D. (2009). Sensitivity to violations of gender agreement in native and nonnative Spanish: An eye-movement investigation. *Language Learning, 59*(3), 503–535.

Knightly, L. M., Jun, S.-A., Oh, J. S. & Au, T., K,-f. (2003). Production benefits of childhood overhearing. *Journal of the Acoustical Society of America, 114*(1), 465–474.

Kramsch, C. (Ed.). (2002). *Language acquisition and language socialization: Ecological perspectives*. London, England: Continuum.

Kroll, J. F., & de Groot, A. M. B. (1997). Lexical and conceptual memory in the bilingual: Mapping form to meaning in two languages. In A. M. B. de Groot, & J. F. Kroll (Eds.), *Tutorials in bilingualism: Psycholinguistic perspectives* (pp. 169–199). Mahwah, NJ: Erlbaum.

Kroll, J. F., & de Groot, A. M. B. (Eds). (2005). *Handbook of bilingualism: Psycholinguistic approaches.* New York, NY: Oxford University Press.

Kuhl, P. K. (2007). Is speech learning "gated" by the social brain? *Developmental Science, 10*(1), 110–120.

Lantolf, J. (2006). Sociocultural theory and L2: State of the art. *Studies in Second Language Acquisition, 28*, 67–109.

Larsen-Freeman, D. (1976). An explanation for the morpheme acquisition order of second language learners. *Language Learning, 26*, 125–134.

Larsen-Freeman, D. (1997). Chaos/complexity science and second language acquisition. *Applied Linguistics, 18*, 141–165.

Larsen-Freeman, D. (2002). Language acquisition and language use from a chaos/complexity theory perspective. In C. Kramsch (Ed.), *Language acquisition and language socialization*. London, England: Continuum.

Lightbown, P. M., & Spada, N. (2006). *How languages are learned.* Oxford, NY: Oxford University Press.

Luk, Z.P.-s., & Shirai, Y. (2009). Is the acquisition order of grammatical morphemes impervious to L1 knowledge? Evidence from the acquisition of plural -s, articles, and possessive 's. *Language Learning, 59*(4), 721–754.

Marian, V., & Spivey, M. (2003). Competing activation in bilingual language processing: Within- and between-language competition. *Bilingualism: Language and Cognition, 6*(2), 97–115. doi: 10.1017/S1366728903001068

Mayer, M. (1969). *Frog, where are you?* New York, NY: Dial Press.

McClelland, J. L., Fiez, J. A., & McCandliss, B. D. (2002). Teaching the /r/-/l/ discrimination to Japanese adults: Behavioral and neural aspects. *Physiology and Behavior*, 77, 657–662.

Nekrasova, T. M. (2009). English L1 and L2 Speakers' knowledge of lexical bundles. *Language Learning*, 59(3), 647–686.

Northwestern University. (2009, May 20). Exposure to two languages carries far-reaching benefits. *ScienceDaily*. Retrieved June 4, 2010, from http://www.science daily.com/releases/2009/05/090519172157.htm

Oh, J. S., Jun, S.-A., Knightly, L. M., & Au, T. K. (2003). Holding on to childhood language memory. *Cognition*, 86(3), B53–B64.

Robinson, P., & Ellis, N. C. (Eds.). (2007). *A handbook of cognitive linguistics and SLA*. Mahwah, NJ: Lawrence Erlbaum.

Schwieter, J., & Sunderman, G. (2009). Concept selection and developmental effects in bilingual speech production. *Language Learning*, 59(4), 897–927.

Tokowicz, N., & MacWhinney, B. (2005). Implicit and explicit measures of sensitivity to violations in second language grammar: An event-related potential investigation. *Studies in Second Language Acquisition*, 27, 173–204.

Treffers-Daller, J. (1994). *Mixing two languages, French-Dutch contact in a comparative perspective*. Berlin, Germany: Mouton de Gruyter.

University of Alberta. (2009, September 24). Lower lexical recall in bilingual kids no cause for alarm. *ScienceDaily*. Retrieved June 4, 2010, from http://www .sciencedaily.com/releases/2009/09/090916133523.htm

Werker, J. F., & Tees, R. C. (1984). Cross-language speech perception: Evidence for perceptual reorganization during the first year of life. *Infant Behavior and Development*, 7, 49–63.

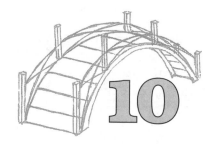

10

Using Psycholinguistics in Testing, Teaching, and Therapy

10.0 Introduction

We start this final chapter with some background on why we do what we do in the clinic and the language classroom, with a focus on evaluation and testing, which are such major activities (like it or not). Next, using our model, we'll analyze the psycholinguistic processes for two very ordinary test tasks, repetition and spelling; this analysis will help us understand in detail why these "simple" tasks can be hard for people with language problems or who don't know the language of the test very well. Then, drawing on more of the material from the earlier chapters of this book, we'll take a deeper look at aphasia testing, including some problems of "translating" tests from one language to another. Finally, we'll look at an example of a teaching/therapy idea based on the results of an experimental aphasia study, and at the special requirements of designing a clinical training experiment to test whether that idea would work in real clinical intervention.

10.0.1 Where do clinical and classroom testing and teaching methods come from?

When you prepare to enter a language profession, nobody tells you that what people do in the clinic and the language classroom—and probably in every other language profession (translating, Internet localization, speech recognition)—has evolved as a mixture of tradition and innovation. But as you work, some things about the history of professional practice in your field begin to dawn on you. In both speech-language pathology and in language teaching, some of what practitioners do is evidence-based (and you can wonder how good the evidence is), and some is theory-based (and you can wonder whether those theories are on the right track). And some turns out to come from old practical considerations; the protocol or method is based on what doctors, teachers, or therapists could do without equipment and with little knowledge of linguistics a hundred or more years ago (so you can wonder how much value it still has—diagnostically, therapeutically, or pedagogically).

When you begin professional training, though, you have to learn so much information and so many ways of doing things that you don't have time to wonder why certain tests are used or why certain procedures are followed. When you become a clinician, teacher, or other language professional, it's your workload that doesn't leave you much time to think, and the need to meet workplace standards can make it risky to try new ideas. But professional practices harden into unexamined traditions if creative newcomers and outsiders (and the leading seniors in the field) don't continually ask: Why do we do this? Does it get to the heart of what we want to know and do? If not, what should we be doing differently?

Great critical writers on science and medicine like Rachel Carson 60-odd years ago and Atul Gawande today are inspiring models, prompting us to ask those questions, and others: Does a particular way that we do things work? If it does, how? What does it really do? How could we do it better? And also: What would be the costs of not doing something that we do? What is the reasoning behind a suggested innovation? How could we get evidence that the new idea would work?

The problem with theories is that, if they are simple enough to understand easily, they are only approximations to the real world, and sometimes they completely miss crucial real-world complications. Because we can't know whether there will be such complications until the theoretical ideas get tested, laboratory schools, university clinics, and funded clinical research are necessary; those settings give people time to think about practices and test whether they can improve them. Incidentally, some things work even though the theory behind them has been discredited. So they must be working for some other reason; finding out what that is should lead us to figure out even better methods.

In this chapter, we look at a few of the standard tests and teaching methods used in language clinics and classrooms, and think about what they tell us. After you have worked through it, you should have some useful tools for thinking about what you are learning or have learned to do as a language professional, and for becoming an informed consumer of new applied linguistics research. Perhaps you yourself will become an innovator, a researcher, and a role model for new members of your profession. In the last section of the chapter, we'll look at an example of an idea that is in the process of being tested to see whether it should be used in the clinic and the language classroom. But before we get into the main part of this chapter, we need a brief look at what is called **PSYCHOMETRICS**, because it applies to all kinds of testing, including testing the effectiveness of clinical and teaching methods in improving language ability.

10.0.2 Psychometrics and language testing: Two basic criteria for a good test

PSYCHOMETRICS is the field of figuring out how to design, give, and score tests that meet two basic criteria. The first criterion is that the test must be **RELIABLE**. Test **RELIABILITY** means that if someone takes that test twice, they will get pretty much the same score each time. Not the same score, necessarily, because near the margins of our abilities for language (or anything else that we do), our performance is variable, like gymnasts or bobsledders pushing their limits in the Olympics. So when you test someone to find the limits of their language abilities, their results will be somewhat variable: There will be some tasks and test items that they can always do, some that they always have trouble with, and a substantial number of tasks and/or items in a gray area: They sometimes get them right and sometimes wrong. Tests are more reliable if they have enough examples of each language behavior so that you can get an idea of a person's average performance, and test design always involves a compromise between the reliability criterion and the need to make tests short enough for people with language problems. You may be able to endure a three-hour exam like the GRE or the TOEFL, but a child or a person with aphasia cannot.

The second criterion is **VALIDITY,** a much harder goal to achieve. A test is **VALID** if (unlike an online social network quiz: *Which Harry Potter character are you?*), it gives you a score or a profile of scores that is a good predictor of your ability to perform some useful real-world task, or to reach some important real-world goal like graduating from college. Your score on a well-made second-language essay test, for example, should predict your ability to write something useful in that language, like an accurate, informative and grammatically correct business e-mail. But, obviously, although your performance on the essay test may show what your limits are (get too many wrong noun genders on the test and you're not ready to be a Portuguese-English bilingual secretary), it doesn't measure all of the information that would be needed to predict how well you will do in a real-world job. Other factors make a big difference in your job performance, for example, the specific job pressures, and how good you are at knowing what your limits are and compensating for them. How resourceful are you at finding other ways to say the same thing? How conscientious are you at checking your accuracy before you click "send"? And will you have the time for those work-arounds?

One of the enduring problems of all kinds of language testing is how hard it is to create materials that are valid in the sense of predicting your real-world performance, because how you actually perform involves so many of these nonlanguage abilities (resourcefulness, patience, conscientiousness) in addition to language skills. As a consequence, creating valid tests is a lively research field in education and in the clinic—and within commercial firms as well; for example, a small Silicon Valley company created by a linguist successfully created software and telephone-based procedures for testing a person's intelligibility in English that seem to have a reasonable amount of validity.

10.1 What Does It Mean to Look "Psycholinguistically" at Language Tests?

10.1.1 Troubleshooting someone's problems on familiar language tests

The first language tests we all took were probably spelling tests, or perhaps circling the right answer in a workbook that had multiple choice questions about pictures. Later, we had to read paragraphs and answer questions about them, define words, and write essays and explanations. In a second or foreign language class, we had to translate words, sentences, and perhaps longer passages from the new language back into the language of the school, and, much harder, from the familiar language into the new one. We also had to read aloud and to carry out memorized practice conversations that made us feel both idiotic and anxious, especially when the teacher and the whole rest of the class were listening: *Hello, my name is Susie!*

What is your name? I am very pleased to meet you. Where are you from? Is this your first visit to Paris/Mexico City/Brazil/China? You also may have written sentences to dictation and done exercises on the comprehension and production of the new language in a language lab. (If you learned a signed language as your new language, you did much more interaction in it, and little or no writing.)

Troubleshooting someone's language processing problems takes two major steps. The first is TASK ANALYSIS, which we've already done for some language tasks in earlier chapters. For example, we did it for repetition in Chapter 7, section 7.1.6 (review that section unless it's still fresh in your mind, because we're about to go further into that topic). Task analysis gets you set to do the second step in troubleshooting, which is ERROR ANALYSIS: thinking about the kinds of errors a person has made and why they might be making those particular errors.

Task analyses are annoyingly pedestrian (like reading a complete analysis of a joke), but they are essential to figuring out what to do in challenging cases. After all, any of the many steps in saying, writing, reading, or understanding a word or sentence can go wrong while other steps are working properly. You want to focus your intervention efforts on the parts of a language task that your clients or students find difficult, and not waste their time (and yours) on the parts that are not part of their problem.

10.1.2 What we can learn from repetition tasks in the clinic and classroom

In Chapter 7, sections 7.1.4, 7.1.6, and 7.1.7, we analyzed the psycholinguistic demands of imitating what you have just heard, and we spent a while looking at McNeill's and Slobin's early studies of two toddlers trying to repeat what someone said to them. We saw that imitating what someone else has said depends on a lot of top-down processing, and that it's almost impossible to repeat something that differs in more than one way from what your own grammar would produce. What you can repeat accurately is either in your grammar already, or it's in your ZONE OF PROXIMAL DEVELOPMENT (ZPD). (It might be a good idea to back and do a quick review of those sections before you read further.) Let's use that analysis from Chapter 7 now to dig into a clinical example in English and in Japanese. The Japanese example is real; I made up the English one to parallel it, and we'll do that one first so that the Japanese example will be easier to understand. The story involves a child with a developmental language disorder, but it could just as well be about a second-language learner or an adult with aphasia.

Here's the made-up English version: A clinician asks a child, let's call him Dylan, to repeat the sentence *He made grandpa laugh*. Dylan responds: *Grandpa laughed*. Assuming that Dylan was paying attention and really trying, it looks as if the English CAUSATIVE CONSTRUCTION *A made B do something* is too hard for him—it's outside his ZPD. But what has Dylan gotten right—what does he know? He seems to be a lot closer to the target than Echo was in section 7.1.7 when she repeated THE BOY THE BOOK HIT WAS CRYING as *boy the book was crying*.

Dylan's *Grandpa laughed* shows that he probably understands that it was Grandpa who laughed, and that the event was in the past. So he it looks like he processed the clinician's verb *made* enough to get the tense marker out of it, as well as picking up on the meanings of *Grandpa*, *laugh*, and the fact that Grandpa is the subject of the verb *laugh* even if he's not the subject of the sentence. On the other hand, we don't know whether Dylan noticed the real subject of the sentence, *he*, and we know he wasn't able to produce the causative construction in this sentence.

The articulatory demands of *He made Grandpa laugh* aren't much greater than those of *Grandpa laughed*, so we'll assume that the problem isn't articulatory. And, although it might be a memory problem, remember that it's much, much easier to remember a sequence of words that makes syntactic sense to you than one that doesn't. So the prime suspect here is Dylan's syntax, not his memory. But there are (at least) three quite different syntactic reasons why Dylan might have failed to produce the whole construction. Each one gives a different picture of Dylan's grammatical ability, so his clinician will have to probe some more to see where he is in his syntactic development and what needs to be worked on.

First, Dylan may not have understood the causative construction, which means that he didn't realize that someone else made Grandpa laugh. That could be checked with a picture-pointing comprehension test; if Dylan flunks it, the clinician could start work with getting him to understand the construction. Second, Dylan might have understood that someone else was involved in Grandpa's laughing, but not yet be able to produce the causative construction. In that case, the clinician doesn't need to work on its comprehension, just its production.

Third, the problem might be in the PRAGMATICS of the test situation, because this sentence (and the Japanese original, as far as I know) was given as an imitation task, with no context. So, if there's no person besides Grandpa around for *he* to refer to, the clinician's sentence would be pragmatically wrong; using a pronoun when your hearer can't figure out who it refers to is not a fair move in a conversation. Maybe Dylan could have used the causative construction if he had had some idea who this mysterious agent *he* was, but because he didn't have a context that would have established this other person, he couldn't quite conceive of what was happening. That would mean he didn't have a mental picture of some person who was making Grandpa laugh; in his understanding (the **MESSAGE LEVEL** in our model), Grandpa was laughing alone.

Now let's follow the logic of production according to this third hypothesis about Dylan's understanding of the clinician's sentence. When it was his turn to say the sentence, his mental picture at the Message Level (the one he's most likely to remember—see Chapter 5, section 5.2.4) didn't have that nameless other person in it. Without that person, the only participant in the event at the Message Level must be Grandpa. So the causative relationship wouldn't have been aroused at his Functional Level of production; in his event structure (Chapter 3, section 3.2.1), the Agent was Grandpa and laughing was the event. That, in turn, means that the causative construction—even if Dylan knew how to say it—wouldn't be aroused at the Positional Level: *Grandpa* would be the subject and *laugh* (past) would be the verb.

To check out whether this third hypothesis—that Dylan can understand the causal construction when he can see who or what is doing the causing—is true, the clinician needs to try telling a story or showing a picture of someone clowning for Grandpa, and see whether Dylan can repeat the construction when he has that contextual support. If he can, he doesn't need to learn the causative construction; he's got it. However, for success at test-taking (and for some situations in the real world), he needs to learn something else: how to imagine contexts that will fit a sentence that comes at him out of the blue.

Here's the actual Japanese version of this story; it's almost the same, including the pragmatics. But it has one new twist, because Japanese and English have an important difference in the way they use pronouns, and I have to explain that first. Where English would use a subject pronoun, Japanese usually just leaves out the subject (Spanish, Italian, and many other languages do that, too). So the Japanese sentence that corresponds to our *He made Grandpa laugh* doesn't have any subject pronoun; the sentence that the Japanese clinician really used would be literally translated *Made Grandpa laugh*, and a normal Japanese adult would infer that there had been another, nameless person who had amused Grandpa, just as we do when we hear *He made Grandpa laugh*. Okay, that's the twist; now we can go on to a few more points of Japanese grammar.

Japanese has an inflectional past tense ending *-ta* or *-da* that's not very different from the English past tense *-t* or *-d* or *-əd*. *Grandpa laughs* is *Ojiisan warau*, and *Grandpa laughed* is *Ojiisan waratta*. A fuller form of this sentence, marking Grandpa explicitly as the subject, would have the function word *ga* as a **CASE-MARKING POSTPOSITION** after *Ojiisan*. We don't have any function words like that in English (although German and Russian have case-marking endings that do a similar job). Japanese often marks the object noun, too, by putting the function word *o* after it (so *o* is another case-marking postposition); that's a bit like the way Spanish marks some objects with the case-marking preposition *à* (*Veo à Juan—I see John*).

Finally, Japanese has a neat way of making a verb causative; instead of using a construction with two verbs, *make* and *laugh*, as we do, it puts a causative suffix (in this case, its form is *-asa*) on the verb *laugh* between the verb stem and the *-ta* ending, and it makes Grandpa the object of this new verb, like this: *Ojiisan o warawasatta*. That's the Japanese clinician's actual original sentence that corresponds to our translation *He made Grandpa laugh*.

What the child—let's call him Kenji—said back to the clinician, however, was just *Ojiisan ga waratta*: *Grandpa laughed*. Everything that made the clinician's sentence causative is gone: there's no *-asa* on the verb, and there's a subject postposition instead of the object postposition after *Ojiisan,* Grandpa. Kenji's *ga* marks Grandpa as the sentence subject, and he is, because he's the agent of the verb *laughed*. The reasoning about why Kenji only said *Ojiisan ga waratta* when he was supposed to be imitating *Ojiisan o warawasatta* is identical to the reasoning we went through for the made-up English example. Maybe Kenji didn't understand the meaning of the causative form; maybe he understood it but couldn't produce it; or maybe he would have been able to understand and produce it if he had heard the sentence in a story or seen a picture that told him who was making Grandpa laugh, but the sentence by itself wasn't enough for him to imagine the existence of this other person who hadn't been mentioned.

So what we see here is that, when someone doesn't imitate a sentence exactly (assuming that there's nothing difficult about the pronunciation of the words), something about that sentence might be either outside the person's grammar for comprehension and production, or understandable but outside their production grammar, or pragmatically inappropriate—in the "Grandpa" case, introducing a new person (the one who made Grandpa laugh) without giving any information about who this person is. But figuring out which of these possibilities is the correct one will take follow-up work.

Here's the take-home lesson for this section: Language test tasks in general, are designed to give reliable (and possibly valid) scores. But they are not designed to figure out what level or levels of processing are impaired, so no single test task can tell you what aspect of language processing is causing your client's or student's problems. To do this, you have to follow up your error analysis with other tasks that can distinguish among the possible causes that you have thought of, as we have imagined doing here.

However, and this goes beyond what we've said so far, that kind of follow-up might not be the right thing to do for your client or student.

Why not? Isn't it best to know as much as possible, if you have the time and the resources? Maybe, but there's something else to consider: Many people with aphasia or developmental disorders have trouble with several different psycholinguistic processes. Any or all of those processes could be involved in a particular error. Similarly, many learners are uncertain about lots of aspects of their new language, from pragmatics to pronunciation. So you may not be able to pinpoint one particular level of difficulty, and you'll need to judge when it's time to stop investing your time and your client's time in what could be a wild goose chase. After a certain point, you might have to work with your client or your student without focusing on any particular level of production, hoping that their language will improve overall with time and practice, just as happens in normal first-language learning.

10.1.3 Psycholinguistics and spelling: An exhausting look at the details

Let's walk through the task analysis for another very familiar language task, spelling a dictated word, so that we can see what needs to be activated in our brains (and muscles!) in order to carry it out. This will also be useful as a review of some other parts of our language-processing model. Spelling is quite hard for most people with language damage, and you'll see why.

What could be stupider than a spelling test? It's just reproducing memorized information, right? Yes—and no. There's no "just" about it. I'm going to show you a moderately detailed task analysis of the process of spelling a word. Figuring out this kind of complex process for yourself can be an exhilarating challenge, but working through somebody else's account of it—in this case, mine—may be both difficult and boring. If you can make this into a game where you read a little, write down your most logical guess as to what I'm going to say next, check the text see if you were right, and then go to on to the next step, it should help make it more interesting, and you'll remember it better, too, because you will have been doing more of the thinking yourself—what pedagogy textbooks call doing more "active processing."

Comprehension

Put yourself mentally back in grammar school, taking a spelling test. First, you had to understand the word that the teacher said, the TARGET WORD. That process started with hearing and attending to the incoming sounds well enough so that they could start to activate the right English phonemes. Those sounds also sent some activation to similar ones, and began to arouse words that sounded similar to the target. If your attention was properly focused, the unwanted words never made it to your consciousness; however, they might have started activating their meanings, and/or the letters in their spellings—letters that don't belong in the word that you were supposed to be spelling. Those other activated letters might affect what you write a few seconds later, if your attention is poor or if you are hesitating between possible spellings. (Attention is controlled by activity in brain structures that we haven't talked about, so we can't go into detail here; see the "neural thermostat" link on the CD in Materials for this chapter. But we can't ignore the effects of attentional problems; as you know, attentional overload from trying to do too much at once (driving and texting!) can get us into serious trouble. Spelling in a classroom instead of on the road isn't going to be deadly, but for people with attentional disorders, it may be difficult.)

When the sound waves of the first phoneme of the spelling word had brought that phoneme to its activation threshold in your brain, in about two-tenths of a second, the activated phoneme started sending activation to all the words in your memory that begin with it. If you saw the teacher's lips move, that visual information also sent activation to your stored knowledge of the English speech sounds, and on to all the relevant phonemes. (You might remember from the information about coarticulation in Chapter 1, section A that the sound waves from each phoneme usually contain information about the one that will be coming next, and that your best information on a speech sound may be its effects in the one that came after it. Lip and jaw movements also contain that kind of information.)

As more of the sounds of the word activated their phonemes above their thresholds, the words in your mental lexicon that contained all of those activated phonemes got the most total activation and got closer to their own thresholds. The most frequent words among them had a head start on actually getting above threshold, because they had higher resting levels of activation than the others (and studying a word would raise its activation level, too). After a certain point—perhaps well before the word ended—the target word would have been the only word form in your mind that matched all the incoming phonemes, and it would have started inhibiting other words that matched only some of those phonemes. As this word form was reaching its threshold, it also sent activation back down to the phonemes that were in it. This INTERACTIVE ACTIVATION—the same kind of process that produces the **WORD SUPERIORITY EFFECT** for recognizing written letters (see Chapter 8, section 8.1.2 and Figure 8.1, along with the Classic Interactive Intervention Model, p. 308)—helped you feel surer that you had heard these sounds and that you had recognized the word.

When the target word form reached its activation threshold, it sent activation on to its LEMMA—your stored information about what it means and how it can be used in making phrases and sentences (Chapter 3, section 3.4). When that lemma became activated above threshold, it sent activation to the concept behind the meaning of the word; you began to understand it. And the concept, when it reached its threshold, sent activation to lots of memories associated with the target word (although they probably didn't get enough activation to break through to your conscious mind, unless your attention sagged and you started daydreaming). If the target word had several meanings, several lemmas would have been aroused by its sound. In that case, of course, the teacher should have used the target word in a phrase or sentence. That context should succeed in sending extra activation to the concept she intended, and inhibition to the others—we'll skip the details of that process, but you can work through it as an exercise.

If you couldn't hear well (you were hard of hearing, or a bell rang, or an airplane roared overhead), or you didn't know the target word, some of the sounds in the incoming word might not have gotten aroused enough. In that case, one of the more frequent words that have most of the same sounds might become activated so much that you thought you heard it instead of the target word.

If you didn't recognize the word, its sounds didn't activate a clear concept. Instead, the concepts of similar sounding words were jostling each other, probably below your level of consciousness. In that case, remembering the sounds long enough to spell the word was hard; you had no mental image to help you hold onto them in your mind. Probably you tried to hold onto the sounds by saying them over and over mentally, and maybe moving your tongue and lips, so that you could guess at the spelling, using the phoneme-grapheme correspondences that link sounds and letters together as well your memories of how similar-sounding words are spelled.

Production of spelling

If all went well, you understood the target word. How did you start to spell it? In several ways at once, actually. Even before you fully understood it, because you had learned the phoneme-grapheme correspondences, the phonemes started activating their associated letters (graphemes). The graphemes, in turn, activated your stored memory of the movement patterns of the various forms of the letter (the "graphs"): uppercase and lowercase print and script, plus your visual memory of what they look like. Assuming you were taking the test in English, most of the vowel sounds and some of the consonant sounds activated several letters and sets of letters. For example, if the target word was *pheasant* ['fɛznt], the graphemes F and PH both got activation from the first phoneme [f], and both E and the EA combination got activation from the first vowel [ɛ]. The second syllable, which was just pronounced [nt] (unless the teacher was speaking hyperdistinctly), could be spelled NT, ANT, INT, ENT, or UNT.

How did you manage to pick the correct letters? In other words, how did the brain fight that was set up by the various possible activated letters and letter sequences get settled properly, so that you didn't write FESINT or FEZENT? Frequency helped: for example, INT and UNT usually spell the syllable [nt] at the beginning of a word, not at the end, so hearing [fɛznt] didn't send much activation to them. And NT, which spells the syllable [nt] if you write it N'T, is tightly linked to words that you'd recognize as contractions. N'T probably got some inhibition, since you knew that [fɛznt] wasn't a contraction. So, the only real competition in how to spell the second syllable of this word was between ANT and ENT. And this was as far as knowing grapheme-phoneme correspondences could get you with figuring out how to spell [fɛznt].

If you had started with the wrong letters and they didn't make a word you'd seen before, what you wrote looked weird: FEZENT?? "Looking weird" means that your visual memory is taking over, as it must for this word at this point. If you'd seen the word *pheasant* often enough, you formed some memory of what letters were in it and in roughly what order, so when the word's lemma reached threshold, it would have sent activation to that whole visual memory: pheasant (with some of the details a little weak). (The concept of *pheasant*, which would have been activated as the teacher was saying the word, helped that lemma stay active.) Because PH is not the usual way to spell the F sound, when you were learning the word, you would have really noticed that *pheasant* is not spelled with an F. (Noticing unusual patterns helps to strengthen links between the concept and the way the word looks.)

The ENT/ANT choice gets some help in the ANT direction because there are two common words that rhyme with *pheasant* and have the same spelling: *peasant* and *pleasant*. Because they have those very similar sounds, they will have been somewhat aroused by the sound of *pheasant* (although they probably won't come to your conscious awareness, as we said a few paragraphs ago). Their spellings will give the ANT some activation. Unfortunately, *present* will give a boost to the spelling ENT in the competition. That kind of thing happens a lot in English, and probably even more in French, which is orthographically deeper than English (see Chapter 8, section 8.1.3), as we've said, although it's much more regular.

Homonyms

Enough about *pheasant*. Let's look at a different problem: Suppose the target word had homonyms, like *steak* and *stake*; how would the activation story go? The teacher would have clarified which one she meant by using it in a phrase or a sentence (*a nice juicy* [steik]), but the lemma and concept of the nontarget word *stake* would still be active, because they got activation from the sound of the word, which was in your working memory. Because the homonyms *steak* and *stake* have different spellings, the spellings would have set up a brain fight. How does a spelling brain fight get settled? How do the right letters get activated in the order that you'll have to write them in?

The target word was *steak*, and the concept of a nice juicy one is active in your mind. Since you know that *stake* means a stick or the amount of money someone puts into a risky deal, the wrong spelling STAKE, although it was activated because it also has the sound [steik], won't send any activation to the lemma of the target word *steak*. The right spelling STEAK, on the other hand, will send activation to the lemma of *steak*, and on to its active concept, and they will send activation back to the spelling STEAK, so STEAK should win the competition. But wait, doesn't the lemma *stake* keep the spelling STAKE active? Sure. What keeps the lemma *stake* and its spelling STAKE under control is the fact that you have the concept of *steak* in your working memory, being kept strong by the fact that a rich set of concepts were aroused when you heard the word in the example phrase. They will help STEAK inhibit STAKE.

If your brain couldn't hang onto the semantics of the target word until you were done writing it, you would be helpless in fighting off the attack of its homonym. (You'd be in exactly the same position as if the teacher had refused to give you a sentence so that you could tell which word she had in mind.) Being unable to hold onto the concept for the target word may be a major source of spelling errors in people with aphasia, attentional disorders, or traumatic brain injury—and if they have aphasia, they probably also have trouble holding onto the sound in memory, making everything worse.

Getting letters in the right order

As our STAKE/STEAK homonym example makes clear, the letters in the word have to come out in the right order. If one of the letters that comes towards the end of the word—let's say the K—happens to beat out its competition and reach its activation threshold early on, it will have to be held in a buffer (called the GRAPHEMIC BUFFER) until all the letters that come before it have settled any fights they might have had. This is the same concept of buffer that we used in Chapter 4, section 4.1.1, only this time it's holding letters instead of words or sounds.

The sound of the word helps to get and keep the letters in the graphemic buffer in the right order: It'll keep the S before the T, and the K after at least one of the vowel letters. For many words, the sounds are even more reliable in getting the order right: If you can match letters with sounds, even roughly, you'll never write WAS for SAW, or KALE for LAKE. Remember from the section on dyslexia in Chapter 8 (section 8.8.1) that the most likely reason that people with dyslexia get letters in the wrong order is that they don't have good phonological activation going from the letters to the sounds and/or from the sounds to the letters, so there's nothing but their visual memory to help them get and keep the letters lined up in the buffer in the right order.

Double letters

If the word has double letters, for example *tomorrow*, typing errors like TOMMOROW or TOMOOROW (which sometimes also show up as aphasic spelling errors) tell us one more interesting thing about how our brains handle spelling: Double letters aren't like other kinds of letter sequences. The "doubleness" is a property that has a kind of autonomy—your brain knows that the word has a double letter in it, separately from knowing which letter is the one that gets doubled. Under stress, "double" can get linked to and then activated by the wrong letter while they all are hanging around in the graphemic buffer; that's our model for how errors like TOMMOROW occur.

The final stages of spelling involve the letters in the graphemic buffer activating your motor memory of how to make the uppercase or lowercase letters, and your visual memory of how they should look—or, if you were typing, your motor memory of which fingers need to move to which keys. If your right hand is paralyzed, as it often is in nonfluent aphasia, you'll have to write with your left hand, which has little or no motor memory of spelling and has to make letters by some kind of visually guided drawing. You know what it feels like to do that; right hand paralysis is an added burden for many people who have brain injuries that affects their language, because the part of the brain that controls the right hand's fine movements is very close to Broca's area, which is deeply involved in language processing and related cognitive activity.

Spelling in L2

If the spelling test is in your second (or 3rd or Nth) language (and at least one of your earlier languages used an alphabet—see writing systems,

Chapter 8, section 8.7), then your brain has a large additional set of brain fights that have to be settled correctly in order for you to spell a word. Walking through the details would take too much space here, but you can figure them out if you like; here's an overview and some examples.

Each written language has its own set of grapheme-phoneme correspondences, so each orthographic system is at least a little different. Grapheme-phoneme relations for vowels typically differ violently across languages (and across dialects within languages). Even the most reliable letter of all, M (or the letter that corresponds to M in another alphabet, like Greek μ), isn't always pronounced /m/: At the ends of words in Portuguese, it's just a signal that the vowel before it is nasalized—you lower your velum but you don't close your lips when you see the M in *Bom dia!* (*Good day*, the usual way to say hello).

So, if English is your second alphabet-using language and you hear a sound or a syllable in a spelling test, the grapheme-phoneme rules from your first alphabetic language will be activated by those sounds, and they'll compete with the rules you have learned (or are trying to learn) for English. If your first language is French, for example, the word *white*— probably pronunced [wajt?]—will arouse a letter sequence something like O U A I T E (French doesn't have the letter W, and a written /t/ that's actually pronounced at the end of a French word has an E written after it, as in *petite*). If your first language is Spanish, the same word sound should arouse G U A I (T?) and J U A I (T?); Spanish doesn't have the letter W either, and the nearest sounds to it are spelled as I've shown. The question marks on the T's are there because Spanish rarely has final Ts or the final /t/ sound, so if you are literate only in Spanish, you may not have a clear idea of what to do with that part of the English word.

If you are a literate speaker of either French or Spanish and do spell the English word correctly, WHITE, and then check what you've written, you'll have more competition in your brain, because the letter I will arouse the wrong vowel sound in your mind—you would pronounce the letter I with the sound /i/ in either of those languages, and so it would look wrong for the /aj/ sound. On the other hand, the silent H should only cause you the minor problem of remembering that it's there. That problem would already be familiar to you, because H is always silent in both French and Spanish; you'd expect to have to memorize where it goes.

So, if you are an L2 teacher, thinking about these problems should help you understand where your students' spellings are coming from, and to design explicit teaching strategies to help their new knowledge of English compete successfully with their established knowledge of spelling in their earlier language or languages.

10.2 Aphasia Testing: Clinical Testing and its Problems

10.2.1 A little history of psycholinguistics and testing

About 50 years ago, the ILLINOIS TEST OF PSYCHOLINGUISTIC ABILITY (ITPA) was published. It was based on the very simple ideas (I am tempted to say "mindless ideas"—that's a pun, as you'll see after you finish this sentence) of the BEHAVIORIST school of psychology, which talked about connections rather like we do, but which didn't deal with—in fact, didn't believe in— the whole idea that people have minds.

What's the difference? There are a lot of technical ones, but here's the main point: The connections that behaviorists talked about were not like the ones in our model. Our model's links are interconnected and cross-connected in an intricate web—a simplified version of the highly branched connections in our brains—but theirs were simple SENSORY-MOTOR LINKS that joined end-to-end, forming direct channels between senses and movements, or movements and senses. The signals running along them couldn't influence each other, combine, or pass their activation along in multiple directions. Behaviorists, who started their work long before electronic computers were invented, had modeled their channels on chains of reflexes— essentially, knee-jerk reactions. Brain researchers of that era, trying to explain more complicated behavior, supplemented the behaviorists' mechanical channels of end-to-end reflexes with "centers" in the brain that supposedly carried out processes like reading and speaking; in other words, this old brain model pretty much treated reading, speaking, and other complex cognitive process as impenetrable mysteries.

In contrast, our spreading-activation-based model analyzes cognitive processes into the work of many thousands of interacting neurons. We now know that activities like reading and speaking are complex; they are not single processes that can be carried out in one chunk of brain tissue. Instead, they have multiple steps and require input and regulation from many parts of our brains. And we talk again about people (and animals) as having minds, because we know now, from the past 50 years of brain research, that our brains do a huge amount of work—of information processing—that doesn't necessarily result in immediately visible behavior. For example, we form mental images, and we can imagine saying words without actually doing so. With today's equipment, researchers can see changes in the brain waves that give observable evidence that those things are really happening when we say they are.

Evidence from slips of the tongue (Chapters 3 and 4), experiments (Chapter 5), and aphasia (Chapter 6), as well as from **FUNCTIONAL BRAIN IMAGING** studies, has confirmed the idea that the brain is a tumultuous place. It's full of activation and inhibition flowing every which way, with signals from different sources combining and competing. And we know that our brains don't operate like reflex chains, because they have to be able to regulate our attention, so that we aren't distracted by currently irrelevant information that might come in handy later. New information coming in from our senses gets integrated with top-down processing that has been shaped by our past experiences; as a result, even in what we think of as pure perception, memory influences what we see and hear. All of this action and interaction—the little bit that we can become aware of and the enormous amount that goes on subconsciously—is what constitutes our minds. Our brains don't have hard-walled channels (though they may have some limited-access superhighways); they are gigantic, constantly changing networks.

How has testing changed to keep up with current understanding of how our minds work? Most of it hasn't; the major innovations are in computer-based testing of attention and other cognitive abilities. It's not easy to figure out how to modify the tasks that researchers use in their labs so that they can be used in the clinic. Although a lot of people are working toward that goal, what we can do in the meantime is to work on how to interpret the information that we get from existing tests. And that begins with looking at test tasks and the kinds of errors that people make, and asking how those errors could happen as we did with slips of the tongue (in Chapters 3 and 4), other language errors (mostly in Chapter 6), and with some kinds of spelling errors just now (section 10.1.2). In this section (10.2), we'll add some more discussion of written language, aphasia tests, and nonlanguage factors affecting test performance.

10.2.2 What aphasia tests are like (and why)

Do you remember the old definition of a camel? "A horse designed by a committee." But as ugly as it is, a camel gets you where you need to go, and a horse might not survive the trek. An aphasia test has to be a camel, because it has several very different jobs to do.

First, it must *establish that the client has aphasia.* We discussed some of what this involves in Chapter 6, and you should review it now if you have a serious interest in aphasia. In the United States until as late as the 1960s, some people who had severe **WERNICKE'S APHASIA** (fluent aphasia with severe comprehension disorder)—the kind of aphasia that ruins their comprehension of all modalities of language and makes them speak an unintelligible jargon—were locked up in insane asylums, because so few psychiatrists and psychologists had been trained on DIFFERENTIAL DIAGNOSIS between a disorder of language and a disorder of thought or emotion, and they apparently didn't even think about consulting a speech-language pathologist.

To be sure of a correct diagnosis these days, speech-language pathologists work with neurologists and also with trained NEUROPSYCHOLOGISTS, the professionals who know how to test the other areas of cognition that may be involved in a puzzling case. For example, Alzheimer's disease and other dementias may have to be ruled out, or someone could have both aphasia and a dementia.

Second, an aphasia test is supposed to *classify* the aphasia, if possible, with one of the kinds of labels that we introduced at the end of Chapter 6 (Broca's aphasia, Wernicke's aphasia, and so on), or with a similar kind of label, because our whole medical/remedial culture is organized around classifications.

Third (and overlapping with the second requirement), an aphasia test should give clinicians a good portrait of their *client's strengths and weaknesses*, so they have some idea of how to start working with the patient. It also needs to give a picture of the client's overall ability to use language, so that they and their family can make practical decisions about what the client is able to do and can be responsible for. We'll explore some aspects of these goals in section 10.2.4.

The last requirement is the economic one (which of course conflicts with the others): The clinician must be able to *give the aphasia examination in a short time*—preferably in one or two office hours—with modest testing apparatus. Until recently, that meant without using a computer to show pictures or play sounds; practical ways to computerize testing are still being worked out.

A typical aphasia test samples the four basic modalities of communication in our society: speaking (or signing, if your client is deaf), understanding spoken (or signed) language, reading, and writing. But this doesn't mean that clinicians and research APHASIOLOGISTS are still using the simple input-to-output model of the ITPA that we just discussed. We look at each modality to help classify the aphasia and also to figure out the best way for each client to communicate. We also need to look at each modality to be sure that the person across the desk actually is aphasic.

How would you make sure that your client's communication problem is aphasia? Brain damage that is severe enough to cause a language disorder probably has affected some other abilities, especially how well your client can control the movements of their articulators (lips, the various parts of the tongue, velum), vocal folds, and hands. Aphasia is also often accompanied by APRAXIA—difficulty with arousing the motor patterns necessary for actions (remember Jenny at 80, attempting to blow out a candle after having had a stroke, in Chapter 2, section 2.4.3). Because aphasia is often accompanied by these motor and motor arousal problems, you have to figure out whether those nonlanguage motor problems in fact are all that's wrong with your client, or whether there's aphasia as well. Remember the definition of aphasia from Chapter 6, section 6.0: an acquired language disorder caused by FOCAL brain damage. What do you need to map out to decide whether that's what your client has, and how does an aphasia test help you do it?

Let's follow the logic: Does this person in front of you have language damage, is damage to some other system impairing communication, or are you seeing the effects of both kinds of damage? Let's suppose that mental illness, massive cognitive damage, serious motor problems, and serious problems with vision and hearing have been ruled out by the neurologist and NEUROPSYCHOLOGIST who have seen your client. What next?

Aphasia tests are designed to compare language performance across the four basic communication modalities, and that comparison should give you the information you need to decide whether your client's communication problem is really a language processing problem, or whether it's more superficial. Here's why: If a person can use one of their production modalities—speech (or sign) or writing—without difficulty, then the language production processing must be working in that modality for *all* the levels we studied in Chapters 3 and 4—the Message Level, the Functional Level of arousing constructions and lemmas, and also the lower levels of arousing word forms and getting the sounds (or hand movements) or letters into the right order. So the production process is going wrong only for the steps that take place after the spoken (or signed) and written modalities have parted company, on their way to their vocal tract and to their writing hand, respectively. In that case, what's wrong with whichever production modality is not working normally is too superficial to be called a language processing problem, and that means that it's not aphasia. (Just a reminder: It's common to have both a superficial output processing problem like dysarthria or apraxia *and* aphasia.)

Similarly, if your client has trouble with one of their comprehension modalities (understanding spoken language or reading) but not with the other one, then the language comprehension process must be working on *all* processing levels for the good modality. So the problem in the troublesome modality must be only at the early input processing stage, before written and spoken input start using the same comprehension processes. What are those early stages? You know them: for written input, identifying the graphemes and having them arouse the words (via grapheme-phoneme correspondences and whole-word visual memory); for spoken input, identifying the phonemes and having them arouse words. Or possibly, a disconnection between the parts of the brain that process visual input and the parts of the brain that process language, as is found in people who can still write after brain damage but can no longer read.

One more example, to make this completely clear: If your client has *no* problem in comprehension and in one of their production modalities, but does have trouble with their other production modality, is that aphasia? Suppose the person you're with has a problem with producing spoken English, but they can read, can understand spoken English, and can write relevant, sensible, grammatical English sentences. In that case, their problem with speaking must be occurring quite late, after lemmas and constructions have been retrieved and integrated into the Positional Level (see Chapter 4, sections 4.1 and 4.2). It must be only the last few stages of spoken language production that are impaired: phonological encoding or articulation (or PHONATION). In our discussions of dyslexia, we've noted that reliable spelling seems to require support from phonology; so if your client has good spelling—the correct letters and in the correct order—their phonology is probably good too. In that case, their production problem is only with speech processing, not with output language processing. They have DYSARTHRIA, DYSPHONIA, or APRAXIA OF SPEECH, but they are not aphasic. (Second reminder: Many people who have these speech processing problems do have aphasia as well, or did. But not all of them.)

In summary: If the brain damage affects *only* the last stages of articulation, the ones that come after the retrieval and organization of the sounds needed to produce a word, that's a speech disorder; it's not aphasia. If someone who is literate has only a speech disorder, they can use writing to communicate normally. Hearing people who really have aphasia have problems with at least two of the four modalities we've been considering: spoken language comprehension, written language comprehension, spoken language production, and written language production. (For sign language users, the logic is the same: Real aphasia will produce disorders in sign production or comprehension (or both). We can't discuss the evaluation of sign aphasia in this book, but the Salk Institute Sign Aphasia Test Battery (http://signaphasiatests.salk.edu/) based on the *Boston Diagnostic Aphasia Examination* (2nd ed.), is the place to start.

10.2.3 We have already used our model to analyze several aphasia test tasks

A typical aphasia test has several kinds of language production and comprehension tasks (including repetition), a few reading tasks, and a bit of writing. In Chapters 6, 7, and 8, as well as this one, we've looked quite closely at the psycholinguistics behind most of the tasks involved in aphasia testing. I won't repeat what we've worked through; I'll just remind you of what we've done in case you want to review it. In this chapter, section 10.1.2, we looked at spelling, which of course is basic to writing; in Chapter 7, section 7.1.6, we analyzed repetition (elicited imitation), and in Chapter 8, reading. In Chapter 6, we analyzed the psycholinguistics behind many of the error patterns that are found in typical language production and comprehension tasks. Section 6.4.1 looked at naming and naming errors, and showed how difficulties at particular stages of language production—arousing the lemma, arousing the word form, maintaining the order of the sounds during assembly—all gave different patterns of errors in naming. In section 6.4.2, we discussed the psycholinguistics behind problems that show up when people are asked to tell stories or talk with someone—too much or too little speech, vagueness, limited variety in their words, syntactic and semantic errors. Section 6.5 turned to the problems involved in comprehending spoken commands, words, and basic sentence structures. If we pull this all together, we get a general picture of aphasic language processing: People with aphasia have problems with activating linguistic forms, structures and/or meanings, and/or problems with resolving competition between the possible meanings that were aroused by what they heard or read, or between possible messages, syntactic structures, word lemmas, and word forms aroused by what they wanted to say or write. If you look at an individual person's errors, you may be able to tell which processes are working fairly well and which are not.

So our model has provided us with a framework for describing what seems to be going wrong in how a person with aphasia processes language, and it does help us see why some disorders of comprehension and production might not really be language disorders. But it doesn't help us very much with assigning people to diagnostic categories or with figuring out how to give numerical values for how well a person is doing. Aphasia tests are supposed to do those jobs, too. How do they do them?

10.2.4 Classifying aphasias: Scores and profiles

Regardless of whether you are comfortable with the Boston system (or any other system) for classifying aphasias into syndromes, the startling differences between different people with aphasia need to be described and evaluated. We need a handle on what kinds of language tasks each client is good at and bad at, whether they are getting better at any of the tasks that were hard for them, and whether a particular treatment has helped or not. The Boston system described at the end of Chapter 6 and other classification systems depend on comparing your client's abilities at tasks measuring their abilities (and sometimes their error patterns) in seven major areas: articulation, fluency/phrase length (apart from word-finding pauses), repetition, word-finding, understanding words, producing words linked into phrases and sentences, and understanding syntax. (In practice, "understanding syntax," for English, just means understanding sentences like *The car was hit by the bus*, where the grammatical morphemes have to be used to override the meaning that you would get from understanding only the content words and their order; see the "Geschwind" link in Materials for Chapter 10 on your CD.) To compare someone's abilities on these different tasks, a test score sheet often includes an APHASIA PROFILE chart (more about that soon) and/or a procedure for deriving a diagnostic category from the shape of that profile or the relative values of the test scores.

The profile of test scores, and possibly your judgment of your client's communicative ability, are also used to give the overall SEVERITY RATING, which is intended to give a rough idea of how well the person can use language to communicate. Some tests, like the **BOSTON DIAGNOSTIC APHASIA EXAMINATION** (BDAE), also have you describe your client's language communication ability on an impressionistic scale—which turns out, amazingly, to be very easy to do reliably with only a short period of clinical training.

A word of caution, though: How well a person can use language to communicate in response to test tasks is not a good predictor of how well they can communicate when they have the freedom to combine their language with gesture, mime, and drawing. Nor does it tell us how well they will do if they have a cooperative and skilful conversation partner, instead of an examiner who is sympathetic but isn't permitted (during the examination) to help them by suggesting possible words that they might be looking for, or by asking them if what they mean is really A or really B. We'll talk more about the difference between language ability and communication ability in section 10.2.5, and you should also check out this chapter's suggested readings on your CD.

Comprehension test tasks

The person whose language you are supposed to evaluate may have language production problems and apraxia, so your comprehension tests must work regardless of how well your client can talk or whether they can act things out. Most comprehension tests ask your client to respond either by pointing to a picture or by answering "yes" or "no." Nods and headshakes are always accepted in place of the words, and sometimes it's clearer if you have your client point to a smiley face for "yes" and a frowning face for "no." What's important is to be able to get a reliable response—one that your client has under control. If their brain damage is so severe that they can't control their voluntary muscles to give even eye-blink responses, brain response measures adapted from experimental studies of aphasia can show whether they have any understanding of spoken language, but that's outside present standard procedures.

You might start by checking whether your client can understand single words when there's a bit of competition—for example, to point to an object ("show me the tree") in an array of six object pictures, to an action/event ("show me 'falling'") in an array of six action pictures, and similarly with such categories as numbers, letters, and colors. Traditionally—and here, you can still see the doctor-at-the-bedside history of our profession—you also ask your clients to point to various parts of their body ("show me your knee; your chin; your left elbow") and to carry out little sequences of actions ("point to the ceiling and then to the floor"). Finally, you look at comprehension of more complex language, which you do by reading little stories aloud to your client and then asking two or more questions about the story that can be answered "yes" or "no."

None of these tasks is psycholinguistically revealing, because there are all kinds of reasons why your client may give you the wrong answer to any of them. But basic clinical tests aren't diagnostic in the sense of telling you where your client's processing is going wrong. What they are designed to do is to allow you to compare your client's scores on each type of task (oral comprehension, naming, repetition, picture description, conversation, and so on) with those of hundreds of other people with aphasia, because it's that comparative profile—better than average on one test, worse on another—that gives the diagnostic label.

Production test tasks

Production testing often uses some of the same words and phrases as comprehension testing, which cuts down the number of stimulus materials you need in your test kit. This time, you point to colors, objects, and so on, and ask your client to name them. (Actually, you do the production testing before the comprehension testing, so that your client doesn't get a boost from just having heard you say the words they'll need.) You may start with single words, with conversation, or with asking your client to describe a complex picture like the Cookie Theft (see Figure 6.1). You'll also test repetition of words and short sentences.

In the production subtests, you'll finally be able to do more than note whether the answer is right or wrong and how long it took your client to respond. Now you'll start classifying the errors and describing the quality of your client's narrative, because the some of the different aphasia syndromes have different types of production problems. Are the errors just "no response"? Semantically related words (SEMANTIC PARAPHASIAS)? Phonologically related forms, either words or nonwords (PHONOLOGICAL/ PHONEMIC PARAPHASIAS)? Phonetically clumsy (DYSARTHRIC) attempts at what seems to be the right phonological target? In CONNECTED SPEECH (conversations and picture descriptions), can your client keep talking in smooth-sounding sentences, and if they leave words out or use incorrect ones, do those problematic words tend to be content words or functors?

Other test tasks

You'll also test your client's written language a little, usually by first asking them to write their name and some letters of the alphabet; if they can do that, you have them go on and try to write the names of some of the objects and colors in the test pictures.

When you've completed all the subtests that your client is able to do, you enter the scores on a chart (or a computerized version does that for you); the resulting pattern of strengths and weaknesses is their APHASIA PROFILE. If your client's profile of speech rate, speech quantity, repetition ability, comprehension scores, and error types matches a syndrome such as one of the seven classical "Boston" syndromes that we described in Chapter 6, section 6.6, you have accomplished the goal of classifying the aphasia as one of the fluent aphasias (anomic, Wernicke's, conduction, transcortical sensory) or one of the nonfluent aphasias (Broca's aphasia, mixed/global aphasia, transcortical motor). As we said, you will also use the subtest scores plus your impressions of your client's speech patterns to get an overall rating of how severe their language problem is.

In the process of scoring the test, you have begun to collect the kind of information that you would need to start looking at your client's problem psycholinguistically: You have begun to classify their production errors. In the exercises for this chapter, you'll get a chance to think about what those errors can tell you about your client's language problem. Word of warning, though: Understanding the source of an error doesn't tell you what kind of therapy will help. At the present state of the art, the main thing it can do is to tell you what kind is probably a waste of time. But the great research clinics keep trying new ideas, and there has been much progress, especially because new computer-based therapies make it possible for clients to practice their language exercises for hours a day if they have the strength. We do know, now, that relearning language requires training up new neural connections in the brain, and that this requires intensive and extensive practice, and a lot of courage; it's comparable, perhaps, to learning to ski or play the violin at 50 or 60 years of age.

10.2.5 Language problems are not *just* language problems: Executive function abilities and other factors affecting language errors

We've already mentioned one of the cognitive problems that can interfere with someone's performance on language tests—or any other task, for that matter: the ability to pay attention and not get distracted. Paying attention is one of a family of self-control skills that neuropsychologists call EXECUTIVE FUNCTION. Another executive function skill is being able to delay your actions until a signal, or until you are sure you are correct (executive control is weak in children who don't have enough self-control to raise their hand and wait for the teacher to call on them: that's called IMPULSIVITY). The neuropsychologist's report should tell you about your client's executive functioning, or you can get training to do some basic executive function testing yourself.

Other executive functions include being able to plan and carry out a series of different actions, and being able to switch from doing one thing to another when you need to change the kind of response you are making (for example, to change your speaking style when you see that you are not being understood). If you are really bad at executive function, you may keep on doing the same thing over and over again when it's no longer appropriate—this is called PERSERVERATING. People with injury to parts of the frontal lobes may perseverate a lot to fill in for responses that they can't produce; for example, if they have severe difficulties activating the names of objects on a test and they also have a tendency to perseverate, they might come up with one name and then give the same name or a garbled version of it to the next half-dozen items. In the exercises for this section, you'll get a chance to analyze perseveration in terms of spreading activation.

Executive function problems are not the only ones that may make it hard for your client to compensate for their aphasia. Difficulty visualizing an action or an object can seriously interfere with your client's ability to use drawing, mime, or gestures to fill in for their missing words; articulation problems can make it hard for them to say a word to themselves clearly enough to help with remembering its spelling. And as we've already said or implied, motor problems, vision problems, and hearing problems can make communication problems worse.

10.2.6 Language ability and communication ability are not the same thing

We've just seen that someone's communication ability may be quite a bit worse than we would expect from their performance on tests of language ability, because other cognitive systems have to be working in order for people to use their language to understand what other people mean, and to judge whether other people have understood them.

On the good side, some people with moderate aphasia and dysarthric, difficult speech, like Shirley (*Shirley Says: Living with Aphasia*, http://spot.colorado.edu/shirley4.pdf), are very effective communicators. They have good executive functioning, plenty of smarts, and use mime and gesture and perhaps drawing. They often can indicate the first letter or two of words they are hunting for, which is enormously helpful in helping you guess what the word is. They have fairly good comprehension of what they hear if there's not too much background noise or conversation, and you speak moderately slowly and don't change the subject without warning. They can hold onto the topic they want to talk about, and they watch us closely to try to figure out whether we really understand what they are trying to say or are just nodding along trying to be agreeable. Shirley, 80 years old, 4 feet, 8 inches tall and in a wheelchair, caught a well-meaning neurology professor "just nodding along" when he was interviewing her in front of an audience of medical students, and scolded him for it right there; I don't think he tried that again. After all, when someone is just nodding at you without really understanding, they are treating the meaning of what you're saying as unimportant; if you have been busting a gut to explain something to them, that's pretty infuriating. This happens in second-language communication situations all the time, too, and it's hard to deal with.

10.3 "Translating" Language Tests and Some Problems With Bilingual Aphasia Testing

When an aphasic person is (or was) bilingual, which language should they begin therapy in? Often, unfortunately, there's no choice; the available therapists are people who speak only the majority language of whatever country the aphasic person is living in. But if there's an option—perhaps including sending the person to live with family in another country—then it's urgent to know which language is stronger after the stroke and offers the best hope for recovery.

However, comparing someone's language ability in two different languages is tricky. It certainly can't be done by translating the test materials from one language to another, getting someone who knows the other language to test your client on that translated set of materials, and seeing which scores are higher. Why not?

There are two very different kinds of problems with a test-translation approach. The first kind of problem is that when you translate a test, the resulting materials may have some additional unexpected differences from the materials you started with; for example, the translated names for things could turn out to be much harder or easier to pronounce in the new language. The second kind of problem is that different kinds of language have different kinds of opportunities for errors, so that a translated test is going to over-test some areas and miss others entirely. And, of course, creating aphasia tests that will help to classify patients and indicate your client's strengths and weakness in other languages isn't just an issue for bilingual people. In countries all over the world, there are people with aphasia who need services. Standard aphasia examinations have been created for most of the languages of Europe, Japan, and parts of China and India, but a lot of the world has no remedial materials and no aphasia examinations. Much needs to be done, and it's not simple to do. Let's look at some of the specifics of the two kinds of problems we just mentioned: unexpected differences between the original and the translated materials, and the two languages having different kinds of opportunities for making errors.

"Translating" a naming test

Let's start with a very simple-looking task, choosing the items to be pictured for a naming test, and look at some of what can go wrong if you start from a naming test that's been created for North American English speakers. Remember that a naming test has to have its items in approximate order of difficulty, so that you can go quickly through the part that's easy for your client, or perhaps skip it, and get to where their problems start to show up. But at least three different things contribute to the order of difficulty: the frequency of the word, the phonological difficulty of pronouncing it, and how hard it is for someone to recognize it from a picture. Word frequency can be checked easily if there's a good-sized computerized collection of written language, and pronunciation difficulty can be judged fairly well by experienced language professionals, but sometimes it's hard to determine whether a picture is easy to recognize—or to misperceive. How all three factors will interact to make a given test item easy or hard is complex.

So what happens if you send a set of Philadelphia Naming Test pictures for a colleague to use in examining clients in Taipei? Each of the now-familiar steps from recognizing a picture to pronouncing its name might raise different obstacles for a person from Philadelphia naming it in English and a person from Taipei naming it in Taiwanese Mandarin. Frequency of the word might differ across languages and cultures, and we know that word frequency plays a role in pretty much every process involved in producing a word (it even affects how easy it is to recognize an item in a picture). Orchids are commoner than roses in humid, subtropical Taipei; American footballs are rare, abacuses are common. So the Taipei naming test needs its items in different orders, and some American items will have to be replaced entirely.

Second, as we've said, there's the effect of phonology. For example, a word that's hard to say in English, like *rhinoceros*, is *xi niu* in Mandarin; there is nothing difficult about its sounds for a Chinese speaker. And third, the pictures that were drawn for Philadelphia might slow up the recognition for a client in Taipei; although *dog* might be a good test item in both languages, a "typical" dog in Taiwan doesn't look like a "typical" dog in America (here, it's usually a golden retriever, in case you are wondering). So the dog picture would have to be redrawn. You get the idea: A naming test must be revamped and checked for word frequency, pronunciation difficulty, and the appropriateness of its drawings for each language and culture that will use it.

"Translating" a repetition test

Repetition tests cannot be translated. You have to start from scratch in each language, figuring out a sequence of items from easy to hard, because there are so many factors—pragmatic, semantic, syntactic, morphological, and phonological—that contribute to how hard it is to repeat a particular item. For the fun of it, here's an example of a possible repetition test item in Mandarin that would be useless in English, the tongue twister *si shi si zhi shi zi,* "forty-four lions." Would anybody translating a test of articulatory control from Chinese into English be literal-minded enough to ask English-speaking clients to say *forty-four lions* instead of replacing it with a comparable English tongue-twister like *She sells seashells*? We'd hope not. But it's good to have a simple example like this around to remind us that if we're making a version of an aphasia test for a speaker a different language (and with the amount of immigration all around the world, people have to do this unofficially all the time), we have to think about what each item on the original test was really trying to get at. Appropriate "translated" items are not translations; they are parallel materials that will get at the same thing that the original test was trying to explore, whether it's articulatory agility or the ability to understand sentences with unexpected combinations of words (like the BDAE's *Pry the tin lid off*).

"Translating" tests of morphology and syntax

When we get to testing syntax and morphology, we may find that tasks that are important for one language may not have parallels in the other one. For Portuguese, Spanish, French, and the other Romance languages, where every noun is either masculine or feminine in gender and the articles and adjectives have to be in the form that matches the gender of the noun, you'd naturally want to check whether a client makes errors in gender agreement. The same kind of task is even harder for Slavic languages and many Germanic languages, which have three grammatical genders—masculine, feminine, and neuter. A test translated from English wouldn't have any task like this, and a test translated from French to German or German to French wouldn't deal with the neuter nouns properly. More problems could arise if you wanted to get a good balance of items in each gender, as many words that are masculine in German, like *der Mond*, the (masculine) moon are feminine in French: *la lune,* the (feminine) moon—and vice versa, like *die Sonne*, the (feminine) sun: *le* (masculine) *soleil.*

In Mandarin and other varieties of Chinese, on the other hand, there is no noun gender and so no noun gender agreement. Even the pronouns are the same for males, females, and things (though the characters for these three pronouns are written with different semantic components— see Figure 10.1). In Mandarin, *ta* means *he, she, it*—and most of the time *ta* is also perfectly fine for *they*, although sometimes the plural form *tamen* is used. Also, Chinese keeps the forms of all of the pronouns constant, whether they are the subject or the object of a clause; to say this in more formal linguistic terms, Chinese has no case-marking on pronouns. So, in Mandarin, *wo* means both *I* and *me*; *ta* means not only *he, she, it*, and *they*, but also *him, her*, and *them*. (Similarly, we use the same pronoun forms for *you* and *it* in English to say both *You want it* and *It wants you.*)

他 *he*   她 *she*   牠 *it*

Figure 10.1. *He, she*, and *it* in Chinese characters; all pronounced /ta/.

In summary, there are major differences across languages in whether their pronouns use separate forms for different genders and cases. These differences have a strong impact on syntax testing. For example, suppose you have a Portuguese test item that gives a choice of a picture of a girl using a pen (*a caneta*, feminine) and another picture with a girl using a pencil (*o lapiz*, masculine) and asks which picture goes with *Ela escreve com ele* (masculine pronoun) and which one goes with *Ela escreve com ela* (feminine pronoun). That's a good test of the ability to use gender knowledge in Portuguese. But if you translate it into English and ask an English-speaking client whether the pen picture or the pencil picture shows *She writes with it,* the question would be meaningless and your client would have every right to be upset.

Or suppose a test item has a picture of a boy chasing a cat, one of a girl chasing a cat, and one of a cat chasing a girl, and you to say to your client *Show me "She chases it."* That's fine—the English sentence matches only one of the pictures. But if this test item is translated into spoken Chinese, the Chinese speech-language therapist is asking her client to show *"Ta zhui ta,"* and that's a correct match for *all three* of the pictures, because the characters for *he, she, her*, and *it* are all pronounced exactly the same—they are all *ta*. So the question of which picture matches *"Ta zhui ta"* is confusing and probably upsetting to a Chinese-speaking client.

Some aphasia tests have been translated without enough attention to between-language differences like these; if you use a test in a language you don't know well, find someone who does know it—a native speaker, if possible—and ask them to go over it and help you throw out any questions that have no right answer, or more than one.

10.4 The Long Road From a Psycholinguistic Idea to a Teaching or Remediation Method

This book should be leaving you full of ideas about how our minds work, and also with the feeling that what teachers do in classrooms and clinicians do in therapy (and what everybody does in testing) isn't very closely related to those ideas. That seems like a bad thing, and in a way, it is. The reasons why people keep on doing things the same way they've always done them are often rather unimpressive. But there are also some good reasons for changing practice slowly. Even ideas that seem to be well grounded, and grounded in theories that make sense, can turn out to be no improvement over tradition when they are translated into real-world practice, for reasons that nobody anticipated. You already know that that's true in medicine—news media often report on promising treatments that passed the early clinical trial phases but turned out to be no better than cheaper, older methods, or even no better than placebos.

The same is true in any area of intervention: If you want to be an innovator or are thinking of following an innovative leader, that's wonderful, but it can be a long haul until your work bears fruit. Why? Let's follow an example of a sensible psycholinguistically based idea (okay, it was my idea) that is still unproven—indeed, untested!—in either teaching or therapy after more than 15 years, and see what some of the problems have been.

10.4.1 Step 1: An idea and where it came from

The idea was this: Specific constructions that are difficult for learners (whether they are delayed L1 learners, normal L2 learners, or aphasic clients) will be learned better if they are taught in a CONTEXT OF USE: that is, in a situation where the learner would really want to express the ideas those constructions are good for. The evolution of this idea, and its justification, draw on most of the material in this book.

From 1995 to 2005, my research team investigated how people with aphasia explain where things are, a task that they can find quite difficult. When things are where they belong, for example, in Figure 10.2 showing a table lamp on a table, we found out that people with nonfluent aphasia leave out prepositions most of the time (*table . . . and lamp*).

But if you ask people with any kind of aphasia to describe a picture where something is in the wrong place, for example, where there's a table lamp on the floor or a footstool behind its chair (Figure 10.3), they usually try really, really hard to tell you where it is, and they can have lots of problems getting it right, like this:

um, uh on the right is . . . light light an' t[ei] tables on on the other half

uh . . . it's on the floor and it should be on the table

The table is uh uh—the—table is in the in the l.lampshade, not on the table.

um, night table and on a dround, lamp.

For a real-world situation where an aphasic person might need to be able to use a preposition, imagine someone in a wheelchair trying to tell a new household helper where to find, say, their private notebook with their daughter's new phone number. If the notebook was *on* the table

Figure 10.2. Lamp on table. Copyright ©
2010 Lise Menn and Michael Gottfried.

Figure 10.3. Table lamp on floor beside table. Copyright ©
2010 Lise Menn and Michael Gottfried.

or the bed, leaving out the preposition would be okay; but suppose it's hidden *under* the bed, *behind* the TV, or in some even less likely safe-keeping place?

Being able to zero in on an appropriate prepositional phrase seems like it might help speakers with aphasia in situations like that. My colleague Gail Ramsberger (a professor of speech-language pathology) and I decided to test the idea—by now we can call it a hypothesis—that if we trained people with aphasia to use prepositions in contexts like the ones where the people in that first study really wanted to use them (describing pictures with objects that were in unexpected places, like a plate under a table), they would learn them faster than if we trained them in contexts where there was nothing remarkable about where the objects were (like a plate on a table; not only boring, but if you left out the preposition and just said *plate . . . table,* someone listening to you would look in the right place anyway).

Why might this idea not work? There are all sorts of reasons—the people with aphasia have too much language damage, there might not be enough training sessions, and so on. And there's one that strikes at the heart of the idea: Sure, normal and aphasic speakers put more effort into describing locations when they are weird. The first time, that is. After you've seen the same weird picture a couple of times, its novelty is bound to wear off. Maybe the urge to explain unexpected locations won't last long enough to make a difference in training. So that's why we have to do experiments before we go out and sell our idea. If this does turn out to be a problem, there might be ways to fix it . . . and so the work continues.

10.4.2 Step 2a: Designing a clinical training experiment

Training someone with aphasia to master a new construction takes time, and if you're trying a new method, you can't just slip it into their regular therapy sessions—it's not ethical to replace a treatment that works with one that hasn't been tested yet. You need aphasic participants who have time to do it outside their regular sessions. Also, if you want to be sure that their improvement (if there is any) is because of your experimental method, it's better to have people who aren't currently enrolled in therapy, because you don't know the possible effect of whatever their regular therapist might have decided to work on.

And as people want their own bright ideas to turn out to be right, there's a problem that we didn't mention in Chapter 5: If the experiment involves face-to-face contact, as this one would, then the therapist who does the teaching shouldn't know the hypothesis that the experiment is designed to test. We couldn't do the experimental therapy ourselves; we'd need to get someone else to do it. Why? Because there's no way to avoid the effects of an unconscious bias in favor of our own idea. For example, we might unconsciously respond with a little more enthusiasm when the aphasic participant supplies the right answer when they are describing the "unexpected" picture than when they are describing the "boring" picture. There's no way to prevent that from happening unless the experimental therapy is being given by a computer or by a person who doesn't know the hypothesis, and computer speech recognition programs are not yet able to judge relative accuracy of speech production for aphasia.

What kind of experimental design would we need to use to test our hypothesis? There are two conditions: training prepositions with expected pictures and training prepositions with unexpected pictures. So we'd need to set up two sets of locative prepositions, Set A and Set B, whose meaning we could clearly show in pictures. Because we wouldn't have any way to be sure that the prepositions and the pictures in the two sets were equally difficult to process, we'd also have to have two groups of participants. The first group of people would learn Set A in the expected condition and Set B in the unexpected condition, and the second group of people would learn Set B in the expected condition and Set A in the unexpected one. Then, if they all did better with the set they had learned in the unexpected condition, we'd know that it wasn't because we had accidentally made one set of prepositions easier to learn than the other set. We would, of course, try to keep the sets of prepositions equal in difficulty, by matching the average frequency of the words in the two sets and making their meanings comparable. Our actual Set A was *behind*, *next to*, and *over*; Set B was *in front of*, *off (of)*, and *under*. (As you see, we had to use some multiword prepositions to get these roughly-balanced picturable lists.)

The typical experiment on normal speakers has at least 10 participants in each condition. But finding 20 aphasic participants with enough time to come to the clinic for several training sessions a week for several weeks is impossible (I don't know of any case, even in the largest cities, where that has been done). And carrying out the training would be a full-time job for several therapists—impossible to fund the personnel for that. Also, because people with aphasia differ from each other in so many ways that might affect whether they can learn a new item, even short-term aphasia studies often don't use groups. When a published paper on aphasia mentions having 10 or 20 participants, it is often (although not always!) a collection of parallel individual studies. This means that each person's performance on a task gets compared to how they themselves performed on other tasks, or the same task under different conditions or at a different time: It's a **MULTIPLE CASE STUDY**. The authors of a multiple case study provide additional information about each participant that may help in understanding their performance (including their age, how long since their brain injury, the severity of their aphasia, and some kind of information about the type of aphasia). You'll remember that studies of normal speakers don't do that—they are GROUP STUDIES, which means that the data from the participants are averaged for each condition and then the averages (and other statistical measures) are compared for each condition.

Okay, now, we have a problem: Two paragraphs ago we talked about how we'd need to have two sets of prepositions, Set A and Set B, and two groups of people with aphasia—one set learning Set A in the expected-picture condition and Set B in the unexpected-picture condition, and the other group learning the two sets in the opposite condition. How can we use "two groups of people" if we can't be sure that the people in one group are really comparable to the people in the other group? This isn't only an aphasia research problem, by the way—it's also a problem for research on new teaching methods in L2 classes when the students have several different language backgrounds and different skills in the target language.

Because of this common problem with getting comparable groups, clinical researchers often use a particular type of training or treatment design that has been developed over the years: a MULTIPLE-PARTICIPANT SINGLE-SUBJECT MULTIPLE BASELINE DESIGN. Let's unpack that: First, let's look at a SINGLE-SUBJECT MULTIPLE-BASELINE experimental design. This kind of design allows us to compare how much each participant individually improves in two or more experimental conditions. That's the "single-subject" part of the name. BASELINE performance on a task is a participant's level of performance before we start their training; that's what we'll compare their post-training performance to.

A typical example of the MULTIPLE-BASELINE procedure is this: First, the clinician who is working with the patient (not us!) tests each person on both sets of materials—here, it's the two sets of prepositions—before they start any training, to establish the baseline for both sets. Then they teach one set of materials, say the Set A prepositions, to Participant 1 in one condition—say the "expected picture" for perhaps five sessions, but they don't teach the other set. At the end of five sessions, they test Participant 1 on both sets again, to get a measure of improvement for Set A plus a new baseline for Set B. (Set B might have improved even though they haven't touched it.)

Now they teach Participant 1 Set B, in the "unexpected picture" condition, for five sessions, and test it again at the end of them. During this time, to keep any gains on Set A from being lost, they don't teach it, but they review it in some low-key way (this is called "maintenance"). Finally, they test Participant 1 on both sets of prepositions again, and compare what Participant 1 got out of learning Set A in the "expected picture" condition to what they got out of learning Set B in the "unexpected picture" condition. The clinician does this by comparing Participant 1's final performance on each set to their baseline performance on that same set. Notice that the clinician uses two different baselines for comparing the participant's performance at the end of the training: The first baseline was Participant 1's performance on Set A at the beginning, and the second baseline was their performance on Set B in the middle, after we had only taught set A. That's what "multiple baselines" means.

Why did we bother having the clinician do that first baseline test on Set B, since we weren't going to use it? Because it allowed us to see whether Set B got better even without being treated. Maybe the ways the clinician treated the Set A prepositions in the dull old "expected picture" condition not only works, but works well enough to generalize from Set A to Set B, which would be wonderful for the participant—who is, after all, also a client.

Are we done? If our Participant 1 did better on Set B, can we conclude that the "unexpected picture" condition was a better learning situation, as we had hypothesized? Nope, not yet. There are two other reasons that this person might have done better with Set B. One we've talked about already: Maybe, in spite of the effort to balance the two sets, Set B is easier. So our clinician needs to start with Participant 2, and switch the conditions in the way we've already described: Go through the same procedure, but now teach Set B first, in the "expected picture" condition, and then Set A, in the "unexpected picture" condition.

If Set A (taught in the "unexpected picture" condition) shows more improvement than Set B (taught in the "expected picture" condition) for Participant 2, can we conclude that the "unexpected picture" condition is better and publish the study so we can move it into clinical practice?

Not yet. There is something else that we haven't yet controlled for (and by the way, this is the point that Prof. Ramsberger and our team have actually reached). Both participants so far have had the dull "expected picture" condition first, and the hopefully more motivating "unexpected picture" condition second. Maybe they just did better on the "unexpected picture" condition because they had gotten a boost from what they learned in the first part of the experiment, the "expected picture" condition? We need our hands-on clinician to get results from two more participants. Participant 3 will, like Participant #1, have the Set A prepositions in the "expected picture" condition and the Set B prepositions in the "unexpected picture" condition, but they'll get treated on "unexpected" Set B first, and then on Set A. And—you could fill this in yourself—Participant 4 will have the same pairing of sets with pictures as Participant 2 did, but they'll be taught Set A prepositions in the "unexpected" condition first, and then set B in the "expected" condition.

If, after all that, the participants all do better on the prepositions that they learned in the "unexpected picture" condition (or if three of them do better and nobody does worse), we can tell our clinician and our participants what our hypothesis was and open the champagne for everybody. Or we could, except that we then have to see whether our results from testing one participant in each of the four conditions hold up with a few more patients (of varied diagnostic types) in each condition. If it does, we would have a good basis for thinking that our procedure will work for most of the aphasic patients most of the time.

10.4.3 Step 2b: Designing an L2 classroom experiment

The same psycholinguistic idea—that people would be better at learning a grammatical form for expressing an idea if they learned it in a context where they actually wanted to communicate that idea—is also plausible in a classroom setting. From very early on in this book, after all, we've talked about the need to get constructions aroused in the real-world context where they'll be needed, like buying a newspaper in another country —not to mention something really scary, like renting an apartment. How would we create a classroom experiment? Here, the ethical issues are less serious, because we know that essentially any kind of practice in using a language helps to teach it. We just have to be sure that our design involves plenty of practice for the students, and the more they actually have to produce the constructions we're trying to teach them, the better.

So let's go right to the two other big questions: What are the variables that we have to control for? What are the logistical problems that we'll be confronted with? We've already mentioned that students in L2 classes have varying skills, and may have varying language backgrounds. The students also may differ a lot in how much they want to learn the language. Is it just a graduation requirement, or are some of them desperate to be able to compete for jobs that require a command of the language? They may also differ in how much time they have to work on it and use it outside of class. Do they have jobs? What kinds of jobs? How many kids are they taking care of? These variations are called **POPULATION VARIABLES** or **DEMOGRAPHIC VARIABLES**. Like the variation between people with different types and severity of aphasia, we can't really control for them; all we can do is to test-teach enough people so that a reasonably broad range of students—a **REPRESENTATIVE SAMPLE**—will have gone through the experimental teaching program. (What a representative sample is supposed to "represent" is the general population of students that you would expect to enroll in a language course roughly like yours.) So that's one logistical component: getting a representative sample of students to participate. But because we seldom have any control over who is in our classes, we usually have to turn this around: we try our method on anyone who enrolls and get information about their demographic status. Then, when we report our study, we make it clear who was in our classes, and make our claims about whether our method has worked very cautiously: This is what we found for these particular people, and those are the only kinds of people that we have learned about. (What's true for a class of Chilean doctors can't be generalized to a class of Korean kindergartners, although it might turn out to be true for the children; you'd need to do another research study, using them as participants, with their parents' permission.)

Another classroom logistical problem is also like one we face in the clinic: Who will be the teacher? And does the teacher know the hypothesis? If you use different teachers for different conditions, differences between those teachers may outweigh the differences between the conditions (especially if some of them are more enthusiastic about helping to test your hypothesis than the others). If you do all the teaching, you can't help being a little biased in favor of your own hypothesis.

How can you design an experiment to compare teaching methods while minimizing unconscious bias effects? Because normal L2 learners can learn much faster than people with aphasia, you can have each person in two experimental conditions at the same time; that way, you could teach all your prepositions in the same lesson, so it should be easier to keep your teaching quality the same for all of them (and you could check that by videotaping yourself and having someone else rate how enthusiastic and how clear you are when you're teaching each of the words). Another thing that's easier about the classroom is that you can get many more participants, enough so that averaging their performances is legitimate, so you don't have to use single-subject procedures. You can teach the whole class three prepositions in the expected condition (that is, with the boring pictures) and three in the unexpected condition (with the weird pictures), let them study, and test them for immediate learning and later, for long-term learning. Next term, you can reverse the conditions, just to make sure that there wasn't something special about the particular pairing of prepositions and conditions that you used.

10.5 Summary/Conclusion

In this final chapter, we've used a lot of what we learned throughout the book to understand a variety of real-world problems: why some very ordinary classroom tasks are so complex for our brains to handle, the difference between reliable tests and valid tests of language ability, how aphasia tests are constructed, how to think about the processing problems underlying some kinds of errors that people with aphasia make on standard clinical tests, some sources of difficulty in extending aphasia tests to speakers of other languages, and why the road from a new idea to clinical or classroom practice can be so long. There are dozens more topics we could look at, but the point of this book is to get you started thinking for yourself about the language problems in your professional or personal world, and thinking about them from a psycholinguistic point of view rather than a purely linguistic, clinical, or pedagogical standpoint. So I'll conclude this chapter by reminding you what it means to look at language problems psycholinguistically—that is, in terms of the way language is understood and created by our brains.

Thinking psycholinguistically about language problems means thinking about them with two things in mind: what language is like and how the brain works. Understanding what language is like starts with getting a basic appreciation of the different levels of language use and language structure, from pragmatics all the way down to phonetics and articulatory gestures. We've sampled the enormous range and detail of information and skill involved in being able to speak, understand, read, and write a language, and we got some perspective on this by looking (a little) at several different languages, not just at English. If you underestimate the complexity of any level of language knowledge, you underestimate the task of your clients, your students, or of programmers who are trying to get computers to react as if they understand spoken commands.

Understanding how the brain works means getting a basic appreciation of how different our brains are from machines that take in chunks of raw material in and grind out a predictable product, how their myriad connections are constantly being strengthened or weakened by new experiences, and how activation comes into a neuron, adds up, and spreads out. And it means appreciating how the strengthening of connections between events happening together or in close succession allows us to pick up on patterns in the language and the world around us, to group objects and events into many cross-cutting types of categories, and to use that information to predict what is likely to happen next. It also means appreciating how those expectations create the top-down processing that is constantly shaping the bottom-up information that we get from our senses, increasing our efficiency when we're dealing with familiar kinds of stimuli, but also making it harder for us to accurately perceive new information (new sounds, new ways of making words, new syntactic patterns) that doesn't match what we have learned to expect.

We started from these basic understandings of language and of our brains, and continued to elaborate both of them as we looked at speech errors: What kind of thing could it be in our heads that makes these mistakes rather than others? Then we got in deeper, following the history of key experiments as they looked at things that happen too fast to be observed in the real world, or that would get swamped by all the other things that happen in natural language use. We saw that psycholinguists need to do experiments and then integrate their results with what happens in real life (which includes the clinic and the classroom), just as ecologists need to bring animals and plants into the laboratory, get to understand them there, and then to look at them again in the real world.

We also stopped to note, at least once in a while, that understanding how people use or struggle with language isn't just a matter of psycholinguistics; that is, it can't be understood by just looking at the knowledge and skills in each individual brain. Our language knowledge and skills are created in an emotional and social context—humans are social animals—and our language problems also need to be looked at in this broader context. But most of that is beyond the scope of this book, which is a beginning, not an end.

We can be more creative and more conscientious language professionals if we think psycholinguistically about what we're doing, why we do it, and how to interpret what our students and our clients respond to what we do. Why do they learn some things and not others? Why do they get confused, and how can we reduce that confusion? Why do they appropriately generalize some of the things that they learn, overgeneralize others, and yet fail to generalize some things to new contexts where they are needed? How can we explain things more clearly, how can we make them easier to remember? Psycholinguistics doesn't give us the answers to these questions on a silver platter, but it does give us some of the picks and shovels that we need for digging them out.

Again: This book is a beginning, not an end.

Acknowledgment. Thanks to Vicky Lai for the Chinese language examples.

Exercises for Chapter 10

10.1. Perseveration—repeating an action or a response when it is not appropriate—is very common in people with brain injury. A specific example mentioned in section 10.2.5 is repeating the name of a picture on a naming test as the response to several pictures that are shown later (particularly likely if the later pictures belong to the same semantic category, such as tools) and another (mentioned in the Glossary) is repeating a double letter in writing not once but many times; for example, spelling need as NEEEE . . .

Explain one of these kinds of perseveration or another one that you know of in terms of spreading activation and response competition within the brain. If you want to do the semantic example, look back at the Belke et al. experiment in Chapter 5, section 5.3.1.

10.2. Write a few paragraphs for caregivers of people with brain injury that clearly explain, with evidence, this statement from section 10.2.1:

> We now know that activities like reading and speaking are complex; they are not single processes that can be carried out in one chunk of brain tissue. Instead they have multiple steps and require input and regulation from many parts of our brains.

If you have access to a university library online or go to some of the links suggested on your CD for Chapter 2, you should be able to find studies from professional journals on the Internet to supplement information from the book.

Sources Consulted

Menn, L., Gottfried, M., Holland, A. L., & Garrett, M. F. (2005). Encoding location in aphasic and normal speech: The interaction of pragmatics with language output processing limitations. *Aphasiology, 19*, 487–519.

Miceli, G., Benvegnu', B., Capasso, R., & Caramazza, A. (1995). Selective disorder in writing double letters. *Cortex, 31*, 161–171.

Revonsuo, A., & Laine, M. (1996). Semantic processing without conscious understanding in a global aphasic: Evidence from auditory event-related brain potentials. *Cortex, 32*(1), 29–48.

Afterword

Other Important Areas for Applying Psycholinguistics

In parting, here are four topic areas where I think that more psycholinguistic thinking and research design would help, areas in which you might be able to help clear away misconceptions, contribute to sensible polices, and get involved in research and product development that could make a difference for literally millions of people, young and old. A lot is being done and there is a lot for you to read about already. These are not new areas of investigation, but much more needs to be done.

First Language Under Stress: Topics in Developmental Difficulty

Politics, ethics, and the diagnosis of first language problems

In dozens of countries around the world, children whose home language is not the language used in schools, and also those who don't speak the majority dialect of the school language, are at a disadvantage in understanding what the teacher is saying and in learning to read. Some of those children who don't speak the teacher's dialect also have developmental language processing problems, but which ones? How can fair and helpful evaluation tools be developed when standardized tests are not available? Or can useful programs be developed for all children who are lagging, regardless of the reason?

415

Developmental processing test design

Developmental tests are like clinical tests: They are designed to show whether a client has a language problem, and they are not designed to give a detailed picture of a person's language processing problems. How could tests, perhaps computer-based tasks, zero in on language processing problems?

The puzzles of specific language impairment and dyslexia

Some children with developmental language disorders have no cognitive, sensory, or motor problems that can be uncovered by the usual clinical tests, or at least, no other problems that are severe enough to explain their language delay. But what a child learns each day becomes information to use in top-down processing, and top-down processing is essential for dealing with the flood of speech sounds and other information that surround us. It seems that minor problems in the way an infant's brain makes and strengthens connections might easily leave her further and further behind. Is this what happens in Specific Language Impairment and/or dyslexia? Can games for young children be developed that would help strengthen the right kinds of connections?

Language, Aging, and Hearing Loss

As people get older, all of our senses seem to work less well. Hearing loss makes it hard to keep up good social connections, but having a good social network is one of the major ingredients in keeping a reasonable level of physical as well as mental health. There's work to be done on improving testing, hearing aids, counseling, and the development of coping strategies for seniors and their families that take advantage of what we have been learning about brain plasticity so that "lip reading" can become an effective supplement to hearing.

Glossary

Note: These definitions and explanations are just sketches of what these words mean; hopefully, they provide enough information so that you can make sense of this textbook as you read it. (Whole books have been written about some of these terms.) You can also find articles about many of them in general dictionaries, medical dictionaries, on-line encyclopedias, and print encyclopedias of linguistics and language disorders. Make sure your sources are recent and reputable. Numbers in parentheses indicate sections where these terms are discussed.

acquired (6.1.0): Acquired disorders are disorders that are caused by damage that happens to a person after they are born; this term is used as the opposite of **DEVELOPMENTAL**.

acquisition (9.0): In **NATIVIST** theories of language development, the term "language acquisition" refers to the way first language develops. Your native language (or languages) are said to be *acquired* with the help of **INNATE UNIVERSAL GRAMMAR**, while later languages are said to be *learned*, with less or no help from this innate ability. In "emergentist" theories of language development, which do not assume that we have an innate grammar, the terms "language learning" and "language acquisition" are considered to be synonyms.

action verb (see also **ACTIVE VOICE**) (6.5.3): A **VERB** that refers to a real-world action. Many grammars focus on action verbs (*hit, kiss, chase, give, run, play, eat,* etc.) as being the most typical, perhaps because they are easy to visualize, but several other kinds of verbs are just as important (see **VERB** for examples).

activate, activation, activation threshold (2.3, 2.4, 3.1, 3.3, 3.4, 4.1, 4.2, 4.3, 5.6.1, 6.2, 6.4.1, 6.4.2, 6.4.3. 6.5.2, 6.5.4, 8.1.2, 8.2, 8.4, 8.7.3, 8.8.2, 9.1.1, 9.1.3, 9.2, 9.2.1, 9.5.2, 9.7, 10.3): Neurons pass electrical impulses from one to another; this process and the impulses themselves are called **ACTIVATION**. Activation that comes into the **DENDRITES** of a neuron from multiple sources at about the same time adds up (unless some of the information coming in is INHIBITORY.) We say that a neuron is ACTI-VATED (or has reached its ACTIVATION THRESHOLD) when it has gotten enough total activation to send new electrical impulses along its AXON.

active voice (1.7.2, 5.2.4, 6.5.3, 8.2): For almost all English ACTION VERBS (verbs that describe one person doing something to another person or a thing, like *kiss* or *carry*), the active voice form is the one where the person doing the action is the SUBJECT of the verb: *Joe **carried** the baby, Susie **is opening** her mail*. The active voice contrasts sharply with the PASSIVE VOICE, where the person or thing being acted on is the subject and the person doing the action may not even be mentioned. In English, passive voice forms are made using the verb's past participle (the verb form used after "have") plus forms of the verb "to be," or, in informal language, "to get": *The baby **was carried** (by his father). The martini **must be shaken**, not stirred. My car **got towed***. Verbs also have other voices, but introductory grammars of most languages deal only with active and passive. Non-action and intransitive verb forms usually are classed as "active" if they are formed in the same way as the active voice of action verbs (*Ollie is **sleeping**, Ella was **running***), pas-sive if they are used with the same "be" or "get" forms as passive action verbs (*Sam **was overheard***).

addressee (1.6.2): See SENTENCE ADDRESSEE. The person that a speaker is talking to, or that a writer has in mind as the reader.

adjective (1.4, 8.2, 8.5.1): An adjective is a word that is not a NOUN and that gives additional information about (MODIFIES) a noun (*the **red** house, an **ancient** monument, her **three** children, the music is **lively***). (In English, nouns frequently also modify other nouns; see MODIFIER.) To be rigorous, we have to state this with more attention to the difference between a word and its REFERENT, that is, the thing the word means. So: An adjective is a word that is not a NOUN and that gives additional infor-mation about the person or thing that the noun refers to. ARTICLES and POSSESSIVE PRONOUNS also modify nouns, but they are different enough from adjectives to be put into another category, DETERMINER.

adverb (3.3.3): "Adverb" is a rather loose category of words in English grammar; what adverbs have in common is that they MODIFY words that are not nouns. Some adverbs modify VERBS (*run **quickly***), some mod-ify ADJECTIVES (***very** bright*), and some modify sentences (***Truthfully**, we're broke*).

affricate (1.2.2.2): You make an affricate speech sound like this: First make an ORAL STOP (a complete oral closure). Then release it slightly so that the air that was dammed up behind it makes an airstream friction noise (a **FRICATIVE**) as it escapes. English has two affricates, /tʃ/ (the sound of *ch* in *church*) and /dʒ/ (the sound of the *j* and of the *dge* combination in *judge*).

Agent (1.2, 3.4, 4.1.2, 5.4, 6.4.3): Agent is a **SEMANTIC ROLE** or function, not a **SYNTACTIC** term. The Agent of an action verb is, in clear cases, a person or animal that carries out the action on purpose (voluntarily): ***Chris*** *sang,* ***Bruce*** *bought some steak.* The boundary between agents and other people or things that cause events to happen is fuzzy, and depends on how many categories of causes a linguist wants to set up; it's especially a problem when something might or might not have been an accident. "Agent" is sometimes used for the subjects of sentences like these: *The* ***wind*** *knocked down some trees;* ***George*** *dropped his laptop.* The subjects of sentences like, *The* ***broom*** *bumped the lamp; The* ***knife*** *cut my hand* are **INSTRUMENTS**, not **AGENTS**. The subjects of *The* ***plane*** *landed safely* and *The* ***car*** *hit the truck* are usually called Agents, for lack of a better word.

agraphia (8.8.2): Difficulty in writing due to brain damage that happens after a person has learned to read and write normally. Also called "dysgraphia."

agrammatic aphasia (6.6): Nonfluent aphasia syndrome; nearly synonymous with **BROCA'S APHASIA**.

agree, agreement (1.6.2): If a word has several forms (e.g., a singular and a plural or a **MASCULINE** and a **FEMININE**) and another word that is used in the same construction must also be used with the same category of form (must also be singular, must also be masculine), then we say that the two words must agree or be in agreement. In English, the most obvious example of agreement is between the **SUBJECT** noun or **THIRD PERSON PRONOUN** and the verb or **VERB PHRASE** of a main clause: *The boy* ***is*** *going, The boys* ***are*** *going; The clock* ***strikes***, *The clocks* ***strike***. We also have number agreement between two of our **DETERMINERS** and the nouns they modify: ***This*** *clock,* ***These*** *clocks;* ***That*** *hat,* ***Those*** *hats*. Most languages of Europe have much more agreement than English, but most languages of East Asia have less.

alexia (8.8.2): Difficulty in reading due to brain damage that happens after a person has become a skilled reader.

allophone (1.2.5.2, 9.1.1): One of the ways a particular **PHONEME** can be pronounced in a specific language. Two sounds are allophones of the same phoneme if they never **CONTRAST** and if speakers treat them as two ways of saying the same sound. In English, the alveolar **FLAP** sound [ɾ] is an allophone of the phoneme /t/ (as in *matter*) and also of the phoneme /d/ (as in *madder*).

alveolar ridge (1.2.2): The gum ridge that holds the tooth sockets in the upper and the lower jaw. As a POSITION OF ARTICULATION, it always means the gum ridge behind your upper teeth; see Figure 1.2.

alveolar stop, alveolar fricative, and alveolar liquid (1.2.2.2): A STOP, FRICATIVE, or LIQUID made by bringing the tip or BLADE of your tongue touching or close to the alveolar ridge (of the upper jaw). English /t, d, s, z/ and "light" [l] are alveolar consonants.

alveopalatal (1.2.2.2): The POSITION OF ARTICULATION between ALVEOLAR and PALATAL; English FRICATIVES /ʃ, ʒ/ and AFFRICATES /tʃ/ and /dʒ/ are alveopalatal. This position also may be called postalveolar, prepalatal, or palatoalveolar.

ambient language (7.2.0): A person's ambient language is one that they hear spoken around them much of the time. There may be more than one.

anomia, anomic aphasia (6.6): Difficulty in finding the CONTENT WORDS needed to name pictures and refer to people and things in conversations. Everyone who has APHASIA has anomia to some extent. If anomia is the most noticeable and troubling aspect of a person's aphasia, the BOSTON SYNDROME classification system describes them as having anomic aphasia.

antonym (3.3.2): As in school grammar, the antonym of a word is a word that means its opposite (*day/night*; *cold/hot*).

aphasia (6.0, 6.6): Aphasia, as used by researchers and in this book, means an ACQUIRED language disorder due to LOCALIZED brain damage. Stroke is one of the major causes of aphasia, and thousands of people become aphasic every year. Clinicians dealing with people who have acquired language disorders because of massive head injuries (motorcycle accidents) or diffuse brain injury (Alzheimer disease) also call their clients' language problems aphasia; children who have developmental language problems are sometimes said to have *dysphasia*. British clinicians sometimes use the term *dysphasia* where Americans would say *aphasia*.

AphasiaBank (6.3.0): AphasiaBank is a Web-based data resource housed at Carnegie Mellon University. If you have a bona fide interest in studying aphasia, you can apply to them via the Web for permission to access their collection of audio and video recordings of people with different kinds of aphasia in various languages.

aphasia profile (10.2.4): Because people with aphasia have strikingly different patterns of ability and disability, diagnostic aphasia tests give their results in terms of a profile of scores showing the client's abilities in comprehension, content word finding, syntactic structure production, FLUENCY, and repetition, and sometimes also other aspects of communication with language.

aphasiologist, aphasiology (6.1.2): Aphasiology is the study of aphasic language and how to improve the language abilities of people with aphasia. Aphasiologists are researchers with backgrounds in speech-language pathology, psychology, linguistics, cognitive science, or neurology who specialize in aphasiology.

apraxia (2.4.3, 10.2.2): A person has apraxia if they can't mime or carry out a movement or set of movements that they once would have been able to do, such as blowing out a candle or hammering a nail, even though they still understand what they are supposed to do and still have voluntary control of the muscles needed to do it. Being unable to mime or demonstrate such actions when there's no real candle or hammer in view is much more common than being unable to do them when the objects or instruments are really present.

apraxia of speech (10.2.2): A person has apraxia of speech if their speech motor control appears to be disordered even though the muscles are capable of making all the necessary movements and coordinating them. It is not the same as DYSARTHRIA, but a client may have both dysarthria and apraxia of speech. The BOSTON SYNDROME classification does not recognize apraxia of speech, but most speech-language pathologists find it a useful way to describe the problems of people who can pronounce short words correctly but have more and more difficulty as the length of the word increases. In our model, the problem might be due to something that interferes with maintaining the information in the PHONOLOGICAL BUFFER (4.3.1).

apraxia, oral (2.4): A person has oral apraxia if they have APRAXIA for motions involving their mouth or tongue (blowing out a candle, licking their lips, smiling), again, they can't carry out the action or they do it abnormally, even though they demonstrably understand the request and have control of the needed muscles. A person may have oral apraxia and yet be able to speak normally, or may have apraxia of speech without any oral apraxia.

articulator (1.2.3. 7.5.1): Any part of your mouth that is used in producing speech. The lower articulators include your lower lip and all of the parts of your tongue from TIP to ROOT; the upper articulators include your upper lip, upper teeth, all of the points on the roof of your mouth, and the back wall of your PHARYNX. When you make a GLOTTAL STOP or GLOTTAL FRICATIVE, your GLOTTIS also acts as an articulator.

articulatory feature (1.2.3, 7.4.1): A term describing which articulators we use to make a speech sound (BILABIAL, ALVEOLAR, GLOTTAL, etc.), whether/how much the airflow is obstructed (STOP, FRICATIVE, etc.), the path of the airflow (NASAL, ORAL), whether the VOCAL FOLDS are vibrating (VOICED, VOICELESS), and other row and column labels on the IPA CHART.

aspect (of a verb) (6.4.2): In English, information about whether the action expressed by the verb is ongoing (*is singing*) or completed (*sang, has just sung*), or other information about the time course of the action; some languages have richer systems and express more aspectual information directly on a verb than English does.

auditory memory, short-term auditory memory (7.1.4): Memory for the exact words or sounds that a person has just heard. The fuller term is "short-term auditory memory."

axon (2.2): An axon is the slender branch of a NEURON that carries electrical signals (ACTIVATION) to the other neurons that receive neural impulses directly from it. Each axon ends in SYNAPSES that link it to the DENDRITES of the neurons that receive activation from that axon.

behaviorist school of psychology (10.2.1): The group of psychologists, notably J. B. Watson and B. F. Skinner and early psycholinguist Charles Osgood, who tried to account for human and animal behavior in terms of reflex-like connections, completely avoiding concepts like "mind" and "thinking."

bilabial (1.2.2.2): Any speech sound articulated with both lips. In English, the bilabial sounds are /p, b/ and /m/. Spanish has the VOICED bilabial FRICATIVE /β/, but English doesn't.

blade (1.2.2): The part of your tongue just behind the very tip. See Figure 1.3. English /t/, /d/ and /s/ are made using your tongue blade as the lower ARTICULATOR and the ALVEOLAR RIDGE as the upper articulator, in contrast to French and Spanish, which use your tongue TIP and the back of your upper teeth to make these sounds.

blend, blend error (3.3.3): A speech error that seems to combine parts from two words (usually, two words that would both be appropriate to say at that moment), or from two (usually appropriate) phrases; for example, *Help all you want!* blending *Help yourself!* and *Take all you want!*

blind spot (5.1.1): The small area just off-center in your retina where the optic nerve connects to it. The blind spot has no rods or cones, so it can't respond to light. You don't experience any blanks in your visual field for two reasons: The blind spots in your two eyes correspond to different parts of your visual field, so one makes up for the other, and also, your brain fills in the missing information on the basis of the rest of what you perceive (TOP-DOWN PROCESSING). You can easily find demonstrations of this on the Web.

Boston classification (of APHASIA), **Boston Diagnostic Aphasia Examination** (6.6, 10.2.4): A system of grouping aphasia symptoms into seven major SYNDROMES, largely shaped by the work of neurologist Norman Geschwind and psychologists Harold Goodglass and Edith Kaplan, working in Boston starting around 1960, and made practical by the successive editions of the Boston Diagnostic Aphasia Examination (BDAE), beginning with Goodglass and Kaplan in 1973.

bottom-up processing (2.5, 3.1.1, 5.1.2, 5.5.2, 6.5.0, 8.1.2, 8.3, 8.4, 8.6, 8.9, 9.3.2, 9.7): Processing based directly on sensory input from your eyes, ears, skin, etc. Pure bottom-up processing probably almost never happens in an experienced organism; it's always modified by TOP-DOWN processing based on previous experience and/or built-in processing mechanisms.

bound morpheme: See MORPHEME

brain (2.1, 6.0, 6.6): Your brain is your body's main information processor, composed of billions of massively interconnected nerve cells. In this book we focus on the parts of the brain that are relatively recently evolved (the neocortex), but everything we do also depends on the smooth working of much older brain structures that we share with other animals, such as the brainstem. See Figure 2.1

Broca's aphasia (6.6): A NONFLUENT (slowed-speech) aphasia, named for early neurologist Paul Broca, although it is not the same kind of aphasia that he originally described. People who show all of the symptoms of Broca's aphasia have limited ability to understand and produce grammatical structures, use fewer FUNCTION WORDS and a smaller variety of BOUND GRAMMATICAL MORPHEMES than normal speakers, use short or one-word phrases (except for some idioms and very frequent phrases like *I don't know*); don't speak much better when they are imitating than they do on their own; and have relatively good comprehension of CONTENT WORDS. Broca's aphasia is one of the classical SYNDROMES (collections of symptoms) of the BOSTON CLASSIFICATION. The term "agrammatic aphasia" is sometimes used interchangeably with Broca's aphasia, depending on the author. YouTube has an excellent example of a speaker with Broca's aphasia; Google "youtube aphasia geschwind" and watch the second part of the video, in which Dr. Geschwind talks with a client named Mr. Landry, who had been a lawyer before his stroke.

Broca's area (2.7): A small part of the lower FRONTAL LOBE on the left side of brain, next to the area that controls face and mouth movements, one of the classical "language areas." See Figure 6.2. Older texts describe Broca's area as responsible for grammar; current work suggests that its importance for grammar may come from the fact that it is heavily involved in getting items into the correct places in complex structures. Broca's aphasia often involves injury to Broca's area, but several other parts of the brain usually are involved as well, and there is no neat correlation of where brain injuries are and what the language symptoms are.

buffer (4.1.1, 5.4): In models of brain function, a temporary storage area for any kind of information, such as the words you are about to say or the sounds you have just heard. (Waiting rooms, inboxes, and laundry baskets are real-world buffers.)

canonical babble (7.4.2, 7.5.1): Babble with a clear consonant + vowel syllable structure; the sounds may be repeated ([mamama . . .]), varied ([bagigu . . .]), or be one-syllable utterances.

cascade model (4.1.1, 5.4): A model of speech production or comprehension in which each processing step is taken as soon as possible instead of waiting for units like words or phrases to be completed. Early models of language comprehension suggested that people waited until the ends of clauses to start processing their meaning, but EYE-TRACKING experiments now show that we don't even wait for the end of a word before we start to process its meaning.

case (of a noun, pronoun, adjective, or article) (6.4.3): The term "case" is a syntactic term, not a semantic one. It is used in two basic ways in grammar. It can mean the syntactic role that a NOUN or PRONOUN has in a clause; for example, being the SUBJECT or OBJECT of the clause. Or it can mean the morphological form of the noun or pronoun (and of modifiers that AGREE with it) that helps to determine its syntactic role; for example, the pronoun *they* is nominative case, used for subjects in English, while the pronoun *them* is accusative (also called "objective") case, used for OBJECTS OF VERBS and of PREPOSITIONS in English.

case-marking postposition (10.1.2): Japanese and many other languages have POSTPOSITIONS, words that do the same sorts of jobs that prepositions do in English and most languages of Europe, but which come after a noun phrase (*Kyoto-toward*) instead of before it (*toward Kyoto*). In Japanese, some of the postpositions show whether the noun phrase that they follow is the SUBJECT (*Mariko ga*) or the OBJECT (*Mariko o*) of the clause; these are the case-marking prepositions.

case study (6.4.1): A study that looks at the behavior of each PARTICIPANT as an individual. Case studies are important when there are many differences between participants that are likely to affect the way they respond to a test task, a treatment, or a curriculum. Researchers try to make up for the small size of the set of people they are studying (often just one person) by providing enough information about that person and how the testing was done so that valid comparisons can be made when similar work is done with other participants at some later time.

categorical perception (5.5.1): The tendency to perceive speech sounds or other stimuli that are near the boundaries of a perceptual category (e.g., a sound that is halfway between a perfect example of a /b/ and a perfect example of a /d/) as belonging to one category or the other instead of being ambiguous, *plus* having a sharpened ability to discriminate between sounds that are near a category boundary if one is slightly on one side of it and the other one is slightly on the other side.

category concept (5.3.1): As we are using it in this book, a category concept is a concept (like "animal" or "food" or "tool") that includes many quite different individual kinds of things (all the kinds of animals, all the kinds of edible things, all the kinds of tools).

causative construction (10.1.2): A grammatical CONSTRUCTION that links an action and something or someone that caused that action to happen; for example, *Susie **made** Ella clean her room.*

cell (5.3.1): (in an experimental design chart) A division in the design chart that represents a single condition in the experiment. See EXPERIMENTAL CONDITION.

cell body (2.4): The main part of any cell in an animal, containing its NUCLEUS.

central sulcus (6.6): The deep, roughly vertical groove (SULCUS) separating the FRONTAL LOBE of your brain from the PARIETAL LOBE. See Figure 2.1.

character (1.1, 8.7, 8.9): In a logographic writing system, like Chinese, a character is a unit of written language corresponding to one MORPHEME of the spoken language. Many very common CONTENT and FUNCTION WORDS in Chinese are written with just one character, like 牛 *cow*, but most Chinese words are COMPOUND WORDS containing two morphemes, so they are written with two characters, like 犀牛 *rhinoceros*; some contain three or more morphemes and are written with the corresponding number of characters.

CHILDES (7.1.1): The Child Language Data Exchange, a database for transcripts and recordings of child language materials (mostly parent-child conversations) from many languages hosted at Carnegie Mellon University (http://childes.psy.cmu.edu/). Anyone with a serious interest in language development may apply for on-line access to these materials and the programs that have been developed at CMU for analyzing the data.

child phonology (7.5.3): The patterns of children's speech sounds as they start to learn to pronounce the words of the language(s) around them. See also PHONOLOGY.

circumlocution (6.3.0): Using a descriptive phrase, like *the place in the place I used to get food,* to substitute for a name or other word that a speaker can't find (the speaker's target was the name of a supermarket); especially characteristic of ANOMIC APHASIA and of the language of elderly speakers.

citation form (of a word) (1.9.2): The way a word is pronounced when we say it slowly and distinctly; this may be quite different from the way we say it in ordinary speech.

clause (1.6.2. 3.3): A syntactic unit that contains at least a VERB and its SUBJECT, like *Ella called* (or a verb with an "understood" subject, like *Get* *down!*). It is not clear whether some very short utterances like *Help!* are clauses—if "help" is a noun here, it's not a clause, but if you think it has the same structure as *Help me!*, it is a clause.

clitic (8.1.3, 8.5.3): A MORPHEME in the "gray area" between FREE MOR- PHEMES and BOUND MORPHEMES; examples are the English possessive morpheme and the casual forms of *is* and *has*, written *-'s* as in *She's here!* and the Romance reflexive pronouns like French or Portuguese *se* in *Il se léve*, Portuguese *Ele se levanta* "He stands up." A clitic is like a bound morpheme because it seems always to be attached to some other word, and it may change form depending on the nearby sounds in the word it is attached to. But most clitics also are like free mor- phemes (words), because other words can be put between the clitic and the word that it logically should attach to; for example the English possessive *-'s* may be a long way from the noun it marks, as in *The kid up the street's new bike*—the bike belongs to the kid, not the street. Many clitics are written as CONTRACTIONS.

coarticulation (1.2.1.2, 4.3.2): Pronouncing part of two different sounds in a word at the same time; for example, in saying *tube*, ROUNDING your lips for the upcoming /u/ while you are making the /t/. Good coarticula- tion is essential for smooth, normal pronunciation. In teaching reading, coarticulated sequences of consonants (especially at the beginnings of words, like the /pl/ of *please*) are, quite reasonably, called "blends."

cochlear implant (3.1.2): An electronic device attached to the skull with wires leading to the cochlea (the sound-sensing organ of the inner ear) that can send partial information about sounds to the auditory nerve. Cochlear implants do not give nearly as much information about sounds as normal hearing does, but they give enough for profoundly deaf infants to learn to speak and function well in school, and for older people who have previously had adequate hearing to interact fairly nor- mally with people speaking their language.

code-switching, code-mixing (9.5.2): In conversations between peo- ple who share knowledge of two or more languages, combining words and structures from two or more of their shared languages. Just put- ting in a few nouns from one language into a sentence in the other language, for example, *I can't take any more of this* mishigass, *I'm leaving,* is the simplest form of code-switching (*mishigass* = Yiddish for "craziness").

Cognitive Grammar (7.2.4): A theory of grammar that starts from the ideas that the purpose of SYNTACTIC STRUCTURE is to convey meanings from one person to another, and that language is organized to make this process reasonably efficient and accurate.

competing hypothesis (5.2.3): Another possible explanation besides the one that you originally thought of for the way people (or other things) behave.

compound word (1.4.5, 8.1.2, 8.7.2): A word made from two or more other whole words (plus perhaps additional MORPHEMES), like *babysitter* or *birthday*.

conditioned sound change (8.1.3): A sound change that may or may not happen to a particular PHONEME, depending on the sounds near it, whether it is in a STRESSED syllable, or other phonological factors.

conduction aphasia (6.6): One of the aphasia SYNDROMES in the BOSTON CLASSIFICATION system. People who have all the symptoms of conduction aphasia have problems repeating what is said to them that are much worse than can be explained just on the basis of their problems in understanding and producing sentences. Typically, they have clear **pronunciation** but much difficulty in getting out the sounds of words in the right order, and the longer the word, the greater the difficulty.

confounding variable (5.3.1): In a psychology experiment, a factor that is not what you want to examine but that might be a cause of the behavior you are observing. For example, if you are testing the hypothesis that long words are harder to remember than short words, and you just pick a list of long words and a list of short words for people to try to remember, it could be that your long words are rarer than your short words or that their meanings are harder to picture than your short words, or perhaps there's some other difference. If you can't or don't set up your lists so that such other possible factors are the same for both lists, one or more of the other factors is a confounding variable and may invalidate your conclusions.

conjunction (1.4.2): A word used to connect two other words or two constructions; for example, the word *or* in the sentence *Are you driving the red Chevy **or** the blue Honda?* and the word *because* in the sentence *He's upset **because** you left without him. And* and *or* are coordinating conjunctions, and *because* is a subordinating conjunction; if you're interested in this distinction and why it's worth making, see a major grammar of English or an encyclopedia of linguistics. (The Wikipedia article, at least as of April 2010, is not very good.)

connected speech (6.4.2, 10.2.4): Typically, a story or other kind of narrative, or a long turn in a conversation, that is, a turn composed of several UTTERANCES in a row by one person. Older research about language production often used the term "spontaneous speech" to refer to descriptions of pictures like the Cookie Theft or explanations (*Tell us how you became ill; Explain how you would change a tire*) that an examiner would request of a patient, because patients had more choice in creating these utterances than when they were asked to name pictures, give short answers to questions, or imitate. The term "connected speech" is used now, because there's usually little or nothing that's "spontaneous" about responding to an examiner's question.

construction (7.2.3, 8.1.2. 8.2): A meaningful pattern of words; that is, an association of a specific pattern of words with a meaning. Constructions may have very specific meanings (the X-er, the Y-er = if the amount of X-ness is larger, then the amount of Y-ness is larger, as in "the more, the merrier"), or very general (see the discussion of the meaning of the construction Noun-transitive verb-Noun in the text).

content morpheme, content word (1.4.1, 3.1.1, 8.7.2): A content word is one that has meaning ("content") on its own, or that does not link other words in a phrase or CLAUSE together. Most NOUNS, VERBS (except LINKING VERBS and MODALS), ADJECTIVES, and many ADVERBS are content words. Although most words in a language are either content words or FUNCTION WORDS (FUNCTORS), some words, like greetings and exclamations (*hello, ouch! dammit!*) are neither, and some, like LOCATIVE ADVERBS/PREPOSITIONS/PARTICLES in English (*in, out, up*) seem to be in a gray area between the two categories. We use the term content morpheme for a BOUND MORPHEME that is highly meaningful, like the *can-* of *canine* or the *fel-* of *feline*; we know that those parts of those words mean "dog" and "cat" even though they can't be used in English without an ending like *–ine* or *–id*.

context of use (10.4.1): The real-world setting in which you would use a word, a formula, or other linguistic structure, for example, buying something, apologizing, trying to land a plane.

contraction (8.5.3): In standard English ORTHOGRAPHY, a contraction is two or more words written together without a space between them, using an apostrophe (') for the letters that are omitted, in order to represent CLITICS in the spoken language more accurately: *can't, haven't, I'd've, that's* (as in, *That's all, folks*). The term also is used for words spelled with apostrophes that no longer seem separable as stem + clitic because their pronunciation has changed over time: *don't, won't*.

contrast (1.2.5): In phonology, two speech sounds (PHONES) contrast with each other if you can find two different words, for example, *wing* and *ring,* that sound exactly alike except that one of them has one of these sounds and one of them has the other sound. If two phones contrast, like English [r] and [w], they belong to different PHONEMES, and speakers need to be able to hear and produce the difference between them. Examples of two phones that do not contrast in English are the

[t] in *top* and the [t] in *stop*. Your CD demonstrates the difference between them, but it's very hard for native speakers of English to hear or control this difference in speech. These two speech sounds belong to the same phoneme in English, but in Thai, they contrast.

control (5.2.3): This word is used for two slightly different key concepts in designing experimental studies, both concerned with making sure that the factor that the researcher is "wiggling" (varying) is really what is causing the change in what the PARTICIPANTS do or what is happening in their brains. When "control" is used for some of the STIMULI in an experiment (the words to be remembered, the sentences to be repeated . . .), it usually means the stimuli that are less tricky and more like what participants might encounter in the real world. When "control" is used to refer to some of the participants in a psycholinguistic study (*the controls, the control subjects*), it means the people who are taken to be normal speakers or who are asked to respond to the control stimuli.

Experimenters also say that they have "controlled for" variables that might affect how the participants respond to the experimental stimuli—that is, they have tried to make sure that these variables can't explain the differences in how the participants respond. For example, experimenters control for the number of years that the participants have studied a particular language by making sure either that they have all studied it for the same amount of time or that each group of participants contains a very similar mix of people who have studied it for different amounts of time.

conventional, conventional phrase (6.3.0, 7.5.3): Something is conventional if it's agreed on by some social group as the right way to do something. In this sense, all words of a language are conventional: the speakers agree that *dog* means a particular kind of animal, and so on. Beyond that, to say that a word or phrase is "conventional" means that it is the usual way to express a particular meaning in a language as it's spoken in a particular time and place, especially one that is used so much that other ways of saying what ought to be the same thing sound weird. Politeness phrases tend to be very conventional; for example, *May I be excused? Good morning, everybody.* (Notice that *Lovely morning, everybody* means something different.)

conversational turn (6.3.0): In a conversation between two or more people, everything that one person says in between the times when another person talks. If people interrupt each other, their turns overlap. A turn may also be a nonverbal sound (a laugh, a grunt) or a gesture (a shoulder shrug, a nod, a raised eyebrow, a point). People with language problems may rely on gestural turns, which is a major reason that videotapes are needed to evaluate their communication abilities.

Cookie Theft picture (6.3.1): The picture used for the "picture description" task in the *Boston Diagnostic Aphasia Examination*. It shows a complicated household scene, and one of its strengths is that it's not just a scene of disconnected activities. This means that it makes fairly complex cognitive and linguistic demands—it can't be properly described without mentioning what is about to happen, what the people in it are thinking, and what they are trying to accomplish.

copula (7.2.1) See LINKING VERB.

corpus (6.4.1): A database of writings or transcribed spoken language that can be studied by researchers. The plural form is either English "corpuses" or Latin "corpora" (stressed on the first syllable: /ˈkɔrpɔrə/). Large shared on-line corpora have made an enormous improvement in the quality and kind of work linguists can do.

critical period hypothesis (9.0): The idea that there is a restricted "critical period" early in a person's life when learning language (or other essential and intricate skills) must take place if it's going to happen normally. Compare SENSITIVE PERIOD HYPOTHESIS.

deep orthography (8.1.3, 8.3, 8.9): A writing system that shows the MORPHOLOGICAL relations between words relatively clearly in spite of sound changes that might make them hard to recognize, because the system has preserved old spellings instead of updating them to match changed pronunciations. French is very deep, preserving many final consonants and vowels that are no longer pronounced (*petit*, "small," masculine form, pronounced [pɛˈti]; *petite*, "small," feminine form, pronounced [pɛˈtit]). English is also deep, preserving spellings of sounds that have not been pronounced for centuries in standard English, like the *gh* in *light*. However, English spelling is not just deep, it is also IRREGULAR, which makes it harder to learn to read than any other language spelled with the Roman alphabet.

definite article (1.4.2): In English, the word *the*, and roughly equivalent words in other languages, for example Spanish *el, la, los, las*. Using the definite article with a noun shows, roughly, that the speaker is thinking of a particular example of that noun and that he or she expects the hearer to know which one they are talking about: *The moon, **the** gold medalist in the downhill event, **the** President at the beginning of World War II*. Definite articles belong to the class of words called "determiners," which also (for English) includes INDEFINITE ARTICLES, possessive pronouns (*my, their*) and demonstrative pronouns (*this, that, these, those*).

demographic variable (10.4.3): Any factor that may make some of the people you are studying different from the others in the way they react to your stimuli or are affected by an injury, such as native language, years of education, age, or gender. Same as POPULATION VARIABLE.

dendrite (2.2): Dendrites are the highly-branched input-side extensions of neurons. The name comes from *dendros*, the Greek word for tree (as in *rhododendron*, literally, rose-tree).

dental, dental stop (1.2.2.2): A position of articulation involving your teeth. English /d/ and /t/ are sometimes called dental stops, even though they are usually made with your tongue touching the ALVEOLAR RIDGE a little behind your teeth, because "dental" is a shorter and more easily understood word. Spanish, French, and Italian /t/ usually really is dental, not alveolar.

dependent variable (5.2.3): In experimental design, what the researchers measure to test their hypothesis, for example, how long it takes participants to push a button in response to a STIMULUS, or how quickly they can read a sentence with a particular structure. Compare INDEPENDENT VARIABLE.

derivational morpheme (1.4.4, 8.1.2, 8.6, 8.7.2. 8.9, 9.2.3): A BOUND MORPHEME (i.e., a meaningful part of a word that can't be used by itself) and seems to make a new word when it's attached to another word or morpheme. Some English examples are the *-ful* of *cupful*, the *-tion/-sion* of *creation* and *tension*, the *un-* and the *-able* of *unbelievable*. Compare INFLECTIONAL MORPHEME.

developmental dysphasia: See DEVELOPMENTAL LANGUAGE DISORDER (6.1.3)

developmental language disorder (6.1.3): A language disorder that apparently occurs without being caused by an identifiable injury or disease as a child is learning his or her first language, presumably because the brain is not developing normally. This term also may be used for language problems associated with more general developmental disorders such as autism or Down syndrome.

developmental psycholinguistics, developmental psycholinguists (7.1.4): Research that studies how language develops in children; the people who do that kind of research. For historical reasons, no distinction is made between studies where researchers only observe and analyze children's language (you might expect those folks to be called "developmental linguists") and those who do experimental studies.

devoice, devoicing (7.5.3): Producing a speech sound that is normally voiced without the normal vocal fold vibration. Especially common at the ends of words (**FINAL DEVOICING**).

diacritic (1.2.6): A mark can be added to letters or other phonetic symbols, to change or to show more detail about the sound that symbol represents. Accent marks, tone marks, cedillas (as in *façon*), and many other diacritics are used to extend what alphabets and syllabaries can show about pronunciation.

dialect (1.9.3, 8.5.2, 8.9): A dialect is a specific way of speaking a language that is used by speakers from a particular place, ethnic group, or social class. We all speak some dialect of our native language(s), but, if our way of speaking is close to a national standard, we usually think that other varieties are "dialects" and that our own way of speaking is just "the language." In many (but not all!) cultures, for that reason, it's insulting if you say that someone is speaking a dialect, and sociolinguists use the term language variety instead. (If you're from the United States or Canada, you would probably not be thrilled if someone from Australia said that you speak the North American dialect of English instead of saying simply that you speak North American English, or an American variety of English.)

Whether a way of speaking is a national language or "just a dialect" is a political matter, not a linguistic one. There is a classic and only slightly humorous definition of a dialect that everyone should know: "A language is a dialect that has an army and a navy" (Max Weinreich, translated from the original Yiddish).

differential diagnosis (10.2.2): Diagnosis of the disorder or disease affecting a client, with specific attention to which of several similar-looking disorders the client might have; for example, schizophrenia or severe WERNICKE'S APHASIA.

diffuse (6.1.2): Diffuse brain damage is damage widespread throughout or to many parts of the brain; the opposite is FOCAL brain damage.

diphthong (1.2.4.3, 8.3): A sequence of two vowel sounds produced in the same syllable; English has the diphthong phonemes /ai/ as in *ride,* /ɔi/ as in *boy*, and /ei/ as in *eight.* We also tend to say the vowel /o/ with a movement towards /w/ at the end, /ow/. Try not to use this term for a sequence of vowel letters that really spell one fairly constant vowel sound, like the *ea* sequence in *read*.

directional preposition (1.4.2): A preposition that says where its object (see OBJECT OF A PREPOSITION) is going to or coming from: *in the garage*, *over the moon*. Because these words have real meanings and also connect their objects to the rest of the sentence they are in, they are in the "gray area" between CONTENT WORDS and FUNCTION WORDS. Many (but not all) of the English directional words also can be directional ADVERBS (when they have no objects: *Take it out!*) and verb PARTICLES (when they have no objects and little or no directional meaning: *Eat it up!*)

diminutive ending (9.1.2): In English, the very common ending spelled *-ie* or *-y*, used to make nicknames for children, like *Debbie, Mikey*, or to modify other words for things we want children to feel comfortable with, for example, *doggie, baffy* (for *bath*). Many other languages, including Italian, Spanish, and Russian, have a much richer set of diminutive endings than English does.

distractor task (5.2.3): To keep participants in an experiment from thinking about the stimuli for a while, or to make it harder for them to respond, experimenters may ask them to do a task that has nothing to do with the experiment itself, like counting backward or moving a cursor to follow a moving point on a screen; these are distractor tasks.

dysarthria, dysarthric (6.2, 6.6, 6.7.2, 10.2.4): A person has dysarthria (or is dysarthric) if he or she has problems getting the articulators (tongue, lips, velum) to the right place at the right time. As a result, their speech sounds clumsy or mushy and may be incomprehensible. Dysarthria is a motor problem, but it is often found in people with aphasia because the part of the brain that controls the movements of our articulators is close to some of the areas that are essential for processing language. A dysarthric pronunciation that is so far off the target that it appears to be an entirely different speech sound may be impossible to distinguish from a **PHONOLOGICAL PARAPHASIA** (the substitution of an incorrect target phoneme).

dysgraphia: See **AGRAPHIA**.

dyslexia (8.8.1): Developmental difficulty in learning to read that is not explained by low intelligence, evident vision problems, or evident hearing problems.

dysphonia (10.2.2): Abnormal vibrations of a speaker's vocal folds, giving his or her voice a strained, hoarse, whispery, or otherwise distracting quality.

elicitation task (6.3.1): A language production task that an examiner or researcher asks clients or research participants to carry out in order to check their abilities and to see what kinds of language production problems they have. Commonly used tasks: describe a complex picture, name a set of pictured objects, retell a fairy tale, describe how to do a familiar task such as making a peanut-butter-and-jelly sandwich. Another common elicitation task is **ELICITED IMITATION**.

elicited imitation (= repetition) (7.1.5, 10.1.2): Asking someone whose language you want to study to repeat what you have just said. This task is very sensitive to all kinds of limitations in a person's language ability; however, it can take quite a bit of work to figure out which limitation is causing the differences between what you said and what the person trying to imitate you managed to say.

empty preposition (1.4.2): A preposition that seems to have no meaning of its own, but just serves to link its object with the rest of the clause. The English preposition *of* is always empty—any meaning that it has is derived from the meanings of the words it links plus what we know about their real-world relationship (compare the meanings of *of* in *a cup **of** milk, a heart **of** stone, the heart **of** a problem*). Other prepositions vary in how much meaning they carry in a particular situation. In general, the easier it would be to guess a word if it were missing, the less meaning it has: compare *I saw the girl _____ brown hair*, where you can fill in the gap with near certainty, to *She left _____ her notebook*, where you could fill in either *with* or *without*, plus other words that aren't prepositions at all, like *them*.

encode (3.5, 4.3.1): In psycholinguistics, to "encode" a meaning means to find the words and SYNTACTIC STRUCTURES needed to express it appropriately in language (spoken, written, or signed).

entrenched knowledge (9.1.1, 9.8): A skill or way of doing things that has become very strongly established in your brain and is very hard to change, such as the way you make speech sounds in your first language(s).

error analysis: In clinical linguistics and NEUROPSYCHOLOGY, to study a person's mistakes (and correct answers) on test tasks in order to figure out where his or her processing difficulties are, instead of just looking at test scores.

error of omission (9.4): The mistake of leaving out a speech sound, MORPHEME or word.

evaluative (6.4.2): An evaluative word or phrase is one that expresses the speaker's attitude towards something; aphasic speakers who can't give much information about an event or a picture may give evaluative responses (*That's all right now*) by way of taking a conversational turn.

event structure (3.2.1, 3.6.1, 4.1.2, 5.2.4, 10.1.2): In semantics and cognitive grammar, the way a real-world event is broken up into clause-sized pieces at the MESSAGE LEVEL so that it can be put into syntactically organized clauses; for example, you could analyze a fight between two cats into "Tigger chased Snowball/ Snowball went under a chair/ Snowball turned around/ Snowball hissed at Tigger," where the event structures could be called, respectively, Transitive Action/ Intransitive Directional Motion/ Intransitive Rotational Motion/ Intransitive Oriented Action. A different set of event structures describing the exactly same scene might be "Tigger chased Snowball under a chair/Snowball faced Tigger / Snowball hissed at Tigger" with structures Transitive Directional Motion/Transitive Static/ Intransitive Oriented Action.

According to the CASCADE MODEL of sentence production, as each event structure is created at the Message Level, it arouses the LEMMAS and SEMANTIC ROLES that will be needed at the FUNCTIONAL LEVEL (which is where it starts to be ENCODED into language).

excitatory (2.4), **excitatory neuron** (2.2): In describing the roles of neurons in the brain or other parts of the nervous system, neuron A is excitatory if the activation it sends to the next neuron down the line B if a signal from A increases B's level of activation. The opposite of excitatory is INHIBITORY.

executive function (6.8, 9.5.2, 10.2.5): A general term for the set of cognitive abilities that we need to keep track of and control our own actions, including the ability to plan the order that we need to do things in, to remember whether we have done them, to stop doing them and then come back to them if something else has to be done in the meantime, to notice whether what we are doing is having the effect we intended, and to modify what we are doing if it's not accomplishing what we had in mind.

Experiencer (7.2.4): The SEMANTIC ROLE label for a person or animal affected by an action or an event. The syntactic SUBJECT of an ACTIVE VOICE SENSORY VERB, for example *Jon* in ***Jon** liked the chocolate*, is an Experiencer (not an AGENT).

experimental condition (5.2.4): In designing an experiment, we need to "wiggle" something—more formally, to vary the STIMULI in some way and see how participants' behavior changes (unless our experimental design is to compare how two different groups of participants behave with the same set of stimuli). For example, we might ask participants to type some handwritten material into a computer while listening to music and while listening to a recording of speech; these two situations would be the called experiment's two conditions.

experimental procedure (5.2.4): Exactly what the participants in an experiment are asked to do; for example, to listen to stimulus sentences through headphones and push a button whenever they hear the sound /s/.

experimental subject (5.2.1): See PARTICIPANT

explicit knowledge (1.9.1): Information that you know you have and that you can put into words or communicate without actually showing someone how to do it, for example, the directions for getting to your home from where you work. The opposite is IMPLICIT or TACIT knowledge.

expressive aphasia (6.6): See BROCA'S APHASIA. This term is not used in the Boston classification.

eye-tracker (5.1.1, 5.4, 5.6.2): A computer-plus-hardware set of equipment that bounces a tiny beam of infrared light off your cornea to detect where you are looking. Eye-trackers have become essential tools for studying how people compose and understand words, phrase, and sentences.

false memory (5.2.4): A memory of an event or a scene that a person feels actually happened, but which, in fact, never took place. False and true memories cannot be distinguished by any known kind of test.

false positive (5.2.4): A mistaken "yes" response in an experiment to a question, for example, "Have you heard this word before?" or "Is this stimulus the same as the one you just heard?"

feature (1.2.3, 5.5.2,): See ARTICULATORY FEATURE

feminine gender (1.10.1): There are two overlapping meanings of this term. In a natural gender system, feminine gender words are nouns and pronouns that specifically refer to female beings; for example, words like *she, her, goddess, lioness, woman*. In GRAMMATICAL GENDER systems, which are found in many languages, especially in the IndoEuropean and Semitic language families, genders are grammatical categories of nouns that correspond only roughly to biological categories. Feminine grammatical gender includes words that refer or modify many biologically female creatures, but not necessarily all of them, and may also include words for objects that are not alive; for example, French *la chaise blanche*, "the white chair," using the feminine definite article *la* and the feminine form, *blanche,* of the adjective meaning "white."

filler: A word or a conventional hesitation noise that a speaker uses to get more time for planning their utterance; for example, *Well, Oh, uh, er . . .* A speaker also may deliberately use fillers in order to sound more tentative or less well rehearsed.

final devoicing (7.5.3): Pronouncing a word that should have a voiced final consonant with the corresponding voiceless consonant. This is a change that children often make in attempting to produce words (see also DEVOICING).

filler stimulus (5.3.1): In experimental design, it is often important to keep the participants from figuring out what the experiment is looking for, because that would affect their responses. To obscure the patterns in the experimental stimuli (the ones whose responses will be analyzed), the experimenters may put in many other stimuli whose responses will not be analyzed. For example, if you wanted to know whether people tend to re-read false statements more often than they re-read true statements, you might mix a large number of filler sentences that are neither true nor false in with your true and false sentences.

flap (1.2.5): In phonetics, a speech sound that is made with a quick flip or tap of the tongue. English has a very frequent alveolar flap PHONE [ɾ]; for American English speakers in casual speech, this is the sound spelled *tt* in *pretty*. The flap is very common in normal rate and fast speech, but it is not a PHONEME by itself; it is an ALLOPHONE of either /t/ or /d/.

fluent (6.6): A technical term in APHASIOLOGY, not to be confused with the ordinary meaning of the word "fluent." Fluent aphasic speech is defined as speech with clear articulation, normal-sounding use of function words, and with phrase length and INTONATION CONTOURS that sound normal except for pauses to try to remember content words. The fluent aphasias in the Boston system are ANOMIC APHASIA, CONDUCTION APHASIA, TRANS-CORTICAL SENSORY APHASIA, and WERNICKE'S APHASIA. Speakers with the first two of these aphasias would not sound "fluent" in the everyday sense of the word; people with anomic aphasia have many pauses for finding CONTENT words, and people with conduction aphasia make multiple attempts at producing long words, hesitating at the beginnings of the words and often scrambling their sounds.

focal (6.1.0): In describing brain damage, focal damage means damage that is restricted to a well-defined part of the brain, and affects some cognitive abilities while leaving others in fairly good shape or even unaffected. The opposite is *diffuse* or *distributed* damage, which will have a general impact on most or all cognitive processes.

formula (4.1.3, 7.2.4, 9.1.3, 9.4); **formulaic utterance** (7.2.4): In linguistics, a CONVENTIONAL EXPRESSION, especially one that leaves a slot or two where the speaker can insert an appropriate word, for example, *I'm happy to be in the fine city of* <CITY NAME> *this* {*morning, afternoon, evening*}.

frame: See VERB FRAME.

free morpheme: See MORPHEME

frequency (1.2.2.1): In acoustics, the rate of vibration of a sound source, usually described in terms of the number of vibrations per second. Higher pitched sounds have a higher frequency, that is, they have more vibrations per second than lower-pitched sounds.

fricative (1.2.2.2): In phonetics, a sound made with airstream frication, like /s/ or/f/; voiced fricatives like /z/ and /v/ have both airstream friction and vocal fold vibration.

frontal lobe (2.1, 6.6): Each HEMISPHERE of the brain is divided into four parts called lobes, which are separated by relatively deep grooves. Your right and left frontal lobes are the farthest forward; they are located directly behind your forehead.

Fronting (7.5.3): In phonetics, making a speech sound using a position of articulation that is closer to your lips. A common kind of fronting, both in young children and in people with some varieties of dysarthria, is using an ALVEOLAR or perhaps a PALATAL speech sound instead of a VELAR sound, for example, saying [tar] for *car*.

functional brain imaging (10.2.1): Making an image of the brain that shows where brain activity is taking place. There are several kinds of functional brain imaging, some looking at blood flow and some at the electrical activity of the brain's neurons; more and more sensitive functional imaging methods are being developed.

Functional Level (of speech production) (3.2, 4.0, 4.1, 5.2.4, 5.4): The first linguistic stage in the production of a clause. In the model of speech production that we are using, the functional level is the one where word LEMMAS are ACTIVATED and TAGGED with their SEMANTIC ROLES.

function word, functor (1.4.2): A function word is a word whose main job in a sentence is to link other words together or to provide very general information about another word. Function words in English include **DEFINITE** and indefinite **ARTICLES**, **CONJUNCTIONS**, **EMPTY PREPO-SITIONS**, **LINKING VERBS**, **MODALS**, and **PRONOUNS**. See **CONTENT WORD** for comparison.

garden path sentence (5.1.2, 8.1.2): A sentence whose early words set you up to think that it has a particular structure, but then its later words don't fit that structure, so you have to stop and rethink how it could all fit together and make sense. Newspaper headlines, like the infamous *Squad Helps Dog Bite Victim* and the more recent *McDonald's Fries the Holy Grail for Potato Farmers, Violinist Linked to JAL Crash Blossoms* (cited by Ben Zimmer in the *New York Times Magazine*, January 31, 2010), are particularly likely to be garden path sentences, because their style of omitting random function words and capitalizing all **CONTENT** words makes it harder to tell which words are being used as nouns and which ones as verbs.

glia, glial cell (2.2): The other major kind of cell in the brain besides **NEURONS**. Until recently, glia were thought to provide just structure and support for the neurons, but there are now hints that they play some more active role in brain function.

glide (1.2.4.2): The English glides are /j/ (*yod*, the sound of *y* in *you*) and /w/. In phonetics, a glide is a speech sound that is produced with the same mouth and pharynx shape as a **HIGH VOWEL** (a vowel that has a very small airflow channel, like [i] or [u]), but is being used as a conso-nant, not as the **NUCLEAR VOWEL** of a syllable. If you keep making a glide sound without changing the position of your articulators, the glide will morph into the corresponding vowel sound; /j/ will sound like /i/ and [w] will sound like [u].

global aphasia (6.6): The most severe aphasia syndrome, with major dam-age to all language modalities in both comprehension and production.

glottal pulse (1.2.2.1): A single puff of air from your lungs that pushes out through the **VOCAL FOLDS** during **VOICING**. If you are making a **VOICED** sound with a fundamental frequency of 200 Hz (200 cycles per second), that means that your vocal folds are releasing 200 tiny puffs of air per second, flapping closed briefly after each one.

glottal stop (1.2.2.1): The consonant made by bringing your vocal folds tightly together so that they close your glottis completely. Like all **VOICE-LESS STOPS**, there is no sound during this closure; you only can tell that someone is making a glottal stop by its effect on the sounds before and after it.

glottis (1.2.2.1): The opening between your **VOCAL FOLDS**. Changing the tension and position of your **VOCAL FOLDS** controls how much air flows through the glottis, from none (during a **GLOTTAL STOP**) to free airflow (during quiet breathing). See also **VOICING**.

Goal (3.2.2, 5.4, 8.1.2): A SEMANTIC ROLE: the destination of something that is moving; for example, the objects of the prepositions in the prepositional phrases *to **Alabama**, onto **the floor***. Sometimes new or intended owners (like the objects of the prepositional phrases *to **Mary**, for **George***) are also called Goals, and sometimes they are called RECIPIENTS. Semantic role labels are capitalized to mark that they are being used in a technical sense.

grain size (8.1.2, 8.1.3, 8.3, 8.9): In analyzing spelling (and many other things), the size of the chunks of raw material that we use as units to analyze our raw data. Choosing the right grain sizes can make patterns much easier to find. In English spelling, we understand that learners should be taught to read using grain sizes that are sometimes bigger than single letters, notably the two-letter units like *sh*, *ch*, *th* that spell single phonemes, but the regularities that appear when we look at larger grain sizes like *igh* and word-final *igm/agm* are often overlooked. French also has large "grains," like *eau* (= /o/).

grammatical gender (1.10.1, 9.2.2): Many languages, especially in the IndoEuropean and Semitic language families, have a GRAMMATICAL GENDER system. Genders are grammatical categories of nouns that correspond only roughly to biological categories; for example, in French, boy (*le garçon*), bridge (*le pont*), and the sun (*le soleil*) are masculine gender, but woman (*la femme*), chair (*la chaise*), and the moon (*la lune*) are feminine. In a language with a full-fledged grammatical gender system, every noun has a gender; articles and adjectives that modify a noun must have the same gender form as the noun (must AGREE with it), and pronouns that refer to it must also have that gender (although this rule weakens for pronouns that are not in the same sentence).

grammatical morpheme (9.5.1) An INFLECTIONAL morpheme or a FUNCTION WORD (FUNCTOR). Most grammatical morphemes have little or no content, but instead give information about how words in a phrase or clause are related to one another

grapheme (8.1.2, 9.7, 10.1.3): Briefly, a letter of an alphabet; more precisely, the class of all the possible ways of writing/printing a letter of an alphabet, regardless of typeface and whether it is capitalized or lowercase.

grapheme-phoneme correspondence (8.1.2, 8.1.3, 8.4. 8.5, 8.8.1, 8.9, 10.1.3): A rule linking a GRAPHEME to how it is pronounced. Readers may have been taught these rules explicitly, may have figured them out, or may only know them subconsciously.

graphemic buffer (10.1.3): In psycholinguistic models of the process of writing, typing, or spelling aloud, the "place" where the letters that the word has activated "wait" until it is their turn to be produced. Models need such a "place" in order to explain errors of getting the letters in the wrong order or doubling the wrong letter in a word.

Great Vowel Shift (8.1.3): In the history of English, the huge change around the year 1400 in how vowels (especially long vowels) were pronounced, so that the pairs of long and short vowels written with the same letter (for example, long *a* and short *a*) no longer sounded similar to one another. The Great Vowel Shift also put the English spelling system out of step with the orthographies of other languages that use the Roman alphabet.

group study (10.4.2): A study that compares the responses of people who belong to different groups, for example, people with different kinds of aphasia or people who have studied a second language in different kinds of curricula. The responses of the people in each group are averaged together (for example, the scores of third-year students in traditional L2 immersion programs versus the scores of third-year students in dual-immersion programs) instead of being analyzed as individual CASE STUDIES.

hard palate (1.2.2): The hard part of the roof of your mouth; behind it is the soft PALATE (VELUM), which is cartilage. You can use your tongue to explore how far back your hard palate extends and where your soft palate begins. See Figure 1.1B, and also the color version of it in the Materials for Chapter 1 on your CD. In phonetics, the word "palate" used by itself means the hard palate.

harmonics (1.2.2.1): Most natural sound sources, for example, your vocal folds, the strings of a stringed instrument, or the air inside a wind or brass instrument, produce complex vibrations, that is, sounds composed of with many different vibrations at the same time. The lowest FREQUENCY of vibration is the sound's fundamental frequency (which we basically experience as the pitch of the sound), and the others are its harmonics.

hemisphere (of the brain) (2.7): The outer layer of the brain has a clear front-to-back dividing groove that divides the brain into left and right sides; these two parts are called its left and right hemispheres.

heritage language learner (9.2.2): A person who comes from a family where a particular language was once spoken but who did not grow up using that language. Most heritage language learners are from immigrant families or native minorities, but some are re-immigrants returning to the country of their parents or grandparents with little or no knowledge of its language.

high vowel: (See also VOWEL.) A vowel made with your tongue fairly close to the roof of your mouth. The highest vowels in English are [i] and [u]; next highest are [ɪ] and [ʊ]. These four speech sounds are called the English high vowels.

hyperdistinct speech (8.5.3): The extra-clear speech that people use when they are pronouncing words as carefully as they can, for example, when they are teaching new words to someone.

hypothesis (5.2.3): In experimental design, the carefully expressed, explicit version of the idea that the experiment is designed to test.

Illinois Test of Psycholinguistic Ability (ITPA) (10.2.1): An influential standardized test of people's ability to use language.

imperative (6.4.2): The form of a verb used for giving direct commands (*Scram!*); an imperative clause is one whose main verb is imperative (*Open the door*; *Get out of there now!*).

impulsivity (10.2.5): General difficulty in controlling impulses to respond to things immediately. We expect to have to teach small children not to be impulsive (not to grab for cookies, not to put all kinds of things into their mouths), but impulsivity caused by certain kinds of brain damage in adolescents or adults is a long-term problem.

indefinite article (1.4.2): In English, the word *a/an* as in *I want* a *new hat*, typically indicating that you know the kind of thing you are talking about, but not exactly which one. You could also say this if you know which one you want, but you don't expect your ADDRESSEE to know which one you have in mind. The plural indefinite article is *some*, as in *I need some new shoes*. See also DEFINITE ARTICLE.

independent variable (5.2.3): In experimental design, the thing that you "wiggle" (i.e., vary systematically) so you can see its effects; for example, if you want to test the hypothesis that it is harder to read words in a scrambled line (*the the cat dog chased*) than the same words in a grammatically correct and semantically plausible sentence (*the cat chased the dog*), your independent variable would be "word order." Compare with DEPENDENT VARIABLE.

inference (5.2.4): In psycholinguistics, information in someone's mental model of a situation that wasn't directly stated in the information that they were given; for example, if a child reads a story that starts *Angie's daddy said goodnight and closed the door*, the writer of the story probably expects his young reader to make inferences such as: it's Angie's bedtime, the door is the door of her bedroom, her daddy expects her to sleep with the door closed, and so on.

infinitive marker (1.4.2): In English, the function word *to* when it is used before a verb form with no ending, as in *I have too much to do*, **To fail** *is not an option*.

inflectional morpheme (1.4.3, 7.2.3, 8.1.2, 8.6, 8.7.2): A BOUND MORPHEME (that is, a meaningful part of a word that can't be used by itself) that adds information without changing the word's basic meaning, signals how the word is used in its clause, or marks its AGREEMENT with another word in the clause. In English, the noun plural ending, the noun possessive ending -'s, the verb past tense ending, and the verb progressive -*ing* ending are inflectional morphemes, and so the are the irregular changes in nouns that mark them plural (as in *woman, women*) and the irregular changes that mark verb past tenses and past participles (as in *sing, sang, sung*).

inhibition (2.2): Inhibition is anything that stops or slows down activity —it "puts on the brakes."

inhibitory, inhibitory neuron (2.2): An inhibitory NEURON is one that sends out signals to reduce the amount of ACTIVATION in the neurons that it connects to.

innate (7.2.0): Relating a characteristic of a living organism, "innate" means genetically preprogrammed, like eye color or anatomical structure, with the environment providing only the minimal support that is necessary for the organism to develop normally. The term is also used for abilities that may be determined genetically, such as a baby's ability to suck or to cry, with the environment playing only a life-maintaining role. There is no question that the brain structures that make language possible are innate, and we also know that our brains require early interaction with users of a spoken or signed language for those brain structures to develop and work properly. The deep controversies about language innateness concern how much else about language is innate, and how much depends on the environment.

intake (7.1.2): The part of the ambient language input that a learner can actually make use of. "Intake" clearly includes whatever the learner picks up on and responds to immediately, but learners also develop some expectations about the new language slowly and subconsciously, so we could consider what they learn subconsciously to be part of their intake also.

interactive activation (8.1.2, 10.1.3): If a model of how our brains work has activation that flows both BOTTOM-UP and TOP-DOWN, so that our past experience can affect (interact with) the information that we perceive, it is called an "interactive activation" model. See Figure 8.1.

interdental (1.2.2.2): The POSITION OF ARTICULATION where the tip your tongue is between your upper and lower teeth, as in the English phonemes /θ/ (the *th* of *think*) and /ð/ (the *th* of *this*).

International Phonetic Alphabet (IPA) (1.2, 8.1.3): A set of alphabet-based symbols for the vast majority of the speech sounds of the world's languages, standardized and occasionally updated by the International Phonetics Association. Their home page is at http://www.langsci.ucl.ac .uk/ipa/, which has a link to the current version of the **IPA CHART**; the last update was in 2005. Links to these pages are on your CD under Materials for Chapter 1.

Internal Review Boards (IRB) (5.2.1): Every academic and medical institution in the United States that gets federal research money has an Internal Review Board, which must make sure that any research done by people who work for the institution meets ethical standards following national guidelines.

intonation, intonation contour (1.4.3, 8.1.1, 9.1.1): The rise and fall of voice pitch (the FREQUENCY of vibration of your vocal folds, *not* the loudness of your voice) in speech production. We recognize some rise-fall patterns as intonation contours appropriate to our native language. These contours may indicate that what someone has said is a complete statement, exclamation, or question (which we would punctuate, respectively, with a period, an exclamation point, or a question mark if we were writing them down). We recognize other intonation contours as indicating that the speaker has trailed off without completing his or her thought (which we might punctuate with a comma, a dash, or three dots) or as interrupted.

IPA: See INTERNATIONAL PHONETIC ALPHABET

IPA chart (1.2.3): The standard two-dimensional arrangement of the INTERNATIONAL PHONETIC ALPHABET. All sounds in the same column have the same PLACE OF ARTICULATION; those in the same row have the same MANNER OF ARTICULATION.

irregular, irregular noun, irregular verb (1.4.3): "Irregular" in grammar means not following the most general pattern or patterns of morphology (changes in word forms). English irregular nouns are the few that make their plurals by doing something other than adding *-s/-z/-es*, like *man, woman, child*, and *ox*. English irregular verbs are a large set, but most of them clump into little groups with "subregular" patterns. Some of those, like *keep/kept, sleep/slept* are only slightly different from the regular verbs that add *-ed*; other groups, like the *sing/sang/sung, ring/rang/rung* group, are quite different from the regular verbs.

irregular orthography (8.1.3, 8.3, 8.5, 8.7.3, 8.9): A writing system in which you cannot tell how a word will be pronounced by looking at how it is spelled. Every writing system probably has a little irregularity, but English has the most irregular Roman-alphabet-based writing system in the world.

ITPA: See ILLINOIS TEST OF PSYCHOLINGUISTIC ABILITY

jargon (7.5.3): In early child language (and also in APHASIOLOGY), "jargon" means utterances that make no sense, but that sound like speech in their INTONATION, loudness, and timing patterns, and that the adult or child producing them seems to expect you to understand by the way they make eye contact with you and how they gesture.

kana (8.7.2, 9.7): A symbol representing a consonant plus a vowel or just a vowel in the Japanese SYLLABARY, which supplements the Chinese-based KANJI characters in the Japanese writing system. There are two parallel sets of kana: *hiragana,* basically used for native Japanese words, and *katakana,* used for words borrowed from Western languages.

kanji (8.7.2, 9.7): A Chinese-based character in the Japanese writing system.

labial, labial stop, labial fricative (1.2.2.2): A speech sound made using at least one lip. The English speech sounds /b/, /p/, and /m/ are labial STOPS, and because we make them using both lips, they are also called BILABIALS. The English fricatives /f/ and /v/ can be called labial fricatives or LABIODENTAL FRICATIVES (see LABIODENTAL). However, the Spanish fricative spelled either *v* as in *Havana* or *b* as in *Cuba* is made with both lips, so it's a BILABIAL fricative; it's written in **IPA** with the symbol /β/ (the Greek letter "beta").

labiodental (1.2.2.2): A speech sound made using your upper lip and your lower teeth. It's hard to make a STOP in that POSITION OF ARTICULATION, but easy to make a FRICATIVE.

labiovelar (1.2.4.2): In a labiovelar speech sound, the airflow from your lungs is restricted or blocked at two places: your lips are close together or touching each other, and at the same time the back of your tongue is raised close to or touching your VELUM. In English, /w/ is a labiovelar GLIDE. The consonant sound at the beginning of *quit,* which we usually write as /kw/ in **IPA**, is a labiovelar STOP, because the /k/ and the /w/ are essentially simultaneous.

language area, language sensitive area (2.7, 6.5.1): Usually, this means the parts of our brains that have long been known to be involved in language comprehension and production: BROCA'S AREA, WERNICKE'S AREA and the long-distance connections between them. Modern FUNCTIONAL BRAIN IMAGING technology shows that many more parts of our brains are involved in language processing, and that the traditional language areas process other kinds of information in addition to language, so some neurolinguists are replacing the term "language area" by the more cautious term "language sensitive area."

language disorder (6.1.1): A difficulty in processing language; someone with a language disorder may or may not have accompanying motor problems in producing speech, sign, or writing. Vision problems and deafness obviously also may interfere with language processing, but they are not language disorders, although they may be adding to the problems of people who have them in addition to a language disorder.

language innateness (2.5): See INNATENESS.

language typology (1.10): Classifying languages by the grammatical and phonological structures that they use; for example, as grammatical gender languages, or as tone/tonal languages. The other way of classifying languages is by whether they are historically related to each other. Related languages may be typologically similar, like Spanish and Italian, or rather different from one another, like English and German.

larynx (1.2.2): The "voice box," the whole sound-producing structure in your throat at the top of your trachea, including the cartilages in front and back, the VOCAL FOLDS, the muscles that control them, and the GLOTTIS (the opening between the vocal folds). See Figures 1.1 and 1.4. There are more good images and diagrams on Wikipedia.

latency: See RESPONSE LATENCY

lateral (1.2.4.2): Anything relating to the side of something; in phonetics, specifically, a sound made by keeping the TIP or BLADE of your tongue touching your teeth or a point on the roof of your mouth, while you allow air to escape from your mouth behind that contact by flowing out over one or both sides of your tongue. The [l] that we say at the beginnings of English words like *light* or *look* ("light L") is a lateral speech sound, but in making the "dark" ALLOPHONES of the English /l/ PHONEME, IPA [ɫ], often found at the ends of syllables, your tongue doesn't touch the roof of your mouth, so strictly speaking, dark [ɫ] is not lateral. Using dark [ɫ] where English requires light [l] is a very common articulatory problem for children, and it was also a characteristic of the speech of actor Peter Falk, best known for the TV detective series *Columbo*.

left hemisphere: See HEMISPHERE (of the brain).

lemma (3.2.1, 3.6.1, 4.1, 4.2, 4.3, 5.2.2, 5.2.4, 5.3, 5.4, 5.6, 6.4.1, 6.4.2, 6.5.4, 8.1.1, 8.1.2, 8.2, 8.4, 8.8.1, 8.8.2, 10.1.3): In current models of language processing, the semantic and grammatical information in your brain about each word that you know, but not the phonological or ORTHOGRAPHIC (word form) information, which appears to be stored separately.

lexical decision (5.6.1): A task used in many psycholinguistic experiments: Participants briefly see a word or a set of letters that looks as if it might be a word, and they are asked to decide whether what they see is a word or not. Usually, they are asked to push a button if what they see is a word; sometimes they are asked to push one button if it is a word and a different button if it's not.

lexical retrieval (3.1.1, 5.3.2, 5.4, 6.4.1); same as "retrieving a word": This term has two slightly different meanings in models of language processing, but they both involve arousing the LEMMA of a word (or morpheme). In language comprehension, it means understanding a word that we hear or see, which happens when the sound, sign, or letters activate the lemma enough so that it activates the concept that it corresponds to. In language production, it usually means succeeding in thinking of both the lemma and the form of the word we need to express a concept.

linking verb (7.2.1, 7.2.3, 7.2.4): A verb that connects the SUBJECT of a CLAUSE with information about it, like English *be, become, seem* in sentences like *Sarah **is** on the stage, Sarah **became** a violinist, Sarah **seemed** excited*. Linking verbs have very little meaning in themselves, so that the most common ones behave like FUNCTORS. They are often omitted by people with NONFLUENT APHASIA. In many languages from all over the world, including Russian, Hebrew, Chinese, and Indonesian, present tense *be*-verbs are rarely used (*She—on stage*), so it can be difficult for native speakers of those languages to remember to use *am/is/are* and their equivalents in speaking languages like English and the other Germanic languages (and Romance languages) that do require them.

lip rounding (1.2.4.2): Moving your lips forwards and towards the center (kissing position), as in saying the English sounds /u/ and /w/.

liquid (1.2.4.2): A rather poetic term for the SEMIVOWELS that aren't GLIDES. In English phonetics, the liquid sounds are /r/ and /l/. Many languages (such as Japanese) have only one liquid PHONEME, either with a sound that is intermediate between /r/ and /l/, or with an [r]-like ALLOPHONE and an [l]-like allophone.

list effect (5.2.3): In experimental phonetics, the way people respond to a stimulus may be different depending on what other stimuli have been seen or heard earlier in the experiment; this is a "list effect." To make sure that your experimental results aren't distorted by list effects, you can make up several different lists of stimuli, each having the same items but in different orders, divide your participants into random groups, and have some of your groups use one list and some another. If you get the same results from all of your groups, you don't have any list effects, but if the results vary, you probably need to redesign your experiment.

localization (2.7): In theories of how our brains are organized, the part of the brain in which a particular process or set of processes takes place. It is still common to talk about very complex multiprocess events like understanding a sentence or reading as being "localized" to a particular area of the brain, but modern high-resolution functional imaging makes it clear that multiple parts of the brain are involved in such activities.

location (1.7, 3.3.3): A SEMANTIC ROLE: the place where something is located (*Your shoes are **under the bed***). In fine-grained semantic analysis, SOURCE (where something is coming from—*The cat jumped* *off the chair*) and GOAL (its destination—*The raccoon disappeared under the porch*) are not lumped in with "location," but in less detailed analyses, all three of these concepts may be called "location."

locative (1.7.3): In grammar, a form that gives information about location, or is usually used to do so.

locative particle: In English grammar, a word that is tightly linked to and used along with a motion or action verb to give information about the direction of the movement of the subject or object: *Pick **up** your toys, Take it **out***. These words can also be used as prepositions and/or as adverbs, but the verb + particle construction is special and tricky. (Notice that we can say *Take out the trash* and *Take the trash out* and *Take it out*, but not *Take out it*.) English also has many verb + particle constructions that use locative words (especially *up*) without their locative meaning, as in **look up** *a phone number*, *hurry **up** and get dressed*. In these cases, the *up* is just called a particle, not a locative particle.

locative prepositional phrase (1.7.3, 5.6.2, 7.2.3): A PREPOSITIONAL PHRASE that gives LOCATION information.

longitudinal study (7.1.1): A research design that follows one or more individual participants over a number of sessions, possibly extending over several years, in order to track changes in each person's behavior.

lowercase letter: In the ROMAN ALPHABET (but not in some others), each letter has two sets of forms: capital or **UPPERCASE** letters, which are used to begin sentences and proper names (and for many other special purposes), and ordinary lower-case letters, used when there is no reason to use upper case.

malapropism (3.1.1): A word that is mistakenly used in place of one that sounds a lot like it, and which the speaker apparently thinks is the right word (so it's not a slip of the tongue). In the play by Sheridan that this word comes from, Mrs. Malaprop says things like "I would have her instructed in geometry, that she might know something of the contagious countries," where the words she needed were "geography" and "contiguous."

manner of articulation (1.2.3): In phonetics, speech sounds are (basically) described by POSITION OF ARTICULATION, manner of articulation, and VOICING. Manner of articulation describes the kind of airflow you use in making the speech sound; common manner descriptors are STOP = zero air leaving your mouth (when you make a consonant like /p/, /b/, or /m/), NASAL = air going out through your nose (when you make a nasal stop like /m/ or a nasal vowel), and FRICATIVE = air flowing turbulently around a partial blockage in your mouth (when you make a fricative like /s/).

masculine gender (1.10.1): See also **GRAMMATICAL GENDER**. There are two overlapping meanings of this term. In a natural gender system, masculine gender words are nouns and pronouns that specifically refer to male beings; for example, words like *he, his, father, bull, man*. In a **GRAMMATICAL GENDER** system, found in many languages, especially in the IndoEuropean and Semitic language families, genders are grammatical categories of nouns that correspond only roughly to biological categories. Masculine grammatical gender includes words that refer or modify many biologically male creatures, but not necessarily all of them, and may also include words for objects that are not alive; for example, French *le tapis blanc,* "the white carpet," using the masculine definite article *le* and the masculine form, *blanc,* of the adjective meaning "white."

mental lexicon (3.1.1): The words you know well enough to understand them in context; your total vocabulary, considered as information stored in your brain.

Message Level (of language production) (3.2, 3.2.1, 3.6.1, 4.1, 4.5, 5.2.4, 5.4): In our model, the prelinguistic stage of organizing what you want to talk about into concepts of people, animals, things, and events, before you start finding the words and the semantic relations between them that you will need to express your thoughts. The first linguistic level of production is the **FUNCTIONAL LEVEL**, which comes right after the Message Level.

minimal pair (1.2.5, 9.1.1): In phonology, a pair of words that differ only by one sound, like *wheel/real, beet/boat,* or *lake/late.*

mirror neurons (2.4.1): Specialized **NEURONS** in the motor area of the brain that become activated when a person or animal sees (or hears) a similar creature performing a familiar action; they probably are essential to really understanding what the other creature is doing.

mixed aphasia (6.6): Aphasia involving considerable difficulty with both comprehension and production, but less severe than **GLOBAL APHASIA**.

modal, modal verb: A verb, like English *might, could, will,* or *should,* that gives information about how certain or necessary the action of another verb or verb phrase is: *She **might** do it, A phone call **would** be better.* Verbs like *ought to* and *have to* have the same kind of meaning but slightly different grammar.

modality (8.8.2): Any of our ways of perceiving or producing language. Hearing speech, reading, and perceiving sign language are different perception modalities; in contrast, producing speech, writing, typing, and signing are production modalities.

modifier, modify (3.3.3, 7.2.3): A modifier is a word that alters or makes more precise the meaning of some other word; number words (*ten, a thousand*), **ADJECTIVES** (*blue, comfortable*), and content **ADVERBS**

(*quickly, happily*) are the clearest examples of modifiers. In English, NOUNS are also used to modify other nouns (**lion tamer, school holiday**), but when people speak of the category of "modifiers," nouns are rarely included.

mondegreen (3.1.1): A misanalysis of the words in a phrase from a song or poem. Google "mondegreen" and enjoy the results.

morph, morpheme, morphology (1.4, 4.2, 5.3.2, 6.2, 6.3, 6.3.2, 6.4.2, 6.4.3, 6.5.3, 6.7.2, 7.1.1, 7.1.4, 7.2.1, 7.2.2, 8.6, 8.7.2, 8.9, 9.1.2): A morpheme is the smallest meaningful part of a word; it may be a whole word (*it, may, be, a, whole*, and *word* are each one-morpheme words), or a part that can't stand alone (*meaningful* has three morphemes: *mean-ing-ful. Mean* can be a word by itself, but *-ing* cannot; *-ful* is on the borderline, as it seems to be a form of the word *full*. A morpheme doesn't have to be a whole syllable; *words* has two morphemes, *word* and the plural ending *-s*. The MORPHOLOGY of a language is the system of how its words are put together from its morphemes. When a morpheme has several different forms depending on what it's attached to, as most of the English bound grammatical morphemes do, each of those forms is a MORPH belonging to that morpheme, and the morphs that belong to a particular morpheme are called its *allomorphs*. For example, the English possessive morpheme has the three allomorphs /-s, -z, and -əz/.

- **bound morpheme** (1.4.3, 1.4.4): A morpheme that can't stand by itself; it must be attached to another morpheme in order to form a word, like the English plural ending *-s* or the three morphemes *in-vis-ible* of the word *invisible*.

- **free morpheme** (1.4.1, 1.4.2): A morpheme that can be a word on its own, like the two morphemes in the COMPOUND WORD *baseline*. A free morpheme can sometimes have several different phonetic forms (allomorphs); in English, [ei], [ə], and [æn] are the allomorphs of the INDEFINITE ARTICLE morpheme.

Motor aphasia (6.6): See BROCA'S APHASIA.

motor neuron (2.3): A neuron that sends activation to muscle fibers.

multiple baseline design (10.4.2): An experimental paradigm designed especially for comparing the effectiveness of therapies. An example for speech therapy: For each participant, their ability to produce several different sounds is measured before treatment; then just one of the sounds is treated, all are tested (to see if any have improved even without treatment), then another one is treated, and so on. A multiple baseline design makes it possible to be sure whether the specific treatment is effective or whether improvement is just a general result of contact with the therapist.

multiple case study (10.4.2): A set of parallel CASE STUDIES with several participants. Like a single case study, a multiple case study includes several kinds of data from each participant, plus DEMOGRAPHIC information about each of them. In this way, each participant can be considered as an individual. Doing multiple case studies instead of an ordinary study of a group is important when there are likely to be major differences among the subjects' patterns of strengths and weaknesses that would be hidden if their scores were just averaged together.

multiple-participant single-subject multiple baseline design (10.4.2): A SINGLE-SUBJECT MULTIPLE BASELINE DESIGN that is carried out with many participants, still considering each person as an individual.

naming latency (5.3.1): The length of time between when a person is shown the picture of an object and when they begin to say its name aloud.

nasal speech sound, nasal stop (1.2.4.1): A speech sound made while air is flowing out of your nose. A nasal stop like /m, n, ŋ/ doesn't let any air out of your mouth; nasal vowels, fricatives, and semivowels allow air to flow out of your mouth as well as your nose.

neighbors (of a word) (8.1.4): The neighbors of a one-syllable word are all the words that differ from it by only one sound (or, for written stimuli, all the words which differ from it only by one letter). For longer words, defining 'neighbors' in a way that makes psycholinguistic sense is difficult.

neural event (2.2): A change in the activation level of a neuron, especially an increase in its activation level that's enough to push it over its ACTIVATION THRESHOLD.

neurolinguistics (5.7): The study of the events in our brains that make it possible for us to understand, learn, and produce language in any of its MODALITIES.

neuron (2.2): A nerve cell. This book focuses on the neurons in the brain (the central nervous system), but nerves run throughout our bodies, carrying sensory information to the brain and motor instructions from it, as well as processing and transmitting other kinds of information.

neuropsychologist, neuropsychology (10.2.2): Neuropsychologists study how our brains process all kinds of information; clinical neuropsychologists are particularly concerned with diagnosing and treating disorders of memory and EXECUTIVE FUNCTIONING, which have such a big impact on clients' ability to function in the real world.

neurotransmitter (2.2): Any of a fairly large set of complex chemicals manufactured in our bodies that transmit electrical information across the SYNAPSES that separate the AXON of each neuron from the DENDRITES of the neurons that it sends ACTIVATION to.

nonfluent aphasia: Aphasia in which the symptoms include slow speech, short phrases, and usually also difficulty in articulating speech sounds clearly (**DYSARTHRIA**).

non-nasal speech sound (1.4.2.1): A speech sound made without letting air flow out through your nose. For almost all speech sounds, you do this by raising your **VELUM** so that it blocks off the connection between your **PHARYNX** and your nasal passages. The only speech sounds that can be non-nasal without raising the velum are the **GLOTTAL STOP** and **PHARYNGEAL STOPS**; look carefully at Figure 1.1B to see why.

noun (1.4, 4.1, 4.2, 4.5, 5.3.1, 6.3.2, 6.4.1, 6.4.3, 7.2.2, 7.3, 7.6): In school grammar, the standard definition is that a noun is the name of a person, place, or thing, but that's not very good. Many names, like *The New York Public Library*, are **NOUN PHRASES**, and many words that are nouns, like *democracy* and *concept*, aren't what we usually mean by "things." Try this as a starting point: A noun is a single word that can be the **SUBJECT** or **OBJECT** of a **VERB** or a **PREPOSITION**, and is not a **PRONOUN**. This is not a complete definition; if you think about it, you can find interesting exceptions.

noun phrase (1.6.2, 4.1, 4.5, 6.4.2, 7.2.2): A construction that syntactically behaves like a noun—specifically, it can be a **SUBJECT** or an **OBJECT**. Examples: a subject or object **PRONOUN** (it, he, she, us . . .), a proper name (*Los Angeles, Martha Stewart*), a noun plus its **MODIFIYING** words or phrases (***Our new friends from across the street** are waving; You have **the right to remain silent***), a **CLAUSE** beginning with "the fact that" or with "that" in the sense of "the fact that" (***The fact that he hasn't called yet** is really bothering me; The reason it's hot in here is **that the furnace is on***).

normal (3.1): Expected; not likely to attract attention. For properties that can be measured and whose measurements form a symmetric bell curve, "normal" is formally defined as being within one standard deviation from the mean (the average). This works out to be the middle 68% of the people whose performance is being measured.

nucleus (plural **nuclei**) (1.3): In anatomy, the nucleus of a cell of a living thing is the part that contains the cell's DNA and controls most of its activities. In phonology, the nucleus of a **SYLLABLE** is its vowel, or some other sound that is being pressed into service if there is no vowel (see **SYLLABLE NUCLEUS**).

object (1.6.2, 4.1.2, 4.5, 7.2.3): In syntax, the object of a **VERB** (in school grammar, the "direct object") is the **NOUN**, **PRONOUN**, or **NOUN PHRASE** that is most strongly linked to the main verb, both syntactically and semantically. In English, there is no preposition before the object of a verb, but in Spanish, there may be. Some verbs have "double-object" constructions, like *give* and *buy* in *We gave her a round of applause, His folks bought him a car.* In school grammar, the RECIPIENT in this construction is called the "indirect object" and the thing the recipient gets is the direct object.

object of a preposition (1.6.2, 3.3.3, 4.1, 7.2.3): In syntax, the object of a PREPOSITION is the NOUN, PRONOUN, or NOUN PHRASE that is linked to the rest of a CLAUSE by the preposition. In a long clause, most of the noun phrases are probably objects of prepositions. In the first sentence of this definition, there are four PREPOSITIONAL PHRASES: *of a preposition*, *to the rest*, *of a clause*, and *by the preposition*. The objects of these prepositional phrases are the words in bold italics.

occipital lobe (6.6): The occipital lobes are at the back of each hemisphere. The "occiput" is the back of your head in Latin, derived from "caput," meaning "head."

oral apraxia (2.4): A person has oral apraxia if they have APRAXIA for motions involving their mouth or tongue (blowing out a candle, licking their lips, smiling)—that is, they can't carry out the action or they do it abnormally, even though they demonstrably understand the request and have control of the needed muscles. A person may have oral apraxia and yet be able to speak normally, or may have apraxia of speech without any oral apraxia

oral cavity (1.2.2): Mouth. Is there any good reason for using the five-syllable Latin-based term instead of a plain English monosyllable? Two that I know of: Making adjectives from nouns is smoother and often less ambiguous with Latin-based words than with English ones, and sometimes Latin gives us the only way to set up a clean parallel structure for expressing comparisons clearly (*oral airflow vs. nasal airflow*).

oral speech sound, oral stop (1.2.2.2): A speech sound that you make without letting any air go out through your nose. In English, all the phonemes are oral except the NASAL STOPS /m, n, ŋ/. The oral stops (/p,t,k,b,d,g/) allow no air out through either your mouth or your nose; the other oral speech sounds let air out through your mouth. When they are next to nasal phonemes, some English oral phonemes have nasal ALLOPHONES.

ordered string (of phonemes) (4.3.1): An ordered string of items—phonemes, words, gestures, and so forth—is a set of those items plus the information about what order they should be in.

orthographic, orthography (8.1.2): "Orthography" or "orthographic system" is usually used to mean the spelling system of a language that is written with some kind of alphabet or SYLLABARY, but it can also be used to refer to other kinds of writing systems, such as hieroglyphics or Chinese characters.

orthographic dazzle (8.5.1): An informal but useful description of the way that TOP-DOWN PROCESSING based on our knowledge of how a word is spelled can mess up our ability to hear the way we really say it.

overgeneralize, overgeneralization (7.2.0, 9.4): Extending a pattern, for example, a syntactic or morphological pattern in a language you are learning, to words or constructions where that language doesn't happen to follow it; for example, saying *goed* instead of *went*, or *That's just what I've been wanting for* (based on the pattern of *wishing for, hoping for*) instead of *That's just what I've been wanting*.

palatal (1.2.4.2): A speech sound made by bringing your tongue up close to or touching your HARD PALATE. The only palatal phoneme in English is the glide /j/ (*yod*).

palate, hard palate (1.2.2): The roof of your mouth. The front part of the palate is called the "hard palate" because it is made of bone (above the lining of your mouth); behind that is the soft palate, which is cartilage. See Figures 1.1A and B and the corresponding color figures of the vocal tract in the Materials for Chapter 1 on your CD.

paragraph (1.1): In many writing systems, a group of sentences, marked off by some kind of spacing, that the writer wants the reader to group together as a step in understanding the meaning of the whole story. In spoken language, we use voice PITCH, tempo, and pauses to group utterances for our hearers in a way that is similar but not identical to paragraphing.

paraphasia (6.3.2, 10.2.4): An error of word choice (SEMANTIC PARAPHASIA, also called "verbal paraphasia") or speech sound target ("phonemic paraphasia", also called PHONOLOGICAL PARAPHASIA) made by a person with aphasia.

parietal lobe (6.6): One of the four lobes that make up each hemisphere of the outer part of our brain (its cortex); the parietal lobe in each hemisphere is on the side of your brain, above the TEMPORAL lobe and just behind the FRONTAL lobe. See Figure 2.1 and the brain figure in Materials for Chapter 2 on your CD. Derived from the Latin word for "wall."

parse (6.5.0): In psycholinguistics, to "parse" a phrase, clause, or sentence means to subconsciously figure out its SYNTACTIC STRUCTURE; for example, in the sentence 1.7.3a. *Sally took her to the zoo* from Chapter 1, section 1.7.3, parsing it means recognizing *Sally* as the SUBJECT, *took* as the main VERB, *her* as the direct object, and *to the zoo* as a prepositional phrase modifying *took*. This is not the same process as recognizing the SEMANTIC ROLES (AGENT, UNDERGOER, GOAL) or the meanings of the words. Parsing and basic SEMANTIC processing (recognizing the meanings and roles of the words) in a sentence probably happen in parallel, each helping the other, although some psycholinguistic models have the syntactic process of parsing happening before semantic processing, using a CASCADE model for comprehension. We may become aware of parsing as a process happening in our heads when we have to reparse a GARDEN PATH SENTENCE.

participant (5.1.2): A person who takes part in an experiment or a study. This word replaces older terms like "experimental subject."

particle: See LOCATIVE PARTICLE.

passive voice (1.7.2, 5.0, 5.2.4, 6.5.3, 8.7.2): In English and many other languages, the passive or the passive voice is a special verb form (and the VERB FRAME that goes with it) that changes the usual SEMANTIC ROLES of the verb's SUBJECT and OBJECT; for example, the active voice sentence *Eddie rode the winning horse brilliantly* has the corresponding passive voice sentence *The winning horse was ridden brilliantly by Eddie.* In a movement (transformational) analysis of grammar, linguists say that the passive voice is formed by moving the object of the active voice verb (*the winning horse*) to subject position, and either removing the subject entirely (so that we get *The winning horse was ridden brilliantly*) or putting it into the *by*-phrase (*by Eddie*).

past tense marker (1.4.3): A MORPHEME—in English, it's the BOUND MORPHEME that's spelled *-ed* for regular verbs—indicating that the action of a verb took place in the past. (It's also used to convey some other meanings, such as unreal conditions, as in *If I were king*).

perseverating, perseveration (10.2.5): Continuing to do something when it is no longer appropriate; for example, a brain-damaged client may start to write a word like *need* that has a repeated letter and then continue making that letter (NEEEEE . . .).

pharynx (1.2.2): The tube behind your nasal passage and mouth that connects them and leads down to your LARYNX. See Figures 1.1A and B. When you speak, you move your tongue root back and forward to change the shape of the lower part of your pharynx; this plays an important role in vowel and semivowel sounds that is only beginning to be appreciated, because it has been hard to see without modern imaging techniques. See the MRI pictures of /r/ articulation in the Materials for Chapter 1 on your CD.

pharyngeal stop (1.2.2.2): A speech sound made by pulling your TONGUE ROOT all the way back so that it touches the back wall of your PHARYNX. Pharyngeal stops are used in only a few languages, but pharyngeal FRICATIVES are found in Arabic. Pharyngeal consonants are also used to substitute for ORAL ones by people who have certain speech disorders, such as cleft palate.

phonate, phonation (7.5.1): Producing sound by making your VOCAL FOLDS vibrate.

phone (See also PHONEME): A speech sound, that is, a particular way in which a PHONEME can be produced. In careful usage, the IPA symbol for a phone is written in square brackets, for example, [a]. Please don't use PHONEME when what you really mean is "speech sound"; use either "speech sound" or "phone."

phoneme (1.2.5, 4.3, 7.4.3, 8.1.2, 9.1.1): The basic unit of phonological analysis. A phoneme is a class of speech sounds (PHONES). In careful usage, the IPA symbol for a phoneme is written between slant lines /a/. Two phones in a language belong to the same phoneme if they don't CONTRAST and if they have some basic phonetic resemblance to one another; for example, the flap [ɾ] and the alveolar stop [t], which are both ways of saying the consonant in the middle of *matter*, both belong to the phoneme /t/. Two phones belong to different phonemes in a particular language if they contrast; for example, the voiced alveolar stop [d] as in *dime* and the voiceless alveolar stop [t] as in *time* belong to two different phonemes, /d/ and /t/, because *dime* and *time* are different words rather than being two different ways to say the same word.

Two phones may belong to the same phoneme in one language or dialect, but different phonemes in some other language or dialect. For example, the speech sounds [a] as in *cot* and [ɔ] as in *caught* are separate phonemes, /a/ and /ɔ/, in most of the Eastern United States, because these two words CONTRAST; that is, they (and dozens of other MINIMAL PAIRS like them) sound quite different to speakers from the Northeast. But the same two words are complete homonyms for most people from the rest of the country; they don't contrast in sound, even though their written forms are different. The phone [ɔ] usually sounds just like /a/ to Westerners, except that before [/r/], it sounds like /o/ (as in *core, pour,* which contrast with *car, par*). So for those speakers, the phone [ɔ] is a member of the /a/ phoneme (it's an ALLOPHONE of /a/), except before /r/, when it's an allophone of /o/.

It is very hard for us to hear the difference between two phones that belong to the same phoneme in our native language/dialect; we've been learning to ignore those differences since we were infants, mostly because they either don't give us cues as to what a word in our dialect means, or they are so predictable from context that we don't learn to control them consciously.

phoneme restoration effect (5.5.2): When a sound in a familiar word in a naturalistic speech context is replaced by a noise, listeners usually report hearing the missing sound (as well as the noise); this is the "phoneme restoration effect."

phonemic awareness: The ability to think about the sounds in a word, for example, to say what's different between the sounds of two rhyming words or to recognize when two words begin with the same **PHONEME**.

phonetic (1.2): Generally, "phonetic" means "concerning speech sounds." In phonology, it is often used to contrast with **PHONEMIC**, like this: "In English, the difference between the flap [ɾ] and the voiced alveolar stop [d] is only phonetic, not phonemic."

phonetic environment (8.1.3): The phonetic environment of a particular speech sound means the speech sounds, around it plus the other phonetic factors that may affect how it is pronounced, particularly whether it is **STRESSED** or not, whether it's at the beginning or end of a **SYLLABLE**, and whether it's at the beginning or end of a word.

phonics (8.1.3): The method of teaching reading (especially English) that focuses on the sounds of the letters (their **GRAPHEME-PHONEME CORRESPONDENCES**).

phonological development (7.5): How children slowly learn to pronounce the sounds of their language(s).

Phonological Encoding Level (of **SPEECH PRODUCTION**) (3.2, 4.3): In our model, the level of production after the **POSITIONAL LEVEL**. At the Phonological Encoding Level, the phonemes of the words have been activated and lined up so that the forms of **REGULAR** affixes (for example, /s/ or /z/ or /əz/) can be chosen.

phonological paraphasia (6.3.2, 10.2.4): In aphasia terminology, an error of substituting an incorrect speech sound for one or several of the phonemes in a target word. Also called "phonemic paraphasia." Contrast this with **DYSARTHRIA**.

phonotactic, phonotactics (1.2.1.3, 9.1.1): Concerning the way sounds can be combined in a particular language. Learning new phonotactic patterns in your first or your second language—for example, being an English speaker and learning to say Russian words beginning with combinations like /rt/ or /zdr/—can be just as challenging as learning to produce new speech sounds.

phrase (1.6.2): A **STRING** of words that a speaker groups together; usually, they form a syntactic **CONSTRUCTION**, but sometimes the grouping is just a matter of timing and **INTONATION CONTOUR**.

pilot study (5.2.3): A try-out experiment, to see whether your method works.

pitch (Box 1-1, 1.2.2.1): In phonetics, the pitch of your voice at each point in time is the number of vibrations per second of the lowest **FREQUENCY** sound wave that your **VOCAL FOLDS** are making at each point; this is the same as the musical concept of pitch. Pitch is not related to loudness; a high-pitched sound may be either loud or soft.

place of articulation (1.2.2.2): The **IPA CHART** organizes each speech sound of the world's languages in terms of several factors; the most important is place of articulation, which means the point at which the airstream is notably narrowed or is closed off entirely. The "place" is defined by both its "upper" articulator (for example, upper lip, ALVEO- LAR RIDGE, UVULA, back wall of the PHARYNX) and its "lower" one (lower lip, lower teeth, TONGUE BLADE, TONGUE ROOT). Some speech sounds, like [w], have two important narrowings or closures. The GLOTTIS also functions as a place of articulation.

plasticity (of the brain) (2.3, 6.9): The ability to be modified by experience. Without plasticity, we couldn't learn anything.

population variables (10.4.3): Differences between people, especially differences that might affect how they respond to a teaching method or in an experimental study; the same as DEMOGRAPHIC VARIABLES.

Positional Level (of SPEECH PRODUCTION) (3.2, 4.1, 4.3): In our model, the level at which words are put into their syntactic slots; this sets up the order in which that we will say them.

possessive (1.4.3, 7.2.2): The form of a NOUN or PRONOUN that we use to indicate the owner of something: *George's car*, *my mother*, *that story of theirs*.

postposition (6.7.2): A word that does the same kinds of job as a preposition but comes after its noun or noun phrase instead of before it. Japanese and many other languages have postpositions instead of prepositions; some languages have mostly prepositions plus a few postpositions.

potential confound (5.3.1): A factor besides the one you are interested in that might be the real explanation for the results you get from your experiment.

pragmatics (1.8, 9.1.4, 10.1.2): The way we choose what to say so that our hearers/readers can understand us, and also so that we can persuade, soothe, amuse, anger or excite them (etc.).

predicate (of a CLAUSE) (1.7.1): Clauses—in their fullest forms—have two main syntactic parts: a SUBJECT noun phrase and a predicate. The predicate is the VERB PHASE (the verb and all the words and phrases that modify its meaning); for example, the **boldface** sections of the following sentences are their predicates:

> *Chris* ***wanted me to come for dinner.***
>
> *The new folks on the block* ***seem to have a Lexus.***
>
> *Olga's* ***out in the garden.***

"Spare parts" that may show up and that don't belong to either the subject or the predicate include SENTENCE ADVERBS, exclamations, and the SENTENCE ADDRESSEE.

predicate adjective (1.7.1): An adjective in the PREDICATE of a sentence that modifies the subject; it's connected to the subject by a LINKING

VERB. Examples in boldface: *Their house is really* **gorgeous**. *The winner looked* **exhausted.**

Preferential Looking (7.3): A way of doing language comprehension experiments that is used when the participants can't reliably control pointing responses and/or are at an early and uncertain state of learning to understand the language structure that is being tested. What is measured (the **DEPENDENT VARIABLE**) is how long the participant spends in looking at one of two or more pictures while they are hearing a stimulus word or sentence like, *Big Bird is tickling Cookie Monster.*

prefix (1.4.3, 8.3): A **MORPHEME** added to the beginning of a word to form a new word (or, in some languages, to mark its number, **GENDER**, etc.). English prefixes include a large number that are originally from Latin: for example, the **boldface** parts of these words: **sub***merge,* **in***flammable,* **retro***fit.*

preposition (1.4.2): A word whose main function is to link a **NOUN PHRASE** into the rest of a **CLAUSE**. Some prepositions, like *of,* have almost no meaning of their own and are pure **FUNCTION WORDS**; others, like *under,* have fairly clear meanings and so they are like both function words and **CONTENT WORDS**. Some languages, like Hindi and Japanese, use postpositions (function words that go after the noun phrase) where English uses prepositions.

prepositional phrase (1.6.2, 7.2.3): A **CONSTRUCTION** that's made up of a **PREPOSITION** and the **NOUN PHRASE** it connects to the rest of a clause; for example, *of our generation, under the car.*

prime, priming (5.6.1, 6.5.4, 8.1.2): Priming is one of the major effects of **SPREADING ACTIVATION**: When we sense a **STIMULUS**, the **NEURONS** that it activates send activation to the neurons that they are linked to, bringing them closer to their **THRESHOLD OF ACTIVATION**. If we then get new sensory information that goes to those same neurons—for example, if we see a similar object or an object that we have learned to associate with the first stimulus—we'll be faster to respond to the new sensory information.

profile (10.2.4): See **APHASIA PROFILE**

progressive (1.4.3, 7.2.2): In English, a verb form indicating explicitly that an action or state of affairs is continuing; it's made with a the progressive ending *-ing* and a form of the verb *to be,* as in *David* **is** *sing***ing**. The progressive *-ing* is one of the first **GRAMMATICAL MORPHEMES** that English-learning children acquire. (Be careful: This ending is also used to make verbs into **NOUNS** and **ADJECTIVES**, as in *His* **singing** *needs work*; *We listened to the* **singing** *birds.*)

projection, to project (1.7.3): In psycholinguistics, we say (somewhat informally) that a word or a phrase projects a structure if it sets up the hearer to expect it; for example, a **TRANSITIVE VERB** like *buy* projects its direct **OBJECT NOUN PHRASE** (*She wants to buy some printer paper*), and some **ADJECTIVES** project **PREPOSITIONAL PHRASES** (*fond of chocolate, kind to his students*).

prompt (10.3): In language testing, a hint to help the person being tested. Most formal naming tests give a carefully specified set of semantic and phonological prompts that the examiner may or must use when the client can't produce the name of a pictured test item.

pronoun (1.4.2, 4.2.1, 7.2.1, 7.2.2): One of a fairly small set of words that speakers can use to replace **NOUN PHRASES** when they expect that the hearer can identify who/what the speaker is referring to, or when it's not necessary or possible to be explicit. (School grammar says that pronouns replace nouns, but that's not accurate; for example, in the sentence *Melissa borrowed my brown leather boots*, we can replace the whole object noun phrase *my brown leather boots* by the pronoun *them* (*Melissa borrowed them*), but we can't say *Melissa borrowed my brown leather them* or *Melissa borrowed my them*. The only English pronoun that can replace just a noun is *one/ones*, as in *Melissa borrowed my brown leather ones*.)

English pronouns are usually divided into several groups; the most important ones are personal pronouns (*he, she, they, them, you . . .*), impersonal pronouns (*It is raining, One might think . . .*), interrogative (question-asking) pronouns (*Who did it? What did they say?*), demonstrative pronouns (*I found that, She bought those*) and relative (linking) pronouns (*I know who did it, She forgot what they said*).

proofreader's error (5.1.2): An error in printed or written materials that has not been detected and corrected before the materials are shared.

protoword (7.5.3): A protoword (proto-word) is a reasonably word-like sound that a child uses with a recognizable meaning during her transition from babble to speech. It may be entirely her own creation, or it may be based on an adult word.

pseudorandom (5.2.3): An order of events; specifically, of **STIMULI** in an experiment that is carefully constructed to seem random to the participants. True random sequences may have some very long runs of the same value (like a coin coming up heads by chance nine times in a row), but such runs don't seem random to the people experiencing them.

psycholinguistics (0.2, 10.5): The study of how our minds understand, learn, and produce all forms of language—written, spoken, or signed.

psychometrics (10.0.2): The study of how to get **RELIABLE** and **VALID** measures of various kinds of mental abilities.

receptive aphasia (6.6): See **WERNICKE'S APHASIA**.

Recipient (1.7, 3.3.3, 3.4, 6.4.3): The **SEMANTIC ROLE** label for the person (or animal) that receives or is intended to receive something: *She gave the kitten some milk*. The term is not used for inanimate objects, as in

*I gave **my car** a new coat of paint*; the best semantic role label for *my car* in this case would probably be Goal or Theme.

reduced relative clause: A RELATIVE CLAUSE that has been condensed by leaving out the words that would explicitly link it to the noun it modifies; for example, *The car **driving by the corner** turned suddenly* (instead of *The car **that was driving by the corner**...*); *A dog **found yesterday behind the supermarket** will be available for adoption.* GARDEN PATH SENTENCES may be created when the verb of a reduced relative clause looks as if it's the verb of the main CLAUSE.

Reduced vowel (8.3): A vowel phone that is produced without stress and is less clearly articulated than a stressed vowel. Many English vowels lose their stress when certain word suffixes are added; for example, the /ei/ of "able" is reduced to schwa [ə] when the suffix morpheme *–ity* is added to make "ability."

referent (3.2.2, 3.6.1, 5.4): The real-world (or imaginary-world) entity (person, animal, thing, idea . . .) that a NOUN PHRASE or PRONOUN means or refers to. In discussing language disorders and language development, it's important to be clear about whether someone has a problem remembering a word for something (for example, a client can't remember his wife's name, but knows perfectly well that he's married to a particular lady), or a problem remembering the real-world referent (the client does not remember that he has a wife, or thinks he is married to someone other than his present wife).

relative clause (7.1.5): A clause used to MODIFY a noun; for example, *The people **you met yesterday**, Some guy **who was in the bar**, The car **that she wanted***.

reliable, reliability (10.0.2): In test design (PSYCHOMETRICS), a test is reliable if it produces essentially the same results each time it is given to a person (assuming that the person's abilities haven't changed between the times they took the test and that they didn't learn the test answers). Compare VALID, VALIDITY.

repetition: See ELICITED IMITATION.

representative sample (10.4.3): If you want to be able to claim that the results of your study are applicable to a general group (all second-graders, all third-year French students whose first language is Spanish), your participants need to be statistically like that larger group; that is, they need to be a representative sample of the larger group. Many controversies about research results arise because study participants may not have been representative of the population that the researchers are really interested in.

response (5.2.3): In an experiment, what a person (or animal) is expected to do when they hear, see, or feel the STIMULUS; for example, push a button, say something, look at something on a screen, or even just blink. Other things they might also do that are not being measured in the particular experiment, like saying *Um*, coughing, or scratching their heads, are not treated as responses.

response latency (5.3.1): In an experiment, how long it takes a participant to make their RESPONSE to a STIMULUS.

resting level (2.4): In our model of the brain, how close a NEURON is to its THRESHOLD LEVEL when it's not getting any input (or any input above random noise level). The higher the resting level, the easier it is to activate the neuron to its threshold.

reversible sentence (7.2.3): A sensible TRANSITIVE sentence that would also make good real-world sense if its SUBJECT and OBJECT were interchanged; for example, *The monkey chased the weasel/The weasel chased the monkey*. A nonreversible sentence would be one like, *The monkey ate the banana*.

right hemisphere: See HEMISPHERE (of the brain).

Roman alphabet (1.2.1): The alphabet used for writing the languages of Western Europe, including English; it's derived from the alphabet used by the Romans over 2000 years ago for writing Latin.

saccade (5.4): Although we are not aware of it as we look at a scene or a page, our eyes move by short jumps rather than smoothly; each jump is called a saccade [sə 'kad].

self-monitoring (4.4, 9.3.4): Staying aware of our own behavior and its effects.

semantic category (3.3.1, 5.2.2, 5.3.1, 5.2.3, 5.6.2): A grouping of words according to what they mean; semantic categories range from very specific (Swiss watchmakers' tools) to very general (artifacts = things made by humans).

semantic function, semantic role (1.7.2, 3.2.2, 4.0, 4.1, 4.5, 5.4, 7.2.3): In analyzing how the words in a clause are combined to get the clause's meaning, the semantic function or role of a NOUN PHRASE—or to be accurate, the function of whatever it refers to, its REFERENT—is what the referent does, what happens to it, or what other kind of information it supplies. Examples of semantic roles that we have discussed are AGENT, UNDERGOER, RECIPIENT, SOURCE, GOAL, and THEME. We figure out the semantic roles of the referents mentioned in a clause by combining the SYNTAX of the clause, the possible frames of the verb (see VERB FRAME), and our knowledge of the real world; for example, in the sentence *Margaret got first prize*, we combine all of those kinds of information to recognize that the SUBJECT Margaret is the RECIPIENT, but in *Margaret got me a cookie*, we combine them to recognize that she is the AGENT. The names of the semantic roles have their first letter capitalized, partly to signal that the words are being used in a technical sense; in contrast, the first letters of names of SYNTACTIC ROLES, like SUBJECT and OBJECT, are lower case (when they're not in all-caps, of course).

semantic paraphasia (6.3.2, 10.2.4): In aphasia terminology, the error of substituting a semantically related word for a target word. Sometimes used (although not as widely) for any aphasic error of substituting one word for another. If there is no semantic relationship between the target word and the erroneous word, many clinical researchers prefer the term "verbal paraphasia."

semivowel (1.2.4.2): A speech sound that has some of the phonetic properties of VOWELS (importantly, smooth rather than turbulent or blocked airflow) and some of the phonological properties of consonants (specifically, not being part of the SYLLABLE NUCLEUS—unless there's no vowel in the syllable to do the job). The English semivowels are /j/ (YOD), /w/, /l/, and /r/.

sensitive period (9.0): A period in the development of children (or young animals) when they seem especially able to tune into particular kinds of patterns around them. These patterns can also be learned outside the sensitive period, but not as readily. A sensitive period hypothesis about the ability to learn something is the "soft" version of a CRITICAL PERIOD HYPOTHESIS about that ability.

sensory-motor link (10.2.1): A sequence of NEURONS that relays information coming in from our sense organs all the way to our muscles, like a more elaborate version of a knee-jerk reflex.

sensory aphasia (6.6): See WERNICKE'S APHASIA.

sensory neuron (2.3): A NEURON in a sense organ that sends information to the brain about the world (or about the state of our body).

sensory verb (7.2.3): In semantics, a verb like *see, hear, feel* that refers to a person or animal's becoming aware of something in the world (or internal to their body). The SUBJECT of a sensory verb like *see* is an UNDERGOER, not an AGENT (think about sentences like *I looked at it but I didn't see it*).

sentence (1.1): In written languages that use capital letters and punctuation, a sentence is fairly easy to recognize: it's a clause or a string of linked clauses with the first word capitalized and a period, question mark, or exclamation point after the last word. Normal spoken language, however, is full of UTTERANCES that are quite appropriate in the context of people interacting with each other but would not be complete clauses or sentences, like *Hello* or *Maybe next year*.

sentence addressee (1.6.2): In semantics and pragmatics, the person the speaker is talking to. ("Utterance **addressee**" would be a more appropriate term.)

severity rating (10.2.4): In aphasia testing, an overall rating of how difficult it is for your client to communicate using language, taking into account both comprehension and production. Different aphasia tests have different rating scales—they may go from 0 to 5, 0 to 100, and so forth.

shallow orthography (8.1.3): A spelling system that is a fairly close representation of the way the words in a language are pronounced.

shape bias (7.6): Young children's assumption, for rigid objects, that the name people give it will also apply to other objects of the same shape, rather than to other objects made of the same stuff.

short-term auditory memory (7.1.4) (See AUDITORY MEMORY): Whatever it is in our minds that makes it possible for us to hold onto the exact words of what we have just heard for a short time if we are not distracted. Sometimes called the "auditory buffer."

single-subject multiple-baseline design (10.4.2): An experimental design that looks at only one participant over time, using a MULTIPLE-BASELINE DESIGN.

SLI: see SPECIFIC LANGUAGE DISORDER (8.8.1)

slip of the ear (3.1.1): A misunderstanding that happens when your brain organizes an incoming sequence of speech sounds into different words from the ones the speaker actually said, for example, hearing *Sistine Chapel* as *Sixteenth Chapel*.

slip of the tongue (3.1.1): A speech error in which the words a person actually says are not the ones they intended to say. (At least, these are the slips that we can document. We also have the experience of errors that seem to be just the same kind of thing but that happen before we actually say the words aloud, and of errors even in our internal, purely mental talking to ourselves, so it's not actually our tongues that slip, it's something earlier in the production process.)

slot (3.5, 4.1.2): In our language production model, the place where a word should go during the creation of the POSITIONAL LEVEL so that it gets produced in the right order for the intended meaning.

sociolinguistics (1.9.3, 9.6): The study of how people in different social categories and social situations use their language(s) to show their status and their relationships with each other.

soft palate (1.2.2): The part of the roof of your mouth that feels slightly soft (because it's made of cartilage) when you touch it with your tongue or your finger; it's behind the hard part (which is made of bone; see Figure 1.1B and the corresponding color figure in Materials for Chapter 1 on your CD). The soft palate is more conveniently called the VELUM.

Source (4.1.2, 7.2.3): A SEMANTIC ROLE: the place (or a person) that a REFERENT is or was moving away from; for example, *I got it off* **the shelf**; *He received an award from* **the governor**.

spreading activation (2.4, 5.2.2, 5.2.3, 5.3.1, 5.3.2, 5.5.2, 5.6.1, 5.6.2, 6.2, 6.5.4, 8.1.2, 8.4, 8.8.2, 9.7): In current models of how our brains work, the idea that electrical activation spreads from NEURON to neuron, being passed on from each neuron that reaches its ACTIVATION THRESHOLD to all the other neurons that it connects to through its SYNAPSES.

Specific Language Impairment/Specific Language Disorder (SLI) (8.8.1): A DEVELOPMENTAL language delay affecting language production, and often also comprehension, with no apparent cause—a child with SLI has normal intelligence, hearing, and oral movement abilities, and no obvious brain damage. The problem must be in how their brain processes language, but there are hot debates about what part of language processing is not working properly.

speech gesture (4.3.2): A movement of your articulators—that is, any part of your VOCAL TRACT from your GLOTTIS on up and out to your lips. See also SPEECH GESTURE LEVEL.

Speech Gesture Level (of speech production) (3.2, 4.3.1): The final stage in our speech production model, where your VOCAL TRACT and your lungs collaborate to actually product the speech sounds that you intend.

speech sound (1.2): A sound that is part of the phonological system of a language. Speech sounds are sounds that you make as part of a word; hesitation noises and grunts, as well as imitations of animal sounds and other natural noises, may be made with sounds that aren't part of the system. In some languages, the boundary between speech sounds and imitative sounds (onomatopoeia) is fuzzy.

stimulable: (7.1.5) In speech-language pathology, a speech sound or a phrase that a client can imitate but cannot say reliably without having just heard it.

stimulus (5.2.3): In an experiment, what the participants are asked to respond to—a picture, a sound, a word, etc. In the real world, any sensory input that we might react to.

stop (1.2.2.2, 7.5.3): A speech sound made by closing off the airflow through your vocal tract at some point. ORAL stops and the GLOTTAL STOP close off the airflow completely, while NASAL stops let air out, but only through your nose.

stopping (7.5.3): In children's phonological development, approximating an adult language fricative or semivowel by using a stop consonant at the same or a nearby PLACE OF ARTICULATION; for example, saying /pɪt/ for *fish*.

stranding error (4.2.1): A SLIP OF THE TONGUE in which an ending, a PARTICLE, or some other GRAMMATICAL MORPHEME is left in the position where it belongs but the word it should have been attached to is produced somewhere else in the sentence; for example, . . . *seven innings in one run* . . . (Fromkin collection).

stress (1.2.2.2, 1.2.4.3, 1.3, 8.1.2): Emphasis on a particular syllable in a word or phrase. Linguists use "stress" rather than "accent" for this meaning.

subconscious (5.3.1, 5.6.2): An event or information in your mind/brain is subconscious if you are not aware that the event has happened or that you know the information. Things that we are "dimly aware of" or have feelings and intuitions about are probably on the boundary between subconscious and conscious knowledge. Most of what we know about how to do things must be subconscious, as we have a very hard time becoming aware enough of that kind of knowledge to explain it, draw it, or even mime it accurately.

subject (1.6.2, 7.2.3): In English syntax, and in other languages that have subject-verb AGREEMENT, the subject is the NOUN PHRASE that the main verb of a clause AGREES with; for example, ***The children*** *were running away,* ***I*** *was sleeping soundly*. In languages without either agreement or CASE-MARKING, the subject can be harder to define.

subject slot (4.1.2): The place in a VERB FRAME where its subject belongs.

subject-verb agreement (1.6.2, 7.2.2): Changes in the form of a verb that depend on the form or meaning of the verb's subject, for example, adding the third person singular ending spelled "s" to a verb if its subject is third person singular, as in the clause *Dan sings*. Most English verbs have only this agreement change, but the verb "to be" has three agreement forms in the present tense: *am, is,* and *are*.

subliminal (8.1.2): Below the level of conscious awareness.

subordinate clause (9.1.2): A clause that cannot stand alone, but has to be used along with another clause that can do so. A subordinate clause in English usually starts with some kind of connecting word; for example, ***Because you're mine***, *I walk the line;* ***That we are here today*** *is reason for celebration; He finished* ***after I did***.

sulcus (6.6): The very evident grooves or wrinkles in the surface of our brains; "sulcus" is Latin for "furrow."

suffix (1.4.3, 8.3, 8.7.2): A BOUND MORPHEME attached to the end of a word. In English and many other languages, long words may be built up of a basic part, called the "stem," plus several suffixes; for example, *alter-**ation**-s, kind-**ness-es**, contain-**er-iz-ation***.

syllabary (1.1, 8.7.2).: A writing system (or part of a writing system), like Japanese KANA or the Cherokee syllabary, whose units stand mostly for whole SYLLABLES like *ka* or *mu*.

syllable (1.3, 7.5.1, 7.7, 8.0, 8.1.2, 8.7.2): Syllable is one of the hardest concepts in phonetics to define. Defining the number of syllables in a word isn't quite so bad, because the sound waves of vowels contain more energy than the sound waves of consonants, especially in the lower **FREQUENCIES**. If you have a computer program that can graph the amount of energy in the low-frequency sound waves of a word from moment to moment as it's being produced, the number of syllables is the number of energy peaks. Words that have sequences of **HIGH VOWELS** and/or **SEMIVOWELS** right next to each other, like *towel* or *hire/higher*, are problems for any definition of syllable, because semivowels and high vowels have about the same amount of energy, and people disagree even about how many syllables words with those consequences have.

syllable nucleus (1.3): The part of a syllable that has the most low-frequency energy; if the syllable has a vowel, the vowel is the nucleus.

synapse, synaptic gap (2.2): The tiny gap between the end of the **AXON** of one **NEURON** and the **DENDRITES** of the neurons it connects to (see Figure 2.4). **ACTIVATION** can get across the synapse because the axon releases **NEUROTRANSMITTER** molecules, which move across this synaptic gap and dock on the other side of it.

syndrome (6.6): A collection of symptoms that seem to co-occur frequently, suggesting that they may all be caused by the same underlying problem. Five to seven aphasia syndromes, including anomia (anomic aphasia), **BROCA'S APHASIA**, **CONDUCTION APHASIA**, **GLOBAL APHASIA**, **WERNICKE'S APHASIA**, and the **TRANSCORTICAL** aphasias, are commonly recognized, although much about them is still controversial.

syntactic role (1.7, 7.2.3): How a word (or a larger unit such as a **PHRASE** or a **CLAUSE**) functions as part of a sentence. **SUBJECT**, **OBJECT OF A VERB**, **OBJECT OF A PREPOSITION**, and **MODIFIER** are the most important syntactic roles. It's important to keep syntactic and **SEMANTIC ROLES** separate as you think about language; sometimes they are closely correlated, but often they are not. For example, **SUBJECTS** aren't always **AGENTS** and **AGENTS** aren't always **SUBJECTS**.

syntactic structure (1.7.3): How a **PHRASE**, **CLAUSE**, or **SENTENCE** has been created from putting words together into larger and larger constructions. For example, the syntactic structure of the sentence *Dumbledore usually let me find out stuff for myself* (Rowling, 2007, p. 433) can be **PARSED** (analyzed) this way: The proper noun *Dumbledore* is the **SUBJECT**, and the rest of the sentence forms the main **VERB PHRASE** (in school grammar, the **PREDICATE**). This verb phrase is made up of the **ADVERB** *usually*, **MODIFYING** the "permission" construction *let me find out stuff for myself*. That construction in turn is made up of the main verb *let*, the direct object *me*, and the "complement" verb phrase *find out stuff for myself*. The complement verb phrase is made up of the verb + **PARTICLE CONSTRUCTION** *find out*, its object *stuff*, and the **PREPOSITIONAL PHRASE** *for myself*.

syntax (1.7, 4.1.1, 4.1.2, 4.5, 5.6.2): How words are put together to make CONSTRUCTIONS, PHRASES, CLAUSES, and SENTENCES. See SYNTACTIC STRUCTURE.

tacit knowledge (1.9.1): Roughly, what you know without being aware that you know it. Skills that have become automatic, like the ability to understand a sentence or tie your shoes, are the clearest examples of tacit knowledge.

tag (3.6.1, 4.1, 4.2): In our model of language production, information about the SEMANTIC ROLE of a referent (AGENT, UNDERGOER, GOAL . . .) that gets attached to its LEMMA at the FUNCTIONAL LEVEL so that it can then be given its proper syntactic SLOT (SUBJECT, OBJECT, OBJECT OF A PREPOSITION . . .) at the POSITIONAL LEVEL.

tap (1.2.5): A speech sound made by quickly hitting your teeth or a point on the roof of your mouth with the tip or blade of your tongue. The alveolar tap used in English is IPA [ɾ] (look carefully—this is not an "r").

target word (4.1.2, 4.2.2, 4.3.1, 4.3.2, 5.2.3, 5.3.1, 5.3.2, 6.3.0, 6.3.2, 6.4.1, 7.5.3, 8.7.2, 10.1.3): In speech production, the word a speaker intends to say; in tests or experiments, the word that the client or participant is expected to say or to recognize (the "'right answer'"). An experiment may also have "target sentences" (5.2.4, 7.1.5) or "target sounds."

task, experimental task, test task (5.6.1): What participants or clients or students are asked to do during an experiment or a test.

task analysis (10.1.1): Thinking step-by-step through what a person carrying out a task really has to be able to do in order to carry it out successfully. Very simple-seeming tasks can turn out to be very complicated when we analyze their demands carefully.

temporal lobe (6.6): In each hemisphere of your brain, the temporal lobe is directly under your ear. The word is related to the word "temple" as used to describe the area of the side of your face between your eye and your ear (the areas under the earpieces of a pair of glasses).

Theme (1.7, 3.4, 4.1.2, 6.4.3): In the semantic analysis of a clause, the REFERENT that is most affected by the action of the verb. For some action verbs, the theme is the OBJECT, as in *I ate **an apple***; for others, it's the SUBJECT, as in ***The apple** fell from the tree*. Theme also seems to be used as the "wastebasket" term for a referent when no other semantic role label is appropriate.

third person singular marker (1.4.3, 7.2.2): In English and many other languages that have subject-verb AGREEMENT, the MORPHEME added to the stem of a verb when the SUBJECT is singular (is a single person or thing) and third person (a person or thing that is not the speaker or the person being addressed).

threshold, threshold level (2.4): The level of activation that a NEURON has to reach before it sends activation on to the neurons it's connected to. See ACTIVATION THRESHOLD.

tip-of-the-tongue state (3.1.1): The stressful feeling we have when we know what word or name we need, but can't quite remember it and just have to wait for it to "come to us"—that is, to accumulate enough ACTIVATION from its concept to make us conscious of its sounds.

toddlers (2.4.1, 7.1.1): An informal but useful term for children from 1 to 3 years of age, when they are learning to speak (and of course, learning many other things as well).

tone (1.4.3): In linguistics, tone is a technical term; it doesn't mean "tone of voice," but rather voice PITCH when it is used as a phoneme. Chinese, most languages of Southeast Asia, and many other languages across the world have MINIMAL PAIRS of words that are the same in all of their consonants and vowels, and differ only in the PITCH of the speaker's voice (the number of vibrations per second of the sound waves), which means that their pitch is PHONEMIC. These languages are called tone languages or tonal languages.

top-down processing ((2.5, 3.1.1, 5.1.2, 5.5.2, 6.1.4, 6.5.0, 7.1.4, 7.1.5, 8.1.2, 8.3, 8.4, 8.5.1, 8.9, 9.3.2, 9.7, 10.5): Processing that uses already-stored information to help with processing incoming data; for example, using your knowledge of the words of your language to help understand what someone else is saying in noisy conditions. Using top-down processing is essential for most purposes and highly automatic, but that makes it hard to inhibit when it is misleading, as in proofreading or in trying to hear the sounds of a new language accurately.

transcortical motor aphasia (6.6): One of the NONFLUENT aphasia syndromes in the Boston classification; people with transcortical motor aphasia have good comprehension and repetition, but tend to speak in short phrases, using as few words as possible, so that what they say may be grammatically and even semantically incomplete.

transcortical sensory aphasia (6.6): One of the FLUENT aphasia syndromes in the Boston classification; people with transcortical sensory aphasia have very poor comprehension but surprisingly good ability to repeat the examiner's words and sentences on request. They typically produce long utterances that may make very little sense (JARGON).

transfer (9.2.1): In learning any new skill, and specifically in learning a new language, applying your existing knowledge to the new situation; depending on how well the situations actually match, transfer can be useful or can cause problems.

transitive, transitive frame; transitive verb, transitive action verb (1.7.3, 7.2.3): A transitive verb is a VERB that has an OBJECT. In the clause

*Martha **hit** the ball*, *hit* is transitive, and *the ball* is its object. Because *hit* is an action verb, it's a transitive action verb in this sentence. Also, some non-action verbs are syntactically transitive, like *miss* in *I **miss** you*. In our production model, if a verb is being used as transitive verb in a clause that is being constructed, it sets up a TRANSITIVE VERB FRAME —that is, one that has a SLOT for an object to be put into at the POSITIONAL LEVEL.

transitive clause (7.2.3): A CLAUSE whose main verb is transitive.

transparent orthography (8.1.3): A spelling system that is a perfect match to the phonology of a language, with each symbol always having the same value, so that readers can accurately pronounce even words that they have never seen before. As language changes, ORTHOGRAPHIES that were once transparent become SHALLOW, then DEEP; if spellings are borrowed from other languages or are created freely, they eventually become IRREGULAR as well.

tree diagram (1.7.3): A type of branching diagram that has become a standard way for linguists to show the interrelationships of parts of a sentence (or main clause), different from the sentence diagramming of school grammar. It begins with the symbol S (for sentence) at the top, and each branching represents a division of the sentence (or of information about a division of it).

Two-word stage (7.2.1): A period of time, commonly found in a child's language development, when there are many two-word utterances as well as one-word utterances, but practically no longer ones.

Undergoer (1.7, 3.5, 4.1.2, 5.4, 6.4.2, 6.5.3, 6.5.4. 7.2.3): In the semantic role analysis of a clause with an ACTION VERB, the Undergoer is the person (or animal) that is most strongly affected by the action of the verb; for example, *Sam* in *Chris pushed **Sam***. An inanimate object of the same kind of verb, like *the car* in *Chris pushed **the car***, would be called the THEME. When people don't want to make such fine distinctions, Undergoers are grouped with Themes. EXPERIENCER is a closely related term, used when the verb is a SENSORY VERB instead of an action verb (notice that the names of SEMANTIC ROLES have their first letter capitalized, to signal that the words are being used in a technical sense).

Universal Grammar (9.0): According to one group of linguistic theories, humans have an innate set of possible types of grammars; this is the Universal Grammar, and it limits the kinds of language patterns that we can find in the language input that we hear, making it possible for us to induce a grammar from the raw data that we are exposed to as infants.

uppercase letter: In the ROMAN ALPHABET (but not in some others), each letter has two sets of forms: capital or UPPERCASE letters, which are used to begin sentences and proper names (and for many other special purposes), and ordinary **LOWERCASE** letters, used when there is no reason to use upper case.

utterance (1.6.1): A unit of spoken language that sounds complete because of its **INTONATION CONTOUR**, roughly corresponding to a sentence in written language. It can be as short as a word or two that a speaker uses as their complete turn, like *Oh* or *Uh-huh*, or it can be many clauses chained together, if the speaker produces them without pausing and doesn't use the kind of intonation contour that sounds complete until getting to the end of the chain.

uvula (1.2.2): The little bit of flesh that hangs down at the back of your throat when you say "aaah"; it's the end of the **VELUM** (see the picture in Materials for Chapter 1 on your CD). "Uvula" is a Latin word meaning "little grape."

valid, validity (10.0.2): In tests of people's abilities, such as language tests, a test (or other measure) is called valid if it successfully predicts (at least roughly) how a person will do in a real-world situation; for example, if a higher score on the test correlates with how much information they can give or get in a telephone conversation, the test is valid as a predictor of their oral/auditory language comprehension and production.

velar, velar stop (1.2.2, 7.5.3): Velar refers to the family of **PLACES OF ARTICULATION** in which the narrowest part of your vocal tract becomes the air channel between the back of your tongue and your **velum** (soft palate): A velar stop is a speech sound (/k/, /g/, or /ŋ/, made when the air channel is closed off because the back of your tongue touches your **VELUM**. See Figure 1.1B.

velum (1.2.2): The back half (roughly) of the roof of your mouth, which is somewhat soft because it's made of cartilage rather than bone. The velum is also called the **SOFT PALATE**, but "velum" is a shorter expression and it lets us use the convenient adjective **VELAR**. See Figure 1.1B.

verb (1.4, 6.2, 6.3.2, 6.3.3, 6.4.2, 6.4.3, 6.5.3, 7.2.1, 7.2.2, 7.3): In school grammar, we are told that a verb is a word that describes "action, being, or a state of being," but this meaning-based definition isn't good enough, because lots of nouns (like *revolution* or *sleepiness*) would also fit that criterion. Problem: Basic terms like verb and **NOUN** are hard to define. One way to do it is to start with common examples, use them to give a "starter" definition (technically, a prototype), and show how to expand the idea from there.

Following that plan, we'll define verb this way: In sentences where one person or animal acts on another, as in *The cat **carried** her kitten to safety*, the word that **ENCODES** the action is the verb. When we look other words that are verbs (according to this starter definition) in clauses that have other nouns or noun phrases before the verb and that are about events at different times, in English (and in many but not all other languages), we find forms like *The cat carries kittens*, *The cat scratched the door*, *They were carrying*, etc. We see from this that (many) English ACTION VERBS have the same kinds of patterns of endings: in the present tense, they add *-s* for a third person singular subject, and *-ed* for a past event.

We then use this MORPHOLOGICAL pattern, saying that other English words that have the same pattern for adding endings are also verbs, even if they don't encode actions (*It **seemed** like a good idea*) or if their actions are aren't actions on something else (*We're **walking** to school*). We can also figure out the SYNTACTIC patterns that these verbs are used with, and finally we can say that any English word that fits those syntactic patterns is a verb, because this move lets us extend the definition to IRREGULAR verbs—ones that have different morphological patterns (*We **sang** all night*). Explaining the syntactic patterns that define verbs in English is well beyond the scope of this book, but here are some important SEMANTIC CATEGORIES of verbs that are not action verbs: SENSORY VERBS (*feel, hear, see*), mental state verbs (*want, hope, miss, love, hate*), state verbs (*sit, sleep, have*), LINKING VERBS (*be, seem, become*). A fair number of verbs belong to more than one of these semantic categories, depending on how they are used: *Smell* can be a state verb (*That cheese **smells** weird*), a sensory verb (*Yuck, I **smelled** it from here*), or an action (***Smell** it carefully and see if you think it's okay to eat*).

verb frame (1.7.3): In syntax, a way of describing the kinds of other words a verb may or must be used with. A verb's frame sets up most of the clause that the verb is being used in; it's made up of SLOTS for these other key words, arranged in the position that they will show up in when the sentence is produced. In our production model, the frame is set up and filled at the POSITIONAL LEVEL. In English, the verb's frame always includes a SUBJECT slot (which gets filled with a noun or a noun phrase); if the verb is transitive, the frame also includes a slot for its object. An example of an English verb that requires a very complicated verb frame is *put*; it has a subject slot, an OBJECT slot, and also a LOCATION slot, which can be filled by a PREPOSITIONAL PHRASE (*They put the tires **in the trunk***), a locative PRONOUN (*They put the tires **there***), or some kinds of locative ADVERB (*They put the tires **away**, They put the tires **back***).

verb + particle construction: See LOCATIVE PARTICLE.

verb phrase (1.6.2): A verb and the words that are closely linked to it. In modern syntax, it usually means the verb of a CLAUSE plus its OBJECT(s) and the words or phrases that modify it—that is, the whole PREDICATE in a clause like *The committee **already sent notifications to the winners and the runners-up in the essay contest***. In school grammar, "verb phrase" is used for what might better be called the "extended verb" or the "verb complex": the main verb of a clause plus the MODALS and AUXILIARY VERBS that MODIFY it. Examples of English verb complexes are *send, is sending, might have sent, could have been sent, shouldn't be sending*, etc.

vocal cords: See VOCAL FOLDS. They are not cords (or chords). However, the term "cord" has become established in the international otorhino-laryngology (ear-nose-throat) medical terminology and in nontechnical writing about the voice.

vocal folds (1.2.2.1): The two flexible flaps of tissue on opposite sides of your LARYNX that will vibrate and produce sound (PHONATION) if you bring them close together in the right range of tensions and let air flow through the opening between them. See Materials for Chapter 1 on your CD for videos of vocal fold vibration.

voiced, voicing (1.2.2.1): A speech sound is voiced if it is made with VOCAL FOLD vibration. *Important:* The term "voiced" is also often used for speech sounds (PHONES) that don't actually have vocal fold vibration during the time you are making them. This is often because the phone you happen to be making is voiceless, but it's one way of pronouncing a PHONEME that's called "voiced" because it has other ALLOPHONES that are actually produced with vocal fold vibration. In English, we typically make "voiced" stop phonemes /b, d, g/ without voicing at the beginnings and ends of phrases and when they are next to VOICELESS speech sounds, but we do make them with voicing when they are between VOWELS and in some other PHONETIC ENVIRONMENTS.

voiced fricative, voiced stop (1.2.2.2): A FRICATIVE made while your VOCAL FOLDS are vibrating; a stop made while your vocal folds are vibrating or one that is often made that way.

voiceless (1.2.2.2): A speech sound is voiceless if it is made (or typically made) without VOCAL FOLD vibration.

voiceless fricative, voiceless stop (1.2.2.2): A FRICATIVE / a STOP made while your VOCAL FOLDS are not vibrating; but see VOICED and VOICED STOP.

vowel (1.2.4.3): A speech sound made with air flowing freely out of your mouth; the sounds on the IPA vowel chart (see Materials for Chapter 1 on your CD). SEMIVOWELS also have free airflow; the boundary between the semivowels and the two highest of the HIGH VOWELS (those made with the narrowest air channel, English /i/ and /u/) is fuzzy.

Wernicke's aphasia (6.6, 10.2.2): A type of APHASIA where the speaker has poor comprehension, difficulty finding all but the commonest CONTENT WORDS, good articulation, long FLUENT phrases, and uses many vague or empty expressions; in the most dramatic cases, the aphasic person uses unintelligible JARGON, which may be made entirely of English words or which may have many nonsense words in place of the content words. Some old books may say that people with Wernicke's aphasia have good syntax, but this is true mostly for the PHRASE level; if you record their speech and look at the sentence level, you can see that syntax is also damaged.

Wernicke's area (6.6): A small area overlapping the boundary of the TEMPORAL and PARIETAL lobes close to the OCCIPITAL lobe the on the left side of brain, near an area responsible for much auditory processing. It is one of the classical "language areas." Older texts describe Wernicke's area as responsible for comprehending words, but there is no neat correlation of where brain injuries are and what the language symptoms are. See Figure 6.2.

whole-phrase strategy (7.2.1): A way that some first-language learners get a start on their language production, by attempting to approximate whole phrases (perhaps at first just the vowels and the INTONATION) instead of learning one word at a time; they seem to take a while to figure out that the phrases they are using are composed of separate words. Most young children use a mix of whole-phrase strategy and WORD-COMBINING STRATEGY. Immersed second-language learners also tend to use a whole-phrase approach.

whole-word method (8.1.3): A way of teaching reading that, in its more extreme forms, asks children to memorize how each word looks as a whole, without showing them any of the ways that the individual letters correspond to sounds or how to use those GRAPHEME-PHONEME CORRESPONDENCES to figure out how the word is pronounced.

word (1.5): Another basic language concept that is very hard to define if you try to do it accurately and seriously—and in fact, there is no agreed-on linguistic definition of "word." A spelling-oriented definition is "a meaningful string of letters with no spaces in it," as when we ask whether *data base* is one word ("database") or two ("data base"), but spelling choices are just matters of convention. Talking about spelling doesn't touch either the linguistic problem of whether a sequence of FREE MORPHEMES like this is one word in the spoken language, or the psycholinguistic problem of whether it's one word in our minds.

word-combining strategy (7.2.1): A way that some first-language learners get a start on their language production, first saying single words, then beginning to use more and more two-word sequences, and then beginning to combine words freely into phrases and clauses. Most young children use a mix of WHOLE-PHRASE STRATEGY and word-combining strategy.

Word Superiority Effect (8.1.2, 10.1.3): Found by experimenters starting with Cattell in 1885, the Word Superiority Effect is the fact that if you flash a word on a screen and ask people whether it contains a particular letter, say "B," they will be faster at answering "yes" or "no" than they will be if you flash just one letter on the screen and ask whether it's the letter B. The INTERACTIVE ACTIVATION MODEL of reading (Chapter 8, section 8.1.2) is the first successful explanation of how the Word Superiority Effect happens.

working memory (6.5.0): In models of memory, language processing, and other mental operations, the mental "workspace" where we hold onto the information we need; for example, a phone number we're dialing, a list of words or a sentence we're supposed to repeat, the results of each successive addition if we're adding a column of numbers in our heads, or what we've computed of a sentence structure at each point as we're creating it or listening to it. There are probably several kinds of working memory for different kinds of mental processes.

yod (1.2.4.2): The name used by linguists to mean the PALATAL speech sound pronounced *y* as in *you* and its IPA written symbol, [j]. ("Yod" is the better name for this symbol when you're using the IPA because calling it *jay* makes it hard to remember that it's pronounced *y*.)

Zone of Proximal Development (ZPD) (7.1.5, 10.1.2): A term created by Soviet psychologist Lev Vygotsky to describe information that's a little more elaborated or skills that are a little more advanced that what a learner has mastered. Material in the ZPD is what a person is ready to learn; it's neither too easy nor too difficult.

Reference

Rowling, J. K. (2007). *Harry Potter and the deathly hallows.* New York, NY: Scholastic.

Index